Guide to LaTeX

Fourth Edition

Addison-Wesley Series on Tools and Techniques for Computer Typesetting

This series focuses on tools and techniques needed for computer typesetting and information processing with traditional and new media. Books in the series address the practical needs of both users and system developers. Initial titles comprise handy references for LaTeX users; forthcoming works will expand that core. Ultimately, the series will cover other typesetting and information processing systems, as well, especially insofar as those systems offer unique value to the scientific and technical community. The series goal is to enhance your ability to produce, maintain, manipulate, or reuse articles, papers, reports, proposals, books, and other documents with professional quality.

Ideas for this series should be directed to the editor: mittelbach@awl.com. Send all other comments to the publisher: awprofessional@awl.com.

Series Editor

Frank Mittelbach
Manager LaTeX3 Project, Germany

Editorial Board

Jacques André
Irisa/Inria-Rennes, France

Barbara Beeton
Editor, TUGboat, USA

David Brailsford
University of Nottingham, UK

Tim Bray
Textuality Services, Canada

Peter Flynn
University College, Cork, Ireland

Leslie Lamport
Creator of LaTeX, USA

Chris Rowley
Open University, UK

Richard Rubinstein
Human Factors International, USA

Paul Stiff
University of Reading, UK

Series Titles

Guide to LaTeX, Fourth Edition, by Helmut Kopka and Patrick W. Daly
The LaTeX Companion, by Michel Goossens, Frank Mittelbach, and Alexander Samarin
The LaTeX Graphics Companion, by Michel Goossens, Sebastian Rahtz, and Frank Mittelbach
The LaTeX Web Companion, by Michel Goossens and Sebastian Rahtz

Also from Addison-Wesley:
LaTeX: A Document Preparation System, Second Edition, by Leslie Lamport
The Unicode Standard, Version 4.0, by the Unicode Consortium

Guide to LaTeX

Fourth Edition

Helmut Kopka
Patrick W. Daly

✦✦Addison-Wesley

Boston • San Francisco • New York • Toronto • Montreal
London • Munich • Paris • Madrid
Capetown • Sydney • Tokyo • Singapore • Mexico City

Many of the designations used by manufacturers and sellers to distinguish their products are claimed as trademarks. Where those designations appear in this book, and Addison-Wesley was aware of a trademark claim, the designations have been printed with initial capital letters or in all capitals.

The authors and publisher have taken care in the preparation of this book, but make no expressed or implied warranty of any kind and assume no responsibility for errors or omissions. No liability is assumed for incidental or consequential damages in connection with or arising out of the use of the information or programs contained herein.

The publisher offers discounts on this book when ordered in quantity for bulk purchases and special sales. For more information, please contact:

U.S. Corporate and Government Sales
(800) 382-3419
corpsales@pearsontechgroup.com

For sales outside of the U.S., please contact:

International Sales
(317) 581-3793
international@pearsontechgroup.com

Visit Addison-Wesley on the Web: www.awprofessional.com

Library of Congress Cataloging-in-Publication Data
Kopka, Helmut.
  Guide to LaTeX/Helmut Kopka, Patrick W. Daly.—4th ed.
    p. cm.
  Include bibliographical references and index.
  ISBN 0-321-17385-6 (pbk. : alk. paper)
  1. LaTeX (Computer file) 2. Computerized typesetting. I. Daly, Patrick W. II. Title
Z253.4.L38K66 2004
686.2'2544536—dc22   2003060364

Text printed on recycled and acid-free paper.

ISBN 0321173856

4 5 6 7 8 9 CRS   07 06 05

4th Printing   March 2005

Contents

Appendices

Preface

A new edition to *A Guide to LaTeX* begs the fundamental question: Has LaTeX changed so much since the appearance of the third edition in 1999 that a new release of this book is justified?

The simple answer to that question is 'Well,....' In 1994, the LaTeX world was in upheaval with the issue of the new version LaTeX 2_ε, and the second edition of the *Guide* came out just then to act as the bridge between the old and new versions. By 1998, the initial teething problems had been worked out and corrected through semiannual releases, and the third edition could describe an established, working system. However, homage was still paid to the older 2.09 version since many users still employed its familiar syntax, although they were most likely to be using it in a LaTeX 2_ε environment. LaTeX has now reached a degree of stability that since 2000 the regular updates have been reduced to annual events, which often appear months after the nominal date, something that does not worry anyone. The old version 2.09 is obsolete and should no longer play any role in such a book. In this fourth edition, it is reduced to an appendix just to document its syntax and usage.

But if LaTeX itself has not changed substantially since 1999, many of its peripherals have. The rise of programs such as pdfTeX and `dvipdfm` for PDF output adds new possibilities, which are realized, not in LaTeX directly, but by means of more modern *packages* to extend the basic features. The distribution of TeX/LaTeX installations has changed, such that most users are given a complete, ready-to-run setup, with all the 'extras' that previously had to be obtained separately. Those extras include user-contributed packages, many of which are now considered indispensable. Today 'the LaTeX system' includes much more than the basic kernel by Leslie Lamport, encompassing the contributions of hundreds of other people. This edition reflects this increase in breadth.

The changes to the fourth edition are mainly those of emphasis.

1. The material has been reorganized into 'Basics' and 'Beyond the Basics' ('advanced' sounds too intimidating) while the appendices contain topics that can be skipped by most everyday users. One exception: Appendix G is an alphabetized command summary that many people find extremely useful (including ourselves).

   This reorganizing is meant to stress certain aspects over others. For example, the section on graphics inclusion and color was originally treated as an exotic extra, relegated to an appendix on extensions; in the third edition, it was moved up to be included in a front chapter along with the `picture` environment and floats; now it dominates Chapter 8 all on its own, the floats come in the following Chapter 9, and `picture` is banished to the later Chapter 16. This is not to say that the `picture` features are no good, but only that they are very specialized. We add descriptions of additional drawing possibilities there too.

2. It is stressed as much as possible that LaTeX is a *markup* language, with separation of content and form. Typographical settings should be placed in the preamble, while the body contains only logical markup. This is in keeping with the modern ideas of XML, where form and content are radically segregated.

3. Throughout this edition, contributed packages are explained at the point in the text where they are most relevant. The `fancyhdr` package comes in the section on page styles, `natbib` where literature citations are explained. This stresses that these 'extensions' are part of the LaTeX system as a whole. However, to remind users that they must still be explicitly loaded, a marginal note is placed at the start of their descriptions.

4. PDF output is taken for granted throughout the book, in addition to the classical DVI format. This means that the added possibilities of pdfTeX and `dvipdfm` are explained where they are relevant. A separate Chapter 13 on PostScript and PDF is still necessary, and the `hyperref` package, the best interface for PDF output with all its bells and whistles, is explained in detail. PDF is also included in Chapter 17 on presentation material.

   On the other hand, the other Web output formats, HTML and XML, are only dealt with briefly in Appendix E, since these are large topics treated in other books, most noticeably the *LaTeX Web Companion*.

5. This book is being distributed with a modified version of one of the CDs from the TeX Live set. It contains a full TeX and LaTeX installation for Windows, Macintosh OSX, and Linux, plus many of the myriad extensions that exist.

We once again express our hope that this *Guide* will prove more than useful to all those who wish to find their way through the intricate world of LaTeX. And with the addition of the included TeX Live CD, that world is brought even closer to their doorsteps.

Helmut Kopka and Patrick W. Daly
September 2003

Part I

Basics

1   Introduction

1.1   Just what is LaTeX?

This book is a manual for LaTeX, a *documentation preparation system* widely used in the fields of mathematics and natural sciences, but which is also spreading to many other disciplines. A brief overview of its features is presented here.

- LaTeX is a comprehensive set of markup commands used with the powerful typesetting program TeX for the preparation of a wide variety of documents, from scientific articles, to reports, to complex books.

- LaTeX, like TeX, is a totally open software system, available free of charge. It is also permissible to modify and redistribute all or any part of it, provided the name is altered, in order to avoid confusion.

- The LaTeX core is maintained by the LaTeX3 Project Group but it also benefits from extensions written by hundreds of user/contributors, with all the advantages and disadvantages of such a democracy.

- A LaTeX document consists of one or more source files containing plain text characters, the actual textual content plus markup commands. These include instructions that can insert graphical material produced by other programs.

- It is processed by the TeX program to produce a binary file in DVI (*device independent*) format containing precise directions for the typesetting of each character. This in turn can be viewed on a monitor, or converted into printer instructions, or some other electronic form such as PostScript, HTML, XML, or PDF.

- A variant of the TeX program called pdfTeX produces PDF output directly from the source file without going through the DVI intermediary. With this, LaTeX can automatically include internal links and bookmarks with little or no extra effort, plus PDF buttons and external links, in addition to graphics in a wide range of common formats.

- TeX activities are coordinated by the TeX Users Group, TUG (www.tug.org), as well as by many other national groups (see www.tug.org/usergroups.html). Contributions are made by anyone who feels he or she has something vital (or simply interesting) to add.

- TeX and LaTeX installations are provided online through the *Comprehensive TeX Archive Network*, CTAN (Section B.4), where all contributed programs and source files may also be found. In addition, there is a set of CDs and a DVD, known as TeX Live, containing the current versions of the installations for various computer types (www.tug.org/texlive/). These are distributed annually to members of the TeX groups.

The rest of this book attempts to fill in the gaps in the previous summary. With the help of the included CD from the TeX Live set, which also contains a directory specific to this book (books→Guide4), we hope to give the user additional pleasure in learning the joys of LaTeX.

1.2   Markup Languages

1.2.1   Typographical markup

In the days before computers, an author would prepare a *manuscript* either by hand or by typewriter, which he or she would submit to a publisher. Once accepted for publication (and after several rounds of corrections and modifications, each requiring a rewrite of the paper manuscript), it would be sent to a copy editor, a human being who would 'decorate' the manuscript with *edits* and *markup*, marginal notes that tell the typesetter (another human being) which fonts, spacing, and other typographical features should be used to convert it to the final printed form of a book or article.

Electronic processing of text today follows a similar procedure, except that the humans have been replaced by computer programs. (So far the author has mainly avoided this fate, but the publishing industry is rapidly working on it.) The markup is normally included directly in the manuscript in such a way that it is converted immediately to its output form and displayed on the computer monitor. This is known as WYSIWYG, or 'what you see is what you get.'

However, what you see is not always what you've got. An alternative that is used more and more by major publishers is *markup languages*, in which the raw text is interspersed with indicators 'for the typesetter.' The result as seen on the monitor is much the same as a typewritten manuscript, except that the markup is no longer abbreviated marginal notes, but cryptic code within the actual text. This *source text*, which can be prepared by a simple, dumb *text editor* program, is converted into typographically set output by a separate program.

For example, to code the line

He took a **bold step** forward.

with HTML, the classical markup language of the World Wide Web, one enters in the source text:

```
He took a <b>bold step</b> forward.
```

In Plain TEX, the same sentence would be coded as:

```
He took a {\bf bold step} forward.
```

The first example is to be processed (displayed) by a Web browser program that decides to set everything between <b> and </b> as boldface. The second example is intended for the TEX program (Section 1.3). The markup in these two examples follows different rules and different syntax, but the functionality is the same.

1.2.2 Logical markup

The above examples illustrate *typographical markup*, in which the inserted commands or tags give direct instructions to alter the appearance of the output, here a change of font. An alternative is to indicate the purpose of the text. For example, HTML recognizes several levels of headings; to place a title into the highest level one enters:

```
<h1>Logical Markup</h1>
```

The equivalent LATEX entry would be:

```
\title{Logical Markup}
```

With this *logical markup*, the author concentrates entirely on the content and leaves the typographical considerations to the experts. One merely marks the structure of the document, without worrying about how the logical elements, such as section titles, are to be rendered typographically. This information is put into HTML style sheets or LATEX classes and packages, which are external to the actual source file or at least restricted to its preamble. It may even be the author who undertakes this task, but such that the typographic design is separated from the actual content.

Today much effort is being put into XML, the Extensible Markup Language, as the ultimate markup system, since it allows the markup, or tags, to be defined as needed, without any indication of how they are to be implemented. That is left to XSL, the Extensible Stylesheet Language. It must be emphasized that neither XML nor XSL are programs at all; they are specifications for how documents and databases may be marked up, and how the markup tags may be translated into real output. Programs still need to be found to do the actual job.

And this is the fundamental idea behind markup languages: that the source text indicates the logical structure of its contents. Such source files, being written in plain ASCII text, are extremely robust, not being married to any particular software package or computer type.

What does all this have to do with LATEX? In the next section we outline the development of TEX and LATEX, and go on to show that LATEX, a product of the mid-1980s, is a programmable markup language that is ideally suited for the modern world of electronic publishing.

1.3   TₑX and its offspring

The most powerful formatting program for producing book-quality text of scientific and technical works is that of Donald E. Knuth (Knuth, 1986a, 1986b, 1986c, 1986d, 1986e). The program is called TₑX, which is a rendering in capitals of the Greek letters $\tau\epsilon\chi$. For this reason the last letter is pronounced not as an *x*, but as the *ch* in Scottish *loch* or German *ach*, or as the Spanish *j* or Russian *kh*. The name is meant to emphasize that the printing of mathematical texts is an integral part of the program and not a cumbersome add-on. In addition to TₑX, the same author has developed a further program called METAFONT for the production of character fonts in electronic form. The standard TₑX program package contains 75 fonts in various design sizes, each of which is also available in up to eight magnification steps. All these fonts were produced with the program METAFONT. With additional applications, additional character fonts have been created, such as for Cyrillic, Chinese, and Japanese, with which texts in these alphabets can be printed in book quality.

The TₑX program is free, and the source code is readily available. Anybody may take it and modify it as they like, provided they call the result something other than TₑX. This indeed has occurred, and several TₑX variants do exist, including pdfTₑX which we deal with later in this chapter. Only Knuth is allowed to alter TₑX itself, which he does only to correct any obvious bugs. Otherwise he considers TₑX to be completed; the current version number is 3.141592, and with his death the code will be frozen for all time, and the version number will become exactly π.

1.3.1   The TₑX program

The basic TₑX program only understands a set of very primitive commands that are adequate for basic typesetting operations and programming functions. However, it does allow more complex, higher-level commands to be defined in terms of the primitive ones. In this way, a more user-friendly environment can be constructed out of the low-level building blocks.

During a processing run, the program first reads in what is known as a *format file*, which contains the definitions of the higher-level commands in terms of the primitive ones as well as the hyphenation patterns for word division. Only then does it read in the author's *source file* containing the actual text to be processed, including formatting commands that are predefined in the format file.

Creating new formats should be left to very knowledgeable programmers. The definitions are written to a source file which is then processed with a special version of the TₑX program called initex. It stores the new format file in a compact manner so that it can be read in quickly by the regular TₑX program.

Although the normal user will almost never write such a format, he or she may be presented with a new format source file that will need to be installed with initex. For example, this is just what must be done to upgrade LATₑX periodically. How to do this is described in Appendix B.

1.3.2 Plain TEX

Knuth has provided a basic format named *Plain TEX* to interact with TEX at its simplest level. This is such a fundamental part of TEX processing that one tends to forget the distinction between the actual processing program TEX and this particular format. Most people who claim to 'work only with TEX' really mean that they only work with Plain TEX.

Plain TEX is also the basis of every other format, something that only reinforces the impression that TEX and Plain TEX are one and the same.

1.3.3 LATEX

The emphasis of Plain TEX is still very much at the typesetter's level rather than the author's. Furthermore, the exploitation of all its potential demands considerable experience with programming techniques. Its application thus remains the exclusive domain of typographic and programming professionals.

For this reason, the American computer scientist Leslie Lamport has developed the LATEX format (Lamport, 1985), which provides a set of higher-level commands for the production of complex documents. With it, even the user with no knowledge of typesetting or programming is in a position to take extensive advantage of the possibilities offered by TEX and to be able to produce a variety of text outputs in book quality within a few days, if not hours. This is especially true for the production of complex tables and mathematical formulas.

As pointed out in Section 1.2.2, LATEX is very much more a *logical* markup language than the original Plain TEX on which it is based. It contains provisions for automatic running heads, sectioning, tables of contents, cross-referencing, equation numbering, citations, and floating tables and figures, without the author having to know just how these are to be formatted. The layout information is stored in additional *class files* that are referred to but not included in the input text. The predefined layouts may be accepted as they are or replaced by others with minimal changes to the source file.

Since its introduction in the mid-1980s, LATEX has been periodically updated and revised, like all software products. For many years the version number was fixed at 2.09 and the revisions were only identified by their dates. The last major update occurred on December 1, 1991, with some minor corrections up to March 25, 1992, at which point LATEX 2.09 became frozen.

1.3.4 LATEX 2ε

The enormous popularity of LATEX and its expansion into fields for which it was not originally intended, together with improvements in computer technology, especially with regard to cheap but powerful laser printers, had created a diversity of formats bearing the LATEX label. In an effort to reestablish a genuine, improved standard, the LATEX3 Project was set up in 1989 by Leslie Lamport, Frank Mittelbach, Chris Rowley, and Rainer Schöpf. Their goal was to construct an optimized and efficient set of basic commands complemented by various *packages* to add specific functionality as needed.

As the name of the project implies, its aim is to achieve a version 3 for LaTeX. However, since that is the long-term goal, a first step towards it was the release of LaTeX 2_ε in mid-1994 together with the publication of the second edition of Lamport's basic manual (Lamport, 1994) and of an additional book, *The LaTeX Companion*, (Goossens et al., 1994) describing many of the extension packages available and LaTeX programming in the new system. Since then, two further books have appeared, Goossens et al. (1997), covering the inclusion of graphics and color, and Goossens and Rahtz (1999), explaining how LaTeX may be used with the World Wide Web. A completely reworked and extended 2nd edition of *The LaTeX Companion* by Mittelbach et al. (2004) has now become available.

Initially, updates to LaTeX 2_ε were issued twice a year, but it has now become so stable that since 2000 new releases have been much less frequent. The latest, dated December 2003, appeared in March 2004, after a break of over two years.

LaTeX 2_ε is now the standard version, and LaTeX 2.09 is considered obsolete, although source files intended for the older version may still be processed with the newer one. In this book, unless otherwise indicated, 'LaTeX' will always mean LaTeX 2_ε.

1.3.5   TeX fonts

TeX initially made use of its own set of fonts, called Computer Modern, generated by Knuth's METAFONT program. The reason for doing this was that printers at that time (and even today) may contain their own preloaded fonts, but they are often slightly different from printer to printer. Furthermore, they lacked the mathematical character sets that are essential to TeX's main hallmark, mathematical typesetting. So Knuth created pixel fonts that could be sent to every printer, thus ensuring the same results everywhere.

Today the situation with fonts has changed dramatically. Outline fonts (also known as type 1 fonts) are more compact and versatile than the pixel fonts (type 3). They also have a far superior appearance and are drawn much faster in PDF files. The original Computer Modern fonts have been converted to outline fonts, but there is no reason to stick with them, except possibly for the mathematical symbols. For example, the 35 standard PostScript fonts are now a basic part of any LaTeX installation (Section 13.1.2). It is LaTeX 2_ε with its New Font Selection Scheme that freed TeX from its rigid marriage to Computer Modern.

1.3.6   The LaTeX bazaar: user contributions

Like the TeX program on which it relies, LaTeX is freeware. There may be a prejudice that what is free is not worth anything, but there are several other examples in the computer world (for example, GNU, Linux) to contradict this statement. And since the LaTeX macros are provided in files containing plain text, there is no problem to exchange, modify, and supplement them. In other words, the user can participate in extending the basic LaTeX system.

Taking advantage of a mechanism in LATEX 2.09 that allowed options to the default layouts to be contained in so-called *style option files*, many users began writing their own 'options' to provide additional features to the basic LATEX. They then made these available to other users via the Internet. Many were intended for very specific problems, but many more proved to be of such general usefulness that they have become part of the standard LATEX installation. In this way, the users themselves have built up a system that meets their needs.

With LATEX 2_ε, these user contributions acquired official status: They became known as *packages*, they could be entered directly into the document and not by the back door, guidelines were issued for writing them, and additional commands were introduced to assist package programming. Package files bear the extension .sty from LATEX 2.09 days, so that the older style option files may still function as packages today.

Contributions may also be made as *class* files, something that defines the overall structure of the document. These correspond to the old LATEX 2.09 main style files, which may not be reused as class files anymore. Most contributed class files start by loading one of the standard ones and then making modifications to it.

Those packages and classes that have established themselves as indispensable for sophisticated LATEX processing are described in this book in those sections where they are most relevant. This does not imply that the others are less worthwhile, but simply that this book does have to make a selection. Many other packages are described fully in *The LATEX Companion* (Mittelbach et al., 2004).

1.3.7 The LATEX Project Public License

The LATEX core and most of the contributions are distributed under the conditions of the LATEX Project Public License (LPPL). The contents of the TEX Live distribution are subject to the terms of this license, a rigid requirement for their inclusion. The main purpose of LPPL is to ensure the free distribution of the software and support files, while guaranteeing the integrity of naming schemes so that all users employing version *n* of package *X* will obtain identical results. Thus it is allowed to modify packages and programs provided they are given a new name.

The current text of LPPL can be found at

```
www.latex-project.org/lppl.txt
```

1.3.8 LATEX and electronic publishing

The most significant development in computer usage in the last decade is the rise of the World Wide Web (or the hijacking of the Internet by the advertising world). LATEX makes its own contribution here with

- programs to convert LATEX files to HTML (Appendix E);

- means of creating PDF output, with hypertext features such as links, book-marks, and active buttons (Chapter 13);

- interfacing to XML both by acting as an engine to render XML documents and with programs to convert LaTeX to XML and vice versa (Appendix E).

All these forms of electronic publishing are alternatives to traditional paper output. We do not expect paper to disappear entirely so quickly, but it is rapidly being replaced by electronic forms, which can always reproduce the paper whenever needed.

1.4   How to use this book

This book is meant to be a mixture of textbook and reference manual. It explains all the essential elements of the current standard LaTeX 2_ε, but compared to Lamport (1985, 1994), it goes into more detail, offers more examples and exercises, and describes many 'tricks' based on the authors' experiences. It explains not only the core LaTeX installation, but also many of the contributed packages that have become essential to modern LaTeX processing, and thus quasi-standard. We necessarily have to be selective, for we cannot go to the same extent as *The LaTeX Companion* (Mittelbach et al., 2004), *The LaTeX Graphics Companion* (Goossens et al., 1997), and *The LaTeX Web Companion* (Goossens and Rahtz, 1999), which are still valid *companions* to this book.

The first part of the book is entitled *The Basics*, and covers the more fundamental aspects of LaTeX: inputting text and symbols, document organization, lists and tables, entering mathematics, and customizations by the user. The second part is called *Beyond the Basics*, meaning it presents concepts that may be more advanced but are still essential to producing complex, sophisticated documents. The distinction is rather arbitrary. Finally, the appendices contain topics that are not directly part of LaTeX itself, but useful for understanding its applications: installation, error messages, creating packages, World Wide Web, and fonts. Appendix G is an alphabetized summary of most of the commands and their use, cross-referenced to their locations in the main text.

1.4.1   Some conventions

In the description of command syntax, `typewriter` type is used to indicate those parts that must be entered exactly as given, while *italic* is reserved for those parts that are variable or for the text itself. For example, the command to produce tables is presented as follows:

`\begin{tabular}{`*col_form*`}`   *lines*   `\end{tabular}`

The parts in typewriter type are obligatory, while *col_form* stands for the definition of the column format that must be inserted here. The allowed values and their combinations are given in the detailed descriptions of the commands. In the above example, *lines* stands for the line entries in the table and are thus part of the text itself.

Package:
`sample`   Sections describing a package, an extension to basic LATEX, have the name of that package printed as a marginal note, as demonstrated here for this paragraph. In this way, you are reminded that you must include it with `\usepackage` (Section 3.1.2) in order to obtain these additional features.

⟦ ! ⟧   Sections of text that are printed in a smaller typeface together with the boxed exclamation mark at the left are meant as an extension to the basic description. They may be skipped over on a first reading. This information presents deeper insight into the workings of LATEX than is necessary for everyday usage, but which is invaluable for creating more refined control over the output.

1.5   Basics of a LATEX file

1.5.1   Text and commands

The *source file* for LATEX processing, or simply the *LATEX file*, contains the *source text* that is to be processed to produce the printed output. Splitting the text into lines of equal width, formatting it into *paragraphs*, and breaking it into *pages* with page numbers and running heads are all functions of the processing program and not of the input text itself.

For example, words in the source text are strings of letters terminated by some non-letter, such as *punctuation*, *blanks*, or *end-of-lines* (*hard* end-of-lines, ones that are really there, not the *soft* ones that move with the window width); whereas punctuation marks will be transferred to the output, blanks and end-of-lines merely indicate a gap between words. Multiple blanks in the input, or blanks at the beginning of a line, have no effect on the interword spacing in the output.

Similarly, a new paragraph is indicated in the input text by an empty line; multiple empty lines have the same effect as a single one. In the output, the paragraph may be formatted either by indentation of the first line or by extra interline spacing, but this is not affected in any way by the number of blank lines or extra spaces in the input.

The source file contains more than just text, however; it is also interspersed with markup commands that control the formatting or indicate the structure. It is therefore necessary for the author to be able to recognize what is text and what is a command. Commands consist either of certain single characters that cannot be used as text characters or of words preceded immediately by a special character, the backslash (\).

The syntax of source text is explained in detail in Chapter 2.

1.5.2   Contents of a LATEX source file

Every LATEX file contains a *preamble* and a *body*.

The preamble is a collection of commands that specify the global processing parameters for the following text, such as the paper format, the height and width of the text, and the form of the output page with its pagination and automatic page heads and footlines. At a minimum, the preamble must contain the command \documentclass to specify the document's overall processing type. This is the first command in the preamble.

If there are no other commands in the preamble, LATEX selects standard values for the line width, margins, paragraph spacing, page height and width, and much more. By default, these specifications are tailored to the American norms. For European requirements, built-in options exist to alter the text height and width to the A4 standard. Furthermore, there are language-specific packages to translate certain headings, such as 'Chapter' and 'Abstract'.

The preamble ends with \begin{document}. Everything that follows this command is interpreted as *body*. It consists of the actual text mixed with markup commands. In contrast to those in the preamble, these commands have only a local effect, meaning they apply only to a part of the text, such as *indentation*, *equations*, temporary change of *font*, and so on. The body ends with the command \end{document}. This is normally the end of the file as well.

The general syntax of a LATEX file is as follows:

```
\documentclass[options]{class}
    Further global commands and specifications
\begin{document}
    Text mixed with additional commands of local effect
\end{document}
```

The possible *options* and *classes* that may appear in the \documentclass command are presented in Section 3.1.1.

A minimal LATEX file named hi.tex contains just the following lines:

```
\documentclass{article}
\begin{document}
    Hi!
\end{document}
```

A more complex sample file is shown in Section 1.7.

1.5.3 Extending LATEX with packages

Packages are a very important feature of LATEX. These are extensions to the basic LATEX commands that are written to files with names that end in .sty and are loaded with the command \usepackage in the preamble. Packages can be classified by their origin.

- **Core** packages are an integral part of the LATEX basic installation and are therefore fully standard.

- **Tools** packages are a set written by members of the LATEX3 Team and should always be in the installation.

- **Graphics** packages are a standardized set for including pictures generated by other programs and for handling color; they are on the same level as the tools packages.

- *A$_{\mathcal{M}}$S*-LATEX packages, published by the American Mathematical Society, should be in any installation.

- **Contributed** packages have been submitted by actual users; certain of these have established themselves as 'essential' to standard LATEX usage, but all are useful.

Only a limited number of these packages are described in this book, those that we consider indispensable. However, there is nothing to prevent the user from obtaining and incorporating any others that should prove beneficial for his or her purposes.

There are more than 1000 contributed packages on the TₑX Live distribution. How can one begin to get an overview of what they offer? Graham Williams has compiled a list of brief descriptions that can be found online and on TₑX Live at

```
texmf→doc→html→catalogue→catalogue.html
```

(Here and elsewhere in this book, we give paths on the CD with → as the directory separator, representing the \ for Windows, / for Unix, and : for Macintosh.)

How to load packages into the LATEX source file is explained in Section 3.1.2.

Documentation of contributed packages is somewhat haphazard depending on how much the author has put into it. The preferred method for distributing packages is to integrate the documentation with the code into a single file with extension .dtx. A special program DocStrip is used to extract the actual package file or files, while LATEXing the original .dtx file produces the instruction manual. Most ready-to-run installations will already have done all this for the user, with the resulting manuals stored as DVI or PDF files somewhere in texmf→doc→latex→.... However, you might have to generate the documentation output yourself by processing the .dtx file, which should be found in texmf→source→latex→.... (Section B.3 explains the organization of the TₑX directory system.)

Some package authors write their manuals as an extra .tex file, the output of which may or may not be prestored in DVI or PDF form. Others provide HTML files. And still others simply add the instructions as comments in the package file itself. (This illustrates some of the joys of an open system.)

1.6   TₑX processing procedure

Since LATEX is a set of definitions for the TₑX program, LATEX processing itself is in fact TₑX processing with the LATEX format. What TₑX does with this is the same as for any other of the many formats available (of which LATEX is perhaps the most popular). All the typesetting work is done by TₑX, while LATEX handles the conversion from the logical markup to the typesetting commands. It also enables cross-referencing, running headlines, table of contents, literature citations and bibliography, indexing, and more. However, the processing of the source file to final output is TₑX's task regardless of the format being used.

1.6.1   In the good old days

TₑX arose more than 20 years ago before there were such things as PCs and graphical displays, and before computers were 'infected' with windows or mice. TₑX and its support programs were invoked from a command line, not with a mouse click. This may sound very old fashioned, but it did guarantee portability to all computer types.

The processing steps that were taken in those days still exist with today's graphical interfaces, but are now executed more conveniently. One can still open a 'command prompt window' and run them from the command line.

The first step is, of course, to use a *text editor* program to write the source file containing the actual text and markup. The rules for entering this source text are explained in Chapter 2. It goes into a text file, or what is often called an ASCII file containing only standard punctuation marks, numbers, unaccented letters, and upper- and lowercase. In other words, the text is that which can be produced from a standard English typewriter.

The name of the source file normally has the extension .tex; it is then processed by TₑX to produce a new file with the same base name and the extension .dvi, for *device independent* file. This is a binary file (all codes possible, not a text file) containing precise instructions for the selection and placement of every symbol, a coded description of the final printed page. The command to invoke TₑX with the source file hi.tex is

```
tex &latex hi
```

meaning run the TₑX program with the format latex. Usually the installation has defined a shortcut named latex to do this, so

```
latex hi
```

should be sufficient. It is only necessary to specify the extension of the source file name if it is something other than .tex.

During the processing, TₑX writes information, warnings, error messages to the computer monitor, and to a *transcript* file with the extension .log. It is well worth inspecting this file when unexpected results appear.

The final step is to produce the printed pages from the DVI file. This requires another program, a *driver*, to generate the instructions specific to the given printer. For example, to produce a PostScript file, run

```
dvips hi
```

to obtain hi.ps from hi.dvi. And then send hi.ps to the PostScript printer with the regular command for that computer system.

Previewing the DVI file on a computer monitor before printing was a later development, requiring high-quality graphics displays. These programs are essentially special drivers that send the output directly to the monitor rather than to a printer or printer file. One very popular previewer is called with

```
xdvi hi
```

to view `hi.dvi` before committing it to paper.

1.6.2   And today

The various steps for LATEX processing described above are still necessary today, and one can open up a command prompt window and carry them out just as before. However, intelligent editors with LATEX-savvy now exist that not only assist writing the source text, but also will call the various programs—TEX, previewer, printer driver, BIBTEX, MakeIndex (these are explained later)—with a mouse click.

One such editor for Windows is called *WinShell*, written by Ingo H. de Boer (`www.winshell.de`). Although free of charge, its author appreciates donations to offset his expenses.

Another such editor and LATEX interface is *WinEdt* by Aleksander Simonic (`www.winedt.com`). A sample window with the text from the demonstration file in Section 1.7 is shown in Figure 1.1. This program is available for a 30-day trial period, after which one must pay a nominal fee to obtain a license. It is the editor that we ourselves use and we can highly recommend it.

An alternative is L_YX, a free open source software for document processing that is almost WYSIWYG, acting as a front-end to LATEX, where the user need not know anything about LATEX. See its home page at `www.lyx.org`.

It must be stressed that all the above are *interfaces* to an existing LATEX installation. On the other hand, there are also commercial packages that include both the TEX/LATEX installation and a graphics interface. These are listed in Section B.1.1.

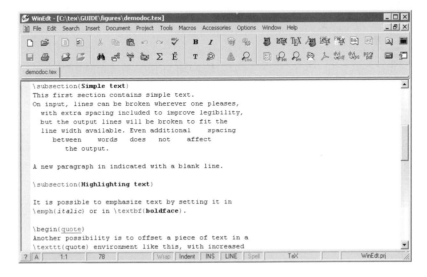

Figure 1.1: Sample display with the WinEdt editor for interfacing to LATEX

1.6.3   Alternative to TEX: pdfTEX

As we mentioned earlier, it is permissible to use the TEX source code to generate something else, as long as it bears another name. One such modification is called pdfTEX, created by Hàn Thế Thành. This program does everything TEX does, but it optionally writes its output directly to a PDF file, bypassing the DVI output of regular TEX. It therefore combines the TEX program with a DVI-to-PDF driver program. Normally this option is also the default.

There are many advantages to producing PDF output directly this way, apart from saving a step. The PDF file is generated in exactly the same way as the DVI file with TEX and can be viewed immediately with the Acrobat Reader or other PDF viewer. The results can be sent directly to a printer without going through the DVI-to-Printer program. It is also much easier to include the hypertext features of a true active PDF file, as we explain in Section 13.2.4.

Adding the LATEX macros to pdfTEX produces something one could call pdfLATEX. This distinction is only meaningful for invoking the program-plus-format to process the LATEX source file. Except for some things that we note in Section 13.2.3, LATEX commands are identical whether used with TEX or with pdfTEX. This makes the conversion extremely easy.

The rest of this book deals essentially with LATEX itself, regardless of what the end product is to be: paper, HTML, XML, or PDF.

1.7   Sample LATEX file

Here we present a more complicated sample LATEX file, which can be found on the TEX Live CD at books→Guide4→demodoc.tex. The annotations in the following source text give the section numbers where the various features are explained in detail. The resulting output is shown in Figure 1.2.

```
\documentclass[a4paper,12pt]{article}
\usepackage{palatino}
\usepackage{graphicx}
\usepackage{amsmath}
\usepackage[margin=1.5cm,
    vmargin={0pt,1cm},
    includefoot]{geometry}

\title{Demonstration Document}
\author{M. Y. Self\\
        At Home}
\date{February 1, 2004}

% End of preamble,
% the body now follows
```

Mandatory, document type and options (Sec. 3.1)

Loading extra features (Sec. 3.1.2):–
Use Palatino fonts (Sec. 13.1.2)
Enable graphics importation (Chap. 8)
Add extra math functions (Chap. 15)
Add page layout specs. (Sec. 3.2.6)

Enter texts for title block (Sec. 3.3.1). The author text contains name with affiliation on 2nd line.

Comment lines beginning with % are ignored in processing (Sec. 4.7).

Demonstration Document

M. Y. Self
At Home

February 1, 2004

1   Introduction

1.1   Simple text

This first section contains simple text. On input, lines can be broken wherever one pleases, with extra spacing included to improve legibility, but the output lines will be broken to fit the line width available. Even additional spacing between words does not affect the output.

A new paragraph in indicated with a blank line.

1.2   Highlighting text

It is possible to emphasize text by setting it in *italic* or in **boldface**.

> Another possibility is to offset a piece of text in a `quote` environment like this, with increased margins on either side.

2   Sophistications

2.1   Mathematics

There are special rules for entering math, and many commands that only exist in math mode. An in-line math formula like $x^2 + \beta$ has automatic spacing between variables and operators, while displayed equations like

$$\vec{A} \times (\vec{B} \times \vec{C}) = (\vec{A} \cdot \vec{C})\vec{B} - (\vec{A} \cdot \vec{B})\vec{C} \tag{1}$$

$$\vec{A} \cdot (\vec{B} \times \vec{C}) = \begin{vmatrix} A_x & A_y & A_y \\ B_x & B_y & B_y \\ C_x & C_y & C_y \end{vmatrix} \tag{2}$$

are given automatic numbers.

2.2   Lists

1. Various lists are possible, to enumerate,

2. to itemize with bullets,

3. or to make descriptive lists.

2.3   Adding graphics

Pictures and graphics ⛤ produced by other programs are easily inserted.

1

Figure 1.2: Output of the demonstration document

```
\begin{document}
```
→ Start of document body

```
\maketitle
```
→ Generates title block (Sec. 3.3.1)

```
\section{Introduction}
\subsection{Simple text}
```
→ Make section headings (Sec. 3.3.3)

```
This first section contains simple text.
On input, lines can be broken wherever one pleases,
  with extra spacing included to improve legibility,
  but the output lines will be broken to fit the
  line width available. Even additional    spacing
     between    words    does    not    affect
        the output.
```
→ Two paragraphs

```
A new paragraph in indicated with a blank line.
```

```
\subsection{Highlighting text}
```

```
It is possible to emphasize text by setting it in
\emph{italic} or in \textbf{boldface}.
```
→ Font styles (Sec. 4.1)

```
\begin{quote}
Another possibility is to offset a piece of text in a
\textttt{quote} environment like this, with increased
margins on either side.
\end{quote}
```
→ Two-sided indenting (Sec. 4.2.3)

```
\section{Sophistications}
```

```
\subsection{Mathematics}
```
→ Math mode, Chapters 7 and 15

```
There are special rules for entering math, and many
commands that only exist in math mode. An
in-line math formula like $x^2+\beta$
```
→ A $ sign toggles math
```
has automatic spacing between variables and
operators, while displayed equations like
```

```
\begin{equation}
```
→ Start displayed, numbered equation (Sec. 7.1)
```
  \vec{A} \times (\vec{B}\times\vec{C}) =
  (\vec{A}\cdot\vec{C})\vec{B} -
  (\vec{A}\cdot\vec{B})\vec{C}
\end{equation}
```
```
\begin{equation}
```
→ Start 2nd equation
```
  \vec{A}\cdot(\vec{B}\times\vec{C}) =
  \begin{vmatrix}
    A_x & A_y & A_y \\
    B_x & B_y & B_y \\
    C_x & C_y & C_y
  \end{vmatrix}
```
→ Matrix produced with $\mathcal{A}_{\mathcal{M}}\mathcal{S}$ extension (Sec. 15.2.4)

```
\end{equation}
are given automatic numbers.
```

```
\subsection{Lists}
```

```
\begin{enumerate}  ───────▶  Start numbered list (Sec. 4.3)
  \item Various lists are possible, to enumerate,
  \item to itemize with bullets,
  \item or to make descriptive lists.  ─▶  Items in list
\end{enumerate}
```

```
\subsection{Adding graphics}
```

```
Pictures and graphics  ──────▶  Insert graphics file (Sec. 8.1.3)
\includegraphics[width=1cm]{demo}
produced by other programs are easily inserted.
\end{document}  ───────▶  End of entire document
```

Write the above source text to a file named `demodoc.tex`, and process it with

```
latex demodoc
dvips demodoc
```

for DVI and PS output, or with

```
pdflatex demodoc
```

for PDF output. The results should look like that in Figure 1.2 (except for possible variations due to different versions of the `geometry` package).

Note: In order to fit the entire output on to a single page, it is necessary to decrease the margins considerably over the standard values. The package `geometry` has been loaded with selected values to do this. You may try removing these lines to see what the output would be like with the standard page layout. And if you are using American letter paper, replace the option `a4paper` with `letterpaper` to center the text properly.

2 Text, Symbols, and Commands

The text that is to be the input to a LaTeX processing run is written to a *source file* with a name ending in .tex, the file name extension. This file is prepared with a *text editor*, either one that handles straightforward plain text or one that is configured to assist the writing and processing of LaTeX files. In either case, the contents of this file are plain ASCII characters only, with no special symbols, no accented letters, preferably displayed in a fixed-width typewriter font, with no frills like bold or italics, all in one size. All these aspects of true typesetting are produced afterwards by the TeX processing program with the help of *markup* commands inserted visibly into the actual text. It is therefore vital to know how commands are distinguished from text that is to be printed and, of course, how they function.

(However, for languages other than English, native keyboard input may indeed be used, as shown in Section 2.5.9.)

2.1 Command names and arguments

A *command* is an instruction to LaTeX to do something special, such as print some symbol or text not available to the restricted character set used in the input file, or change the current typeface or other formatting properties. There are three types of command names:

- the single characters # \$ & ~ _ ^ % { } all have special meanings that are explained later in this chapter;

- the backslash character \ plus a single non-letter character; for example, \\$ to print the \$ sign; all the special characters listed above have a corresponding two-character command to print them literally;

- the backslash character \ plus a sequence of letters, ending with the first non-letter; for example, \large to switch to a larger typeface. Command names are case sensitive, so \large, \Large and \LARGE are distinct commands.

Many commands operate on some short piece of text, which then appears as an *argument* in curly braces following the command name. For example, \emph{stress} is given to print the word stress in an emphasized typeface (here italic) as *stress*. Such arguments are said to be *mandatory* because they must always be given.

Some commands take *optional* arguments, which are normally employed to modify the effects of the command somehow. The optional arguments appear in square brackets.

In this book we present the general syntax of commands as

name[*optional*]{*mandatory*}

where typewriter characters must be typed exactly as illustrated and italic text indicates something must be replaced. Optional arguments are put into square brackets [ ] and the mandatory ones into curly braces { }. A command may have several optional arguments, each one in its set of brackets in the specified sequence. If none of the optional arguments is used, the square brackets may be omitted. Any number of blanks, or even a single new line, may appear between the command name and the arguments to improve legibility.

Some commands have several mandatory arguments. Each one must be put into a { } pair and their sequence must be maintained as given in the command description. For example,

\rule[*lift*]{*width*}{*height*}

produces a black rectangle of size *width* and *height*, raised by an amount *lift* above the current baseline. A rectangle of width 10 mm and height 3 mm is made with \rule{10mm}{3mm}. Since the optional argument *lift* is omitted, the rectangle is set on the baseline with no lifting, as ▮▮▮▮. The arguments must appear in the order specified by the syntax and may not be interchanged.

Some commands have a so-called *-form in addition to their normal appearance. A * is added to their name to modify their functionality somehow. For example, the \section command has a *-form \section* which, unlike the regular form, does not print an automatic section number. For each such command, the difference between the normal and *-form will be explained in the description of the individual commands.

Command names consist only of letters, with the first non-letter indicating the end of the name. If there are optional or mandatory arguments following the command name, then it ends before the [or { bracket, since these characters are not letters. Many commands, however, possess no arguments and are composed of only a name, such as the command \LaTeX to produce the LaTeX logo. If such a command is followed by a punctuation mark, such as comma or period, it is obvious where the command name ends. *However, any blanks following the command name will also terminate it, but are then swallowed up:* The \LaTeX logo results in 'The LaTeXlogo', that is, the blank was seen only as the end of the command and not as spacing between two words. This is a result of the special rules for blanks, described in Section 2.5.1.

To insert a space after a command that consists only of a name, either an empty structure {} or a space command (\ and blank) must be placed after the command. The proper way to produce 'The LaTeX logo' is to type either The \LaTeX{} logo or

The \LaTeX\ logo. Alternatively, the command itself may be put into curly braces, as The {\TeX} logo, which also yields the right output with the inserted blank: 'The TeX logo'. Incidentally, the LaTeX 2ε logo is produced with \LaTeXe. Can you see why this logo command cannot be named \LaTeX2e?

2.2 Environments

An *environment* is initiated with the command \begin{*name*} and is terminated by \end{*name*}.

An environment affects the text within it by treating it differently according to the environment parameters. It is possible to alter (temporarily) certain processing features, such as indentation, line width, typeface, and much more. The changes apply only within the environment. For example, with the quote environment

> *previous text*
> \begin{quote}
> *text1* \small *text2* \bfseries *text3*
> \end{quote}
> *following text*

the left and right margins are increased relative to those of the previous and following texts. In the example, this applies to the three texts *text1*, *text2*, and *text3*. After *text1* comes the command \small, which has the effect of setting the next text in a smaller typeface. After *text2*, there is an additional command \bfseries to switch to boldface type. Both commands only remain in effect up to the \end{quote}.

> The three texts within the quote environment are indented on both sides relative to the previous and following texts. The *text1* appears in the normal typeface, the same one as outside the environment. The *text2* and *text3* appear in a smaller typeface, and *text3*, **furthermore, appears in boldface.**

After the end of the quote environment, the subsequent text appears in the same typeface that was in effect beforehand.

Note that if the names of the environment in the \begin{..} \end{..} pair do not match, an error message will be issued on processing.

Most declaration command names (see next section) may also be used as environment names. In this case the command name is used *without* the preceding \ character. For example, the command \em switches to an emphatic typeface, usually *italic*, and the corresponding environment \begin{em} will set all the text in *italic* until \end{em} is reached.

A nameless environment can be simulated by a {...} pair. The effect of any command within it ends with the closing curly brace.

You can even create your own environments, as described in Section 10.4.

2.3   Declarations

A *declaration* is a command that changes the values or meanings of certain parameters or commands without printing any text. The effect of the declaration begins immediately and ends when another declaration of the same type is encountered. However, if the declaration occurs within an environment or a {...} pair, its scope extends only to the corresponding \end command or to the closing brace }. The commands \bfseries and \small mentioned in the previous section are examples of such nonprinting declarations that alter the current typeface.

Some declarations have associated arguments, such as the command \setlength, which assigns a value to a *length parameter* (see Sections 2.4 and 10.2).

Examples:

{\bfseries This text appears in boldface}   The \bfseries declaration changes the typeface: **This text appears in boldface**. The effect of this declaration ends with the closing brace }.

\setlength{\parindent}{0.5cm} The paragraph indentation is set to 0.5 cm. The effect of this declaration ends with the next encounter of the command \setlength{\parindent} or at the latest with the \end command that terminates the current environment.

\pagenumbering{roman} The page numbering is to be printed in Roman numerals.

Some declarations, such as the last example, are global; that is, their effects are not limited to the current environment. The following declarations are of this nature, the meanings of which are given later:

\newcounter	\pagenumbering	\newlength
\setcounter	\thispagestyle	\newsavebox
\addtocounter		

Declarations made with these commands are effective right away and remain so until they are overridden by a new declaration of the same type. In the last example above, page numbering will be done in Roman numerals until countermanded by a new \pagenumbering{arabic} command.

2.4   Lengths

2.4.1   Fixed lengths

Lengths consist of a decimal number with a possible sign in front (+ or -) followed by a mandatory dimensional unit. Permissible units and their abbreviated names are:

cm   centimeter
mm   millimeter
in   inch (1 in = 2.54 cm)
pt   point (1 in = 72.27 pt)
bp   big point (1 in = 72 bp)
pc   pica (1 pc = 12 pt)
dd   didôt point (1157 dd = 1238 pt)
cc   cicero (1 cc = 12 dd)
em   a font-specific size, the width of the capital M
ex   another font-related size, the height of the letter x

Decimal numbers in TeX and LaTeX may be written in either the English or European manner, with a *period* or a *comma:* both 12.5cm and 12,5cm are permitted.

Note that 0 is not a legitimate length since the unit specification is missing. To give a zero length it is necessary to add some unit, such as 0pt or 0cm.

Values are assigned to a length parameter by means of the LaTeX command \setlength, which is described in Section 10.2 along with other commands for dealing with lengths. Its syntax is:

\setlength{*length_name*}{*length_spec*}

For example, the width of a line of text is specified by the parameter \textwidth, which is normally set to a default value depending on the class, paper type, and font size. To change the line width to be 12.5 cm, one would give:

\setlength{\textwidth}{12.5cm}

2.4.2   Rubber lengths

Some parameters expect a *rubber* length. These are lengths that can be stretched or shrunk by a certain amount. The syntax for a rubber length is:

nominal_value   plus *stretch_value*   minus *shrink_value*

where the *nominal_value, stretch_value,* and *shrink_value* are each a length. For example,

\setlength{\parskip}{1ex plus0.5ex minus0.2ex}

means that the extra line spacing between paragraphs, called \parskip, is to be the height of the *x* in the current font, but it may be increased to 1.5 or reduced to 0.8 times that size.

One special *rubber* length is \fill. This has the natural length of *zero* but can be stretched to any size.

2.5   Special characters

2.5.1   Spaces

The *space* or *blank* character has some properties that are different from those of normal characters, some of which have already been mentioned in Section 2.1. During processing, blanks in the input text are replaced by rubber lengths (Section 2.4.2) to allow the line to fill up to the full line width. As a result, some peculiar effects can occur if one is not aware of the following rules:

- One blank is the same as a thousand, only the first one counts.

- Blanks at the beginning of an input line are ignored.

- Blanks terminating a command name are removed.

- The end of a line is treated as a blank.

Some of the consequences of these rules are that there may be as many blanks as desired between words or at the beginning of a line (to make the input text more legible) and that a word may come right at the end of a line without the spacing between it and the next word disappearing. To force a space to appear where it would otherwise be ignored, one must give the command \␣ (a \ followed by a space character, made visible here by the symbol ␣).

To ensure that certain words remain together on the same line, a *protected space* is inserted between them with the ˜ character (Section 2.7.1, page 32). Multiple protected spaces are all printed, in contrast to normal spaces.

Sometimes it is necessary to suppress the space that appears because of the new line. In this case, the last character in the line must be the *comment* character % (Section 4.7).

Paragraphs are separated in the source text by blank lines. As for blank characters, one blank line is the same as a thousand. Instead of a blank line, the command \par may also be used to indicate the end of a paragraph.

2.5.2   Quotation marks

The *quotation marks* found on the typewriter, ", are not used in book printing. Instead, different characters are used at the beginning and end, such as 'single quotes' and "double quotes". Single quotes are produced with ' and ', while double quotes are made by typing the respective characters twice: '' for " and '' for ". Furthermore, the typewriter character " will also generate the double closing quote ". However, it should be avoided since it can lead to confusion.

2.5.3   Hyphens and dashes

In book printing, the character that appears on the typewriter as - comes in various lengths: -, –, —. The smallest of these, the *hyphen*, is used for compound words such as *father-in-law* and for word division at the end of a line. The middle-sized one, the *en dash*, is used in ranges of numbers, for example, pages 33–36. And the largest one, the *em dash*, is used as punctuation—what is normally called the *dash*. These are generated by typing the hyphen character one, two, or three times, so that - yields -, while -- makes –, and --- produces —. A fourth type of dash is the minus sign −, which is entered in math mode as $-$ (Chapter 7).

2.5.4 Printing command characters

As mentioned in Section 2.1, the characters # $ & _ % { } are interpreted as commands. To print them as text, one must give a command consisting of \ plus that character.

= \# $ = \$ & = \&   _ = _   % = \%   { = \{   } = \}

2.5.5 The special characters §, †, ‡, ¶, ©, and £

These special characters do not exist on the computer keyboard. They can, however, be generated by special commands as follows:

§ = \S   † = \dag   ‡ = \ddag   ¶ = \P   © = \copyright   £ = \pounds

The production of Greek letters and other mathematical symbols is described in Chapter 7.

2.5.6 Non-English letters

Special letters that exist in languages other than English can also be generated with TEX. These are:

œ={\oe}   Œ={\OE}   æ={\ae}   Æ={\AE}   å={\aa}   Å ={\AA}   ¡=!`
ø ={\o}   Ø ={\O}   ł ={\l}   Ł ={\L}   ß={\ss}   SS={\SS}   ¿=?`

Ångstrøm may be written as {\AA}ngstr{\o}m while *Karlstraße* can be input as Karlstra{\ss}e. The 'letter' \SS is the uppercase equivalent of \ss, used for automatic conversion between upper- and lowercase.

However, see Section 2.5.9 for the possibility of entering such characters directly.

2.5.7 Accents

In non-English languages, there is a multiplicity of *diacritical marks* or *accents*, most of which can be printed with TEX:

ò =\'{o}   ó=\'{o}   ô=\^{o}   ö=\"{o}   õ=\~{o}
ō =\={o}   ȯ=\.{o}   ŏ=\u{o}   ǒ=\v{o}   ő=\H{o}
ôo=\t{oo}   ǫ=\c{o}   ọ=\d{o}   o̲=\b{o}   o̊=\r{o}

The *o* above is given merely as an example: any letter may be used. With *i* and *j* it should be pointed out that the dot must first be removed. This is carried out by prefixing these letters with a backslash: the commands \i and \j yield ı and ȷ. In this way ĭ and ĵ are formed by typing \u{\i} and \H{\j}.

The accent commands consisting of a non-letter may also be given without the curly braces:

$$\grave{o}=\verb|\'o| \quad \acute{o}=\verb|\'o| \quad \hat{o}=\verb|\^o| \quad \ddot{o}=\verb|\"o| \quad \tilde{o}=\verb|\~o| \quad \bar{o}=\verb|\=o| \quad \dot{o}=\verb|\.o|$$

The letter accent commands should always be used with the curly braces.

2.5.8   The euro symbol

The euro symbol € (or €) is too new to be part of the original LaTeX, but it can be produced with the help of some additional fonts and contributed packages. Just which package you may use depends on your installation and whether you have access to these additional fonts.

Package: textcomp   The *Text Companion* fonts, described in Section A.3.2, do contain a euro symbol. Since these fonts should be part of every modern LaTeX installation, you should be able to use their euro symbol if all else fails.

The package textcomp must be loaded in the preamble with

```
\usepackage{textcomp}
```

which defines many commands including \texteuro to print the symbol €. Since the European Commission originally dictated that it should only be printed in a sans serif font, it is better to issue \textsf{\texteuro} to produce €. (The font selection commands are described in Section 4.1.4.) If you are going to use this very frequently, you might want to define a shortcut named \euro with

```
\newcommand{\euro}{\textsf{\texteuro}}
```

as described in Section 10.3 on defining commands.

Package: eurosym   A better solution is presented by the eurosym package by Henrik Theiling and the associated fonts that come with it, which bear the names feymr10, feybr10, and so on. This package defines the \euro command to print €, which changes automatically to bold € and slanted € as needed.

Package: europs   The europs package by Joern Clausen interfaces to the type 1 (PostScript) euro fonts published by Adobe. For licensing reasons, these fonts may only be obtained from Adobe directly, though free of charge (see Section B.2). This package provides the command \EUR for a symbol that varies with font family (Roman €25, sans serif €25, and typewriter €25) as well as for bold €25 and slanted *€25*. There is also a command \EURofc for the invariable symbol €.

Package: eurosans   Finally, the package eurosans by Walter Schmidt also addresses the Adobe euro fonts, again with the command \euro, with the same behavior as that of eurosym: always the sans serif family, but it changes with the other font attributes.

The following table summarizes the above packages:

Package	Command	Fonts	Notes
textcomp	\texteuro	Text Companion	Nonstandard symbol
eurosym	\euro	Eurosym	Sans serif, variable
europs	\EUR	PostScript	Varies with font family
	\EURofc		Invariable, official
eurosans	\euro	PostScript	Sans serif, variable

So which package should one use? That really depends on the fonts available. Since the Adobe fonts can never be distributed with a TeX installation, they must be actively fetched and installed. However, it is worth doing so, because the European Commission has revised its initial directive and now allows the euro symbol to be typographically matched to the text, which is also standard practice in Europe today. This strengthens the case for the europs package and the \EUR command for €, at least for Roman fonts.

2.5.9 Typing special symbols directly

!

The commands for producing the special characters and accented letters in the previous sections may be suitable for typing isolated 'foreign' words, but become quite tedious for inputting large amounts of text making regular use of such characters. Most computer systems provide non-English keyboards with appropriate fonts for typing these national variants directly. Unfortunately, the coding of such extra symbols is by no means standard, depending very much on the computer system.

For example, the text Gauß meets Ampère entered with an MS-DOS editor (using IBM code page 437 or 850) appears in a Windows application as Gauá meets AmpŠre and on a Macintosh as Gau· meets Ampäre. Since LaTeX is intended to run on all systems, it simply ignores all such extra character codes on the grounds that they are not properly defined.

Package: The inputenc package solves this problem. It not only informs LaTeX which input coding
inputenc scheme is being used, it also tells it what to do with the extra characters. One invokes it with

\usepackage[*code*]{inputenc}

where *code* is the name of the coding scheme to be used. The current list of allowed values for *code* (more are added with each LaTeX update) can be found in Table D.1 on page 443. For most users, the most interesting codes are:

cp437   IBM code page 437 (DOS, North America)
cp850   IBM code page 850 (DOS, Western Europe)
applemac Macintosh encoding
ansinew   Windows ANSI encoding

In short, you should select applemac for a Macintosh, and ansinew for Windows, and one of the others if you are working with DOS.

Documents making use of this package are fully portable to other computer systems. The source text produced with a DOS editor may still look very strange to a human user reading it on a Macintosh, but when the Macintosh LaTeX processes it, the proper DOS interpretations will be applied so that the end result is what the author intended.

See Section D.4 for more details.

2.5.10 Ligatures

In book printing, certain combinations of letters are not printed as individuals but as a single symbol, called a *ligature*. TeX processes the letter combinations `ff`, `fi`, `fl`, `ffi`, and `ffl` not as

ff, fi, fl, ffi, ffl   but rather as   ff, fi, fl, ffi, ffl

Ligatures may be broken, that is, forced to be printed as separate letters, by inserting `\/` between the letters. This is sometimes desired for such words as *shelfful* (`shelf\/ful`), which looks rather strange when printed with the normal *ff* ligature, *shelfful*.

2.5.11 The date

The current date can be placed at any point in the text with the command `\today`. The standard form for the date is the American style of month, day, year (for example, July 15, 2003). The British form (15th July 2003) or the date in other languages can be generated with the help of the TeX commands `\day`, `\month`, and `\year`, which return the current values of these parameters as numbers. Examples of how such a new `\today` command may be made are shown on page 442 in Section D.3.2.

Package: *babel*   A more convenient way to do this is with the `babel` system for multilingual LaTeX (Chapter 14), which automatically redefines `\today` for the current language or dialect. The British form is activated for the 'languages' `english`, `UKenglish`, and `canadian`, while the American style appears with the selections `american` and `USenglish`.

It is indeed better to enter the date explicitly, rather than to rely on `\today`. Reprocessing a two-year-old LaTeX source file will yield a document with the current date, not the date when the text was written.

2.6   Exercises

Solutions to all the exercises in this book can be found on the enclosed TeX Live CD in `books→Guide4→exercises`.

Exercise 2.1: This exercise tests the basic operations of running the LaTeX program with a short piece of text. A few simple commands are also included. Use a text editor to produce the following source text and store it in a file named exer.tex.

```
\documentclass{article}
\begin{document}
Today (\today) the rate of exchange between the British
pound and American dollar is \pounds 1 = \$1.71, an
increase of 1\% over yesterday.
\end{document}
```

Process this source file with LATEX by clicking the appropriate icon, or by issuing `latex exer` *in a command window. If the processing occurs without any error messages, the* `.dvi` *file* `exer.dvi` *will have been successfully created and may be viewed by a dvi previewer or sent to a printer. The final printed result should look as follows except that your current date will appear:*

Today (July 15, 2003) the rate of exchange between the British pound and American dollar is £1 = $1.71, an increase of 1% over yesterday.

Note the following points about the commands used:

- *No blank is necessary after* \today *because the)* suffices to terminate it.
- *The blank after* \pounds *is optional, and it is not printed in the output.*
- *The commands* \$ *and* \% *do not require blanks to terminate them; if blanks are given, they will be printed.*

Exercise 2.2: *Take some text of about 3/4 of a page long out of a book or journal article and type it into a LATEX source file. Pay attention that the paragraphs are separated by blank lines. Use the same set of commands as in Exercise 2.1; that is, put the text between the commands* \begin{document}...\end{document} *and repeat the procedures for obtaining the output.*

Exercise 2.3: *If you are likely to need the euro symbol in your work, try redoing Exercise 2.1 as follows:*

```
\documentclass{article}
\usepackage{eurosym}
\begin{document}
Today (\today) the rate of exchange between the British
pound and European euro is \pounds 1 = \euro1.44, an
increase of 1\% over yesterday.
\end{document}
```

If this fails, try using one of the other packages described in Section 2.5.8, substituting \textsf{\texteuro} *or* \EUR *for* \euro *as required.*

2.7 Fine-tuning text

The subject of this section concerns pure typographical markup and has nothing to do with the logical markup that we wish to stress in this book. Unfortunately, there are times when the author or editor does have to help the typesetting program to achieve good appearance.

2.7.1 Word and character spacing

The spacing between words and characters is normally set automatically by TEX, which not only makes use of the natural width of the characters but also takes into account alterations for certain character combinations. For example, an A followed by a V does not appear as AV but rather as AV; that is, they are moved together slightly for a more pleasing appearance. Interword spacing within one line is uniform and is chosen so that the right and left ends match exactly with the side margins. This is called left and right *justification*. TEX also attempts to keep the word spacing for different lines as nearly the same as possible.

TEX adheres to traditional typesetting rules according to which there should be extra spacing between sentences. Words that end with a punctuation mark are given extra spacing depending on the character: Following a period '.' or exclamation mark '!', there is more space than after a comma ','. In certain cases, the automatic procedures do not work properly, or it is desirable to override them, as described in the next sections. (Except in this paragraph and the next section, this book inserts no extra spacing between sentences.)

Sentence termination and periods

TEX interprets a period following a lowercase letter to be the end of a sentence where additional interword spacing is to be inserted. This leads to confusion with abbreviations such as *i. e., Prof. Jones*, or *Phys. Rev.*, where the normal spacing is required. This can be achieved by using the characters ˜ or \␣ instead of the normal blank. (The character ␣ is simply a symbol for the blank that is otherwise invisible.) Both these methods insert the normal interword spacing; in addition, ˜ is a *protected space* that prevents the line from being broken at this point. The above examples should be typed in as i.˜e., Prof.˜Jones, and Phys.\ Rev., producing *i. e., Prof. Jones*, and *Phys. Rev.* with the correct spacing and forcing the first two to be all on one line. In the third case, there is nothing wrong with putting *Phys.* and *Rev.* on different lines.

A period following an uppercase letter is not interpreted as the end of a sentence, but as an abbreviation. If it really is the end of a sentence, then it is necessary to add \@ before the period in order to achieve the extra spacing. For example, this sentence ends with NASA. It is typed in as This sentence ends with NASA\@.

French spacing

The additional interword spacing between sentences can be switched off with the command \frenchspacing, which remains in effect until countermanded with \nonfrenchspacing. In this case, the command \@ is ignored and may be omitted. This paragraph has been printed with \frenchspacing turned on so that all word spacings within one line are the same. It corresponds to the general usage in contemporary typesetting.

Character combinations "' and '"

A small spacing is produced with the command \,. This may be used, for example, to separate the double quotes " and " from the corresponding single quotes ' and ' when they appear together. For example, the text ''\,'Beginning' and 'End'\,'' produces "'Beginning' and 'End'".

Inserting arbitrary spacing

Spacing of any desired size may be inserted into the text with the commands

    \hspace{*space*}
    \hspace*{*space*}

where *space* is the length specification for the amount of spacing, for example, 1.5cm or 3em. (Recall that one *em* is the width of the letter M in the current typeface.)

    This command puts blank space of width *space* at that point in the text where it appears. The standard form (without *) has no effect if it should come at the beginning of an output line, just as normal blanks are removed at the beginning of lines. The *-form, on the other hand, inserts the spacing no matter where it occurs.

    A blank before or after the command will also be included:

`This is\hspace{1cm}1cm`	This is	1cm
`This is \hspace{1cm}1cm`	This is	1cm
`This is \hspace{1cm} 1cm`	This is	1cm

    The length specification may be negative, in which case the command works as a backspace for overprinting characters with other ones or moving them closer together. For example, there is an energy unit in physics called *electron volt*, abbreviated 'eV', which looks much better if the two letters are nearer together, as 'eV', with `e\hspace{-.12ex}V`.

    The command `\hfill` is an abbreviation for `\hspace{\fill}` (see Section 2.4.2). It inserts enough space at that point to force the text on either side to be pushed over to the left and right margins. With `Left\hfill Right` one produces

Left   Right

    Multiple occurrences of `\hfill` within one line will each insert the same amount of spacing so that the line becomes left and right justified. For example, the text `Left\hfill Center\hfill Right` generates

Left   Center   Right

    If `\hfill` comes at the beginning of a line, the spacing is suppressed in accordance with the behavior of the standard form for `\hspace`. If a rubber space is really to be added at the beginning or end of a line, `\hspace*{\fill}` must be used instead. However, LaTeX also offers a number of commands and environments to simplify most such applications (see Section 4.2.2).

    A number of other fixed horizontal spacing commands are available:

    \quad   and   \qquad

The command `\quad` inserts a horizontal space equal to the current type size, that is, 10 pt for a 10 pt typeface, whereas `\qquad` inserts twice as much.

Inserting variable ...... and ＿＿ sequences

Two commands that work exactly the same way as `\hfill` are

    `\dotfill` and `\hrulefill`

Instead of inserting empty space, these commands fill the gap with dots or a ruled line, as follows:

```
Start \dotfill\ Finish\\                              and
Left \hrulefill\ Center \hrulefill\ Right\\  produce
```

Start .... Finish
Left _____ Center _____ Right

Any combination of `\hfill`, `\dotfill`, and `\hrulefill` may be given on one line. If any of these commands appears more than once at one location, the corresponding filling will be printed that many more times than for a single occurrence.

```
Departure \dotfill\dotfill\dotfill\ 8:30 \hfill\hfill
Arrival \hrulefill\ 11:45\\
```

Departure .... 8:30   Arrival _____ 11:45

2.7.2   Line breaking

Breaking text into lines is done automatically in TeX and LaTeX. However, there are times when a line break must be forced or encouraged, or when a line break is to be suppressed.

The command \\

A new line with or without additional line spacing can be achieved with the command `\\`. Its syntax is

    `\\[`*space*`]`
    `\\*[`*space*`]`

The optional argument *space* is a length that specifies how much additional line spacing is to be put between the lines. If it is necessary to start a new page, the additional line spacing is not included and the new page begins with the next line of text. The *-form prevents a new page from occurring between the two lines.

With `\\*[10cm]`, the current line is ended and a vertical spacing of 10 cm is inserted before the next line, which is forced to be on the same page as the current line. If a page break is necessary, it will be made before the current line, which is then positioned at the top of the new page together with the 10 cm vertical spacing and the next text line.

The command `\newline` is identical to `\\` without the option *space*. That is, a new line is started with no additional spacing and a page break is possible at that point.

Both commands may be given only within a paragraph, and not between them where they would be meaningless.

Further line-breaking commands

The command \linebreak is used to encourage or force a line break at a certain point in the text. Its form is

\linebreak[*num*]

where *num* is an optional argument, a number between 0 and 4 that specifies how important a line break is. The command recommends a line break, and the higher the number the stronger the recommendation. A value of 0 allows a break where it otherwise would not occur (such as in the middle of a word), whereas 4 compels a line break, as does \linebreak without *num*. The difference between this command and \\ or \newline is that the current line will be fully justified; that is, interword spacing will be added so that the text fills the line completely. With \\ and \newline, however, the line is filled with empty space after the last word and the interword spacing remains normal.

The opposite command

\nolinebreak[*num*]

discourages a line break at the given position, with *num* specifying the degree of discouragement. Again, \nolinebreak without a *num* argument has the same effect as \nolinebreak[4]; that is, a line break is absolutely impossible here.

Another way of forcing text to stay together on one line is with the command \mbox{*text*}. This is convenient for expressions such as 'Voyager-1' to stop a line break at the hyphen.

2.7.3 Vertical spacing

It is possible to add extra vertical spacing of amount *space* between particular paragraphs using the commands

\vspace{*space*}
\vspace*{*space*}

The *-form will add the extra space even when a new page occurs or when the command appears at the top of a new page. The standard form ignores the extra vertical spacing in these situations.

If these commands are given within a paragraph, the extra space is inserted after the current line, which is right and left justified as usual.

The *space* parameter may even be negative in order to move the following text higher up on the page than where it would normally be printed.

The command \vfill is an abbreviation for \vspace{\fill} (see Section 2.4.2). This is the equivalent of \hfill for vertical spacing, inserting enough blank vertical space to make the top and bottom of the text match up exactly with the upper and lower margins. The comments on multiple occurrences of \hfill also apply to \vfill. If this command is given at the beginning of a page, it is ignored, just like the standard form of \vspace{\fill}. If a rubber space is to be put at the top of a page, the *-form \vspace*{\fill} must be used.

Further commands for increasing the spacing between paragraphs are

\bigskip   \medskip   \smallskip

which add vertical spacing depending on the font size declared in the document class.

2.7.4   Page breaking

Breaking text into pages occurs automatically in TeX and LaTeX, just as for line breaking. Here again, it may be necessary to interfere with the program's notion of where a break should take place.

Normal pages

The commands

\pagebreak[*num*]
\nopagebreak[*num*]

are the equivalents of \linebreak and \nolinebreak for page breaking. If the command \pagebreak appears between two paragraphs, a new page will be forced at that point. If it comes within a paragraph, the new page will be implemented after the current line is completed. This line will be right and left justified as usual.

The command \nopagebreak has the opposite effect: Between paragraphs it prevents a page break from occurring there, and within a paragraph it stops a page break that might take place at the end of the current line.

Optional numbers between 0 and 4 express the degree of encouragement or discouragement for a page break. The analogy with the command \linebreak goes further: Just as the line before the break is left and right justified with extra interword spacing, the page before the break is expanded with interline spacing to make it top and bottom justified.

The proper command to end a page in the middle, fill it with blank spacing, and go on to a new page is

\newpage

which is equivalent to \newline with regard to page breaking.

Pages with figures and tables

If the text contains tables, pictures, or reserved space for figures, these are inserted at the location of the corresponding command provided that there is enough room for them on the current page. If there is not enough space, the text continues and the figure or table is stored to be put on a following page.

The command

`\clearpage`

ends the current page like `\newpage` and, in addition, outputs all the pending figures and tables on one or more extra pages (Chapter 9).

Two-column pages

If the document class option `twocolumn` has been selected, or the command `\twocolumn` has been issued, then the two commands `\pagebreak` and `\newpage` end the current *column* and begin a new one, treating columns as pages. On the other hand, `\clearpage` and `\cleardoublepage` (see below) terminate the current page, inserting an empty right column if necessary.

Two-sided pages

An additional page-breaking command is available when the document class option `twoside` has been selected:

`\cleardoublepage`

It functions exactly the same as `\clearpage` (the current page is terminated, all pending figures and tables are output) but, in addition, the next text will be put onto an *odd*-numbered page. If necessary, an empty page with an even number is printed to achieve this.

Controlling page breaks

LaTeX provides the possibility of increasing the height of the current page slightly with commands

`\enlargethispage{`*size*`}`
`\enlargethispage*{`*size*`}`

which add the length *size* to `\textheight` for this one page only. Sometimes the difference of a few points is all that is necessary to avoid a bad page break. The *-form of the command also shrinks any interline spacing as needed to maximize the amount of text on the page.

2.8   Word division

When a line is to be right and left justified, it often happens that the break cannot be made between whole words without either shoving the text too close together or inserting huge gaps between the words. It is then necessary to split a word. This fundamental task is performed by TeX, the underlying basis of LaTeX, by means of a word-dividing algorithm that works (almost) perfectly for English text, which is more than can be said for most authors. Nevertheless, even it makes mistakes at times, which need to be corrected by human intervention.

If normal TeX/LaTeX is used for other languages, or if foreign words appear in English text, incorrect hyphenations are very likely to appear. (See Section 2.8.4 and Chapter 14 for more about LaTeX with other languages.) In these cases too, something must be done to override TeX's hyphenation rules, as described below.

2.8.1   Manual hyphenation

The simplest way to correct a wrongly divided word is to include a \- command at the right place within the word. The word *manuscript*, for example, will not be hyphenated at all, so if it causes problems with breaking a line, write it as man\-u\-script. This tells TeX to divide the word as necessary either as *man-uscript* or as *manu-script*, and to ignore its normal rules.

The \- command merely makes hyphenation possible at the indicated locations; it does not force it. If the author absolutely insists on dividing a word at a certain point, say between the *u* and *s* in *manuscript*, he or she can type manu-\linebreak script to achieve this. However, this brute-force method is not recommended, because the line break will always occur here even if the text is later changed.

For English text, the spelling of a word remains the same when it is hyphenated, something that is not true in other languages. In traditional German spelling, for example, if *ck* is split, it becomes *k-k*. TeX allows such behavior with the general hyphenation command

```
\discretionary{before}{after}{without}
```

where *before* and *after* are the letters (with hyphen) that come on either side of the break if division takes place, and *without* is the normal text with no hyphenation. Thus Boris Becker's name should be typed as

```
Boris Be\discretionary{k-}{k}{ck}er
```

something that one only wants to do in exceptional situations. Incidentally, the \- command is shorthand for \discretionary{-}{}{}.

Note: In today's new German spelling, *ck* is never split. This reformed spelling is still controversial, however.

2.8.2   Hyphenation list

Words that are incorrectly hyphenated and that appear frequently within the document can be put into a *list of exceptions* in the preamble, to avoid laboriously inserting \- every time:

```
\hyphenation{list}
```

The *list* consists of a set of words, separated by blanks or new lines, with the allowed division points indicated by hyphens. For example,

```
\hyphenation{man-u-script com-pu-ter gym-na-sium
             coun-try-man re-sus-ci-tate ... }
```

The list may contain only words with the normal letters *a–z*, with no special characters or accents. However, if the `inputenc` package is loaded, then the directly typed letters are also included in the automatic hyphenation.

2.8.3   Suppressing hyphenation

Another means of avoiding bad word divisions is to turn hyphenation off, at least for a paragraph or two. Actually, the environment

> `\begin{sloppypar}` *paragraph text* `\end{sloppypar}`

does not prevent word division, but it does permit larger interword spacings without giving a warning message. This means that practically all lines are broken between words. It is also possible to put the command `\sloppy` in the preamble or in the current environment to reduce the number of word divisions in the whole document or within the environment scope. This is recommended when the line width is rather narrow.

When the command `\sloppy` is in effect, it is possible to undo it temporarily and to turn hyphenation back on with the command `\fussy`.

2.8.4   Word division with multilingual text

!

Multiple hyphenation lists may be included in the TEX format, making it possible to switch hyphenation schemes within one document, using the TEX command `\language`. This command may be used as part of language-specific adaptations to translate certain explicit English words in the output (such as 'Contents'), to simplify accents or punctuation, and to alter the definition of the date command `\today`. This topic is treated in more detail in Chapter 14.

3 Document Layout and Organization

3.1 Document class

The first command in the preamble of a LaTeX file determines the global processing format for the entire document. Its syntax is:

    \documentclass[*options*]{*class*}

where some value of *class* must be given, while [*options*] may be omitted if default values are acceptable.

Class:
article
report
book

The standard values of *class*, of which one and only one may be given, are book, report, article, or letter. (The properties of the letter class are explained in Chapter 18.) The basic differences between these classes lie not only in the page layouts, but also in the organization. An article may contain *parts*, *sections*, *subsections*, and so on, while a report can also have *chapters*. A book also has chapters, but treats even and odd pages differently; also, it prints running heads on each page with the chapter and section titles.

Other classes besides the standard ones exist, as contributions for specific journals or for book projects. These will have their own set of *options* and additional commands, which should be described in separate documentation or instructions. However, since they are normally modifications of one of the standard classes, most of the following options apply to them too.

3.1.1 Standard class options

The *options* available allow various modifications to be made to the formatting. They can be grouped as follows.

Selecting font size

The basic font size is selected with one of the options

    10pt   11pt   12pt

This is the size of the font in which the normal text in the document will be set. The default is 10pt, which means that this is the value assumed if no size option is specified. All other font-size declarations are relative to this standard size so that the section titles, footnotes, and so on will all change size automatically if a different basic font size is selected.

Specifying paper size

LaTeX calculates the text line width and lines per page according to the selected font size and paper mode. It also sets the margins so that the text is centered both horizontally and vertically. To do this, it needs to know which paper format is being used. This is specified by one of the following options:

letterpaper (11×8.5 in)	a4paper (29.7×21 cm)
legalpaper (14×8.5 in)	a5paper (21×14.8 cm)
executivepaper (10.5×7.25 in)	b5paper (25×17.6 cm)

The default is letterpaper, American letter-size paper, 11×8.5 in.

Normally, the paper format is such that the longer dimension is the vertical one, the so-called *portrait* mode. With the option

landscape

the shorter dimension becomes the vertical one, the *landscape* mode. (One still has to ensure that the output is printed as landscape; see, for example, page 242.)

Page formats

The text on the page may be formatted into one or two columns with the options

onecolumn   twocolumn

The default is onecolumn. In the case of the twocolumn option, the separation between the columns as well as the width of any rule between them may be specified by \columnsep and \columnseprule, described below.

The even- and odd-numbered pages may be printed differently according to the options

oneside   twoside

With oneside, all pages are printed the same; however, with twoside, the running heads are such that the page number appears on the right on odd pages and on the left on even pages. *It does not force the printer to output double-sided.* The idea is that when these are later printed back to back, the page numbers are always on the outside where they are more easily noticed. This is the default for the book class. For article and report, the default is oneside.

With the book class, chapters normally start on a right-hand, odd-numbered page. The options openright openany

control this feature: With openany, a chapter always starts on the next page, but with openright, the default, a blank page may be inserted if necessary.

Normally the title of a book or report will go on a separate page, while for an article it is placed on the same page as the first text. With the options

notitlepage titlepage

this standard behavior may be overruled. See Sections 3.3.1 and 3.3.2.

Further options

The remaining standard options are:

leqno   Equation numbers in displayed formulas will appear on the left instead of the normal right side (Section 7.1).

fleqn   Displayed formulas will be set flush left instead of centered (Section 7.1). The amount of indentation may be set with the parameter \mathindent described below.

openbib
    The format of bibliographies may be changed so that segments are set on new lines. By default, the texts for each entry are run together.

draft   If the LaTeX line-breaking mechanism does not function properly and text must stick out into the right margin, then this is marked with a thick black bar to make it noticeable.

final   The opposite of draft and the default. Lines of text that are too wide are not marked in any way.

If multiple options are to be given, they are separated by commas, as for example, \documentclass[11pt,twoside,fleqn]{article}. The order of the options is unimportant. If two conflicting options are specified, say oneside and twoside, it is not obvious which one will be effective. That depends entirely on the definitions in the class file itself, so it would be best to avoid such situations.

Parameters associated with some options

Some options make use of parameters that have been given certain default values:

\mathindent
    specifies the indentation from the left margin for the equation numbers when fleqn is selected (Section 7.1);

\columnsep
    specifies the space between the two columns for the twocolumn option (see Figure G.2 on page 555);

`\columnseprule`
> determines the width of the vertical line between the two columns for the `twocolumn` option. The default is zero width; that is, no vertical rule (see Figure G.2).

The standard values of these parameters may be changed with the LaTeX command `\setlength`. For example, to change `\mathindent` to 2.5 cm, give

> `\setlength{\mathindent}{2.5cm}`

These parameters may be assigned values either in the preamble or at any place in the document. Parameters in the preamble apply to the entire document, whereas those within the text are in effect until the next change or until the end of the environment in which they were made (Section 2.3). In the latter case, the previous values become effective once more.

Exercise 3.1: Take your text file from Exercise 2.2 and change the initial command `\documentclass{article}` *first to* `\documentclass[11pt]{article}` *and then to* `\documentclass[12pt]{article}` *and print the results of each LaTeX processing. Compare the line breaking of these outputs with that of Exercise 2.2.*
Note: If there are some improper word divisions, you can tell LaTeX where the correct division should occur with the command `\-`, *for example,* `man\-u\-script`. *(This is one of the few words that the TeX English word divider does not handle properly.) Additional means of modifying word division are given in Section 2.8.*
If there are warnings of the sort `Overfull \hbox ...` *during the LaTeX processing, TeX was not able to break the lines cleanly. In the output, these lines will extend beyond the right margin. The usual cause is that TeX was not able to divide some word, either because it is indivisible or because TeX's word division routines were not adequate. Here again a suggested hyphenation in the text can solve the problem. Other solutions will be given shortly.*

Exercise 3.2: Now employ `\documentclass[twocolumn]{article}` *in your text file. If you now receive a number of warnings with* `Underfull \hbox ...`, *then these lines will indeed be left and right justified but will have too much empty space between the words. Check the output yourself to see whether the word spacing is acceptable. If not, try giving some hyphenation suggestions in the first words of the next line.*
Note: If you use the classes book *or* report *instead of* article *in the preceding exercises, you will notice no difference in the outputs. These classes affect the subsequent structural elements of the document. Basically, you should use* article *for short articles (say, 10–20 pages) and* report *for longer reports that are to be organized into chapters. The chapters always begin on a new page. The class* book *is available for producing books.*

3.1.2   Loading packages

In Section 1.5.3 we explained how LaTeX can be extended by *packages*, which are either part of the core installation or contributed by engaged users. How to write your own packages is described in Appendix D.

A package is nothing more than a set of LaTeX (or TeX) commands stored in a file with the extension `.sty`, although there are some special commands that may only appear within them. To invoke a package, simply call

```
\usepackage{package}
```

in the preamble, where *package* is the root name of the file. More than one package may be loaded with one call to \usepackage. For example, two packages provided with standard LATEX are stored in files makeidx.sty (Section 11.4.3) and ifthen.sty (Section 10.3.5). They may be read in together with

```
\usepackage{makeidx,ifthen}
```

A package may have options associated with it, which may be selected in the same way as for document classes: by including the option names within square braces. The general syntax is:

```
\usepackage[opt1,opt2...]{package1,package2,...}
```

where all the listed options will be applied to all the selected packages. If any of the packages does not understand one of the options, a warning message is output to the monitor.

3.1.3   Global and local options

! One interesting feature about options specified with the \documentclass command is that they also apply to any packages that follow. This means that if several packages take the same option, it is only necessary to declare it once in \documentclass. For example, one might design a package to modify article for generating a local house style that might do different things for single- or double-column text; this package could make use of the class options onecolumn and twocolumn to achieve this. Or, it could elaborate on the draft option to produce double line spacing, as for a manuscript. Alternatively, several packages might have language-dependent features that could be activated with options like french or german; it is sufficient to list such options only in \documentclass to apply them to all packages. Such options are called *global*, for they are passed on to all subsequent packages automatically.

Global options need not be limited to the standard class options listed in Section 3.1.1. A warning message is printed only if neither the class nor any of the packages understand one or more of them. By contrast, any options specified with \usepackage will be applied only to those packages listed in that one command, and it is applied to all of them. A warning is printed if one or more of those packages does not recognize any one of these *local* options.

3.1.4   Class and package versions

! Class and package files normally have an internal version specification in the form of their release date, as *yyyy/mm/dd*. If you wish to make use of some feature that you know was added on a certain date, you include that date in square brackets after the class or package name. An example of this is shown in Section 3.2.4 on page 50.

The version date may also be added to the \documentclass command to ensure that the right version of the class file is being employed. The reason for doing this is to ensure that the source files are processed properly, say, on other systems.

3.2   Page style

The basic page format is determined by the *page style*. With one exception, this command is normally given in the preamble. Its form is:

> \pagestyle{*style*}

The mandatory argument *style* takes on one of the following values:

plain   The page head is empty; the foot contains the centered page number. This is the default for the article and report classes when no \pagestyle is given in the preamble.

empty   Both head and footlines are empty; no page numbers are printed.

headings
>   The head contains the page number as well as title information (chapter and section headings); the foot is empty. This is the default for book class.

myheadings
>   The same as headings except that the page titles in the head are not chosen automatically but rather are given explicitly by the commands \markright or \markboth (see below).

The command

> \thispagestyle{*style*}

functions exactly as \pagestyle except that it affects only the current page. For example, the page numbering may be suppressed for just the current page with the command \thispagestyle{empty}. It is only the *printing* of the page number that is suppressed; the next page will be numbered just as though the command had never been given.

3.2.1   Heading declarations

For the page styles headings and myheadings, the information appearing in the headline may be given with the declarations

> \markright{*right_head*}
> \markboth{*left_head*}{*right_head*}

The declaration \markboth is used with the document class option twoside, with even-numbered pages considered to be on the *left* and odd-numbered pages on the *right*. Furthermore, the page number is printed on the left side of the head for a left page and on the right side for a right page.

For one-sided output, all pages are considered to be right-handed. In this case, the declaration \markright is appropriate. It may also be used with two-sided output to overwrite the *right_head* given in \markboth.

With the page style headings, the standard titles in the page headline are the chapter, section, or subsection headings, depending on the document and page style, according to the following scheme:

Style		Left Page	Right Page
`book, report`	one-sided	—	*Chapter*
	two-sided	*Chapter*	*Section*
`article`	one-sided	—	*Section*
	two-sided	*Section*	*Subsection*

If there is more than one \section or \subsection on a page, the heading of the last one appears in the page head.

3.2.2 Customized head and footlines

Package:
fancyhdr
The standard page styles described in Section 3.2 select how the head and footlines are to appear, and what information they contain. This is a very limited choice, and the fancyhdr package by Piet van Oostrum offers the user considerably more flexibility.

This package makes available an additional page style named fancy that the user can easily redefine. Head and footlines consist each of three parts—left, center, and right—each of which can be individually defined with

\lhead{*Left head*}   \chead{*Center head*}   \rhead{*Right head*}
\lfoot{*Left foot*}   \cfoot{*Center foot*}   \rfoot{*Right foot*}

where the various texts may be explicit, or a command such as \thepage to print the current page number. Both head and footlines may be decorated with a rule, the widths of which are set by commands \headrulewidth and \footrulewidth. By default, the fancy head and footlines are much the same as for the headings page style, but the head rule is set to 0.4 pt and the foot rule set to 0 (no rule). The rules may be redefined with, for example,

\renewcommand{\footrulewidth}{0.4pt}

to turn on the foot rule.

The above defining commands are in fact specific examples of the more general commands \fancyhead and \fancyfoot, where

\lhead{..} is \fancyhead[L]{..}
\cfoot{..} is \fancyfoot[C]{..}

and so on, with L C R standing for 'left', 'center', 'right'.

For two-sided output with the twoside option, one normally wants the left and right parts to alternate with the page number. The easiest way to do this is with

\fancyhead[LE,RO]{*Text 1*}   \fancyhead[LO,RE]{*Text 2*}

to put the same *Text 1* in the left part of even pages, and right part of odd pages, and *Text 2* for the other way around. With \fancyhead{}, all headline parts are set to blanks, something that should be done before resetting them explicitly. Similarly, \fancyfoot{} sets all foot entries to blank.

The default (two-sided) definitions for the fancy page style are

```
\fancyhead[EL,OR]{\textsl{\rightmark}}
\fancyhead[ER,OL]{\textsl{\leftmark}}
```

where \rightmark and \leftmark contain the automatic texts for the headings page style generated by the \chapter, \section, \subsection commands (Section 3.3.3), while \textsl (Section 4.1.4) sets its argument in a slanted typeface. The user may also make use of these to redefine the headline with automatic texts.

There is also the most general \fancyhf command taking optional arguments [H] and [F] to apply to head or footlines. Thus \fancyhf[HL]{..} is the same as \fancyhead[L]{..}. Clearly, \fancyhf{} resets everything.

In many classes, the first page of a chapter, or the very first page of the document, is switched to plain automatically. If the user wants to change this, he or she must redefine that page style. The fancyhdr package simplifies this task with

```
\fancypagestyle{plain}{definitions}
```

where *definitions* consist of \fancyhead, \fancyfoot, and/or rule redefinitions that are to apply to the revised plain style. In fact, any existing page style can be redefined in this way.

3.2.3   Page numbering

The declaration that specifies the style of the page numbering has the form

```
\pagenumbering{num_style}
```

The allowed values of *num_style* are:

arabic	for normal (Arabic) numerals,
roman	for lowercase Roman numerals,
Roman	for uppercase Roman numerals,
alph	for lowercase letters,
Alph	for uppercase letters.

The standard value is arabic. This declaration resets the page counter to 1. To paginate the foreword of a document with Roman numerals and the rest with Arabic numbers beginning with page 1 for chapter 1, one must declare \pagenumbering{roman} at the start of the foreword and then reset the page numbering with \pagenumbering{arabic} immediately after the first \chapter command. (See Section 3.3.5 for the preferred method.)

Pages may be numbered starting with a value different from 1 by giving the command

```
\setcounter{page}{page_num}
```

where *page_num* is the number to appear on the current page.

Exercise 3.3: Expand your exercise text file so that it fills more than one page of output and include the following preamble:

```
\documentclass{article}
\pagestyle{myheadings} \markright{Exercises}
\pagenumbering{Roman}
\begin{document}
```

3.2.4 Paragraph formatting

The following parameters affect the appearance of a paragraph and may be given new values with `\setlength` as explained in Section 10.2:

`\parskip`
> The distance between paragraphs, expressed in units of `ex` so that it will automatically change with character font size. This should be a *rubber* length.

`\parindent`
> The amount of indentation for the first line of a paragraph.

`\baselinestretch`
> This is a number that magnifies the normal distance between *baselines*, the line on which the letters sit. This number is initially 1, for standard line spacing. It may be changed to another number with

> `\renewcommand{\baselinestretch}{`*factor*`}`

> where *factor* is any decimal number, such as 1.5 for a 50% increase. This then applies to all font sizes. If this command is given outside the preamble, it does not come into effect until another font size has been selected (Section 4.1.2).

These parameters may be set either in the preamble or anywhere in the text of the document. In the latter case, the changes remain in effect until the next change or until the end of the environment in which they were made (Section 2.3).

To suppress indentation for one paragraph, or to force it where it would otherwise not occur, place

> `\noindent` or `\indent`

at the beginning of the paragraph to be affected.

Package: indentfirst Normally, the first paragraph of a section is not indented, not even with `\indent`. However, by including the package `indentfirst` one ensures that all paragraphs are indented.

Package: parskip By default, LaTeX indicates paragraphs by indenting the first line. An alternative is without indentation but with extra spacing between paragraphs. One could redefine `\parindent` and `\parskip` accordingly, or one could employ one of the oldest and simplest packages dating back to LaTeX 2.09 days: `parskip`, written by H. Partl. For consistency, this package also makes some changes in the parameters for lists (Section 4.3). One loads this package with

```
\usepackage{parskip}
```

There is a recent update to the parskip package by Robin Fairbairns that includes the option parfill, given as

```
\usepackage[parfill]{parskip}
```

that avoids ugly-looking rectangular paragraphs by ensuring that there is always space at the end of the last line. This update is dated April 9, 2001, so to be sure that this package version is loaded, add this date as

```
\usepackage[parfill]{parskip}[2001/04/09]
```

as explained in Section 3.1.4. A warning will be issued on processing if the actual version of parskip is earlier than this. There will also be a warning about the unknown option parfill.

Exercise 3.4: Add the following to the preamble of your exercise file:

```
\usepackage{parskip}
\renewcommand{\baselinestretch}{1.2}
```

After processing this exercise, repeat it with another value for \baselinestretch, say 1.5, to get a feeling for how it works. Remove these lines from the exercise file afterwards.

3.2.5   Page format

Each page consists of a *head*, the *body* containing the actual text, and a *foot*. The selection of the page style determines what information is to be found in the head and footlines.

LaTeX uses default values for the distances between the head, body, and foot, for the upper and left margins, and for the text line width and heights of the head, body, and foot. These formatting lengths are illustrated in Figure 3.1 on the opposite page. They may be changed by declaring new values for them, preferably in the preamble, with the command \setlength (Section 10.2). For example, give

```
\setlength{\textwidth}{12.5cm}
```

to make the text line width 12.5 cm.

There is also a parameter \linewidth equal to the text line width in whatever environment one is currently in. This must never be changed, but is used when one needs to know this width.

More detailed diagrams of the page formats for one- and two-column outputs are shown in Figures G.1 and G.2 in Appendix G.

Package: You can examine your own page layout with the layout package from the tools
layout collection. Simply issue the command \layout and a diagram similar to that in Figure 3.1 will be drawn at that point, together with a list of the current values of the layout parameters. Naturally, you would not do this in the middle of the final version of a document, but only as a diagnostic check.

\oddsidemargin
  left margin for odd pages,
\evensidemargin
  left margin for even pages
\topmargin
  upper margin to top of head
\headheight
  height of head
\headsep
  distance from the bottom of headline
  to top of body
\topskip
  distance from top of body to baseline
  of first line of text
\textheight, \textwidth
  height and width of main text
\footskip
  distance from the bottom of body to
  bottom of foot
\paperwidth, \paperheight
  total width and height of paper as
  given by paper size option, including
  all margins

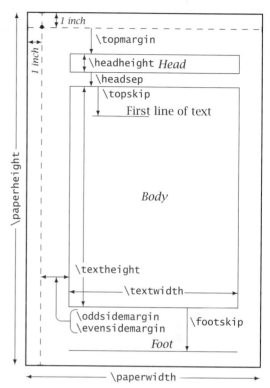

Figure 3.1: Page layout parameters

In order to calculate the page layout precisely, bear in mind that LaTeX measures all distances from a point one inch from the top of the paper and one inch from the left edge. Thus the total left margin is \oddsidemargin plus one inch. The LaTeX parameters \paperwidth and \paperheight, which include this extra inch, are given their values by the paper size option in the \documentclass command; they are used internally to calculate the margins so that the text is centered. The user may also take advantage of them for calculations.

With document class book or with the option twoside, the bottom edge of the body will always appear at exactly the same position on every page. In the other classes or options, it will vary slightly. In the first two cases, the constant bottom edge is produced by the internal command \flushbottom, whereas the varying bottom is produced by the command \raggedbottom. The user may apply these declarations to change the behavior of the bottom edge at any time, independent of document class and options.

Exercise 3.5: *You can change the page format of your text by altering the above parameters. Add the following to the preamble of your text:*

  \setlength{\textwidth}{15cm}   *\setlength{\textheight}{23cm}*

The upper and left margins of your output will now seem too large. Select new values for \oddsidemargin and \topmargin to correct this. Note: Do not forget the 1-inch margin *at the left and top from which additional margins are measured. You must take this into account when you select \oddsidemargin and \topmargin.*

Exercise 3.6: *Expand your text so that the output requires more than two full pages with the increased page format. Add \flushbottom to the preamble and check that the last line of all pages is at exactly the same location.*

Exercise 3.7: *Remove the command \flushbottom and select the document class \documentclass[twoside]{article}. Now the last lines are at the same location without the \flushbottom command. On the other hand, the left margin of the odd pages probably does not agree with the right margin of the even pages. Adjust the value of \evensidemargin to correct this.*

3.2.6   Simplified page formatting

Package: geometry

Getting the page layout to be exactly the way you want it can be very tedious. Just centering the text on the page involves a complex set of settings that are not at all intuitive. The geometry package by Hideo Umeki offers considerable assistance.

With this package, one can easily give values for some layout parameters, and the rest will be set automatically, taking into account the total paper size. For example, to set \textwidth to 15 cm and \textheight to 25 cm on A4 paper, one gives

```
\usepackage{geometry}
\geometry{a4paper,textwidth=15cm,textheight=25cm}
```

which also sets \oddsidemargin and \topmargin to appropriate values.

Rather than using the \geometry command, one may also place the parameters as options to \usepackage, for example as

```
\usepackage[letterpaper,left=3cm,right=2cm]{geometry}
```

to set the margins to definite values, and \textwidth to whatever is left over on the U.S. letter paper.

In general, all the parameters in Figure 3.1 may be specified by geometry by giving their names (without the backslash character). However, the package is far more powerful than that. Here we describe the essentials of version 3.2 from 2002/07/08.

- The paper size is either inherited from the \documentclass option, given as a predefined option such as a4paper, given explicitly as paperwidth=*pwidth* and paperheight=*pheight*, or as papersize={*pwidth*, *pheight*}.

- By default, \textwidth and \textheight are set to be 70% of \paperwidth and \paperheight. They may be set explicitly with width=*width* and height=*height*, or with body={*width*, *height*}.

- With the option includeheadfoot, the height calculation includes the parameters \headheight + \headsep + \footskip; options includehead and includefoot include head and foot parameters separately.

- With includemp, the width calculation includes the marginal note parameters \marginparwidth + \marginparsep (Section 5.2.5). With reversemp, the marginal notes appear in the left margin.

- The option includeall adds all the parameters to height and width. For each include.. option, there is a corresponding ignore.. option to remove the parameters from the calculations.

- With nohead, nofoot, noheadfoot, the corresponding head and foot parameters are set to zero.

- Margins are set by default such that top and bottom are in the ratio 2:3; similarly, with twoside, the inner and outer margins are also in the ratio 2:3, while, with oneside, the left and right margins are equal. These ratios may be reset with hmarginratio=m:n, vmarginratio=m:n, or both together with marginratio={mh:nh,mv:nv}, where m and n are integers under 100. One may also give vcentering, hcentering, or centering to set the corresponding ratios to 1:1.

- Margins may be set explicitly with left=$lmarg$ and right=$rmarg$, or with hmargin={$lmarg$,$rmarg$}; similarly, with top=$tmarg$ and bottom=$bmarg$, or vmargin={$tmarg$,$bmarg$}; inner and outer are synonyms for left and right, respectively. Set all margins to a common value with margin=$marg$.

- The text width and height may be set to a fraction of the paper size with hscale=h and vscale=v, or scale={h,v}. With scale=s, both h and v are set to s. For example, \geometry{scale=0.8} sets width and height to 80% of \paperwidth and \paperheight, respectively.

- For two-sided output, add the option twoside. In this case, the values of the left and right margins will switch for even page numbers. There is an option asymmetric for two-sided output but without switching margins. A length given by bindingoffset=$boff$ is added to the inner margin.

- One can specify the text height as a number of lines of text with lines=n. Or, with heightrounded, the existing \textheight is rounded to be exactly an integral number of text lines.

Version 3.2 has many additional features over the earlier version 2.3, but it also exhibits different default behavior; the option compat2 restores those older calculation rules. Without this option, which must be the first one, documents written for the previous version, such as demodoc.tex on the included CD, behave differently under the new version. (The modified demodoc.tex is listed on page 16.)

3.2.7   Single- and double-column pages

The document class option twocolumn sets the entire document in two columns per page. The default is one column per page. Individual pages may be output in one or two columns with the declarations:

\twocolumn[*header text*]
>   Terminates the current page, starting a new one with *two columns* per page. The optional *header text* is written at the top of the page in one column with the width of the whole page.

\onecolumn
>   Terminates the current two-column page and continues with one column per page.

! The option twocolumn automatically changes certain page style parameters, such as indentation, compared with the one-column format. This does not occur with the command \twocolumn. These additional changes must be made with the corresponding \setlength declarations if they are desired. If the bulk of the document is in two-column format, the class option is to be preferred.

! An additional page style parameter is \columnwidth, the width of one column of text. For single-column text, this is the same as \textwidth, but when twocolumn has been selected, LaTeX calculates it from the values of \textwidth and \columnsep. The author should never change this parameter, but he or she may make use of it, for example, to draw a rule the width of a column of text.

! The length \linewidth is even more general, always containing the text line width in the current environment, minipage, or parbox. Within a single column, it is the same as \columnwidth. It too may never be changed.

3.2.8   Multicolumn text

Package: The commands \twocolumn and \onecolumn always start a new page, and when two-
multicol column text is terminated, the two columns are of unequal length. These problems are solved with the multicol package in the tools collection, written by Frank Mittelbach, which also allows up to 10 columns of text. Once this package has been loaded, one can switch the number of columns in the middle of a page with

>   \begin{multicols}{*num_cols*}[*header text*][*pre_space*]
>   *Text set in* num_cols *columns*
>   \end{multicols}

where the optional *header text* is written across all the columns before switching to multicolumns.

Some automatic control for page breaking before and after switching to multicolumns is offered by the two lengths \premulticols and \postmulticols: If the remaining space on the current page is less than \premulticols, a new page is started before switching to multicolumns. Similarly, if, at the end of the environment, there is less than \postmulticols on the page, a page break is inserted before continuing. The standard values of these lengths may be altered by the user with \setlength, or in the case of \premulticols they may be overridden by the second optional argument *pre_space*.

The lengths \columnsep and \columnseprule that apply to two-column texts are also in effect for the multicols environment, to set the widths of the gap between columns and a possible separating rule, respectively.

There is also a *-version \begin{multicols*}{*num_cols*}...\end{multicols*} for which the columns on the last page are not balanced, with all the remaining space put into the final column.

Note: For historical reasons the multicol package copyright, though distributed under the LaTeX Project Public License, contains an additional 'moral obligation' clause that asks commercial users to consider paying a license fee to the author or the LaTeX3 fund for their use of the package. Details are to be found in the head of the package file itself.

3.3 Parts of the document

Every document is subdivided into chapters, sections, subsections, and so on. There can be an appendix at the end and a title page, table of contents, abstract, and so forth at the beginning. LaTeX has a number of markup commands available to indicate these structures. In addition, sequential numbering and sub-numbering of headings take place automatically. Even a table of contents may be produced with a single command.

The effects of some sectioning commands depend on the selected document class, and not all commands are available in every class.

3.3.1 Title page

A title page can be produced in a preprogrammed LaTeX style with the commands

> \title{*Title text*}
> \author{*Author names and addresses*}
> \date{*Date text*}
> \maketitle

In the standard LaTeX layout for the title page, all entries are centered on the lines in which they appear. If the title is too long, it will be broken up automatically. The author may select the break points himself with the \\ command, that is, by giving \title{...\\...\\...}.

If there are several authors, their names may be separated with \and from one another, such as \author{G. Smith \and J. Jones}. These names will be printed next to each other in one line. The sequence

> \author{*Author1**Institute1**Address1*
> \and *Author2**Institute2**Address2*}

separately centers the entries, one per line, in each of the sets *Author1, Institute1, Address1* and *Author2, Institute2, Address2* and places the two blocks of centered entries beside each other on the title page.

Instead of printing the author names next to each other, one may position them on top of one another by replacing \and with the \\ command, together with an optional length specification [*space*] to adjust the vertical spacing.

```
\title{%
   How to Write DVI Drivers}

\author{%
   Helmut Kopka\thanks{Tel.
      [+49] 5556--401--451}\\
   Max--Planck--Institut\\
   f\"ur Aeronomie
 \and
   Phillip G. Hardy
      \thanks{Tel.
      [+1] 319--824--7134}\\
   University\\of Iowa}

\maketitle
```

> ## How to Write DVI Drivers
>
> Helmut Kopka[1]   Phillip G. Hardy[2]
> Max–Planck–Institut   University
>   für Aeronomie   of Iowa
>
> July 15, 2003
>
> [1] Tel. [+49] 5556-401-451
> [2] Tel. [+1] 319-824-7134

Figure 3.2: Sample title page and the text that produced it

If the command \date is omitted, the current date is printed automatically below the author entries on the title page. On the other hand, the command \date{*Date text*} puts the text *Date text* in place of the current date. Any desired text may be inserted here, including line break commands \\ for more than one line of centered text.

The command

   \thanks{*Footnote text*}

may be given at any point in the *title, author*, or *date text*. This puts a marker at that point where the command appears and writes *footnote text* as a footnote on the title page.

The title page is created using the entries in \title, \author, \date, and \thanks when the command

   \maketitle

is issued. The title page itself does not possess a page number, and the first page of the following document is number 1. (For book, the page numbering is controlled by the special commands in Section 3.3.5.) A separate title page is produced only for document classes book and report. For article, the command \maketitle creates a title heading on the first page using the centered entries from the \title,

\author, and, if present, \date and \thanks declarations. If the document class option titlepage has been given, the title appears on a separate page even for the article class.

An example of a title page in the standard LaTeX format is shown in Figure 3.2 on the facing page. Note that the current date appears automatically since the command \date is missing in the definition of the title page. This command may be used to put any desired text in place of the date.

Alternatively, one can produce a free-format title page with

> \begin{titlepage} *Title page text* \end{titlepage}

Here the commands \title and \author are left out and the entire title page is designed according to the author's specifications within the environment. To this end, he or she may make use of all the structuring commands described in Chapter 4. In this case, the printing of the title page is implemented at the end of the titlepage environment, so the command \maketitle is also left out.

Exercise 3.8: *Remove the declarations for changing the page format in Exercises 3.5 through 3.7. Add to your exercise text a title heading with the title 'Exercises', your name as author, and your address, together with a date entry in the form 'place, date'. To do this, write the following commands after \begin{document}:*

> *\title{Exercises} \author{Your name\\Your address}*
> *\date{Your town, \today} \maketitle*

Make sure that you have selected document class article. *After printing the document, change the document class command to*

> *\documentclass[titlepage]{article}*

to put the title information onto a title page instead of a title heading. Deactivate these commands by putting the comment character % at the beginning of each of the lines. In this way you avoid getting a title page in the following exercises, but you can easily reactivate the commands simply by removing the % characters.

3.3.2 Abstract

The abstract is produced with the command

> \begin{abstract} *Text for the abstract* \end{abstract}

In document class report, the abstract appears on a separate page without a page number; in article, it comes after the title heading on the first page, unless the document class option titlepage has been selected, in which case it is also printed on a separate page. An abstract is not possible in document class book.

3.3.3 Sections

The following commands produce automatic, sequential sectioning:

```
\part       \chapter       \subsection       \paragraph
            \section       \subsubsection    \subparagraph
```

With the exception of \part, these commands form a sectioning hierarchy. In document classes book and report, the highest sectioning level is \chapter. The chapters are divided into sections using the \section command, which are further subdivided by means of \subsection, and so on. In document class article, the hierarchy begins with \section since \chapter is not available.

The syntax of all these commands is

\sec_command[*short title*]{*title*}   or
\sec_command*{*title*}

In the first case, the section is given the next number in the sequence, which is then printed together with a heading using the text *title*. The text *short title* becomes the entry in the table of contents (Section 3.4) and the page head (provided that page style headings has been selected). If the optional *short title* is omitted, it is set equal to *title*; this is the normal situation unless *title* is too long to serve for the other entries.

In the second (*-form) case, no section number is printed and no entry in the table of contents is made (however, see Section 3.4.3).

The size of the title heading and the depth of the numbering depend on the position of the sectioning command within the hierarchy. For document class article, the \section command generates a single number (say, 7), the \subsection command a double number with a period between the two parts (say, 7.3), and so on.

In document classes book and report, the chapter headings are given a single number with the \chapter command, the \section command creates the double number, and so on. Furthermore, the command \chapter always starts a new page and prints **Chapter n** over the chapter title, where **n** is the current chapter number. At this point in this book, we are in *Chapter 3, Section 3.3, Subsection 3.3.3*.

For each sectioning command there is an internal counter that is incremented by one every time that command is called, and it is reset to zero on every call to the next higher sectioning command. These counters are not altered by the *-forms, a fact that can lead to difficulties if standard and *-forms of the commands are mixed such that the *-forms are higher in the hierarchy than the standard forms. There are no problems, however, if the *-forms are always lower than the standard forms. The sequence

```
\section ... \subsection ... \subsubsection* ...
```

numbers the headings for \section and \subsection while leaving the headings for \subsubsection without any numbering.

The sectioning command \part is a special case and does not affect the numbering of the other commands.

The automatic numbering of sections means that the numbers might not necessarily be known at the time of writing. The author may be writing them out of their final order, or might later introduce new sections or even remove some. If he or she wants to refer to a section number in the text, some mechanism other than typing the number explicitly will be needed. The LaTeX cross-reference system, described in detail in Section 11.2.1, accomplishes this task with the two basic commands

> \label{*name*}   \ref{*name*}

the first of which assigns a keyword *name* to the section number, while the second may be used as reference in the text for printing that number. The keyword *name* may be any combination of letters, numbers, or symbols. For example, in this book the command \label{sec:xref} has been typed in at the start of Section 11.2.1, so that this sentence contains the input text at the start of Section \ref{sec:xref}.

A second referencing command is \pageref for printing the page number where the corresponding \label is defined.

The referencing commands may be used in many other situations for labeling items that are numbered automatically, such as figures, tables, and equations.

!   Every sectioning command is assigned a level number such that \section is always level 1, \subsection level 2, ... \subparagraph level 5. In document class article, \part is level 0 while in book and report classes, \part is level −1 and \chapter becomes level 0. Section numbering is carried out down to the level given by the number secnumdepth. This limit is set to 2 for book and report, and to 3 for article. This means that for book and report, the section numbering extends only to the level of \subsection and for article to \subsubsection.

To extend (or reduce) the level of the section numbering, it is necessary to change the value of secnumdepth. This is done with the command

> \setcounter{secnumdepth}{*num*}

(The command \setcounter is explained in Section 10.1.3.) In article, *num* may take on values from 0 to 5, and in book and report from −1 to 5.

It is possible to change the initial value of a sectioning command within a document with the command

> \setcounter{*sec_name*}{*num*}

where *sec_name* is the name of the sectioning command without the preceding \ character. This procedure may be useful when individual sections are to be processed by LaTeX as single files. For example,

> \setcounter{chapter}{2}

sets the \chapter counter to 2. The counter will be incremented on the next call to \chapter which then produces **Chapter 3**.

3.3.4   Appendix

An appendix is introduced with the declaration

> \appendix

It has the effect of resetting the section counter for `article` and the chapter counter for `book` and `report` and changing the form of the numbering for these sectioning commands from numerals to capital letters A, B, ... Furthermore, the word 'Chapter' is replaced by 'Appendix' so that subsequent chapter headings are preceded by 'Appendix A', 'Appendix B', and so on. The numbering of lower sectioning commands contains the letter in place of the chapter number, for example, A.2.1.

3.3.5   Book structure

To simplify the structuring of a book, the commands

> `\frontmatter`
> *preface, table of contents*
> `\mainmatter`
> *main body of text*
> `\backmatter`
> *bibliography, index, colophon*

are provided in the book class. The `\frontmatter` command switches page numbering to Roman numerals and suppresses the numbering of chapters; `\mainmatter` resets the page numbering to 1 with Arabic numbers and reactivates the chapter numbering; this is once again turned off with `\backmatter`.

Exercise 3.9: *Insert at the beginning of your exercise text the command* `\section{Title A}` *and at some appropriate place near the middle* `\section{Title B}`. *Select some suitable text for Title A and Title B. Insert at appropriate places some* `\subsection` *commands with reasonable subtitles. Remove the commands included from Exercise 3.3:*

> `\pagestyle{myheadings}  \markright{Exercises}`
> `\pagenumbering{Roman}`

and print the results.

Exercise 3.10: *Include the additional command* `\chapter{Chapter title}` *with your own appropriate Chapter title before your first* `\section` *command. Change the document class command to* `\documentclass[twoside]{report}` *and call the page style command* `\pagestyle{headings}` *in the preamble. Note the twofold effect of the sectioning commands in the headings and in the page headlines. Compare the results with the table in Section 3.2.1.*

Exercise 3.11: *Change the chapter command to*

> `\chapter[Short form]{Chapter title}`

by putting an abbreviated version of Chapter title for Short form. Now the page head contains the shortened title where the full chapter title previously appeared.

3.4   Table of contents

3.4.1   Automatic entries

LaTeX can prepare and print a table of contents automatically for the whole document. It will contain the section numbers and corresponding headings as given in the standard form of the sectioning commands, together with the page numbers on which they begin. The sectioning depth to which entries are made in the table of contents can be set in the preamble with the command

    \setcounter{tocdepth}{num}

The value *num* has exactly the same meaning and effect as it does for the counter secnumdepth described above, by which the maximum level of automatic subsectioning is fixed. By default, the depth to which entries are included in the table of contents is the same as the standard level to which automatic sectioning is done: to level \subsection for book and report and to level \subsubsection for article.

3.4.2   Printing the table of contents

The table of contents is generated and printed with the command

    \tableofcontents

given at the location where the table of contents is to appear, which is normally after the title page and abstract.

This leads to a paradox, for the information in the table of contents is to be printed near the beginning of the document, information that cannot be known until the end. LaTeX solves this problem as follows: The first time the document is processed, no table of contents can be included, but instead LaTeX opens a new file with the same name as the source file but with the extension .toc; the entries for the table of contents are written to this file during the rest of the processing.

The next time LaTeX is run on this document, the \tableofcontents command causes the .toc file to be read and the table of contents is printed. As the processing continues, the .toc file is updated in case there have been major changes since the previous run. This means that the table of contents that is printed is always the one corresponding to the previous version of the document. For this reason, it may be necessary to run LaTeX more than once on the final version.

3.4.3   Additional entries

! The *-form sectioning commands are not entered automatically in the table of contents. To insert them, or any other additional entry, the commands

    \addcontentsline{toc}{sec_name}{entry text}
    \addtocontents{toc}{entry_text}

may be used.

With the first command, the entries will conform to the format of the table of contents, whereby `section` headings are indented more than those for `chapter` but less than those for `subsection`. This is determined by the value of the argument *sec_name*, which is the same as one of the sectioning commands without the \ character (for example, `section`). The *entry_text* is inserted in the table of contents along with the page number. This command is most useful to enter unnumbered section headings into the table of contents. For example,

```
\section*{Author addresses}
\addcontentsline{toc}{section}{Author addresses}
```

The \addtocontents command puts any desired command or text into the .toc file. This could be a formatting command, \newpage, for example, which takes effect when the table of contents is printed.

3.4.4   Other lists

!

In addition to the table of contents, lists of figures and tables can also be generated and printed automatically by LaTeX. The commands to produce these lists are

```
\listoffigures   reads and/or produces file .lof
\listoftables    reads and/or produces file .lot
```

The entries in these lists are made automatically by the \caption command in the `figure` and `table` environments (see Section 9.4). Additional entries are made with the same commands as for the table of contents, the general form of which is

```
\addcontentsline{file}{format}{entry}
\addtocontents{file}{entry}
```

where *file* stands for one of the three types `toc` (*table of contents*), `lof` (*list of figures*), or `lot` (*list of tables*). The argument *format* is one of the sectioning commands for the table of contents, as described above, or `figure` for the list of figures, or `table` for the list of tables. The argument *entry* stands for the text that is to be inserted into the appropriate file.

Exercise 3.12: In your exercise file, insert after the deactivated title page commands

```
\pagenumbering{roman}
\tableofcontents \newpage
\pagenumbering{arabic}
```

Process your exercise file <u>twice</u> *with LaTeX and print out the second results. Deactivate the above commands with % before doing the next run.*

Displaying Text

4

There are a variety of ways to display or emphasize the text: changing font style or font size, centering, indentation, making lists, and so on. LaTeX supplies us with commands for the most common forms of such highlighting.

Many parts of this chapter violate the concept of logical markup, especially those dealing with selection of font properties. The author should not attempt to decorate the document with arbitrary switches of font size and style, but should pack his or her source text into a structure that indicates its purpose. The exercises in this book are an example of this. Rather than starting each one with the word 'Exercise' in boldface followed by an explicit number and then shifting to a slanted font, we defined an `exercise` environment to do all that automatically. This not only ensures consistency, it also allows a change of style to be easily implemented simply by redefining the environment. This is where the font style commands come into play. They should not appear in the main text at all, but rather in the preamble as part of the definitions of environments and commands.

On the other hand, many of the topics in this chapter really do involve logical markup, such as the `verse`, `quote`, and `quotation` environments, lists, bibliographies, and theorems.

4.1 Changing font style

In typography, a set of letters, numbers, and characters of a certain size and appearance is called a *font*. The standard font in LaTeX for the main body of text is an *upright, Roman* one of *medium* weight, in the size specified in the \documentclass statement at the start. The three possible basic sizes are 10, 11, and 12 pt, depending on the size options `10pt` (default), `11pt`, and `12pt`. (Recall that there are 72.27 points per inch, or about 28.45 pt per cm.) The parenthesis characters ( ) extend the full height and depth of the font size.

The differences in the visual appearance of the three standard sizes are greater than would be expected from the ratios of the numbers:

This is an example of the 10 pt font. ( )

And this is the 11 pt font for comparison. ( )
And finally, this is a sample of 12 pt font. ( )

4.1.1   Emphasis

The usual way to emphasize text in a typewritten manuscript is by <u>underlining</u>. The typesetter will transform underlined text into *italics* for the printed version. Switching from standard to *emphasized* text is carried out in LaTeX with the command \emph or the declaration \em.

The \em declaration functions just as the other font declarations described below: The change of font remains in effect until negated by another appropriate declaration (which can be \em itself) or until the end of the current *environment* (Section 2.2). An environment may also be created with a pair of curly braces {...}. The command \emph, on the other hand, operates only on the text in the following argument. This is the easiest way to *emphasize* short pieces of text, as, for example:

```
This is the easiest way to \emph{emphasize} short ...
```

The \em declaration is more appropriate for longer text that is enclosed in an environment, *named or nameless.*

```
...enclosed in an environment, {\em named or nameless.}
```

Note carefully the difference between the *declaration* that remains in effect until the local environment is ended with the closing curly brace and the *command* that operates on an argument enclosed in curly braces. Another more subtle difference is that the command \emph automatically inserts extra spacing at the end if necessary, the so-called *italic correction*, to improve the appearance at the interface between sloping and upright fonts.

Both the declaration and the command switch to an emphasizing font. This means that if the current font is upright it switches to *italics, whereas if the text is already slanted, an* upright *font is selected.*

Nested emphasis is possible and is simple to understand:

```
The \emph{first, \emph{second, and \emph{third font switch.}}}
```

produces 'The *first,* second, and *third font switch.*'

4.1.2   Choice of font size

The following declarations are available in LaTeX for changing the font size:

\tiny	smallest	\Large	larger
\scriptsize	very small	\LARGE	even larger
\footnotesize	smaller		
\small	small	\huge	still larger
\normalsize	normal		
\large	large	\Huge	largest

all of which are relative to the standard size selected in the document class option. In this book, the standard size is 10 pt, which is then the size selected with `\normalsize`.

The font size declarations behave as all other declarations: They make an immediate change that remains in effect until counteracted by another size declaration or until the current environment comes to an end. If issued within curly braces `{..}`, the effect of the declaration extends only to the closing brace, as in a nameless environment:

normal {\large large \Large larger} normal again

normal large larger normal again

Changing the font size with one of the above commands also automatically changes the interline spacing. For every font size, there is a corresponding *natural* line spacing `\baselineskip`. This may be altered at any time. If the natural line spacing is 12 pt, the command `\setlength{\baselineskip}{15pt}` will increase it to 15 pt.

The value of `\baselineskip` that is in effect at the end of the paragraph is used to make up the whole paragraph. This means that if there are several changes to `\baselineskip` within a paragraph, only the last value given will be taken into account.

With every change in font size, `\baselineskip` is reset to its natural value for that size. Any previous setting with `\setlength` will be nullified.

To create a change in the line spacing that is valid for all font sizes, one must make use of the factor `\baselinestretch`, which has a normal value of 1. The true interline spacing is really

\baselinestretch×\baselineskip

which maintains the same relative spacing for all font sizes. The user may change this spacing at any time with:

\renewcommand{\baselinestretch}{*factor*}

where *factor* is any decimal number. A value of 1.5 increases the interline spacing (baseline to baseline) by 50% over its natural size for all font sizes.

The new value of `\baselinestretch` does not take effect until the next change in font size. To implement a new value in the current font size, it is necessary to switch to another size and back again immediately. If the present font size is `\normalsize`, the sequence

\small\normalsize

will do the trick. Any size command may be used in place of `\small`.

4.1.3   Font attributes

The size of a font is only one of several *attributes* that may be used to describe it. With the New Font Selection Scheme (NFSS), which was introduced as part of LaTeX 2_ε, it is possible to select fonts strictly by these attributes, as described in Appendix A. However, for normal usage there are some declarations and corresponding commands to simplify this procedure.

For the Computer Modern fonts provided with TeX and LaTeX, the following attributes and values exist:

Family: for the general overall style. Traditional typographical families have names such as *Baskerville*, *Bodoni*, *Times Roman*, *Helvetica*, and so on. The standard LaTeX installation provides three families with declarations

\rmfamily to switch (back) to a Roman font,
\ttfamily to switch to a typewriter font, and
\sffamily to select a sans serif font.

Shape: for the form of the font. The shape declarations available with the standard installation are

\upshape to switch (back) to an upright font,
\itshape to select an *italic* shape,
\slshape to choose a font that is *slanted*, and
\scshape to switch to CAPS AND SMALL CAPS.

Series: for the width and/or weight (boldness) of the font. The declarations possible are

\mdseries to switch (back) to medium weight, and
\bfseries to select a **boldface** font.

These do not exhaust all the possible attribute settings, but they do cover the most standard ones, especially for the Computer Modern fonts. For other fonts, especially PostScript ones, additional attribute values exist. See Section A.1 for more details.

These declarations are used just like any others, normally enclosed in a pair of curly braces {...}, such as {\scshape Romeo and Juliet} producing ROMEO AND JULIET. For longer sections of text, an environment is preferable:

\begin{*font_style*} ... *text in new font* ... \end{*font_style*}

This keeps better track of the beginning and end of the switch-over. For *font_style*, any of the above font commands may be used, leaving off the initial \ character.

Since changing any one attribute leaves the others as they were, all possible combinations may be obtained. (However, this does not mean that a font exists for each possible combination; if not, a substitution will be made.) If we first select a bold series with \bfseries, and then a slanted shape with \slshape, we obtain a bold, slanted font.

normal and {\bfseries bold and
    {\slshape slanted} and back} again.

produces: normal and **bold and *slanted* and back** again.

Finally, the declaration \normalfont resets all the attributes (except size) back to their defaults: Roman, upright, medium weight. It is often useful to issue this command just to be sure of the font in effect.

4.1.4   Font commands

For each of the font declarations listed above, there is a corresponding *font command* that sets its argument in a font with the specified attribute.

Family:	`\textrm{`*text*`}`	`\texttt{`*text*`}`	`\textsf{`*text*`}`
Shape:	`\textup{`*text*`}`	`\textit{`*text*`}`	`\textsl{`*text*`}`
	`\textsc{`*text*`}`		
Series:	`\textmd{`*text*`}`	`\textbf{`*text*`}`	
Default:	`\textnormal{`*text*`}`		
Emphasis:	`\emph{`*text*`}`		

Note that the `\emph` command is included here, corresponding to the declaration `\em`. The argument of `\textnormal` is set in the standard font selected with `\normalfont`.

The use of such commands to change the font for short pieces of text, or single words, is much more logical than placing a declaration inside an implied environment. The previous example now becomes

```
normal and \textbf{bold and \textsl{slanted}
    and back} again.
```

to make: normal and **bold and *slanted* and back** again.

As for the `\emph` command, these font commands automatically add any necessary *italic correction* between upright and slanted/italic fonts.

The old two-letter TeX declarations such as `\bf` and `\tt`, which were part of LaTeX 2.09, are still available but are now considered obsolete and should be avoided. They are listed for reference in Appendix F.

4.1.5   Additional fonts

!

It is likely that your computing center or your TeX installation has even more fonts and sizes than those listed above. If so, they may be made available for use within a LaTeX document either by referring to them by name, or by their attributes, if they have been set up for NFSS.

To load a new font explicitly by name, the command

```
\newfont{\fnt}{name scaled factor}    or
\newfont{\fnt}{name at size}
```

is given, which assigns the font to the new command named `\fnt`. In the first case, *factor* is a number 1000 times the scaling factor that is to be used to magnify or reduce the font from its basic or design size. In the second case, the font is scaled to be of the *size* specified. To install a slanted, sans serif font of size 20.74 pt, as `\sss`, we load `cmssi17` at 20.74pt with

```
\newfont{\sss}{cmssi17 at 20.74pt}
```

Now the declaration `\sss` switches directly to this font but without altering the baseline separation.

4.2   Centering and indenting

4.2.1   Centered text

The environment

> \begin{center} *line 1* \\ *line 2* \\ ... *line n* \end{center}

centers the sections of text that are separated by the \\ command. (An optional
additional line spacing may be inserted with \\[*len*].) If the text is too long for one
line, it is split over several lines using uniform word spacing, filling the whole line
width as best it can, except for the last line. Word division does not occur.

Within an environment, the command \centering may be used to center the
following text, again with \\ as the line divider. The effect of this declaration lasts
until the end of that environment.

A single line may be centered by typing its text as the argument of the TeX
command \centerline{*text*}.

4.2.2   One-sided justification

The environments

> \begin{flushleft} *line 1* \\ *line 2* \\ ... *line 2* \end{flushleft}
> \begin{flushright} *line 1* \\ *line 2* \\ ... *line 2* \end{flushright}

produce text that is left (flushleft) or right (flushright) justified. If a section of
text does not fit on to one line, it is spread over several with fixed word spacing, the
same as for the center environment. Again, word division does not occur.

The same results may be produced within an environment with the declarations

> \raggedright   replacing the flushleft   environment, and
> \raggedleft   replacing the flushright environment.

4.2.3   Two-sided indentation: quotations

A section of text may be prominently displayed by indenting it by an equal amount
on both sides, with the environments

> \begin{quote}   *text*   \end{quote}
> \begin{quotation}   *text*   \end{quotation}

An example of the quote environment is:

> Additional vertical spacing is inserted above and below the displayed text
> to separate it visually from the normal text.
>
> The text to be displayed may be of any length; it can be part of a sentence,
> a whole paragraph, or several paragraphs.
>
> Paragraphs are separated as usual with an empty line, although no empty
> lines are needed at the beginning and end of the displayed text since
> additional vertical spacing is inserted here anyway.

And here is an example of the quotation environment:

In the `quotation` environment, paragraphs are marked by extra indentation of the first line, whereas in the `quote` environment, they are indicated with more vertical spacing between them.

The present text is produced within the `quotation` environment, while the sample above was done within the `quote` environment.

The `quotation` environment is only really meaningful when the regular text makes use of first-line indentation to show off new paragraphs.

4.2.4   Verse indentations

For indenting rhymes, poetry, verses, and so forth on both sides, the environment

> `\begin{verse}`   *poem*   `\end{verse}`

is more appropriate.

> Stanzas are separated by blank lines
> while the individual lines of the stanza are divided by the \\ command.
>
> If a line is too long for the reduced text width, it will be left and right
>   justified and continued on the next line, which is indented even further.

The above indenting schemes may be nested inside one another. Within a `quote` environment there may be another `quote`, `quotation`, or `verse` environment. Each time, additional indentations are created on both sides of the text and vertical spacing is added above and below; these quantities, however, decrease as the depth of nesting increases. A maximum of six such nestings is allowed.

Exercise 4.1: *Put some appropriate sections of text in your exercise file into the* quote *and* quotation *environments; that is, enclose these sections within these commands:*

> `\begin{quote}` . . . . . . `\end{quote}`   *or*
> `\begin{quotation}` . . . . . `\end{quotation}`

Exercise 4.2: *Make up a new file with the name* poem.tex, *and type your favorite poem in the* verse *environment. Select* 12pt *as the standard font size and italic as the typeface. Put the title of the poem before the* verse *environment in a larger bold typeface, such as* \Large\bfseries. *Include the name of the poet, set right justified.*
Note: Remember that you may include declarations to change the font style or size within an environment and that these remain in effect only until the end of that environment.

Exercise 4.3: *Make up another file with the name* title.tex. *Do you recall the* titlepage *environment for producing a free-form title page? If not, refer to Section 3.3.1. Create a title page with this environment using font sizes and styles of your choice, centering all the entries.*
Note: Within the titlepage *environment you may, of course, make use of the* center *environment. But it is also sufficient to give the* \centering *declaration instead, since this will remain in effect only until the end of the* titlepage *environment.*

Choose the individual line spacings with the command \\[len] using an appropriate value for the spacing len. Remember that vertical spacing before the first line of text must be entered with the *-form of the command \vspace*[len] (see Section 2.7.3).

Experiment with different font sizes and styles for the various parts of the title page, such as title, author's name, and address, until you are satisfied with the results.

Compare your own title page with that of Exercise 3.8. If your creation appeals to you more, include it in your standard exercise file by replacing the commands \title, \author, \date, and \maketitle with the titlepage environment and your own entries.

4.3   Lists

There are three environments available for producing formatted lists:

\begin{itemize}	*list text*	\end{itemize}
\begin{enumerate}	*list text*	\end{enumerate}
\begin{description}	*list text*	\end{description}

In each of these environments, the *list text* is indented from the left margin and a label, or marker, is included. What type of label is used depends on the selected list environment. The command to produce the label is \item.

4.3.1   Sample itemize

- The individual entries are indicated with a black dot, known as a *bullet*, as the label.

- The text in the entries may be of any length. The label appears at the beginning of the first line of text.

- Successive entries are separated by additional vertical spacing.

The above text was produced as follows:

```
\begin{itemize}
\item The individual entries are indicated with a black dot,
      known as a \emph{bullet}, as the label.
\item The text in the entries may be of any length. The label
      appears at the beginning of the first line of text.
\item Successive entries are separated from one another by
      additional vertical spacing.
\end{itemize}
```

4.3.2   Sample enumerate

1. The labels consist of sequential numbers.

2. The numbering starts at 1 with every call to the enumerate environment.

The above example was generated with the following text:

```
\begin{enumerate}
\item The labels consist of sequential numbers.
\item The numbering starts at 1 with every call to the
      \texttt{enumerate} environment.
\end{enumerate}
```

4.3.3   Sample description

purpose This environment is appropriate when a number of words or expressions are to be defined.

example A keyword is used as the label and the entry contains a clarification or explanation.

other uses It may also be used as an author list in a bibliography.

The above sample was created using the following:

```
\begin{description}
\item[purpose] This environment is appropriate when a number of
      words or expressions are to be defined.
\item[example] A keyword is used as the label and the entry
      contains a clarification or explanation.
\item[other uses] It may also be used as an author list in a
      bibliography.
\end{description}
```

The \item[*option*] command contains an optional argument that appears in boldface as the label.

4.3.4   Nested lists

The above lists may be included within one another, either mixed or of one type, to a depth of four levels. The type of label used depends on the depth of the nesting. The indentation is always relative to the left margin of the enclosing list. A fourfold nesting of the itemize environment appears as follows:

- The label for the first level is a black dot, a *bullet*.
  - That of the second level is a long dash.
    - That of the third level is an asterisk.
      - And the label for the fourth level is a simple dot.
      - At the same time, the vertical spacing is decreased with increasing depth.
    - Back to the third level.

> — Back to the second level.

- And here we are at the first level of `itemize` once again.

The `enumerate` environment is similar, where the style of the numbering changes with the nesting level:

1. The numbering at the first level is with Arabic numerals followed by a period.

   (a) At the second level, it is with lowercase letters in parentheses.

      i. The third level is numbered with lowercase Roman numerals with a period.
         A. At the fourth level, capital letters are used.
         B. The label style can be changed, as described in the next section.
      ii. Back to the third level.

   (b) Back to the second level.

2. And we are at the first level of `enumerate` again.

Here is an example of a nested list with mixed types:

- The `itemize` label at the first level is a bullet.

   1. The numbering is with Arabic numerals since this is the first level of the `enumerate` environment.
      — This is the third level of the nesting, but the second `itemize` level.
         (a) And this is the fourth level of the overall nesting, but only the second of the `enumerate` environment.
         (b) Thus the numbering is with lowercase letters in parentheses.
      — The label at this level is a long dash.
   2. Every list should contain at least two points.

- Blank lines ahead of an `\item` command have no effect.

The above mixed list was produced with the following text:

```
\begin{itemize}
  \item The \texttt{itemize} label at the first level is a ...
  \begin{enumerate}
    \item The numbering is with Arabic numerals since this ...
    \begin{itemize}
      \item This is the third level of the nesting, but the ...
      \begin{enumerate}
        \item And this is the fourth level of the overall ...
        \item Thus the numbering is with lowercase letters ...
      \end{enumerate}
      \item The label at this level is a long dash.
    \end{itemize}
```

```
    \item Every list should contain at least two points.
\end{enumerate}

    \item Blank lines ahead of an \verb+\item+ command ...
\end{itemize}
```

Exercise 4.4: Produce a nested list using the `itemize` and `enumerate` environments as in the above example, but with a different sequence of these commands.

Exercise 4.5: Prepare a list of conference participants with their place of residence using the `description` environment, where the name of the participant appears as the argument in the `\item` command.

Note: For all three types of lists, any text before the first `\item` command will yield an error message on processing.

4.3.5   Changing label style

The labels, or markers, used in the `itemize` and `enumerate` environments can be easily changed by means of the optional argument in the `\item` command. With `\item[+]` the label becomes +, and with `\item[2.1:]` it is 2.1:. The optional argument takes precedence over the standard label. For the `enumerate` environment, this means that the corresponding counter is *not* automatically incremented and the user must do the numbering manually.

The optional label appears right justified within the area reserved for the label. The width of this area is the amount of indentation at that level less the separation between label and text; this means that the left edge of the label area is flush with the left margin of the enclosing level.

It is also possible to change the standard labels for all or part of the document. The labels are generated with the internal commands

```
\labelitemi ,\labelitemii ,\labelitemiii ,\labelitemiv
\labelenumi ,\labelenumii ,\labelenumiii ,\labelenumiv
```

The endings `i`, `ii`, `iii`, and `iv` refer to the four possible levels.

These commands may be altered with `\renewcommand`. For example, to change the label of the third level of the `itemize` environment from * to +, give

```
\renewcommand{\labelitemiii}{+}
```

Similarly, the standard labels for the `enumerate` environment may be changed. However, here there is an additional complication because there is a counter for each `enumerate` level, named `enumi`, `enumii`, `enumiii`, and `enumiv`. As explained in Section 10.1.4, the value of a counter can be printed using one of the commands `\arabic`, `\roman`, `\Roman`, `\alph`, or `\Alph`, where the style of each command should be obvious from its name. That is, `\Roman{xyz}` prints the current value of the counter xyz in uppercase Roman numerals, whereas `\alph{xyz}` prints it as a lowercase letter (with a corresponding to 1 and z to 26).

These counters, together with the counter style commands, must be used in the redefinitions of the label commands. For example, to change the second-level label to Arabic numerals followed by '.)', it is necessary to give

```
\renewcommand{\labelenumii}{\arabic{enumii}.)}
```

which redefines \labelenumii to the value of counter enumii printed in Arabic, plus the characters '.)'. In this way, all the numbering levels may be changed. It is even possible to include more than one counter:

```
\renewcommand{\labelenumii}{\Alph{enumi}.\arabic{enumii}}
```

which will produce for every call to \item at level two the value of the counter enumi as a capital letter followed by the value of counter enumii as a number: that is, in the form A.1, A.2, ..., B.1, B.2, ... and so on.

If the new standard labels are to apply to the whole document, the redefining commands should be included in the preamble. Otherwise they are valid only within the environment in which they appear.

Exercise 4.6: *Change the standard labels for the* itemize *environment into a long dash —* (written ---) for the first level, to a medium dash - (--) for the second level, and to a hyphen - for the third level.

Exercise 4.7: *Change the standard labels for the* enumerate *environment for the first level to (I), (II), ..., and for the second level to the Roman numerals of the first level followed by the number for the second level in the form I-1:, I-2:, ..., II-1:, II-2:, ...*

Package: enumer- ate

Another method of customizing the enumeration labels is with the enumerate package in the tools collection (Section B.5.4). Once this package has been loaded, the enumerate environment accepts an optional argument specifying the text of the label. The characters A a I i 1 represent the number in alphabetical, Roman, Arabic styles. If these characters appear elsewhere in the label text, they must be in { }. For example,

```
\begin{enumerate}[{Case} A]
 \item Witness tells the truth
 \item Witness is lying
\end{enumerate}
```

$\Longrightarrow$

Case A Witness tells the truth
Case B Witness is lying

4.4   Generalized lists

Lists like those in the three environments itemize, enumerate, and description can be formed in a quite general way. The type of label and its width, the depth of indentation, spacings for paragraphs and labels, and so on may be wholly or partially set by the user by means of the list environment:

```
\begin{list}{stnd_lbl}{list_decl} item_list \end{list}
```

Here *item_list* consists of the text for the listed entries, each of which begins with an \item command that generates the corresponding label.

The *stnd_lbl* contains the definition of the label to be produced by the \item command when the optional argument is missing (see below).

The list parameters described in Section 4.4.2 are set by *list_decl* to whatever new values the user wishes.

4.4.1   Standard label

The first argument in the list environment defines the *stnd_lbl*, that is, the label that is produced by the \item command when it appears without an argument. In the case of an unchanging label, such as for the itemize environment, this is simply the desired symbol. If this is to be a mathematical symbol, it must be given as $*symbol_name*$, enclosed in $ signs. For example, to select ⇒ as the label, *stnd_lbl* must be defined to be $\Rightarrow$.

However, the label is often required to contain a sequential numeration. For this purpose, a counter must be created with the \newcounter{*name*} command, where *name* is its designation. This command must appear before the first application of the counter in a list environment. If a counter named marker has been defined for this use, then the argument *stnd_lbl* could be any of the commands for printing counters described in Section 10.1.4; for example, \arabic{marker} produces a running Arabic number.

Even more complex labels can be made up in this way. If the sequential labels are to be A-I, A-II, . . . , *stnd_lbl* is set to A--\Roman{marker}.

Before a counter can function properly within the standard label, it must be associated with that list by including the command \usecounter{*counter*} in *list_decl*, where *counter* is the name of the counter to be assigned (marker in the above example).

The standard label is actually generated by the command \makelabel{*label*}, which is called by the \item command. The user can redefine \makelabel with the aid of the \renewcommand in the list declaration:

> \renewcommand{\makelabel}{*new_definition*}

If the standard label is defined in this manner, the corresponding entry in the list environment is left blank. This is because \makelabel is the more general command and overrides the other definition.

4.4.2   List style parameters

There are a number of style parameters used for formatting lists that are set by LaTeX to certain standard values. These values may be altered by the user in the *list_decl* for that particular list. The assignment is made in the usual way with the \setlength command. However, if the assignment is made outside the list environment, in most cases it will simply be ignored. This is because there are preset default values for each parameter at each level that can only be overridden by *list_decl*.

The style parameters are listed below and are also illustrated in Figure 4.1 on the next page, which is based on one taken from Lamport (1985, 1994).

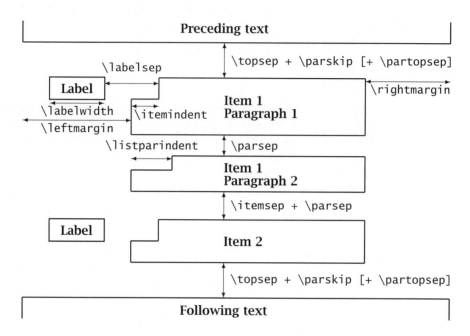

Figure 4.1: The `list` parameters

`\topsep`
> is the vertical spacing in addition to `\parskip` that is inserted between the list and the enclosing text above and below. Its default value is set at each list level and cannot be globally redefined outside the *list_decl*.

`\partopsep`
> is the vertical spacing in addition to `\topsep` + `\parskip` that is inserted above and below the list when a blank line precedes the first or follows the last `\item` entry. It may be redefined globally, but only for the first and second levels.

`\parsep`
> is the vertical spacing between paragraphs of a single `\item`. Its default value is reset at each level, as for `\topsep`.

`\itemsep`
> is the vertical spacing in addition to `\parsep` that is inserted between two `\item` entries. As for `\topsep` and `\parsep`, its default value is reset at each level and cannot be globally changed.

`\leftmargin`
> is the distance from the left edge of the current environment to the left margin of the list text. There are default values for it at each level that may

be globally redefined, as described in Section 4.4.6.

`\rightmargin`
> is the distance from the right edge of the current environment to the right margin of the list text. Its standard value is 0 pt, which can only be altered in *list_decl*.

`\listparindent`
> is the indentation depth of the first line of a paragraph within an `\item` with respect to the left margin of the list text. It is normally set to 0 pt so that no indentation occurs. This can only be changed in *list_decl*.

`\labelwidth`
> is the width of the box reserved for the label. The text of the label is printed right justified within this space. A new default value may be set globally, which then applies to all list levels.

`\labelsep`
> is the spacing between the label box and the list text. A new value may be assigned globally, but it is only effective at the first level.

`\itemindent`
> is the distance by which the label and the first line of text in an `\item` are indented to the right. It is normally set to 0 pt and thus has no effect. This value can only be redefined in *list_decl*.

When changing the vertical spacings from their standard values, it is recommended that a rubber length (Section 2.4.2) be used.

The label created by the `\item` command normally appears right justified within a box of width `\labelwidth`. It is possible to make it left justified, as in the following list of parameters, by putting `\hfill` at the end of the definition of the standard label or in the `\makelabel` command.

4.4.3 Example of a user's list

List of Figures:

> **Figure 1:** *Page format with head, body, and foot, showing the meaning of the various elements involved.*
>
> **Figure 2:** *Format of a general list showing its elements.*
>
> **Figure 3:** *A demonstration of some of the possibilities for drawing pictures with LaTeX.*

This list was produced with the following input:

```
\newcounter{fig}
\begin{list}{\bfseries\upshape Figure \arabic{fig}:}
  {\usecounter{fig}
\setlength{\labelwidth}{2cm}\setlength{\leftmargin}{2.6cm}
```

```
\setlength{\labelsep}{0.5cm}\setlength{\rightmargin}{1cm}
\setlength{\parsep}{0.5ex plus0.2ex minus0.1ex}
\setlength{\itemsep}{0ex plus0.2ex} \slshape}
\item Page format with head, body, and foot, showing the
      meaning of the various elements involved.
\item Format of a general list showing its elements.
\item A demonstration of some of the possibilities for
      drawing pictures with \LaTeX.
\end{list}
```

The command `\newcounter{fig}` sets up the counter `fig`. The standard label is defined as the word **Figure** in upright, boldface, followed by the running Arabic number, terminated by :. This label is printed for each `\item` command.

The list declaration contains `\usecounter{fig}` as its first command, which makes the counter `fig` operational within the list. The width of the label box (`\labelwidth`) is set to 2.0 cm, the left margin of the list text (`\leftmargin`) to 2.6 cm, the distance between the label and the text (`\labelsep`) to 0.5 cm, and the right edge of the list (`\rightmargin`) is set to be 1 cm from that of the enclosing text.

The vertical spacing between paragraphs within an item (`\parsep`) is 0.5 ex but can be stretched an extra 0.2 ex or shrunk by 0.1 ex. The additional spacing between items (`\itemsep`) is 0 ex, stretchable to 0.2 ex.

Standard values are used for all the other list parameters. The last command in the list declaration is `\slshape`, which sets the list text in a *slanted* typeface.

Note: If `\upshape` were not given in the label definition, the text of each `\item` would also be slanted, as *Figure 1:*.

4.4.4   Lists as new environments

If a particular type of list is employed several times within a document, it can become tiresome typing the same *stnd_lbl* and *list_decl* into the `list` environment every time. LaTeX offers the possibility of defining a given list as an environment under its own name. This is achieved by means of the `\newenvironment` command.

For example, the list in the above example can be stored so that it may be called at any time with the name `figlist`:

```
\newenvironment{figlist}{\begin{list}
   {\bfseries\upshape Figure \arabic{fig}:}
   {\usecounter{fig} ... {0ex plus0.2ex}\slshape}}
   {\end{list}}
```

It can then be called with

```
\begin{figlist} item_list \end{figlist}
```

so that it behaves as a predefined list environment.

Exercise 4.8: Define a new environment with the name `sample` that produces a list in which every call to `\item` prints labels Sample A, Sample B, and so on. The labels are to be left justified within a box of width 20mm, and the distance between the label box and the item text is to be 2mm, with a total left margin of 22mm. The right edge of the text is to be moved in 5mm from that of the enclosing text. The extra vertical spacing between two items is to be `1ex plus0.5ex minus0.4ex` in addition to the normal paragraph spacing. Secondary paragraphs within an item are to be indented by `1em`. The normal paragraph separation should be `0ex`, expandable to `0.5ex`.

!

LATEX itself makes frequent use of the list environment to define a number of other structures. For example, the `quote` environment is defined as

```
\newenvironment{quote}{\begin{list}{}
    {setlength{\rightmargin}{\leftmargin}}
    \item[]}{\end{list}}
```

This environment is thus a list in which the value of `\rightmargin` is set to the current value of `\leftmargin`, which has a default value of 2.5 em. The list itself consists of a single `\item` call with an *empty* label, a call that is automatically included in the definition of `quote` with the entry `\item[]`.

In the same way, LATEX defines the `quotation` and `verse` environments internally as special `list` environments. The left margins and the vertical spacings around the structures are left as the standard values for the `list` environment, and are therefore changed only when the standard values themselves are altered.

Finally, as an example of a possible user-defined special list we offer

```
\newenvironment{lquote}{\begin{list}{}{}\item[]}{\end{list}}
```

which creates an `lquote` environment that does nothing more than indent its enclosed text by the amount `\leftmargin`, with the right edge flush with that of the normal text, since `\rightmargin` has the standard value of 0 pt.

4.4.5   Trivial lists

!

LATEX also contains a `trivlist` environment, with syntax

```
\begin{trivlist} enclosed text \end{trivlist}
```

in which the arguments *stnd_lbl* and *list_decl* are omitted. This is the same as a `list` environment for which the label is empty, `\leftmargin`, `\labelwidth`, and `\itemindent` are all assigned the value 0 pt, while `\listparindent` is set equal to `\parindent` and `\parsep` to `\parskip`.

LATEX uses this environment to create further structures. For example, the call to the `center` environment generates internally the sequence

```
\begin{trivlist} \centering \item[] enclosed text \end{trivlist}
```

The environments `flushleft` and `flushright` are similarly defined.

4.4.6   Nested lists

Lists can be nested within one another with the environments `itemize`, `enumerate`, and `description`, to a maximum depth of six. At each level, the new left margin is indented by the amount `\leftmargin` relative to that of the next higher one.

!

As mentioned earlier, it is only possible to change the standard values of a limited number of the `list` parameters with declarations in the preamble. One exception is the indentations of the left margins for the different nesting levels. These are set internally by the parameters `\leftmargin`n, where n stands for i, ii, iii, iv, v, or vi. These values can be changed by the user; for example, by declaring `\setlength{\leftmarginiv}{12mm}`, the left margin of the fourth-level list is shifted 12 mm from that of the third. These declarations must be made *outside* of the `list` environments and not in the *list_decl*.

At each level of list nesting, the internal macro `\@list`n (n being i to vi) is called. This sets the value of `\leftmargin` equal to that of the corresponding `\leftmargin`n, unless `\leftmargin` is explicitly declared in the `list` environment. That is, there does not exist a single standard value for `\leftmargin` externally, but rather six different ones. The parameter `\leftmargin` has meaning only within a `list` environment.

4.5   Theorem-like declarations

In scientific literature one often has text structures such as

Theorem 1 (Balzano–Weierstrass) *Every infinite set of bounded points possesses at least one maximum point.*

or

Axiom 4.1 *The natural numbers form a set S of distinct elements. For any two elements a, b, they are either identical, a = b, or different from one another, a ≠ b.*

Similar structures frequently appear with names such as *Definition, Corollary, Declaration, Lemma* instead of *Theorem* or *Axiom*. What they have in common is that a keyword and a running number are printed in **boldface** and the corresponding text in *italic*.

Of course, these could be generated by the user by explicitly giving the type styles and appropriate number, but if a new structure of that type is later inserted in the middle of the text, the user would have the tedious job of renumbering all the following occurrences. With the command

   `\newtheorem{`*struct_type*`}{`*struct_title*`}[`*in_counter*`]`

LaTeX will keep track of the numbering automatically. Here *struct_type* is the user's arbitrary designation for the structure, while *struct_title* is the word that is printed in boldface followed by the running number (for example, **Theorem**). If the optional argument *in_counter* is missing, the numbering is carried out sequentially throughout the entire document. However, if the name of an existing counter, such as `chapter`, is given for *in_counter*, the numbering is reset every time that counter is augmented, and both are printed together, as in **Axiom 4.1** above.

The predefined structures are called with the command

   `\begin{`*struct_type*`}[`*extra_title*`]`   *text*   `\end{`*struct_type*`}`

which also increments the necessary counter and generates the proper number. The above examples were produced with

```
\newtheorem{theorem}{Theorem} \newtheorem{axiom}{Axiom}[chapter]
. . . . . . . . . . . . . . .
\begin{theorem}[Balzano--Weierstrass] Every .... \end{theorem}
\begin{axiom} The natural numbers form .......... \end{axiom}
```

The optional *extra_title* also appears in boldface within parentheses ( ) following the running number.

Occasionally a structure is not numbered on its own but together with another structure. This can be included in the definition with another optional argument

$$\newtheorem\{\textit{struct\_type}\}\,[\textit{num\_like}]\,\{\textit{struct\_name}\}$$

where *num_like* is the name of an existing theorem structure that shares the same counter. Thus by defining `\newtheorem{subthrm}[theorem]{Sub-Theorem}`, the two structures `theorem` and `subthrm` will be numbered as a single series: **Theorem 1**, **Sub-Theorem 2**, **Sub-Theorem 3**, **Theorem 4**, and so on.

For more powerful theorem tools, see the $\mathcal{A}_{\mathcal{M}}\mathcal{S}$ `amsthm` package (Section 15.3.1) and the `theorem` package in the tools collection (Section B.5.4).

4.6   Printing literal text

Occasionally it is necessary to print text exactly as it is typed, with all special characters, blanks, and line breaks appearing literally, unformatted, and in a typewriter font. Lines of computer code or samples of LaTeX input text are examples of such literal text. This is accomplished with the environments

```
\begin{verbatim}    text  \end{verbatim}
\begin{verbatim*}   text  \end{verbatim*}
```

A new line is inserted before and after these environments.

With the *-form, blanks are printed with the symbol ␣ to make them visible.

As an example, on page 97 some input text is printed to demonstrate the use of footnotes in forbidden modes. This is done with

```
\begin{verbatim}
 \addtocounter{footnote}{-1}\footnotetext{Small insects}
 \stepcounter{footnote}\footnotetext{Large mammals}
\end{verbatim}
```

Literal text may also be printed within a line using the commands `\verb` and `\verb*`, as for example

```
\verb=\emph{words of text}=    \emph{words of text}
\verb*=\emph{words of text}=   \emph{words␣of␣text}
```

where the first character after `\verb` or `\verb*` (here =) is the delimiter, such that all text up to the next occurrence of that character is printed literally. This character may not appear in the literal text, obviously.

In contrast to the behavior in the verbatim environment, the literal text must be all on one line in the input text, otherwise an error message is printed. This is to indicate that you may have forgotten to repeat the delimiting character.

Important: Neither the verbatim environment nor the \verb command may be used in an argument of any other command!

Exercise 4.9: Reproduce some input lines from this book as literal text.

4.6.1   Extension packages for literal text

Package:
alltt

The standard package alltt (Section B.5.3, page 386) provides an alltt environment that also prints its contents literally in a typewriter font, except that the characters \ { } retain their normal meaning. Thus LaTeX commands can be included within the literal text. For example,

```
\begin{alltt}
Underlining \underline{typewriter}
text is also possible.
Note that dollar ($) and
percent (%) signs are
treated \emph{literally}.
\end{alltt}
```

Underlining <u>typewriter</u>
text is also possible.
Note that dollar ($) and
percent (%) signs are
treated *literally*.

Package:
shortvrb

The standard package shortvrb (Section B.5.3, page 386) offers a shorthand for the \verb command. After issuing \MakeShortVerb{\|}, one can print short literal text with |*text*|. The countering command \DeleteShortVerb{\|} then restores the original meaning to |. Any character may be temporarily turned into a literal switch this way.

Package:
verbatim

One problem with the verbatim environment is that the entire literal text is input and stored before processing, something that can lead to memory overflows. The verbatim package in the tools collection (Section B.5.4, page 389) re-implements the environment to avoid this problem. A minor drawback is that *there must not be any other text on the same line as the* \end{verbatim}.

The verbatim package offers two other extra features. It provides a comment environment that simply ignores its contents, as though each line started with a % sign (Section 4.7). And it adds a command \verbatiminput{*filename*} to input the specified file as literal text. This is useful for listing actual computer programs rather than copying them into the LaTeX file.

4.6.2   E-mail and Internet addresses

Package:
url

E-mail and Internet addresses present some special problems that are solved with the url package by Donald Arseneau. These addresses are best listed in a typewriter font, often contain special symbols, and should never be hyphenated, because the hyphen could be interpreted as part of the address. The obvious solution would be to use the \verb command, which fulfills all these conditions but suppresses all line breaks. Thus, if the address does not fit on the current line, it will stick out into the right margin. Using \texttt instead means that special symbols must be preceded by a backslash and hyphenation is suppressed, although line breaks can still occur at spaces, something that should not be present in any decent address.

Inserting the address with the \url command allows it to be broken at non-letters between words, without a hyphen. Moreover, its argument is treated literally, so all special characters are printed as given, just as with \verb. In fact, the argument of the \url command may be either enclosed in curly braces, as usual, or delimited by some arbitrary character, just as with \verb.

An Internet address may be given as \url{http://address.edu/home/page/} or an e-mail address might be given as \url=fred.smith@general.services.gov=	An Internet address is given as http://address.edu/home/page/ or an e-mail address might be given as =fred.smith@general.services.gov=

The \url command is to be preferred for another reason: It conforms to logical markup indicating the purpose of its argument. In fact, the hyperref package of Section 13.2.4 will even turn the argument into an active link, something it does not do for \verb arguments.

The printed appearance of the address can be set by specifying \urlstyle{*style*}, where *style* is one of tt (default), rm, sf, or same, for typewriter, Roman, sans serif, or unchanged font, respectively.

A fixed address can be predefined with, for example,

```
\urldef{\myurl}\url{myname@mydomain.uk}
```

Now \myurl is used to print myname@mydomain.uk.

There is also a \path command for giving directory/folder names, with the same syntax as \url. As logical markup, it has a different significance; for example, the hyperref package does not turn it into a link.

For further information on advanced uses of this package, see the comments at the end of the file url.sty.

4.7   Comments within text

All computer languages provide a means of inserting comments into the code, including explanatory notes, documentation, history of development, or alternative text or code that has been temporarily deactivated. Comment lines are completely ignored during processing. They are only intended for human readers inspecting the source text.

In LaTeX, the comment character is the percent sign, %. When this character appears in the text, it and the rest of the line are ignored. If a comment is several lines long, each line must be prefixed with %.

As for other single character commands, the percent sign itself is printed with the command \%, as explained in Section 2.5.4.

The comment character % is also useful for experimenting with text or definitions of user commands or formatting parameters, to try alternatives without deleting the old versions. By 'commenting out' selective lines, one can play around with variations without losing them.

Large sections of text may be more effectively commented out with the `comment` environment from the `verbatim` package (see page 82).

Finally, the % character has an important role to play in suppressing implied blanks at the end of a line. This is especially desirable in user definitions wherein unexpected blanks can creep in between otherwise invisible declarations with arguments. See Section 10.5.2.

Exercise 4.10: Add some comment lines to your Exercise 4.9 explaining where the text has been taken from. The result should be the same as when those lines were absent.

Text in Boxes

5

Regular text is formatted into lines and paragraphs that are used to fill up the full width and height of the main page. However, there are occasions when a segment of text is to be set in a box on its own, possibly with differing line width, to be placed as a unit somewhere on the page, perhaps with a frame around it, or as two paragraphs side by side. LaTeX provides several structures for doing this, described in the next section.

Footnotes and marginal notes, other methods for repackaging a piece of text to be placed as a block at a certain spot on the page, are also treated in this chapter.

5.1 Boxes

A *box* is a piece of text that TeX treats as a unit, like a single character. A *box* (along with the text within it) can be moved left, right, up, or down. Since the box is a unit, TeX cannot break it up again, even it was originally made up of smaller individual boxes. It is, however, possible to put those smaller boxes together as one pleases when constructing the overall box.

This is exactly what TeX does internally when it carries out the formatting: The individual characters are packed in *character* boxes, which are put together into *line* boxes horizontally with rubber lengths inserted between the words. The *line* boxes are stacked vertically into *paragraph* boxes, again with rubber lengths separating them. These then go into the *page body* box, which with the *head* and *foot* boxes constitutes the *page* box.

LaTeX offers the user a choice of three *box types*: LR boxes, paragraph boxes, and rule boxes. The LR (left–right) box contains material that is ordered horizontally from *left* to *right* in a single line. A paragraph box will have its contents made into vertically stacked lines of a given width. A rule box is a rectangle filled solidly with black, usually for drawing horizontal and vertical lines.

5.1.1 LR boxes

To create LR boxes containing text in a single line, one can make use of the commands

> \mbox{*text*}   and   \makebox[*width*][*pos*]{*text*}
> \fbox{*text*}   and   \framebox[*width*][*pos*]{*text*}

The two commands at the left produce an LR box with a width exactly equal to that of the *text* given between the braces { }. The \fbox command is the same as \mbox except that the ‎ text ‎ is also framed.

   With the two commands at the right, the width is predetermined by the optional length argument *width*. The other optional argument *pos* specifies how the text is positioned within the box. With no value given, the *text* is centered. Otherwise *pos* may be

   l   to left justify the *text*,
   r   to right justify it,
   s   to stretch it to fill up the full width.

Thus \makebox[3.5cm]{centered text} creates a box of width 3.5 cm in which the text is centered, as   centered text   , filled with white space, while with \framebox[3.5cm][r]{right justified} the text is pushed to the right inside a framed box of width 3.5 cm: ‎ right justified ‎. One may also give

> \framebox[3.5cm][s]{stretched\dotfill text}

to fill up the box, as ‎ stretched . . . . text ‎, in which case some rubber length (Section 2.4.2) or other filler (page 33) must be added where the stretching is to occur.

   If the *text* has a natural width that is larger than that specified in *width*, it will stick out of the box on the left, right, or both sides, depending on the choice of *pos*. For example,

> \framebox[2mm]{centered} produces   cent‎e‎red

   The above application may appear rather silly for \framebox, but it can indeed be very useful for \makebox. A width specification of 0 pt for \makebox can generate a centered, left-, or right-justified positioning of text in diagrams made with the picture environment (see Chapter 16 for examples). It may also be used to cause two pieces of text to overlap, as \makebox[0pt][l]{/}S prints a slash through an S, as $\not\!S$.

Note: Length specifications must always contain a dimensional unit, even when they are zero. Thus 0pt must be given for the width, not 0.

   It is also possible to specify the *width* of an LR box relative to its natural dimensions (those produced by the simple \mbox command):

   \width   is the natural width of the box.
   \height   is the distance from baseline to top.
   \depth   is the distance from baseline to bottom.
   \totalheight   is \height plus \depth.

To make a framed box such that the width is six times the total height, containing centered text, use the command

`\framebox[6\totalheight]{Text}` | Text |

Note: These special length parameters only have meaning within the *width* specification of an LR box, or within the *height* specification of a paragraph box, as shown below. In any other context, they will produce an error message.

If a set piece of text is to appear in several places within the document, it can be stored by first giving the command

    `\newsavebox{\`*boxname*`}`

to create a box with the name *boxname*. This name must conform to LaTeX command name syntax (letters only) with an initial \\. The name must not conflict with any existing LaTeX command names. After such a box has been initiated, the commands

    `\sbox{\`*boxname*`}{`*text*`}` or
    `\savebox{\`*boxname*`}[`*width*`][`*pos*`]{`*text*`}`

will store the contents *text* for future use. The optional arguments *width* and *pos* have the same meanings as for `\makebox` and `\framebox`. Now with the command

    `\usebox{\`*boxname*`}`

the stored contents are inserted into the document text wherever desired, as a single unit.

The contents of an LR box may also be stored with the environment

    `\begin{lrbox}{`*boxname*`}`
     text
    `\end{lrbox}`

This is equivalent to `\sbox{\`*boxname*`}{`*text*`}`. Its advantage is that it allows text within a user-defined environment (Section 10.4) to be stored for future use with `\usebox`.

5.1.2   Vertical shifting of LR boxes

The command

    `\raisebox{`*lift*`}[`*height*`][`*depth*`]{`*text*`}`

produces an `\mbox` with contents *text*, raised above the current baseline by an amount *lift*. The optional arguments tell LaTeX to treat the box as though its extension above the baseline were *height* and that below were *depth*. Without these arguments, the box has its natural size determined by *text* and *lift*. Note that *lift*, *height*, and *depth* are lengths (Section 2.4.1). If *lift* is negative, the box is lowered below the baseline.

For example:

    `Baseline \raisebox{1ex}{high} and \raisebox{-1ex}{low}`
    `and back again`

produces: Baseline ^{high} and $_{\text{low}}$ and back again.

The values for *height* and *depth* can be totally different from the actual ones of the *text*. Their effect is to determine how far away the previous and next lines of text should be from the current line, based on the heights and depths of all the boxes (characters are also boxes) in the line. By raising a box but specifying *height* to be the regular character size, the raised box will overprint the line above, and similarly for *depth* when a box is lowered.

5.1.3   Parboxes and minipages

Whole paragraphs can be put into separate *vertical* boxes (or *parboxes* in the LaTeX jargon) with the command

> \parbox[*pos*]{*width*}{*text*}

or with the environment

> \begin{minipage}[*pos*]{*width*}   *text*   \end{minipage}

Both produce a vertical box of width *width*, in which the lines of text are stacked on top of each other as in normal paragraph mode.

The optional positioning argument *pos* can take on the values

>   b   to align the bottom edge of the box with the current baseline,
>   t   to align the top line of text with the current baseline.

Without any positioning argument, the parbox is centered vertically on the baseline of the external line of text.

The positioning argument is only meaningful when the \parbox command or the minipage environment occurs within a line of text, otherwise the current line and its baseline have no meaning. If the parbox is immediately preceded by a blank line, it begins a new paragraph. In this case, the vertical positioning of the parbox is made with reference to the following elements of the paragraph. These could be further parboxes. If the paragraph consists of only a single parbox or minipage, the positioning argument is meaningless and has no effect.

Examples:

```
\parbox{3.5cm}{\sloppy This is a 3.5 cm wide parbox. It is
    vertically centered on the}
\hfill CURRENT LINE \hfill
\parbox{5.5cm}{Narrow pages are hard to format. They usually
    produce many warning messages on the monitor. The command
    \texttt{\symbol{92}sloppy} can stop this.}
```

This is a 3.5 cm wide parbox. It is vertically centered on the	CURRENT LINE	Narrow pages are hard to format. They usually produce many warning messages on the monitor. The command \sloppy can stop this.

```
\begin{minipage}[b]{4.3cm}
 The minipage environment creates a vertical box like the parbox
 command. The bottom line of this minipage is aligned with the
\end{minipage}\hfill
\parbox{3.0cm}{middle of this narrow parbox, which in turn is
  aligned with}
\hfill
\begin{minipage}[t]{3.8cm}
 the top line of the right-hand minipage. It is recommended that
 the user experiment with the positioning arguments to get used
 to their effects.
\end{minipage}
```

The minipage environment creates a vertical box like the parbox command. The bottom line of this minipage is aligned with the

middle of this narrow parbox, which in turn is aligned with

the top line of the right-hand minipage. It is recommended that the user experiment with the positioning arguments to get used to their effects.

In Section 5.1.7 we demonstrate how parboxes can be vertically stacked in any desired manner relative to one another.

The \parbox command produces a vertical box containing the *text* just like the minipage environment. However, the latter is more general. The *text* in a \parbox may not contain any of the centering, list, or other environments described in Sections 4.2 through 4.5. These may, on the other hand, appear within a minipage environment. That is, a minipage can include centered or indented text as well as lists and tabbings.

5.1.4   Problems with vertical placement

Vertical positioning of minipages and parboxes can often lead to unexpected results, which can be explained by showing more graphically how a box is treated by LaTeX. Suppose we want to place two parboxes of different heights side by side, aligned on their first lines, and the two together set on the current line of text at the bottom. The 'obvious' way of doing this is

```
\begin{minipage}[b]{..}
   \parbox[t]{..}{..} \hfill  \parbox[t]{..}{..}
\end{minipage}
```

which does not work, for it produces instead the following results:

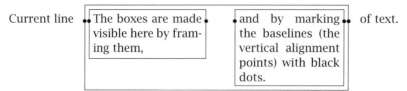

The reason for this is that each parbox or minipage is treated externally as a single character with its own height and depth above and below the baseline. As far as the outer minipage is concerned, it contains only two 'characters' on the same line, and that line is both the top and bottom one. Thus the bottom line of the outer minipage is indeed aligned with the line of text, but that bottom line is simultaneously the top line. The solution is to add a dummy second line to the outer box, as

> \parbox[t]{..}{..} \hfill \parbox[t]{..}{..} \\ \mbox{}

The dummy line may not be entirely empty, hence the \mbox.

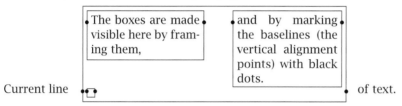

A similar problem occurs if two boxes are to be aligned with their bottom lines, and the pair aligned at the top with the current line of text. Here there are two possibilities to add a dummy *first* line.

> \mbox{} \\   aligns with the very top, or
> \mbox{} \\[-\baselineskip] aligns with the first text line.

An example of the first case is shown on page 176. Dummy lines are also needed for the solution of Exercise 5.1 on page 93.

5.1.5   Paragraph boxes of specific height

The complete syntax of the \parbox command and minipage environment includes two more optional arguments:

> \parbox[*pos*][*height*][*inner_pos*]{*width*}{*text*}

> \begin{minipage}[*pos*][*height*][*inner_pos*]{*width*}
>   *text*
> \end{minipage}

In both cases, *height* is a length specifying the height of the box; the parameters \height, \width, \depth, and \totalheight may be employed within the *height* argument in the same way as in the *width* argument of \makebox and \framebox (page 86).

The optional argument *inner_pos* states how the text is to be positioned *internally*, something that is only meaningful if *height* has been given. Its possible values are:

> t   to push the text to the top of the box,
> b   to shove it to the bottom,
> c   to center it vertically,
> s   to stretch it to fill up the whole box.

In the last case, rubber lengths (Section 2.4.2) should be present where the vertical stretching is to take place.

Note the difference between the external positioning argument *pos* and the internal one *inner_pos*: The former states how the box is to be aligned with the surrounding text, while the latter determines how the contents are placed within the box itself.

Example:

```
\begin{minipage}[t][2cm][t]{3cm}
   This is a minipage of height 2~cm with the text
   at the top.
\end{minipage}\hrulefill
\parbox[t][2cm][c]{3cm}{In this parbox, the text
   is centered on the same height.}\hrulefill
\begin{minipage}[t][2cm][b]{3cm}
   In this third paragraph box, the text is at the bottom.
\end{minipage}
```

This is a minipage of height 2 cm with the text at the top.   In this parbox, the text is centered on the same height.   In this third paragraph box, the text is at the bottom.

The `\hrulefill` commands between the boxes show where the baselines are. All three boxes are the same size and differ only in their values of *inner_pos*.

5.1.6   Rule boxes

A rule box is a basically a filled-in black rectangle. The syntax for the general command is:

> `\rule[`*lift*`]{`*width*`}{`*height*`}`

which produces a solid rectangle of width *width* and height *height*, raised above the baseline by an amount *lift*. Thus `\rule{8mm}{3mm}` generates ▬. Without the optional argument *lift*, the rectangle is set on the baseline of the current line of text.

The parameters *lift*, *width*, and *height* are all lengths (Section 2.4.1). If *lift* has a negative value, the rectangle is set below the baseline.

It is also possible to have a rule box of zero width. This creates an invisible line with the given *height*. Such a construction is called a *strut* and is used to force a horizontal box to have a desired height or depth that is different from that of its contents. For this purpose, \vspace is inappropriate because it adds additional vertical space to that which is already there.

For example: `\fbox{Text}` produces Text. In order to print Text, one has to tell TEX that the box contents extend above and below the baseline by the desired amounts. This was done with `\fbox{\rule[-2mm]{0cm}{6mm}Text}`. This says that the text to be framed consists of 'an invisible bar beginning 2 mm below the baseline, 6 mm long, followed by the word *Text*'. The vertical bar indeed remains unseen, but it determines the upper and lower edges of the frame.

5.1.7   Nested boxes

The box commands described above may be nested to any desired level. Including an LR box within a parbox or a minipage causes no obvious conceptual difficulties. The opposite, a parbox within an LR box, is also possible, and is easy to visualize if one keeps in mind that every box is a unit, treated by LATEX as a single character of the corresponding size.

> A parbox inside an \fbox command has the effect that the entire parbox is framed. The present structure was made with
>
> `\fbox{\fbox{\parbox{10cm}{A parbox...}}}`
>
> This is a parbox of width 10 cm inside a framebox inside a second framebox, which thus produces the double-framing effect.

Enclosing a parbox inside a \raisebox allows vertical displacements of any desired amount. The two boxes here both have positioning [b], but the one at the right has been produced with:

```
\raisebox{1cm}{\begin{minipage}[b]{2.5cm}
        a b c d e ... x y z\\
        \underline{baseline}
      \end{minipage} }
```

a b c d e f g h i
j k l m n o p q r
s t u v w x y z
<u>baseline</u>

which displaces it upwards by 1 cm.   <u>baseline</u>

A very useful structure is one in which `minipage` environments are positioned relative to one another inside an enclosing `minipage`. The positioning argument of the outside `minipage` can be used to align its contents as a unit with the neighboring text or boxes. An example of this is given in Exercise 5.1.

Finally, vertical boxes such as \parbox commands and `minipage` environments may be saved as the *text* in an \sbox or \savebox command, to be recalled later with \usebox, as described in Section 5.1.1.

5.1.8   Box style parameters

!

There are two style parameters for the frame boxes \fbox and \framebox that may be reset by the user:

\fboxrule determines the thickness of the frame lines,

\fboxsep sets the amount of spacing between the frame and enclosed text.

New values are assigned to these length parameters in the usual LaTeX manner with the command \setlength: The line thickness for all the following \framebox and \fbox commands is set to 0.5 mm with \setlength{\fboxrule}{0.5mm}.

The scope of these settings also obeys the usual rule: If they are found in the preamble, then they apply to the entire document; if they are within an environment, then they are valid only until the end of that environment.

These parameters do *not* influence the \framebox command that is employed within the picture environment (Section 16.1.4) and which has different syntax and functionality from those of the normal \framebox command.

Exercise 5.1: How can the following nested structure be generated? (Note: Font size is \footnotesize.)

The first line of this 3.5 cm wide minipage or parbox is aligned with the first line of the neighboring minipage or parbox.

This 5 cm wide minipage or parbox is positioned so that its top line is at the same level as that of the box on the left, while its bottom line is even with that of the box on the right. The naïve notion that this arrangement may be achieved with the positioning arguments set to t, t, and b is incorrect. Why? What would this selection really produce?

The true solution involves the nesting of two of the three structures in an enclosing minipage, which is then separately aligned with the third one.

Note: There are two variants for the solution, depending on whether the left and middle structures are first enclosed in a minipage, or the middle and right ones. Try to work out both solutions. Incidentally, the third minipage is 3 cm wide.

Note: The problems of correctly aligning two side-by-side boxes as a pair on a line of text (Section 5.1.4) arises here once more. It will be necessary to add a dummy line to get the vertical alignment correct.

Exercise 5.2: Produce the framed structure shown below and store it with the command \sbox{\warning}{structure}. You will first have to create a box named \warning with the \newsavebox{\warning} command. Print this warning at various places in your exercise file by giving \usebox{\warning}.

> Vertical placement of minipages and parboxes can lead to surprising results, which may be corrected by the use of dummy lines.

Note: The parbox width is 10 cm. There should be no difficulty producing the framed structure if one follows the previous example for the double-framed box. Watch out when writing \sbox{\warning}{structure} that you have the correct number of closing braces at the end.

Next, change the values for the line thickness (\fboxrule) and frame spacing (\fboxsep) and print your results once more.

5.1.9 Further framed boxes

Package:
fancybox The fancybox package, by Timothy van Zandt, allows additional framed boxes of various styles. These make use of the length \fboxsep to set the distance between frame and text, the same as for \fbox and \framebox. Depending on the box type, additional new lengths are also applicable. They may be changed with \setlength to modify the box appearance. These new framed boxes are:

\shadowbox{*text*}
The width of the shadow is given by the length \shadowsize, default 4 pt. Multiline *text* must be placed in a minipage environment, the same as for \fbox.

\doublebox{*text*}
The width of the inner frame is 0.75\fboxrule, that of the outer frame is 1.5\fboxrule, and the spacing between the frames is 1.5\fboxrule plus 0.5 pt.

\ovalbox{*text*}
The thickness of the frame is that of \thinlines (Section 16.1.4); the diameter of the corners is set with the command \cornersize{*frac*}, to *frac* times the smaller of the box width or height, or with \cornersize*{*size*} to the length *size*. The default is *frac*=.5.

\Ovalbox{*text*}
The frame thickness is set by \thicklines, but otherwise is the same as \ovalbox.

This package also allows all pages to be boxed as part of the page style. This is done by issuing \fancypage{*cmds1*}{*cmds2*}, where *cmds1* and *cmds2* are commands setting box parameters, terminated by one of the box commands \fbox, \shadowbox, and so on. The first set, *cmds1*, forms a box with the head- and foot-lines outside, while the second set draws a box including them. Normally one would only specify one set, leaving the other blank, such as:

```
\fancypage{\setlength{\fboxsep}{5pt}
   \setlength{\shadowsize}{3pt}\shadowbox}{}
```

for a shadow box on each page excluding head and footlines. There is also the command \thisfancypage{*cmds1*}{*cmds2*} to box just the current page.

5.2 Footnotes and marginal notes

5.2.1 Standard footnotes

Footnotes are generated with the command

\footnote{*footnote_text*}

which comes immediately after the word requiring an explanation in a footnote. The text *footnote_text* appears as a footnote in a smaller typeface at the bottom of the page. The first line of the footnote is indented and is given the same footnote marker as that inserted in the main text. The first footnote on a page is separated from the rest of the page text by means of a short horizontal line.

The standard footnote marker is a small, raised number,[1] which is sequentially numbered. This footnote is produced with:

```
... raised number,\footnote{Normal American practice is to
place the footnote number ... punctuation mark.} which is ...
```

The footnote numbering is incremented throughout the whole document for the article class, whereas it is reset to 1 for each new chapter in the report and book classes.

The \footnote command may only be given within the normal paragraph mode, and not within math or LR modes. In practice, this means it may not appear within an LR box (Section 5.1.1) or a parbox (Section 5.1.3). However, it may be used within a minipage environment, in which case the footnote text is printed beneath the minipage and not at the bottom of the actual page.[2]

The \footnote command must immediately follow the word that is to receive the note, without any intervening blanks or spacing. A footnote at the end of a sentence can be given after the period, as in the last example above:

```
... of the actual page.\footnote{With nested ... wrong place.}
```

5.2.2 Nonstandard footnotes

If the user wishes the footnote numbering to be reset to 1 for each \section command with the article class, this may be achieved with

---

[1] Normal American practice is to place the footnote number after any punctuation, whereas in Europe it is more usual to place it immediately after the word, preceding any punctuation mark.

[2] With nested minipages, the footnote comes after the next \end{minipage} command, which could be at the wrong place.

```
\setcounter{footnote}{0}
```

just before or after a \section command.

The internal footnote counter has the name footnote. Each call to \footnote increments this counter by one and prints the new value in Arabic numbering as the footnote marker. A different style of marker can be implemented with the command

```
\renewcommand{\thefootnote}{\number_style{footnote}}
```

where *number_style* is one of the counter print commands described in Section 10.1.4: \arabic, \roman, \Roman, \alph, or \Alph. However, for the counter footnote, there is an additional counter print command available, \fnsymbol, which prints the counter values 1 through 9 as one of nine symbols:

$$* \quad \dagger \quad \ddagger \quad \S \quad \P \quad \| \quad ** \quad \dagger\dagger \quad \ddagger\ddagger$$

If more than 10 \footnote calls are issued before the footnote counter is reset, there will be trouble: Author beware!

An optional argument may be added to the \footnote command

```
\footnote[num]{footnote_text}
```

where *num* is a positive integer that is used instead of the value of the footnote counter for the marker. In this case, the footnote counter is not incremented. For example,**

```
\renewcommand{\thefootnote}{\fnsymbol{footnote}}
For example,\footnote[7]{The 7th symbol ... marker.}
\renewcommand{\thefootnote}{\arabic{footnote}}
```

where the last line is necessary to restore the footnote marker style to its standard form. Otherwise, all future footnotes would be marked with symbols and not with numbers.

5.2.3   Footnotes in forbidden modes

A footnote marker can be inserted in the text with the command

```
\footnotemark[num]
```

even where the \footnote command is normally not allowed, that is, in LR boxes, tables, and math mode. The marker is either the optional argument *num* or, if it is omitted, the incremented value of the footnote counter. The footnote itself is not generated. This must be done external to the forbidden mode with the command

```
\footnotetext[num]{footnote_text}
```

**The 7th symbol appears as the footnote marker.

If the optional argument has been used for the footnote marker, the same *num* must be given as the option for the text command. Similarly, if no option was used for the marker, none may appear with the text. The footnote will be generated with the value of *num* or with that of the footnote counter.

This counter is incremented by a call to \footnotemark without an optional argument. The corresponding \footnotetext command, on the other hand, does not alter the counter.

If there are a number of \footnotemark commands without optional arguments appearing before the next \footnotetext command, it is necessary to adjust the counter with the command

```
\addtocounter{footnote}{dif}
```

where *dif* is a negative number saying how many times the counter must be set back. Then before every \footnotetext command, the counter must be incremented by one. This can be done either with the command \addtocounter, with *dif*=1, or with the command

```
\stepcounter{footnote}
```

which adds 1 to the given counter.

For example: | mosquitoes[3] and elephants[4] |

```
For example: \fbox{mosquitoes\footnotemark\ and
    elephants\footnotemark}
```

generates the footnote markers [3] and [4]. Now the counter has the value 4. For the first \footnotetext outside the framed box to operate with the correct counter value, it must first be decremented by one. The two footnote texts are made with

```
\addtocounter{footnote}{-1}\footnotetext{Small insects}
\stepcounter{footnote}\footnotetext{Large mammals}
```

immediately following the \fbox{} command. The footnote counter now has the same value as it did on leaving the \fbox.

5.2.4 Footnotes in minipages

As mentioned in Section 5.2.1, footnote commands are allowed inside the minipage environment. However, the footnote appears underneath the minipage, not below the main page.

---

[3]Small insects
[4]Large mammals

Footnote commands within a minipage[a] have a different marker style. The footnote comes after the next \end{minipage} command.[b] Minipage footnotes have a counter separate from that of the main page, called mpfootnote, counting independently of footnote.

```
\begin{minipage}{6cm}
Footnote commands within
a minipage\footnote{The
marker is a raised
lowercase letter.} have
a different...
\end{minipage}
```

---

[a]The marker is a raised lowercase letter.
[b]Watch out for nested minipages.

> ! Footnotes within a tabular environment can normally only be generated with the commands described above: \footnotemark within the table and \footnotetext outside the environment. However, if the tabular environment is inside a minipage, normal \footnote commands may also be used inside the table. The footnote appears below the table where the minipage comes to an end.

Exercise 5.3: Produce a number of footnotes in your standard exercise file by inserting them where you think fit and by selecting some appropriate footnote text.

Exercise 5.4: Redefine the command \thefootnote so that the footnote markers become the symbols illustrated in Section 5.2.2. Add the redefinition to the preamble of your standard exercise file.

5.2.5   Marginal notes

Notes in the page margin are produced with the command

    \marginpar{note_text}

This is a margin-al note

which puts the text *note_text* into the margin beginning at the level of the line where the command is given. The marginal note appearing here was generated with

```
... The marginal note \marginpar{This\\ is a\\ margin-\\al note}
    appearing here ...
```

The text is normally enclosed in a parbox of width 1.9 cm (0.75 in). Such a narrow box causes great difficulties with line breaking, which is why the lines are manually broken with the \\ command in the above example. Such a box is far more ⟹ appropriate for marginal notes in the form of a single symbol, such as the arrow shown here.

The width of the marginal note can be changed with a style parameter described in the next section. The user must be sure that the total page width does not become too big for the printer.

By default, marginal notes appear in the right-hand margin of the page or in the outer margin when the twoside option has been selected. 'Outer' refers to the right margin for odd pages, and the left margin for even ones. With the twocolumn option, they are placed in the outside margins: left for the left column and right for the right one.

This leads to a problem for marginal markings such as the arrow illustrated on the previous page. On this page, it must point in the opposite direction. In fact, its $\Longleftarrow$ direction depends on which side of the page it is to appear, and that in turn depends on the page number or column. Since these are not known at the time of writing (and may even change with later revisions) it is necessary to have another solution. This is provided by the extended syntax of the `\marginpar` command

```
\marginpar[left_text]{right_text}
```

This form of the command contains two versions of the marginal text, *left_text* to go into the left margin and *right_text* for the right margin, depending on which one is selected. Both arrows on this and the previous page were generated with the same command

```
\marginpar[\hfill$\Longrightarrow$]{$\Longleftarrow$}
```

(The mathematical arrow commands are explained in Section 7.3.5.)

$\Longrightarrow$ Without the `\hfill` command in the above `\marginpar` example, the arrow in the left margin appears as it does at the side of this paragraph, too far over to the left. The reason for this is that the `\marginpar` command sets its contents flush with the left edge of the narrow margin box. This left edge is aligned with the main text only when the note is put on the right side; however, in the left margin, it is displaced from the main text. The `\hfill` command has the effect of setting the contents flush with the right edge of the margin box, which is then properly aligned with the main text.

A similar device was used to make the first marginal note in this section. The actual command given was

```
\marginpar[\flushright This\\ is a\\ margin-\\al note]
    {This\\ is a\\ margin-\\al note}
```

Here `\flushright` (Section 4.2.2) is equivalent to putting an `\hfill` on each line.

The standard positioning of the marginal notes can be switched with the command `\reversemarginpar`. When this command has been given, marginal notes will appear in the left margin, or in the 'inner' margin for the `twoside` option. The command `\normalmarginpar` restores normal behavior. These commands have no effect with the `twocolumn` option.

If the note appears at the bottom of a page, it will extend downwards below the last line of regular text. For this reason, and because of the difficulties with line breaking for narrow columns, marginal notes should be kept short, limited to a few words or a symbol.

5.2.6   Style parameters for footnotes and marginal notes

There are two footnote style parameters that may be changed as needed, either in the preamble or locally within an environment.

`\footnotesep`

> The vertical spacing between two footnotes. This is a length that can be changed with the `\setlength` command.

`\footnoterule`

> The command that draws a horizontal line between the page text and the footnotes. It should not add any net vertical spacing. It may be changed, for example, by

$$\texttt{\textbackslash renewcommand\{\textbackslash footnoterule\}}$$
$$\texttt{\{\textbackslash rule\{\textit{wth}\}\{\textit{hght}\}\textbackslash vspace\{-\textit{hght}\}\}}$$

> A value of 0 cm for the *hght* produces an invisible line of zero thickness.

The following style parameters may be changed to redefine how marginal notes appear:

`\marginparwidth`

> determines the width of the margin box;

`\marginparsep`

> sets the separation between the margin box and the main text;

`\marginparpush`

> is the smallest vertical distance between two marginal notes.

These parameters are all lengths and are assigned new values as usual with the `\setlength` command.

6 Tables

Arranging information in tabular form is a very important part of any text formatting system. In this chapter, we explain the two LaTeX environments available for this task: `tabbing`, which is similar to the way a typewriter works, and `tabular`, a far more sophisticated and powerful environment.

In Chapter 9 we show how tables (and figures) can be made to 'float' to a convenient position on the current or following page without producing ugly page breaks. However, that is a separate mechanism; the contents of such a floating `table` environment must still be produced with the structures described here.

6.1 Tabulator stops

6.1.1 Basics

In the days of typewriters, it was possible to set *tabulator stops* at various positions within a line; then by pressing the tab key the print head or carriage jumps to the next tab location.

A similar possibility exists in LaTeX with the `tabbing` environment:

> `\begin{tabbing}`   *lines*   `\end{tabbing}`

One can think of the set tab stops as being numbered from left to right. At the beginning of the `tabbing` environment, no tabs are set except for the left border, which is called the *zeroth* tab stop. The stops can be set at any spot within a line with the command `\=`, and a line is terminated by the `\\` command.

> `Here is the \=first tab stop, followed by\= the second\\`

sets the first tab stop after the blank following the word *the*, and the second immediately after the word *by*.

After the tab stops have been set in this way, one can jump to each of the stops in the subsequent lines, starting from the left margin, with the command `\>`. A new line is started with the usual `\\` command.

Example:

Type	Quality	Color	Price
Paper	med.	white	low
Leather	good	brown	high
Card	bad	gray	med.

```
\begin{tabbing}
Type\qquad\= Quality\quad\=
Color\quad\= Price\\[0.8ex]
Paper   \> med. \> white \> low\\
Leather \> good \> brown \> high\\
Card    \> bad  \> gray  \> med.
\end{tabbing}
```

6.1.2   Sample line

It is often advantageous or even necessary to set the tab stops in a sample line that is not actually printed. It could contain, for example, the widest entries in the various columns that appear later or the smallest intercolumn spacing between stops. The sample line may also contain \hspace commands to force the distance between stops to be a predetermined amount.

To suppress the printing of the sample line, it is ended with the command \kill instead of the \\ terminator.

```
\hspace*{3cm}\=sample column \=\hspace{4cm}\= \kill
```

In addition to the left border, the above statement sets three tab stops:

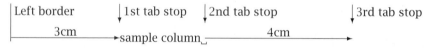

An \hspace command at the beginning of a sample line must be of the *-form, otherwise the inserted spacing will be deleted at the line margin.

6.1.3   Tab stops and the left margin

The left border of each line of the tabbing environment is at first identical to the left margin of the enclosing environment, and is designated the *zeroth* stop. By activating the 'tab key' \> at the start of a line, one sets the following text beginning at the first tab stop. However, the command \+ has the same effect, putting the left border permanently at the first stop, for all subsequent lines. With \+\+ at the beginning or end of a line, all of the following lines will start two stops further along. There can be as many \+ commands as there are tab stops set on the line.

The command \- has the opposite effect: It shifts the left border for the following lines one stop to the left. It is not possible to set this border to be to the left of the *zeroth* stop.

The effect of the \+ commands may be overridden for a single line by putting \< at the start for each tab to be removed. This line then starts so many tabs to the left of the present border. With the next \\ command, the new line begins at the current left border determined by the total number of \+ and \- commands.

6.1.4   Further tabbing commands

Tab stops can be reset or added in every line. The command \= will add a stop if there have been sufficient \> commands to have jumped to the last stop; otherwise it will reset the next stop. For example:

<table>
<tr><td>Old column 1 Old column 2</td><td><code>Old column 1 \= Old column 2\\</code></td></tr>
<tr><td>Left column   Middle col Extra col</td><td><code>Left column \> Middle col</code></td></tr>
<tr><td>New col 1 New col 2   Old col 3</td><td><code>   \= Extra col\\</code></td></tr>
<tr><td>Column 1 Column 2   Column 3</td><td><code>New col 1 \= New col 2 \></code></td></tr>
<tr><td></td><td><code>   Old col 3\\</code></td></tr>
<tr><td></td><td><code>Column 1\> Column 2 \> Column 3</code></td></tr>
<tr><td></td><td><code>\end{tabbing}</code></td></tr>
</table>

Occasionally it is desirable to be able to reset the tab stops and then to reuse the original ones later. The command \pushtabs accomplishes this by storing the current tabs and removing them from the active line. All the tab stops can then be set once again. The stored stops can be reactivated with the command \poptabs. The \pushtabs command may be given as many times as needed, but there must be the same number of \poptabs commands within any one tabbing environment.

It is possible to position text on a tab stop with *left_text* \' *right_text*, where *left_text* goes just before the current tab (or left border) with a bit of spacing, while *right_text* starts exactly at the stop. The amount of spacing between the *left_text* and the tab stop is determined by the tabbing parameter \tabbingsep. This may be changed by the user with the \setlength command as usual.

Text may be right justified up against the right border of a line with the command \' *text*. There must not be any more \> or \= commands in the remainder of the line.

The commands \=, \', and \' function as accent commands outside of the tabbing environment (Section 2.5.7). If these accents are actually needed within tabbing, they must be produced with \a=, \a', and \a' instead. For example, to produce ó, ò, or ō inside a tabbing environment, one must give \a'o, \a'o, or \a=o. The command \- also has another meaning outside of the tabbing environment (suggested word division), but since lines are not broken automatically within this environment there is no need for an alternative form.

Here is an example illustrating all the tabbing commands:

<table>
<tr><td>Apples: consumed by: people</td><td><code>\begin{tabbing}</code></td></tr>
<tr><td>   horses</td><td><code>Grapefruits: \= \kill</code></td></tr>
<tr><td>   and sheep</td><td><code>Apples: \> consumed by: \= people\+\+\\</code></td></tr>
<tr><td>   reasonably juicy</td><td><code>horses \\</code></td></tr>
<tr><td>Grapefruits: a delicacy</td><td><code>and \' sheep\-\\</code></td></tr>
<tr><td>(see also: melons</td><td><code>reasonably juicy\-\\</code></td></tr>
<tr><td>   pumpkins)</td><td><code>Grapefruits: \> a delicacy\\</code></td></tr>
<tr><td>Horses   feed on   apples</td><td><code>\pushtabs</code></td></tr>
<tr><td></td><td><code>(see also: \= melons\\</code></td></tr>
<tr><td></td><td><code> \> pumpkins)\\</code></td></tr>
<tr><td></td><td><code>\poptabs</code></td></tr>
<tr><td></td><td><code>Horses \> feed on \> apples</code></td></tr>
<tr><td></td><td><code>\end{tabbing}</code></td></tr>
</table>

6.1.5   Remarks on tabbing

TEX treats the `tabbing` environment like a normal paragraph, breaking a page if necessary between two lines within the environment. However, the commands `\newpage` and `\clearpage` are not allowed within it, and the command `\pagebreak` is simply ignored. If the user wishes to force a page break within the `tabbing` environment, there is a trick that he or she may employ: Specify a very large interline spacing at the end of the line where the break should occur (for example, `\\[10cm]`). This forces the break, and the spacing disappears at the start of the new page.

Each line of text is effectively within a { } pair so that any size or font declarations remain in force only for that one line. The text need not be put explicitly inside a pair of curly braces.

It is not possible to nest `tabbing` environments within one another.

Beware: The tab jump command `\>` always moves to the next logical tab stop. This could actually be a move backwards if the previous text is longer than the space available between the last two stops. This is in contrast to the way the tabulator used to work on a typewriter.

There is no automatic line breaking within the `tabbing` environment. Each line continues until terminated by a `\\` command. The text could extend beyond the right margin of the page. The user must take care that this does not happen.

The commands `\hfill`, `\hrulefill`, and `\dotfill` have no effect inside a `tabbing` environment, since no *stretching* takes place here.

Exercise 6.1: Generate the following table with the `tabbing` *environment.*

```
Project: Total Requirements = $900 000.00
        of which      2003 = $450 000.00
                      2004 = $350 000.00
                      2005 = $100 000.00

        2003 approved: $350 000.00   Deficiency: $100 000.00
        2004           $300 000.00               $150 000.00
        2005           $250 000.00   Surplus:    $150 000.00
        tentative      2004 = $100 000.00 for deficiency 2003
                       2005 = $  50 000.00              2004
                            + $100 000.00      excess for  2003 in 2004
Commitments            2003 = $100 000.00
                       2004 = $150 000.00                signed: H. André
```

Hint: The first line in the `tabbing` *environment should read*

> `Project: \=Total Requirements\= = \$900\,000.00 \+\\`

What is the effect of the `\+` *command at the end of this line? How do you arrange, using these tab stops, for the years 2003, 2004, and 2005 in the second to fourth lines all to be positioned before the second tab stop? Which command should be at the end of the second line just before the* `\\` *terminator?*

Lines 1–4 and 8–12 all use the same set of tab stops, even though there are additional stops set in the eighth line. With `\$\=00\,000.00` *one can align the entry* `\$\>50\,000.00` *in the ninth line to match the decimal places of the lines above.*

Lines 5–7 have their own tab stops. Use the save and recall feature to store the preset tab stops and to bring them back. The left border of lines 5–7 correspond to the first stop of the first group. What command is at the end of the fourth line to ensure that the left border is reset to one stop earlier? How is the left border of the second-to-last line reset?

The last line contains 'signed: H. André' right justified. With what tabbing *command was this produced? Watch out for the accent é in this entry within the* tabbing *environment!*

6.2 Tables

With the *box* elements and tabbing environment from the previous sections it would be possible to produce all sorts of framed and unframed tables. However, LaTeX offers the user far more convenient ways to build such complicated structures.

6.2.1 Constructing tables

The environments tabular, tabular*, and array are the basic tools with which tables and matrices can be constructed. The syntax for these environments is

```
\begin{array}[pos]{cols}           rows  \end{array}
\begin{tabular}[pos]{cols}         rows  \end{tabular}
\begin{tabular*}{width}[pos]{cols} rows  \end{tabular*}
```

The array environment can only be applied in *mathematical mode* (see Chapter 7). It is described here only because its syntax and the meaning of its arguments are exactly the same as those of the tabular environment. All three environments actually create a minipage. The meaning of the arguments is as follows:

pos Vertical positioning argument (see also the explanation of this argument for parboxes in Section 5.1.3). It can take on the values

  t   the top line of the table is aligned with the baseline of the current external line of text;

  b   the bottom line of the table is aligned with the external baseline;

      with no positioning argument given, the table is centered on the external baseline.

width This argument applies only to the tabular* environment and determines its overall width. In this case, the *cols* argument must contain the @-expression (see below) @{\extracolsep{\fill}} somewhere after the first entry. For the other two environments, the total width is fixed by the textual content.

cols The column formatting argument. There must be an entry for every column, as well as possible extra entries for the left and right borders of the table or for the intercolumn spacings.

  The possible *column formatting symbols* are

  l   the column contents are *left* justified;

  r   the column contents are *right* justified;

c   the column contents are *centered*;

p{*wth*} the text in this column is set into lines of width *wth*, and the top line is aligned with the other columns. In fact, the text is set in a parbox with the command \parbox[t]{*wth*}{*column text*};

*{*num*}{*cols*} the *column format* contained in *cols* is reproduced *num* times, so that *{5}{|c}| is the same as |c|c|c|c|c|.

The available *formatting symbols* for the left and right borders and for the intercolumn spacing are

| draws a vertical line;

|| draws two vertical lines next to each other;

@{*text*} referred to as an *@-expression*, inserts *text* in every line of the table between the two columns where it appears.

   An @-expression removes the intercolumn spacing that is automatically put between each pair of columns. If white space is needed between the inserted text and the next column, this must be explicitly included with \hspace{ } within the *text* of the @-expression. If the intercolumn spacing between two particular columns is to be something other than the standard, this may be easily achieved by placing @{\hspace{*wth*}} between the appropriate columns in the formatting argument. This replaces the standard intercolumn spacing with the width *wth*.

   An \extracolsep{*wth*} within an @-expression will put extra spacing of amount *wth* between all the following columns until countermanded by another \extracolsep command. In contrast to the standard spacing, this additional spacing is not removed by later @-expressions. In the tabular* environment, a command @{\extracolsep{\fill} must occur somewhere in the column format so that all the subsequent intercolumn spacings can stretch out to fill the predefined table width.

   If the left or right borders of the table do not consist of a vertical line, spacing is added there of an amount equal to half the normal intercolumn spacing. If this spacing is not wanted, it may be suppressed by including an empty @-expression @{} at the beginning or end of the column format.

rows These contain the actual entries in the table, each horizontal row being terminated with a \\ command. These rows consist of a sequence of column entries separated from each other by the & symbol. Thus each row in the table contains the same number of column entries as in the column definition *cols*. Some entries may be empty. The individual column entries are treated by LATEX as though they were enclosed in braces { } so that any changes in type style or size are restricted to that one column.

\hline This command may only appear before the first row or immediately after a \\ row termination. It draws a horizontal line the full width of the table below the row that was just ended, or at the top of the table if it comes at the beginning.

   Two \hline commands together draw two horizontal lines with a little space between them.

\cline{*m* – *n*} This command draws a horizontal line from the left side of column *m* to the right side of column *n*. Like \hline, it may only be given just after a \\ row termination, and there may be more than one after another. The command \cline{1-3} \cline{5-7} draws two horizontal lines from column 1 to 3 and from column 5 to 7, below the row that was just ended. In each case, the full column widths are underlined.

\multicolumn{*num*}{*col*}{*text*} This command combines the following *num* columns into a single column with their total width including intercolumn spacings. The argument *col* contains exactly one of the positioning symbols l, r, or c, with possible @-expressions and vertical lines |. A value of 1 may be given for *num* when the positioning argument is to be changed for that column in one particular row.

In this context, a 'column' starts with a positioning symbol l, r, or c, and includes everything up to but excluding the next one. The first column also includes everything before the first positioning symbol. Thus |c@{}rl| contains three columns: the first is |c@{}, the second r, and the third l|.

The \multicolumn command may only come at the start of a row or right after a column separation symbol &.

\vline This command draws a vertical line with the height of the row at the location where it appears. In this way, vertical lines that do not extend the whole height of the table may be inserted within a column.

! If a p-type column contains \raggedright or \centering, the \\ forces a new line *within the column entry* and not the end of the whole row. If this occurs in the last column, then \\ cannot be used to terminate the row; instead, one must use \tabularnewline to end such a row.

Since a table is a vertical box of the same sort as parbox and minipage, it may be positioned horizontally with other boxes or text (see examples in Section 5.1.3). In particular, the table must be enclosed within

\begin{center} *table* \end{center}

to center it on the page.

6.2.2   Table style parameters

! There are a number of style parameters used in generating tables, which LaTeX sets to standard values. These may be altered by the user, either globally within the preamble or locally inside an environment. They should not be changed within the tabular environment itself.

\tabcolsep is half the width of the spacing that is inserted between columns in the tabular and tabular* environments;

\arraycolsep is the corresponding half intercolumn spacing for the array environment;

\arrayrulewidth is the thickness of the vertical and horizontal lines within a table;

\doublerulesep is the separation between the lines of a double rule.

Changes in these parameters can be made with the \setlength command as usual. For example, to make the line thickness 0.5 mm, give \setlength{\arrayrulewidth}{0.5mm}. Furthermore, the parameter

\arraystretch can be used to change the distance between the rows of a table. This is a multiplying factor, with a standard value of 1. A value of 1.5 means that the inter-row spacing is increased by 50%. A new value is set by redefining the parameter with the command

\renewcommand{\arraystretch}{*factor*}

6.2.3   Table examples

Creating tables is much easier in practice than it would seem from the above list of formatting possibilities. This is best illustrated with a few examples.

The simplest table consists of a row of columns in which the text entries are either centered or justified to one side. The column widths, the spacing between the columns, and thus the entire width of the table are automatically calculated.

Position	Club	Games	W	T	L	Goals	Points
1	Amesville Rockets	33	19	13	1	66:31	51:15
2	Borden Comets	33	18	9	6	65:37	45:21
3	Clarkson Chargers	33	17	7	9	70:44	41:25
4	Daysdon Bombers	33	14	10	9	66:50	38:28
5	Edgartown Devils	33	16	6	11	63:53	38:28
6	Freeburg Fighters	33	15	7	11	64:47	37:29
7	Gadsby Tigers	33	15	7	11	52:37	37:29
8	Harrisville Hotshots	33	12	11	10	62:58	35:31
9	Idleton Shovers	33	13	9	11	49:51	35:31
10	Jamestown Hornets	33	11	11	11	48:47	33:33
11	Kingston Cowboys	33	13	6	14	54:45	32:34
12	Lonsdale Stompers	33	12	8	13	50:57	32:34
13	Marsdon Heroes	33	9	13	11	50:42	31:35
14	Norburg Flames	33	10	8	15	50:68	28:38
15	Ollison Champions	33	8	9	16	42:49	25:41
16	Petersville Lancers	33	6	8	19	31:77	20:46
17	Quincy Giants	33	7	5	21	40:89	19:47
18	Ralston Regulars	33	3	11	19	37:74	17:49

The above table is made up of eight columns, the first of which is right justified, the second left justified, the third centered, the next three right justified again, and the last two centered. The column formatting argument in the tabular environment thus appears as

{rlcrrrcc}

The text to produce this table is

```
\begin{tabular}{rlcrrrcc}
Position & Club & Games & W & T & L & Goals & Points\\[0.5ex]
  1  & Amesville Rockets & 33 & 19 & 13 &  1 & 66:31 & 51:15 \\
  2  & Borden Comets     & 33 & 18 &  9 &  6 & 65:37 & 45:21 \\
```

```
... & .....                & .. & .. & .. & .. & ... & ...  \\
17  & Quincy Giants        & 33 & 7 &  5 & 21 & 40:89 & 19:47 \\
18  & Ralston Regulars     & 33 & 3 & 11 & 19 & 37:74 & 17:49
\end{tabular}
```

In each row, the individual columns are separated from one another by the symbol &, and the row itself is terminated with the \\ command. The [0.5ex] at the end of the first row adds extra vertical spacing between the first two rows. The last row does not need the termination symbol since it is ended automatically by the \end{tabular} command.

The columns may be separated by vertical rules by including the symbol | in the column formatting argument. Changing the first line to

    \begin{tabular}{r|l||c|rrr|c|c}

results in

Position	Club	Games	W	T	L	Goals	Points
1	Amesville Rockets	33	19	13	1	66:31	51:15
2	Borden Comets	33	18	9	6	65:37	45:21
⋮	⋮						⋮
17	Quincy Giants	33	7	5	21	40:89	19:47
18	Ralston Regulars	33	3	11	19	37:74	17:49

The same symbol | before the first or after the last column format generates a vertical line on the outside edge of the table. Two symbols || produce a double vertical line. Horizontal lines over the whole width of the table are created with the command \hline. They may only appear right after a row termination \\ or at the very beginning of the table. Two such commands \hline\hline draw a double horizontal line.

```
\begin{tabular}{|r|l||c|rrr|c|c|} \hline
Position & Club & Games & W & T & L & Goals & Points\\
 \hline\hline
 1  & Amesville Rockets & 33 & 19 & 13 &  1 & 66:31 & 51:15 \\
 \hline
 . . . . . . . . . . . . . . . . . . . . . . . . . . . .
18  & Ralston Regulars  & 33 &  3 & 11 & 19 & 37:74 & 17:49 \\
 \hline
\end{tabular}
```

The table now appears as

Position	Club	Games	W	T	L	Goals	Points
1	Amesville Rockets	33	19	13	1	66:31	51:15
2	Borden Comets	33	18	9	6	65:37	45:21
⋮	⋮						⋮
17	Quincy Giants	33	7	5	21	40:89	19:47
18	Ralston Regulars	33	3	11	19	37:74	17:49

In this case, the row termination \\ must be given for the last row too because of the presence of \hline at the end of the table.

In this example, all rows contain the same entry in the third column, that is, 33. Such a common entry can be automatically inserted in the column format as an @-expression of the form @{*text*}, which places *text* between the neighboring columns. This could be accomplished for our example by changing the column format to

        {rl@{ 33 }rrrcc} or {|r|l||@{ 33 }|rrr|c|c|}

so that the text ' 33 ', blanks included, appears between the second and third columns in every row. This produces the same table with slightly different row entries: for example, the fourth row would now be given as

        4   & Daysdon Bombers & 14 & 10 &   9 & 66:50 & 38:28 \\

The column format now consists of only seven column definitions, rlrrrcc. The previous third column c has been removed, so each row contains one less column separation symbol &. The new third column, the number of games won, begins with the second & and is separated from the club name by the contents of @{ 33 }, which is entered automatically without any additional & symbol.

The last two columns give the relations between goals and points won and lost as a centered entry of the form *m:n*. The colons ':' are only coincidentally ordered exactly over one another since two-digit numbers appear in every case on both sides of the colon. If one entry had been 9:101, the colon would have been shifted slightly to the left as the entire entry was centered.

A vertical alignment of the ':' independent of the number of digits can also be achieved using an @-expression of the form r@{:}l in the column format. This means that a colon is placed in every row between a right- and a left-justified column. The column formatting argument in the example now becomes

        {rl@{ 33 }rrrr@{:}lr@{:}l} or
        {|r|l||@{ 33 }|rrr|r@{:}l|r@{:}l|}

and the row entry is

4 & Daysdon Bombers & 14 & 10 &   9 & 66 & 50 & 38 & 28 \\

Each of the former c columns has been replaced by the two columns in r@{:}l. An @-expression inserts its text between the neighboring columns, removing the intercolumn spacing that would normally be there. Thus the r column is justified flush right with the ':' and the following l column flush left.

The same method can be employed when a column consists of numbers with decimal points and a varying number of digits.

The entries for the goal and point relationships are now made up of two columns positioned about the ':' symbol. This causes no problems for entering the number of goals won and lost or for the number of plus and minus points, since each entry has its own column. The column headings, however, are the words 'Goals' and 'Points', stretching over two columns each and without the colon. This is accomplished with the \multicolumn command, which merges selected columns in a particular row and redefines the column format. The first row of the unframed soccer table is then

```
Position& Club & W & T & L & \multicolumn{2}{c}{Goals}
                    & \multicolumn{2}{c}{Points}\\[0.5ex]
```

Here `\multicolumn{2}{c}{Goals}` means that the next two columns are to be combined into a centered column, containing the text 'Goals'. For the framed table, the new formatting argument in the `\multicolumn` commands must be `{c|}` since the vertical line symbol | was also removed when the old columns were combined. In deciding what belongs to a given column, use the rule that a column 'owns' everything up to but excluding the next r, l, or c.

The table of final results for our soccer league 2002/03 is to have a title created with the following commands:

```
\begin{tabular}{|r|l||rrr|r@{:}l|r@{:}l||c|}\hline
  \multicolumn{10}{|c|}{\bfseries 1st Regional Soccer League ---
  Final Results 2002/03}\\ \hline
&\itshape Club &\itshape W &\itshape T &\itshape L &
  \multicolumn{2}{c|}{\itshape Goals}
  & \multicolumn{2}{c||}{\itshape Points}
  & \itshape Remarks \\ \hline\hline
```

. . . .

1st Regional Soccer League — Final Results 2002/03							
	Club	*W*	*T*	*L*	*Goals*	*Points*	*Remarks*
1	Amesville Rockets	19	13	1	66:31	51:15	League Champs
2	Borden Comets	18	9	6	65:37	45:21	Trophy Winners
3	Clarkson Chargers	17	7	9	70:44	41:25	Candidates
4	Daysdon Bombers	14	10	9	66:50	38:28	for
5	Edgartown Devils	16	6	11	63:53	38:28	National
6	Freeburg Fighters	15	7	11	64:47	37:29	League
7	Gadsby Tigers	15	7	11	52:37	37:29	
8	Harrisville Hotshots	12	11	10	62:58	35:31	
9	Idleton Shovers	13	9	11	49:51	35:31	
10	Jamestown Hornets	11	11	11	48:47	33:33	
11	Kingston Cowboys	13	6	14	54:45	32:34	Medium Teams
12	Lonsdale Stompers	12	8	13	50:57	32:34	
13	Marsdon Heroes	9	13	11	50:42	31:35	
14	Norburg Flames	10	8	15	50:68	28:38	
15	Ollison Champions	8	9	16	42:49	25:41	
16	Petersville Lancers	6	8	19	31:77	20:46	Disbanding
17	Quincy Giants	7	5	21	40:89	19:47	Demoted
18	Ralston Regulars	3	11	19	37:74	17:49	

The horizontal lines for positions 3–5, 7–14, and 17 were made with the command `\cline{1-9}` while all the others used `\hline`:

```
11  & Kingston Cowboys  & 13 &  6 & 14 & 54&45 & 32&34 &
    Medium Teams \\ \cline{1-9}
```

!

The last two rows of the table deserve a comment. The remark 'Demoted' is vertically placed in the middle of the two rows. This is accomplished by typing

```
18  & Ralston Regulars  &  3 & 11 & 19 & 37&74 & 17&49
    & \raisebox{1.5ex}[0pt]{Demoted}\\ \hline
```

The \raisebox command lifts the text 'Demoted' by 1.5 ex. If the optional argument [0pt] had been left out, this lifting of the box would have increased the total height of the last row by 1.5 ex. This would have resulted in correspondingly more vertical spacing between the horizontal line of row 17 and the text of row 18. This additional spacing is suppressed by the optional argument *height* = [0pt]. (See Section 5.1.2 for a description of the \raisebox command.)

Occasionally one wants to increase the vertical spacing between horizontal lines and enclosed text. The soccer table would look better if the heading were thus:

1st Regional Soccer League — Final Results 2002/03					
Club	*W T L*	*Goals*	*Points*	*Remarks*	

This is done by inserting an invisible vertical rule, a *strut* (Section 5.1.6), into the heading text:

```
\multicolumn{10}{|c|}{\rule[-3mm]{0mm}{8mm}\bfseries 1st
    Regional Soccer League ---  Final Results 2002/03}\\ \hline
```

The included rule has a width of 0 mm, which makes it invisible, extends 3 mm below the baseline, and is 8 mm high. It thus stretches 5 mm (8 − 3) above the baseline. It effectively pushes the horizontal lines away from the baseline in both directions. If a row consists of more than one column, it is sufficient to include a *strut* in only one of them since the size of the whole row is determined by the largest column.

Exercise 6.2: *Produce your own table for the final results of your favorite team sport in the same manner as for the soccer results above. Watch out that the colons ':' are properly aligned for the goals and points relationships.*

Exercise 6.3: *Generate the following timetable.*

Day	6.15–7.15 pm		7.20–8.20 pm		8.30–9.30 pm	
	Subj.	Teacher / Room	Subj.	Teacher / Room	Subj.	Teacher / Room
Mon.	UNIX	Dr. Smith / Comp. Ctr	Fortran	Ms. Clarke / Hall A	Math.	Mr. Mills / Hall A
Tues.	LaTeX	Miss Baker / Conf. Room	Fortran	Ms. Clarke / Conf. Room	Math.	Mr. Mills / Hall A
Wed.	UNIX	Dr. Smith / Comp. Ctr	C	Dr. Jones / Hall B	ComSci.	Dr. Jones / Hall B
Fri.	LaTeX	Miss Baker / Conf. Room	C++	Ms. Clarke / Conf. Room	canceled	

The entries 'Day' and 'Subj.' are raised in the same way as 'Demoted' was in the soccer table. To simplify its application, one can introduce a user-defined command with

`\newcommand{\rb}[1]{\raisebox{1.5ex}[0pt]{#1}}`   (see Section 10.3.2)

so that `\rb{entry}` behaves the same as `\raisebox{1.5ex}[0pt]{entry}`. This can be used, for example, as `\rb{ Mon. }` or `\rb{UNIX}` to elevate the entries by the necessary amount.

In all the above examples, the entries in the individual columns are each a single line. Some tables contain certain columns with several lines of text that are somewhat separated from the rest of the row:

Model	Description	Price
FBD 360	**Desktop**: XP3600+ Processor, 512 MB DDR-RAM, 80 GB hard disk, 16x DVD drive, 32x CDRW drive, 64 MB TV output, Windows XP, 15" monitor	999.00
FBD 480	**Desktop DeLuxe**: Same as FBD 360 but with XP4800+ Processor, 48x CDRW drive, 17" monitor	1399.00
FBT 240	**Laptop**: XP2400+, 512 MB RAM, 40 GB hard disk, 56 kb modem, 32x speed DVD/CD-RW drive, 2x USB, 15" display, Windows XP, Infrared interface	1299.00

The above table is made up of three columns, the first left justified, the third right justified. The middle column contains several lines of text with a line width of 7.5 cm. This is generated with the column formatting symbol p{width}. The whole column formatting argument in this example is {lp{7.5cm}r}.

```
\begin{tabular}{lp{7.5cm}r}
\bfseries Model & Description & \bfseries Price \\[1ex]
FBD 360 &\small{\bfseries Desktop}: XP3600+ Processor,
512~MB DDR-RAM, 80~GB hard disk, 16x DVD drive,
32x CDRW drive, 64~MB TV~output,
Windows~XP, 15'' monitor & 999.00\\

    . . . . . . . . . . .
```

```
15'' display, Windows~XP, Infrared interface& 1299.00
\end{tabular}
```

The text for the middle column is simply typed in, being broken up into lines of width 7.5 cm automatically. The column is separated from the others with the & symbol in the usual way.

Warning: The line termination command \\ is ambiguous within a p column, for it can either start a whole new row or, if \raggedright or \centering have been given, it ends a line of text within that column entry. In this case, if this is the last column in the row, the only way to terminate the row is with \tabularnewline, which always starts a new row.

Exercise 6.4: Produce the following table.

Course and Date	Brief Description	Prerequisites
Introduction to LSEDIT March 14 – 16	Logging on — explanation of the VMS file system — explanation and intensive application of the VMS editor LSEDIT — user modifications	none
Introduction to LaTeX March 21 – 25	Word processors and formatting programs — text and commands — environments — document and page styles — displayed text — math equations — simple user-defined structures	LSEDIT

The final example describes a blank form produced as a framed table. The difficulty here is to set the heights and widths of the empty boxes, since these are normally determined automatically by the text entries. The example shows how this may be accomplished with the help of *struts* and \hspace commands.

```
\newsavebox{\k}\newsavebox{\kkk}
\sbox{\k}{\framebox[4mm]{\rule{0mm}{3mm}}}
```

```
\sbox{\kkk}{\usebox{\k}\usebox{\k}\usebox{\k}}
\begin{tabular} {|l|c|c|c|}\hline
  \multicolumn{4}{|c|}{\rule[-0.3cm]{0mm}{0.8cm}\bfseries
      Budget Plan 2003--2004}\\
  \hline\hline
  \rule[-0.4cm]{0mm}{1cm}Project
  & \multicolumn{3}{l|}{Nr. \usebox{\kkk}\hspace{0.5cm}
 \vline\hspace{0.5cm}Name\usebox{\kkk}\usebox{\kkk}\usebox{\kkk}
   \usebox{\kkk}}\\ \hline
  \multicolumn{1}{|r|}{Year} & 2003 & 2004 & 2005 \\
  \cline{2-4}
  & \euro\ \vline\  \$ & \euro\ \vline\  \$
    & \euro\ \vline\  \$ \\ \hline
  Investment & \hspace{2.5cm}& \hspace{2.5cm}& \hspace{2.5cm}\\
  Costs    & & & \\ \hline
  Operating & & & \\
  Costs    & & & \\ \hline
  Industrial& & & \\
  Contracts & & & \\ \hline
  \multicolumn{4}{|l|}{\rule[-10mm]{0mm}{13mm}Signature
      \hspace{5cm}\vline~Authorization} \\ \hline
\end{tabular}
```

The first three lines are only indirectly related to the table construction. They arrange for three empty boxes ☐☐☐ to be drawn when the command \usebox{\kkk} is given (see Section 5.1.1).

Except for the command \hspace{2.5cm} to set the column widths of the last three columns and the command \vline to draw a vertical line within a column, this example contains nothing new that was not in the previous examples. It is only necessary to give a brief explanation of the last row in the table: The command \multicolumn{4}{|l|} merges all four table columns into one, in which the text is set flush with the left margin. This text consists first of a strut \rule[-10mm]{0mm}{13mm} that says the height of the last row begins 10 mm below the baseline and is a total of 13 mm high. Then, beginning at the left margin, comes the word Signature, followed 5 cm later by \vline, a vertical line. The word Authorization is separated from the vertical line by a blank space (~).

The above examples clearly illustrate how the column widths and row heights are automatically determined for tables. These sizes, however, may be influenced by *struts* and \hspace commands. In addition, the commands described in Section 6.2.2 permit the *intercolumn* and *inter-row* spacings as well as *line thickness* to be altered. For example,

```
\setlength{\tabcolsep}{5mm}
```

inserts 5 mm of spacing before and after every column; that is, it produces an intercolumn spacing of 10 mm. Section 6.2.2 gives more information about the use of these *table style* parameters.

6.2.4   Extension packages for tables

As powerful as the `tabular` environment is, it does have limitations. For this reason, there are a number of tools packages (Section B.5.4) that add additional features for constructing tables.

Package: array
The `array` package extends the normal functionality of the `tabular` and `array` environments by adding several column formatting arguments, shown below, and by allowing the user to be able to define his or her own such arguments.

m{*wth*} produces a column of width *wth* that is aligned vertically in the middle. (The standard p{*wth*} aligns the text with the top line.)

b{*wth*} is like p and m but aligns the text on the bottom line.

>{*decl*} inserts *decl* before the next column; thus >{\bfseries} sets the entire column in boldface without having to type \bfseries in each row.

<{*decl*} inserts *decl* after the last column; to have a centered column in math mode, give >{$}c<{$}.

!{*decl*} inserts *decl* between two columns without removing the normal intercolumn spacing, as for @{*decl*}.

With \newcolumntype{*type*}{*decl*} one can define new column specifiers for multiple applications. For example, to have C defined as a centered math column, give

    \newcolumntype{C}{>{$}c<{$}}

The height of all rows can be increased by setting \extrarowheight to some value with \setlength; this is useful to prevent horizontal lines from being too close to the text below them.

With \firsthline and \lasthline, horizontal lines can be issued before the first and after the last rows, respectively, without interfering with the vertical alignment of the table.

Package: dcolumn
The `dcolumn` package loads the `array` package and defines a column specifier D to align a column of numbers on a decimal point. Its syntax is

    D{*in_char*}{*out_char*}{*number*}

where *in_char* is the input character for the decimal point (say, .), *out_char* is the character that is output (say, \cdot), and *number* is the maximum number of decimal places. If *number* is negative, the column is centered on the decimal point, otherwise it is right justified. Later versions allow *number* to specify the number of digits on both sides of the decimal point, for example as 3.2.

Package: tabularx
The `tabularx` package loads the `array` package and defines an environment `tabularx` that makes a table of a desired total width, like `tabular*`, but in which the columns expand, not the intercolumn spacings. The column specifier X is used to indicate the expandable columns and is equivalent to p{*wth*}, where *wth* is adjusted to the necessary size. For example,

    \begin{tabularx}{10cm}{c X l X} ... \end{tabularx}

produces a table of width 10 cm with columns 2 and 4 expandable.

Package:
delarray   The delarray package loads the array package and redefines the array environment so that it may be enclosed in brackets that are automatically adjusted in size, as with the \left and \right commands of Section 7.4.1. The brackets surround the column specifier. For example,

$$\verb|\begin{array}[{cc}] a & b \\ c & d \end{array}| \Rightarrow \begin{bmatrix} a & b \\ c & d \end{bmatrix}$$

Package:
long-
table   The longtable package produces tables extending over several pages. It does not require the array package, but does recognize its extra features if loaded. The longtable environment takes the same column formatting argument as tabular and array, but has additional row entries at the start to determine:

- those rows that appear at the start of the table, terminated by \endfirsthead; this often includes the main \caption;

- those at the top of every continuation page, terminated by \endhead; these normally include an additional \caption and the column headers;

- those at the bottom of each page, terminated by \endfoot; and

- those rows at the end of the table, terminated by \endlastfoot.

An example of a long table is:

```
\begin{longtable}{|l|c|r|}
   \caption[Short title]{Demonstration of a long table}\\
   \hline
   Left & Center & Right \\
   \hline \endfirsthead
   \caption[]{\emph{continued}}\\
   \hline
   Left & Center & Right \\
   \hline \endhead
   \hline
   \multicolumn{3}{r}{\emph{continued on next page}}
   \endfoot
   \hline\endlastfoot
   Twenty-two & fifty & A hundred and eighty \\
   22 & 50 & 180 \\
   .  .  .  .  .  .
\end{longtable}
```

The \caption command normally may only appear within table and figure environments (Section 9.4) but may also be used within longtable; in a continued row, \caption must have an empty optional argument [] to prevent multiple entries in the list of tables.

A \newpage command forces a new page within the long table.

Up to four LaTeX runs may be needed to get the correct column widths.

Primary Energy Consumption

Energy Source	1975	1980	1986
Total Consumption			
(in million tons of BCU[a])	347.7	390.2	385.0
of which (percentages)			
petroleum	52.1	47.6	43.2
bituminous coal	19.1	19.8	20.0
brown coal	9.9	10.0	8.6
natural gas	14.2	16.5	15.1
nuclear energy	2.0	3.7	10.1
other[b]	2.7	2.3	3.0

[a]BCU = Bituminous Coal Unit (1 ton BCU corresponds to the heating equivalent of 1 ton of bituminous coal = 8140 kwh)
[b]Wind, water, solar energy, and so forth

Source: Energy Balance Study Group, Essen 1987.

6.2.5 Floating tables

In Chapter 9 we explain how figures and tables can be made to *float*, that is, to move to the top or bottom of a page, or to a separate page altogether. The reason for doing this is that the author does not know in advance where the page breaks will occur, and therefore does not know whether there is enough room on the current page for such a large object. The float mechanism allows the material to be saved and then placed later at an appropriate location. It also allows for table and figure captions and automatic numbering.

Table material is made to float with the environment:

\begin{table} *head_text*   *table*   *foot_text* \end{table}

where *table* stands for the entire table as defined in a tabular environment, *head_text* for whatever text appears above the table, and *foot_text* for that below. Widths, spacing, and positioning of the texts relative to the table are all matters for the user to arrange.

Everything that appears between \begin{table} and \end{table} is normally placed at the start of the current page. If a table already occupies the top of the page, an attempt is made to place it at the page bottom if there is enough space for it. Otherwise, it will be placed on the next page where further tables may be accumulated. The surrounding text is printed as though the table were not there. For further details about floats in general, including automatic sequential numbering, see Chapter 9.

The table at the top of this page was generated within the text at this location with the following (excluding the footnotes, which are described in Section 5.2.4):

```
\begin{table} {\bfseries Primary Energy Consumption}\\[1ex]
  \begin{tabular*}{118mm}{@{}ll...rr@{}}
```

```
  . . . . . . . . . . . . . . . . . . . .
  \end{tabular*}\\[0.5ex]
  \emph{Source:} Energy Balance Study Group, . . .
\end{table}
```

There are a number of formatting parameters that may be used in connection with the `table` environment, which are described together with those for figures in Section 9.3.

Exercise 6.5: Complete the above text for the table on the facing page (see Section 5.2.3 for the footnotes). Pay attention to the following questions (check the explanations for the @-expressions in Section 6.2.1):

1. *What is the effect of the @{} entries at the beginning and end of the formatting definition?*

2. *The `tabular*` environment generates a table with a given width, here 118 mm. What would be the effect of @{extracolsep{\fill}} at the beginning of the formatting definition?*

3. *Where in the formatting definition should @{extracolsep{\fill}} and the countermanding @{\hspace{1em}}@{\extracolsep{1em}} appear in order to format the table as it is printed here? How would the table appear if only @{\extracolsep{1em}} were given as countermand?*

7

Mathematical Formulas

Mathematics is the soul of TeX. It was because the setting of mathematical formulas is so complicated in normal printing, not to mention on a typewriter, that Donald Knuth invented his text formatting system. On the other hand, the soul of LaTeX is logical markup. Nevertheless, all the power of TeX's math setting is also available in LaTeX, offering an unbeatable combination.

In this chapter we confine ourselves to the elements of mathematical typesetting available in standard LaTeX. The simplifications and additional elements provided by *AMS*-LaTeX are reserved for Chapter 15.

Mathematical formulas are produced by typing special descriptive text. This means that LaTeX must be informed that the *following text* is to be interpreted as a *mathematical formula*, and it must also be told when the *math text* has come to an end and normal text recommences. The processing of *math text* is carried out by switching to *math mode*. Mathematical environments serve this purpose.

7.1 Mathematical environments

Mathematical formulas may occur within a line of text, as $(a + b)^2 = a^2 + 2ab + b^2$, or separated from the main text as

$$\int_0^\infty f(x)\,\mathrm{d}x \approx \sum_{i=1}^n w_i \mathrm{e}^{x_i} f(x_i)$$

These two types are distinguished by referring to them as *text* and *displayed formulas*, respectively.

Text formulas, or equations, are generated with the environment

> \begin{math} *formula_text* \end{math}

Since text formulas are often very short, sometimes consisting of only a single character, a shorthand version is available as \(*formula_text* \). However, most authors prefer the very short form, $*formula_text*$, which is actually the TeX method. All three are essentially the same, and there is no reason not to use the $ sign.

The contents of the formula, *formula_text*, consist of math constructs, which are described in the following sections.

Displayed formulas, or equations, are produced in the environments

```
\begin{displaymath}   formula_text   \end{displaymath}
\begin{equation}       formula_text   \end{equation}
```

The difference between these two is that the `equation` environment automatically adds a sequential equation number. The `displaymath` environment may be given with the shorthand forms \[... \] or $$...$$.

By default, displayed formulas are centered horizontally with the equation number, if it is present, and set flush with the right margin. By selecting the document class option `fleqn` (Section 3.1.1), the formulas are set left justified with an adjustable indentation. This option remains valid for the entire document whereas the amount of indentation may be changed with \setlength{\mathindent}{*indent*}, where *indent* is a length specification. Moreover, the document class option `leqno` sets the equation numbers flush with the left margin throughout the whole document.

Finally, multiline formulas can be created with the environments

```
\begin{eqnarray}    formula_text   \end{eqnarray}
\begin{eqnarray*}   formula_text   \end{eqnarray*}
```

where the standard form adds a sequential equation number for each line and the *-form is without equation numbers.

7.2   Main elements of math mode

7.2.1   Constants and variables

Numbers that appear within formulas are called *constants*, whereas *simple variables* are represented by single letters. The universal practice in mathematical typesetting is to put constants in Roman typeface and variables in *italics*. LaTeX adheres to this rule automatically in math mode. Blanks are totally ignored and are included in the input text simply to improve the appearance for the writer. Spacing between constants, variables, and operators such as $+$, $-$, $=$ are set automatically by LaTeX. For example, `$z=2a+3y$`, and `$ z = 2 a + 3 y $` both produce $z = 2a + 3y$.

Mathematical symbols that are available on the keyboard are

$$+ \quad - \quad = \quad < \quad > \quad / \quad : \quad ! \quad ' \quad | \quad [\quad] \quad (\quad)$$

all of which may be used directly in formulas. The curly braces { } serve the purpose of logically combining parts of the formula and therefore cannot act as printable characters. To include braces in a formula, the same commands \{ and \} are used as in normal text.

$M(s) < M(t) < |M| = m$ `$M(s)<M(t)<|M| = m$`

$y'' = c\{f[y', y(x)] + g(x)\}$ `$y'' = c\{f[y',y(x)] + g(x)\}$`

Preparation: Create a new LaTeX file with the name math.tex containing at first only the commands \documentclass{article}, \begin{document}, and \end {document}.

Exercise 7.1: Produce the following text with your math exercise file: 'The derivative of the indirect function $f[g(x)]$ is $\{f[g(x)]\}' = f'[g(x)]g'(x)$. For the second derivative of the product of $f(x)$ and $g(x)$ one has $[f(x)g(x)]'' = f''(x)g(x) + 2f'(x)g'(x) + f(x)g''(x)$.' Note: Higher derivatives are made with multiple ' symbols: y''' yields y'''.

7.2.2   Exponents and indices

Mathematical formulas often contain exponents and indices, characters that are either raised or lowered relative to the main line of the formula, and printed in a smaller typeface. Although their mathematical meanings are different, superscripts and subscripts are typographically the same as exponents and indices, respectively. It is even possible that exponents themselves have exponents or indices, and so on. These are produced by multiple applications of the raising and lowering operations.

LaTeX and TeX make it possible to create any combination of exponents and indices with the correct type size in a simple manner: The character command ^ sets the next character as an exponent (raised), while the character command _ sets it as an index (lowered).

$$x^2 \quad \text{x\textasciicircum2} \qquad a_n \quad \text{a\_n} \qquad x_i^n \quad \text{x\textasciicircum n\_i}$$

When exponents and indices occur together, their order is unimportant. The last example above could also have been given as x_i^n.

If the exponent or index contains more than one character, the group of characters must be enclosed in braces { }:

$$x^{2n} \quad \text{x\textasciicircum\{2n\}} \qquad x_{2y} \quad \text{x\_\{2y\}} \qquad A_{i,j,k}^{-n!2} \quad \text{A\_\{i,j,k\}\textasciicircum\{-n!2\}}$$

Multiple raisings and lowerings are generated by applying ^ and _ to the exponents and indices:

$$x^{y^2} \quad \text{x\textasciicircum\{y\textasciicircum2\}} \qquad x^{y_1} \quad \text{x\textasciicircum\{y\_1\}}$$
$$A_{j_{n,m}^{2n}}^{x_i^2} \qquad \text{A\textasciicircum\{x\_i\textasciicircum2\}\_\{j\textasciicircum\{2n\}\_\{n,m\}\}}$$

Note: The raising and lowering commands ^ and _ are only permitted in math mode.

7.2.3   Fractions

Short fractions, especially within a text formula, are best represented using the slash character /, as in $(n+m)/2$ for $(n + m)/2$. For more complicated fractions, the command

\frac{*numerator*}{*denominator*}

is employed to write the *numerator* on top of the *denominator* with a horizontal fraction line of the right width between them.

$$\frac{1}{x+y}$$

`\[ \frac{1}{x+y} \]`

$$\frac{a^2 - b^2}{a + b} = a - b$$

`\[ \frac{a^2 - b^2}{a+b} = a-b \]`

Fractions may be nested to any depth within one another.

$$\frac{\frac{a}{x-y} + \frac{b}{x+y}}{1 + \frac{a-b}{a+b}}$$

`\[ \frac{\frac{a}{x-y} + \frac{b}{x+y}}`
`{1 + \frac{a-b}{a+b}}   \]`

LaTeX sets fractions within fractions in a smaller typeface. Section 7.5.2 describes how the automatic type sizes may be overridden if LaTeX's choice is unsuitable.

7.2.4   Roots

Roots are printed with the command

  `\sqrt[n]{arg}`

as in this example: $\sqrt[3]{8} = 2$ produces $\sqrt[3]{8} = 2$. If the optional argument n is omitted, the square root is generated: `$\sqrt{a}$` yields $\sqrt{a}$.

The size and length of the root sign are automatically fitted to *arg*: `$\sqrt{x^2 + y^2 + 2xy} = x+y$` $\sqrt{x^2 + y^2 + 2xy} = x + y$, or

$$\sqrt[n]{\frac{x^n - y^n}{1 + u^{2n}}}$$

`\[ \sqrt[n]{\frac{x^n - y^n}{1 + u^{2n}}} \]`

Roots may be nested inside one another to any depth:

$$\sqrt[3]{-q + \sqrt{q^2 + p^3}}$$

`\[ \sqrt[3]{-q + \sqrt{q^2 + p^3}} \]`

7.2.5   Sums and integrals

Summation and integral signs are made with the two commands `\sum` and `\int`, which may appear in two different sizes depending on whether they occur in a text or displayed formula.

Sums and integrals very often possess upper and lower limits. These are printed with the exponent and index commands ^ and _. The positioning of the limits also depends on whether the formula is in text or displayed.

In a text formula `\sum_{i=1}^n` and `\int_a^b` produce $\sum_{i=1}^n$ and $\int_a^b$, whereas in a displayed formula they appear as at the left on the next page:

$$\sum_{i=1}^{n} \int_a^b \qquad\qquad \int_{x=0}^{x=1}$$

Some authors prefer the limits for the integral to be placed above and below the integral sign, the same as for summation. This is achieved with the command \limits immediately following the integral sign: \int\limits_{x=0}^{x=1}

The rest of the formula text coming before and after the sum and integral signs is correctly aligned with them.

$$2 \sum_{i=1}^{n} a_i \int_a^b f_i(x)g_i(x)\,\mathrm{d}x$$

```
\[ 2\sum_{i=1}^n a_i \int^b_a
   f_i(x)g_i(x)\,\mathrm{d}x \]
```

!

Two points must be made regarding integrals such as $\int y\,\mathrm{d}x$ and $\int f(z)\,\mathrm{d}z$. First, there should be a little extra spacing between the differential operators $\mathrm{d}x$ and $\mathrm{d}z$ and the integrands preceding them. This is achieved with the small spacing command \, , mentioned on page 32, not with a blank, which is ignored in math mode. Second, the differential operator should be written upright, not italic, as explained in Section 7.4.10. This is accomplished by setting it within a \mathrm command (Section 7.4.2). Thus \int y\,\mathrm{d}x and \int f{z}\,\mathrm{d}z produce the desired results shown above, whereas \int y dx and \int f(z) dz yield $\int y dx$ and $\int f(z)dz$.

7.2.6 Continuation dots—ellipsis

Formulas occasionally contain a row of dots $\ldots$, meaning *and so on*. Simply typing a period three times in a row produces an undesirable result: ..., that is, the dots are too close together. Therefore, LATEX provides several commands

| \ldots | ... | *low dots* | \cdots | $\cdots$ | *center dots* |
| \vdots | $\vdots$ | *vertical dots* | \ddots | $\ddots$ | *diagonal dots* |

to space the dots correctly. The difference between the first two commands is best illustrated by the examples $a_0, a_1, \ldots, a_n$ and $a_0 + a_1 + \cdots + a_n$, which are produced with $a_0,a_1,\ldots,a_n$ for the first and $a_0 + a_1 + \cdots + a_n$ for the second.

The command \ldots is also available in normal text mode, whereas the other three are only allowed in math mode. In text mode, the command \dots may be used in place of \ldots with the same effect.

Exercise 7.2: Generate the following output:
The reduced cubic equation $y^3 + 3py + 2q = 0$ has one real and two complex solutions when $D = q^2 + p^3 > 0$. These are given by Cardan's formula as

$$y_1 = u + v, \quad y_2 = -\frac{u+v}{2} + \frac{i}{2}\sqrt{3}(u-v), \quad y_3 = -\frac{u+v}{2} - \frac{i}{2}\sqrt{3}(u-v)$$

where

$$u = \sqrt[3]{-q + \sqrt{q^2 + p^3}}, \qquad v = \sqrt[3]{-q - \sqrt{q^2 + p^3}}$$

Note: The spacings between the parts of the displayed equations are made with the spacing commands \quad *and* \qquad.

Exercise 7.3: *Select the option* fleqn *in the document class command and include the specification* \setlength{\mathindent}{2cm} *in the preamble. Redo the three* y *equations above, each as a separate displayed formula, using the* equation *environment instead of* displaymath *or* \[...\] *brackets.*

Exercise 7.4: *Create the following text:*
Each of the measurements $x_1 < x_2 < \cdots < x_r$ occurs $p_1, p_2, \ldots, p_r$ times. The mean value and standard deviation are then

$$x = \frac{1}{n} \sum_{i=1}^{r} p_i x_i, \qquad s = \sqrt{\frac{1}{n} \sum_{i=1}^{r} p_i (x_i - x)^2}$$

where $n = p_1 + p_2 + \cdots + p_r$.

Exercise 7.5: *Although this equation looks very complicated, it should not present any great difficulties:*

$$\int \frac{\sqrt{(ax+b)^3}}{x}\, dx = \frac{2\sqrt{(ax+b)^3}}{3} + 2b\sqrt{ax+b} + b^2 \int \frac{dx}{x\sqrt{ax+b}}$$

The same applies to $\int_{-1}^{8} (dx/\sqrt[3]{x}) = \frac{3}{2}(8^{2/3} + 1^{2/3}) = 15/2$.

7.3   Mathematical symbols

There is a very wide range of symbols used in mathematical text, of which only a few are directly available from the keyboard. LaTeX provides many of the mathematical symbols that are commonly used. They are called with the symbol name prefixed with the \ character. The names themselves are derived from their mathematical meanings.

7.3.1   Greek letters

The Greek letters are made simply by putting the command character \ before the name of the letter. Uppercase (capital) letters are distinguished by capitalizing the first letter of the name. Greek letters that do not appear in the above list are identical to some corresponding Latin letter. For example, uppercase ρ is the same as Latin P and therefore needs no special symbol.

LaTeX normally sets the uppercase Greek letters in Roman (upright) type within a mathematical formula. If they need to be in italics, this can be done with the *math alphabet command* \mathnormal: $\mathnormal{\Gamma\Pi\Phi}$ appears as *ΓΠΦ*.

Greek letters may only be used in math mode. If they are needed in normal text, the command must be enclosed in $...$ signs.

lowercase letters

α	\alpha	θ	\theta	o	o	τ	\tau
β	\beta	ϑ	\vartheta	π	\pi	υ	\upsilon
γ	\gamma	ι	\iota	ϖ	\varpi	ϕ	\phi
δ	\delta	κ	\kappa	ρ	\rho	φ	\varphi
ϵ	\epsilon	λ	\lambda	ϱ	\varrho	χ	\chi
ε	\varepsilon	μ	\mu	σ	\sigma	ψ	\psi
ζ	\zeta	ν	\nu	ς	\varsigma	ω	\omega
η	\eta	ξ	\xi				

Uppercase letters

Γ	\Gamma	Λ	\Lambda	Σ	\Sigma	Ψ	\Psi
Δ	\Delta	Ξ	\Xi	Υ	\Upsilon	Ω	\Omega
Θ	\Theta	Π	\Pi	Φ	\Phi		

7.3.2 Calligraphic letters

The following 26 *calligraphic* letters may also be used in math formulas:

$$\mathcal{A}, \mathcal{B}, \mathcal{C}, \mathcal{D}, \mathcal{E}, \mathcal{F}, \mathcal{G}, \mathcal{H}, \mathcal{I}, \mathcal{J}, \mathcal{K}, \mathcal{L}, \mathcal{M}, \mathcal{N}, \mathcal{O}, \mathcal{P}, \mathcal{Q}, \mathcal{R}, \mathcal{S}, \mathcal{T}, \mathcal{U}, \mathcal{V}, \mathcal{W}, \mathcal{X}, \mathcal{Y}, \mathcal{Z}$$

These are called with the math alphabet command \mathcal:

```
$\mathcal{A, B, C,...,Z}$
```

7.3.3 Binary operators

Two mathematical quantities combined with one another to make a new quantity are said to be joined by a *binary operation*. The symbols that are available for use as binary operators are

$\pm$	\pm	$\cap$	\cap	$\circ$	\circ	$\bigcirc$	\bigcirc
$\mp$	\mp	$\cup$	\cup	$\bullet$	\bullet	$\Box$	\Box
$\times$	\times	$\uplus$	\uplus	$\diamond$	\diamond	$\Diamond$	\Diamond
$\div$	\div	$\sqcap$	\sqcap	$\lhd$	\lhd	$\bigtriangleup$	\bigtriangleup
$\cdot$	\cdot	$\sqcup$	\sqcup	$\rhd$	\rhd	$\bigtriangledown$	\bigtriangledown
$\ast$	\ast	$\vee$	\vee	$\unlhd$	\unlhd	$\triangleleft$	\triangleleft
$\star$	\star	$\wedge$	\wedge	$\unrhd$	\unrhd	$\triangleright$	\triangleright
$\dagger$	\dagger	$\oplus$	\oplus	$\oslash$	\oslash	$\setminus$	\setminus
$\ddagger$	\ddagger	$\ominus$	\ominus	$\odot$	\odot	$\wr$	\wr
$\amalg$	\amalg	$\otimes$	\otimes				

Package:
latexsym
amsfonts
The underlined symbol names in the above and following tables are only available if one of the packages latexsym (Section B.5.3) or amsfonts (Section 15.4.3) has been loaded.

7.3.4   Relations and their negations

When two mathematical quantities are compared, they are connected by a *relation*. The different types of relational symbols for the various comparisons are

$\le$	\le \leq	$\ge$	\ge \geq	$\neq$	\neq	$\sim$	\sim
$\ll$	\ll	$\gg$	\gg	$\doteq$	\doteq	$\simeq$	\simeq
$\subset$	\subset	$\supset$	\supset	$\approx$	\approx	$\asymp$	\asymp
$\subseteq$	\subseteq	$\supseteq$	\supseteq	$\cong$	\cong	$\smile$	\smile
$\sqsubset$	\sqsubset	$\sqsupset$	\sqsupset	$\equiv$	\equiv	$\frown$	\frown
$\sqsubseteq$	\sqsubseteq	$\sqsupseteq$	\sqsupseteq	$\propto$	\propto	$\bowtie$	\bowtie
$\in$	\in	$\ni$	\ni	$\prec$	\prec	$\succ$	\succ
$\vdash$	\vdash	$\dashv$	\dashv	$\preceq$	\preceq	$\succeq$	\succeq
$\models$	\models	$\perp$	\perp	$\parallel$	\parallel |	$\mid$	\mid |

A number of the above symbols may be called by more than one name. For example, $\le$ may be produced with either \le or \leq.

The opposite, or negated, meaning of the relation is indicated in mathematics with a slash / through the symbol: = and $\neq$ mean *equals* and *not equals*. One may put a slash through any of the above symbols by prefixing its name with \not. Thus \not\in yields $\notin$. The same is true for the keyboard characters: \not=, \not>, and \not< produce $\neq$, $\not>$, and $\not<$. For \not= there is also the special command \neq, which produces $\neq$, a symbol on its own and not the combined $\neq$.

The following symbols may be negated in this manner. Note that the last two, \not\in and \notin, are not exactly the same: $\notin$ and $\notin$. The latter form is the preferred one.

$\not<$	\not<	$\not>$	\not>	$\neq$	\not=
$\not\le$	\not\le	$\not\ge$	\not\ge	$\not\equiv$	\not\equiv
$\not\prec$	\not\prec	$\not\succ$	\not\succ	$\not\sim$	\not\sim
$\not\preceq$	\not\preceq	$\not\succeq$	\not\succeq	$\not\simeq$	\not\simeq
$\not\subset$	\not\subset	$\not\supset$	\not\supset	$\not\approx$	\not\approx
$\not\subseteq$	\not\subseteq	$\not\supseteq$	\not\supseteq	$\not\cong$	\not\cong
$\not\sqsubseteq$	\not\sqsubseteq	$\not\sqsupseteq$	\not\sqsupseteq	$\not\asymp$	\not\asymp
$\notin$	\not\in	$\notin$	\notin		

7.3.5   Arrows and pointers

Mathematical manuscripts often contain arrow symbols, also called *pointers*. The following arrow symbols are available:

← \leftarrow \gets	⟵ \longleftarrow	↑ \uparrow	
⇐ \Leftarrow	⟸ \Longleftarrow	⇑ \Uparrow	
→ \rightarrow \to	⟶ \longrightarrow	↓ \downarrow	
⇒ \Rightarrow	⟹ \Longrightarrow	⇓ \Downarrow	
↔ \leftrightarrow	⟷ \longleftrightarrow	↕ \updownarrow	
⇔ \Leftrightarrow	⟺ \Longleftrightarrow	⇕ \Updownarrow	
↦ \mapsto	⟼ \longmapsto	↗ \nearrow	
↩ \hookleftarrow	↪ \hookrightarrow	↘ \searrow	
↼ \leftharpoonup	⇀ \rightharpoonup	↙ \swarrow	
↽ \leftharpoondown	⇁ \rightharpoondown	↖ \nwarrow	
⇌ \rightleftharpoons	⤳ \leadsto		

Here again the symbols → and ← may also be referred to under the names \to and \gets. Furthermore, the command \Longleftrightarrow may be substituted by \iff, although the latter (⟺) has slightly more spacing on either side than the former (⟺).

7.3.6 Various other symbols

The above lists by no means exhaust the complete repertoire of mathematical symbols. However, the following are additional characters that standard LaTeX does make available. (Even more symbols are possible with the $\mathcal{AMS}$ symbol fonts and amssymb package, Section 15.4.3.)

ℵ	\aleph	′	\prime	∀	\forall	□	\Box
ℏ	\hbar	∅	\emptyset	∃	\exists	◇	\Diamond
ι	\imath	∇	\nabla	¬	\neg	△	\triangle
ȷ	\jmath	√	\surd	♭	\flat	♣	\clubsuit
ℓ	\ell	∂	\partial	♮	\natural	♦	\diamondsuit
℘	\wp	⊤	\top	♯	\sharp	♥	\heartsuit
ℜ	\Re	⊥	\bot	∥	|	♠	\spadesuit
ℑ	\Im	⊢	\vdash	∠	\angle	⋈	\Join
℧	\mho	⊣	\dashv	\	\backslash	∞	\infty

7.3.7 Symbols with two sizes

The following symbols are printed in different sizes depending on whether they appear in text or displayed formulas:

Σ	\sum	∩	\bigcap	⊙	\bigodot		
∫	\int	∪	\bigcup	⊗	\bigotimes		
∮	\oint	⊔	\bigsqcup	⊕	\bigoplus		
∏	\prod	∨	\bigvee	⊎	\biguplus		
∐	\coprod	∧	\bigwedge				

The symbols \int and \sum have already been introduced in Section 7.2.5. There it was shown how these symbols may take on upper and lower limits; in the same way, all the above symbols may also be assigned upper and lower limits using the shifting commands ^ and _. The positioning of the limits varies for some symbols depending on whether they occur in text or displayed formulas. As indicated in Section 7.2.5, the command \limits forces the limits to be written above and below the symbol where they would otherwise be placed beside it. Similarly, the complementary command \nolimits sets them beside the symbol when the standard positioning is above and below.

$$\oint_0^\infty \qquad \oint\limits_0^\infty$$

\[\oint^\infty_0 \oint\limits^\infty_0   \]

$$\prod_{\nu=0}^n \qquad \prod\nolimits_{\nu=0}^n$$

\[\prod^n_{\nu=0} \prod\nolimits^n_{\nu=0} \]

7.3.8   Function names

The universal standard for mathematical formulas is to set variable names in *italics* but the names of functions in Roman. If one were simply to write the function names *sin* or *log* in math mode, LaTeX would interpret these as variables s i n and l o g and write them as sin and log. To tell LaTeX that a function name is wanted, it is necessary to enter a command consisting of the backslash \ plus the function name. The following names are recognized by LaTeX:

\arccos	\cosh	\det	\inf	\limsup	\Pr	\tan
\arcsin	\cot	\dim	\ker	\ln	\sec	\tanh
\arctan	\coth	\exp	\lg	\log	\sin	
\arg	\csc	\gcd	\lim	\max	\sinh	
\cos	\deg	\hom	\liminf	\min	\sup	

Some of these functions may also appear with limits attached to them. This is easily achieved by means of the subscript command after the name of the function:

\lim_{x\to\infty} yields $\lim_{x\to\infty}$ in text formulas and

$$\lim_{x\to\infty}$$ in displayed formulas

The following function names may accept a limit with the lowering (index) command _:

\det \gcd \inf \lim \liminf \limsup \max \min
\Pr   \sup

Finally, there are the function commands \bmod and \pmod{*arg*}, both of which produce the function *mod* in one of two forms:

$ a \bmod b $ ⇒ $a \bmod b$
$ y \pmod{a+b} $ ⇒ $y \pmod{a+b}$.

With $\mathcal{A}_{\mathcal{M}}S$-LaTeX (Section 15.2.5) it is possible to define additional function names.

7.3.9   Mathematical accents

The following mathematical accents are available within math mode:

$\hat{a}$ \hat{a}	$\breve{a}$ \breve{a}	$\grave{a}$ \grave{a}	$\bar{a}$ \bar{a}
$\check{a}$ \check{a}	$\acute{a}$ \acute{a}	$\tilde{a}$ \tilde{a}	$\vec{a}$ \vec{a}
$\dot{a}$ \dot{a}	$\ddot{a}$ \ddot{a}	$\mathring{a}$ \mathring{a}	

The letters i and j should be printed without their dots when they are given an accent. To accomplish this, type the symbols \imath and \jmath instead of the letters, as in

$\vec{\imath}$ + \tilde{\jmath}$: $\vec{\imath} + \tilde{\jmath}$

There are wider versions of \hat and \tilde available with the names \widehat and \widetilde. In this way, these accents may be placed over parts of a formula:

$\widehat{1-x} = \widehat{-y}$ $\widehat{1-x}=\widehat{-y}$
$\widetilde{xyz}$ $\widetilde{xyz}$

Exercise 7.6: The union of two sets $\mathcal{A}$ and $\mathcal{B}$ is the set of all elements that are in at least one of the two sets and is designated as $\mathcal{A} \cup \mathcal{B}$. This operation is commutative $\mathcal{A} \cup \mathcal{B} = \mathcal{B} \cup \mathcal{A}$ and associative $(\mathcal{A} \cup \mathcal{B}) \cup \mathcal{C} = \mathcal{A} \cup (\mathcal{B} \cup \mathcal{C})$. If $\mathcal{A} \subseteq \mathcal{B}$, then $\mathcal{A} \cup \mathcal{B} = \mathcal{B}$. It then follows that $\mathcal{A} \cup \mathcal{A} = \mathcal{A}$, $\mathcal{A} \cup \{\varnothing\} = \mathcal{A}$ and $\mathcal{J} \cup \mathcal{A} = \mathcal{J}$.

Exercise 7.7: Applying l'Hôpital's rule, one has

$$\lim_{x\to 0} \frac{\ln \sin \pi x}{\ln \sin x} = \lim_{x\to 0} \frac{\pi \frac{\cos \pi x}{\sin \pi x}}{\frac{\cos x}{\sin x}} = \lim_{x\to 0} \frac{\pi \tan x}{\tan \pi x} = \lim_{x\to 0} \frac{\pi / \cos^2 x}{\pi / \cos^2 \pi x} = \lim_{x\to 0} \frac{\cos^2 \pi x}{\cos^2 x} = 1$$

Exercise 7.8: The gamma function $\Gamma(x)$ is defined as

$$\Gamma(x) \equiv \lim_{n\to\infty} \prod_{v=0}^{n-1} \frac{n!\,n^{x-1}}{x+v} = \lim_{n\to\infty} \frac{n!\,n^{x-1}}{x(x+1)(x+2)\cdots(x+n-1)} \equiv \int_0^\infty e^{-t}t^{x-1}\,dt$$

The integral definition is valid only for $x > 0$ (2nd Euler integral).

Exercise 7.9: Remove the option fleqn from the document class command in Exercise 7.3 and redo the output.

Exercise 7.10:
$$\alpha \vec{x} = \vec{x} \alpha, \qquad \alpha \beta \vec{x} = \beta \alpha \vec{x}, \qquad (\alpha + \beta)\vec{x} = \alpha \vec{x} + \beta \vec{x}, \qquad \alpha(\vec{x} + \vec{y}) = \alpha \vec{x} + \alpha \vec{y}.$$
$$\vec{x}\vec{y} = \vec{y}\vec{x} \quad \text{but} \quad \vec{x} \times \vec{y} = -\vec{y} \times \vec{x}, \qquad \vec{x}\vec{y} = 0 \quad \text{for} \quad \vec{x} \perp \vec{y}, \qquad \vec{x} \times \vec{y} = 0, \quad \text{for} \quad \vec{x} \parallel \vec{y}.$$

Exercise 7.11: Reproduce Equations 7.1 and 7.2 from the next section.

7.4   Additional elements

The math elements described in the previous sections already permit the construction of very complex formulas, such as

$$\lim_{x\to 0}\frac{\sqrt{1+x}-1}{x}=\lim_{x\to 0}\frac{(\sqrt{1+x}-1)(\sqrt{1+x}+1)}{x(\sqrt{1+x}+1)}=\lim_{x\to 0}\frac{1}{\sqrt{1+x}+1}=\frac{1}{2} \tag{7.1}$$

$$\frac{\partial^2 U}{\partial x^2}+\frac{\partial^2 U}{\partial y^2}=0 \implies U_M=\frac{1}{4\pi}\oint_\Sigma\frac{1}{r}\frac{\partial U}{\partial n}\,ds-\frac{1}{4\pi}\oint_\Sigma\frac{\partial\frac{1}{r}}{\partial n}U\,ds \tag{7.2}$$

$$I(z)=\sin(\frac{\pi}{2}z^2)\sum_{n=0}^{\infty}\frac{(-1)^n\pi^{2n}}{1\cdot 3\cdots(4n+1)}z^{4n+1}-\cos(\frac{\pi}{2}z^2)\sum_{n=0}^{\infty}\frac{(-1)^n\pi^{2n+1}}{1\cdot 3\cdots(4n+3)}z^{4n+3} \tag{7.3}$$

By reading the formulas from left to right, it should not be difficult to reconstruct the text that produced them. For example, the last equation is generated with

```
\begin{equation}
I(z) = \sin( \frac{\pi}{2} z^2 ) \sum_{n=0}^\infty
    \frac{ (-1)^n \pi^{2n} }{1 \cdot 3 \cdots (4n+1) } z^{4n+1}
   -\cos( \frac{\pi}{2} z^2 ) \sum_{n=0}^\infty
    \frac{ (-1)^n \pi^{2n+1} }{ 1 \cdot 3 \cdots (4n+3) } z^{4n+3}
\end{equation}
```

The above examples were made using the `equation` environment instead of the `displaymath` environment or its abbreviated form \[...\], which has the effect of adding the equation numbers automatically. In the document classes `book` and `report`, equations are sequentially numbered within the chapter, the number being preceded by the chapter number and set within parentheses ( ), as illustrated above. For document class `article`, the equations are numbered sequentially throughout the entire document.

By default the equation number appears right justified and vertically centered with the equation. If there is not enough room for it on the same line, it is printed right justified below the equation. If the document class option `leqno` has been selected, the equation numbers are set left justified for the entire document.

The automatic numbering of equations means that the author may not know at the time of writing just what the equation number is. The LaTeX cross-reference system described in Section 11.2.1 has already been explained for referring to section numbers (Section 3.3.3) and may also be used for equation numbers. By including a command \label{*name*} within the `equation` environment, one can print the unknown equation number in the text with the command \ref{*name*}, where *name* is a keyword consisting of any combination of letters, numbers, or symbols.

Examining Equation 7.3 more closely, one notices that the two parentheses pairs ( ) in cos() and sin() could be somewhat larger. Furthermore, this equation just fills the line width, and if it were any longer, it would have to be broken at some appropriate spot and the parts positioned in a meaningful way relative to one another. None of the math elements described so far can accomplish these requirements.

Even something so simple as including some normal text within a formula has not yet been mentioned. The rest of this section addresses these problems.

Finally, there are times when one is not happy with the sizes that TeX has chosen, as for example in the last integral of Equation 7.2, where $\partial\dfrac{1}{r}$ would be more desirable than $\partial\frac{1}{r}$. This and other formatting aids, such as adjusting horizontal spacing between parts of formulas, are dealt with in Section 7.5.

7.4.1   Automatic sizing of bracket symbols

Mathematics often contains bracketing symbols, usually in pairs that enclose part of the formula. When printed, these bracket symbols should be the same size as the included partial formula. LaTeX provides a pair of commands

`\left` *lbrack*   *sub_form* `\right` *rbrack*

to accomplish this. The command `\left` is placed immediately before the opening (left-hand) bracket symbol *lbrack* while `\right` comes just before the closing (right-hand) symbol *rbrack*.

$$\left[\int + \int\right]_{x=0}^{x=1}$$

`\[ \left[ \int + \int \right]_{x=0}^{x=1} \]`
The pair of brackets [ ] is adjusted to the size of the enclosed formula, as are the raised exponent and lowered index.

The commands `\left` and `\right` must appear as a pair. For every `\left` command there must be a corresponding `\right` command somewhere afterwards. The pairs may be nested. The first `\left` is paired with the last `\right`; the following `\left` with the second last `\right`, and so on. There must be the same number of `\right` as `\left` commands in a nesting.

The corresponding bracket symbols *lbrack* and *rbrack* may be perfectly arbitrary and do not need to be a logical pair.

$$\vec{x} + \vec{y} + \vec{z} = \left(\begin{matrix} a \\ b \end{matrix}\right.\Big[$$

This set of brackets is admittedly unusual but permissible.

`\[ \vec{x} + \vec{y} + \vec{z} =`
`\left( ... \right[ \]`

Sometimes a formula contains only a single opening or closing bracket without a corresponding counterpart. However, the `\left...\right` commands must still be given as a pair, but with a period '.' as an *invisible* bracket symbol.

$$y = \left\{ \begin{array}{r@{\quad:\quad}l} -1 & x < 0 \\ 0 & x = 0 \\ +1 & x > 0 \end{array}\right.$$

`\[  y = \left\{ \begin{array}`
`{r@{\quad:\quad}l}`
`-1 & x<0 \\ 0 & x=0 \\ +1 & x>0`
`\end{array} \right.    \]`

The `array` environment in the above example is described in Section 6.2.1 and produces a table in math mode.

The `\left...\right` commands may be applied to a total of 22 different symbols. These are

(`(`	) `)`	⌊ `\lfloor`	⌋ `\rfloor`
[`[`	] `]`	⌈ `\lceil`	⌉ `\rceil`
{ `\{`	} `\}`	⟨ `\langle`	⟩ `\rangle`
| `|`	‖ `|`	↑ `\uparrow`	⇑ `\Uparrow`
/ `/`	\ `\backslash`	↓ `\downarrow`	⇓ `\Downarrow`
		↕ `\updownarrow`	⇕ `\Updownarrow`

For example, `\left|...\right|` produces two vertical bars adjusted in height to contain the enclosed formula text.

Exercise 7.12: *In Equation 7.3, generate* $\cos\left(\dfrac{\pi}{2}z^2\right)$ *and* $\sin\left(\dfrac{\pi}{2}z^2\right)$ *instead of* $\cos(\dfrac{\pi}{2}z^2)$ *and* $\sin(\dfrac{\pi}{2}z^2)$.

7.4.2   Ordinary text within a formula

It is often necessary to include some *normal* text within a formula, for example, single words such as *and*, *or*, *if*, and so on. In this case one must switch to LR mode (Section 5.1.1) while staying in math mode. This is carried out with the command `\mbox{`*normal text*`}` given inside the formula, together with horizontal spacing commands such as `\quad` or `\hspace`. For example:

$$X_n = X_k \qquad \text{if and only if} \qquad Y_n = Y_k \quad \text{and} \quad Z_n = Z_k$$

```
\[  X_n = X_k \qquad\mbox{if and only if}\qquad
    Y_n = Y_k \quad\mbox{and}\quad Z_n = Z_k        \]
```

To set a longer piece of text beside a displayed formula, as in some of the above examples, it is more appropriate to put both the formula and the text in their own parboxes or minipages, placed side by side with the proper vertical positioning.

On the other hand, if letters from text fonts are required as mathematical symbols, they should be entered with the *math alphabet commands*:

```
\mathrm    \mathtt    \mathbf
\mathsf    \mathit    \mathcal
```

We have already met `\mathcal` in Section 7.3.2 on calligraphic letters. All these commands function the same way: They set their argument in the corresponding font.

$\mathbf{B}^0(x)$ T^i_j `$\mathbf{B}^0(x)$ \quad $\mathsf{T}^i_j$`

The command `\mathnormal` in Section 7.3.1 also belongs to this group. The difference between it and `\mathit` is that it sets its argument in the regular *math* italic font, while the latter uses the normal *text* italic. The letters are the same, but the spacing is different.

$\mathnormal{differ} \ne \mathit{differ}$
differ ≠ differ

All the math alphabet commands set their text in math mode, which means that spaces are ignored as usual. This is not the case for text placed in an \mbox.

7.4.3   Matrices and arrays

$$
\begin{array}{cccc}
a_{11} & a_{12} & \cdots & a_{1n} \\
\vdots & \vdots & \ddots & \vdots \\
a_{n1} & a_{n2} & \cdots & a_{nn}
\end{array}
$$

Structures like the one at the left are the basis for matrices, determinants, system of equations, and so on. They will all be referred to here as *arrays*.

Arrays are produced by means of the array environment, whose syntax and construction are described in Section 6.2.1 on tables. The array environment generates a table in math mode; that is, the column entries are interpreted as formula text. For example:

$$
\begin{array}{*{3}{c@{{}+{}}}c@{{}={}}c}
a_{11}x_1 + a_{12}x_2 + \cdots + a_{1n}x_n = b_1 \\
a_{22}x_1 + a_{22}x_2 + \cdots + a_{2n}x_n = b_2 \\
\hdotsfor{5} \\
a_{n1}x_1 + a_{n2}x_2 + \cdots + a_{nn}x_n = b_n
\end{array}
$$

```
\[ \begin{array}{*{3}{c@{{}+{}}}c@{{}={}}c}
      a_{11}x_1 & a_{12}x_2 & \cdots & a_{1n}x_n & b_1 \\
      a_{22}x_1 & a_{22}x_2 & \cdots & a_{2n}x_n & b_2 \\
         \multicolumn{5}{c}{\dotfill}                   \\
      a_{n1}x_1 & a_{n2}x_2 & \cdots & a_{nn}x_n & b_n
   \end{array}      \]
```

!

As a reminder of the table construction elements (Section 6.2.1): @{*t*} inserts the contents of *t* between the adjacent columns. In the above example, this is {}+{} and {}={}. The {} before and after the symbols forces normal math spacing to be inserted with them, otherwise they are abutted directly on the adjacent columns. Further, *{3}{c@{{}+{}}} is an abbreviation for three repetitions of the column definition c@{{}+{}}; c defines the column to be one of centered text; \multicolumn{5}{c} says that the next five columns are to be merged and replaced by one with centered text; and the command \dotfill fills the column with dots.

It is possible to nest array environments:

$$
\left(\begin{array}{c}
\left| \begin{array}{cc}
x_{11} & x_{12} \\ x_{21} & x_{22}
\end{array} \right| \\
y \\ z \end{array} \right)
$$

```
\[ \left( \begin{array}{c}
      \left| \begin{array}{cc}
         x_{11} & x_{12} \\ x_{21} & x_{22}
      \end{array} \right| \\
      y \\ z \end{array} \right)      \]
```

The outermost array consists of one column with centered text (c). The first entry in this column is also an array, with two centered columns. This array is surrounded left and right by vertical lines with adjusted sizes.

The array environment is structurally the same as a vertical box. This means that it is treated as a single character within the surrounding environment so that it may be coupled with other symbols and construction elements.

$$\sum_{p_1<p_2<\cdots<p_{n-k}}^{(1,2,\ldots,n)} \Delta_{\begin{array}{l} p_1p_2\cdots p_{n-k} \\ p_1p_2\cdots p_{n-k} \end{array}} \sum_{q_1<q_2<\cdots q_k} \left| \begin{array}{llcl} a_{q_1q_1} & a_{q_1q_2} & \cdots & a_{q_1q_k} \\ a_{q_2q_1} & a_{q_2q_2} & \cdots & a_{q_2q_k} \\ \multicolumn{4}{c}{\dotfill} \\ a_{q_kq_1} & a_{q_kq_2} & \cdots & a_{q_kq_k} \end{array} \right|$$

```
\[ \sum_{p_1<p_2<\cdots<p_{n-k}}^{(1,2,\ldots,n)}
   \Delta_{\begin{array}{l}
            p_1p_2\cdots p_{n-k} \\ p_1p_2\cdots p_{n-k}
          \end{array}}
   \sum_{q_1<q_2<\cdots q_k} \left| \begin{array}{llcl}
            a_{q_1q_1} & a_{q_1q_2} & \cdots & a_{q_1q_k} \\
            a_{q_2q_1} & a_{q_2q_2} & \cdots & a_{q_2q_k} \\
            \multicolumn{4}{c}{\dotfill}\\
            a_{q_kq_1} & a_{q_kq_2} & \cdots & a_{q_kq_k}
            \end{array} \right|        \]
```

In this example, an array environment is used as an index on the Δ. However, the indices appear too large with respect to the rest of the formula. Section 7.4.6 presents a better solution for array indices.

As for all table environments, an optional vertical positioning parameter b or t may be included with the array environment. The syntax and results are described in Sections 5.1.3 and 6.2.1. This argument is included only if the array is to be positioned vertically relative to its top or bottom line rather than its center.

$$x - \begin{array}{c} a_1 \\ \vdots \\ a_n \end{array} - u-v \quad \begin{array}{cl} 10 \\ 12 \\ -120 \end{array}$$

```
\[ x - \begin{array}{c}
       a_1 \\ \vdots \\ a_n \end{array}
   - \begin{array}[t]{cl}
       u - v & 10\\
       u + v & \begin{array}[b]{r}
               12\\-120  \end{array}
       \end{array}           \]
```

We suggest that the user try to deduce how the various arrays are structured with the help of the generating text on the right.

Exercise 7.13: The solution for the system of equations

$$F(x,y) = 0 \quad \text{and} \quad \begin{vmatrix} F''_{xx} & F''_{xy} & F'_x \\ F''_{yx} & F''_{yy} & F'_y \\ F'_x & F'_y & 0 \end{vmatrix} = 0$$

yields the coordinates for the possible inflection points of $F(x,y) = 0$.
Note: The above displayed formula consists of two sub-formulas, between which the word

'and' plus extra spacing of amount \quad *are inserted. Instead of enclosing the* array *environment within size-adjusted vertical lines with* \left|... \right|, *one may use a formatting argument* {|... |} *(Section 6.2.1) to produce the vertical lines. Such a structure is called a* determinant *in mathematics.*

Exercise 7.14: The shortest distance between two straight lines represented by the equations

$$\frac{x - x_1}{l_1} = \frac{y - y_1}{m_1} = \frac{z - z_1}{n_1} \quad \text{and} \quad \frac{x - x_2}{l_2} = \frac{y - y_2}{m_2} = \frac{z - z_2}{n_2}$$

is given by the expression

$$\pm \frac{\begin{vmatrix} x_1 - x_2 & y_1 - y_2 & z_1 - z_2 \\ l_1 & m_1 & n_1 \\ l_2 & m_2 & n_2 \end{vmatrix}}{\sqrt{\begin{vmatrix} l_1 & m_1 \\ l_2 & m_2 \end{vmatrix}^2 + \begin{vmatrix} m_1 & n_1 \\ m_2 & n_2 \end{vmatrix}^2 + \begin{vmatrix} n_1 & l_1 \\ n_2 & l_2 \end{vmatrix}^2}}$$

If the numerator is zero, the two lines meet somewhere.
Note: We do not recommend using {|cc|} *in the formatting argument of the three determinants in the denominator under the root sign. Here the* \left|... \right| *pair should be applied. Try out both possibilities for yourself and compare the results.*

Exercise 7.15: *Laurent expansion: Using* $c_n = \frac{1}{2\pi i} \oint (\zeta - a)^{-n-1} f(\zeta) \, d\zeta$, *for every function* $f(z)$ *the following representation is valid* ($n = 0, \pm 1, \pm 2, \dots$)

$$f(x) = \sum_{n=-\infty}^{+\infty} c_n (z - a)^n = \begin{cases} c_0 + c_1(z - a) + c_2(z - a)^2 + \cdots + c_n(z - a)^n + \cdots \\ \qquad + c_{-1}(z - a)^{-1} + c_{-2}(z - a)^{-2} + \cdots \\ \qquad\qquad + c_{-n}(z - a)^{-n} + \cdots \end{cases}$$

Tip: The right-hand side of the equation can be created with an array *environment consisting of only one column. What is its formatting argument?*

7.4.4 Lines above and below formulas

The commands

\overline{*sub_form*} and \underline{*sub_form*}

can be used to draw lines over or under a formula or sub-formula. They may be nested to any level:

$$\overline{a^2 + \underline{xy} + \overline{\overline{z}}}$$

```
\[ \overline{\overline{a}^2 + \underline{xy}
        + \overline{\overline{z}}}    \]
```

The command \underline may also be employed in normal text mode to underline text, whereas \overline is allowed only in math mode.

Exactly analogous to these are the two commands

\overbrace{*sub_form*} and \underbrace{*sub_form*}

that put horizontal curly braces above or below the sub-formula.

$$\overbrace{a + \underbrace{b+c} +d}$$

`\overbrace{a + \underbrace{b+c} + d}`

In displayed formulas, these commands may have exponents or indices attached to them. The (raised) exponent is set above the *overbrace* while the (lowered) index is placed below the *underbrace*.

$$\underbrace{a + \overbrace{b + \cdots + y}^{123} + z}_{\alpha\beta\gamma}$$

```
\[  \underbrace{a + \overbrace{b + \cdots +
      y}^{123} + z}_{\alpha\beta\gamma}   \]
```

Exercise 7.16: The total number of permutations of n elements taken m at a time (symbol P_n^m) is

$$P_n^m = \prod_{i=0}^{m-1} (n - i) = \underbrace{n(n - 1)(n - 2)\ldots(n - m + 1)}_{\text{total of } m \text{ factors}} = \frac{n!}{(n - m)!}$$

7.4.5   Stacked symbols

The command

`\stackrel{`*upper_sym*`}{`*lower_sym*`}`

places the symbol *upper_sym* centered on top of *lower_sym*, whereby the symbol on top is set in a smaller typeface.

$$\vec{x} \stackrel{\mathrm{def}}{=} (x_1,\ldots x_n)$$ `$ \vec{x} \stackrel{\mathrm{def}}{=} (x_1,...$`

$$A \stackrel{\alpha'}{\longrightarrow} B \stackrel{\beta'}{\longrightarrow} C$$ `$ A \stackrel{\alpha'}{\longrightarrow} B ... $`

By making use of math font size commands (Section 7.5.2) it is possible to construct new symbols with this command. For example, some authors prefer to have the `\le` symbol appear as $\stackrel{<}{=}$ instead of $\leq$. This is achieved by combining $<$ and $=$ with `$\stackrel{\textstyle<}{=}$`. If the command `\textstyle` were omitted, the symbol would be printed as $\stackrel{<}{=}$.

7.4.6   Additional TeX commands for math

The TeX math commands `\atop` and `\choose` are useful additions to the set of commands and may be applied within any LaTeX document. (In fact, all TeX math commands except `\eqalign`, `\eqalignno`, and `\leqalignno` may be used in a LaTeX manuscript.) Their syntax is

{*top* `\atop` *bottom*}
{*top* `\choose` *bottom*}

Both commands produce a structure that looks like a fraction without the dividing line. With the \choose command, this structure is also enclosed within round brackets (in mathematics this is called a *binomial coefficient*).

$$\binom{n+1}{k} = \binom{n}{k} + \binom{n}{k-1}$$

```
\[ {n+1 \choose k} =
   {n \choose k} + {n \choose k-1} \]
```

$$\prod_{j\geq0}\left(\sum_{k\geq0} a_{jk}z^k\right) = \sum_{n\geq0} z^n \left(\sum_{\substack{k_0,k_1,\dots\geq0\\k_0+k_1+\cdots=0}} a_{0k_0}a_{1k_1}\cdots\right)$$

```
\[ \prod_{j\ge0}\left( \sum_{k\ge0} a_{jk}z^k \right) =
   \sum_{n\ge0} z^n \left(\sum_{k_0,k_1\ldots\ge0 \atop
      k_0+k_1+\cdots=0} a_{0k_0} a_{1k_1}\ldots \right)    \]
```

Similar structures can be generated with the LaTeX environments

```
\begin{array}{c}   upper_line \\ lower_line \end{array}          (atop)
\left(\begin{array}{c} upper \\ lower \end{array}\right)        (choose)
```

The difference between these `array` structures and those of the TeX commands is that the former are always printed in the size and style of normal text formulas, whereas the latter will have varying sizes depending on where they appear within the formula.

For comparison

$$\Delta_{\substack{p_1p_2\cdots p_{n-k}\\p_1p_2\cdots p_{n-k}}}$$ The index array is produced using \atop

$$\Delta \begin{array}{c} p_1p_2\cdots p_{n-k}\\ p_1p_2\cdots p_{n-k}\end{array}$$ The index array is produced using \array

The above TeX commands may also be employed to produce small matrices within text formulas, such as $\binom{1\,0}{0\,1}$ or $\left(\begin{smallmatrix}a&b&c\\l&m&n\end{smallmatrix}\right)$. Here the first matrix was typed in with

```
${1\,,0\choose0\,,1}$
```

and the second with

```
$\left({a\atop l}{b\atop m}{c\atop n}\right)$
```

! The syntax of these Plain TeX commands is radically different from that normally used by LaTeX. See Example 1 on page 189 for a way to correct this.

7.4.7 Multiline equations

A multiline equation is one that is developed over several lines in which the relation symbols (for example, = or ≤) in each line are all vertically aligned with each other. For this purpose, the environments

```
\begin{eqnarray}  line_1\\  ...  \\ line_n end{eqnarray}
\begin{eqnarray*} line_1\\  ...  \\ line_n end{eqnarray*}
```

are used to set several lines of formulas or equations in displayed math mode. The individual lines of the equation or formula are separated from one another by \\. Each entry line has the form

left_formula & *mid_formula* & *right_formula* \\

When printed, all the *left_formula*s appear right justified in a left column, the *right_formula*s left justified in a right column, and the *mid_formula*s centered in between. The column separation character & designates the various parts of the formula. Normally the *mid_formula* is a single math character, the relation operator mentioned above. The individual lines thus have the same behavior as they would in a \begin{array}{rcl}...\end{array} environment.

The difference between the array and eqnarray environments is that in the latter the lines are set as displayed formulas. This means that for those symbols listed in Section 7.3.7 the larger form will be selected, and that the numerator and denominator of fractions will be in normal size. On the other hand, for the array environment the column entries will be set as text formulas, the smaller form of these symbols will be chosen and the parts of the fraction will appear in a smaller type size.

The standard form of the eqnarray environment adds an automatic sequential equation number, which is missing in the *-form. To suppress the equation number for a single line in the standard form, add the command \nonumber just before the line termination \\.

The equation numbers may be referred to within the text with the command \ref{*name*} once the keyword *name* has been assigned to the equation number with the \label{*name*} command somewhere in the line of the equation. See Section 11.2.1 for more details.

Examples:

$$
\begin{aligned}
(x+y)(x-y) &= x^2 - xy + xy - y^2 \\
&= x^2 - y^2 \\
(x+y)^2 &= x^2 + 2xy + y^2
\end{aligned}
$$

$$(7.4)$$
$$(7.5)$$

```
\begin{eqnarray}
    (x+y)(x-y) & = & x^2-xy+xy-y^2 \nonumber\\
               & = & x^2 - y^2 \\
    (x+y)^2    & = & x^2 + 2xy + y^2
\end{eqnarray}
```

$$
\begin{aligned}
x_n u_1 + \cdots + x_{n+t-1} u_t &= x_n u_1 + (ax_n + c)u_2 + \cdots \\
&\quad + \left(a^{t-1}x_n + c(a^{t-2} + \cdots + 1)\right)u_t \\
&= (u_1 + au_2 + \cdots + a^{t-1}u_t)x_n + h(u_1, \ldots, u_t)
\end{aligned}
$$

```
\begin{eqnarray*}
  x_nu_1 + \cdots + x_{n+t-1}u_t
      & = & x_nu_1 + (ax_n + c)u_2 + \cdots\\
      &   & + \left(a^{t-1}x_n + c(a^{t-2} + \cdots+1)\right)u_t\\
      & = & (u_1 + au_2 + \cdots + a^{t-1}u_t)x_n + h(u_1,\ldots,u_t)
\end{eqnarray*}
```

The second example requires some explanation. In the second line there is a $\left(\ldots\right)$ pair for the automatic sizing of the (). Such a pair may only appear within a single line; that is, it may *not* be broken by the \\ line terminator! If automatic bracket sizing is to occur in a multiline equation, it may only be found within a single line.

If bracket pairs must appear on different lines, one can try using the construction $\left(\cdots\right. \\ \left.\cdots\right)$. In the first line, the \left(is paired with the *invisible* bracket \right., while the second begins with the invisible \left. that is paired with the closing \right). However, this will only work satisfactorily if both parts of the equation have roughly the same height so that the two automatic sizings yield much the same results. Section 7.5.3 describes how to select bracket sizes manually in the event that the automatic method fails.

The + sign at the beginning of the second line also requires a remark. The signs + and − have two meanings in mathematics: Between two math quantities they act as a coupling (*binary operator*), but coming before a math symbol they serve as a sign designation (positive or negative). LaTeX stresses this difference by inserting different spacing in the two cases (for example, compare $+b$ with $a + b$).

$$y \quad = \quad a + b + c + d$$
$$+e + f + g$$
$$+ h + i + j$$

If a long formula is broken into several lines and one of them begins with + or −, LaTeX regards it as a sign designation and moves it closer to the next character.

The solution is to introduce an *invisible* character of *zero* width at the beginning of such a line. This may be the empty structure {}. Compare the effects of && +e+f+g and &&{}+h+i+j in the above equation.

Since the extra spacing is always inserted between + and an opening parenthesis (, it was not necessary to give the {} at the beginning of the second line of the eqnarray* example on this page.

Occasionally it is better to break long multiline equations as follows:

$$w + x + y + z =$$
$$a + b + c + d + e + f +$$
$$g + h + i + j + k + l$$

that is, the second and subsequent lines are not aligned with the equals sign but are left justified with a certain indentation from the beginning of the first line.

```
\begin{eqnarray*}
\lefteqn{w+x+y+z = } \\
   & & a+b+c+d+e+f+  \\
   & & g+h+i+j+k+l
\end{eqnarray*}
```

The command $\lefteqn{w+x+y+z =}$ \\ in the first line has the effect that the contents of the argument are indeed printed out, but that LaTeX considers them to have *zero* width. The left-hand column then contains only intercolumn spacing, which produces the indentation for the rest of the lines.

The indentation depth may be altered by inserting \hspace{*depth*} between the \lefteqn{...} and the \\ line termination. A positive value for *depth* increases the indentation, a negative value decreases it.

Exercise 7.17: *The following equations are to be broken as shown:*

$$
\begin{aligned}
\arcsin x \;\; &= \;\; -\arcsin(-x) = \frac{\pi}{2} - \arccos x = \left[\arccos \sqrt{1 - x^2} \; \right] \\
&= \;\; \arctan \frac{x}{\sqrt{1 - x^2}} = \left[\arccot \frac{\sqrt{1 - x^2}}{x} \right]
\end{aligned}
\tag{7.6}
$$

$$
\begin{aligned}
f(x + h, y + k) &= f(x, y) + \left\{ \frac{\partial f(x, y)}{\partial x} h + \frac{\partial f(x, y)}{\partial y} k \right\} \\
&+ \frac{1}{2} \left\{ \frac{\partial^2 f(x, y)}{\partial x^2} h^2 + 2 \frac{\partial^2 f(x, y)}{\partial x \partial y} kh + \frac{\partial^2 f(x, y)}{\partial y^2} k^2 \right\} \\
&+ \frac{1}{6} \{ \cdots \} + \cdots + \frac{1}{n!} \{ \cdots \} + R_n
\end{aligned}
\tag{7.7}
$$

A note regarding possible error messages:

Long formulas with many sets of logical brackets, especially deeply nested ones, will almost always contain errors at first. The cause is often brackets that have been incorrectly ordered or overlooked.

If LATEX produces error messages during formula processing, which the beginner is not able to interpret correctly (error messages are described in detail in Appendix C), he or she should check the bracket pairing very carefully in the formula text. Some text editors can do the search for the matching bracket, which greatly simplifies the task.

If the error is not found in this way, one can try pressing the return key at the error message in order to proceed with the processing. The resulting printout can indicate where things may have gone wrong.

Exercise 7.18: *The* eqnarray *environment inserts additional spacing where the column separation character & appears. This is undesirable when an equation is to be broken and aligned on + or − within a long summation. For example:*
The inverse function of the polynomial expansion $y = f(x) = ax + bx^2 + cx^3 + dx^4 + ex^5 + fx^6 + \cdots$ $(a \neq 0)$ *begins with the elements*

$$
\begin{aligned}
x = \varphi(y) = \frac{1}{a} y \;\; &- \;\; \frac{b}{a^3} y^2 + \frac{1}{a^5} (2b^2 - ac) y^3 \\
&+ \;\; \frac{1}{a^7} (5abc - z^2 d - fb^3) y^4 \\
&+ \;\; \frac{1}{a^9} (6a^2 bd + 3a^2 c^2 + 14b^4 - a^3 e - 21ab^2 c) y^5 \\
&+ \;\; \frac{1}{a^{11}} (7a^3 be + 7a^3 cd + 84ab^3 c - a^4 f - \\
& \quad\;\; 28a^2 b^2 d - 28a^2 bc^2 - 43b^5) y^6 + \cdots
\end{aligned}
$$

Select a value for the declaration \arraycolsep *(Section 6.2.2) such that the distance between the + and − and the break points are as near as possible to those in the rest of the formula.*

7.4.8 Framed or side-by-side formulas

> [!] Displayed formulas or equations may be put into vertical boxes of appropriate width, that is, in a \parbox command or minipage environment. Within the vertical box, the formulas are horizontally centered or left justified with indentation \mathindent according to the selected document class option.

Vertical boxes may be positioned relative to one another just like single characters (Sections 5.1.3 and 5.1.7). In this way the user may place displayed formulas or equations side by side.

$$\alpha = f(z) \quad (7.8)$$
$$\beta = f(z^2) \quad (7.9)$$
$$\gamma = f(z^3) \quad (7.10)$$

$$x = \alpha^2 - \beta^2$$
$$y = 2\alpha\beta$$

The left-hand set of equations is set in a \parbox of width 4 cm, the right-hand set in one of width 2.5 cm, while this text is inside a minipage of width 4.5 cm.

```
\parbox{4cm}{\begin{eqnarray} \alpha &=& f(z)...\end{eqnarray}}
\hfill  \parbox{2.5cm}{\begin{eqnarray*}
  x &=& \alpha^2 - \beta^2\\ y &=& 2\alpha\beta \end{eqnarray*}}
\hfill  \begin{minipage}{4.5cm} The left-hand ... \end{minipage}
```

> [!] Vertical boxes can also be useful when equation numbers are placed in an unconventional manner. The eqnarray environment generates an equation number for every line, which may be suppressed with \nonumber. To add a vertically centered equation number to a set of equations, for example,

$$P(x) = a_0 + a_1x + a_2x^2 + \cdots + a_nx^n$$
$$P(-x) = a_0 - a_1x + a_2x^2 - \cdots + (-1)^n a_nx^n$$

$$(7.11)$$

the following text may be given:

```
\parbox{10cm}{\begin{eqnarray*} ... \end{eqnarray*}} \hfill
\parbox{1cm}{\begin{eqnarray}\end{eqnarray}}
```

The actual set of equations is produced here in the eqnarray* environment, within a vertical box of width 10 cm, followed by an empty eqnarray environment in a box of width 1 cm that generates the equation number. Both boxes are vertically aligned along their center lines.

> [!] Emphasizing formulas by framing requires no new construction elements. It is sufficient to put them into an \fbox (Section 5.1.7). Text formulas $\boxed{a + b}$ are simply framed with \fbox{$a+b$}. For displayed formulas, \displaystyle (Section 7.5.2) must be issued, otherwise they are set as text formulas.

$$\boxed{\int_0^\infty f(x)\,\mathrm{d}x \approx \sum_{i=1}^n w_i e^{x_i} f(x_i)}$$

is produced with

```
\[\fbox{$\displaystyle \int^\infty_0 f(x)\,\mathrm{d}x ..$}\]
```

An alternative method to frame displayed equations is with the $\mathcal{A}_{\mathcal{M}}\mathcal{S}$-LaTeX \boxed command; see page 281.

7.4.9   Chemical formulas and boldface in math formulas

In mathematics it is sometimes necessary to set individual characters or parts of the formula in boldface. This can be achieved simply with the math alphabet command \mathbf that we met in Section 7.4.2:

$\mathbf{S^{-1}TS = dg(\omega_1,\ldots,\omega_n) = \Lambda}$

produces $\mathbf{S^{-1}TS = dg(\omega_1,\ldots,\omega_n) = \Lambda}$.

In this example, the entire formula has been set as the argument of \mathbf so that everything should be set in boldface. In fact, only numbers, lower- and uppercase Latin letters, and uppercase Greek letters are set in **bold Roman** with \mathbf. Lowercase Greek letters and other math symbols appear in the normal *math* font.

If only part of the formula is to be set in boldface, that part must be given as the argument of the \mathbf command.

$\mathbf{2\sqrt{x}/y} = z$ $\mathbf{2\sqrt{x}/y} = z$

The math font style command \boldmath will set all characters in boldface, with the following exceptions:

- raised and lowered symbols (exponents and indices)
- the characters + : ; ! ? ( ) [ ]
- symbols that exist in two sizes (Section 7.3.7)

The \boldmath declaration may not appear in math mode. It must be called before switching to math mode or within a parbox or minipage. The countercommand \unboldmath resets the math fonts back to the normal ones.

$$\oint\limits_C V\,\mathrm{d}\tau = \oint\limits_\Sigma \nabla\times V\,d\sigma$$

```
\boldmath \[ \oint\limits_C V
\,\mathrm{d}\tau =\oint\limits_\Sigma
\nabla\times V\,d\sigma \] \unboldmath
```

If \boldmath has been turned on outside the math mode, it may be temporarily turned off inside with \mbox{\unboldmath$...$}.

\boldmath\(P = \mbox{\unboldmath$m$}b\)\unboldmath

yields $\boldsymbol{P} = m\boldsymbol{b}$. Similarly, \boldmath can be temporarily turned on within math mode with the structure \mbox{\boldmath$...$}: $W_r = \int M\,\mathrm{d}\varphi = r^2 m\omega^2/2$

\(W_r = \int\mbox{\boldmath$M\,\mathrm{d}\varphi$} =..\)

Package: bm   An alternative method of printing single symbols in boldface is provided by the bm package described on page 387.

Chemical formulas are normally set in Roman type, not in italics as for mathematical formulas. This may be brought about by setting the formula as the argument of the font command \mathrm:

$\mathrm{Fe_2^{2+}Cr_2O_4}$ $\mathrm{Fe_2^{2+}Cr_2O_4}$

7.4.10 Mathematical typesetting conventions

The International Standards Organization (ISO) has established the recognized conventions for typesetting mathematics, the essential elements of which are presented in an article by Beccari (1997), along with a description of how they may be realized with LaTeX. Some of these rules have already been mentioned and demonstrated in the examples. Here are the major points.

1. Simple variables are represented by italic letters, as $a\ b\ c\ x\ y\ z$.
2. Vectors are written in boldface italic, as $\boldsymbol{B}\ \boldsymbol{v}\ \boldsymbol{\omega}$.
3. Tensors of 2nd order and matrices may appear in a sans serif font, as M D I.
4. The special numbers e, i, π, as well as the differential operator d, are to be *written in an upright font* to emphasize that they are not variables.
5. A measurement consisting of a number plus a dimension is an indivisible unit, with a smaller-than-normal space between them, as 5.3 km and 62 kg. The dimension is in an upright font.

Point 1 is fulfilled automatically by LaTeX. Point 5 is easily achieved by inserting the small space `\,` command between the number and dimension, as `5.3\,km` and `62\,kg`. Using the protected space `~` instead is very common practice among LaTeX users, which ensures that the two parts are not split, but with regular, not small spacing: 5.3 km and 62 kg.

Point 2 is not satisfied with the `\vec` command, which produces $\vec{B}$. Nor does `\mathbf` help, for this yields **B**, in an upright font. The best solution is to use the `\boldsymbol` command from the $\mathcal{AMS}$ package amsbsy (Section 15.2.1) or the `\bm` command from the tools package bm (Section B.5.4). Otherwise one must resort to defining

```
\renewcommand{\vec}[1]{\mbox{\boldmath$#1$}}
```

for a revised `\vec` command.

Similarly, point 3 can be met with the math alphabet command `\mathsf`.

Point 4 is the one that is most often violated, especially for the differential d. We have demonstrated it in the examples in this book and have shown how it may be achieved with the `\mathrm` math alphabet command. However, to simplify the application, it is recommended to create some user-defined commands, such as

```
\newcommand{\me}{\mathrm{e}}      for math e
\newcommand{\mi}{\mathrm{i}}      for math i
\newcommand{\dif}{\mathrm{d}}     for differential operator d
```

An upright π is not so easy since this is not provided in the usual math fonts.

With these new commands, the equation on page 121 is more conveniently set with

```
\[ \int^{\infty}_0 f(x)\,\dif x \approx
          \sum^n_{i=1}w_i \me^{x_i} f(x_i) \]
```

7.5   Fine-tuning mathematics

7.5.1   Horizontal spacing

Even though TeX has a thorough knowledge of the rules of mathematical typesetting, it cannot hope to understand the mathematical meaning. For example, $y\ dx$ normally means the joining of the variable y with the differential operator dx, and this joining is designated by a small space between the two. However, TEX removes the blank in the entry y dx and prints $y dx$, the product of three variables y, d, and x. At this point, LATEX needs some fine-tuning assistance. (And the d should really be upright, the \dif or \mathrm{d} of the previous section.)

Small amounts of horizontal spacing can be added in math mode with the commands

\,	small space	= 3/18 of a quad
\:	medium space	= 4/18 of a quad
\;	large space	= 5/18 of a quad
\!	negative space	= −3/18 of a quad

In the following examples taken from Knuth (1986a), the third column contains the results without the additional horizontal spacing command.

$\sqrt{2}\,x$	$\sqrt{2}\,x$	$\sqrt{2}x$
$\sqrt{\,\log x}$	$\sqrt{\log x}$	$\sqrt{\log x}$
$0\left(1/\sqrt{n}\,\right)$	$O\left(1/\sqrt{n}\right)$	$O\left(1/\sqrt{n}\right)$
$[\,0,1)$	$[\,0,1)$	$[0,1)$
$\log n\,(\log\log n)^2$	$\log n\,(\log\log n)^2$	$\log n(\log\log n)^2$
$x^2\!/2$	$x^2/2$	$x^2/2$
$n/\!\log n$	$n/\log n$	$n/\log n$
$\Gamma_{\!2}+\Delta^{\!2}$	$\Gamma_2+\Delta^2$	$\Gamma_2+\Delta^2$
$R_i{}^j{}_{\!kl}$	$R_i{}^j{}_{kl}$	$R_i{}^j{}_{kl}$
$\int_0^x\!\int_0^y \mathrm{d}F(u,v)$	$\int_0^x\int_0^y \mathrm{d}F(u,v)$	$\int_0^x\int_0^y \mathrm{d}F(u,v)$
\[\int\!\!\!\!\int_D \mathrm{d}x\,\mathrm{d}y \]	$\iint_D \mathrm{d}x\,\mathrm{d}y$	$\int\!\int_D \mathrm{d}x\mathrm{d}y$

Note: In the third last example above, R_i{}^j is so constructed that an invisible character of zero width comes after the index of R_i, and it is this dummy character that receives the following exponent. The result is $R_i{}^j$, instead of R_i^j, which is produced by R_i^j.

There are no hard and fast rules for applying the math spacing commands. Some candidates are the differential operator, small root signs in text formulas followed by a variable, the dividing sign /, and multiple integral signs. The above examples illustrate many suitable situations.

7.5.2   Selecting font size in formulas

It is possible to alter the font sizes that TEX selects for the various parts of the formula. First we must explain what sizes are available in math mode and what TEX's selection rules are.

In math mode there are four font sizes that may be chosen, their actual sizes being relative to the basic font size of the document class:

`\displaystyle`	D	Normal size for displayed formulas
`\textstyle`	T	Normal size for text formulas
`\scriptstyle`	S	Normal size for first sub-, superscript
`\scriptscriptstyle`	SS	Normal size for later sub-, superscripts

From now on we shall make use of the symbolic abbreviations D, T, S, and SS. When math mode is switched on, the active font size becomes D for displayed and T for text formulas. Their only difference lies in those symbols that appear in two sizes, plus the corresponding style of those superscripts and subscripts (Section 7.3.7). The larger symbols belong to D, the smaller to T.

Starting from these base sizes, various math elements will be set in other sizes. Once another size has been chosen for an element, it remains the active size within that element. The table below shows the selection rules:

Active size	Fractions upper	lower	Super-, subscripts
D	T	T	S
T	S	S	S
S	SS	SS	SS
SS	SS	SS	SS

If the active size is D, size T is selected for both parts of the fraction. That is, for both numerator and denominator, T becomes the active size. If they in turn contain further fractions, these will be set in S. If the active size is D or T, superscripts and subscripts (exponents and indices) appear in S; within them S is the active size, and any fractions or shiftings inside them will be set in SS.

The TeX elements { \atop } and { \choose } are treated as fractions.

The active font size inside an `array` environment is T.

The smallest available math font size is SS. Once it has been reached, no further reduction is possible, so that all subsequent superscripts and subscripts appear in SS as well.

From the table one easily sees that

```
\[ a_0 + \frac{1}{a_1 + \frac{1}{a_2
     + \frac{1}{a_3 + \frac{1}{a_4}}}} \]
```

$$a_0 + \cfrac{1}{a_1 + \cfrac{1}{a_2 + \cfrac{1}{a_3 + \frac{1}{a_4}}}}$$

will appear as shown at the right.

This math structure, called a *continued fraction*, is usually printed as:

$$a_0 + \cfrac{1}{a_1 + \cfrac{1}{a_2 + \cfrac{1}{a_3 + \cfrac{1}{a_4}}}}$$

```
\[ a_0 + \frac{1}{\displaystyle a_1
     + \frac{1}{\displaystyle a_2
     + \frac{1}{\displaystyle a_3
     + \frac{1}{a_4}}}}        \]
```

By explicitly giving the font size within each element, one makes that size active rather than relying on the internally selected size. In this example, D is chosen for each denominator. Thus the next fraction acts as though it were outermost. The \displaystyle command may be omitted in the last fraction. (Can you see why?)

The selection table allows one to predict precisely which math font size will be applied at any part of the formula so that an explicit specification may be made if necessary. The effects of such a choice may also be calculated for the following math elements.

In the examples below, the right-hand column shows how the formulas would appear if the math font size is not explicitly specified.

$$\cfrac{\dfrac{a}{x-y}+\dfrac{b}{x+y}}{1+\dfrac{a-b}{a+b}}$$

```
\[ \frac{\displaystyle\frac{a}{x-y}
             +\frac{b}{x+y}}
   {\displaystyle 1+\frac{a-b}{a+b}} \]
```

$$\cfrac{\frac{a}{x-y}+\frac{b}{x+y}}{1+\frac{a-b}{a+b}}$$

$$e^{-\frac{x_i-x_j}{n^i+n^j}}$$

```
\[    e^{\textstyle -
   \frac{x_i-x_j}{n^i+n^j}}    \]
```

$$e^{-\frac{x_i-x_j}{n^i+n^j}}$$

$$\left(\begin{pmatrix}ab\\cd\end{pmatrix}\quad\dfrac{e+f}{g-h}\right.$$
$$\left.\quad 0 \quad\quad \begin{vmatrix}ij\\kl\end{vmatrix}\right)$$

```
\[ \left(\begin{array}{cc}
\displaystyle{ab\choose cd} &
\displaystyle\frac{e+f}{g-h}\\
0 & \displaystyle \left|
   {ij\atop kl} \right|
\end{array}\right)        \]
```

$$\left(\begin{pmatrix}ab\\cd\end{pmatrix}\quad\frac{e+f}{g-h}\right.$$
$$\left.\quad 0 \quad\quad \begin{vmatrix}ij\\kl\end{vmatrix}\right)$$

If an explicit size specification is to be given frequently within a document—say, within every entry in an array environment—then considerable writing effort may be avoided by adding this to the preamble:

```
\newcommand{\D}{\displaystyle}\newcommand{\T}{\textstyle}...
```

In this way, the size command may be given simply by typing \D or \T, and so forth.

The math font size selection rules given above are, in fact, a simplification. Here we present the complete description.

For each of the four math font sizes D, T, S, and SS there is a modified version D', T', S', and SS'. The difference is that with D, T, S, and SS the superscripts (exponents) are somewhat higher than they are with D', T', S', and SS'. Compare the positions of the exponent 2 above and below the line: $\frac{x^2}{x^2}$.

Otherwise, the primed and unprimed font sizes are identical. The true selection rules are given in the table at the right.

Active size	Fractions upper	lower	Superscripts	Subscripts
D	T	T'	S	S'
D'	T'	T'	S'	S'
T	S	S'	S	S'
T'	S'	S'	S'	S'
S, SS	SS	SS'	SS	SS'
S', SS'	SS'	SS'	SS'	SS'

When the font size is explicitly stated within a numerator or superscript, it is the unprimed version that is selected, while in the denominators and subscripts, it is the primed fonts.

7.5.3   Manual sizing of bracket symbols

The \left...\right commands preceding one of the 22 bracket symbols listed in Section 7.4.1 adjust the symbol size automatically according to the height of the enclosed formula text. However, it is possible to select a size explicitly by placing one of the TEX commands \big, \Big, \bigg, or \Bigg before the bracket symbol.

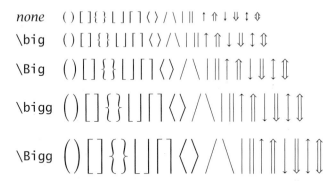

In contrast to the \left...\right pairs, the explicit bracket size commands do not have to be contained within one line of a multiline formula. The opening and closing brackets may appear on different lines. This applies also to the commands described in the next paragraph.

7.5.4   Math style parameters

The mathematical style parameters listed below are set to standard values by LATEX. The user may alter them at any time with the \setlength command in the usual manner.

\arraycolsep
> Half the width of the intercolumn spacing for the array environment (see also Section 6.2.2).

\jot   Extra vertical spacing that appears between the rows of multiline equations in the eqnarray and eqnarray* environments.

\mathindent
> The amount of indentation for math formulas when the document class option fleqn has been selected.

\abovedisplayskip
> The vertical spacing above displayed formulas when the left side of the formula is closer to the left margin than the end of the preceding line of text. Such a formula is designated *long*.

\belowdisplayskip
> The vertical spacing inserted below a *long* displayed formula.

\abovedisplayshortskip
> Vertical spacing added above a *short* displayed formula. In this case, the left edge is to the right of the end of the preceding line of text.

`\belowdisplayshortskip`

> Vertical spacing inserted after a *short* displayed formula.

`\topsep`

> The above four spacings are not used with the document class option `fleqn` where, instead, `\topsep` is inserted above and below displayed formulas (see Section 4.4.2).

All the above parameters except `\jot` should be rubber lengths (Section 2.4.2).

7.5.5   Some further advice

Sometimes authors want horizontal and vertical alignments of their formulas that just cannot be achieved using the means described so far. They should consider placing their formulas inside horizontal or vertical boxes that may then be positioned wherever they please.

Similarly, the `array` environment, together with explicit size declarations and the table construction and style elements from Sections 6.2.1 and 6.2.2, should be able to accomplish just about any horizontal and vertical alignment.

Exercise 7.19: *Generate this continued fraction. Note: In contrast to the example on page 147, the 1 here in the numerator appears left justified. Hint: Do you remember the command* `\hfill`?

$$a_0 + \cfrac{1}{a_1 + \cfrac{1}{a_2 + \cfrac{1}{a_3 + \cfrac{1}{a_4}}}}$$

Exercise 7.20: *Produce the following set of equations with the* `array` *environment.*

$$
\begin{array}{ll}
\sin 2\alpha = 2\sin\alpha\cos\alpha, & \cos 2\alpha = \cos^2\alpha - \sin^2\alpha \\
\sin 3\alpha = 3\sin\alpha - 4\sin^3\alpha & \cos 3\alpha = 3\cos^3\alpha - 3\cos\alpha \\
\sin 4\alpha = 8\cos^3\alpha\sin\alpha - 4\cos\alpha\sin\alpha & \cos 4\alpha = 8\cos^4\alpha - 8\cos^2\alpha + 1
\end{array}
$$

Hint: Recall that @{...} *expressions in the formatting field of the* `array` *environment can be used to insert horizontal spacing and/or mathematical text between the columns (see the first example in Section 7.4.3).*

Exercise 7.21: *Create the table on the following page with the* `array` *environment. Hints for the solution:*

1. *Define abbreviations, such as* `\D` *for* `\displaystyle` *and* `\bm` *for* `\boldmath` *and possibly even* `\ba` *and* `\ea` *for* `\begin{array}` *and* `\end{array}`.

2. *Build the table in stages. Start with the head and only proceed further when it looks reasonable. Remember that normal text within the* `array` *environment must be included inside an* `\mbox`.

3. *Continue with the first mathematical row. Here the first entry in the second column is also an* `array` *environment that is aligned with the rest of the row by means of the* [t] *positioning argument. Do not forget to activate the size* `\D` *at the necessary places in the inner structures. Insert a possible strut (Section 5.1.6) to generate the right distance from the head. The distance to the next row can be adjusted with a length specification added to the row terminating command* \\[..].

4. *After this row has been completed successfully, the next should pose no difficulties.*

5. *In the third mathematical row, both the first column and the left side of the second column consist of* array *environments. The third column contains three fractions whose denominators may be produced either with* array *or with the TeX* {...\atop...} *command; the fractions themselves are placed in two rows with another* array *environment.*

6. *The second and third columns of the last mathematical row again contain* array *environments. Some of the sub-formulas in this row appear in* \boldmath. *Recall that this command may only be invoked within text mode, that is, within an* \mbox.

7. *In the last row, all three columns of the outer* array *environment are merged together and the text is set within a parbox of appropriate width:*

> \multicolumn{3}{|c|}{\parbox{..}{......}}

<table>
<tr><td colspan="3" align="center">Equations for the tangential plane and surface normal</td></tr>
<tr><td>Equation for the surface</td><td align="center">Tangential plane</td><td align="center">Surface normal</td></tr>
<tr>
<td>$F(x,y,z) = 0$</td>
<td>$\dfrac{\partial F}{\partial x}(X-x) + \dfrac{\partial F}{\partial y}(Y-y)$
 $+ \dfrac{\partial F}{\partial z}(Z-z) = 0$</td>
<td>$\dfrac{X-x}{\dfrac{\partial F}{\partial x}} = \dfrac{Y-y}{\dfrac{\partial F}{\partial y}} = \dfrac{Z-z}{\dfrac{\partial F}{\partial z}}$</td>
</tr>
<tr>
<td>$z = f(x,y)$</td>
<td>$Z-z = p(X-x) + q(Y-y)$</td>
<td>$\dfrac{X-x}{p} = \dfrac{Y-y}{q} = \dfrac{Z-z}{-1}$</td>
</tr>
<tr>
<td>$x = x(u,v)$
 $y = y(u,v)$
 $z = z(u,v)$</td>
<td>$\begin{vmatrix} X-x & Y-y & Z-z \\ \dfrac{\partial x}{\partial u} & \dfrac{\partial y}{\partial u} & \dfrac{\partial z}{\partial u} \\ \dfrac{\partial x}{\partial v} & \dfrac{\partial y}{\partial v} & \dfrac{\partial z}{\partial v} \end{vmatrix} = 0$</td>
<td>$\dfrac{X-x}{\begin{vmatrix} \frac{\partial y}{\partial u} & \frac{\partial z}{\partial u} \\ \frac{\partial y}{\partial v} & \frac{\partial z}{\partial v} \end{vmatrix}} = \dfrac{Y-y}{\begin{vmatrix} \frac{\partial z}{\partial u} & \frac{\partial x}{\partial u} \\ \frac{\partial z}{\partial v} & \frac{\partial x}{\partial v} \end{vmatrix}}$
 $= \dfrac{Z-z}{\begin{vmatrix} \frac{\partial x}{\partial u} & \frac{\partial y}{\partial u} \\ \frac{\partial x}{\partial v} & \frac{\partial y}{\partial v} \end{vmatrix}}$</td>
</tr>
<tr>
<td>$\boldsymbol{r} = \boldsymbol{r}(u,v)$</td>
<td align="center">$(\boldsymbol{R} - \boldsymbol{r})(\boldsymbol{r}_1 \times \boldsymbol{r}_2) = 0$
 or $\quad (\boldsymbol{R} - \boldsymbol{r})\boldsymbol{N} = 0$</td>
<td align="center">$\boldsymbol{R} = \boldsymbol{r} + \lambda(\boldsymbol{r}_1 \times \boldsymbol{r}_2)$
 or $\quad \boldsymbol{R} = \boldsymbol{r} + \lambda\boldsymbol{N}$</td>
</tr>
<tr>
<td colspan="3">In this table, x, y, z and $\boldsymbol{r}$ are the coordinates and the radius vector of a fixed point M on the curve; X, Y, Z, and $\boldsymbol{R}$ are the coordinates and radius vector of a point on the tangential plane or surface normal with reference to M; furthermore, $p = \frac{\partial z}{\partial x}$, $q = \frac{\partial z}{\partial y}$ and $\boldsymbol{r}_1 = \partial\boldsymbol{r}/\partial u$, $\boldsymbol{r}_2 = \partial\boldsymbol{r}/\partial v$.</td>
</tr>
</table>

Note: If you succeed in reproducing this mathematical table, you should have no more problems with positioning formulas and their parts!

7.6 Beyond standard LaTeX

The typesetting elements presented in this chapter should be able to handle many of the everyday problems of mathematical composition. The American Mathematical

Society, $\mathcal{A}_{\mathcal{M}}\mathcal{S}$, which has supported TeX from its beginning, has developed a set of packages to assist authors in composing even more complicated formulas with LaTeX. Known as $\mathcal{A}_{\mathcal{M}}\mathcal{S}$-LaTeX, it includes many extra commands, further environments to supplement `eqnarray`, and many additional symbols. This system is presented in Chapter 15.

In any event, typesetting mathematics is a very complicated issue. It was for this reason that Donald Knuth selected the $ sign as the switch to math mode: In the old days of movable lead type, setting mathematical formulas was an expensive business because of the extra workload it entailed. Even today, electronic typesetting is far more involved for math than for simple text.

8 Graphics Inclusion and Color

The two topics of this chapter have one thing in common: Neither is handled by TeX at all, and thus neither by LaTeX. Outputting graphics files produced by other programs, or printing in color, are functions of the output device, that is, the printer, the monitor, and the electronic output file. These are controlled by the DVI driver program that converts the DVI output of LaTeX into the final output form. For each output type, a different set of commands is needed to switch color or to send an image.

TeX does have a way of sending special driver-specific commands to the driver by placing them in the .dvi file; the command to do this is even named \special. LaTeX exploits this feature to pass driver commands to the .dvi file, but to do so it needs to know which driver is going to be used for the further processing.

With the advent of LaTeX 2_ε, a standardized syntax was introduced, replacing the driver-specific commands that abounded with LaTeX 2.09 and caused much confusion. At last, the importation of external images had become a basic part of LaTeX usage and was no longer an exotic, magical art. Well . . . , nearly.

It is still necessary to tell LaTeX which driver will be used afterwards, as an option to the graphics and color packages, but once that is done, all the driver-specific special commands are loaded from a corresponding .def file, which the user does not have to worry about. The top-level syntax remains the same for all types.

It is also important to realize that not all image formats can be handled by every driver. PostScript drivers, for example, will only accept PostScript images, and then only as *encapsulated* PostScript. Image format conversion may be required.

8.1 The graphics packages

Strictly speaking, these packages, referred to as the *graphics collection*, are extensions to the basic LaTeX installation. We describe them here because of their indispensability in producing professional documents and camera-ready copy. Provided by Sebastian Rahtz and David Carlisle and many other contributors, they can be expected to be part of every LaTeX installation. A basic manual is provided in a file named grfguide.tex, which may already be preprocessed to .dvi or some other form. Even more details about these packages and advanced applications of PostScript to LaTeX are to be found in the book *The LaTeX Graphics Companion* (Goossens et al., 1997).

The commands defined by these packages are the building blocks for other packages that either emulate the older driver-specific ones or provide a more comfortable syntax for these functions. As long as these other packages are based on `graphics` and `color`, they should be equally compatible with all the supported drivers.

These features are not limited to PostScript drivers. As long as a driver can support the inclusion and manipulation (scaling, rotation) of graphics, and/or the use of color, a `.def` file can be written to enable it to make use of the standardized graphics and color commands.

Driver names that may be used as options are:

dvipdf	dviwin◆□⇑	pctexhp◆□⇑	tcidvi□⇑
dvipdfm	emtex◆□⇑	pctexps	textures
dvips	oztex	pctexwin◆□⇑	truetex□⇑
dvipsone	pctex32	pdftex	vtex

(Limited functionality: ◆no color support; □no scaling; ⇑no rotation.)

The `xdvi` previewer (and its Windows equivalent `windvi`) work with PostScript graphics; although there is also an `xdvi` option, it is only an alias for `dvips`.

A driver option *must* be specified when loading the `graphics` and `color` packages, for example, as

```
\usepackage[dvips]{graphics,color}
```

However, it is possible to establish a default for the local configuration, as described in Section 8.1.7. It is conceivable that your installation has already done this, so it is worth doing an experiment to determine whether a default driver option already exists.

8.1.1   Importing external graphics

We wish to have a graphics file produced by some other program included in the document, possibly scaled to a desired size or rotated by 90°. Essentially, we want to do by computer what used to be done with scissors and glue.

There are two packages available for importing and manipulating external graphics files: the basic `graphics` package and the more extended `graphicx` one. They both offer identical functionality, differing only in their syntax.

In addition to the driver names, some other options may be invoked when the packages `graphics` or `graphicx` are loaded:

draft   does not import but places a framed box where the graphic would appear, with the file name printed inside; this speeds up the processing considerably when one is only working on the text;

final   counteracts `draft`; needed when the `draft` option has been issued globally in \documentclass;

`hidescale`

>   leaves blank space where scaled text should be;

`hiderotate`

>   leaves blank space where rotated text should be; this and the option `hidescale` are useful if the previewer cannot handle scaling or rotation;

`hiresbb`

>   look for the bounding box values in `%%HiResBoundingBox` instead of the normal `%%BoundingBox` line.

8.1.2 Importing with the graphics package

Package:
graphics

The basic importing command with the `graphics` package is

>   `\includegraphics[`*llx,lly*`][`*urx,ury*`]{`*file_name*`}`

where *llx, lly* are the coordinates of the lower-left corner, and *urx, ury* those of the upper-right corner of the *bounding box* containing the part of the picture that is to be included. In other words, they say where the scissors are to be applied. Units may be specified (like `[3cm, 2in]`), but if they are omitted, big points (bp, 72 per inch, 28.3464... per cm) are assumed. If only one optional argument is given, it is the upper-right corner, and the lower left is assumed to be `[0,0]`.

If no bounding box coordinates are given, the driver will obtain them some other way, depending on the type of graphics file. For example, for the very common *encapsulated PostScript* files with extension `.eps`, the bounding box information is extracted from the graphics file itself. The figure at the right is stored in such a file and is included simply with the command

>   `\includegraphics{clock}`

(It is not necessary, nor recommended, to include the file extension `.eps` in the file name designation; LaTeX will automatically test for all the extensions allowed by the selected driver option, something that permits greater flexibility in the source text.)

With `\includegraphics*`, the figure is clipped, so that any drawing outside the specified bounding box is suppressed. This is useful if only part of a figure is to be reproduced. It is also vital with some perverse figures that paint the whole page white!

Scaling

The graphics file in the above commands is transferred to the document in its original size. To rescale it, two commands are available:

>   `\scalebox{`*h_scale*`}[`*v_scale*`]{`*text*`}`

which applies horizontal and vertical scale factors to the contents *text*; if *v_scale* is omitted, it is the same as *h_scale*;

> \resizebox{*h_length*}{*v_length*}{*text*}

adjusts the figure to fit into the specified horizontal and vertical sizes; if either length is given as !, the one scale factor is used for both dimensions. A *-form allows *v_length* to refer to the height + depth of the box, rather than just to the height. In both cases, the contents *text* may be an \includegraphics command, but it may also be any arbitrary text.

Reflection

The contents of a box may be reflected horizontally with

> \reflectbox{*text*}

Rotation

Rotation of a box about the left-hand end of its baseline is done with

> \rotatebox{*angle*}{*text*}

where *angle* is in degrees, and the rotation is counterclockwise.

To illustrate this, we have scaled the previous clock figure to a height of 2 cm and then rotated it by 30°, using the commands

```
\rotatebox{30}{\resizebox{!}{2cm}{%
    \includegraphics{clock}}}
```

For demonstration purposes, we have added framed boxes around the figure before and after the rotation. It is the inner (tilted) box that is 2 cm high, while the overall outer box is somewhat higher and broader due to its inclined contents. Without these frames, the figure seems to have extraneous space above and to the left, something that can be very puzzling even to experienced users. (The frames would not normally appear with the above commands.)

Exercise 8.1: Copy the lines at the right to a file named demo.eps and then include it in a LaTeX document, with some normal text above and below it. The result should appear as:

```
%!PS-Adobe-3.0 EPSF-3.0
%%BoundingBox: 169 158 233 242
220 200 moveto
200 200 20 0 360 arc
170 170 moveto
230 220 lineto
170 210 lineto
225 160 lineto
205 240 lineto
170 170 lineto
stroke
showpage
```

Note: The file demo.eps can be copied from the enclosed CD in the directory books →Guide4, where it is also available as demo.pdf.

8.1.3 Importing, scaling, and rotating with the graphicx package

Package:
graphicx If one selects the graphicx rather than the graphics package, a different interface is available for both importing and rotation, one making use of keys and values:

\includegraphics[*key=value*,...]{*file_name*}

The keys are of two types: those that take a numerical value and those that are flags with the values true or false. Simply giving the name of a flag without a value is equivalent to setting it to true. Possible keys and their values are:

scale= *number*; enters the number by which the figure size should be magnified over its natural size;

width= *length*; specifies the width to which the figure should be scaled; if height not given, it is scaled with the same factor as the width;

height= *length*; specifies the height to which the figure should be scaled; if width is not given, it is scaled with the same factor as the height;

totalheight= *length*; like height but specifies the height plus depth of the figure; should always be used in place of height if the figure has been rotated;

keepaspectratio (=true|false); if both height and width are specified, this flag ensures that the original height/width ratio remains unchanged; the figure will not exceed either of the given dimensions;

angle= *number*; the angle by which the figure is to be rotated counterclockwise, in degrees; any height or width specifications coming before this key are also rotated so that the height becomes the width and the width becomes either the height (positive angle) or depth (negative angle);

origin= *loc*; determines the point about which the rotation occurs; default is bl for bottom-left corner; also possible are c for center, t for top, r for right, and B for baseline; any sensible combination, such as tr, is allowed;

draft (=true|false); like the draft package option but applied to the one graphics file; the figure is not imported, but rather a framed box of the correct size is printed containing the name of the file;

clip (=true|false); suppresses the printing of any graphic outside the bounding box;

bb= *llx lly urx ury*; enters the coordinates of the bounding box manually if they are missing or incorrect in the graphics file, or are to be deliberately altered; the specifications are four lengths separated by blanks; units may be given, but if omitted, big points (bp) are assumed; this option should never be used with pdfTeX;

`viewport=` *llx lly urx ury*; specifies the bounding box but relative to the lower-left corner of the existing one; this is the preferred method for correcting the bounding box or (with `clip`) to select only a portion of the whole figure; with pdfTeX, this option must be used rather than bb;

`trim=` *dllx dlly durx dury*; reduces the existing bounding box by the amounts specified;

`hiresbb` (=`true|false`); like the `hiresbb` package option but applied to one graphics file; reads bounding box information from the %%HiResBoundingBox line in the graphics file.

The keys are all optional; they are included as needed. Their order is not important other than that `angle` interchanges any previous `height` and `width` meanings. The sets of key/values are separated from each other by commas. It is often best to set `width` relative to the current line width \linewidth, say, as `width=0.8\linewidth`.

With the key/value syntax, the tilted, scaled graphic on page 156 is produced with

> `\includegraphics[height=2cm,angle=30]{clock}`

For compatibility with the `graphics` package, there is also a starred version, `\includegraphics*`, that clips the imported figure; this is equivalent to including the key `clip`.

With the `graphicx` package, the \rotatebox command is similarly redefined to accept the optional key `origin`.

Exercise 8.2: *Include the graphics file* demo.eps *from Exercise 8.1 scaled by a factor of 2 and rotated by* 45° *using the* \includegraphics *command with the* graphicx *package. Experiment with various keys, in particular with* height *and* width *together.*

8.1.4   Additional graphics packages

Package: epsfig

Sebastian Rahtz has provided a package `epsfig` that not only updates the earlier (LaTeX 2.09) version, but also re-implements Rokicki's `epsf` package by means of the `graphics` commands. This is helpful for users who are accustomed to those syntaxes. For `epsf`, this is

> \epsfysize=*y_size*   or   \epsffxsize=*x_size*
> \epsf[*llx lly urx ury*]{*file_name*}

The `epsfig` package also defines an importing command that makes use of the regular keys and values to enter its parameters:

> \epsfig{file=*file_name*,*key=value*,...}

For compatibility with some older versions, there is a \psfig command that is synonymous with the above.

The `epsfig` package is included in the bundle of `graphics` packages and drivers.

Package:
lscape
Another extra package in the graphics bundle is lscape, by David Carlisle. This defines a landscape environment that prints its contents rotated 90° on a page for itself. Head- and footlines remain as normal. This is intended primarily for inserting figures that are in landscape mode, that is, wider than they are high.

Package:
rotating
The rotating package by Sebastian Rahtz and Leonor Barroca tries to make the interface for rotation somewhat simpler. It defines

> \begin{sideways} *text* \end{sideways}
> \begin{turn}{*angle*} *text* \end{turn}
> \begin{rotate}{*angle*} *text* \end{rotate}
> \turnbox{*angle*}{*text*}

where sideways rotates *text* by 90° and turn by an arbitrary angle. The environment rotate and command turnbox are equivalent; they rotate, but in a box of zero size so that the contents overlap the surroundings.

This package is not part of the graphics bundle and must be obtained separately.

8.1.5 Superimposing images

!

Sometimes one may want to superimpose an image file over part of another, say, to add an inset in a corner. Or one may want to add text elements, or even lines and arrows pointing to some feature in the image. One might even want to make some area of the image into a link to another document. The picture environment described in Section 16.1 can be used to allow exact placement of such objects.

For example, in Figure 8.1 on the next page, we embellish the TeX Live welcome image from Figure B.1 on page 377 by adding a blow-up of a small section, pointing a labeled arrow to it, and making the area around the text 'TeX Live!' into a link. We do this with the following input:

```
\setlength{\unitlength}{0.01\linewidth}
\setlength{\fboxsep}{0pt}
\setlength{\fboxrule}{1.5pt}
\begin{picture}(80,80)
 \thicklines
 \put(0,0){\includegraphics[width=80\unitlength]{texlive}}
 \put(57,26){\framebox(14.2,14.6){}}
 \drawline(57,26)(-10,36.7)
 \drawline(71.2,26)(20.5,36.7)
 \drawline(71.2,40.6)(20.5,67.2)
 \drawline(57,40.6)(-10,67.2)
 \put(-10,37){\fbox{\includegraphics[width=30\unitlength,
               viewport=390 180 490 280,clip]{texlive}}}
 \put(-9,19){\vector(1,4){4}}
 \put(-9,18){\makebox(0,0)[t]{\large Blow-Up}}
 \put(43,2){\hyperlink{info}{\makebox(30,7){}}}
\end{picture}
```

Here the unit length for the picture placement has been set to 1/100 of the current line width \linewidth, so we can conveniently use 100 units for the full width. The picture

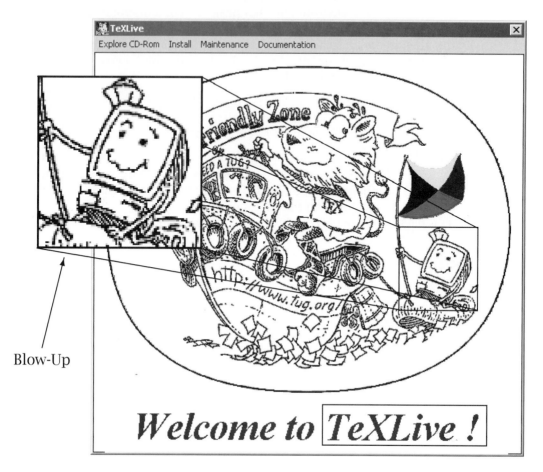

Blow-Up

Figure 8.1: An embellished image

environment reserves a space of 80×80 units; the image file `texlive` is placed at the lower-left corner (location 0,0) and set to a width of 80 units. We then draw a framed box around a portion of this image and add that portion as a second image (selected with `viewport` and clipped) as a blow-up. The `\drawline` commands (from the `epic` package) join the corners of the original and blown-up areas. The order here is important since later images overwrite the earlier ones. Then we add an arrow (`\vector`) and the text 'Blow-up' (with `\makebox`). Finally, the `\hyperlink` command from the `hyperref` package turns the 30×7 unit area around the text '$T_{E}X$ Live!' into a active link to the target named `info`.

One can also place objects outside of the reserved `picture` area, so arrows could be added pointing from the main text to some part of an image. This is more appropriate for the production of slides (Chapter 17), when one wants rigid control over the relative locations of graphics and text.

8.1.6   How importation can go wrong

!

In order to understand better what can go wrong when a graphics file is imported, and to know what to do about it, it is important to realize how the interplay between LaTeX and the driver program functions.

LaTeX has no idea what is in the graphics file; for it, the figure is simply a box of a given height, width, and depth, as indeed are all the characters that LaTeX processes. The information on the graphic's natural size is somehow obtained, either by information in the graphics file itself or through the optional entries in the \includegraphics command or equivalent. After scaling and rotating, LaTeX knows the final size that it must reserve in the output text for the figure.

What is then written to the .dvi file is the name of the graphics file and information on how it should be transformed. Just how this information is coded depends on the graphics driver selected. When the printer driver program processes the .dvi file, it interprets these special instructions, reads in the specified graphics file, performs the transformations, and places the result where LaTeX has said it should go. The end result is that the area inside the designated bounding box coincides with the box that LaTeX has reserved for it. If the bounding box information is incorrect, the figure is obviously going to be misplaced.

PostScript output

Graphics inclusion was originally developed for PostScript graphics adhering to the *encapsulated* specification that was designed to allow PostScript code to be included within another PostScript file. Tomas Rokicki and his dvips driver broke the ground in this field and thus established the standards. It is for this reason that we place so much emphasis on PostScript graphics here. Encapsulated PostScript files may not contain any commands that reset the whole graphics page, and furthermore, they must contain a comment line of the form

%%BoundingBox: *llx lly urx ury*

giving the coordinates of the lower-left and upper-right corners of the bounding box. The units are never specified, always being big points.

PDF output

Today PDF is an important alternative to PostScript, and the pdfTeX program (Section 13.2.3) is the most convenient way to produce it with LaTeX. However, pdfTeX is not only a replacement for the classical TeX program, producing identical output, it also combines the functionality of a DVI-to-PDF driver. Thus, no intermediate .dvi file is generated at all, with the .pdf file being generated directly from the LaTeX source file in one operation. This has consequences for graphics inclusion with pdfTeX. First of all, the number of allowed graphics formats is increased: Images may be PNG (.png files), JPEG (.jpg or .jpeg files), or even a single image in a one-page PDF file. Ironically, PostScript images are absolutely out! Second, the concept of bounding box does not really apply to these formats, since they have a natural size anyway. The viewport option should therefore be used to make a cutout from the original rather than bb.

An alternative method of obtaining PDF output is to employ the true DVI-to-PDF driver, dvipdfm, written by Mark A. Wicks. In this case, a .dvi file is produced as usual (with the graphics option dvipdfm), and then the PDF output is generated with this conversion program. The same set of graphics formats is allowed as for pdfTeX, for much the same reasons.

The third method would be to generate DVI, then PostScript, and then convert it to PDF. As far as the graphics are concerned, this is the same as PostScript.

Having pointed out how the importation takes place, we can now discuss what can go wrong along this chain of processes.

Problems with importation: pdfTeX

The single most common error when importing a graphics file with pdfTeX is that it does not exist in one of the permitted formats. Many users who are used to using classical TeX with PostScript simply switch to pdfTeX and are astonished to get the error message:

```
! LaTeX Error: Unknown graphics extension: .eps.
```

As explained above, pdfTeX cannot handle PostScript files, so the graphics must be converted to, or regenerated in, another format.

The above error message will appear only if one has specified the full name of the graphics file including the extension .eps. If the extension is absent, which we recommend, the error message will report that the file cannot be found. This means that it cannot be found with any of the allowed extensions. It might very well be that it exists with the extension .eps, but since that is not allowed for pdfTeX, it will not be sought.

To maintain flexibility, one can have the same graphics file available both as an .eps and as a .pdf file. Leaving the extension off in the \includegraphics command means one does not need to make any changes to the file name when switching between regular TeX and pdfTeX.

Problems with importation: PostScript

The most common problems encountered when importing encapsulated PostScript files are listed here.

No bounding box. If the bounding box information is totally missing from the graphics file, LaTeX issues the error message

```
! LaTeX Error: Cannot determine size of graphic
                         in ... (no BoundingBox).
```

The solution is to determine the bounding box coordinates somehow (see next point) and to include them, either in the \includegraphics command or by editing the graphics file itself. However, if there really is no bounding box information in the file, it is unlikely to conform to the encapsulated standard and will cause other problems.

The placement is incorrect. Both LaTeX and the driver process without error messages, but the figure is either displaced from the expected position or is far too small.

Most likely the bounding box information is incorrect. Many applications that produce PostScript files are too lazy to calculate the true bounding box, or they think they are generating a whole page with a figure somewhere in the middle. In either case, the bounding box corresponds to the full page even though the printed figure occupies only a portion of it.

Find the true bounding box by one of the following methods:

1. Print the figure, mark the lower-left and upper-right corners of the box containing the figure, and measure their distances from the left and bottom edges. Enter these distances in the `\includegraphics` command, or edit the PostScript file. In the latter case, convert to big points.

   Difficulties with this are that some encapsulated PostScript files cannot be printed on their own, and that the left and bottom edges of the paper need not be the exact lines from which the printer really measures.

2. Include the figure in a short LaTeX file such as

   ```
   \setlength{\fboxsep}{-\fboxrule}
   \fbox{\includegraphics{test.eps}}
   ```

   and print the output. The apparent bounding box appears as a framed box. Measure the true bounding box relative to the left and bottom edges of the apparent one, and enter the values in the `\includegraphics` command with the `viewport=` key. If necessary, scale down the figure to fit on the page, but then remember to increase the measurements by the same scale factor.

3. Use the GhostView program to fix the bounding box, either automatically or manually. This is the most convenient method if you have this utility for viewing and manipulating PostScript files.

Immovable graphic. It does not shift, nor scale nor rotate, no matter what is specified. In this case, it violates the encapsulated PostScript rules and contains some global plotting commands. Graphics produced by word-processing programs are notorious for this. Often the offending command is `setpagedevice`.

There is little that can be done to correct this, other than trying to regenerate the graphics file with an option for encapsulated PostScript. Judicious editing can remove the troublesome lines, but this could result in the file becoming totally unreadable.

8.1.7   Configuring graphics importation

!

Although the graphics syntax has been standardized and most of the driver-specific coding hidden in the `.def` files, a number of items still must be set up for any particular installation and operating system. These are most conveniently placed in the local configuration file graphics.cfg, which is read in if it is present.

Many installations come with a ready-made configuration file, so there may not be any need to make up your own. On the other hand, you may want to edit or replace it for your own purposes.

Default driver

The choice of driver option must always be given, but a local default can be specified in the configuration file. For example, if dvips is the standard graphics driver, you may add

```
\ExecuteOptions{dvips}
```

to graphics.cfg, and you do not need to give the option dvips when loading graphics or graphicx. You may still specify any other graphics driver option if you wish.

Many supplied configuration files go further and determine whether pdfTeX is activated or not; if so, the default graphics option is set to pdftex, otherwise to dvips.

The rest of the configuring commands in this section can be issued either in the graphics.cfg file or in the document.

Search path for graphics files

One can specify the directories where LaTeX is to look for graphics files with

```
\graphicspath{dir_list}
```

where *dir_list* is a list of directory names, each enclosed in brackets { }, with no other separator. The syntax of the local operating system must be used. Without this command, LaTeX searches for graphics files in the same directories as for all other TeX files. For example,

```
\graphicspath{{figs/}{eps/}}      for Unix, DOS, Windows
\graphicspath{{:figs:}{:eps:}}    for Macintosh
\graphicspath{{[.figs]}{[.eps]}}  for VMS
```

Note: The Unix syntax works even with DOS and Windows, since the normal backslash in the directory names must be replaced by a slash / to avoid looking like a command name.

Default extensions

A list of default extensions for the graphics files can be defined with

```
\DeclareGraphicsExtensions{ext_list}
```

This means that only the root name of the file must be given and LaTeX will attempt to find it by attaching all the possible extensions. For PostScript drivers, the *ext_list* is usually set to .eps, .ps. At our installation, we also include the nonstandard extension .psc. Note that the above command does not add to the list of extensions but rewrites it anew; if you wish to add to the list, you must include all the allowed extensions in the one declaration.

Graphics types

Defining the extensions is only part of the task: One must also associate each extension with a graphics type so that LaTeX knows how to process it. PostScript recognizes only one type, eps, encapsulated PostScript, but other types do exist such as bmp and pcx for other drivers. For the nonstandard .psc extension above, we must also give

> `\DeclareGraphicsRule{.psc}{eps}{}{}`

to inform LaTeX that this extension belongs to type eps. The other two (empty) arguments specify that the bounding box information is to be read from the file itself and that no other program needs to be applied to the file.

Compressing graphics files

Since PostScript files are often extremely large, it makes sense to try to compress them with either the zip or gzip programs. In such a case, the .eps file is replaced by a file with extension .zip, .eps.gz, or .eps-gz. Two problems now arise: First, LaTeX cannot read such files to obtain the bounding box information, and second, the driver needs to unpack such a file to include it in the final output. This can be accomplished with, for example,

> `\DeclareGraphicsRule{.eps.gz}{eps}{.eps.bb}{'gunzip -c #1}`

This establishes that the graphics type is eps, with the bounding box information in the file of the same name and extension .eps.bb, and that the operating system command gunzip -c must be applied to the file (represented as #1). The single quote ' is required to indicate a system command. The %%BoundingBox line of the original file must be copied and stored in the .eps.bb file.

Such decompression rules are system dependent and thus need to be configured for the local installation. For example, under the VMS operating system, the gzip program produces files with extension .eps-gz, and decompression is performed with gzip -d rather than with gunzip. The corresponding rule becomes

> `\DeclareGraphicsRule{.eps-gz}{eps}{.bb}{'gzip -d -c #1}`

8.2   Adding color

The `color` package accepts the same driver options listed on page 154 for the `graphics` package. In addition, it also recognizes the options:

monochrome
> Converts all color commands to black and white, for previewers that cannot handle color;

dvipsnames
> makes the named color model of dvips (Section 8.2.1) available to other drivers;

nodvipsnames
> disables the named model for dvips, to save memory;

usenames

> loads all the named colors as defined ones; again, see Section 8.2.1 for
> details.

!

A local configuration file color.cfg can be set up in the same way as for the graphics package. The default driver option is specified in exactly the same way as in Section 8.1.7.

Colors are specified either by a defined name or by the form

[*model*] {*specs*}

where *model* is one of rgb (red, green, blue), cmyk (cyan, magenta, yellow, black), gray, or named. The *specs* is a list of numbers from 0 to 1 giving the strengths of the components in the model. Thus [rgb]{1,0,0} defines red, [cmyk]{0,0,1,0} yellow. The gray model takes only one number. The named model accesses colors by internal names that were originally built into the dvips driver, but which may now be used by some other drivers too. This model is described in Section 8.2.1.

A color can be defined with

\definecolor{*name*}{*model*}{*specs*}

and then the *name* may be used in all of the following color commands. Certain colors are automatically predefined for all drivers: red, green, blue, yellow, cyan, magenta, black, white.

In the following color commands, *col_spec* is either the name of a defined color, like {blue}, or [*model*]{*spec*}, like [rgb]{0,0,1}.

\pagecolor *col_spec* sets the background color for the current and following pages;

\color *col_spec* is a declaration to switch to setting text in the given color;

\textcolor *col_spec*{*text*} sets the text of its argument in the given color;

\colorbox *col_spec*{*text*} sets its argument in a box with the given color as background;

\fcolorbox *col_spec1* *col_spec2*{*text*} like \colorbox, with a frame of *col_spec1* around a box of background color *col_spec2*; the two specifications must either both be defined ones, or both use the same model, which is given only once; for example, \fcolorbox{red}{green}{Text} sets 'Text' in the current text color on a green background with a red frame;

\normalcolor switches to the color that was active at the end of the preamble. Thus placing a \color command in the preamble can change the standard color for the whole document. This is the equivalent to \normalfont for font selection.

Normally one would try to define all the colors needed as names for the *col_spec* entries. This simplifies changing the color definition everywhere should fine-tuning be required after the initial printed results are seen. The same color definition can produce quite different effects on different printers. Even the display on the monitor is no reliable guide as to how the output will appear on paper.

8.2.1 The named color model

One very useful color model is called named and is based on the 68 predefined internal colors of the dvips PostScript driver. Sample names are BurntOrange and DarkOrchid. This model can be activated for other drivers with the option dvipsnames, in which case one can define colors as, for example

```
\definecolor{titlecol}{named}{DarkOrchid}
```

The color titlecol can then be used as *col_spec* in the various color commands.

The named colors can be defined with their own names if one invokes the option usenames, which effectively declares

```
\definecolor{BurntOrange}{named}{BurntOrange}
```

and so on, for all 68 colors.

It is possible to generate a palette of the named colors by processing the following short LaTeX file and sending the output to the desired printer.

```
\documentclass[12pt,a4paper]{article}
\usepackage[dvipsnames]{color}
\usepackage{multicol}
\pagestyle{empty}
\setlength{\oddsidemargin}{0pt}
\setlength{\textwidth}{16cm}
\setlength{\textheight}{22cm}
\setlength{\parindent}{0pt}
\setlength{\parskip}{0pt}

\begin{document}
\renewcommand*{\DefineNamedColor}[4]{%
   \textcolor[named]{#2}{\rule{7mm}{7mm}}\quad
   \texttt{#2}\strut\\}

\begin{center}\Large Named colors in \texttt{dvipsnam.def}
\end{center}
\begin{multicols}{3}
\input{dvipsnam.def}
\end{multicols}
\end{document}
```

Remember, each printer can reproduce the colors differently, so it is important to test this table with every color printer that might be used.

Exercise 8.3: *Copy the above lines to a file named palette.tex or copy it from the enclosed CD from books→Guide4. Process it and view the output on a color monitor or send it to a color printer.*

9 Floating tables and figures

Whether a figure is imported with \includegraphics (Chapter 8) or produced with the picture environment of Chapter 16, it is inserted in the text where the drawing or importing commands are issued, coming between the previous and following texts. This can present the same difficulties as for tables, described in Section 6.2.5: if the figure is so high that it no longer fits on the current page, that page is prematurely terminated and the figure is placed at the top of the next page, with too much empty space left on the original page.

In Section 6.2.5 we explore how this problem is solved for tables. Now we give a complete description of the *float* procedures that apply to both figures and tables.

9.1 Float placement

LATEX does make it possible to *float* figures and tables, together with their headlines and captions, to an appropriate location without interrupting the text. This is invoked with the environments

```
\begin{figure}[where]     figure   \end{figure}
\begin{figure*}[where]    figure   \end{figure*}
\begin{table}[where]      table    \end{table}
\begin{table*}[where]     table    \end{table*}
```

The *-forms apply only to the two-column page format, and insert the figure or table across both columns instead of the normal single column. They function exactly like the standard forms when the page format is single column.

In the above syntax, *figure* and *table* are the texts for the contents of the float, either a picture or tabular environment or an \includegraphics command, together with a possible \caption command, as described later in Section 9.4.

The argument *where* specifies the allowed locations for the figure or table. There are several possibilities, so *where* consists of from zero to four letters with the following meanings:

h *here*: The float may appear at that point in the text where the environment is typed in; this is not permitted for the *-form. See also the `here` package and the H parameter, page 179.

t *top*: The float may appear at the top of the current page, provided there is enough room for both it and the previous text; if this is not the case, it is added at the top of the next page. The subsequent text continues on the current page until the next normal page break (for two-column format, read *column* in place of *page*).

b *bottom*: The float may be placed at the bottom of the page; the subsequent text continues until the room left on the current page is just enough for the float. If there is already insufficient room, the float will be put at the bottom of the next page; this is not permitted for the *-form.

p *page*: The float may be put on a special page (or column) containing only figures and/or tables.

! Used together with any combination of the other letters, this suspends all the spacing and number restrictions described in Section 9.3.

The argument values may be combined to allow several possibilities. If none is given, LaTeX assumes the standard combination `tbp`.

There is also an H placement parameter for 'absolutely here', which is made available by some packages. See Section 9.7.2 on page 179.

The placement arguments permit certain possibilities for locating the float, but the actual insertion takes place *at the earliest possible point* in accordance with the following rules:

- No float appears on a page prior to the one on which it is defined.

- Figures and tables are output in the order in which they were defined in the text, so that no float appears before a previously defined float of the same type; figures and tables may, however, be mixed in their output sequence. In two-column format, the double column *-floats may also appear out of sequence.

- Floats will be located only at one of the allowed positions given by the placement argument *where*; without an argument, the standard combination `tbp` is used.

- Unless the ! is included in *where*, the positioning obeys the limitations of the style parameters described in Section 9.3.

- For the combination ht, the argument h takes priority. The float is inserted at the point of its definition even if there is enough room for it at the top of the page.

When any one of \clearpage, \cleardoublepage, or \end{document} is given, all floats that have not yet been output will be printed on a separate page or column regardless of their placement arguments.

Package: **after-** **page**

Sometimes LaTeX gets stuck on a float that holds up the entire queue until the end of the document. One way to clear the queue is to issue \clearpage right after the troublesome float. However, that would insert a new page at that point, something that may not be desired. The package afterpage in the tools collection (Section B.5.4) provides the command \afterpage that executes its argument at the end of the current page. Thus \afterpage{\clearpage} solves this problem by delaying the \clearpage command until the actual page break.

9.2 Postponing floats

Occasionally one wants to prevent floats from appearing on a certain page, for example, at the top of a title page. (LaTeX automatically corrects that case.) However, there are other situations in which a float should be suppressed temporarily. One might want it at the top of a page, but not before the start of the section that refers to it. The command

> \suppressfloats[*loc*]

sees to it that *for the current page only* no further floats of the specified placement *loc* should appear. If the optional *loc* is omitted, all floats are suppressed; otherwise *loc* may be either t or b, but not both.

Note that \suppressfloats does not suppress all floats for the current page, but only *further* ones that come between the issuing of this command and the end of the page. Thus it is still possible for floats from a previous section to appear on the page.

Package: **flafter**

Alternatively, the package flafter (Section B.5.3) may be loaded to ensure that *all* floats appear only after their position in the text.

The command \suppressfloats and the location parameter ! are attempts to give the author more control over the sometimes capricious actions of float placement.

9.3 Style parameters for floats

⚠

A number of style parameters influence the placement of floats, which may be altered by the user as desired.

topnumber
> The maximum number of floats that may appear at the top of a page.

bottomnumber
> The maximum number of floats that may appear at the bottom of a page.

totalnumber
> The maximum number of floats that may appear on any page regardless of position.

dbltopnumber

> The same as topnumber but for floats that extend over both columns in two-column page format.

The above parameters are all *counters* and may be reset to new values with the command \setcounter{*ctr*}{*num*}, where *ctr* is the name of the counter and *num* the new value that it is to take on.

\topfraction

> A decimal number that specifies what fraction of the page may be used for floats at the top.

\bottomfraction

> A decimal number that specifies what fraction of the page may be used for floats at the bottom.

\textfraction

> The fraction of a page that must be filled with text. This is a minimum, so that the fraction available for floats, whether top or bottom, can never be more than 1−\textfraction.

\floatpagefraction

> The smallest fraction of a float page that is to be filled with floats before a new page is called.

\dbltopfraction

> The same as \topfraction but for double-column floats in two-column page format.

\dblfloatpagefraction

> The same as \floatpagefraction but for double-column floats in two-column page format.

These style parameters are altered with \renewcommand{*cmd*}{*frac*} where *cmd* stands for the parameter name and *frac* for the new decimal value, which in every case must be less than 1.

\floatsep

> The vertical spacing between floats appearing either at the top or at the bottom of a page.

\textfloatsep

> The vertical spacing between floats and text, for both top and bottom floats.

\intextsep

> The vertical spacing above and below a float that appears in the middle of a text page with the h placement argument.

\dblfloatsep

> The same as \floatsep but for double-column floats in two-column page format.

\dbltextfloatsep

> The same as \textfloatsep but for double-column floats in two-column page format.

This group of style declarations are rubber lengths that may be changed with the \setlength command (Section 2.4.2).

\topfigrule

> A command that is executed after a float at the top of a page. It may be used to add a rule to separate the float from the main text. Whatever it adds must have zero height.

`\botfigrule`

> Similar to `\topfigrule`, but is executed before a float that appears at the bottom of a page.

`\dblfigrule`

> Similar to `\topfigrule`, but for double-column floats.

These three commands normally do nothing, but they may be redefined if necessary. For example, to add a rule of thickness 0.4 pt below a top float,

```
\renewcommand{\topfigrule}{\vspace*{-3pt}
    \rule{\columnwidth}{0.4pt}\vspace{2.6pt} }
```

Because of the negative argument in `\vspace*`, the total vertical spacing is zero, as required.

All the one-column style parameters also function within the two-column page format, but they apply only to floats that fill up one column.

If the style parameters are set to new values within the preamble, they apply from the first page onwards. However, if they are changed within a document, they do not take effect until the next page.

9.4 Float captions

A figure caption or table title is produced with the command

> `\caption[`*short_title*`]{`*caption_text*`}`

inside the `figure` or `table` environment. The *caption_text* is the text that is printed with the float and may be fairly long. The *short_title* is optional and is the text that appears in the list of figures or tables (Section 3.4.4). If it is missing, it is set equal to *caption_text*. The *short_title* should be given if the *caption_text* is longer than about 300 characters or if it is more than one line long.

In the `table` environment, the `\caption` command generates a title of the form 'Table *n*: *caption_text*', and in the `figure` environment 'Figure *n*: *caption_text*', where *n* is a sequential number that is automatically incremented. In document class `article`, the figures and tables are numbered from 1 through to the end of the document. For the `report` and `book` classes, they are numbered within each chapter in the form *c.n*, where *c* is the current chapter number and *n* is the sequential number reset to 1 at the start of each chapter. Figures and tables are numbered independently of one another.

The `\caption` command may be omitted if numbering is unwanted, since any text included in the *float* environment will accompany the contents. The advantages of `\caption` over simple text are the automatic numbering and entries in the lists of figures and tables. However, a manual entry in these lists may be made as described in Section 3.4.4 using

> `\addcontentsline`   and   `\addtocontents`

A *title*, or *headline*, is produced with `\caption` when the command comes at the beginning of the material in the *float* environment: The number and text are printed above the table or figure. A *caption* is added below the object if the command comes

Table 9.1: Computer Center Budget for 2004

Nr.	Item	51505	52201	53998	Total
1.1	Maintenance	130 000		15 000	145 000
1.2	Network costs	5 000		23 000	28 000
1.3	Repairs	25 000	6 000		31 000
1.4	Expendables		68 000		68 000
1.	Total	160 000	74 000	38 000	272 000

after all the other float commands. In other words, the \caption is just another item within the float, and whether its text appears at the top (as *title*) or below (as *caption*) depends on how the user places it.

The *caption_text* will be centered if it is shorter than one line, otherwise it is set as a normal paragraph. The total width may be adjusted to that of the table or figure by placing the command inside a parbox or minipage. For example,

\parbox{*width*}{\caption{*caption_text*}}

The following demonstrations contain further examples of how text, table, and picture commands may be combined in floats.

9.5   Float examples

The first two tables are produced with the following texts:

```
\begin{table} \caption{Computer Center Budget for 2004}
  \begin{tabular}{|l|l||r|r|r|r|} ... ...   \end{tabular}
\end{table}
```

(This text was typed in before the last paragraph of the previous section. The second table is entered here in the current text.)

```
\begin{table}
  \caption{\textbf{Estimates for 2004} \emph{A continuation...}}
  \begin{tabular}{|l|l||r|r|r|r|} ... ... ...  \end{tabular}
\end{table}
```

Because the placement argument is missing from the table environments, the standard values tbp are used. The first was placed at the top of this page because it was typed in early enough (during the last section) for there still to be room for it there. Then the command \suppressfloats (Section 9.2) was issued to prevent any more floats appearing on the same page. The second table is therefore forced to float to the top of the next page.

Narrow figures or tables may be set beside each other, as shown in the following example (which appears at the bottom of the next page). (The picture environment is explained in Chapter 16.)

Table 9.2: Estimates for 2004. *A continuation of the previous budget is no longer practical since, with the installation of the new computing system in 2003, the operating conditions have been completely overhauled.*

Nr.	Item	51505	52201	53998	Total
1.1	Maintenance	240 000			240 000
1.2	Line costs	12 000	8 000	36 000	56 000
1.3	Training			50 000	50 000
1.4	Expansion	80 000	3 000		83 000
1.5	Expendables		42 000		42 000
1.	Total	332 000	53 000	86 000	471 000

```
\begin{figure}[b]
\setlength{\unitlength}{1cm}
\begin{minipage}[t]{5.0cm}
\begin{picture}(5.0,2.5) ... ... \end{picture}\par
\caption{Left}
\end{minipage}
\hfill
\begin{minipage}[t]{6.0cm}
\begin{picture}(6.0,3.0) ... ... \end{picture}\par
\caption{Right}
\end{minipage}
\end{figure}
```

The two figures along with their captions are each set in a `minipage` environment of widths 5 and 6 cm. The minipages are separated from one another by an `\hfill` space. The positioning argument t has the effect that the minipages are aligned along their first lines (Section 5.1.3). The entire structure within the `figure` environment floats as a single entity.

The question might now arise as to why, since the two figures have unequal heights and are supposedly aligned vertically along their top lines, their bottom edges are at the same level. The explanation is that a `picture` environment establishes an LR box (Section 5.1.1) to contain all the picture commands, and that is viewed by LaTeX

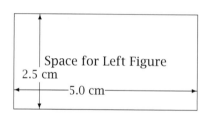

Figure 9.1: Left

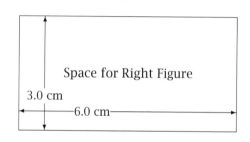

Figure 9.2: Right

as a single line of output text with the baseline at the bottom edge of the picture. In both minipages, the `picture` environment is the first entry and is therefore the first logical line of text. These baselines are taken for the vertical alignment of the minipages.

If the two pictures were to be aligned along their top edges, it would be necessary to include a dummy first line (Section 5.1.4) in each minipage before the `picture` environments. This could be something like `\mbox{}`, for example.

The application of box commands within a float permits completely free positioning. If the caption text is to appear, say, beside the table or figure, instead of above or below it, the objects may be put into minipages or parboxes with suitable alignment arguments. Here is an example:

```
\begin{table}[b]
  \centerline{\bfseries Results and Seat Distribution of the...}
  \mbox{\small
  \begin{minipage}[b]{7.7cm}
    \begin{minipage}[t]{4.4cm}
      \mbox{}\\ \setlength{\unitlength}{0.75cm}
      \begin{picture}(5.75,5.0) ... ... ... \end{picture}
    \end{minipage} \hfill
    \parbox[t]{3.2cm}{\makebox[0cm]{}\\\{\bfseries Seat ...} ...}
  \end{minipage}
  \hspace{-3cm}
  \begin{minipage}[b]{7cm}
    \parbox[b]{2.5cm}{{\bfseries Results:}\\ General Election..}
    \hfill
    \begin{tabular}[b]{|l||r|r|} ... ... \end{tabular}
  \end{minipage} }
\end{table}
```

Here the vertical boxes are nested inside one another. The left side, consisting of graphics and a title at the upper right, is contained in a minipage of width 7.7 cm, in which the picture is in another minipage of width 4.4 cm while the text is in a parbox of width 3.2 cm. Both are aligned with the top lines. A dummy line containing `\mbox{}` (Section 5.1.4) is added before the first `picture` to provide a top line with which the second parbox can be aligned.

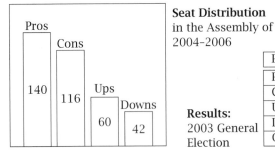

Results and Seat Distribution of the 2003 General Election

Seat Distribution
in the Assembly of
2004–2006

Party	Votes	%
Pros	15 031 287	37.7
Cons	12 637 418	31.7
Ups	6 499 210	16.3
Downs	4 486 514	11.3
Others	1 201 078	3.0

The right-hand side consists of a minipage of width 7 cm, shifted to the left by 3 cm, aligned with the left-hand minipage along the bottom lines. It contains a parbox of width 2.5 cm for the text as well as a table, which is automatically a vertical box. Both of these are aligned with the bottom lines.

9.6 References to figures and tables in text

The automatic numbering of tables and figures means that the author does not know the numbers at the time of writing. Since he or she would like to be able to refer to these objects by number, as 'see Figure 3' or 'Table 5 illustrates', another means of referencing must be found. It is not sufficient to keep track of the number of \caption calls that have been made, since the document may not be written in the order in which it finally appears, and new figures or tables may be inserted during revision, or some removed.

These problems are solved with the LATEX cross-reference system, described in more detail in Section 11.2.1. The basic commands are

> \label{*name*}   \ref{*name*}

which assign a keyword *name* to the figure or table number that may be used as reference in the text. The keyword *name* may be any combination of letters, numbers, or symbols. The assignment is made with the \label command given anywhere within the caption text of the \caption command; in the main text, the command \ref inserts the number that is associated with its keyword.

This is best shown with an example. The budget table on page 174 was actually written as

> \caption{\label{budget04} Computer Center ... }

so that Table \ref{budget04} produces 'Table 9.1' when used in the main text.

There is a second referencing command \pageref to generate the page number where the referenced object is to be found. For example, a few lines up, the input text on page \pageref{budget04} was used to create the text '...on page 174'.

9.7 Some float packages

9.7.1 Defining new floats and styles

Package: float

For authors who are not satisfied with the standard float style or who need additional floating environments, we recommend the float package by Anselm Lingnau. With this package, one defines a new float type with

> \newfloat{*name*}{*loc*}{*ext*}[*within*]

where *name* is the name of the new float environment, *loc* is the default placement letters (selection of tbhpH), *ext* is the extension of the file containing the list of this float type, and the optional *within* is the name of a counter (e.g., chapter) within which the numbering is reset.

For example, to define a plate environment that behaves just like figure but which is numbered separately as *Plate xxx*, with the numbers reset within each chapter, give

```
\newfloat{plate}{p}{lop}[chapter]
\floatname{plate}{Plate}
```

The first line defines the new environment, with default placement on a float page. The second states that the captions associated with this float are to start with the word 'Plate'; without this, they would be labeled as 'plate', the same as the environment name itself.

The information for the list of plates is stored in a file with extension .lop, in the same way that the list of figures is in a file with extension .lof (Section 3.4.4). This list is printed by reading in this file with the command

```
\listof{plate}{List of Plates}
```

where 'List of Plates' is the list title.

The default placement parameters for any float environment, including the standard figure and table ones, can be redefined with

```
\floatplacement{name}{loc}
```

The float package also defines four *float styles*:

plain   much like standard LATEX except the caption is always *below* the float contents;

plaintop
        like plain but with the caption always *above* the contents;

boxed   in which the contents are in a framed box with the caption below it;

ruled   with the caption above, and with rules above, below, and between caption and float contents.

One selects a float style by issuing \floatstyle{*style*}, where *style* is one of the above possibilities. The style then applies to all new float environments defined with \newfloat until a new style is issued.

Note: The style selection affects the subsequent float *definitions*, not the float environments that are then used. To change the float style for the standard figure and table floats, issue

```
\floatstyle{ruled}
\restylefloat{figure}
\restylefloat{table}
```

9.7.2   Placing a float right here

The float placement parameter h, described on page 169, only permits a float to be placed at the current location; it does not force it to appear there. The float package provides an additional placement parameter H to insert the float immediately where it appears in the source text. If there is not enough room on the current page, a \pagebreak command is first issued. This will likely lead to an ugly page break.

Package: There is a package by David Carlisle named here that also provides the H par-
here ameter, but it is considered to be obsolete.

9.7.3   Flowing text around a float

Package: The package floatflt by Mats Dahlgren (based on the earlier and now obsolete
floatflt floatfig by Thomas Kneser) permits one to mix text and floats side by side, with the text flowing around the float at the end, as in the next paragraph.

A figure is placed within the text as shown in the box at the right. Here *pos* determines on which side the figure is to appear; it may be r (right), l (left), p (right for odd, left for even pages), or v (like p unless a package option is

```
\begin{floatingfigure}[pos]{wth}
Figure commands with or without a
\caption command
\end{floatingfigure}
```

given, in which case it is used). The mandatory argument *wth* is the width of the figure itself; in fact, some additional space will be included for a border between text and figure. It is advisable to include a \centering command at the start of the figure material.

The material in the floatingfigure environment need not actually be a figure. In the above example, some boxed text in a minipage was used for demonstration purposes. However, if the \caption command is included in the environment, then a figure number will be printed, in sequence with those of the regular figure environment.

Rather than giving the *pos* parameter each time, one can specify a default value as an option when loading the package with \usepackage: rflt (right), lflt (left), or vflt (variable, i.e., p). If no option is given, the default is vflt.

```
\begin{floatingtable}[pos]{
\begin{tabular}{table specs}
table entries
\end{tabular}}
Optional \caption command
\end{floatingtable}
```

To include a table with text, the usage is slightly different, as shown at the left. That is, the entire table appears in place of the *wth* for a figure, and only the caption is placed in the environment itself.

Both these environments are to be placed at the start of the paragraph that is to flow around the figure or table. The flowing can-not start in the middle of a paragraph.

There is some very tricky coding to get the flowing text to work properly, and needless to say, there are many things that can go wrong. Please read the package's accompanying manual for more details.

User Customizations

10

LaTeX allows the user to define his or her own commands and environments. However, since these make extensive use of the LaTeX counters and lengths, we will first present a more detailed discussion of these objects and how they may be manipulated.

10.1 Counters

10.1.1 LaTeX counters

LaTeX manages a number of counters by giving them initial values at the start and by changing these values when certain commands are called. Most of these counters have the same name as the commands that alter them:

part	chapter	paragraph	figure	enumi
	section	subparagraph	table	enumii
	subsection	page	footnote	enumiii
	subsubsection	equation	mpfootnote	enumiv

The meanings of most of these counters are obvious from their names and need no further explanation. The counters `enumi...` `enumiv` refer to the four levels of the `enumerate` environment (Sections 4.3.4 and 4.3.5), while the counter `mpfootnote` controls the footnote numbering within the `minipage` environment (Section 5.2.4).

The value of a counter is an integer number, usually non-negative. A command may output several numbers at once: The current `\subsection` command outputs 10.1.1, which addresses three counters in all. For example, the `\subsection` command increments the value of the `subsection` counter by one and prints the values of the `chapter`, `section`, and `subsection` counters, separated by periods. At the same time, this command sets the `subsubsection` counter to zero.

10.1.2 User-defined counters

The user may create new counters with the command

> \newcounter{*counter_name*}[*in_counter*]

where *counter_name* is the name of the newly established counter. This may be any combination of letters that is not already the name of an existing counter. Thus none of the names of the LaTeX counters listed above may be used as *counter_name* nor any name of a previously defined user counter.

The optional argument *in_counter* is the name of another counter that already exists (LaTeX or user defined) and has the effect that the newly defined counter is reset to zero whenever *in_counter* is incremented by one of the commands \stepcounter or \refstepcounter (see below). For example, the subsection counter is reset to zero whenever the section counter is incremented.

The \newcounter command may not appear in any file that is read in with the \include command (Section 11.1.2). It is therefore best to put all \newcounter commands into the preamble.

10.1.3 Changing counter values

Every counter, whether LaTeX or user defined, has an initial value of zero; this can be altered with the following commands:

\setcounter{*counter*}{*num*}
> This command is self-explanatory; the specified *counter* is assigned the integer value *num*.

\addtocounter{*counter*}{*num*}
> With this command, the value of the *counter* is increased by the integer *num*, which may be positive or negative.

\stepcounter{*counter*}
> The value of the *counter* is increased by one and, at the same time, all its sub-counters (that is, those that have this counter as their *in_counter*) are reset to zero (see above).

\refstepcounter{*counter*}
> This command has the same effect as \stepcounter but also makes *counter* the current counter for the cross-referencing command \label (see Section 11.2.1).

This last command may be applied, for example, within the figure or table environments when the \caption command is missing and yet there is to be a reference in the text to the figure or table number using the \ref command. Then \refstepcounter{figure} or \refstepcounter{table} is given within that float environment to bring the corresponding counter to the right value and to allow that value to be assigned a keyword with the \label command (Section 11.2.1).

The value of a counter may be treated as a number with the command

> \value{*counter*}

which does not change the value at all. This command is mostly used in connection with \setcounter or \addtocounter. For example, if the user-defined counter mypage has been created, it may be set to the same value as the page counter page by giving \setcounter{mypage}{\value{page}}.

10.1.4 Printing counter values

The numerical value in a counter can be printed with the commands

\arabic{*counter*}	as an Arabic number
\Roman{*counter*}	as a capital Roman numeral
\roman{*counter*}	as a lowercase Roman numeral
\alph{*counter*}	as a lowercase letter
\Alph{*counter*}	as a capital letter
\fnsymbol{*counter*}	as a footnote symbol

For the commands \alph and \Alph, the numbers $1 \ldots 26$ correspond to the letters $a \ldots z$ and $A \ldots Z$. It is up to the user to ensure that the counter value lies within this range. For \fnsymbol, the numbers $1 \ldots 9$ are output as the symbols * † ‡ § ¶ ∥ ** †† ‡‡. Here again, the user must take care that the counter does not reach a value of 10 or more.

For each counter, a command of the form

\the*counter*

is also available, consisting of \the immediately followed by the name of that counter, such as \thepage. These commands are initially set to \arabic{*counter*} but may redefined to be composed of several counter commands. In the document classes book and report, for example, the command \thesection is defined in terms of both the chapter and section numbers: \arabic{chapter}.\arabic {section}. Here is the result of printing \thesection at this point: 10.1.

The automatic printing of counter values such as the page, equation, or sectioning numbers is accomplished by means of calls to the appropriate \the*counter* commands. If a different format for some automatic numbering is desired, say alphabetical equation numbers, the definition of the corresponding \the*counter* command can be altered using the methods described in Section 10.3.

Exercise 10.1: Take your standard exercise.tex *file and print out the final values of the LATEX counters with* \arabic{counter} *commands at the end. Change some the values with the* \setcounter *and* \addtocounter *commands and print the values out once more.*

10.2 Lengths

It has been constantly pointed out in all the descriptions of the length parameters such as \parskip or \textwidth that new values may be assigned with the \setlength command. Some of these parameters expect rubber length values that may stretch or shrink. These are mainly parameters that produce vertical spacing. The types of length units, both fixed and rubber, are described in detail in Section 2.4. This will not be repeated here but, rather, additional commands for assigning and handling lengths are discussed in this section.

The standard LaTeX method for assigning a value to a length parameter is with the command

>   `\setlength{`*\length_cmd*`}{`*length_spec*`}`

where *length_spec* may be a length specification (with units) or another length parameter. In the latter case, *\length_cmd* takes on the current value of that other parameter. Thus with `\setlength{\rightmargin}{\leftmargin}` the right-hand margin in a `list` environment is set to the same value as that of the left-hand margin.

Lengths may be increased with

>   `\addtolength{`*\length_cmd*`}{`*length_spec*`}`

which adds *length_spec* to the value of the length parameter *\length_cmd*. A negative value for *length_spec* decreases *\length_cmd* by that amount. Once again, another length parameter may be used for *length_spec*, with or without a preceding minus sign, and its value will be added or subtracted. A decimal number just before a length parameter multiplies its value by that quantity: `0.5\textwidth` means half the width of the text column and `2\parskip` twice the inter-paragraph spacing.

With the command

>   `\settowidth{`*\length_cmd*`}{`*text*`}`

the length parameter *\length_cmd* is set equal to the natural length of a piece of text.

Similarly the commands

>   `\settoheight{`*\length_cmd*`}{`*text*`}`
>   `\settodepth{`*\length_cmd*`}{`*text*`}`

set the *\length_cmd* equal to the height and depth of the *text* above and below the baseline, respectively.

Finally, the command

>   `\stretch{`*decimal_num*`}`

yields a rubber length that is *decimal_num* times as stretchable as `\fill` (Section 2.4.2).

A user-defined length parameter is created with

>   `\newlength{`*\new_len_cmd*`}`

which establishes *\new_len_cmd* as a length with a value of `0pt`. All the above commands may be used to manipulate its value further.

The command

>   `\addvspace{`*length_spec*`}`

!

inserts extra vertical spacing of the amount *length_spec* at the point where it appears. If more than one such command is given, the total inserted spacing will be that of the largest argument and not the sum of them all. This command may only be given *between* paragraphs. Its application for user-defined commands and environments lies in the generation of structures that should behave like paragraphs.

10.3 User-defined commands

New commands may be defined or redefined under LaTeX with the commands

$$\newcommand{\com\_name}[narg][opt]{def}$$
$$\renewcommand{\com\_name}[narg][opt]{def}$$

The first version is used to define a command \com_name that does not yet exist. Its name may be any combination of letters that do not form the name of another command. The second version redefines an already existing command \com_name. In both cases, an error message is printed if the incorrect variant is called. The first optional argument *narg* is a number between 1 and 9 specifying how many arguments the new or altered command is to have. A second optional argument *opt* gives the default value for an optional argument that the new command may take. The actual definition of the command is contained in the text *def.*

10.3.1 Commands without arguments

We will first illustrate the use of the \newcommand without the optional argument [*narg*]. This form is applied when a fixed combination of LaTeX or user commands is to be repeated frequently as a command with its own name. For example, the structure $x_1, \ldots, x_n$, called an x-vector, often occurs in mathematical formulas and is formed in math mode with x_1,\ldots,x_n. Typing

$$\newcommand{\xvec}{x\_1,\ldots,x\_n}$$

creates a new command named \xvec that may be called and used just like any other command. When called, it inserts the sequence of text and commands, in this case x_1,\ldots,x_n, into the current text exactly as if one had typed it oneself. In fact, this is precisely what happens: When \xvec is called, its definition goes into the LaTeX processing.

Since the new command \xvec contains a math command (the subscript command _), it may only be called within math mode. Thus $\xvec$ is required to produce $x_1, \ldots, x_n$ in text mode. It might therefore seem a good idea to include the switching to math mode in the definition itself, as

$$\newcommand{\xvec}{\$x\_1,\ldots,x\_n\$}$$

Now \xvec yields $x_1, \ldots, x_n$. However, this command may only be applied in text and never in math mode. There is a trick to enable the command to be called in both modes: Define it as

```
\newcommand{\xvec}{\ensuremath{x_1,\ldots,x_n}}
```

Now both \xvec and $\xvec$ are allowed, both with the same result.

The above text mode example was actually written as \xvec{}, since TeX treats it as a command without arguments, terminating its name with the first non-letter that it finds. If this character is a blank, it only ends the command name and does not insert interword spacing (Section 2.1). Thus \xvec and ... produces '$x_1,\ldots,x_n$and ...' without any spacing between. This problem is solved by adding a space command \␣ (\ plus space) or the empty structure {} after the command name, in this case as \xvec\␣ or \xvec{}.

It would also have been possible to include the blank in the definition of \xvec, as {\ensuremath{x_1,\ldots,x_n} }. Now the blank following the command name is still removed, but the command itself inserts one to make up for it. However, this is not recommended practice since this 'programmed' blank will always be present, even when some punctuation or other symbol directly follows the command.

Package: A better solution is provided by the xspace package in the tools collection **xspace** (Section B.5.4). With this package, one adds the command \xspace at the end of a definition where a space may appear:

```
\newcommand{\xvec}{\ensuremath{x_1,\ldots,x_n}\xspace}
```

This command prints a blank unless it is followed by punctuation, in which case it does nothing.

The different versions of the above example were all illustrated with the command \newcommand, although in fact this command may only be used once to initiate a user-defined command that does not already exist. Once \xvec has been created, a revised definition can only be given with the command \renewcommand. This was indeed done with the second and subsequent definitions of \xvec.

Following this example, the user may employ \newcommand (or alternatively \renewcommand) to combine any set of commands and text to form a command under a new name that may then be called whenever necessary. In this way, a considerable amount of typing can be avoided and the possibility of error reduced, especially for complex mathematical structures.

If it is not known whether a command with the chosen name already exists, one may use instead

```
\providecommand{\com_name}[narg][opt]{def}
```

which has the same syntax as \newcommand and \renewcommand. The difference is that if the command already exists, the new definition will be ignored. The opposite effect (overwriting the current definition of a command without knowing if it already exists) can be achieved by first calling \providecommand to ensure the command exists, and then issuing the true definition with \renewcommand. However, this should be done only with great care!

Exercise 10.2: *Define the commands* \iint, \iiint, *and* \idotsint, *to make the multiple integrals shown at the right as displayed formulas, or as the following text formulas:* $\iint, \iiint, \int\cdots\int$

$$\iint \quad \iiint \quad \int\cdots\int$$

Exercise 10.3: Change the \thechapter, \thesection, and \thesubsection commands so that for the document classes book and report, the chapter numbering is done with capital letters, such as B, the section numbering with capital Roman numerals after the chapter letter, in the form B-III, and the subsection numbering with lowercase Roman numerals following a comma: B-III,v.
Hint: The original versions of these commands in book and report are defined as

```
\newcommand{\thechapter}{\arabic{chapter}}
\newcommand{\thesection}{\thechapter.\arabic{section}}
\newcommand{\thesubsection}{\thesection.\arabic{subsection}}
```

Now apply \renewcommand to make the required changes.

10.3.2 Commands with arguments

In addition to the vector $x_1,\ldots,x_n$, there are equivalent vectors $y_1,\ldots,y_n$ and $z_1,\ldots,z_n$ in mathematics. It would be possible to define commands \yvec and \zvec following the pattern for \xvec. However, it is also possible to define a generalized vector command and to specify the variable part as an argument. In the present example, the variable part is the letter x, y, or z. A command with *one* variable part is created with the optional argument [1]. For example,

```
\newcommand{\avec}[1]{\ensuremath{#1_1,\ldots,#1_n}}
```

defines the general vector command \avec{*arg*}. Calling \avec{x} yields $x_1,\ldots,x_n$ while invoking \avec{y} prints out $y_1,\ldots,y_n$. The character #1 in the command definition is a dummy argument representing the text of *arg* that replaces all occurrences of #1 when the command is called. By imagining an x or a y at each location of the #1 in the definition, the desired structures in each case can be recognized.

The digit 1 in the dummy argument #1 seems at first to be rather pointless. In fact, for a command with only one argument it really has no meaning. However, its function becomes more obvious for commands with *multiple* arguments. Let us say, for example, that we want a command to generate structures such as $u_1,\ldots,u_m$ as well as $v_1,\ldots,v_n$. This requires two arguments, one to specify the letter u, v, and so on, and a second to determine the last subscript n, m, and so on. Such a command is created with

```
\newcommand{\anvec}[2]{\ensuremath{#1_1,\ldots,#1_#2}}
```

and invoked as \anvec{u}{n} for $u_1,\ldots,u_n$ and as \anvec{v}{m} for $u_1,\ldots,u_m$. The optional argument [2] for \newcommand says that the command being defined contains two arguments; in the definition part, #1 is replaced by the first argument and #2 by the second. By imagining u or v in place of #1 and n or m where #2 stands, one can see how the command \anvec{*arg1*}{*arg2*} operates.

This pattern may be carried on for even more arguments. With

```
\newcommand{\subvec}[3]{\ensuremath{#1_#2,\ldots,#1_#3}}
```

a command \subvec is defined with three arguments. It should be clear from the definition that calling \subvec{a}{i}{j} produces $a_i, \ldots, a_j$.

!

A command argument that consists of only a single character need not be put into curly brackets { } but may be given directly. If it is the first argument, it must be separated from the command name with a blank, as usual. Thus the sequence \subvec aik is the same as \subvec{a}{i}{k}, and \subvec x1n produces the same structure $x_1, \ldots, x_n$ as our first user-defined example \xvec.

Arguments must be enclosed in curly brackets { } when they contain more than one character, since the brackets indicate that the contents are to be treated as a unit. Thus \subvec{A}{ij}{lk} prints out $A_i j, \ldots, A_l k$. The three replacement arguments are A for #1, ij for #2, and lk for #3.

Why does \subvec{A}{ij}{lk} produce $A_i j, \ldots, A_l k$ and not the expected $A_{ij}, \ldots, A_{lk}$? The answer is that, although the arguments within curly brackets are set as units into the definition text, the brackets themselves are not. The command text after replacement is \ensuremath{A_ij,\ldots,A_lk} so that only the first characters following the subscript symbols _ are actually lowered. In order for both letters to be lowered, they must be seen as a unit within the command text, that is, as A_{ij},...,A_{lk}. This may be achieved with the \subvec command by including an extra set of brackets in the arguments: \subvec{A}{{ij}}{{lk}}. A better solution, however, is to put the brackets in the definition to begin with:

    \renewcommand{\subvec}[3]{\ensuremath{#1_{#2},\ldots,#1_{#3}}}

which will always produce the desired result with only a single set of brackets per argument: \subvec{A}{ij}{lk} prints $A_{ij}, \ldots, A_{lk}$.

10.3.3 Commands with an optional argument

!

As we have seen, many LaTeX commands may take *optional* arguments, including the command \newcommand itself. It is also possible to define user commands with one optional argument. The advantage of this is that, although an argument is provided, in most applications it will usually take some standard value that need not be given explicitly.

As an example, the user-defined vector command \subvec in the last section has three arguments, for the letter and for the first and last subscripts. However, it may be that the letter is normally x, so it makes sense to include it as an optional argument, which is to be specified only for a different letter. This is accomplished with

    \renewcommand{\subvec}[3][x]
        {\ensuremath{#1_{#2},\ldots,#1_{#3}}}

The difference between this and the previous definition is the addition of [x] after the [3] argument. This states that the *first* of the three arguments is to be optional, and its standard value is x. Now \subvec{i}{j} prints $x_i, \ldots, x_j$ while \subvec[a]{1}{n} produces $a_1, \ldots, a_n$.

There may only be one optional argument in the user-defined command, and it will always be the first one, the #1 in the definition.

10.3.4 Additional examples of user-defined commands

In the above explanation of user-defined commands, a very simple case of a vector structure was taken as an example. We would now like to demonstrate some more complex situations, in which counters, lengths, and even some special TeX commands are applied.

Example 1: In Section 7.4.6, the TeX commands \atop and \choose were presented as useful mathematical commands even for LaTeX applications. Unfortunately, the syntax of these commands deviates considerably from that of the similar LaTeX command \frac. However,

    \newcommand{\latop}[2]{{#1\atop#2}}   and
    \newcommand{\lchoose}[2]{{#1\choose#2}}

define two commands \latop and \lchoose that yield the same results with a syntax like that of LaTeX: \latop{*upper*}{*lower*}.

Example 2: The command \defbox{*sample_text*} sets a box width equal to the length of the text *sample_text*. A subsequent call to the command \textbox{*text*} centers *text* within a frame with the same width as *sample_text*.

    \newlength{\wdth}
    \newcommand{\defbox}[1]{\settowidth{\wdth}{#1}}
    \newcommand{\textbox}[1]{\framebox[\wdth]{#1}}

First, a new length parameter \wdth is created, then \defbox is defined so that \wdth is set equal to the length of its argument (Section 10.2), and finally, \textbox makes a framed box of that same width containing its argument, centered. (Do not name the length parameter \width, for this already exists; see Section 5.1.5.)

    as wide as this text\\
    \defbox{as wide as this text}\textbox{}\\
    \textbox{text}\\
    \textbox{longer text}

as wide as this text

text
longer text

Example 3: A footnote command \myftnote is to behave as the normal command \footnote{*text*} by putting *text* into a footnote, but instead of using numbers as the marker, it should take the symbols * † ‡ § ¶ ‖ ** †† ‡‡ one after the other, starting again with the symbol * on each new page. First, a new counter must be established that will be reset to zero every time the **page** counter is incremented. This is done with (see Section 10.1.2)

    \newcounter{myfn}[page]

making a user-defined counter **myfn** that is set to zero every time the **page** counter is incremented.* Next the command

    \renewcommand{\thefootnote}{\fnsymbol{footnote}}

redefines the footnote marker to be that symbol in the sequence given by the counter **footnote** (Sections 5.2.2 and 10.1.4). Now the actual new footnote command can be constructed with

---

*Actually the page counter is not incremented exactly at the end of the page; LaTeX reads in the whole paragraph before it decides if and where a page break should occur. This can cause problems with resetting the **myfn** counter near the top of a page.

```
\newcommand{\myftnote}[1]{\setcounter{footnote}{\value{myfn}}%
   \footnote{#1}\stepcounter{myfn}}
```

yielding the desired results. The user-defined command \myftnote possesses one argument, which is passed to the LATEX \footnote command after the LATEX counter footnote has been set equal to the value of the user counter myfn. Once the command \footnote has been executed, the counter myfn is then incremented by one with \stepcounter{myfn}. This counter, however, is reset to zero whenever the page counter is incremented, that is, whenever a new page begins.

The footnote on the previous page was generated with the command \myftnote as described. It is now used here* and again here†, demonstrating how the symbols have been reset on a new page.

Example 4: A command \alpheqn is to be set up so that once it has been called, the subsequent equations will all have the same number but be followed by letters *a*, *b*, ..., separated by a hyphen '-' from the number. The command \reseteqn restores the numbering scheme to its original style. Thus a sequence of equation numbers could be 4, 5, 6-a, 6-b, 7.

```
\newcounter{saveeqn}
\newcommand{\alpheqn}{\setcounter{saveeqn}{\value{equation}}%
   \stepcounter{saveeqn}\setcounter{equation}{0}%
   \renewcommand{\theequation}
       {\mbox{\arabic{saveeqn}-\alph{equation}}}}
\newcommand{\reseteqn}{\setcounter{equation}{\value{saveeqn}}%
   \renewcommand{\theequation}{\arabic{equation}}}
```

The example should be easy to comprehend with the help of the commands and counters in Section 10.1. The current value of counter equation is saved in the counter saveeqn and then incremented, while equation itself is set to zero. The form of the equation marker, \theequation, is redefined using these two counters. The equation numbering routines will operate on equation as usual, leaving saveeqn unchanged. The resetting command \reseteqn puts the value of saveeqn back into equation and restores the definition of \theequation.

This example is only appropriate for the document class article. For report and book, the definition of \theequation is

```
\arabic{chapter}.\arabic{equation}
```

The necessary modifications are left as an exercise for the user.

The \mbox command in the first \renewcommand{\theequation} defining the combined equation number is necessary because the result will be printed in *math mode*, where the hyphen '-' is interpreted as a binary operator (minus sign) with extra spacing between it and its two 'operands', \arabic{saveeqn} and \alph{equation}. Thus $6 - a$ would be output instead of 6-a. The \mbox command causes a temporary switch out of math into text mode.

Example 5: In Section 7.4.10, several new commands are suggested to simplify typing math according to the ISO standard. These are:

---

*another footnote
†and yet another footnote

```
\newcommand{\me}{\mathrm{e}}
\newcommand{\mi}{\mathrm{i}}
\newcommand{\dif}{\mathrm{d}}
\renewcommand{\vec}[1]{\boldsymbol{#1}}
```

These permit the *constants* e, i, and differential operator d to be printed upright, not italic. The redefinition of the \vec command requires the $\mathcal{A}_{\mathcal{M}}\mathcal{S}$ math package amsbsy, either directly or as part of the amsmath package (Chapter 15).

Here one could also include the abbreviation for the *electron volt*, mentioned on page 33, and its multiples:

```
\newcommand{\eV}{\mbox{e\hspace{-.12em}V}}
\newcommand{\keV}{\mbox{k\eV}}
\newcommand{\MeV}{\mbox{M\eV}}
```

If these commands are used frequently in many different documents, we recommend saving them in a separate file, say, isomath.tex, to be input at the start of those documents, with \input{isomath}.

Exercise 10.4: Define LaTeX commands \Lbrack and \Lbrace in the same manner as in *Example 1 for* \latop *and* \lchoose *corresponding to the TeX commands* \brack *and* \brace. *These TeX commands behave as* \choose *from Section 7.4.6 except that they enclose their contents in square brackets [*\Lbrack*] or curly braces {* \Lbrace*}. (Note that the names* \lbrack *and* \lbrace *are already defined, so they should not be used for these commands.)*

Exercise 10.5: Generalize Example 4 with a command \vareqn{num}{type} to make the subsequent equation numbers have the value num followed by a running number in square brackets printed as \alph ... \Roman, as given by the argument type. For example, 33[A], 33[B], would result from calling \vareqn{33}{\Alph}.

Exercise 10.6: Generalize the integral commands in Exercise 10.2 to include an argument to represent the area of integration set centered below the entire symbol. Thus \iint{(D)}, \iiint{V}, and \idotsint{G} should produce what is shown at the right.

$$\iint\limits_{(D)} \quad \iiint\limits_{V} \quad \int\cdots\int\limits_{G}$$

Hint: The second command can be made simply with a subscript on the middle integral (but see \limits *in Section 7.2.5). For the other two, negative horizontal shifting of the subscripted symbol is needed using* \hspace{-..}.

Exercise 10.7: Define a command \mtrx to produce a matrix name in an upright, sans serif font. (Note that you cannot call this command \matrix because that already exists to produce matrices, not their variable names.)

10.3.5 Conditional text

Package: ifthen

Practiced TeX users will be familiar with the conditional commands that are available, both for TeX and LaTeX. However, their usage is not always straightforward and often requires extensive knowledge of TeX's deeper principles. Leslie Lamport has provided a package named ifthen, extended by David Carlisle, which not only simplifies their application but also gives them a LaTeX syntax.

The package is loaded as usual with the command

```
\usepackage{ifthen}
```

in the preamble. It then makes available the two commands \ifthenelse and \whiledo, which have the following syntaxes:

```
\ifthenelse{test}{then_text}{else_text}
\whiledo{test}{do_text}
```

In both cases, *test* is a logical statement (explained below); for the first command, *then_text* or *else_text* is inserted into the text depending on whether *test* is ⟨true⟩ or ⟨false⟩. For the second command, the *do_text* is inserted (executed) as long as *test* evaluates to ⟨true⟩. (The *do_text* must alter the inputs to *test* or it will never stop!) The texts may also contain commands, or even define or redefine commands.

There are four types of basic logical statements that may be combined to form more complicated ones.

Testing numbers

To compare two numbers or commands that evaluate to numbers, simply put one of the relational operators <, =, or > between them, which stand for *less than*, *equals*, and *greater than*, respectively. The value of a counter may be tested by putting its name as the argument of the \value command. Examples:

```
\newcommand{\three}{3}
\ifthenelse {\three = 3} {O.K.} {What?}
\ifthenelse {\value{page} < 100 }
    {Page xx} {Page xxx}
```

The first case prints 'O.K.' since \three is equal to 3; in the second case *Page xx* is printed if the current page number is less than 100, otherwise it prints *Page xxx*. (The blanks above are added for clarity, since spaces between arguments are always ignored.)

Whether a number is even or odd can be tested with \isodd

```
\ifthenelse {\isodd{\value{page}}
    {odd} {even}
```

Testing text

To test whether two commands evaluate to the same piece of text or whether a command is defined as a certain *string* of text, use

```
\equal{string1}{string2}
```

where *string1* and *string2* are texts or commands that reduce to text. For example, with

```
\ifthenelse {\equal{\name}{Fred}} {Frederick} {??}
```

the text Frederick is inserted if \name has been defined as Fred (with \newcommand), otherwise two question marks are printed.

Testing lengths

Another logical statement compares two lengths.

```
\lengthtest{relation}
```

where *relation* consists of two lengths or length commands separated by a relational operator <, =, or >. For example,

```
\newlength{\horiz} \newlength{\vert}
\newlength{\min}
. . . . . .
\ifthenelse {\lengthtest{\horiz > \vert}}
   {\setlength{\min}{\vert}} {\setlength{\min}{\horiz}}
```

sets \min to be the smaller of \horiz and \vert.

Testing switches

A *boolean switch* is a parameter that is either ⟨*true*⟩ or ⟨*false*⟩, also called a *flag*. Three commands exist to handle them:

\newboolean{*string*}	creates a new switch
\setboolean{*string*}{*value*}	assigns a value true or false
\boolean{*string*}	tests its value

The last of these is used as *test* in \ifthenelse and \whiledo.

There are a number of internal LaTeX switches that may also be tested (but never reset!). The most useful of these are @twoside and @twocolumn for checking whether two-side or two-column modes are active. Since they contain the character @, they may only be used inside a class or package file (Appendix D).

Combining logical statements

Any of the above logical statements may be combined to form a more complex statement by means of the logical operators

```
\and    \or    \not    \(    \)
```

which should be straightforward to anyone familiar with boolean logic. For example, to set \textwidth to 10 cm if two-column mode is active or if \paperwidth is greater than 15 cm and the page counter is below 100,

```
\ifthenelse {\lengthtest{\textwidth > 10cm} \or
      \( \lengthtest{\paperwidth > 15cm} \and
         \value{page} < 100 \) }
      {\setlength{\textwidth}{10cm}} {}
```

will accomplish this.

Such conditionals are fairly complicated, and they are most appropriate for defining new commands that may have alternative actions.

Here is a relatively simple example: Suppose one is uncertain whether British or American spelling is wanted by the publisher. One can write the document with both included in the text, with a switch in the preamble to make the final selection.

```
\newboolean{US}
\setboolean{US}{true} %For American spelling
%\setboolean{US}{false} %For British spelling
\newcommand{\USUK}[2]{\ifthenelse{\boolean{US}}{#1}{#2}}
```

Now \USUK is a command that prints its first or second argument according to the setting of the flag US. Thus, in the text one may write

```
... the \USUK{color}{colour} of music ...
```

which will yield American spelling if \setboolean{US}{true} has been specified, otherwise the British version. In fact, different sections of the work could have different spelling simply by changing the value of the switch at the appropriate point.

As an example of \whiledo: One wishes to write some text n times, where both the text and n are to be variable.

```
\newcounter{mycount}
\newcommand{\replicate}[2]{\setcounter{mycount}{#1}
    \whiledo{\value{mycount}>0}{#2\addtocounter{mycount}{-1}}}
```

Now \replicate{30}{?} will print 30 question marks.

10.4   User-defined environments

Environments may be created or changed with the commands

\newenvironment{*env_name*}[*narg*][*opt*]{*beg_def*}{*end_def*}
\renewenvironment{*env_name*}[*narg*][*opt*]{*beg_def*}{*end_def*}

where the arguments have the following meanings:

env_name: the name of the environment; for \newenvironment, it may not be the same as any existing environment or command name, whether LaTeX or user-defined. For \renewenvironment, on the other hand, there must already be an environment bearing this name. Any changes to LaTeX environments should only be undertaken if the user knows what he or she is doing.

narg: a number between 1 and 9 that states how many arguments the environment is to have; if the optional argument *narg* is omitted, the environment is to have no arguments.

opt: the default text for the first argument (#1) if it is to be optional; this behaves the same as for \(re)newcommand (page 185).

beg_def: the *initial* text to be inserted when \begin{*env_name*} is called; if this text contains entries of the form #*n*, with *n* = 1,...,*narg*, then when the environment is started with the call

\begin{*env_name*}{*arg_1*}...{*arg_n*}...

each occurrence of #*n* within *beg_def* is replaced by the text of the argument *arg_n*.

end_def: the *final* text that is inserted when \end{*env_name*} is called; here the dummy arguments #*n* are not allowed since they are only to appear in the *beg_def* text.

10.4.1 Environments without arguments

Just as for user-defined commands, environments without the optional argument *narg* will be illustrated first. A user-defined environment named sitquote is created with

```
\newenvironment{sitquote}{\begin{quote}\small
    \itshape}{\end{quote}}
```

which sets the text *appearing between* \begin{sitquote} text \end{sitquote} *in the typeface* \small\itshape *and indented on both sides from the main margins, as demonstrated here.*

In this case, *beg_def* consists of the command sequence \begin{quote}\small \itshape while *end_def* is simply \end{quote}. Now the call

```
\begin{sitquote} text \end{sitquote}    is the same as
\begin{quote}\small\itshape text \end{quote}
```

which produces the desired result.

This example does not appear to be very practical since the same effect can be achieved with less typing by adding \small\itshape at the beginning of the quote environment. However, it is more consistent with the concept of *logical markup* introduced in Section 1.2.2. This special quotation environment may be used throughout the document without worrying about its typographical details, which are specified in its definition located in the document preamble. Doing it this way not only ensures consistency, it also simplifies any substitution that may be demanded later by a typographical expert.

Let us expand the previous example somewhat as follows:

```
\newcounter{com}
\newenvironment{comment}
{\noindent\slshape Comment:\begin{quote}\small\itshape}
{\stepcounter{com}\hfill(\arabic{com})\end{quote}}
```

where now *beg_def* contains the text and commands

```
\noindent\slshape Comment:\begin{quote}\small\itshape
```

and *end_def* is

```
\stepcounter{com}\hfill(\arabic{com})\end{quote}
```

where com is a user counter created by the \newcounter command. Now, since the command \begin{comment} inserts the text *beg_def* at the start of the environment and \end{comment} the text *end_def* at the finish, it should be clear that

```
\begin{comment} This is a comment.
   Comments should ...
   ... in round parentheses.
\end{comment}
```

will generate the following type of structure:

Comment:

> *This is a comment. Comments should be preceded by the word 'Comment:', the text being in a small, italic typeface, indented on both sides from the main margins. Each comment receives a running comment number at the lower right in round parentheses.*   *(1)*

The user should examine the sequence of commands with the replacement text of this example to see precisely what the effect of this environment is. Two weaknesses should become apparent: What would happen if \begin{comment} were called in the middle of a line of text without a blank line before? And what would happen if the last line of the comment text were so long that there was no more room for the running comment number on the same line?

The following revision removes these two problems:

```
\renewenvironment{comment}
{\begin{sloppypar}\noindent\slshape Comment:
    \begin{quote}\small\itshape}
{\stepcounter{com}\hspace*{\fill}(\arabic{com})\end{quote}
    \end{sloppypar}}
```

With the \begin{sloppypar} command, the call to the environment always starts a new paragraph in which no *overfull* line can occur upon line breaking. If the comment number does not fit on the last line of text, a new line begins with the number right justified because of the command \hspace*{\fill}. Again the user should examine carefully just what is inserted into the processing between the \begin{comment} and the \end{comment}.

10.4.2 Environments with arguments

Passing arguments over to an environment is carried out exactly as for commands. As an example, the comment environment will be modified so that the name of the person making the comment is added after the word '*Comment:*', and this name will be an argument when the environment is invoked.

```
\renewenvironment{comment}[1]
{\begin{sloppypar}\noindent\slshape Comment: #1
        \begin{quote}\small\itshape}
{\stepcounter{com}\hspace*{\fill}(\arabic{com})%
        \end{quote}\end{sloppypar}}
```

The text
```
\begin{comment}{Helmut Kopka} This is a modified ...
    ... environment argument \end{comment}
```
now produces

Comment: Helmut Kopka

> *This is a modified comment. Comments should be preceded by the word 'Comment:', followed by the name of the commenter, with the text of the comment being in a small, italic typeface, indented on both sides from the main margins. Each comment receives a running comment number at the lower right in round parentheses. The name of the commenter is transferred as an environment argument.*
>
> *(2)*

This example will now be modified once again by interchanging the comment number and the name of the commenter. Placing the running number after the word '*Comment:*' is no problem, for it is simply necessary to insert those commands from {*end_def*} at the location of the #1 dummy argument. However, putting the symbol #1 where the comment number used to be will produce an error message during the LaTeX processing since this violates the syntax of the \newenvironment command: '*No dummy arguments shall appear within the {end_def}.*' If the dummy argument comes after \begin{quote}, the name will be printed at the wrong place, at the beginning of the comment text.

There is a trick to solve this problem:

```
\newsavebox{\comname}
\renewenvironment{comment}[1]
{\begin{sloppypar}\noindent\stepcounter{com}\slshape
   Comment \arabic{com}\sbox{\comname}{#1}
   \begin{quote}\small\itshape}
{\hspace*{\fill}\usebox{\comname}\end{quote}\end{sloppypar}}
```

The commands \newsavebox, \sbox, and \usebox are described in Section 5.1.1. Here \comname is the name of a box that has been created with \newsavebox, in which the first argument, the commenter's name, is stored. With this new definition, a comment now appears as follows:

Comment 3

> *In this form, every comment is assigned a sequential number after the word Comment. The comment text appears as before, while the name of the commenter is entered as the environment argument and is placed at the right of the last line.*
> *Helmut Kopka*

The implementation of more than one argument for environments is the same as for commands and needs no further explanation.

10.4.3 Environments with an optional argument

Similarly, environments may be defined with an optional argument, just as commands. To take our last example once more, if we feel that most comments will be made by Helmut Kopka, we could alter the first line of the definition to

```
\renewenvironment{comment}[1][Helmut Kopka]{..}{..}
```

Now it is only necessary to specify the name of the commenter if it is someone else. With

```
\begin{comment}[Patrick W. Daly]More than ...
... appropriate.\end{comment}
```

we obtain

Comment 4

> *More than one person may want to make a comment, but perhaps one person makes more than others do. An optional argument for the name is then appropriate.*   *Patrick W. Daly*

Exercise 10.8: *Extend the definition of the comment environment so that a page break cannot occur either between the heading 'Comment n' and the comment text or between the comment text and the commenter's name.*

Exercise 10.9: *Create a new environment making use of the* minipage *environment, to be named* varpage *and possessing one argument that is a sample text to determine the width of the minipage. The call*

```
\begin{varbox}{'As wide as this sample text'}
. . . . . . . . . . . . . . . . . . . .\end{varbox}
```

should pack the enclosed text into a minipage that has a width equal to that of the text 'As wide as this sample text'.
Hint: A user-defined length parameter must first be established, say \varwidth. *See Section 10.2 for details on assigning lengths to text widths.*

Exercise 10.10: *Generate an environment named* varlist *with two arguments that behaves as a generalization of the sample list in Section 4.4.3. The first argument is to be the item word that is printed on each call to* \item; *the second is the numbering style of the item numeration. For example, with the call*

```
\begin{varlist}{Sample}{\Alph} . . . . . \end{varlist}
```

every \item *command within the environment should produce the sequence 'Sample A', 'Sample B', ... The indentation should be 1 cm larger than the width of the item word, which itself should be left justified within the label box.*
Hint: Once again a user-defined length, say \itemwidth, *is necessary for this solution. After the length of the item word has been stored with* \settowidth, *the indentation may be set with*

```
\setlength{\leftmargin}{\itemwidth}
```

to be equal to the width of the item word, and then with

> `\addtolength{\leftmargin}{1cm}`

to be 1 cm larger. Length assignments for `\labelwidth` *and* `\labelsep` *may be similarly set to appropriate values.*
All further details may be obtained from Section 4.4.

10.5 Some comments on user-defined structures

10.5.1 Reusing sets of definitions

User definitions are created to alter page formats, to reorganize the document layout, to invent new structures, and to define shortcuts. That is, they either directly specify typographical elements such as the text width, or indicate how new or existing logical elements are to be rendered typographically. As such, they belong in the preamble, where they can be conveniently redefined as needed, affecting the entire document.

Once a set of user definitions has been established, what is the best way to reuse them? There are several possibilities:

1. Write a new class file based on an existing one, incorporating your own changes. This should be reserved for major changes to the layout or document organization, which will be used very frequently.

2. Write your definitions to a package file with the extension `.sty` to be loaded with the `\usepackage` command. You can take advantage of special package features, such as internal commands and options.

3. Write the definitions to a file with the extension `.tex` and load it with `\input {filename}`. No extra features are possible, and the file can be loaded anywhere within the source file.

4. Simply copy the definitions from one source file to the next.

Methods 1 and 2 are more sophisticated, and should be considered for user definitions that have a wide generality. They are explained in Appendix D. Method 3 is perfectly good for a personal collection of shortcut commands or common (re)definitions that are applied to many documents. By having one depository for all such customizations, it is easier to maintain them centrally.

Finally, method 4 is applicable for a short list of uncomplicated definitions.

10.5.2 Unwanted spaces

Occasionally user-defined structures generate spacing where none was expected, or more spacing than was desired. This is almost always due to blanks or new lines in the definition, included only to improve the legibility of the input text but interpreted as spacing when the structure is invoked.

For example, if the % character had been left out of the first line of the \myftnote definition on page 190, a new line would have been added to the command text at that point, and converted into a blank. This blank would be inserted between the previous word which should receive the footnote marker and the call to the \footnote command that actually generates the marker, with the result that it would be displaced from that word (for example, wrong * instead of right*).

!

At this point we would like to point out that many LaTeX commands are *invisible*, in that they do not produce any text at the point where they are called. If such an invisible command is given separated by blanks from the surrounding text, it is possible that two blanks will appear.

```
For example \rule{0pt}{0pt} produces
```

'For example produces' twice the interword spacing between 'example' and 'produces'. Invisible commands without arguments do not present this problem since the trailing blank acts solely as a command name terminator and disappears. Furthermore, the following LaTeX commands and environments always remove the subsequent blanks even when arguments are present.

```
\pagebreak      \linebreak      \label  \glossary  \vspace  figure
\nopagebreak    \nolinebreak    \index  \marginpar          table
```

10.5.3 Identical command and counter names

In the previous examples, a number of counters were introduced for application to specific commands or environments, such as myfn for the command \myfootnote on page 190, or com for the environment comment on page 195. In these cases, the counter and the corresponding command or environment were given different names. This was not necessary: *Counters may have a name that is identical to that of a command or environment.* LaTeX knows from the context whether the name refers to a counter or to a command/environment.

The different names were chosen in the examples in order to avoid confusion for the beginner. In fact, it is reasonable to give a counter the same name as the command or environment with which it is coupled, a practice that LaTeX itself constantly employs (Section 10.1.1). In the above-mentioned examples, the counters could just as easily have been named myfootnote and comment to emphasize their interdependence with the command and environment of the same names.

10.5.4 Scope of user definitions

User structures that are defined within the preamble are valid for the entire document. Command and environment definitions that are made inside an environment remain in effect only until its end. Even their names are unknown to LaTeX outside the environment in which they were defined. Thus if they are to be defined once again in another environment, \newcommand or \newenvironment must be used and not the \renew versions.

For command and environment names that have been globally defined, that is, in the preamble, all further new definitions of these names must be made with the \renew version. However, these subsequent definitions will apply only locally within the environment in which they are declared; outside, the previous global definitions will be valid once more.

The same applies to structure definitions within nested environments. A definition in the outer environment is effective within all inner ones, but a new definition must be made at the deeper levels with \renewcommand or \renewenvironment. On leaving the inner environment, the new definition will no longer be operative, but rather the old one will be reestablished.

Warning: Structures that have been created with \newsavebox or with \newcounter are globally defined. If they are given within an environment, their definitions remain effective even outside that environment. Similarly, \setcounter functions globally, although \savebox does not.

Local definitions are really not to be recommended. It is far better to place all user definitions at the beginning, in the preamble, where they are most easily visible. A local redefinition of a standard command can lead to puzzling effects that are difficult for others, or even for the author, to trace down. Of course, some special effects might just be wanted.

10.5.5 Order of definitions

User-defined structures may be nested within one another. If one user definition contains another user-defined structure, it is often the case that the inner one has already been defined. However, this is not necessary. *User definitions may contain other user structures that are defined afterwards.* What is important is that the other structure is defined before the first command is invoked.

For example, a normal sequence of definitions would be

```
\newcommand{\A}{defa}
\newcommand{\B}{defb}
\newcommand{\C}{\A \B}
```

where \C is defined in terms of \A and \B. However, it is also permissible to write

```
\newcommand{\C}{\A \B}
normal text, but without calling \C
\newcommand{\B}{defb}
\newcommand{\A}{defa}
further text with any number of calls to \A, \B and \C
```

10.5.6 Nested definitions

! User definitions may be nested inside one another. A structure such as

```
\newcommand{\outer}{{\newcommand{\inner}...}}
```

is permissible. The command that is defined with the name {\inner} is valid and known only within the command {\outer}, according to the remarks on the scope of definitions on page 200. Although the TeX macros make copious use of nested command definitions to limit the lifetime of temporary commands, it is not recommended to nest LaTeX definitions excessively since it is too easy to lose track of the bracketing. A forgotten bracket pair will produce an error message on the *second* call to the outer command, since the inner definition still exists as a leftover from the first call. Nevertheless, here is an example:

```
\newcommand{\twentylove}
  {{\newcommand{\fivelove}
    {{{\newcommand{\onelove}
        {I love \LaTeX!}%
        \onelove\ \onelove\ \onelove\ \onelove\ \onelove}}}
    \fivelove\\ \fivelove\\ \fivelove\\ \fivelove}}
```

The entry My opinion of \LaTeX:\\ \twentylove now produces:

My opinion of LaTeX:

I love LaTeX! I love LaTeX! I love LaTeX! I love LaTeX! I love LaTeX!
I love LaTeX! I love LaTeX! I love LaTeX! I love LaTeX! I love LaTeX!
I love LaTeX! I love LaTeX! I love LaTeX! I love LaTeX! I love LaTeX!
I love LaTeX! I love LaTeX! I love LaTeX! I love LaTeX! I love LaTeX!

Indenting the lines of the definition, as shown above, can help to keep track of the nesting levels; each line of the same level starts in the same column, ignoring braces.

If both the *inner* and *outer* definitions are to be provided with arguments, the symbols for the inner and outer dummy arguments must be distinguished. The symbols for the *inner* definition are ##1 ... ##9, while those for the *outer* one are the normal #1 ... #9. For example:

```
\newcommand{\thing}[1]{{\newcommand{\colored}[2]{The ##1 is ##2.}
  \colored{#1}{red} \colored{#1}{green} \colored{#1}{blue}}}
```

The entry The colors of the objects are\\
  \thing{dress}\\ \thing{book}\\ \thing{car}   produces
The colors of the objects are

The dress is red. The dress is green. The dress is blue.
The book is red. The book is green. The book is blue.
The car is red. The car is green. The car is blue.

The separate definition and calling as in Section 10.5.5 is easier to follow and would be:

```
\newcommand{\thing[1]}{\colored{#1}{red} \colored{#1}{green}
                      \colored{#1}{blue}
\newcommand{\colored}[2]{The #1 is #2.}
```

If one were ever to go to a third level of definitions, the dummy arguments are given as ####1 ... ####9. And for the fourth level, one writes eight # signs!

Part II

Beyond the Basics

11 Document Management

This chapter describes those features of LaTeX that justify the subtitle of Leslie Lamport's original book, *A Document Preparation System*. Whereas in the previous chapters we have concentrated more on markup, logical and typographical, we now present topics that are essential for producing large, complex documents in an efficient manner. The subjects included here are the splitting of a document into several files; selective processing of parts of a document; cross-references to sections, figures, and equations; and automated production of bibliographies, indices, and glossaries.

11.1 Processing parts of a document

As is often pointed out, a LaTeX document consists of a preamble and the actual text part. Short documents, such as those that a beginner might have, are written to a single file by means of a text editor and might be corrected after the first trial printing. As the user gathers experience and confidence, the LaTeX documents will rapidly expand in length until one is faced with the task of producing an entire book of more than a hundred pages.

Such long documents could theoretically be kept in one file, although that would make the whole operation increasingly clumsy. The file editor functions less efficiently on longer files and the LaTeX processing takes correspondingly more time. A better idea is to split the work into several files that LaTeX then merges during the processing.

11.1.1 The \input command

The contents of another file may be read into a LaTeX document with the command

    \input{*filename*}

where the name of the other file is *filename*.tex. It is only necessary to specify the full name of the file if the extension is something other than .tex. During the LaTeX processing, the text contained in this second file is read in at that location in the first file where the command is given.

The result of the \input command is the same as if the contents of the file *filename*.tex had been typed into the document file at that position. The command may be given anywhere in the document, either in the preamble or within the text part.

Since the \input command may be given in the preamble, it is possible to put the whole preamble text itself into a separate file. The actual LaTeX processing file could even be reduced to simply \begin{document} ... \end{document} with a number of \input commands. A preamble file makes sense if one has a series of documents all of the same type requiring a common preamble. This also simplifies any later change to the specifications that must be made in *all* the documents. Different preamble files may be prepared for various types of processing and may then be selected with \input{*proc_type*}.

A file that is read in by means of the \input command may also contain further \input commands. The nesting depth is limited only by the capacities of the computer.

To obtain a listing of all extra files read in, give the command

> \listfiles

in the preamble. The list appears both on the computer monitor and in the transcript file at the end of the processing run. The version numbers and any other loading information are also printed. This provides a check as to which files have been input. See Section D.2.9 for a demonstration.

Exercise 11.1: Put the preamble of your standard exercise file exercise.tex *into a separate file,* preamble.tex. *Split the text part into three files* exer1.tex, exer2.tex, *and* exer3.tex. *What should the main file now contain to ensure that LaTeX processes the whole exercise text?*

> [!]

The \input command has been inherited from Plain TeX where the syntax is slightly different: The name of the file is *not* placed within curly braces but simply appears after the command, as \input *filename*. This TeX syntax is permissible even in LaTeX, that is, the braces are actually optional, something that has led to consternation for some users.

11.1.2 The \include command

Splitting the document into several files may be practical for writing and editing, but when the files are merged with the \input commands, it is still the entire document that is processed. Even if only one file contains a small correction, all files will be read in and processed once again. It would therefore be desirable to be able to reprocess only the corrected file.

One rough-and-ready method is to write a temporary main file containing only the preamble (which may be read in) and an \input command to read in that specific file. The disadvantage is that all automatic numbering of page numbers, sections, figures, equations, and so on, will start from 1, since all the information from the previous files will be missing. Furthermore, all cross-references from other files will be absent.

A much better method is to employ the LaTeX command

> \include{*filename*}

which is only allowed within the text part of the document, together with

> \includeonly{*file_list*}

in the preamble, containing a list *file_list* of those files that are to be read in. The file names are separated by commas and the extension .tex is left off.

If *filename* is in the *file_list* or if \includeonly is missing from the preamble, the command \include{*filename*} is identical to

> \clearpage \input{*filename*} \clearpage

However, if *filename* is not contained within the *file_list*, \include is equivalent to \clearpage and the file contents are not read in. However, an auxiliary .aux file is read in that sets all the counters and cross-referencing information for that file.

Since \include always begins a new page, the document must be split into files at those points where a new page occurs, such as between chapters. Furthermore, \include commands may not be nested: They may only appear in the main processing file. However, an \input command may be given within a file that is \included.

The great advantage of the \include command is that the additional information about page, section, and equation numbers will be supplied by the .aux files that are read in in place of the .tex files so that the selective processing takes place with the correct values of these counters. Cross-reference information from the other files is also available so that the \ref and \pageref commands (Section 11.2.1) yield the correct results. All these values will have been determined during a previous processing of the entire document.

If the changes in the file that is being selectively processed lead to an increase or reduction in the number of pages, the following files will also have to be reprocessed to correct their page numbers. The same is true if sections are added or removed, or if the number of equations, footnotes, figures, and so on is altered.

For example, suppose *file_3* ends on page 17, but after the selective processing it now extends to page 22. The following *file_4* still begins on page 18, and all further files also have their original starting page numbers. If *file_4* is now selectively processed, it will receive the correct number for its first page, 23, based on the stored information in the revised *file_3*. So far so good. However, if instead *file_6* were to be selectively processed right after *file_3*, it would receive its starting page number from *file_5*, which has not yet been corrected and would be in error by 5. The same applies to all other structure counters. Their correct values can only be guaranteed when the files have been reprocessed in their proper order.

In spite of these restrictions, the \include command is extremely useful for large documents, saving considerable computation time. Longer documents are normally written and edited in many stages. The \include command permits one to reprocess selective alterations in a short time, even if the numbering systems temporarily go awry. This can be repaired later on with a complete reprocessing of the entire document by temporarily removing the \includeonly command in the preamble.

A file that is read in with \include may not contain any \newcounter declarations. This is not much of a restriction, since they should normally be given in the preamble.

For example, each chapter of a book might be written to a separate file with names chap1.tex, chap2.tex, ... The processing file itself contains the text

```
\documentclass{book}
   . . . . . . . . . . . . . . . .
   \includeonly{...}
\begin{document}
   \frontmatter
    \include{toc}
   \mainmatter
    \include{chap1}
    \include{chap2}
     . . .
   \backmatter
    \include{back}
\end{document}
```

where the file toc.tex contains only commands for the title page, table of contents, and other listings:

```
\begin{titlepage} ... \end{titlepage}
\tableofcontents \listoftables \listoffigures
```

and back.tex for the bibliography and index:

```
\bibliography{..}
\printindex
```

The chapters to be processed are selected by adding them to the argument of \includeonly, not by changing the \include commands, which must always be present to ensure that all the .aux are input every time. For example, by giving \includeonly{toc,chap3}, one processes the table of contents and chapter 3.

Package:
exclude-
only
The excludeonly package by Donald Arseneau can produce just the opposite effect: With \excludeonly{*filenames*}, all files are processed except those listed. If both \includeonly and \excludeonly are given, only those files are processed that are permitted by both. Thus,

```
\includeonly{file1, file2}
\excludeonly{file1, file3}
```

will include only file2. By adding the package option only, this behavior is altered so that \includeonly is overridden and all files, except file1 and file3, are included.

11.1.3 Interactive messages

There are times when LaTeX should write a message to the computer monitor. This can be achieved with the command

> `\typeout{`*message*`}`

where *message* stands for the text that is to appear on the monitor. This text is printed when the LaTeX processing reaches this command. It is also written to the transcript file, but does not appear in the processed output.

If *message* contains a user-defined command, it will be interpreted, and its translation appears on the monitor. The same thing applies to LaTeX commands. This could have dire consequences if the commands, either user or LaTeX, are not really printable. To print the command name literally, precede it with the command `\protect`.

The command

> `\typein[\`*com_name*`]{`*message*`}`

also writes the *message* text to the monitor, but then it waits for the user to enter a line of text from the keyboard, terminated by typing the ⟨*return*⟩ key. If the optional argument `\`*com_name* is missing, the line of text is inserted directly into the processing. In this way, one could, for example, reuse the same text for a letter for several addressees, entering the name each time from the keyboard. Suppose the text contains

> `Dear \typein{Name:}\\ ...`

then what appears on the monitor is:

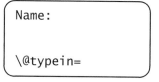

At this point, one enters the name of the recipient. If on successive processings 'George', 'Fred', and 'Mary' are entered, the result will be a set of identical letters differing only in their salutations as 'Dear George', 'Dear Fred', and 'Dear Mary'.

If the `\typein` command contains the optional argument `\`*com_name*, this is treated the same as

> `\typeout{`*message*`} \newcommand{\`*com_name*`}{`*entered definition*`}`

In this case the definition is stored under the command name `\`*com_name* interactively and may be invoked and executed in the rest of the document like any other LaTeX command.

With some experience in LaTeX methodology, it soon becomes obvious that *interactive* processing with the `\typein` command can be very practical. For example, if the preamble contains

> `\typein[\files]{Which files?}`
> `\includeonly{\files}`

the following appears on the monitor:

```
Which files?


\files=
```

Now LATEX waits for the user to type in the names of one or more files (separated by commas) to be processed. This avoids having to modify the main processing file with an editor every time.

A similar procedure may be employed when a form letter is to be sent to various recipients. One can enter the name and address and even the salutation interactively. Complete forms may be processed by LATEX in this way, with the entries being made from the keyboard.

Warning: The \typein command may not be used as the argument of another LATEX command! It may, however, be given in environments such as minipage.

Exercise 11.2: Change the main file from Exercise 11.1 so that the files exer1.tex, exer2.tex, and exer3.tex may be read in with the \include command. Arrange it so that you can determine interactively which of the files is to be processed.

Exercise 11.3: Generate output of the form

Certificate
Olympic Spring Games
Walterville 1992

Finger Wrestling

Gold	A. T. Glitter	AUR	7999.9	Points
Silver	S. Lining	ARG	7777.7	Points
Bronze	H. D. Tarnish	CUP	7250.0	Points

so that the following enquiries appear on the monitor one after the other:

Message	Command=	Input
Sport:	\@typein=	Finger Wrestling
Unit:	\unit =	Points
Gold:	\@typein=	A. T. Glitter
Country:	\@typein=	AUR
Value:	\@typein=	7999.9
Silver:	\@typein=	S. Lining
. . .	. . . =	. . .

and the appropriate entries are made interactively. The third column contains the answers necessary to produce the above sample output. Repeat the program with different entries. Let your imagination run wild.

11.2   In-text references

In a longer text, one often wants to refer to other chapters, sections, tables, and figures, or to pages where some other description has been given. One also needs an index of certain keywords that occur throughout the document. In the days before electronic text processing, such cross-references and indices meant an enormous amount of extra work for the author or secretary. Today the computer can alleviate much of this burden.

In the old days, referring to earlier parts of the text by page number was tedious but feasible. Referencing future parts that had not yet been written had to be limited to section numbers since the page numbers were not yet known, or space had to be left for the page number to be entered at a later date.

The production of a book is usually a progressive and constantly shifting process. The manuscript may not necessarily be written in the order in which it is to appear, and even once the initial draft version is finished, there will be major changes due to new considerations by the author or to knowledgeable advice from reviewers. Revisions, deletions, and insertions of entire sections or even chapters are commonplace, not to mention possible reordering of parts of the text.

LaTeX relegates all the problems associated with such major alterations to the past. No matter what changes the author makes, the information necessary for the cross-references and keyword index is stored for use at any point in the text.

11.2.1 Cross-references

As is already pointed out in several places, the command

> \label{*marker*}

is used to store the current value of the relevant counter (`section`, `equation`, etc.) at that point in the text, which may then be referred to at other places. The value is assigned to the key *marker*, which may be any combination of letters, numbers, and characters, even those that are normally special symbols.

The page number on which the \label command was issued can be printed with

> \pageref{*marker*}

at any point earlier or later in the document.

If the \label command is given after a sectioning command; within an `equation`, `eqnarray`; or `enumerate` environment; or inside the argument of a \caption within the `figure` or `table` environments, the command

> \ref{*marker*}

prints the number of that section, equation, figure, table, or enumeration that was current when *marker* was defined, and in the correct format. For `enumerate`, the same number is printed as is generated by the \item command where the \label appeared. Reference may also be made to theorem-like structures created by a \newtheorem command if the \label is given within the text of that theorem command. For example, a \label with marker text bo-wei was issued in the text of the Bolzano–Weierstrass theorem on page 80:

```
\begin{theorem}[Balzano--Weierstrass]
          \label{bo-wei}...\end{theorem}
```

so that the input text

```
Theorem~\ref{bo-wei} on page~\pageref{bo-wei}
```

generates the output 'Theorem 1 on page 80'. Similarly, the input text

```
for Table~\ref{budget04} on page~\pageref{budget04},
see also Section~\ref{sec:figref}
```

produces 'for Table 9.1 on page 174, see also Section 9.6', since that section contains the marker `\label{sec:figref}`.

Note that the counter whose value is stored by the `\label` command depends on the context in which the command is given. This is normally fairly self-evident. Within regular text, it will be the counter and its value for the last-issued sectioning command, which might not be immediately visible. Therefore, when reference to a section number is desired, it is best to place the `\label` command immediately after the appropriate sectioning command, or even within its argument, as part of the title text. This is in fact the recommended method. Put the `\label` command within the body of the text only when you want to refer to the page number at that point.

A list of all label markers, their translations, and page numbers may be produced by processing the file `lablst.tex`, provided with the LaTeX installation.

11.2.2 How cross-referencing works

!

It is useful to know how the cross-referencing information is managed. What the `\label` command actually does is to write the key name together with the current value of the appropriate counter(s) and the current page number to an auxiliary file with the root name of the document file plus the extension `.aux`. The `\ref` and `\pageref` commands obtain their information from this `.aux` file, which is read in at the beginning of the next processing by the `\begin{document}` command. The same situation as for the table of contents (Section 3.4.2) also applies here: On the first run, the `.aux` file does not exist so that no cross-reference information can be output; instead, the information is gathered and written to a new `.aux` file at the end of the run. A warning message is printed at the end if the auxiliary information has changed and a new run is necessary.

If selective processing is being done with `\includeonly` and a set of `\include` commands, then an `.aux` file exists for each included files, as well as for the main source file. These `.aux` files are read in on every processing run whether or not the corresponding `.tex` file is input. In this way, counter and cross-referencing information for the entire document is maintained even when only parts of it are processed.

11.2.3 Referencing parts of other documents

Package:
xr

It is possible to refer to the marker keys in another LaTeX document by means of David Carlisle's xr package, which is part of the tools collection (Section B.5.4). With

```
\externaldocument{filename}
```

all the keys in the specified file become available in the current document, to be printed with \ref{*key*} as usual. Difficulties arise if there are duplicate key names in any of the external or current files. To circumvent this problem, an optional argument can be given, for example, as \externaldocument[x-]{*filename*}, in which case all the markers in the external file will be prefixed with x-. Thus the external key intro is referred to with \ref{x-intro}.

11.2.4 Smart referencing: the varioref package

Package:
varioref
When the object being referenced is so close that you know it will be on the same or adjacent page, you very likely will want to alter the text accordingly. However, it might later switch from 'same' to 'adjacent' after another revision and then you will have to change that text once more. The tools package varioref by Frank Mittelbach does this for you. It defines a command \vref{*key*}, which is almost the same as '\ref{*key*} on page \pageref{*key*}'. However, if \label{*key*} is on the current, previous, or next page, it prints appropriate text. Thus depending on the relative locations, Fig. \vref{f1} automatically produces one of the following:

Fig. 5	*when \label on same page,*
Fig. 5 on the preceding page	*on previous page,*
Fig. 5 on the next page	*on following page,*
Fig. 5 on the facing page	*on opposite page with twoside option,*
Fig. 5 on page 24	*when two or more pages away.*

The command \vpageref prints only the page part of the text, or 'on this page' if \label{*key*} is on the current page. It may also take one or two optional arguments: the texts for the current page and non-current pages. For example, the example \vpageref[above]{f1} prints one of these texts:

the example above	*when \label on same page,*
the example on the next page	*on following page,*
the example on page 24	*when two of more pages away,*

while the \vpageref[above example][example]{f1} outputs one of these:

the above example	*when \label on same page,*
the example on the next page	*on the following page,*
the example on page 24	*when two of more pages away.*

A range of numbers and pages can be produced with the command \vrefrange, which takes two mandatory arguments, both label keys. It prints text like '5 to 7 on pages 212–214', or '5 to 7 on the next page', and so on. It takes one optional argument, the text to print when both labels are on the current page.

The page part of \vrefrange only is printed with \vpagerefrange, which also takes two mandatory (label key) arguments and one optional (text) one. If both labels are on the same page, it behaves like \vpageref; the optional argument is printed if both are on the current page.

Since English text is automatically printed by the above commands, they would not be very useful for documents, say, in Italian. The `varioref` package therefore accepts all the language options recognized by the `babel` system (Chapter 14) to reprogram the texts. With the option `italian`, one will get texts such as *in questa pagina* for 'on this page' and *nella pagina precedente* for 'on the preceding page', and so on.

All the texts are stored in special commands that can be redefined by the user:

`\reftextbefore`	previous but non-facing page
`\reftextfacebefore`	previous but facing page
`\reftextafter`	next but non-facing page
`\reftextfaceafter`	next but facing page
`\reftextfaraway{`*key*`}`	more than one page away
`\reftextpagerange{`*key1*`}{`*key2*`}`	page range of 2 labels
`\reftextlabelrange{`*key1*`}{`*key2*`}`	range of 2 different labels.

The last three must be redefined with 1 or 2 arguments, as

```
\renewcommand{\reftextfaraway}[1]{on page \pageref{#1}}
\renewcommand{\reftextpagerange}[2]{on pages \pageref{#1}%
                                      --\pageref{#2}}
\renewcommand{\reftextlabelrange}[2]{\ref{#1} to \ref{#2}}
```

There is also `\reftextvario{`*text1*`}{`*text2*`}` to provide alternating texts for the above commands so that the same text is not printed every time.

11.3 Bibliographies

Academic publications normally include a list of references, or bibliography, containing the names of other works that are cited within the text by means of a running number. This is the system supported by standard LATEX, described in the next section. The alternative citation method, with author name and year of publication, can be achieved with various extension packages, as described in Section 11.3.4.

Often the bibliography has not been finalized before the main text is started. Especially for numerical bibliographies, it would be a great nuisance to have to go through the whole text and change all the numbering every time something was added to the bibliography. Therefore, LATEX is programmed not only to format the bibliography but also to keep track of its alterations and additions in order to modify the references in the text automatically.

The bibliography is generated most conveniently and efficiently from a general database with the help of the BibTEX program that should be part of the LATEX installation. How to prepare such databases is explained in Chapter 12. The advantage of a database is that its entries can be reused again and again for all future documents, while the formatting style in each bibliography listing can vary according to the requirements of each document. One can, however, write it by hand without BibTEX.

11.3.1 Bibliography by hand

The actual bibliography, whether created by BibTeX or by hand, is placed inside the environment

```
\begin{thebibliography}{sample_label}
   entries
\end{thebibliography}
```

The individual *entries* in the bibliography each begin with the command

```
\bibitem[label]{key} entry_text
```

Without the optional argument *label*, \bibitem produces a running number in square brackets as the label for the reference in the text. With *label*, one can give whatever indicator one wishes, such as an abbreviation of the author's name or an arbitrary reference number. The mandatory argument *key* is a reference key, much like that for the cross-referencing \label command (page 211), which is used to make the actual citation in the main text. The key name can be made up of any combination of letters, numbers, and symbols except commas.

The bibliography information itself is contained in *entry_text*, such as 'author, title, publisher, year, edition, page numbers', possibly in various typefaces. The output text will be indented after the first line by a width equal to that of the *sample_label*, so this should be as large as the longest label in the bibliography. For the standard application with running numbers, *sample_label* should be a dummy number with as many digits as the largest label (for example, 99 if there are more than 10 but less than 100 entries).

For bibliographies with author–year citations (Section 11.3.4) the entries in the thebibliography are the same, except that the optional *label* must be present, taking a special form that will transfer the author and year texts to the citation commands.

A sample (numerical) thebibliography environment could look as follows:

```
\begin{thebibliography}{99}
 \bibitem{lamport} Leslie Lamport. \textsl{\LaTeX\ -- A Document
    Preparation System}, 2nd edition.  Addison-Wesley,
    Reading, MA, 1994
    . . . . . . . .
 \bibitem{knuth} Donald E. Knuth. \textsl{Computers and
    Typesetting Vol.\ A--E}. Addison-Wesley,
    Reading, MA, 1986
\bibitem[6a]{knuth:a} Vol A: \textsl{The {\TeX}book}, 1986
    . . . . . . . .
 \bibitem[6e]{knuth:e} Vol E: \textsl{Computer Modern
    Typefaces}, 1986
\end{thebibliography}
```

Here lamport, knuth, and knuth:a have been chosen as keys. The sample label is given as 99 since a two-digit number produces sufficient indentation for the standard form of \bibitem. The entry with the key knuth is the sixth in the list and thus it automatically receives the label [6]; in order for its sub-entries `knuth:a` ... `knuth:e` to be printed as [6a] ... [6e], it is necessary to set their optional *label* arguments to `6a` ... `6e`. (Yes, this does violate the automatic labeling system.)

The bibliography is normally printed near the end of the document by placing the `thebibliography` environment at the desired location. For document classes `book` and `report`, the word **Bibliography** appears as an unnumbered chapter title at the beginning, whereas for `article` the word **References** is written as an unnumbered section heading. The above sample bibliography appears as:

[1] Leslie Lamport. *LaTeX – A Document Preparation System*, 2nd edition. Addison-Wesley Co., Inc., Reading, MA, 1994

. . . .

[6] Donald E. Knuth. *Computers and Typesetting Vol. A–E*. Addison-Wesley Co., Inc., Reading, MA, 1986

[6a] Vol A: *The TeXbook*, 1986

. . . .

[6e] Vol E: *Computer Modern Typefaces*, 1986

Exercise 11.4: *Produce a bibliography with the `thebibliography` environment, with a label consisting of the first three letters of the author's name followed by the last digits of the year of publication. If the same author has more than one work in a given year, add a running letter to distinguish them, for example, knu86c, knu86d. With such labels, it is appropriate to make the reference keys the same as the labels. The indentation depth should be 1.5 cm. Note: The indentation depth is determined by the argument sample_label in the `thebibliography` environment. This is usually a dummy text with the right width. This width can be given precisely with \hspace{width}.*

Exercise 11.5: *Copy the `thebibliography` environment from the above exercise to the end of your standard exercise file (but ahead of the \end{document} command). Refer to the entries in the bibliography by inserting \cite commands into your text. Make sure that the key in the \cite command is written exactly as in the \bibitem command in the `thebibliography` environment.*

11.3.2 Bibliography with BibTeX

Bibliographic databases and the BibTeX program are fully described in Chapter 12. Here we just review the essential aspects for the LaTeX source file.

- All the information for the literature references is placed in one or more databases. Each entry is given an identifying key (the *key* in the \bibitem argument), which is the handle to refer to it.

- In the source text, citations to the references are made with various commands, such as \cite, \citet, \citep, taking the *key* as argument.

- The *bibliography style* must be specified somewhere in the document with \bibliographystyle{*bib_style*}; the *bib_style* determines how the bibliography is to be formatted; the basic style is `plain` for numerical citations or `plainnat` with the `natbib` package.

- Give the command \bibliography{*database*} where the bibliography is to appear; *database* is a list of all databases to be searched.

- Process the source file with LaTeX; run BibTeX and then LaTeX twice.

BibTeX writes a bibliography following the formatting specifications of *bib_style* into a thebibliography environment, storing it in a file with extension .bbl; this file is input by the \bibliography command.

11.3.3 Numerical citations

Standard LaTeX can only handle numerical bibliographies and citations. In this case, the citation in the text is made with the command

```
\cite[extra]{key}
```

where *key* is the reference key that appears in the \bibitem command. With the sample bibliography on page 215, the source text

```
For additional information about \LaTeX\ and \TeX\ see
\cite{lamport} and \cite{knuth,knuth:a}.
```

yields: For additional information about LaTeX and TeX see [1] and [6, 6a].

If the optional argument *extra* is included in the \cite command, this text is added after the label(s) but still inside the square brackets.

```
The creation of a bibliographic database is described in
\cite[Appendix B]{lamport}, while the program \BibTeX\
itself is explained in \cite[pages 74, 75]{lamport}.
```

The creation of a bibliographic database is described in [1, Appendix B], while the program BibTeX itself is explained in [1, pages 74, 75].

11.3.4 Author-year bibliographies with natbib

An alternative bibliographic citation style, used in this book and in many scientific journals, makes reference to other published works by citing the author's name and year of publication. In this case, the entries in the bibliographic listing are not numbered. The citation itself may be either parenthetical [*Jones et al.*, 1999] or textual, as shown by *Jones et al.* [1999]. There may be some variations within this style: For example, in this book parentheses are used in place of square brackets and the name is left in normal type. None of this is supported by standard LaTeX, but rather by additional packages.

There are a number of packages developed to deal with this situation, each requiring a different syntax for the optional *label* argument in the \bibitem command in order to transfer the author and year information to the citation commands. And each has its own bibliography style (.bst) file to allow BibTeX to accomplish this.

Package: natbib   The natbib package by Patrick W. Daly is the most universal of these, being compatible with the \bibitem syntaxes, and thus with the .bst files, of other author-year packages such as `apalike`, `chicago`, and `harvard`, to name just a few. Furthermore, `natbib` can even produce numerical or superscript citations as well, and it will also function with the standard (numerical) bibliography styles and \bibitem syntax, albeit only with numerical citations.

Furthermore, `natbib` is integrated with the `hyperref` package (Section 13.2.4) to make citations into automatic links to the bibliographic entry.

The author-year \bibitem

The required `natbib` form of the 'optional' *label* argument to \bibitem within the thebibliography environment is

\bibitem [*short(year)long*] {*key*} ...

where *short* is the short author list (for example, `Jones et al.`) and *long* is an optional full author list. A sample bibliography might be:

```
\begin{thebibliography}{99}
\bibitem[James et al.(2001)James, Jones, and Smith]{JAM01}
   P. R. James, F. J. Jones, and R. T. Smith, ... 2001.
\bibitem[Jones et al.(1999)Jones, Baker, and Toms]{JON99}
   F. J. Jones, H. P. Baker, and W. V. Toms, ... 1999.
\bibitem[Jones et al.(2000a)Jones, Toms, and Baker]{JON00}
   F. J. Jones, W. V. Toms, and H. P. Baker, ... 2000a.
\bibitem[Jones et al.(2000b)Jones, Toms, and Baker]{JON00b}
   F. J. Jones, W. V. Toms, and H. P. Baker, ... 2000b.
\end{thebibliography}
```

Such bibliographies will be automatically produced by BIBTEX when a bibliography style is invoked with the \bibliographystyle command that is compatible with `natbib`. Three such .bst files are provided with `natbib`, as substitutes for three of the four basic BIBTEX styles: `plainnat`, `unsrtnat`, and `abbrvnat` (Section 12.1). However, many others also exist as contributions for specific publishers and journals.

Author-year citations

There is a flexible citation syntax permitting parenthetical (\citep) and textual (\citet) citations, with the abbreviated or full author list, and with optional notes both before and after the citations. For example,

\citet{JON99}	⇒	Jones et al., (1999)
\citet[pg.˜22]{JON99}	⇒	Jones et al., (1999, pg. 22)
\citep{JON99}	⇒	(Jones et al., 1999)
\citep[pg.˜22]{JON99}	⇒	(Jones et al., 1999, pg. 22)
\citep[e.g.,][]{JON99}	⇒	(e.g., Jones et al., 1999)
\citep[e.g.,][pg.˜22]{JON99}	⇒	(e.g., Jones et al., 1999, pg. 22)
\citet*{JON99}	⇒	Jones, Baker, and Toms (1999)
\citep*{JON00}	⇒	(Jones, Toms, and Baker, 2000)

The citation punctuation (type of brackets, points between multiple citations, dates, and so on) can be selected by options when loaded, specified by declarations, or programmed to be associated with the bibliography style. See below.

Multiple citations are available as usual, with compression of repeated authors:

`\citet{JON99,JAM01}`	⇒	Jones et al. (1999); James et al. (2001)
`\citep{JON99,JAM01}`	⇒	(Jones et al., 1999; James et al., 2001)
`\citep{JON99,JON00}`	⇒	(Jones et al., 1999, 2000a)
`\citep{JON00,JON00b}`	⇒	(Jones et al., 2000a,b)

In numerical citation mode, the command `\citep` behaves like the standard `\cite` command, printing the reference's number in brackets, while `\citet` gives the authors' names followed by the reference's number. This is textual citation in numerical mode, allowing the author to use the same syntax for both citation modes.

`\citet{JON99}`	⇒	Jones et al. [21]
`\citet[pg.~22]{JON99}`	⇒	Jones et al. [21, pg. 22]
`\citep{JON99}`	⇒	[21]
`\citep[pg.~22]{JON99}`	⇒	[21, pg. 22]
`\citep[e.g.][]{JON99}`	⇒	[e.g. 21]
`\citep[e.g.][pg.~22]{JON99}`	⇒	[e.g. 21, pg. 22]
`\citep{JON00,JON00b}`	⇒	[21, 32]

The commands `\citeauthor{`*key*`}` and `\citeyear{`*key*`}` print just the author names and year, respectively; a starred version `\citeauthor` prints the full author list.

There also exist capitalized variants of these citation commands, `\Citet`, and so on, for use at the beginning of a sentence, when the first author name begins with something like 'von'.

`\citet{delaM89}` has shown ...	⇒	de la Mar has shown ...
`\Citet{delaM89}` has shown ...	⇒	De la Mar has shown ...

Package options

Many aspects of formatting the citations can be controlled by options specified when loading `natbib` with the `\usepackage` command:

`round`   citations in round parentheses (default)

`square`   citations in square brackets

`curly`   citations in curly braces

`angle`   citations in angle brackets

`colon`   to separate multiple citations with semicolons (default)

`comma`   to use commas as separators

`authoryear`
> for author-year citations (default)

`numbers`
> for numerical citations

`super`   for superscripted numerical citations

`sectionbib`
> puts the bibliography in a section instead a chapter; for use with the `chapterbib` package (Section 11.3.5)

`sort`   orders multiple citations into the sequence in which they appear in the list of references

`sort&compress`
> as `sort` but in addition multiple numerical citations are compressed if possible (as 3–6, 15)

`longnamesfirst`
> makes the first citation of any reference the equivalent of the starred variant (full author list) and subsequent citations normal (abbreviated list)

Note: `natbib` defaults to author-year citations, but if any single `\bibitem` command does not conform to any of the recognized author-year syntaxes, it will switch automatically to numerical citations.

Further customizations

There are several formatting commands in `natbib` that may be (re)defined by the author to achieve special effects in the bibliography, such as font or spacing between entries. In standard LaTeX, these are all fixed.

`\bibsection`
> can be redefined to the desired sectioning command for introducing the list of references. This is normally `\section*` or `\chapter*`.

`\bibpreamble`
> is printed after the bibliography heading but before the actual list of references; it is normally undefined, but can be defined to insert any desired leading text.

`\bibfont`
> can be a font declaration, for example, `\small` to apply to the whole list of references; it is normally undefined.

`\citenumfont`
> can be a font declaration or command such as `\itshape` or `\textit` for formatting numerical citations; it is normally undefined.

`\bibnumfmt`

> is a command with an argument to format the numbers in the list of references; the default definition is [#1].

`\bibhang`

> is the indentation after the first line of each reference; change this with the `\setlength` command.

`\bibsep`

> is the vertical spacing between references; change this with the `\setlength` command.

There are many other customization possibilities and specialized features to `natbib` that can be found in the supplied documentation (process `natbib.dtx` if is it not already provided as a `.dvi` or `.pdf` file) or in the short summary `natnotes.tex`.

11.3.5 Multiple bibliographies

Package:
chapter-
bib

In standard LaTeX, with or without BibTeX, there can only be one bibliography per document. However, it is not uncommon for a book to consist of independent chapters, each with its own bibliography and local citations.

The `chapterbib` package by Donald Arseneau solves this problem. It requires that the document be broken up into individual source files that are read into the main file with the `\include` command of Section 11.1.2. Each such file must contain its own `thebibliography` environment, or its own `\bibliographystyle` and `\bibliography` commands if BibTeX is to be used. The citation commands will work locally within each file. Even if the same reference appears in several bibliographies, with a different number each time, the citations will refer to the one in the local file.

One must process BibTeX individually on each of the separate files, creating a series of `.bbl` files. Then the document is reprocessed with LaTeX, at least twice; the `.bbl` files are read in by the individual `\bibliography` commands.

If you cannot make use of the `\include` commands because you do not want each file to begin on a new page, you can still localize the bibliographies and their citations with the `cbunit` environment. This does not work with BibTeX, however. In that case, you must still put the bibliographic units into separate files, and then read them in with the `\cbinput{file}` command. Set the package option `draft` when loading `chapterbib`, and process with LaTeX, process each file with BibTeX, remove the `draft` option, and process with LaTeX at least twice.

With classes `book` and `report`, the bibliography is placed in an unnumbered chapter; this is undesirable if each chapter is to have its own bibliography. In this case, add the package option `sectionbib` to change the bibliography to an unnumbered section instead.

The `chapterbib` package is compatible with `natbib` except for the `sectionbib` option. The two packages clash on their redefinitions of bibliography. In this case, add the option to `natbib` instead of to `chapterbib`.

11.4   Keyword index

LaTeX itself does not produce a keyword index automatically as it does a table of contents, but it can prepare input data for the MakeIndex program (Section 11.4.3) that does generate such an index in a form that LaTeX can use on a later run.

11.4.1   The index environment

A keyword index is formatted in the environment

> \begin{theindex} *index_entries* \end{theindex}

that switches to a two-column page format with a running head *INDEX*. The first page of the index carries the heading **Index** in the same size as a chapter heading for the book and `report` document classes, and as a section heading for the `article` class. (More precisely, the actual word printed is contained in the command \indexname that may be redefined for other languages.) The individual entries are made with commands

> \item \subitem \subsubitem and \indexspace

followed by the keywords and their page numbers. For example,

commands, 18	`\item commands, 18`
arguments, 19, 101	`\subitem arguments, 19, 101`
multiple, 103, 104	`\subsubitem multiple, 103, 104`
replacement symbol, 20	`\subsubitem replacement symbol, 20`
as environments, 42	`\subitem as environments, 42`
used as arguments for sec-	`\subitem used as arguments for`
tioning commands, 41, 42	`sectioning commands, 41, 42`
	`\indexspace`
displayed text, 21-32	`\item displayed text, 21--32`

If the text entry is too long for one line, it is broken and continued on the next line, indented deeper than all other lines, as in the above example 'used as argument for sectioning commands, 41, 42'. The command \indexspace leaves a blank line in the index.

11.4.2   Preparing the index entries

The `theindex` environment only sets up a suitable format for the index. The entries themselves, as well as their page numbers, are generated by the MakeIndex program described in Section 11.4.3. This program requires input information from the LaTeX file in the form of unsorted keywords and page numbers. The author enters this information in the text file with the command

> \index{*index_entry*}

where *index_entry* is the text to be entered into the index. It may contain any combination of letters, numbers, and symbols *including even command characters and blanks*. This means that even commands may be included in the *index_entry*, such as \index{\LaTeX\ logo}. Even the one command that may otherwise never be used as an argument, \verb, may be included. However, if *index_entry* does contain a command, \index may not be used as an argument of another command.

Normally all the \index commands are ignored by LaTeX and do absolutely nothing. They are activated only when the preamble contains the command

\makeindex

in which case, a file with the document's root name plus the extension .idx is opened. Now the \index commands write *index_entry* and the current page number to this file in the form

\indexentry{*index_entry*}{*pagenumber*}

It is this .idx file that is the input to the MakeIndex program. There are special symbols that may be used in the *index_entry* to indicate main and subitems and other refinements.

The MakeIndex program expects the \index entries to be of one of the three forms:

\index{*main_entry*}
\index{*main_entry*!*sub_entry*}
\index{*main_entry*!*sub_entry*!*sub_sub_entry*}

The individual main and subentries may contain any combination of characters with the exceptions of !, @, and |. The exclamation point is the divider between the various entry fields. If the \index command contains only a main entry, this will become the text for an \item command. The main entries will be in alphabetical order.

If the \index command contains a main and a subentry, the text *sub_entry* will be assigned to a \subitem command underneath the corresponding *main_entry*. The texts for the \subitem will also be in alphabetical order. Similarly the text of a *sub_sub_entry* will appear following a \subsubitem command, alphabetically ordered, below the appropriate *sub_entry* text.

The main and subentries may also contain special characters and even LaTeX commands that are to be neglected during alphabetization. This is indicated by an entry of the form *lex_entry*@*print_entry*, in which *lex_entry* is used for the alphabetical ordering while *print_entry* is the actual text to be output. For example, in the keyword index in this book, which was generated with MakeIndex, all the command names appear as input text and are ordered without the preceding \ character. These entries were made in the text as \index{put@\verb=\put=}.

An entry may be terminated with the character sequences |(or |) to designate the beginning and end of a range of page numbers. For example,

\index{table|(}   on page 105
\index{table|)}   on page 119

produces the entry 'table' with page numbers given as 105–119.

Instead of having the page number printed after the entry, a reference may be made to another index entry. For example, with

```
\index{space|see{blank}}
\index{table|seealso{array}}
```

the entries 'space, *see* blank' and 'table, *see also* array' are made in the index.

The three characters !, @, and | therefore have special functions for the MakeIndex program. To print these characters literally as text without their functions, the *quote* character " must precede them. For example, "! represents a literal exclamation point and not the entry divider.

The quote character itself is thus a fourth special symbol and must be entered literally as "". However, there is a special rule in MakeIndex syntax that says a quote character preceded by a backslash will be interpreted as part of a command: Thus \" may be used to put a German umlaut in an entry (as in \index{Knappen, J\"org}). This special rule can lead to additional problems at times: In this book the index entry \! had to be typed as "\"!.

It is possible to specify varying fonts for the page number. For example, in the index of this book, page numbers are set in boldface to indicate the page where a command is defined or first explained. This is achieved with an entry of the form

```
\index{blank}            on page 11, and
\index{blank|textbf}     on page 26
```

which in the second case puts the page number for this entry as the argument of a command \textbf. The line in the theindex environment becomes

```
\item blank, 11, \textbf{26}
```

Note: The vertical bar in the \index entry is not a typing error, but must replace the backslash as the LaTeX command symbol under these circumstances.

There is a file idx.tex in the LaTeX installation, which can improve the readability of the .idx files. By processing the idx.tex file (that is, calling latex idx), the user is prompted for the name of the .idx file to list:

```
**********************************
* Enter idx file's first Name. *
**********************************

\filename=
```

After the root name of the .idx file has been entered from the keyboard, a two-column page format is output containing the *index_entry* texts listed under page headings of the form **Page n**. No further information is obtained through such a formatted listing, but it is far easier to work with than a straightforward output of the .idx file alone.

Even if the \index commands have no effect without the \makeindex command in the preamble, it is a good idea to include them in the text from the initial development of the document. The \makeindex command can be included later when the final version of the document is ready. At this point, the MakeIndex program can be run to produce the theindex environment from the data in the .idx file just as BibTeX produces thebibliography environments. This tool is described in the next section.

Package:
showidx
The LaTeX installation also contains the package showidx, which prints the index entries from the \index commands as marginal notes, beginning at the top of the page on which they occur. This is useful for going through a preliminary version of the document to check that all index entries are really on the proper page or whether additional entries have to be made.

If showidx is used, it is a good idea to increase the width of the marginal note box with the declaration \marginparwidth (Section 5.2.6) in the preamble. Unfortunately, the present book format is not suitable for such a demonstration.

11.4.3 Running MakeIndex

The tiresome drudgery of making up the theindex environment for a keyword index can be dispensed with if the program MakeIndex is available. This program was written by Pehong Chen with the support of Leslie Lamport. We will give only an abbreviated description of its use here. More details are in the documentation accompanying the program package.

The program MakeIndex processes the .idx file, producing as output another file with the root name of the document and the extension .ind, containing the complete theindex environment. It is run by clicking the appropriate icon in the editor shell or from a command line with

makeindex *root_name*.idx or simply makeindex *root_name*

Package:
makeidx
The next LaTeX processing outputs the index at the location of the \printindex command which, together with the \see command, is defined in the package makeidx. Thus the production of an index in this way requires the package file makeidx to be loaded with the \usepackage command.

The alphabetical ordering of MakeIndex normally follows the standard ASCII code, first *symbols*, then *digits*, and finally *letters*, where uppercase comes before lowercase. Blanks are included as symbols. There are a number of options that allow these rules to be changed. How the options are invoked when the program is called depends on the computer type, but we assume here a hyphen preceding the option letter, as in

makeindex -g -l *root_name*

The most important options are:

-l   Letter ordering: Blanks are ignored when sorting.

-c   Compress blanks: Multiple and leading blanks are removed as they are in normal LaTeX,

-g   German ordering: Following the German rules in which *symbols* precede *letters* (*lower-* before *upper*case) which precede *numbers*; the sequences "a, "o, "u, and "s (the codes for ä, ö, ü, and ß in the usual LaTeX adaptations for German) are treated as though they were ae, oe, ue, and ss, which is standard German practice,

-s   Style specification: Allows the name of an index formatting file to be in-
          cluded to redefine the functioning of MakeIndex.

The -s option reads in an index style file containing commands to define both the
input and output of the MakeIndex program. For example, it is possible to change
the special symbols !, @, |, and " so that different characters execute their functions
and they themselves revert to being pure text.

The style-defining file consists of a list of pairs in the form *keyword attribute*. The
attribute is either one character in single quotes (for example, 'z') or a character
string in double quotes (for example, "a string"). The most important keywords,
together with their default definitions, are:

quote   '"' defines the quote symbol,

level   '!' defines the entry separation symbol,

actual   '@' defines the lexical switch symbol,

encap   '|' defines the dummy command symbol for page formatting.

There are many more keywords for defining complicated output structures. These
are described in the documentation that should be included with the MakeIndex
program package.

The file makeindex.tex contains a short manual by Leslie Lamport (but without
mentioning style definitions).

11.4.4 Glossary

A 'glossary' is a special index of terms and phrases alphabetically ordered together
with their explanations. To help set up a glossary, LaTeX offers the commands

> \makeglossary   in the preamble and
> \glossary{*glossary_entry*}   in the text part

which function just like the commands for making a keyword index. The entries are
written to a file with extension .glo after the command \makeglossary has been
given in the preamble. The form of these file entries from each \glossary command
is

> \glossaryentry{*glossary_entry*}{*pagenumber*}

The information the .glo file can be used to establish a glossary. However, there is
no equivalent to the theindex environment for a glossary, but a recommended structure is the description environment (Section 4.3.3) or a special list environment
(Section 4.4).

12 Bibliographic Databases and BIBTeX

In academic publications, a bibliography or list of references is standard procedure. In Section 11.3 we describe how a bibliography can be formatted with the `thebibliography` environment and how its entries are referred to within the text. Often authors find that they are constantly referring to the same publications in most of their own papers. Similarly, researchers working in the same field will frequently be referring to the same set of papers. This means that many of the entries in the `thebibliography` environment will be repeated from one work to the next, or even among co-workers at one institute.

It would be very useful if the bibliographic entries could be stored in one database file once and for all to be available for all documents with a list of references in that field. Such a database system is possible with the BIBTeX program supplied with the LaTeX installation. The information about the various publications is stored in one or more files with the extension `.bib`. For each publication there is a *key* that identifies it, and which may be used in the text document to refer to it. Such a file is called a *bibliographic database*.

12.1 The BIBTeX program

BIBTeX is an auxiliary program to LaTeX that automatically constructs a bibliography for a LaTeX document by searching one or more databases. To this end, the LaTeX file must contain the command

> `\bibliography{`*database1, database2, . . .*`}`

at that point in the text where the bibliography is to appear. Here the argument *database1, database2, . . .* is a list of root names, separated by commas, of the bibliographic database files that are to be searched. The extension `.bib` is not explicitly written.

Reference can be made to a publication in one of the databases at any place in the text with the commands

> `\cite{`*key*`}`

```
\citep{key}
\citet{key}
```

as is explained in Sections 11.3.3 and 11.3.4. The *key* is the database identifier for that publication, which of course the user must know beforehand. After the first LATEX processing, the BɪʙTᴇX program must be run either by clicking the appropriate icon in the editor shell or from a command line with `bibtex` plus the root name of the LATEX file. Supposing this source file name is `comets.tex`, the call

```
bibtex comets
```

produces a new file with the name `comets.bbl`, containing the extracted information for those publications for which there was a `\cite` reference, packaged in a `thebibliography` environment to be input into the document on the next LATEX run.

Occasionally the bibliography is to include publications that were *not* referenced in the text. These may be added with the command

```
\nocite{key}
```

given anywhere within the main document. It produces no text at all but simply informs BɪʙTᴇX that this reference is also to be put into the bibliography. With `\nocite{*}`, *every* entry in all the databases will be included, something that is useful when producing a list of all entries and their keys.

After running BɪʙTᴇX to make up the .bbl file, it is necessary to process LATEX *at least twice* to establish both the bibliography and the in-text reference labels. The bibliography will be printed where the `\bibliography` command is issued; it in fact inputs the .bbl file.

The formatting of the bibliography may be selected with the declaration

```
\bibliographystyle{style}
```

which may be issued anywhere in the document. Its only function is to inform BɪʙTᴇX what bibliography style file (.bst) is to be loaded to determine the resulting format. Many contributed .bst files exist, designed for specific journals and publishing houses, and it is possible to create one's own (Section 12.3). However, the supplied standard ones for numerical citation only are:

plain   The entries in the bibliography are ordered alphabetically; each is assigned a running number in square brackets as the in-text reference marker, printed where the `\cite` commands are issued.

unsrt   The entries are ordered according to their first references by the `\cite` and `\nocite` commands. The entry for the first `\cite` receives the number 1, that of the next `\cite` with a different key the number 2, and so on. The markers and listings are otherwise the same as for `plain`.

alpha   The listings are the same as for `plain` but the markers are an abbreviation of the author's name plus year. A reference to Smith (1987) appears as [Smi87]. The entries are ordered alphabetically by marker.

abbrv The ordering and markers are the same as for plain, but the bibliographic
listing is shortened by abbreviating first names, months, and journal names.

For author-year citations and the natbib package (Section 11.3.4), there exist
the bibliographic styles plainnat, unsrtnat, and abbrvnat, producing the same
bibliography format as the corresponding standard styles, but with natbib compatibility.

12.2 Creating a bibliographic database

Creating a bibliographic database might seem like more work than typing up a list of
references with the thebibliography environment; the great advantage is that the
entries need to be included in the database once and only once and are then available
for all future publications. Even if a different bibliography style is demanded in later
works, all the information is already on hand in the database for BibTeX to write a
new thebibliography environment in another format. In fact, we feel that even
for a single document, it is simpler to make an entry into the database than to
adhere to the very precise and fiddly requirements of a literature list, especially
regarding punctuation and positioning of the authors' initials. The database entry
proceeds very quickly and easily if one has a generalized template, as illustrated in
Section 12.2.6.

The entries in a bibliographic database are of the form

```
@BOOK{knuth:86a,
   AUTHOR = "Donald E. Knuth",
   TITLE = {The \TeX{}book},
   EDITION = "third",
   PUBLISHER = "Addison--Wesley",
   ADDRESS = {Reading, Massachusetts},
   YEAR = 1986
}
```

The first word, prefixed with @, determines the *entry_type*, as explained in the
next section. The *entry_type* is followed by the reference information for that entry
enclosed in curly braces { }. The very first entry is the *key* for the whole reference
by which it is referred to in the \cite command. In the above example, this is
knuth:86a. The *key* may be any combination of letters, numerals, and symbols,
except commas. The actual reference information is then entered in various *fields*,
separated from one another by commas. Each *field* consists of a *field_name*, an =
sign, with optional spaces on either side, and the *field text*. The *field_names* shown
above are AUTHOR, TITLE, PUBLISHER, ADDRESS, and YEAR. The *field text* must be
enclosed either in curly braces or in double quotation marks. However, if the text
consists solely of a number, as for YEAR above, the braces or quotation marks may
be left off.

For each entry type, certain fields are *required*, others are *optional*, and the rest are
ignored. These are listed with the descriptions of the various entry types below. If a

required field is omitted, an error message will occur during the B<small>IB</small>T_EX run. Optional fields will have their information included in the bibliography if they are present, but they need not be there. Ignored fields are useful for including extra information in the database that will not be output, such as a comment or an abstract of the paper. Ignored fields might also be ones that are used by other database programs.

The general syntax for entries in the bibliographic database reads

> @*entry_type*{*key*,
> *field_name* = {*field text*},
> . . . .
> *field_name* = {*field text*} }

The names of the *entry_types* as well as the *field_names* may be written in capitals or lowercase letters, or in a combination of both. Thus @BOOK, @book, and @bOOk are all acceptable variations.

The outermost pair of braces for the entire entry may be either curly braces { }, as illustrated, or parentheses ( ). In the latter case, the general syntax reads

> @*entry_type*(*key*, ...)

However, the *field text* may only be enclosed within curly braces {...} or double quotation marks "..." as shown in the example above.

12.2.1 The entry types

The following is a list of the standard entry types in alphabetical order, with a brief description of the types of works for which they are applicable, together with the required and optional fields that they take. The meanings of the fields are explained in the next section.

@article Entry for an article from a journal or magazine.
> *required fields*   author, title, journal, year.
> *optional fields*   volume, number, pages, month, note.

@book Entry for a book with a definite publisher.
> *required fields*   author or editor, title, publisher, year.
> *optional fields*   volume or number, series, address, edition, month, note.

@booklet Entry for a printed and bound work without the name of a publisher or sponsoring organization.
> *required fields*   title.
> *optional fields*   author, howpublished, address, month, year, note.

@conference Is the same as @inproceedings below.

@inbook Entry for a part (chapter, section, certain pages) of a book.
> *required fields*   author or editor, title, chapter and/or pages, publisher, year.
> *optional fields*   volume or number, series, type, address, edition, month, note.

@incollection Entry for part of a book that has its own title.
  required fields   author, title, booktitle, publisher, year.
  optional fields   editor, volume or number, series, type, chapter, pages, address, edition, month, note.

@inproceedings Entry for an article in conference proceedings.
  required fields   author, title, booktitle, year.
  optional fields   editor, volume or number, series, pages, address, month, organization, publisher, note.

@manual Entry for technical documentation.
  required fields   title.
  optional fields   author, organization, address, edition, month, year, note.

@mastersthesis Entry for a Master's thesis.
  required fields   author, title, school, year.
  optional fields   type, address, month, note.

@misc Entry for a work that does not fit under any of the others.
  required fields   none.
  optional fields   author, title, howpublished, month, year, note.

@phdthesis Entry for a PhD thesis.
  required fields   author, title, school, year.
  optional fields   type, address, month, note.

@proceedings Entry for conference proceedings.
  required fields   title, year.
  optional fields   editor, volume or number, series, address, month, organization, publisher, note.

@techreport Entry for a report published by a school or other institution, usually as part of a series.
  required fields   author, title, institution, year.
  optional fields   type, number, address, month, note.

@unpublished Entry for an unpublished work with an author and title.
  required fields   author, title, note.
  optional fields   month, year.

Each entry type may also have the optional fields key and crossref. The former provides additional information for alphabetizing the entries, especially when the author information is missing. The author information is normally found in the author field but may also be in the editor or even organization fields. This key field has nothing to do with the *key* for identifying the entry in the \cite command. The crossref field gives the *key* for another entry in the database that shares many of the information fields, as illustrated in Section 12.2.3.

12.2.2 The fields

The fields that may be used within a bibliographic entry are listed below together with their meanings. They are always given in the form:

> *field_name* = {*field text*}   or
> *field_name* = "*field text*"

address
> The address of the publisher or other institution. For major publishing houses, it is sufficient to give just the city. For smaller publishers, giving the full address is recommended.

annote An annotation that may be used by nonstandard bibliography styles to produce an annotated bibliography. The standard BⁱᵦTₑX styles ignore it.

author The name(s) of the author(s) as described in Section 12.2.4.

booktitle
> The title of a book when only part of it is being cited. See Section 12.2.4 for special considerations on capitalization.

chapter
> A chapter or section number.

crossref
> The key of another entry in the database that shares many of the same field entries. See Section 12.2.3.

edition
> The edition of a book, usually written in full and capitalized, as 'Second'. The standard styles will change it to lowercase as necessary.

editor The name(s) of the editor(s) as described in Section 12.2.4. If there is also an author field, then this gives the editor of the book or collection in which the citation appears.

howpublished
> States anything unusual about the method of publishing. Should be capitalized. Example: 'Privately published'.

institution
> The name of the sponsoring institution for a technical report.

journal
> The name of a journal or magazine. Abbreviations are provided for the most common ones (see Section 12.2.5).

key
> An addition for alphabetizing purposes when the author information is missing. This is not the same as the *key* for identifying the entry to a \cite command.

month   The month in which the work was published or, if unpublished, when it was written. Abbreviations exist in the form of the first three letters of the (English) names.

note   Any additional information that should be added. Capitalize the first letter.

number The number of a journal, magazine, technical report, or work in a series. Journals are usually identified by volume and number; technical reports are issued a number by the institution; books in series sometimes have a number given to them.

organization
     The sponsoring organization for a conference or a manual.

pages   A page number or a range of pages, in the form 32,41,58 or 87--101 or 68+. The last form indicates page 68 and following pages. A single hyphen given for a range will be converted by the standard styles to the double hyphen to produce a dash, as '87-101'.

publisher
     The publisher's name.

school The name of the academic institution where a thesis was written.

series The name of a series or set of books. When citing a book from a series, the title field gives the name of the book itself while the optional series specifies the title of whole set.

title   The title of the work, obeying the capitalization rules listed in Section 12.2.4.

type   The type of technical report, for example, 'Research Note'.

url   The *universal resource locator*, or Internet address, for online documents; this is not standard but supplied by more modern bibliography styles.

volume The volume number of a journal or multivolume book.

year   The year in which the work was published or, if unpublished, in which it was written. It should normally consist of four numerals, such as 1993.

  Additional field names may be included, which BibTeX will simply ignore. For example, to add the abstract of an article in the database,

     abstract = {*text of an abstract*}

This can be of use in other applications as well as for database management.

12.2.3 Cross-referencing fields

If many entries in the bibliographic database share a common set of field information, such as for a number of works all appearing in the same conference proceedings, it is possible to refer to another entry containing that common set with the `crossref` field. For example,

```
@INPROCEEDINGS{xyz-1,
  crossref = {xyz-proceedings},
  author = {J. S. Jones},
  title = {The First Results from the {Appleville Experiment}},
  pages = {34--38}  }
. . . . . . . . . . . .
@PROCEEDINGS{xyz-proceedings,
  editor = {C. H. Kelvin},
  title = {Proceedings of the First Conference on the
           {Appleville Experiment}},
  booktitle = {Proceedings of the First Conference on the
               {Appleville Experiment}}
  year = 1991    }
```

The first entry, with key `xyz-1`, is to obtain all its missing fields from the second entry, by means of the `crossref` field referring to the entry with key `xyz-proceedings`. The missing fields are `editor`, `booktitle`, and `year`, those that are common to all articles in the conference proceedings. Note that `booktitle` is an ignored field for `@PROCEEDINGS` but needs to be included here since it is required for `@INPROCEEDINGS`.

If an entry is referred to by two or more other entries, then it too will be included in the bibliography, even though its key never appeared as the argument of a `\cite` or `\nocite` command.

In order for this system to function properly, the entry that is referred to must appear in the database(s) *after* all those that refer to it. It is therefore recommended to put all such referenced entries at the end of the database. Cross-references may not be nested.

12.2.4 Special field formats

There are some special rules for entering the texts to the fields `author`, `editor`, `title`, and `booktitle`. B<small>IB</small>T_EX will process names, putting surnames first, abbreviating given names with initials, and so on, according to the instructions in the style file. Thus it is important that the program knows what a given name is and what a surname is. Similarly for titles, capitalization may change depending on style and/or entry type, so B<small>IB</small>T_EX must know what words are always capitalized.

Names

The names in the `author` and `editor` fields may be typed in either in the form {*Given Names Surname*} or as {*Surname, Given Names*}. That is, BIBTEX assumes that if there is no comma, the last capitalized name is the surname or family name; otherwise, what comes before the comma is taken to be the surname. Thus the name texts "John George Harrison" and "Harrison, John George" are equivalent for Mr. J. G. Harrison. However, if a person has a double surname, without a separating hyphen, the second form must be employed, or the double name must be enclosed in braces, as

"San Martino, Maria" or "Maria {San Martino}"

for Ms. M. San Martino.

Auxiliary words to a surname that are not capitalized, such as *von* or *de*, may be entered in either form:

"Richard von Mannheim" or "von Mannheim, Richard"
"Walter de la Maire" or "de la Maire, Walter"

Anything enclosed in braces will be treated as a single item, something that is used in ambiguous cases, or when the name contains a comma or the word *and*. An example is

"{Harvey and Sons, Ltd}"

If the name contains a *Junior* or some other addition, it must be entered {*Surname, Junior, Given Name*}, for example as

"Ford, Jr, Henry" or "Ford, III, Henry"

However, if there is to be no comma, then the *Jr* must be treated as part of a double surname, *something that is not recommended at all*:

"{Filmore Jr}, Charles" or "Charles {Filmore Jr}"

Accents within a name formed with a backslash command should be enclosed in braces *with the backslash as the first character after the opening brace*. In this way, the alphabetization and the formation of labels with the `alpha` bibliography style will function properly. For example,

author = "Kurt G{\"o}del",
year = 1931

will produce the label [Göd31] as desired. The accent text must not be enclosed any deeper than shown here.

Accents should be formed with the backslash command to ensure portability. Some language modifications have shorthands for accented letters (like "a instead of \"a for German), but these should be avoided in the database to ensure that the results will be universally understood.

Hyphenated first names are properly abbreviated. Thus "Jean-Paul Sartre" becomes 'J.-P. Sartre'.

If an `author` or `editor` field is to contain more than one name, the names are separated by the word `and`. For example,

```
author = "Helmut Kopka and Daly, Patrick William"  or
AUTHOR = {Peter C. Barnes and Tolman, Paul and Mary Smith}
```

If the `and` is actually part of the name, the whole name must be enclosed in braces, as pointed out above.

Do not insert any ˜ characters between names or initials; BibTeX will do this automatically as it deems fit.

If only initials are given for the authors' given names, insert a blank between them, as `P. W. Daly`, not `P.W. Daly`. The latter will be interpreted as a single given name and will be abbreviated as 'P. Daly'.

If the author list is too long to type in all the names, it may be terminated with `and others`. This will be converted to the form of *et al.* prescribed in the style file.

Titles

The capitalization of the title depends on the bibliography style: Usually book titles are capitalized while article titles are not. The text in the fields `title` and `booktitle` should be written in the capitalized form so that BibTeX can change to lowercase as required.

The general rules for capitalizing titles in English state that the first word of the title, the first word after a colon, and all other words are capitalized except articles and unstressed prepositions and conjunctions. For example:

```
title="The Right Way to Learn: A Short-Cut to a Successful Life"
```

Words that are always to be capitalized, such as proper nouns, must be enclosed in braces. It is sufficient to enclose only the letter that must be capitalized. The two following examples are equivalent:

```
title = "The {Giotto} Mission to Comet {Halley}"  or
TITLE = {The {G}iotto Mission to Comet {H}alley}
```

12.2.5 Abbreviations

It is always possible to use an abbreviation in the field text in place of actual text. Some abbreviations, such as the names of the months and some standard journal names, are already available, and the user is free to define new ones for his or her personal use.

The name of an abbreviation consists of any combination of letters, numbers, and symbols except

```
" # % ' ( ) , = { }
```

An abbreviation is defined with the command

```
@string{abbrev_name = {text}}      or
@string(abbrev_name = {text})
```

where *abbrev_name* stands for the name of the abbreviation and *text* is the replacement text. For example, if the abbreviation

```
@string{JGR = {Journal of Geophysical Research}}
```

has been defined, the following two field statements are identical:

```
journal = JGR
journal = {Journal of Geophysical Research}
```

The name of the abbreviation is *not* enclosed in braces or double quotes, otherwise the name itself will be interpreted literally as the field text. In both the @string command and the name of the abbreviation, the case of the letters is unimportant. The above abbreviation could just as well be defined as

```
   @STRING{jgr = {Journal of Geophysical Research}}
or @StrinG{jGr = {Journal of Geophysical Research}}
```

and it may be referred to in the fields as JGR, JGr, JgR, Jgr, jGR, jGr, jgR, or jgr.

Abbreviations may be concatenated with the symbol # between them. Thus, after giving

```
@string{yrbk = {Institute Yearbook}}
```

this abbreviation may be combined with other abbreviations and text, as in

```
title = "Max-Planck~" # yrbk # 2000
```

to produce 'Max-Planck Institute Yearbook 2000'.

Standard abbreviations exist for the months of the year, the names consisting of the first three letters of the name, as jan, feb, and so on. These are actually included within the .bst file and can change their definition for styles intended for other languages. However, the name of the abbreviation remains the same, the first 3 letters of the English name.

Further predefined abbreviations are available (in the .bst file) for some standard journal names. Those produced with custom-bib are especially extensive. See Section 12.3.

The @string commands may be issued anywhere in the database between two bibliographic entries, but must already be defined before they are used. Therefore, it makes most sense to insert all the abbreviation definitions at the beginning of the database file.

12.2.6 Using a template

Typing the text for bibliographic entries into a database might seem to be rather complicated since there are so many things to remember, such as which fields are required and which are optional, what their formats are, and so on. One way to simplify this task is to make up *templates* for the most common entry types that you use. A template is basically a complete entry with all the fields left blank. It is stored in a separate file on its own, to be inserted into the database file whenever a new entry of that type is to be made. Then the field texts are written in.

An appropriate template for the entry type `@article` could be

```
@ARTICLE{<key>,
     AUTHOR  = {},
     TITLE   = {},
     YEAR    = {},
     JOURNAL = {},
     volume  = {},
     number  = {},
     month   = {},
     pages   = {},
     note    = {}
}
```

in which the <key> is a reminder that the keyword is to go here, the required fields come first and are capitalized, while the optional fields are in lowercase.

Finally, we mention that BibTeX has been written by Oren Patashnik, Stanford University, in close association with Leslie Lamport. The BibTeX installation should contain the two files `btxdoc.tex` and `btxhak.tex` for additional information about BibTeX. In particular, `btxhak.tex` contains instructions for writing bibliographic style files. Process these files with LaTeX, if the resulting `.dvi` or `.pdf` files are not already there.

12.3 Customizing bibliography styles

It seems that every journal and publishing house has its own set of rules for formatting bibliographies. The differences are really minor, such as whether to use commas or colons here, or to put volume numbers in bold or italic typeface. Nevertheless, in spite of this triviality, the rules are rigid for each house.

Standard LaTeX provides only four bibliography styles, and their differences have more to do with sorting and labeling than with such fussy details. It is possible to design one's own `.bst` file by modifying existing ones; however, this requires a knowledge of the peculiar BibTeX programming language, something that puzzles even experienced LaTeX users. There are some 50 `.bst` files in the BibTeX directories of the TeX file servers and probably many more in contributed LaTeX directories. Each is designed for a specific journal, and there is no guarantee that it would be accepted by another one. What is a user to do if his or her publisher demands a certain format that just is not to be found? How can one seek a given format anyway among those offered?

Some help can be found in the `custom-bib` application written by Patrick W. Daly. The heart of this package is a generic (or master) bibliography style `merlin.mbs` containing alternative coding for a multitude of different bibliographic features or options. It is processed with the DocStrip program that is capable of including alternative coding according to selected options.

Because of the large number of options offered (well over 100), a menu-guided interface is provided, called makebst.tex. When processed under TeX or LaTeX, this 'program' first asks which .mbs file is to be read and then interactively constructs a DocStrip batch job to produce the selected bibliographic features according to menu information contained in the .mbs file itself. This means that there could be a number of .mbs files to choose from, each one explaining its set of options to the user via makebst.

Support for other languages is provided by means of additional .mbs files, one for each language, which contain the translations for such words as *volume*, *editor*, *edition*, and so on.

Some of the features provided by the supplied generic bibliographic style file are:

- numerical or author-year citations; in the latter case, one may also choose which \bibitem style is to be used;

- order of references: by citation order, alphabetical by all authors, alphabetic by author-year label;

- format of authors' names: first name plus surname, initials plus surname, surname plus initials, reversed initials only for first author, and more;

- number of author names to include before giving *et al.*;

- typeface to be used for the author names;

- position of date, parentheses, or brackets around the year;

- format of volume, number, and pages for journals;

- capitalization of article titles as sentence or title style;

- whether to use the word *and* or an ampersand &;

- placement of commas with the word *and*;

- whether to abbreviate *editor*, *volume*, *chapter*, and so on;

- first and last page numbers or only first.

Abbreviations for many journal names in physics, optics, and geophysics can be provided in those .bst files produced by custom-bib, which then may be used in BibTeX databases. It is unfortunate that these are to be found in the .bst files themselves, which means that they may not be universally present. Which ones are present depends on the options chosen by the producer of the style file. The file shorthnd.tex in the custom-bib installation lists all the current possible abbreviations. (Actually, it is generated by running LaTeX on shorthnd.ins, which then produces the most current list from the existing .mbs files.) To check what any particular .bst file contains, open it and look for the MACRO commands.

13   PostScript and PDF

PostScript is a printing and plotting language developed by the Adobe Systems Inc. Unlike the printing instructions for other types of printers, the PostScript code may be written to an ASCII file, viewed on a computer monitor, put online, downloaded, or included in e-mails. It therefore represents a type of electronic paper.

It is also a programming language and thus offers enormous possibilities for including special effects that cannot easily be inserted with other output formats. Several packages exist to exploit these, packages that are then limited to PostScript output. However, the PostScript advantages are so attractive that this can be justified.

Portable Document Format, PDF, is another Adobe specification, a companion to PostScript, inheriting many of its properties. However, PDF includes many features to make it applicable to true electronic documents: internal and external links, bookmarks, animation, encryption, and so on, features that have no correspondence in paper. It represents a revolutionary new type of information medium.

PostScript has played a very important role in the development of LaTeX, setting the standards for graphics inclusion and offering additional font families over the standard Computer Modern set. Now PDF carries on that tradition. With the pdfTeX program, PDF is actually married to TeX and thus to LaTeX.

In the next sections we describe the generation of PostScript output with LaTeX, the usage of PostScript (type 1) fonts, and then the production of PDF output with all its bells and whistles.

13.1   LaTeX and PostScript

PostScript output is best produced with the dvips driver program written by Tomas Rokicki, available with most TeX installations. This very powerful and flexible program has set the standard for DVI conversion programs.

Its two most significant features are the inclusion of graphics as *encapsulated* PostScript images, as described in Chapter 8, and the capability of making use of PostScript fonts in place of the Computer Modern ones (Section 13.1.2). There are also enhanced drawing capabilities, as demonstrated in Sections 16.2.2 and 16.3.2.

13.1.1 The dvips driver

The `dvips` driver program operates on the DVI result from TeX, with or without LaTeX, to generate PostScript output, which may be written to a file or sent directly to a printer. One either clicks the appropriate icon in the editor shell or issues the command from a command line prompt:

```
dvips myfile
```

to process `myfile.dvi` and generate `myfile.ps`. (The LaTeX source text was, of course, in `myfile.tex`.) The PostScript file may be viewed with a PostScript viewer such as GhostView, sent to a PostScript printer, or included in an e-mail.

There are many options that may be included in the command line, appearing between `dvips` and the file name. For example, to output five pages starting at the 10th page, and then send them to a file named `p5-15.ps`, give

```
dvips -p 10 -n 5 -o p5-15 myfile
```

You may also specify the first (-p) and last (-l) page numbers, whether only odd (-A) or even (-B) pages are to be printed, or in reverse order (-r). The page numbers with -p and -l refer to the actual page numbers in the document, or rather to its first occurrence. Hence -p 8 might start with page *viii* rather than page 8. Specifying -p =8 will start with the 8th page, regardless of its actual number. The list of options can be printed to the monitor with `dvips --help`.

One useful option is `t landscape` to rotate the output into landscape mode, which should be done if the document has been processed with the `landscape` option in `\documentclass`. However, `dvips` has another way of accomplishing this: Add the driver-specific command

```
\special{landscape}
```

in the source text itself and `dvips` will automatically print in landscape mode.

The output is written to a file with the same root name as the input, but with extension `.ps`, unless the option -o *filename* is given. To send the output directly to a printer, specify that printer as the output 'file', as -o `\lpt1`. But beware: If that printer is not a PostScript printer, it will simply output the PostScript code directly as text, something that normally uses a considerable amount of paper.

A full manual for `dvips` should be available as `dvips.ps` or `dvips.pdf`; otherwise the source file `dvips.tex` can be processed (with TeX, not LaTeX!).

The program is configured to the local installation by means of a file `config.ps` that should be located in `texmf→dvips→config`. This sets up certain parameters for the default printer, as well as various paper formats, indicating which is to be the default (European A4 or American letter). This can be overridden with -t a4 or -t letter. Another important configuration item is a list of font-mapping files (Section 13.1.5) to associate TeX font names with actual PostScript fonts and their files.

Additional configuration files are usually provided, for specific printers or other font mappings, all with the name `config` plus a different extension. They may be invoked on the command line with the option -P plus extension. For example, `config.cx` contains lines for a generic PostScript printer with resolution of 300 dpi; with -P cx, this file is input, overriding the default values in `config.ps`. Another example for adding PostScript fonts is given in Section 13.1.5.

Of course, the `dvips` driver manages not only PostScript fonts but also the standard TEX pixel fonts generated by the METAFONT program. These bitmaps are stored in .pk files that need to be generated for the desired printer, size, and resolution. Originally, the user had to ensure that they were present before the driver program could address them. Fortunately, `dvips` has revolutionized this process by calling METAFONT itself if the needed .pk files are missing.

However, it is the use of PostScript fonts that make `dvips` especially interesting. We describe in some detail how they are integrated into the TEX/LATEX system in the next sections since almost all of this applies equally well to PDF output.

13.1.2 Invoking PostScript fonts

Under the New Font Selection Scheme of Appendix A, it is relatively simple to invoke the PostScript fonts if the font definition .fd files are provided. These are normally found in the directory `psnfss` in the standard installations. It also contains packages for the 35 standard PostScript fonts, plus those for a number of other commercially available fonts. These packages are actually quite simple; for example, the `times.sty` file contains only three lines, which are listed on page 366. All these packages do is redefine the three font families: \rmdefault, \sfdefault, and \ttdefault.

The packages for the 35 standard fonts, and the three assignments that they make, are listed in Table 13.1. (The 35 fonts include italic and bold variants of these.)

These packages are only meaningful when the resulting DVI output is to be transformed with `dvips` to PostScript or PDF files, or when the LATEX source is to be processed with pdfTEX to generate PDF directly. Other drivers can only handle the TEX pixel fonts (also known as type 3 fonts). Some drivers, in particular the monitor previewers `xdvi` and `windvi`, will also invoke programs to generate the bitmap .pk files from the PostScript .pfb source files.

Table 13.1: The `psnfss` packages and their fonts

Package	\rmfamily	\sffamily	\ttfamily
`times.sty`	Times-Roman	Helvetica	Courier
`palatino.sty`	Palatino	Helvetica	Courier
`newcent.sty`	NewCenturySchlbk	AvantGarde	Courier
`bookman.sty`	Bookman	AvantGarde	Courier
`avant.sty`		AvantGarde	
`helvet.sty`		Helvetica	

Why bother to use these packages when `dvips` is capable of including the pixel fonts just as well? The answer is that the standard PostScript fonts are well known from other applications, and that there are additional commercially available fonts in PostScript format; they therefore offer a wider choice than simply the traditional Computer Modern fonts that are limited to TeX and LaTeX.

13.1.3 Math fonts with PostScript

Loading any one of the above packages will only replace the text fonts with the corresponding PostScript ones. Since the TeX math fonts are separate from the text ones, these will remain as the standard Computer Modern math fonts of Section A.3.1.

Package:
`mathtime`
This is not really desirable. The Computer Modern characters are somewhat thinner and lighter than Times-Roman, so that with the `times` package, the math symbols will not properly match with the text characters. This can be corrected by using the set of math fonts called MathTimes, which are explicitly intended to be used with the Times family. There is a `mathtime` package that loads and activates these fonts.

Package:
`lucidabr`
The set of Lucida Bright fonts used in this book also have a corresponding set of math fonts designed to harmonize with the text. Both the text and math fonts are invoked with the `lucidabr` package.

The MathTimes and Lucida fonts are commercial products available from Y&Y Inc.

13.1.4 Naming scheme for PostScript fonts

To be compatible with all possible operating systems, it is necessary to reduce the names of the PostScript font files to a maximum of eight characters. This makes for an extremely abbreviated and cryptic nomenclature.

The most commonly used scheme is that of Karl Berry. Here, the first letter of the name specifies the supplier of the font. Examples are p for Adobe (stands for PostScript), h for Bigelow & Holmes (who designed the Lucida fonts used in this book), m for Monotype, l for Linotype, and so on.

A two-letter typeface code follows the supplier letter, such as tm for Times-Roman. Next come various letters to specify weight, for example, r for regular (upright Roman) or b for bold; and variant, such as i for italic or o for oblique (slanted). Next come a number plus letter to indicate the encoding scheme, followed by possible width code letters. The Berry names for the 35 standard PostScript fonts that should be loaded in every printer are listed in Table 13.2 on the opposite page, without the encoding suffixes.

The most important encoding suffixes for our purposes are listed in Table 13.3. The 7-bit encodings are the traditional TeX Computer Modern ones, while 8t corresponds to the newer T1 encoding with 256 characters per font. The other 8-bit schemes are the raw encoding, 8r, and the Adobe standard encoding, 8a, which is the default for most type 1 fonts if no re-encoding is specified. This scheme plays absolutely no role in the NFSS installation for PostScript fonts.

The 8r raw encoding supplies the symbol pool for constructing *virtual* fonts. For example, TeX is aware of the two virtual fonts `ptmr7t` and `ptmr8t`, but they in fact do not really exist.

Table 13.2: Root names of the 35 standard PostScript fonts

pagd	AvantGarde-Demi	phvrrn	Helvetica-Narrow
pagdo	AvantGarde-DemiOblique	phvron	Helvetica-Narrow-Oblique
pagk	AvantGarde-Book	pncb	NewCenturySchlbk-Bold
pagko	AvantGarde-BookOblique	pncbi	NewCenturySchlbk-BoldItalic
pbkd	Bookman-Demi	pncr	NewCenturySchlbk-Roman
pbkdi	Bookman-DemiItalic	pncri	NewCenturySchlbk-Italic
pbkl	Bookman-Light	pplb	Palatino-Bold
pbkli	Bookman-LightItalic	pplbi	Palatino-BoldItalic
pcrb	Courier-Bold	pplr	Palatino-Roman
pcrbo	Courier-BoldOblique	pplri	Palatino-Italic
pcrr	Courier	psyr	Symbol
pcrro	Courier-Oblique	ptmb	Times-Bold
phvb	Helvetica-Bold	ptmbi	Times-BoldItalic
phvbo	Helvetica-BoldOblique	ptmr	Times-Roman
phvbrn	Helvetica-Narrow-Bold	ptmri	Times-Italic
phvbon	Helvetica-Narrow-BoldOblique	pzcmi	ZapfChancery-MediumItalic
phvr	Helvetica	pzdr	ZapfDingbats
phvro	Helvetica-Oblique		

Table 13.3: A selection of the encoding suffixes in the Berry nomenclature

Suffix	Encoding	NFSS designation	Page
7t	7-bit TEX text encoding	OT1	367
7m	TEX math italics encoding	OML	368
7v	TEX math extension encoding	OMX	
7y	TEX math symbols encoding	OMS	368
8t	8-bit Cork encoding	T1	370
8a	Adobe standard encoding		
8r	TeXBase1Encoding		

Rather, their .vf files instruct the driver to take the symbols from various locations in the same raw font ptmr8r to emulate the two different encoding schemes. There are also raw fonts that are modifications of the basic fonts. For example, ptmro8t is an oblique Times-Roman virtual font, based on ptmro8r, the raw version. However, there is no such font in the repertoire of Table 13.2. This pseudo font is generated by applying a PostScript slanting operation to Times-Roman, as demonstrated in Section 13.1.7.

13.1.5 Installing PostScript fonts

!

The packages listed in the previous section invoke the PostScript fonts by means of the NFSS system, provided they have been properly included in the installation. This means that the following files must be present:

.tfm the font metric files for both the virtual and raw fonts;

.fd the NFSS font definition files associating the font attributes to precise virtual font names; these and the `.tfm` files are the only ones read by LATEX itself;

.vf   virtual font files that instruct the DVI driver how to produce the characters; usually this refers to characters in a real font with different encoding;

.map   mapping files that tell the `dvips` driver the true internal names of the real fonts, plus any re-encodings or distortions that must be undertaken.

The .map files are a feature of `dvips` that has been taken over by pdfTEX and other programs that make use of PostScript fonts. They translate the LATEX font names into the internal ones used by PostScript itself. For example, the line

```
ptmr8r Times-Roman "TeXBase1Encoding ReEncodeFont" <8r.enc
```

says that the font known to LATEX as `ptm8r` is really the *Times-Roman* font. Furthermore, the text in quotes is also inserted into the PostScript output; in this case, it is a command to state that the symbol assignments (the encoding) should be that of the `TeXBase1Encoding` vector. The definition of this encoding vector is to be found in the file `8r.enc`, which must also be inserted, since it is not part of basic PostScript.

Note that type 1 fonts are essentially a collection of symbols identified by name, whereas application programs like LATEX address characters by positional number. It is the encoding vector that associates these numbers with symbol names for the sake of the application. They are not intrinsic to the font itself.

For fonts other than the 35 standard ones included in every PostScript output device, additional files must also be input. For example,

```
hlhr8r LucidaBright "TeXBase1Encoding ReEncodeFont" <8r.enc <hlhr8a.pfb
```

says that the file `hlhr8a.pfb` must also be inserted into the PostScript output, containing the drawing instructions for the LucidaBright font.

The .pfb (or non-compressed .pfa) file is what one obtains from the supplier, along with corresponding .afm *font metric* files in Adobe format. If this is all one has, then it is necessary to obtain the equivalent TEX .tfm and .vf files; if they are not available from CTAN (Section B.4), they can be generated from the .afm files with the help of the `fontinst` program by Alan Jeffrey and Rowland McDonnell. This program is actually written in TEX code, so it is fully portable to any system on which TEX runs. It reads in the .afm files and writes the .fd files plus human-readable (ASCII) versions of the .tfm and .vf files, the .pl and .vpl files. These are then converted to their binary forms with the programs `pltotf` and vptovf, which are part of the regular TEX installation.

The .map files are listed in the `config.ps` file that configures `dvips`. Often there is a single mapping file named `psfonts.map`, included with the line

```
p psfonts.map
```

in `config.ps`, or individual mapping files are listed, as

```
p psnfss.map
p +pazo.map
p + ....
```

prefixed with a + sign after the first one.

In some cases, the map file listings are also included in additional `config` files, such as `config.cms` for the PostScript versions of the standard Computer Modern fonts. If these are not already contained in `config.ps` or in `psfonts.map`, they may be added on the `dvips` command line with the option `-P cms`. Other families of PostScript fonts can be included in the same manner.

13.1.6 Computer Modern as PostScript fonts

The traditional pixel fonts produced by METAFONT have served us well in the days when the emphasis was on printed paper output. Even for PostScript output, the pixel fonts are perfectly acceptable. However, they become very tedious when viewed in PDF output because they appear very fuzzy and require a long time to draw. (This situation has been improved with Acrobat version 6.) For this reason, PDF output, whether produced with pdfTEX, dvipdfm, or converted from PostScript, should use type 1 fonts exclusively. To this end, the Computer Modern fonts themselves have been converted to type 1 fonts.

The first such undertaking was carried out by Basil Malyshev, whose set of font files are known as bakoma. However, the set that is more often used today is the result of a joint project by Y&Y Inc. and Blue Sky Research. Originally part of their commercial TEX installations, these fonts are now available free of charge. They are included on the TEX Live distribution under texmf→fonts→type1→bluesky in several subdirectories as .pfb files. They bear the same names and have the same font metrics as the corresponding pixel fonts and therefore do not need any additional .tfm files. However, one must also get the mapping file bsr.map from texmf→dvips→bluesky and add it to the list of mapping files in config.ps.

The Bluesky fonts are incomplete in that certain less-often-used fonts are missing in some sizes. One can either include the map file bsr-interpolated.map, which substitutes the missing sizes with the nearest approximation, or employ the bakoma fonts that fill the gaps, with the map file bakomaextra.map. The TEX Live distribution does not include the complete bakoma set, but only those fonts that are missing in the Bluesky ensemble.

Together, Bluesky and bakoma provide PostScript-encoded versions for all the Computer Modern fonts described in Section A.3.1—for text, math, symbols, decoration, and pictures, along with the additional $\mathcal{A}_{\mathcal{M}}\mathcal{S}$ fonts for additional symbols and Cyrillic. However, these are only for the OT1 encoding with 128 characters per font.

A more recent effort to apply PostScript to the Extended Computer (EC) fonts with the T1 encoding has been successfully completed by Vladimir Volovich with his cm-super collection. Each of the basic .pfb files contains from 468 to 585 characters, which by means of encoding vectors and mapping files can be used to emulate all the EC fonts (Section A.3.2) including the text companion fonts with TS1 encoding, and many other additional encoding schemes. They were generated from the original METAFONT .mf source files and should therefore produce exactly the same results as the corresponding pixel fonts.

The cm-super fonts are not provided on the TEX Live CD included with this book; they are, however, to be found on the 'installable' CD and on the DVD of the complete set of TEX Live 2003. They may also be obtained from CTAN (Section B.4).

13.1.7 Long road from input code to output character

!

Let us illustrate with an example how LaTeX translates an input character with given font attributes into a particular symbol in a specific font. Suppose we have the following attributes (Section A.1):

> Encoding: OT1   Family: ptm   Series: b   Shape: sl

The encoding and family indicate the font definition file that associates these attributes with real font names, in this case ot1ptm.fd. In that file, one finds this set of attributes to be assigned to font ptmbo7t; this is the Berry name for *Times-BoldOblique, 7-bit-text* (see Tables 13.2 and 13.3 on page 245).

Our sample input code is \AE; according to file ot1enc.def, this corresponds to character 29 in the OT1 encoding. LaTeX thus writes instructions to the .dvi file to output the symbol in position 29 of font ptmbo7t. And with that, LaTeX is finished with its part of the operation.

The next step is to process the .dvi file with the dvips driver. When this program searches for a font, it first looks in the map files, then it seeks the .vf virtual font files, and finally it tries to find it as a .pk pixel file. In our case, it discovers the virtual font ptmbo7t.vf, which tells the driver that character 29 is to be symbol 198 of font ptmbo8r. This is the same basic font but with 8-bit raw encoding. Again dvips searches for this next font and finds it in a mapping file, containing the line

```
ptmbo8r Times-Bold ".167 SlantFont TeXBase1Encoding ReEncodeFont" <8r.enc
```

This tells the driver that it is to use the font with the internal name *Times-Bold* slanted by a factor 0.167 and encoded according to the TeXBase1Encoding encoding vector. The file 8r.enc must also be copied into the output.

Finally, the output .ps file is sent to a PostScript printer or other PostScript interpreter. The specified encoding vector indicates that character 198 is the symbol with the internal name AE, which is then printed from the Times-Bold font, distorted as required. The long road has come full circle.

13.2   Portable Document Format (PDF)

In 1993, Adobe Systems Inc. published the *Portable Document Format*, or PDF, as a page-oriented format for electronic documents. As a successor to PostScript, which is also an Adobe creation, it combines fixed textual contents with hypertext elements, graphics, movies, sound clips, as well as compression methods and security measures. It corresponds to true electronic publishing with a fixed layout but still with hard-copy possibilities. Compared to PostScript files, the PDF output is considerably smaller, especially when graphics are included. Today it is considered the ideal medium for storage and transmitting large documents electronically in final format.

13.2.1 Producing PDF output

Adobe has made the PDF specification public and freely available so that anyone is entitled to write software to produce and to read files in this format. They have also made available a free reader program, *Acrobat Reader*, so it is hardly worthwhile writing another one, at least not commercially. (Ghostscript can also interpret PDF as well as PostScript.)

Where Adobe makes its money is in the sales of programs to produce and manipulate PDF files. Of these, the main ones are:

- Acrobat Distiller to convert PostScript into PDF, and

- Acrobat program to modify existing PDF files.

In the latter case, 'modification' means adding links, changing colors, including navigational aids, and inserting notes; it does not mean altering the actual textual content in any way.

Today most graphical and text-processing programs are capable of generating PDF output. For the LaTeX user, there are three routes that may be taken to produce PDF output. The obvious one is .tex → .dvi → .ps → .pdf using dvips to generate the PostScript and then Distiller or Ghostscript to create the PDF file.

The other two methods are to employ a DVI-to-PDF driver, or the pdfTeX program to go directly to PDF, bypassing the intermediate DVI output. We describe each of these in the next sections.

Used on their own, all of these methods produce a simple PDF file containing nothing more than the text itself, a sort of electronic paper. The hypertext features that make an electronic document really live can be added automatically with the help of the hyperref package described in Section 13.2.4.

13.2.2 The dvipdfm driver

The driver program dvipdfm by Mark A. Wicks is the equivalent of dvips for PDF output. As its name implies, it converts DVI to PDF output. (The m suffix is to distinguish it from a previously announced dvipdf program that never came to fruition.)

Graphics input can be included with the graphics or graphicx packages (Section 8.1) by specifying the option dvipdfm. The allowed graphics formats are JPEG, PNG, and PDF.

The program is called from a command line with

```
dvipdfm myfile
```

to convert myfile.dvi to myfile.pdf. As for dvips, there are many options that may be included. It is best to read the provided manual in dvipdfm.pdf or dvipdfm.dvi, or produce it by processing dvipdfm.tex with TeX.

The configuration is set up by means of a file named config in the dvipdfm directory. This is set up similarly to the config.ps file for dvips, including the list of mapping files, although these have a different syntax from those of dvips.

Hypertext features and other PDF additions can be added with the hyperref package (Section 13.2.4).

13.2.3 The pdfTeX program

The most direct method of getting PDF output is to process the LaTeX file with pdfTeX, a variation on the TeX program developed by Hàn Thế Thành. The following points should be noted:

- pdfTeX behaves just like the regular TeX program unless \pdfoutput=1 is issued before the first page is output; in this case, it generates PDF instead of DVI output and activates many new TeX-like commands for including PDF features.

- Since pdfTeX combines the functionality of both the TeX program and a DVI driver, it must be able to deal with fonts in the way that a driver program would. Originally this meant that it could only handle PostScript type 1 fonts, but now it can also cope with METAFONT bitmap fonts (type 3) as well as TrueType fonts. The bitmap fonts, however, look very bad when viewed, but this is a viewer problem that may be overcome soon.

- When started, the program reads a configuration file `pdftex.cfg` that can set many parameters, such as page size, offsets, and PDF compression level, and specifies the names of font-mapping files. It may also set the default output to PDF, avoiding having to set \pdfoutput in the source text.

- The font map files are identical to those used by `dvips` (page 248); they relate the TeX name for the font to various characteristics, encoding scheme, true name, and specify the file containing the character drawing instructions.

- New TeX-like commands exist to include PDF features, such as compression level, page attributes, document information, opening setup, forms, annotations, links, bookmarks, and article threads.

- Graphics can be included in PNG or JPEG formats; TIFF are no longer supported; PDF files may be inserted provided they contain only a single page without any fonts or bitmaps. The graphics packages (Section 8.1) support pdfTeX by means of a `pdftex` graphics option.

To run pdfTeX with LaTeX (often referred to as pdfLaTeX), it is necessary to generate a LaTeX format (Section B.1.3) using pdfTeX instead of TeX, with the `-ini` option, renaming the resulting `latex.fmt` to `pdflatex.fmt`; it is then called with the command

```
pdftex &pdflatex
```

Most installations contain a command `pdflatex` that translates to this combination. The editor shell should also have an icon that invokes this command.

We do not describe the new TeX-like commands to add PDF features to the output, preferring to use the LaTeX-like commands of the `hyperref` package. For information on the intrinsic new pdfTeX commands, see *The LaTeX Web Companion* (Goossens and Rahtz, 1999), which also explains the `hyperref` package in detail. The pdfTeX manual should also be available on your system under `texmf→doc→pdftex` in various formats.

So which of the above methods is to be recommended? The PostScript + Distiller is the most inelegant, involving two intermediate steps (DVI and PS) and requiring purchase of the Distiller program. Alternatively, one can use the free Ghostscript program for the conversion to PDF, but there are still the intermediate steps. And if this route is selected, one must be certain that `dvips` uses the PostScript version of the Computer Modern fonts by setting up the mapping files accordingly.

The `dvipdfm` program is in the original spirit of TeX, using DVI as a universal intermediate format for all outputs. Purists might tend to respect this ideal. After all, no one ever considered rewriting TeX to produce PostScript output directly. That said, one must consider that TeX was invented in the days when no one printer specification dominated the field. Today, PDF is much more than a printer format; it is *the* means of representing documents electronically. That alone would not justify preferring pdfTeX over a DVI-to-PDF converter, nor would the fact that it saves a processing step; the deciding argument is that pdfTeX has established itself as reliable, robust, and flexible.

In the end, it is likely a question of which program one is more comfortable with, and which one has given better results for the user.

13.2.4 The `hyperref` package

Package:
`hyperref` Sebastian Rahtz has written an ambitious package `hyperref`, now maintained by Heiko Oberdiek, to add automatic hypertext links to LaTeX documents that are intended to become HTML (using LaTeX2HTML, Section E.1.1 or TeX4ht, Section E.1.2) or PDF files (using any of the methods described above). Not only do all internal cross-references link to their reference points, citations are linked to the list of references, table of contents to the section headings, and index listings to the original text. Additional links to external documents are possible by means of a single syntax for all types of output. And it does this with a uniform syntax even though all the conversion methods have their own syntaxes.

Because this package redefines many aspects of the LaTeX kernel and of many other packages, it should always be loaded as the very last one to be sure that it has the final word.

This package is especially useful for PDF output, whether by means of PostScript plus Distiller, with `dvipdfm`, or directly with pdfTeX. Figure 13.1 on the next page gives an example of such a PDF file, where it should be noted that the contents entries are all links to their sections, as are the entries in the left-hand outline, which is also generated automatically. The package provides LaTeX-like commands for the PDF features.

Before we go any further, we should explain certain terms that are used below.

Links are indicated in various ways—as a piece of text in a different color, or surrounded by a frame, or maybe an image—which when clicked cause the viewer to jump to another document or some other place in the current document.

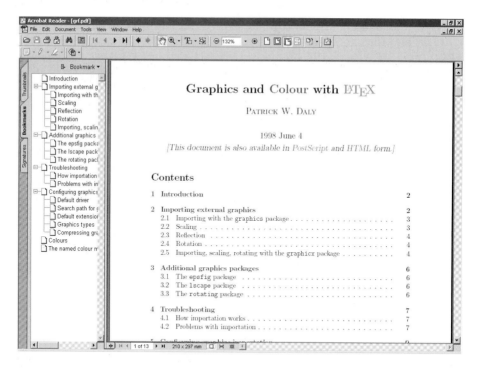

Figure 13.1: Output produced by pdfTeX with the `hyperref` package for automatic links, with an outline list at the left

Anchors (also called *targets*) are the destinations for links. They are provided with an identifying name so that the link can find them. Some anchors are meant only for internal linking within the document, while others are visible from outside.

Thumbnails are small images of the pages that are displayed in a thumbnail window by the viewer. They may be used to locate a certain page more quickly, especially if it has an obviously different appearance because of a figure it contains. Double-clicking the page image causes the viewer to jump to that page.

Bookmarks are special links to places in the document, associated with a *view*, usually meaning a zoom factor, or a specification such as 'fit page to width of window'. The bookmark window displays all these, and by double-clicking them one jumps to that location and view. Bookmarks are ordered within a tree, with sub-bookmarks and so on. The bookmark display may have the tree opened or closed.

Outline is the usual use for bookmarks, building a table of contents, or outline, for the whole document. The word 'outline' is used here, but the PDF viewers refer to 'bookmarks'. The latter is really far more general.

Options for `hyperref`

There are a large number of parameters that may be configured for the package, either as options in the `\usepackage` command, with the `\hypersetup` command, or with a configuration file. An example of setting options with the first method is:

```
\usepackage[pdftex,
   pdftitle={Graphics and Color with LaTeX},
   pdfauthor={Patrick W Daly},
   pdfsubject={Importing images and use of color in LaTeX},
   pdfkeywords={LaTeX, graphics, color},
   pdfpagemode=UseOutlines,
   bookmarks,bookmarksopen,
   pdfstartview=FitH,
   colorlinks,linkcolor=blue,citecolor=blue,
   urlcolor=red,
]
{hyperref}
```

Options that take a value are given with an equals sign and the value; for multiple values, or text, the values must be placed within curly braces, as shown in the example. Options that are either `true` or `false` are simply given (to make them `true`) or equated to `false`. Options may also be given with the `\hypersetup` command, as for example:

```
\hypersetup{colorlinks, linkcolor=blue}
```

Values that are colors must be a name of a defined color, as explained in Section 8.2; the name must be defined before it is first used. However, some color values must be the three numbers of the `rgb` model. The colors of link borders may only be given as `rgb`. The `hyperref` package automatically loads the `color` package if `colorlinks` is given.

One option must specify the driver name for which the output is intended; in the above example this is `pdftex`, but other possibilities are:

```
dvipdf     dvipdfm dvips   dvipsone dviwindo hypertex
latex2html pdftex  tex4ht  textures vtex
```

The option `hypertex` is not for any particular driver, but rather for any that conforms to the HyperTeX guidelines, such as `dvips`. There is also a `draft` option that turns off all hypertext features.

The next four options in the example (`pdftitle`-`pdfkeywords`) are entries for the PDF document information stored in the file and displayed only when the viewer shows the document summary. The complete set of such options is:

```
pdfauthor   pdfcreator pdfkeywords
pdfproducer pdfsubject pdftitle
```

The standard paper size options of Section 3.1.1 are all recognized and one of them must be given, either as an option to `hyperref` or as a global option in the

\documentclass command. This is necessary to set up the size of the PDF page. As a reminder, these are:

a4paper   a5paper   b5paper
executivepaper legalpaper letterpaper

Here is a list of all of the remaining options, with the default value in brackets.

4   (false) use Acrobat 4 features

anchorcolor
        (black) set color of anchors (targets of internal links)

backref
        (false) adds links in the bibliography pointing back to the citation; with pagebackref, a list of pages is added to the bibliography, each being a link back to the citation

baseurl
        determines the prefix for URLs given with \href

bookmarks
        (true) make bookmarks out of sectioning commands

bookmarksnumbered
        (false) include section numbers in bookmark text

bookmarksopen
        (false) start document with bookmarks tree opened

bookmarksopenlevel
        (*max*) the level to which bookmarks are opened

bookmarkstype
        (toc) specifies which 'contents' file used for bookmarks

breaklinks
        (false) allows link text to break over lines

citebordercolor
        (0 1 0) the color of the border around citations

citecolor
        (green) color of citation links when colorlinks given

colorlinks
        (false, but true for tex4ht and dviwindo) link and anchor texts are to be colored, according to color specifications for the various types of links; without this, link text is surrounded by a frame

debug   (false) output diagnostic messages

draft   (false) turn off all hyperlinking

extension
> (dvi) default extension of linked files using the xr package (Section 11.2.3); the package tries to guess whether the file specified by \externaldocument should be .dvi or .pdf; with PDF output, the viewer will open that external file and switch to it

filebordercolor
> (0 .5 .5) color of the border around file links

filecolor
> (cyan) color of file links when colorlinks given

frenchlinks
> (false) use small caps instead of color for links

hyperfigures
> (false) make figures into hyperlinks

hyperfootnotes
> (true) make footnotes into hyperlinks

hyperindex
> (true) make index entries into links back to referenced text

hypertexnames
> (true) use guessable (obvious) names for links

implicit
> (true) redefine LaTeX internal commands

linkbordercolor
> (1 0 0) color of the border around links

linkcolor
> (red) color of link text when colorlinks given

linktocpage
> (false) the page numbers in the table of contents (or list of figures/tables) are the links, rather than the text itself

menubordercolor
> (1 0 0) color of the border around Acrobat menu links

menucolor
> (red) color for Acrobat menu links when colorlinks given

naturalnames
> (false) use LaTeX-computed names for links

nesting
> (false) links are allowed to be nested, although none of the existing drivers support this

pageanchor
>   (true) an anchor (target) is placed automatically on every page, something
>   that is necessary if the table of contents is to act as links

pagebackref
>   (false) adds to each entry in the bibliography a list of page numbers linked
>   to their citations

pagebordercolor
>   (1 1 0) color of the border around page links

pagecolor
>   (red) color of page links when colorlinks given

pdfborder
>   (0 0 1, but 0 0 0 with colorlinks) width of the border around links
>   in PDF files; the first two numbers are always zero, the third is the line
>   thickness in points

pdfcenterwindow
>   (false) positions the document window in the center of the computer
>   monitor when the PDF file is opened

pdffitwindow
>   (false) resizes the document window to fit the first page when the PDF file
>   is opened

pdfhighlight
>   (/I) determines how the Acrobat menu buttons behave when clicked; /I for
>   inverse, /N for none, /O for outline, /P inset highlighting

pdfmenubar
>   (true) makes the menu bar in the PDF viewer visible

pdfnewwindow
>   (false) a new window is opened when the PDF viewer switches to another
>   file

pdfpagelayout
>   (SinglePage) determines the page layout for the PDF viewer; other values
>   are OneColumn (all pages in a continuous column), TwoColumnLeft (two
>   columns, with odd numbers on the left), TwoColumnRight (two columns,
>   with odd numbers on the right)

pdfpagelabels
>   (false) makes the page numbers displayed by the PDF viewer to be the
>   same as those printed on the page, something that is very useful if both
>   Roman and Arabic page numbers are employed; otherwise, the displayed
>   page numbers are sequence numbers starting at 1

pdfpagemode
> (None) determines the initial display in the PDF viewer; other values are UseThumbs (to show thumbnails), UseOutline (to show bookmarks), or FullScreen (no tool or menu bars, window is in full screen mode)

pdfpagescrop
> a set of four numbers determining the crop box when the the PDF file is opened, similar to a bounding box

pdfpagetransition
> (R) determines how the pages are changed; possible values are Split (like opening a curtain), Blinds (like Venetian blinds), Box (a rectangle opens from the center), Wipe (vertical line moves across page), Dissolve (old page dissolves into new), Glitter (variation on dissolve), R (replace); additional parameters can be added where appropriate: /Dm (with Split and Blinds) followed by /H (horizontal) or /V (vertical), /Di (with Wipe and Glitter) followed by 90, 180, 270 for the direction of motion, /M (with Split and Box) followed by /I (inwards), /O (outwards); see page 340 for a simplified interface to this feature

pdfstartpage
> (1) the first page number to be displayed when the PDF file is opened

pdfstartview
> (Fit) determines the initial view when the PDF file is opened; takes values of Fit (fit page to window), FitH (fit to width), FitV (fit to height), FitB (fit to bounding box), FitBH (fit to bounding box width), FitBV (fit to bounding box height), XYZ (no change)

pdftoolbar
> (true) makes the tool bar in the PDF viewer visible

pdfusetitle
> (false) obtains the PDF document information for author and title from the \author and \title commands

pdfview
> (XYZ) determines the page view when a link moves to a new page; takes same values as pdfstartview

pdfwindowui
> (true) makes the user interface elements (bookmarks, thumbnails) in the PDF viewer available; if false, they are permanently switched off

plainpages
> (true) makes the anchors for the pages to be their Arabic form; if false, the page anchors are as the page numbers are formatted, highly recommended if the document contains both Roman and Arabic page numbers

raiselinks
>   (false) with the hypertex driver, makes the border around links the actual
>   height of their contents, rather than the current baseline separation

runbordercolor
>   (0 .7 .7) color of the border around 'run' links

unicode
>   (false) enables Unicode encoded PDF strings

urlbordercolor
>   (0 1 1) color of the border around URL links

urlcolor
>   (magenta) color of URL links when colorlinks given

verbose
>   (false) issues many extra messages

Using a configuration file

Very often a user will find that he or she needs the same set of options in almost every document. Rather than issuing that set again and again, it is possible to prepare a configuration file named hyperref.cfg containing a \hypersetup command with all the option settings that one normally wants. One effectively resets the default values. Any settings in the LaTeX source text itself will override those defaults.

The hyperref.cfg file must be located where it will always be found by the LaTeX processing. It might very well be that a file of that name already exists and will be read in instead of yours. To check which location is being used, examine the transcript .log file for the full path name, and then edit that version of hyperref.cfg.

Linking commands

The main purpose of the hyperref package is to add the automatic links between cross-referencing commands and tables of contents. However, it also enables access to PDF features with LaTeX-style commands. One of these is the ability to add manual links within the file and to other documents, locally or on the Web. The commands to achieve this are:

\hyperbaseurl{url_pre}
>   sets a prefix for all external URLs specified by other commands, so that the
>   common part of a set of URLs need only be given once; this is the same as
>   the baseurl option, but can be changed within the document

\href{url}{text}
>   makes *text* into a link to the full URL given by *url* prefixed with the current
>   base URL; special characters like # and & can be type in *url* directly

\hyperimage{url}{image_url}
>   inserts the image referenced by *image_url*

\hyperdef{*category*}{*name*}{*text*}
   establishes *text* as a target (anchor) with name *category.name*

\hyperref{*url*}{*category*}{*name*}{*text*}
   makes *text* a link to *url#category.name*

\hyperref[key]{*text*}
   makes *text* an internal link to the location marked with \label{*key*}

\hypertarget{*name*}{*text*}
   establishes *text* as an internal target (anchor) with the name #*name*

\hyperlink{*name*}{*text*}
   makes *text* a link to the internal target #*name*

The cross-referencing commands \ref{*key*} and \pageref{*key*} (Section 11.2.1) automatically create links to the corresponding \label{*key*} location. As pointed out above, one can also create a manual link with \hyperref[key]{*text*}.

The hyperref package also provides starred versions \ref* and \pageref* that function as the regular ones but without creating a link.

Adding Acrobat buttons

An electronic document is active, as indicated by the links within it for jumping to other sections. But it is also possible to insert other types of 'actions' in the form of buttons which, when clicked, do something, such as flipping to the next page, opening another document, or even quitting.

The hyperref package can add such functionality for the Acrobat viewers by means of the command

   \Acrobatmenu{*action*}{*text*}

where *text* becomes a button to execute *action* when clicked. Of course, *text* can be more than mere text—it is often a graphic that really does look like a button.

The actions available are those provided by the Acrobat and Acrobat Reader programs. These are not documented by Adobe, but are listed in Table 13.4 on the next page, which is taken from Goossens and Rahtz (1999), who credit Merz (1998) for having figured them out. These actions are therefore specific to these viewers only and may change with later versions. They may all be executed by the viewers themselves, by means of pull-down menus in the menu bar, indicated in the left column of Table 13.4.

The main purpose of this command is to set up navigational controls on each page of a document that is meant essentially for screen viewing. The regular tool bar may be turned off, which is why the document itself must provide it. This is best put into a footline, and that is most conveniently done with the fancyhdr package (Section 3.2.2).

```
\documentclass[a4paper]{article}
\usepackage{fancyhdr}
```

Table 13.4: Actions available from the Acrobat menus (after Goossens and Rahtz, 1999, page 48)

Acrobat Menu	Available options for \Acrobatmenu
File	Open, Close, Scan, Save, SaveAs, Optimizer:SaveAsOpt, Print, PageSetup, Quit
File→Import	ImportImage, ImportNotes, AcroForm:ImportFDF
File→Export	ExportNotes, AcroForm:ExportFDF
File→DocProps	GeneralInfo, OpenInfo, FontsInfo, SecurityInfo, Weblink:Base, AutoIndex:DocInfo
Edit	Undo, Cut, Copy, Paste, Clear, SelectAll, Ole:CopyFile, TouchUp:TextAttributes, TouchUp:FitTextToSelection, TouchUp:ShowLineMarkers, TouchUp:ShowCaptureSuspects, TouchUp:FindSuspect, Properties
Edit→Prefs	GeneralPrefs, NotePrefs, FullScreenPrefs,Weblink:Prefs, AcroSearch:Preferences(Windows)or, AcroSearch:Prefs(Mac), Cpt:Capture
Edit→Search	AcroSrch:Query, AcroSrch:Indexes, AcroSrch:Results, AcroSrch:Assist, AcroSrch:PrevDoc, AcroSrch:PrevHit, AcroSrch:NextHit, AcroSrch:NextDoc
Edit→Fields	AcroForm:Duplicate, AcroForm:TabOrder
Document	Cpt:CapturePages, AcroForm:Actions, CropPages, RotatePages, InsertPages, ExtractPages, ReplacePages, DeletePages, NewBookmark, SetBookmarkDest, CreateAllThumbs, DeleteAllThumbs
View	ActualSize, FitVisible, FitWidth, FitPage, ZoomTo, FullScreen, FirstPage, PrevPage, NextPage, LastPage, GoToPage, GoBack, GoForward, SinglePage, OneColumn, TwoColumns, ArticleThreads, PageOnly, ShowBookmarks, ShowThumbs
Tools	Hand, ZoomIn, ZoomOut, SelectText, SelectGraphics, Note, Link, Thread, AcroForm:Tool, Acro_Movie:MoviePlayer, TouchUp:TextTool, Find, FindAgain, FindNextNote, CreateNotesFile
Window	ShowHideToolBar, ShowHideMenuBar, ShowHideClipboard, Cascade, TileHorizontal, TileVertical, CloseAll
Help	HelpUserGuide, HelpTutorial, HelpExchange, HelpScan, HelpCapture, HelpPDFWriter, HelpDistiller, HelpSearch, HelpCatalog, HelpReader,Weblink:Home
Help(Windows)	About

```
\usepackage[pdftex,colorlinks,
pdftoolbar=false,pdfmenubar=false,
pdfwindowui=false,
pdfpagemode=FullScreen,
]{hyperref}
\pagestyle{fancy}
\cfoot{\navbar}

\newcommand{\navbar}{%
 \Acrobatmenu{FirstPage}{$\Leftarrow$}
 \Acrobatmenu{PrevPage}{$\leftarrow$}
 \Acrobatmenu{NextPage}{$\rightarrow$}
 \Acrobatmenu{LastPage}{$\Rightarrow$}
 \Acrobatmenu{Close}{$\bullet$}
 }
```

The above produces a footline containing

$$\Leftarrow \; \leftarrow \; \rightarrow \; \Rightarrow \; \bullet$$

(by default in red) as clickable buttons to jump to the first page, to the previous page, to the next page, and to the last page, respectively. And clicking the bullet • closes the document. Of course, it looks even better if icons are made up and inserted with \includegraphics.

14 Multilingual LaTeX

The original versions of TeX and LaTeX were set up for the English language, American variant. The built-in hyphenation patterns were for English only, and several English words such as 'Figure' and 'Bibliography' were included explicitly in certain commands. This in fact violates the rules of good programming that forbid doing anything explicitly. In Europe, LaTeX users quickly made customizations for their particular languages. The adaptation for German, `german.sty`, is a set of macros from many contributors collected together by H. Partl of the Technical University of Vienna, and it has become the standard for the German-speaking TeX Users Group (DANTE). It contains some facilities for other languages, including French and English.

The key to the `german` package and other language adaptations is that the standard LaTeX document styles (and later classes for LaTeX 2$_\varepsilon$) had been altered so that explicit English words in the output were replaced by reprogrammable command names. These names had become standardized among European users for application to all languages. The modified LaTeX version by J. Schrod from Darmstadt was known as ILaTeX, for International LaTeX. These names and their standard English values are to be found in Section D.3.1.

As of December 1, 1991, these naming features became part of the LaTeX standard. They represent good programming practice, since they allow even English-speaking users to change certain titles easily, for example 'Abstract' into 'Summary' or 'Contents' into 'Table of Contents'. Naturally, they were taken over, and extended upon, by LaTeX 2$_\varepsilon$.

Another important feature for multilingual usage is the TeX `\language` counter that allows more than one set of hyphenation patterns to be stored in the format with initex (Section B.1.3). Different patterns are activated by setting `\language` to the appropriate number. This is now standard for all TeX versions later than 3.0, which should now be universal.

Individual language packages such as `german` maintained by Bernd Raichle and `french` by Bernard Gaulle have now been superseded to a large extent today by the universal multilanguage system: `babel`.

14.1   The babel system

The babel system has been developed by Johannes Braams at the Dutch PTT Research Laboratories. Its main purpose is to provide LaTeX with a standard means of switching languages with a flexible method for loading the hyphenation patterns.

The three main requirements for a single language adaptation are translation of the explicit English words, special commands to simplify certain features of that language, and selection of the appropriate hyphenation patterns. To these, babel adds removal of the special commands and testing for the current language. The language-specific files must conform to the babel selection command structure. The concept of 'dialects' is also included, that is, two 'languages' that share a common set of hyphenation patterns. Examples are German and Austrian as well as British and U.S. English, which only differ in the form of the dates.

At present, the babel package contains definition files for the following languages (more can be added at any time):

> Afrikaans, Bahasa, Basque, Breton, Bulgarian, Catalan, Croatian, Czech, Danish, Dutch, English, Esperanto, Estonian, Finnish, French, Galician, German, Greek, Hebrew, Hungarian, Icelandic, Irish Gaelic, Italian, Latin, Lower Sorbian, North Sami, Norwegian, Polish, Portuguese, Romanian, Russian, Scottish Gaelic, Spanish, Slovakian, Slovenian, Swedish, Serbian, Turkish, Ukrainian, Upper Sorbian, Welsh

The necessary definition files are delivered with the installation. The hyphenation patterns for the various languages must be obtained from another source, however. For most of these files, there are no special commands for accents or punctuation; they only redefine the naming commands for those words that normally print English text.

The german.sty package has been a great inspiration for babel. However, because of the name conflict, it was necessary to create a new germanb.sty (and ngermanb.sty for the new German grammar rules) for babel applications, which contains the same set of special commands, but with a few babel additions. Similarly, the babel French file had to be named frenchb.sty to distinguish it from the existing french.sty.

To exploit the babel features most fully, one should produce a LaTeX format (Section B.1.3) that incorporates it directly. To this end, the hyphen.cfg supplied with babel must be used with the language.dat file configured for the local languages and hyphenation patterns that are to be pre-loaded. Only in this way can one conveniently get the right word division for each language.

Alternatively, one can use a normal LaTeX format and load babel as a regular package, as illustrated below. The switching of hyphenation patterns will then be questionable.

The babel files

The babel installation provides the following files for its implementation:

babel.def contains some of the basic macros for running babel and must be loaded by the first language file read in; the remaining macros are either already in the format itself (loaded from hyphen.cfg) or read in from switch.def; babel.def determines which is the case and reacts accordingly.

switch.def contains the additional babel macros, to be read in if these macros are not already stored in the LaTeX format.

hyphen.cfg contains the same macro definitions as in switch.def, plus some more that are to be run by initex; if this file is available during the creation of the LaTeX format (Section B.1.3), these macros are built into that format and file switch.def is not necessary at run time.

babel.sty is a master package that loads the language files specified as options.

language.dat contains a list of languages and the file names of their hyphenation patterns; this file is read in by hyphen.cfg during the initex run; it is the only file that may (must!) be edited for the particular installation (Section 14.2).

*.ldf are language definition files.

*.sty are language package files that read in the .ldf files.

Invoking babel

The babel package is loaded with the desired languages as options:

```
\usepackage[english,esperanto]{babel}
```

Alternatively, the language names may be used as global options, which is recommended if there are other packages that take the languages as options, as

```
\documentclass[english,esperanto]{article}
\usepackage{babel,varioref}
```

In both cases, the last named language is the one that is immediately active.
  The recognized language names that may be used as options are:

afrikaans	english	=francais	=polutoniko-
bahasa	=USenglish	=canadien	greek
basque	=american	=acadian	hebrew
breton	=UKenglish	galician	magyar
bulgarian	=british	german	=hungarian
catalan	=canadian	=germanb	icelandic
croatian	esperanto	=ngerman	irish
czech	estonian	=austrian	italian
danish	finnish	=naustrian	latin
dutch	french	greek	lowersorbian

samin	=portuguese	scottish	serbian
norsk	=brazilian	spanish	turkish
=nynorsk	=brazil	slovak	ukrainian
polish	romanian	slovene	uppersorbian
portuges	russian	swedish	welsh

Those names preceded by = are synonyms for the language option above them. (The equals sign is *not* part of the option name.) For example, both `hungarian` and `magyar` load the file `magyar.ldf`.

If the `babel` package is loaded, all it does is read in the specified language packages; they in turn read in `babel.def` and possibly `switch.def` (if its macros are not already in the format).

Language switching commands

The normal user needs to know very little about the `babel` internal operations. The new high-level user commands are:

```
\selectlanguage{language}
\begin{otherlanguage}{language} text \end{otherlanguage}
\begin{otherlanguage*}{language} text \end{otherlanguage*}
\foreignlanguage{language}{text}
\iflanguage{language}{yes_text}{no_text}
```

The `\selectlanguage` command and the `otherlanguage` environment are two ways to switch to another language, with all its features and translations. The `\foreignlanguage` command and the `otherlanguage*` environment also switch to *language* but without the translations or date changes; they are meant for setting short sections of text in a language different from the regular one.

The `\iflanguage` executes *yes_text* if *language* is current, otherwise it executes *no_text*.

In addition, `\languagename` contains the name of the currently selected language.

Of course, each language definition file can also have its own special commands to assist typing accented and special characters. For example, in German, one may type "a as a shorthand for \"a. To find out what special commands are available for each language, and any other special considerations, one must read the documentation for that language. Documentation should be found in the texmf→doc→tex→generic →babel directory, or you can process the desired *language*.dtx file in the texmf→ source→tex→generic→babel directory. (These paths might be different on your system.)

Contents of a language definition file

Although one does not normally need to know how the switching mechanism functions, we will outline it here for the interested user.

Two additional internal `babel` commands are:

\addlanguage{*lang_num*} and
\adddialect{*lang_num_1*}{*lang_num_2*}

where *lang_num* is an internal language number for specifying the set of hyphenation patterns. The command \addlanguage sets its argument equal to the next available language number. The form of *lang_num* used in babel is \l@*language*, for example, \l@english. This command is executed on those language names listed in language.dat during the initex run. The command \adddialect sets the first argument equal to the second so that the two languages make use of the same set of hyphenation patterns. For example, in english.ldf there is the command \adddialect{\l@american}{\l@english}.

A language definition file must provide four commands:

1. \captions*lang* to redefine the naming commands such as \tablename (see Section D.3.1);

2. \date*lang* to define \today (see Section D.3.2).;

3. \extras*lang* to define any language-specific commands;

4. \noextras*lang* to remove the language-specific commands.

If the language *lang* is not one with prestored hyphenation patterns in the current format file (that is, if \l@*lang* is undefined), it is set to be a 'dialect' of language number 0.

Finally, the language definition file calls \selectlanguage{*lang*} to activate that language. This is accomplished by

- calling \language\l@*lang* to select the set of hyphenation patterns,

- invoking \originalTeX in order to remove any existing language-specific commands,

- activating \captions*lang*, \date*lang*, and \extras*lang* to set the language-specific names, date, and commands, and

- redefining \originalTeX to be \noextras*lang* so that the next language switch will remove those features specific to *lang*.

14.2 Contents of the `language.dat` file

As has been mentioned before, with TeX version 3.0 and later it is possible to store more than one set of hyphenation patterns in the format file. The counter \language is used to switch between them by setting it to a different number.

However, there is no standard to dictate which languages belong to which numbers. If a package were to assume a certain ordering, it would most certainly function incorrectly at installations other than the one for which it was designed. The babel system invokes a more reliable procedure.

During the production of the format by initex (Section B.1.3), the file hyphen.cfg is input, which in turn reads in language.dat, the only file to be tailored to the local installation. This file contains a list of languages to add as well as the name of the file with the hyphenation patterns and the name of any additional file to be included. It also indicates names of dialects that use the same hyphenations by prefixing the name with an equals sign. For example, if language.dat contains

```
=USenglish
american  ushyphen.tex
english   ukhyphen.tex
=UKenglish
=british
french    frhyphen.tex
german    dehypht.tex
ngerman   dehyphn.tex
```

then the hyphenation patterns stored in the files ushyphen.tex, ukhyphen.tex, frhyphen.tex, dehypht.tex, and dehyphn.tex are loaded under the language numbers 0 to 4, respectively; and \l@american, \l@english, \l@french, \@german, and \l@ngerman are defined as 0 through 4 for use with the \selectlanguage command. Languages \l@USenglish and \l@UKenglish are synonyms for the current language, in this case 0 and 1, respectively. Similarly \l@british is identical to \l@UKenglish.

15 Math Extensions with $\mathcal{A}_{\mathcal{M}}S$-LATEX

The American Mathematical Society, $\mathcal{A}_{\mathcal{M}}S$, has supported the development and usage of TEX since its first release. Shortly after TEX 82 became available, the $\mathcal{A}_{\mathcal{M}}S$ produced a macro package for generating a special format `amstex`, described in *The Joy of TEX* by Spivak (1990). The macros in this $\mathcal{A}_{\mathcal{M}}S$-TEX complement the mathematical typesetting features of Plain TEX by adding additional ones and simplifying others.

However, $\mathcal{A}_{\mathcal{M}}S$-TEX is not a documentation preparation system like LATEX, describing the logical layout of a document by means of markup commands, but rather is simply an extension to Plain TEX.

The great popularity of TEX as a text formatting program is due primarily to the availability of LATEX as a user-friendly interface to the underlying TEX machinery. Many authors therefore asked the $\mathcal{A}_{\mathcal{M}}S$ to provide LATEX with the same mathematical features as in $\mathcal{A}_{\mathcal{M}}S$-TEX. The $\mathcal{A}_{\mathcal{M}}S$-LATEX project was thus launched in 1987, with version 1.0 completed three years later by Frank Mittelbach and Rainer Schöpf, together with Michael Downes of the $\mathcal{A}_{\mathcal{M}}S$. $\mathcal{A}_{\mathcal{M}}S$-LATEX has been fully converted to LATEX 2_ε with version 1.2 in 1995.

The $\mathcal{A}_{\mathcal{M}}S$-LATEX collection consists of three parts: packages for extending mathematical typesetting; extra classes for articles and books published by the $\mathcal{A}_{\mathcal{M}}S$; and supplemental fonts for additional symbols, math alphabets, and Cyrillic fonts.

In the next sections, we give an overview of the math extensions available in the package `amsmath`; a more detailed user's manual is delivered with the collection, in the file `amsldoc.tex`. How to invoke the additional fonts is described below in Section 15.4 or in the $\mathcal{A}_{\mathcal{M}}S$-supplied manual found in the file `amsfndoc.tex`. The extra classes will not be described in this book; $\mathcal{A}_{\mathcal{M}}S$ authors should refer to the instructions in the document `instr-l.tex` provided with $\mathcal{A}_{\mathcal{M}}S$-LATEX.

15.1 Invoking $\mathcal{A}_{\mathcal{M}}S$-LATEX

Package:
amsmath

If the `\documentclass` statement at the beginning of the LATEX document selects one of the $\mathcal{A}_{\mathcal{M}}S$ classes `amsbook`, `amsart`, or `amsproc`, then most of the $\mathcal{A}_{\mathcal{M}}S$-LATEX features are loaded automatically. These features may still be employed with other classes by including the main extension package amsmath by means of

\usepackage[*options*]{amsmath}

in the document's preamble. The list of allowable options is described below in Section 15.2.8.

The amsmath package defines many of the new math typesetting features itself, but it also loads a number of other packages from the $\mathcal{A}_{\mathcal{M}}\mathcal{S}$-LATEX collection that contain further extensions, such as amsopn, amstext, and amsbsy. These packages could be loaded separately without amsmath if only their limited features are wanted. On the other hand, the packages amscd and amsthm are not included in amsmath and must be loaded explicitly if their features are desired. Simply add their names to the list of packages in \usepackage.

The following section describes the new commands and environments made available with amsmath and its associated packages. We call these the standard features of $\mathcal{A}_{\mathcal{M}}\mathcal{S}$-LATEX. Further extensions added by other packages are explained afterwards.

The examples in this chapter employ the user-defined commands \mi, \me, and \dif, defined in Section 7.4.10, for printing upright i, e, and d in math mode.

!

15.2 Standard features of $\mathcal{A}_{\mathcal{M}}\mathcal{S}$-LATEX

This relatively long section presents those standard features of $\mathcal{A}_{\mathcal{M}}\mathcal{S}$-LATEX that are activated by loading the amsmath package or by selecting one of the $\mathcal{A}_{\mathcal{M}}\mathcal{S}$ classes amsart, amsbook, or amsproc.

15.2.1 Additional font switching commands

Package: Standard LATEX provides the math alphabet commands \mathcal, \mathrm, \mathbf, amsbsy \mathsf, \mathit, \mathtt for changing fonts within math mode (Section 7.4.2). With $\mathcal{A}_{\mathcal{M}}\mathcal{S}$-LATEX, one may also use the commands

\boldsymbol{*symbol*}   and   \pmb{*symbol*}

to print *symbol* in a boldface, provided there is an appropriate bold font for it. Whereas the command \mathbf sets only Latin letters, numbers, and Greek upper-case letters in bold, these commands also affect math symbols and Greek lowercase letters. Compare the result of $\mathbf{\nabla\times V\,d\sigma}$ ($\nabla \times \mathbf{V}\mathrm{d}\sigma$) with that of $\boldsymbol{\nabla\times V\,d\sigma}$ ($\boldsymbol{\nabla \times V\, d\sigma}$). With the standard LATEX command \mathbf, only the letters V and d appear bold, while the other characters remain in normal weight. Not only that, these letters are upright, not italic as required by international standards. With \boldsymbol, all symbols are bold and italic.

Those symbols for which no boldface font exists will remain in normal weight with the \boldsymbol command. Such symbols are, for example, those that come in two sizes (Section 7.3.7) like $\sum$, $\int$, $\bigcup$, and so on. The command `\pmb` (poor man's bold) simulates a boldface even for these symbols by printing them several times slightly displaced. The result of `$\pmb{\sum\;\int\;\bigcup}$` is $\pmb{\sum \int \bigcup}$.

These commands are defined in the package `amsbsy`, which may be loaded separately without `amsmath`.

Package:
amstext
A short piece of normal text can be given within a formula with

> `\text{`*short_text*`}`

In contrast to `\mbox{`*short_text*`}` for standard LaTeX, the `\text` command switches font size when used as superscript or subscript. Thus `.._{\text{Word}}` sets Word lower and changes to `\scriptstyle` font size. To achieve the same effect in standard LaTeX, the font size must be given explicitly, as `.._{\mbox{\scriptstyle Word}}`. Furthermore, the name `\text` is more precise than `\mbox`.

This command is defined in the package `amstext`. Like `amsbsy`, it may be loaded on its own without `amsmath` if none of the other $\mathcal{A}_{\mathcal{M}}S$-LaTeX features are wanted.

Another command to insert normal text inside a displayed equation is

> `\intertext{`*insert_text*`}`

The *insert_text* is inserted as a left-justified line of text between those of the formula. The alignment of the formula lines remains unaffected, something that is not guaranteed if one closes the displayed equation, inserts text, and reopens the equation. For example:

$$(x + iy)(x - iy) = x^2 - ixy + ixy - i^2y^2$$
$$= y^2 + y^2 \quad \text{since} \quad i^2 = -1 \quad \text{is true.}$$

On the other hand

$$(x + iy)^2 = x^2 + 2ixy + i^2y^2 = x^2 + 2ixy - y^2$$
$$(x - iy)^2 = x^2 - 2ixy + i^2y^2 = x^2 - 2ixy - y^2$$

```
\begin{align*}
 (x+\mi y)(x-\mi y) & = x^2 - \mi xy + \mi xy - \mi ^2y^2\\
            & = y^2 + y^2\quad\text{since}\quad \mi ^2=-1
            \quad\text{is true.}\\
\intertext{On the other hand}
 (x +\mi y)^2 & = x^2 + 2\mi xy +\mi ^2y^2 = x^2 + 2\mi xy-y^2\\
 (x -\mi y)^2 & = x^2 - 2\mi xy +\mi ^2y^2 = x^2 - 2\mi xy-y^2
\end{align*}
```

The alignment of the lines on the first equals sign is maintained through the interruption with the line of text 'On the other hand'. The environment `align` (Section 15.2.6) is one of several new ones provided by $\mathcal{A}_{\mathcal{M}}S$-LaTeX to replace the standard LaTeX environment `eqnarray`. Note that `\intertext` may only be issued immediately after the `\\` for starting a new line.

15.2.2 Multiple mathematical symbols

Mathematical formulas often require the same symbol to appear several times, such as multiple integral signs, or symbols and arrows to be stacked above or below a mathematical expression. Usually the distances between these symbols depends on the mathematical meaning, something that LaTeX cannot automatically recognize. $\mathcal{A}_{\mathcal{M}}\mathcal{S}$-LaTeX provides a number of structures to help the user find the right spacing without tedious trial and error.

Multiple integrals

With $\mathcal{A}_{\mathcal{M}}\mathcal{S}$-LaTeX, the commands \iint, \iiint, \iiiint, and \idotsint output multiple integrals, with upper and lower limits being added in the usual manner. In text formulas, they are printed as $\iint$, $\iiint$, $\iiiint$, $\int\cdots\int$, while in displayed formulas, they appear as

$$\iint\limits_S f(x,y)\,\mathrm{d}S$$ \[\iint\limits_S f(x,y)\,\dif S \]

$$\iiint\limits_V f(x,y,z)\,\mathrm{d}V$$ \[\iiint\limits_V f(x,y,z)\,\dif V\]

$$\iiiint\limits_G f(x,y,z,t)\,\mathrm{d}G$$ \[\iiiint\limits_G f(x,y,z,t)
                                                            \,\dif G \]

$$\int\cdots\int\limits_U f(x_1,\ldots,x_k)\,\mathrm{d}U$$ \[\idotsint\limits_U
                                                                   f(x_1,\ldots,x_k)\,\dif U \]

whereby the command \limits may be left off if the option intlimits has been specified when amsmath was loaded (see Section 15.2.8).

Multiline limits

One often needs multiline limits or indices for summations, as in the examples below.
$$\Delta_{\substack{p_1p_2\cdots p_{n-k}\\ q_1q_2\cdots q_{n-k}}} \qquad \sum_{\substack{k_0,k_1,\ldots\geq0\\ k_0+k_1+\cdots=0}} a_{0k_0}a_{1k_1}\cdots$$

$\mathcal{A}_{\mathcal{M}}\mathcal{S}$-LaTeX provides a command \substack for this purpose, with syntax

    \substack{1st line\\2nd line\\...\\ last line}

where the command must immediately follow the ^ or _ shifting commands, and be entirely enclosed in curly braces { }. The index for the left-hand example above was generated with

    \Delta_{\substack{p_1p_2\cdots p_{n-k}\\q_1q_2\cdots q_{n-k}}}

The lines of text printed by \substack are centered horizontally, as is apparent in the right-hand example above. This was produced with

```
\[ \sum_{\substack{k_0,k_1,\ldots\ge0\\ k_0+k_1+
      \cdots=0}}a_{0k_0} a_{1k_1}\cdots \]
```

On the other hand, the environment subarray offers more control over the horizontal alignment:

```
\begin{subarray}{pos} 1st line\\2nd line\\...\\ last line
\end{subarray}
```

The argument *pos* may be c for centered or l for left-justified lines.

$$\sum_{\substack{i\in\Lambda\\i<j<n}} P(i,j)$$

```
\[ \sum_{\begin{subarray}{l} i\in\Lambda\\
      i<j<n \end{subarray}} P(i,j) \]
```

Special limits

To add a differential prime sign to a summation symbol without a lower limit, such as $\sum' E_n$, in a displayed formula, one can easily give

```
\[ \sum\nolimits' E_n \]
```

$$\sum' E_n$$

However, if there is to be an upper limit as well, the prime can only be added with much fiddling. The \sideset command simplifies this task considerably.

$$\sideset{}{'}\sum_{n=0}^\infty (2n+1)E_{2n+1}$$

```
\[ \sideset{}{'}\sum_{n=0}^\infty
      (2n+1) E_{2n+1} \]
```

The complete syntax for this command is

```
\sideset{pre}{post}\symbol
```

where *pre* and *post* are the superscripts and subscript commands to be added before and after the *symbol*, respectively. They must contain the raising and lowering operators ^ and _.

The product symbol $\prod$ is given daggers above and asterisks below with \sideset{_\dag^*}{_\dag^*}\prod, as shown at the right.

$$\sideset{_\dagger^*}{_\dagger^*}\prod$$

Additional shifting commands are

```
\overset{char}{\symbol}   and   \underset{char}{\symbol}
```

which place the arbitrary *char* above or below the *symbol* in the size appropriate for superscripts and subscripts. Thus $\overset{*}{X}$ produces $\overset{*}{X}$ and $\underset{*}{X}$ yields $\underset{*}{X}$.

Extended arrows

The amsmath package provides a number of commands to produce extra long arrows for combining with mathematical expressions. The commands

```
\overleftarrow{expr}            \underleftarrow{expr}
\overrightarrow{expr}           \underrightarrow{expr}
\overleftrightarrow{expr}       \underleftrightarrow{expr}
```

produce lengthened arrows pointing left and right, as well as double arrows above and below the mathematical expression *expr*.

$$\overrightarrow{ABCD} = \underrightarrow{AB} + \underrightarrow{BC} + \underrightarrow{CD}$$

$$\overleftarrow{ABCD} = \underleftarrow{DC} + \underleftarrow{CB} + \underleftarrow{BA}$$

$$\overleftrightarrow{ABCD} = \underrightarrow{DCAB}$$

```
\begin{eqnarray*}
  \overrightarrow{ABCD} & = &
    \underrightarrow{AB} +
    \underrightarrow{BC} +
    \underrightarrow{CD} \\
  \overleftarrow{ABCD} & = &
    \underleftarrow{DC} ...
\end{eqnarray*}
```

The lower arrows are actually too close to the expression, as is seen on the right-hand side of the last example. This should also be the case for all the other examples with a lower arrow, except that we have added a strut to push them down somewhat:

```
\underrightarrow{\rule[-2pt]{0pt}{2pt}AB} ...   and
\underleftarrow{\rule[-2pt]{0pt}{2pt}DC} ...
```

A smaller font size will be used for the arrows when they appear in exponents, indices, superscripts, and subscripts:

$$\int_{\overrightarrow{0.2\pi}} r\, d\varphi = 2\pi r$$

```
\int_{\overrightarrow{0.2\pi}}
  r\,d\varphi = 2\pi r
```

There are two more commands for horizontal arrows of variable length:

```
\xleftarrow[below]{above}   \xrightarrow[below]{above}
```

which place the mandatory *above* in superscript size over the arrow and the optional *below* in subscript size beneath it.

$$A \xleftarrow{n+\mu-1} B \xrightarrow[T]{n\pm i-1} C$$

```
\[ A \xleftarrow{n+\mu-1} B
   \xrightarrow[T]{n\pm i-1} C \]
```

The package `amscd` (Section 15.3.2) offers further possibilities for combining arrows and text.

Multiple dots over symbols

Three or four dots in a row over a symbol are often used for time derivatives of third and fourth order. They can be placed with the commands

```
\dddot{sym}   and   \ddddot{sym}
```

In this way $\dddot{u}$ and $\ddddot{u}$ are produced with $\dddot{u}$ and $\ddddot{u}$.

Continuation dots

In standard LATEX, one has the commands \ldots and \cdots for printing three continuation dots, either on the baseline or raised to the center of the line. $\mathcal{A}_{\mathcal{M}}S$-LATEX offers a number of additional possibilities. The most general of these is the \dots command that adjusts the vertical height according to the symbol that follows it. If this is an equals sign or binary operator, such as $+$ or $-$, the dots are raised, as with \cdots, otherwise they are on the baseline, as with \ldots.

$a_0+a_1+\dots+a_n$ $\Longrightarrow$ $a_0 + a_1 + \cdots + a_n$
$a_0,a_1,\dots,a_n$ $\Longrightarrow$ $a_0, a_1, \ldots, a_n$

If the continuation dots come at the end of a formula, there is no following symbol to determine the height of the dots. In this case, one must manually indicate the height by means of one of the commands \dotsc (comma), \dotsb (binary), \dotsm (multiplication), or \dotsi (integral).

The \dotsc command is to be used with commas, so $A_1,A_2,\dotsc$ produces $A_1, A_2, \ldots$; the \dotsb command sets them for a binary operator, thus $A_1+A_2+\dotsb$ yields $A_1 + A_2 + \cdots$; the command \dotsm is actually identical to \dotsb, but it is logically meant to be applied to multiplication, $A_1A_2\dotsm$ makes $A_1 A_2 \cdots$; finally \dotsi places the dots at the mean height of an adjacent integral sign.

\[\int_{A_1}\int_{A_2}\dotsi \] $\int_{A_1} \int_{A_2} \cdots$

15.2.3 Fractions

The TEX fraction commands \atop, \choose, and others may be allowed in standard LATEX, but not in $\mathcal{A}_{\mathcal{M}}S$-LATEX. With the amsmath package, only those fraction commands described here may be used.

Basic fraction commands

In addition to the regular LATEX command \frac{over}{under}, $\mathcal{A}_{\mathcal{M}}S$-LATEX provides the commands \tfrac and \dfrac with the same syntax. These are effectively the same as \frac but with the font set to \textstyle or \displaystyle, respectively (Section 7.5.2). We demonstrate their effects with some examples from the $\mathcal{A}_{\mathcal{M}}S$-LATEX user's manual.

\[\frac{1}{k}\log_2 c(f)\qquad
   \tfrac{1}{k}\log_2 c(f)\qquad
   \sqrt{\frac{1}{k}\log_2 c(f)}\qquad
   \sqrt{\dfrac{1}{k}\log_2 c(f)}   \]

$$\frac{1}{k}\log_2 c(f) \qquad \tfrac{1}{k}\log_2 c(f) \qquad \sqrt{\frac{1}{k}\log_2 c(f)} \qquad \sqrt{\dfrac{1}{k}\log_2 c(f)}$$

Binomial expressions

A binomial expression looks something like a fraction but is enclosed in round parentheses and is missing the horizontal rule. The basic command in the amsmath package is

    \binom{over}{under}

which functions in the same way as \frac and the other fraction commands.

    \[\binom{n+1}{k} = \binom{n}{k}
       + \binom{n}{k-1 \]

$$\binom{n+1}{k} = \binom{n}{k} + \binom{n}{k-1}$$

Similarly, the commands \tbinom and \dbinom are analogous to \tfrac and \dfrac.

User-defined fractions

The amsmath package provides a powerful tool for defining fraction-like structures:

    \genfrac{left_brk}{right_brk}{thickness}{mathsize}{over}{under}

where *left_brk* and *right_brk* are the parenthesis characters on the left and right, *thickness* is the thickness of the horizontal line, and *{mathsize}* is a number 0–3 representing the math sizes \displaystyle, \textstyle, \scriptstyle, and \scriptscriptstyle, respectively. The last two arguments, *over* and *under*, are the texts in the two parts of the fraction, the same arguments as in \frac and \binom.

If the *thickness* is left blank, the standard thickness for LaTeX fractions is used. If *mathsize* is empty, the font size is determined automatically by the normal rules in Section 7.5.2.

Rather than repeating \genfrac with the same first four arguments time and again, one should define new fraction commands with it. For example, the following definitions are given in amsmath.sty:

    \newcommand{\frac}[2]{\genfrac{}{}{}{}{#1}{#2}}
    \newcommand{\dfrac}[2]{\genfrac{}{}{}{0}{#1}{#2}}
    \newcommand{\tfrac}[2]{\genfrac{}{}{}{1}{#1}{#2}}
    \newcommand{\binom}[2]{\genfrac{(}{)}{0pt}{}{#1}{#2}

As a further example, consider the redefinition of the command \frac

    \renewcommand{\frac}[3][]{\genfrac{}{}{#1}{}{#2}{#3}}

in which the line thickness is now an optional first argument; without this optional argument, the command behaves as normal. Thus

    \[\binom{n}{m} =
       \frac[2pt]{n!}{M!(n-m)!} \]

yields $$\binom{n}{m} = \frac{n!}{M!(n-m)!}$$

Continued fractions

Continued fractions can be made in $\mathcal{A}_{\mathcal{M}}S$-LaTeX with the command

```
\cfrac[pos]{over}{under}
```

whereby the denominator *under* may contain further \cfrac commands.

```
\[ a_0 + \cfrac{1}{a_1 + \cfrac{1}{a_2 +
      \cfrac{1}{a_3 + \cfrac{1}{a_4 +
      \dotsb }}}}   \]
```

produces

$$a_0 + \cfrac{1}{a_1 + \cfrac{1}{a_2 + \cfrac{1}{a_3 + \cfrac{1}{a_4 + \cdots}}}}$$

If the optional argument *pos* is missing, the numerator *over* is centered on the horizontal rule; otherwise it may take values of l or r to left or right justify the numerator.

15.2.4 Matrices

Standard LaTeX possesses the environment array for producing arrays and matrices. The amsmath package provides the additional environments pmatrix, bmatrix, Bmatrix, vmatrix, and Vmatrix, which automatically add the enclosing braces (), [], {}, | |, and ‖ ‖ around the array, and in the right size. For completeness, there is also a matrix environment with no braces.

In contrast to the standard array environment (Section 6.2.1), these matrix environments do not require an explicit column specification as argument. By default, up to 10 centered columns may be used without any argument. (This maximum number may be changed by giving the special counter MaxMatrixCols a new value with either \setcounter or \addtocounter.) Otherwise the matrix environments are used in the same way as the array environment.

The following example is taken from Section 7.4.3 on page 136 and is recast here using $\mathcal{A}_{\mathcal{M}}S$-LaTeX constructs.

$$\sum_{p_1<p_2<\cdots<p_{n-k}}^{(1,2,\dots,n)} \Delta_{p_1 p_2 \dots p_{n-k}}^{p_1 p_2 \dots p_{n-k}} \sum_{q_1<q_2<\cdots<q_k} \begin{vmatrix} a_{q_1 q_1} & a_{q_1 q_2} & \cdots & a_{q_1 q_k} \\ a_{q_2 q_1} & a_{q_2 q_2} & \cdots & a_{q_2 q_k} \\ \cdots\cdots\cdots\cdots\cdots\cdots\cdots \\ a_{q_k q_1} & a_{q_k q_2} & \cdots & a_{q_k q_k} \end{vmatrix}$$

```
\[ \sum_{p_1<p_2<\dots<p_{n-k}}^{(1,2,\dots,n)}
   \Delta_{\substack{p_1p_2\dots p_{n-k}\\p_1p_2
   \dots p_{n-k}}}
```

```
\sum_{q_1<q_2<\dots<q_k}
\begin{vmatrix}
  a_{q_1q_1} & a_{q_1q_2} & \dots & a_{q_1q_k}\\
  a_{q_2q_1} & a_{q_2q_2} & \dots & a_{q_2q_k}\\
  \hdotsfor[2.0]{4}\\
  a_{q_kq_1} & a_{q_kq_2} & \dots & a_{q_kq_k}
\end{vmatrix}                 \]
```

Comparing this input text with that on page 136, one sees that it is simpler and easier to follow. The only new command used here is \hdotsfor, which has the syntax

> \hdotsfor[*stretch*]{*n*}

and which prints a continuous line of dots through *n* columns. The optional argument *stretch* is a multiplicative number to increase the dot density, being 1.0 by default.

```
\[ \begin{matrix} a & b & c & d & e\\
            x & \hdotsfor{3} & z
\end{matrix}   \]
```

$$
\begin{matrix} a & b & c & d & e\\ x & \cdots & z \end{matrix}
$$

Compare the standard dot spacing above with that from \hdotsfor[2.0] in the previous example.

The initial letter of each of the xmatrix environments indicates the type of braces that enclose it: pmatrix for (round) parentheses, bmatrix for (square) brackets, Bmatrix for (curly) braces, vmatrix for vertical lines, and Vmatrix for double vertical lines. They appear as

$$
\begin{matrix} r & s & t\\ u & v & w\\ x & y & z \end{matrix} \quad
\begin{pmatrix} r & s & t\\ u & v & w\\ x & y & z \end{pmatrix} \quad
\begin{bmatrix} r & s & t\\ u & v & w\\ x & y & z \end{bmatrix}
$$

$$
\begin{Bmatrix} r & s & t\\ u & v & w\\ x & y & z \end{Bmatrix} \quad
\begin{vmatrix} r & s & t\\ u & v & w\\ x & y & z \end{vmatrix} \quad
\begin{Vmatrix} r & s & t\\ u & v & w\\ x & y & z \end{Vmatrix}
$$

where each matrix has been produced with

```
\[ \begin{xmatrix} r & s & t\\ u & v & w\\ x & y & z
\end{xmatrix}   \]
```

where xmatrix is set to matrix, pmatrix, bmatrix, Bmatrix, vmatrix, and Vmatrix one after the other.

To generate a small array within a text formula, one can apply the smallmatrix environment. In this way $\left(\begin{smallmatrix} a & b & c\\ e & m & r \end{smallmatrix}\right)$ can be made with

```
$ \bigl( \begin{smallmatrix} a & b & c\\ e & m & r
         \end{smallmatrix} \bigr) $
```

15.2.5 User extensions and fine adjustments

Function names

Package: Standard LATEX recognizes a number of predefined function names (Section 7.3.8) that
amsopn are printed in math made by placing a backslash in front of that name: arccos, arcsin,
arctan, arg, cos, cosh, cot, coth, csc, deg, det, dim, exp, gcd, hom, inf, ker, lg, lim,
liminf, limsup, ln, log, max, min, Pr, sec, sin, sinh, sup, tan, tanh. Not only do these
names appear in an upright font, as is required for function names, but the spacing
with adjacent parts of the mathematical expression is adjusted automatically.

$\mathcal{A}_{\mathcal{M}}$S-LATEX provides some more function names, as variations on the standard
\lim name:

\varlimsup	$\varlimsup$	\varinjlim	$\varinjlim$
\varliminf	$\varliminf$	\varprojlim	$\varprojlim$

These functions may take on limits with the raising and lowering operators ^ and _;
for example, \varliminf_{n\to\infty} for $\varliminf_{n\to\infty}$.

It is also possible to define new function names with the same font and spacing
properties as the predefined ones. The command

$$\texttt{\textbackslash DeclareMathOperator\{\textbackslash}\textit{cmd}\}\{\textit{name}\}$$

which may only be issued in the preamble, before \begin{document}, defines a
command \cmd that prints the function name *name*. For example, to define a
function name \doit, give

$$\texttt{\textbackslash DeclareMathOperator\{\textbackslash doit\}\{doit\}}$$

and then $A=3\doit^2(B)$ yields $A = 3\,\text{doit}^2(B)$. Note that superscripts and subscripts are printed beside the operator; if they are to be printed as limits, that is,
above and below the operator in displayed math mode, use the *-form to define
them. For example:

$$\texttt{\textbackslash DeclareMathOperator*\{\textbackslash Lim\}\{lim\}}$$
$$\texttt{\textbackslash[\textbackslash Lim\_\{n\textbackslash to-\textbackslash infty\}\^\{n\textbackslash to+\textbackslash infty\}\textbackslash]}$$

$$\lim_{n\to-\infty}^{n\to+\infty}$$

The *name* text need not be identical to the command name. In particular, it may
contain special characters not allowed in command names.

Modulo expressions are printed in standard LATEX with \bmod and \pmod com-
mands, and are complemented in $\mathcal{A}_{\mathcal{M}}$S-LATEX by \mod and \pod. The possibilities
are:

$z \equiv x + y \bmod n^2$	z \equiv x+y \bmod{n^2}
$z \equiv x + y \pmod{n^2}$	z \equiv x+y \pmod{n^2}
$z \equiv x + y \mod n^2$	z \equiv x+y \mod{n^2}
$z \equiv x + y \pod{n^2}$	z \equiv x+y \pod{n^2}

The automatic parentheses are missing with \mod, while with \pod the name 'mod' is
omitted. Furthermore, \pmod is redefined for text formulas to reduce the preceding
space: $y\pmod{a+b}$: $y \pmod{a + b}$.

The `\DeclareMathOperator` command and additional function names are defined in the `amsopn` package, which may be loaded on its own without `amsmath`.

Fine-tuning roots

The positioning of an index to a root sign is not always ideal under standard LaTeX. In $\sqrt[\beta]{k}$, for example, the β could be somewhat higher and shifted slightly to the right. The $\mathcal{A}_{\mathcal{M}}S$-LaTeX commands

    \leftroot{*shift*}   \uproot{*shift*}

cause such manual displacements, where *shift* is a number specifying the size in small, internal units. Negative numbers represent a shift in the opposite direction. Compare the above standard result with that of

    $\sqrt[\leftroot{-1}\uproot{3}\beta]{k}$ $\sqrt[\beta]{k}$

The size of the root sign depends on its contents. If they hang below the baseline, the root sign extends lower down than for contents that have no depth. Note the differences between $\sqrt{x}$, $\sqrt{y}$, and $\sqrt{z}$. Some publishers want all root signs to be at the same height, as $\sqrt{x} + \sqrt{y} + \sqrt{z}$. This is accomplished with the TeX command `\smash`, which places its argument in a box of zero height and depth. The $\mathcal{A}_{\mathcal{M}}S$-LaTeX version of this command allows an optional argument b or t to zero only the depth or height, respectively. The above example is produced with `$\sqrt{\smash[b]{y}}$`. The option b is taken because we want only the depth to be ignored, not the height of the letter *y*.

Spacing adjustment

With standard LaTeX, there are a number of commands to fine-tune the spacing in a math formula (Section 7.5.1). These are `\`, `\:`, `\;`, `\quad`, and `\qquad` for increasing amounts of positive spacing, and `\!` for negative spacing. With the `amsmath` package, the first three still exist, but may also be called with the more obvious names `\thinspace`, `\medspace`, and `\thickspace`. There is also `\negthinspace` as an alias for `\!`.

The complete set of spacing commands are summarized in the table below taken from the $\mathcal{A}_{\mathcal{M}}S$-LaTeX manual.

Short form	Command name	Demo	Short form	Command name	Demo
\,	\thinspace	⌐L	\!	\negthinspace	⊥
\:	\medspace	⌐L		\negmedspace	⊥
\;	\thickspace	⌐L		\negthickspace	⊥
	\quad	⌐ L			
	\qquad	⌐ L			

The general math spacing command is

```
\mspace{mu}
```

which inserts space in mathematical spacing units 'mu' (=1/18 em). For example, `\mspace{-9mu}` puts in negative spacing of 1/2 em.

Vertical bars

In standard LᴬTEX, the commands | and \| are used for single and double vertical bars, | and ‖. However, these symbols are often used as delimiters (that is, like braces), in which case different spacing requirements are needed. In particular, a distinction must be made between the left and right delimiter in expressions like $|a|$ and $\|v\|$. The LᴬTEX commands are only appropriate for single appearances, like $p|q$ or $f(t,x)|_{t=0}$.

The amsmath package defines the delimiter commands \lvert, \rvert for a single bar, and \lVert, \rVert for a double bar. They are useful for defining commands that set their arguments in such delimiters, as

```
\newcommand{\abs}[1]{\lvert#1\rvert}
\newcommand{\norm}[1]{\lVert#1\rVert}
```

Now $\abs{a}$ produces $|a|$ and $\norm{v}$ $\|v\|$.

A similar recommendation can be made for the standard commands \langle and \rangle. By defining

```
\newcommand{\mean}[1]{\langle#1\rangle}
```

one gives $\mean{x}$ to generate $\langle x\rangle$, rather than $<x>$ which produces $< x >$.

Boxed formulas

A formula may be placed in a box with the command

```
\boxed{formula}
```

For example,

```
\[ \boxed{\int_0^\infty f(x)\,\dif x \approx
     \sum_{i=1}^n w_i \me^{x_i} f(x_i)}  \]
```

produces

$$\boxed{\int_0^\infty f(x)\,\mathrm{d}x \approx \sum_{i=1}^n w_i \mathrm{e}^{x_i} f(x_i)}$$

15.2.6 Multiline equations

Equations consisting of several lines that are horizontally aligned at set points, such as the equals sign, can be generated in standard LᴬTEX with the eqnarray and eqnarray* environments (Section 7.4.7). Many authors consider these to be far too limited for publications with complicated multiline equations. $\mathcal{A}_{\mathcal{M}}S$-LATEX therefore provides a range of further alignment environments for formulas extending over a single line:

    align   gather   falign   multline   alignat   split

With the exception of split, all exist in a standard and a *-form. As for eqnarray, the standard form adds an automatic equation number to each line, while the *-form does not. The standard LATEX equation environment for single-line formulas is also available in $\mathcal{A}_{\mathcal{M}}S$-LATEX in a *-form. It may be used in combination with multiline environments.

Common features of alignment environments

All the alignment, or multiline, environments switch to math mode at the start and back to text mode at the end, except for split, which must be called in math mode. A new line is forced in the formula with the \\ command, as usual; an optional argument \\[len] can be added to increase the line spacing by *len*, again as usual.

   The automatic numbering with the standard forms can be suppressed for single lines by adding \notag before the \\ line break. Alternatively, the line can be given a desired marker with \tag{*mark*}. For example, with \tag{$\dag$}, the marker is (†). Using the *-form instead, the marker text is printed without the parentheses.

   The vertical position of the equation number or marker is shifted automatically if there is not enough room on the line for it. This shift can be manually adjusted with the command

    \raisetag{*len*}

which moves the marker upwards by *len* for that line only. A negative value moves it downwards.

The multline environment

The multline environment is a variant of the equation environment for *single* formulas that are too long for one line. The line breaks occur where the user forces them with the \\ command. The first line is left justified, the last right justified, and lines in between are centered. However, if the option fleqn has been given, all the lines appear left justified.

   The equation number, if present, appears at the right of the *last* line by default or if the option reqno has been selected; if the option leqno has been chosen, the number is placed at the left of the *first* line. (See Section 15.2.8 for the amsmath options.)

   The $\mathcal{A}_{\mathcal{M}}S$ classes (not dealt with here) put equation numbers at the left by default, something that leads to some confusion.

   It is possible to shift individual lines fully to the left or right with the commands \shoveleft{*formula*} and \shoveright{*formula*}. The entire formula text for that line, except the terminating \\, is placed in their arguments.

The left and right margins for the formula are set by the length parameter \multlinegap, which is initially 10 pt. This may be altered by the user with the \setlength or \addtolength commands.

An equation with five lines could be broken to look as follows:

$$\boxed{\text{First line — left justified}}$$
$$\boxed{\text{Second line — horizontally centered}}$$
$$\boxed{\text{Third line — pushed to the left}}$$
$$\boxed{\text{Fourth line — pushed to the right}}$$
$$\boxed{\text{Last line — right justified}} \qquad (15.1)$$

```
\begin{multline}
  \framebox[.75\columnwidth]{First line --- left justified}\\
  \framebox[.6\columnwidth]{Second line --- horizontally
      centered}\\
  \shoveleft{\framebox[.6\columnwidth]{Third line --- pushed
      to the left}}\\
  \shoveright{\framebox[.6\columnwidth]{Fourth line --- pushed
      to the right}}\\
  \framebox[.75\columnwidth]{Last line --- right justified}
\end{multline}
```

A real equation would contain mathematical expressions and not the \framebox commands in the above demonstration.

The split environment

Like multline, the split environment is meant for a single equation that does not fit on one line. Line breaks are again forced with the \\ command; the difference is that in each line there is an alignment marker & such that the lines are horizontally positioned to line up the markers.

The split environment does not switch into math mode, nor does it produce an equation number. It is intended to be applied within another math environment, such as equation or gather. This is why there is an equation* environment in $\mathcal{A}_{\mathcal{M}}S$-LATEX.

The equation number, if present, is provided by the outer environment. It is applied to the entire multiline formula, which by default, or with the option centertags, is centered on the group of lines. With the option tbtags, it is placed either at the left of the first line, or at the right of the last line, depending on the further options leqno and reqno, respectively. (See Section 15.2.8.)

$$
H_c = \frac{1}{2n} \sum_{l=0}^{n} (-1)^l (k-l)^{p-2} \sum_{l_1+\dots+l_p=l} \prod_{i=1}^{p} \binom{n_i}{l_i}
$$

$$
\times \left[(k-l) - (k_i - l_i) \right]^{k_i - l_i} \times \left[(k-l)^2 - \sum_{j=1}^{p} (k_i - l_i)^2 \right] \tag{15.2}
$$

```
\begin{equation}\begin{split}
  H_c={}&\frac{1}{2n}\sum_{l=0}^n (-1)^l (k-l)^{p-2}
    \sum_{l_1+\dots+l_p=l} \prod_{i=1}^p \binom{n_i}{l_i}\\
    &\times[(k-l) - (k_i-l_i)]^{k_i-l_i}\times
    \Bigl[(k-l)^2 - \sum_{j=1}^p (k_i-l_i)^2\Bigr]
\end{split}\end{equation}
```

The alignment has been chosen to be just after the equals sign. In order not to interfere with the normal spacing around equals signs, a dummy {} has been inserted afterwards, before the &. If the equation consists of several lines all beginning with =, then it would be better to put the alignment character before the = so that all equals signs align. Note the centered equation number at the right.

The gather environment

The gather environment switches to math mode, centering each of its formula lines without any alignment. The formula lines are separated by \\ commands. Each line receives an equation number, unless the *-form has been used or \notag has been issued in that line.

$$
\frac{1}{2} + \left(\frac{2}{3}\right)^4 + \left(\frac{3}{4}\right)^9 + \cdots + \left(\frac{n}{n+1}\right)^{n^2} + \cdots = \sum_{n=1}^{\infty} \left(\frac{n}{n+1}\right)^{n^2} \tag{15.3}
$$

$$
\text{converges since} \quad \lim_{n\to\infty} \sqrt[n]{\left(\frac{n}{n+1}\right)^{n^2}} = \lim_{n\to\infty} \left(\frac{1}{1+\frac{1}{n}}\right)^n = \frac{1}{e} < 1 \quad \text{root condition}
$$

$$
2 + \frac{3}{4} + \frac{4}{9} + \cdots + \frac{n+1}{n^2} + \cdots = \sum_{n=1}^{\infty} \frac{n+1}{n^2} \tag{15.4}
$$

$$
\text{diverges since} \quad \int_c^\infty \frac{x+1}{x^2} \, dx = \left[\ln x - \frac{1}{x}\right]_c^\infty = \infty \quad \text{(integral condition)}
$$

```
\begin{gather}
  \frac{1}{2} + \left(\frac{2}{3}\right)^4 + \left(\frac{3}{4}
  \right)^9 + \dots + \left(\frac{n}{n+1}\right)^{n^2} + \dotsb
  = \sum_{n=1}^\infty \left(\frac{n}{n+1}\right)^{n^2} \\
  \text{converges since}\quad\lim_{n\to\infty}
```

```
    \sqrt[n]{\left(\frac{n}{n+1}\right)^{n^2}} = \lim_{n\to\infty}
    \left(\frac{1}{1 + \dfrac{1}{n}}\right)^n = \frac{1}{\me} < 1
    \tag*{root condition}\\
    2 + \frac{3}{4} + \frac{4}{9} + \dots + \frac{n+1}{n^2} +
    \dotsb = \sum_{n=1}^\infty \frac{n+1}{n^2}\\
    \text{diverges since}\quad\int_c^\infty \frac{x+1}{x^2}\,
    \dif x = \left[ \ln x -\frac{1}{x}\right]_c^\infty = \infty
    \tag{integral condition}
  \end{gather}
```

Note the use of \tag* and \tag (page 282) to add text as markers to the second and fourth lines.

The align environment

The align environment is intended for multiple equations with horizontal alignment, usually on an equals sign or equivalent. New lines are indicated with \\ as usual. Each line is split into aligned columns such that the first column is right justified against the & character; the second left justified; the third column is right justified against the *third* &; the fourth column left justified again, and so on. This is the same as an array environment with column specification {rl rl rl ...}.

$$
\begin{array}{lll}
(x^n)' = nx^{n-1} & (e^x)' = e^x & (\sin x)' = \cos x \\[2mm]
\left(\dfrac{1}{x^n}\right)' = -\dfrac{n}{x^{n+1}} & (a^x)' = a^x \ln a & (\cos x)' = -\sin x \\[2mm]
(\sqrt[n]{x})' = \dfrac{1}{n\sqrt[n]{x^n-1}} & (\ln x)' = \dfrac{1}{x} & (\tan x)' = \dfrac{1}{\cos^2 x} \\[2mm]
 & (\log_a x)' = \dfrac{1}{x\ln a} & (\cot x)' = -\dfrac{1}{\sin^2 x}
\end{array}
$$

```
\begin{align*}
  \left(x^n\right)' &= nx^{n-1} & \left(\me^x\right)' &= \me^x &
  (\sin x)'        &= \cos x    \\
  \left(\frac{1}{x^n}\right)' &= -\frac{n}{x^{n+1}} &
  \left(a^x\right)' &= a^x\ln a & (\cos x)'          &= -\sin x\\
  \left(\sqrt[n]{x}\right)'   &= \frac{1}{n\sqrt[n]{x^n -1}} &
  (\ln x)'         &= \frac{1}{x} & (\tan x)'
                    &= \frac{1}{\cos^2 x}\\
  & &   (\log_a x)' &= \frac{1}{x\ln a} & (\cot x)'
                    &= -\frac{1}{\sin^2 x}
\end{align*}
```

The align* environment is used here to prevent the lines from being numbered, something that is not appropriate for such a collection of formulas. The alignment within each of the three column pairs is on the equals sign. The input for the last line begins with a double && to produce an empty column pair.

Occasionally a set of formulas is to be aligned on several equals signs in one line, as in the equations below for the volume V, inertial moment I_z, and mass M of an arbitrary body, in Cartesian, cylindrical, and spherical coordinates. In this case, the second and third parts are separated by a double && so that the left-hand sides of these column pairs are empty: The equals signs are always on an odd-numbered alignment marker.

$$V = \int\limits_V dv \quad = \iiint dx\, dy\, dz \qquad = \iiint \rho\, dx\, d\rho\, d\phi$$

$$= \iiint r^2 \sin\theta\, dr\, d\theta\, d\phi \qquad (15.5)$$

$$I_z = \int\limits_V \rho^2\, dv = \iiint (x^2 + y^2)\, dx\, dy\, dz = \iiint \rho^3\, dz\, d\rho\, d\phi$$

$$= \iiint r^4 \sin^3\theta\, dr\, d\theta\, d\phi \qquad (15.6)$$

$$M = \int\limits_V \delta\, dv \quad = \iiint \delta\, dx\, dy\, dz \qquad = \iiint \delta\rho\, dz\, d\rho\, d\phi$$

$$= \iiint \delta r^2 \sin\theta\, dr\, d\theta\, d\phi \qquad (15.7)$$

```
\begin{align}
V    &= \int\limits_V\dif v         &&= \iiint\dif x\,\dif y\,\dif z
    &&= \iiint \rho\,\dif x\,\dif \rho\,\dif \phi \notag \\
&&&&= \iiint r^2 \sin\theta\,\dif r\,\dif\theta\,\dif\phi\\
I_z &= \int\limits_V \rho^2\,\dif v &&=\iiint(x^2 + y^2)
                    \,\dif x\,\dif y\,\dif z
    &&= \iiint \rho^3\,\dif z\,\dif \rho\,\dif \phi \notag \\
&&&&= \iiint r^4\sin^3\theta\,\dif r\,\dif\theta\,\dif\phi\\
M    &= \int\limits_V \delta\,\dif v &&= \iiint \delta
                    \,\dif x\,\dif y\,\dif z
    &&= \iiint \delta\rho\,\dif z\,\dif\rho\,\dif\phi\notag \\
&&&&=\iiint\delta r^2\sin\theta\,\dif r\,\dif\theta\,\dif\phi
\end{align}
```

There are two variations on the `align` environment, `falign` and `alignat`. The first has exactly the same syntax as `align` but it inserts so much spacing between the column pairs that the entire line is filled out. The `alignat` environment is just the opposite: No spacing is inserted automatically between the column pairs. It must take the number of column pairs as a mandatory argument, otherwise the syntax of the contents is the same as that for `align`. The example above with the volume, inertial moment, and mass of a body could just as well have been given with

\begin{alignat}{3} *formula_text* \end{alignat}

(In fact, this is precisely what was done in order to fit it within the line width of this book.)

If one or more columns are empty, as in this example, it is possible to control their widths precisely in the alignat environment by adding explicit spacing between the two & characters in one of the lines. See Section 7.5.1 for spacing in math mode.

In summary, for the align environment and its variants, the first, third, fifth, ... & characters are alignment markers, while the second, fourth, sixth, ... are column pair separators.

Nested alignment environments

We have already pointed out on page 283 how the split environment is to be placed inside an equation environment. The same is true for the environments aligned and gathered, which may be used as building blocks within formulas. Their contents and behavior are otherwise the same as their related environments.

Both of these environments take an optional argument *pos*

\begin{aligned}[*pos*]   *lines* \end{aligned}
\begin{gathered}[*pos*]   *lines* \end{gathered}

which takes values of t or b to determine the vertical alignment (top or bottom) when they appear beside other elements. When no *pos* is given, they are centered. In this way

$$
\begin{aligned}
\alpha &= aa\\
\beta &= bbbbb\\
\gamma &= g
\end{aligned}
\qquad \text{versus} \qquad
\begin{aligned}
\delta &= dd\\
\eta &= eeeee\\
\varphi &= f
\end{aligned}
\qquad \text{versus} \qquad
\begin{gathered}
s = x+y\\
d = u - v - w\\
p = x \circ y
\end{gathered}
$$

is produced with

```
\begin{equation*}
  \begin{aligned} \alpha&=aa\\ \beta&=bbbbb\\ \gamma&=g
  \end{aligned}
  \qquad\text{versus}\qquad
  \begin{aligned}[t] \delta&=dd\\ \eta&=eeeeee\\ \varphi&=f
  \end{aligned}
  \qquad\text{versus}\qquad
  \begin{gathered}[b] s= x+y\\ d= u - v - w\\ p = x\circ y
  \end{gathered}
\end{equation*}
```

The cases environment

Although it is possible with standard LATEX to produce structures of the form

$$P_{r-j} = \begin{cases} 0 & \text{if } r - j \text{ is odd,} \\ r! \, (-1)^{(r-j)/2} & \text{if } r - j \text{ is even.} \end{cases} \tag{15.8}$$

as demonstrated by a similar example in Section 7.4.1 on page 133, the $\mathcal{A}_{\mathcal{M}}\mathcal{S}$-LATEX cases environment allows a simpler input:

```
\begin{equation}
 P_{r-j}=\begin{cases} 0 & \text{if $r-j$ is odd,}\\
        r!\,(-1)^{(r-j)/2} & \text{if $r-j$ is even.}
           \end{cases}
\end{equation}
```

There may be more than two cases in the environment, as in the example reproduced here from page 133:

$$y = \begin{cases} -1 & : & x < 0 \\ 0 & : & x = 0 \\ +1 & : & x > 0 \end{cases}$$

```
\[ y = \begin{cases} -1 &:\quad x<0\\
       \hfill 0 &:\quad x=0\\ +1 &:\quad x>0
          \end{cases} \]
```

15.2.7 Equation numbering

Numbering hierarchy

With the standard LATEX classes book and report, equations are given a double number with the chapter designation and then a sequential number starting at 1 for each new chapter. For the article class, the equations are numbered sequentially throughout the work.

With the amsmath package, it is possible to alter this hierarchy. For example, if an article is to have the equations numbered within each section, with the section number give

```
\numberwithin{equation}{section}
```

to redefine the equation numbers to include the section number and to make the equation counter reset every time the section counter is incremented. This is as though the equation counter had been created with \newcounter{equation} [section] (Section 10.1.2), something that the user cannot normally bring about. Furthermore, \theequation is redefined to be \thesection.\arabic{equation}, something that is in the user's power but is not much use if the equation counter is never reset.

Subnumbering equations

On page 190 we give an example of how equations may be subnumbered; that is, the main equation number stays the same and a letter is appended to it, as 1.8a, 1.8b, 1.8c. ... The `amsmath` package provides this feature with the `subequations` environment. Numbered equations appearing within

```
\begin{subequations}   ...   \end{subequations}
```

will all have the same main number, which is one more than that of the previous one, with sequential, lowercase letters attached.

Within the environment, the `equation` counter refers to the subnumber, that is, to the letters, while the main number is to be found in the `parentequation` counter. To change the format of the subnumber, say, to 1.8-A, 1.8-B, ..., give

```
\begin{subequations}
\renewcommand{\theequation}
            {\theparentequation-\Alph{equation}}
. . .
\end{subequations}
```

Referencing equation numbers

The LaTeX cross-reference system is described in Section 11.2.1 and works exactly the same way with $\mathcal{A}_{\mathcal{M}}\mathcal{S}$-LaTeX: When `\label{`*marker*`}` is issued in a mathematical formula that receives an automatic equation number, that number can be printed anywhere in the text with `\ref{`*marker*`}`, where *marker* is arbitrary text to identify that equation.

The `amsmath` package adds a command `\eqref{`*marker*`}` to print the equation number in parentheses, as it appears beside the math formula. For example, the cases equation on page 288 is referred to as equation 15.8 with `\ref` or as equation (15.8) with `\eqref`.

If `\label` is given immediately after the start of a `subequations` environment, the corresponding `\ref` commands will print the main equation number without the extra letter. In this way one can refer to the entire group of equations. Later `\label` commands are associated with individual equation lines and reference them with the letters.

Page breaks within multiline formulas

Unlike the standard LaTeX `eqnarray` environment, the $\mathcal{A}_{\mathcal{M}}\mathcal{S}$-LaTeX multiline math environments do not normally allow any page breaks to occur within them. The idea is that the author should have more control over where such breaks may occur. To allow or force a page break within a multiline equation, one gives

```
\displaybreak[num]
```

just before the line-breaking command \\. Here the optional *num* has the same meaning as for the standard \pagebreak command (page 36): Without it, a new page is forced, but it may take values of 0–4 to allow a break with increasing degrees of encouragement, whereby 4 also forces the page break.

Alternatively, one can issue \allowdisplaybreaks in the document preamble to allow LATEX to break pages automatically within multiline formulas as necessary. This command also takes an optional argument *num* with possible values between 0 and 4, which make it progressively easier for automatic page breaks to occur.

Once \allowdisplaybreaks has been given in the preamble, it is still possible to suppress page breaks within a formula by ending an equation line with * instead of with \\.

15.2.8 Package options for amsmath

The main amsmath package for $\mathcal{A}_{\mathcal{M}}S$-LATEX recognizes a number of options that may be given when it is loaded with

\usepackage[*options*]{amsmath}

They are listed here as pairs with opposing effects. The member of each pair that is assumed if neither is given, the default, is indicated by underlining.

centertags | tbtags The equation number for a split environment (page 283) is centered vertically by default. With tbtags, it is placed either to the left of the first line or to the right of the last line, depending on the side on which numbers are to appear.

sumlimits | nosumlimits In displayed formulas, initial and final limits appear below and above the $\sum$ sign with the sumlimits option. With nosumlimits, they are placed beside the sign, raised and lowered with the usual ^ and _ characters.

Other symbols that are affected by these options are $\sum \prod \coprod \bigcup \biguplus \bigcap \bigsqcup \bigvee \bigwedge \bigodot$ $\bigotimes$ and $\bigoplus$. On the other hand, integral signs are not influenced by them.

sumlimits $\qquad\qquad\qquad\qquad$ nosumlimits

$$\sum_{n=0}^{\infty} \frac{1}{2^n} = 2; \quad \prod_{i=0}^{m-1} n - i = \frac{n!}{(n-m)!} \qquad \sum_{n=0}^{\infty} \frac{1}{2^n} = 2; \quad \prod_{i=0}^{m-1} n - i = \frac{n!}{(n-m)!}$$

The input text is the same for both of the above cases.

intlimits | nointlimits Integral signs normally have their limits at the side; these options allow them to be placed above and below as for summations.

intlimits

$$\int_{0}^{a} \sqrt{a^2 - x^2}\, dx = \int_{0}^{1} a^2 \sqrt{1 - \sin^2 t}\, d\sin t = a^2 \int_{0}^{\pi/2} \cos^2 t\, dt = \frac{\pi a^2}{4}$$

`nointlimits`

$$\int_0^a \sqrt{a^2 - x^2}\,\mathrm{d}x = \int_0^1 a^2\sqrt{1 - \sin^2 t}\,\mathrm{d}\sin t = a^2\int_0^{\pi/2}\cos^2 t\,\mathrm{d}t = \frac{\pi a^2}{4}$$

where again the input text is the same for both cases. As a reminder, the standard LATEX treatment of limits on integral signs is the same as for `nointlimits`.

`namelimits` | `nonamelimits` The functions \det, \gcd, \inf, \lim, \liminf, \limsup \max, \min, \Pr, and \sup frequently take lower limits that normally appear below the name in displayed formulas. With `nonamelimits`, they are placed at the lower right.

namelimits   nonamelimits

$$\lim_{x\to\infty}\left(1 + \frac{1}{x}\right)^x = e = 2.7182\ldots \qquad\qquad \lim_{x\to\infty}\left(1 + \frac{1}{x}\right)^x = e = 2.7182\ldots$$

The above options determine the standard placement of limits for the entire document. It is still possible to change the behavior in any particular case with the \limits and \nolimits commands, as in normal LATEX.

The remaining package options select the side for equation numbers and the horizontal positioning of equations.

`leqno` | `reqno` The standard location for equation numbers is on the right side, at the margin; with `leqno`, they are placed on the left side of the equation. For the $\mathcal{A}_{\mathcal{M}}S$ classes, the default is `leqno`.

`fleqn` With this option, all displayed equations are printed flush left, set off from the left margin by an amount \mathindent. Without this option, equations are centered. (This is like the `fleqn` class option for the standard classes, page 43.)

15.3 Further $\mathcal{A}_{\mathcal{M}}S$-LATEX packages

The $\mathcal{A}_{\mathcal{M}}S$-LATEX packages described in this section must be loaded explicitly if their features are to be exploited. Unlike the amsbsy and amstext packages, they are not loaded automatically with amsmath. They may, however, be used on their own, independently of the main package.

15.3.1 Extended theorem declarations

Package:
amsthm
The amsthm package offers many additional possibilities for generating theorem-like declarations described for standard LATEX in Section 4.5.

As for standard LATEX, a new theorem declaration is created with a statement like

```
\newtheorem{com}{Comment}
```

where the first argument is the name of the theorem type (here `com`) and the second is the title that is printed when the theorem declaration is invoked. For example,

```
\begin{com}
    Theorem declarations can have any name.
\end{com}
```

produces the declaratory text

    Comment 1. *Theorem declarations can have any name.*

In addition to the two mandatory arguments, the `\newtheorem` command may have one of two optional ones. The complete syntax is

    `\newtheorem{`*type*`}[`*num_like*`]{`*title*`}`
        or
    `\newtheorem{`*type*`}{`*title*`}[`*in_counter*`]`

where *num_like* is the name of an existing theorem-like declaration, which is to be numbered in the same sequence as *type*, and *in_counter* is a counter name like `chapter` or `section` to reset the numbers of the *type* declarations.

All this is standard LATEX so far. The `amsthm` package adds the following features:

- A `\newtheorem*` is provided that defines an unnumbered theorem structure.

- Three predefined theorem styles are available:
  - `plain`, in which the title and number are in boldface and the text italic;
  - `definition`, with title and number in boldface and the text in normal font;
  - `remark`, for title and number in italic and the text normal.

  The desired style is activated by first issuing `\theoremstyle{`*style*`}`; all subsequent `\newtheorem` statements will have this style until a new one is activated.

- A `\swapnumbers` can be issued to cause all following new theorem types to have the numbers appear before the title, as **1 Comment.**

- New theorem styles may be defined by means of the `\newtheoremstyle` command, or additional predefined styles may be loaded with package options. Since this is fairly specialized and complex, it is best to examine the example file `thmtest.tex` or read the documentation in `amsthm.dtx`.

- A `proof` environment is available for presenting short proofs. It is an unnumbered structure with the title *Proof*. The text is terminated automatically with the Q.E.D. symbol □. This symbol may be altered by redefining the command `\qedsymbol`; it may be printed at any time by issuing `\qed`.

  There is also a `\qedhere` command to be given within a displayed equation or a list at the end of the proof. This moves the symbol to the end of that line; otherwise it appears below the displayed equation or list, and possibly on the next page.

The `amsthm` package has much in common with Frank Mittelbach's `theorem` package in the tools collection of Section B.5.4.

15.3.2 Commutative diagrams

Package:
`amscd`

The extra $\mathcal{A}\mathcal{M}S$-LaTeX package `amscd` makes it easier to generate commutative diagrams like the one here at the right.

$$S^{W_\Lambda} \otimes T \xrightarrow{\ \ j\ \ } T$$
$$\downarrow \qquad\qquad \downarrow \text{End } P$$
$$(S \otimes T)/I \xlongequal{\quad\quad} (Z \otimes T)/J$$

These diagrams are created within the CD environment using some additional arrow commands. These bear the rather unusual names: @>>> @<<< @AAA and @VVV for arrows pointing right, left, upwards, and downwards, respectively. The command @= draws a horizontal double rule, a lengthened equals sign.

Any text or symbols between the first and second > or < characters will appear above the horizontal arrow in \scriptstyle font. Similarly, any text or symbols between the second and third characters will be printed below the arrow.

For vertical arrows, text or symbols between the first and second A or V are placed to the left; those between the second and third to the right, again in \scriptstyle.

The above example diagram, taken from the $\mathcal{A}\mathcal{M}S$-LaTeX manual `amsldoc.tex`, was produced with

```
\[ \begin{CD}
Sˆ{\mathcal{W}_\Lambda}\otimes T @>j>>  T\\
@VVV                          @VV{\End P}V\\
(S\otimes T)/I               @= (Z\otimes T)/J
\end{CD}  \]
```

The command \End to print the function name 'End' is not standard. It must be previously defined with \DeclareMathOperator{\End}{End} (see page 279).

15.3.3 References with upref package

Package:
`upref`

Normally the numbers printed with the \ref and \pageref commands are in the current font, whether that be bold, italic, or upright. To ensure that the numbers are always upright, load the extra $\mathcal{A}\mathcal{M}S$-LaTeX package `upref`.

15.4 The $\mathcal{A}\mathcal{M}S$ fonts

The $\mathcal{A}\mathcal{M}S$ makes a number of fonts available to complement the regular Computer Modern fonts provided with the standard TeX/LaTeX installation. They include extra math alphabets, supplemental CM bold math italic and symbol fonts in smaller sizes than 10 pt, Cyrillic fonts, and additional symbol fonts.

In the next sections we describe these various fonts and how to take advantage of them.

15.4.1 Extra CM math fonts

Standard TEX installations of Computer Modern fonts provide bold math italic cmmib10, the bold symbols cmbsy10, and math extensions cmex10 fonts only in 10 pt size, as indicated by the suffix 10 to their names. The $\mathcal{A}_{\mathcal{M}}\mathcal{S}$ has supplemented these with versions in sizes 5–9 pt.

cmmib5	cmmib6	cmmib7	cmmib8	cmmib9
cmbsy5	cmbsy6	cmbsy7	cmbsy8	cmbsy9
		cmex7	cmex8	cmex9

The small caps font cmcsc10 is also given companions cmcsc8 and cmcsc9.

The normal LATEX installation automatically assumes that these fonts are on the system and incorporates them into the necessary NFSS font definition files. Substitutions will be made if they are missing.

15.4.2 Cyrillic fonts

The $\mathcal{A}_{\mathcal{M}}\mathcal{S}$ Cyrillic fonts were originally used in reviews of books published in Russian and other Slavic languages in which the titles were to be rendered in the original language. In 1988, the Humanities and Arts Computing Center of the University of Washington redesigned them for general-purpose Slavic studies, adding the pre-Revolutionary and accented letters. The overall appearance was also greatly enhanced.

These fonts all bear the prefix wncy, followed by the style designation r (upright), b (bold), i (italic), sc (small caps), or ss (upright sans serif), and the design size in points.

The best way to enable the Cyrillic fonts is simply to select font encoding OT2 under NFSS, as illustrated in Section A.2 on page 365. The .fd (font definition) files for the Cyrillic fonts have been set up such that the other font attributes fully parallel those of the Latin fonts. This means wncyr10 has all the same attributes as cmr10, except for the encoding: family cmr, shape n, series m. (Of course, if the CM fonts are not the current standard ones, it will require more than just selecting the OT2 encoding to activate these Cyrillic fonts.)

The layout of the Cyrillic fonts has been chosen in such a way that the input text may be entered following the regular English transliteration scheme. Thus Cyrillic C is in position 83 where Latin S is normally situated. Typing S when a Cyrillic font is active outputs the correct equivalent C. Numerals and punctuation are to be found in the standard locations, so they may be typed in as usual. 'Санкт-Петербург 10?' is thus generated by {\cyr Sankt-Peterburg 10?}.

Since the Cyrillic alphabet possesses more letters than the Latin, many of them must be transliterated with multiletter combinations. These are automatically programmed into the fonts using TEX's ligature system. For example, Ch is treated as a ligature for symbol 81 Ч just as fi is for fi in a Latin font. This means that multiletter transliterations are simply typed in. The input for 'Хрущев' is {\cyr Khrushchev}, where Kh → Х and shch → щ. The transliteration scheme is that for English; other languages have their own systems to reproduce the original pronunciation. For example, 'Горбачёв' is *Gorbatschow* in German, *Gorbaciov* in Italian, and *Gorbachev* in English. These other schemes do *not* work with these fonts.

Not all letters can be produced so automatically (for example, the ё in Горбачёв), and for this reason the $\mathcal{A}_{\mathcal{M}}S$ provides a file `cyracc.def` containing macro definitions for accented letters and other special features, such as the hard and soft signs. When these macros are given in a Latin font, additional transliteration symbols appear.

15.4.3 Extra math symbols

Package:
amsfonts
amssymb

The set of symbols in the CM math symbol fonts by no means exhausts the fantasies of active mathematicians. To overcome this deficiency, the $\mathcal{A}_{\mathcal{M}}S$ has produced two fonts, `msam10` and `msbm10`, containing only symbols, arrows, and the blackboard characters. They are also available in sizes 5–9 pt. Since these fonts originated in the days when TeX could only handle 128 characters in any font, that is exactly how many they contain. Today they could be combined into one font of 256 characters.

Two packages permit access to this treasure trove of hieroglyphs:

amsfonts enables the \mathbb math alphabet command for the blackboard characters, and defines those symbol names that are otherwise only provided in the latexsym package (Section 7.3.3).

amssymb is the more convenient package, which loads amsfonts and then defines names for all the symbols in the two fonts.

For example,

```
\[ \circlearrowright \Cup \lessapprox \lll \varpropto \because
     \circeq \vDash \blacktriangle \sphericalangle \]
```

$$\circlearrowright \quad \Cup \quad \lessapprox \quad \lll \quad \propto \quad \because \quad \circeq \quad \vDash \quad \blacktriangle \quad \sphericalangle$$

The 'blackboard' characters are selected with the math alphabet command \mathbb. Thus, $\mathbb{A\ B\ C\ ..}$ produces

$$\mathbb{A\ B\ C\ D\ E\ F\ G\ H\ I\ J\ K\ L\ N\ M\ O\ P\ Q\ R\ S\ T\ U\ V\ W\ X\ Y\ Z}$$

All the symbols and their associated names from the amssymb package are to be found in Tables G.20 through G.26 on pages 551–553.

15.4.4 Euler fonts

The *Euler* fonts, named after the eighteenth-century mathematician Leonhard Euler, were designed by Hermann Zapf. Their main purpose in mathematics is to be a substitute for the CM calligraphic math alphabets.

Package:
eucal

The package eucal redefines the \mathcal command to use the Euler script characters in place of the CM calligraphic letters. If this package is loaded with the option `mathscr`, the command `\mathcal` is left unchanged and, instead, `\mathscr` is defined to invoke these letters. In this case, `$\mathscr{A B C ..}$` produces

$$\mathcal{A\ B\ C\ D\ E\ F\ G\ H\ I\ J\ K\ L\ N\ M\ O\ P\ Q\ R\ S\ T\ U\ V\ W\ X\ Y\ Z}$$

Package:
eufrak
   On the other hand, the package `eufrak` defines the math alphabet command `\mathfrak`, with which `$\mathfrak{A B C ..}$` yields

$$\mathfrak{A\ B\ C\ D\ E\ F\ G\ H\ I\ J\ K\ L\ N\ M\ O\ P\ Q\ R\ S\ T\ U\ V\ W\ X\ Y\ Z}$$

This math alphabet is also enabled with the `amsfonts` package.

Drawing with LaTeX

16

The inclusion of graphical material from other programs is treated in Chapter 8. Such 'foreign' files do add some complications (which are greatly reduced today with LaTeX 2_ε) and can cause portability problems. What would be desirable is a means to do graphics with LaTeX itself so that the source text file is fully self-contained.

Standard LaTeX does contain the means to make somewhat primitive drawings on its own. The word 'primitive' should not be considered derogatory, for simple building blocks are the basic units for constructing very complicated, sophisticated structures. They are also useful for superimposing imported graphics or for adding embellishments to them, as demonstrated in Section 8.1.5.

This chapter describes the intrinsic LaTeX drawing capabilities and then explains some extensions that are available to enhance them.

Many more possibilities exist for adding specialized diagrams, from chemistry, to music, to chess positions. These are described in detail in *The LaTeX Graphics Companion* by Goossens et al. (1997).

16.1 The picture environment

16.1.1 Picture coordinates

The picture building blocks can only be put in place once a *coordinate system* has been established for that picture. This consists of a *reference point* or *origin*, and two mutually perpendicular *coordinate axes*, as well as a *length unit* for the coordinates. The origin is the lower-left corner of the picture and the axes are its lower and left edges. These edges are referred to as the *x-axis* (lower) and *y-axis* (left).

Once the unit of length (UL) has been specified, every point within the picture area can be uniquely referred to with two decimal numbers: The first is the number of length units along the x-axis, the second the number along the y-axis.

The coordinate numbers are generally positive, meaning that the point lies to the right and above the reference point. Since this point is the lower-left corner of the picture, all other points should be more to the right and higher than it. However, negative values are also possible. A negative x value (a negative number for the first member of a coordinate pair) defines a point *left* of the origin, while a negative y value (the second member of the pair is negative) specifies a point below the reference point.

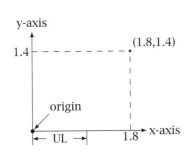
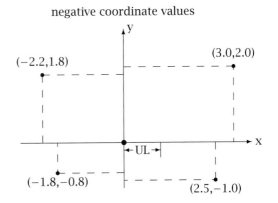

The unit length is selected with the command

`\setlength{\unitlength}{`*length*`}`

In the left-hand example above, the unit length was set to a value of 1.5 cm with the command `\setlength{\unitlength}{1.5cm}`. The point (1.8,1.4) then lies 1.8 times the unit length (= 2.7 cm) to the right and 1.4 times (= 2.1 cm) above the origin. In the right-hand example, the unit length is set to 1 cm.

The unit of length is normally set to a convenient size such as 1 cm, 1 mm, or 1 in, and the picture is built up accordingly. Once it has been completed, it is possible to rescale the whole thing simply by changing the value of the length unit. A picture that was originally designed with `\unitlength` set to 1 cm can be enlarged by a factor 1.2 by redefining its length unit to be 1.2 cm.

16.1.2 The picture environment

Pictures are constructed within the `picture` environment, which is started with

```
\begin{picture}(x_dimen,y_dimen)
  picture_commands
\end{picture}
```

where (*x_dimen*, *y_dimen*) is a pair of numbers that specifies the size (dimensions) of the picture in the *x-direction* (horizontal) and *y-direction* (vertical). This pair of numbers is enclosed in *round* parentheses! The unit of length is that previously selected by `\unitlength`.

```
\setlength{\unitlength}{1.5cm}
\begin{picture}(4,5) ... ... ... \end{picture}
```

produces a picture that is 4 length units wide and 5 units high. Since the length unit has been set to 1.5 cm, the actual size is 6 cm wide and 7.5 cm high.

Picture commands are those commands described below that are used to produce and position the individual picture elements. These are the only commands that are allowed within the picture environment, other than font style and size declarations (Section 4.1) and the line thickness commands \thicklines and \thinlines. These last determine which of the two available line thicknesses will become current for drawing lines, and one may switch back and forth as desired. Initially, *thin* lines are active.

The value of the parameter \unitlength must not be altered within the picture environment, for it must remain the same for the entire picture. It may, however, be changed between pictures.

If the \unitlength specification together with the picture environment are enclosed within another environment, such as \begin{center} ... \end{center}, then that value of \unitlength is valid only until the end of the environment. A picture environment without a preceding \unitlength command uses the standard value of 1 pt.

16.1.3 The positioning commands

Picture elements are generated and positioned by means of the two commands \put and \multiput, which have the syntaxes:

> \put(x,y){*pic_elem*}
> \multiput(x,y)($\Delta x,\Delta y$){*num*}{*pic_elem*}

The *pic_elem* is one of the picture element commands described in the next section. The arguments (x,y) are the *placement coordinates*, designating the location of the picture element within the picture coordinate system, in units of \unitlength. If this is 1 cm, then (2.5,3.6) means that the element is to be positioned 2.5 cm to the right and 3.6 cm above the lower-left corner of the picture.

The \multiput command generates the same picture element *num* times, moving it $(\Delta x,\Delta y)$ each time. Thus the element is drawn at

> (x, y), $(x + \Delta x, y + \Delta y)$,
> $(x + 2\Delta x, y + 2\Delta y)$, ... up to
> $(x + [num - 1]\Delta x, y + [num - 1]\Delta y)$

The coordinate pair (x, y) is incremented by $(\Delta x, \Delta y)$ for each successive placement. The values of the incrementing pair may be positive or negative.

Thus \multiput(2.5,3.6)(0.5,-0.6){5}{*pic_elem*} produces the *pic_elem* a total of five times, first at the location (2.5,3.6) and then at (3.0,3.0), (3.5,2.4), (4.0,1.8), and finally (4.5,1.2).

Note that the numbers for the *coordinate* and *increment* pairs are given in round parentheses (,) and that the two numbers within each pair are separated by a comma. The *num* and *pic_elem* entries, on the other hand, are enclosed in curly brackets { } as usual.

Warning: Since the comma separates the two numbers in a coordinate pair, it may *not* be used in place of a decimal point. *For coordinate entries, decimal numbers must be written with a period, not a comma.*

16.1.4 Picture element commands

Text within pictures

The simplest picture element of all is a piece of text, positioned at the desired location within the picture. This is accomplished by putting text in place of *pic_elem* in the `\put` or `\multiput` command.

An arrow

(1.8,1.2)

The arrow points to the location (1.8,1.2). The command `\put(1.8,1.2){An arrow}` inserts the text 'An arrow' so that its lower-left corner is at the specified position.

The text as picture element may also be packed into a `\parbox` or a `minipage` environment, and the reference point for the coordinate entry in the `\put` command depends on the positioning arguments of that box:

`\parbox[b]{..}{..}`	`\parbox{32mm}{...}`	`\parbox[t]{..}{..}`
Reference point is the lower-left corner of the last line in the parbox.	For a standard parbox, the reference point is the vertical center of the left edge.	Reference point is the lower-left corner of the top line in the parbox.

Exercise 16.1: Produce a picture 100 mm wide and 50 mm high with `\unitlength` equal to 1 mm. Place the given texts at the following locations: (0,0) 'The First Picture', (0,47) 'upper left', (70,40) 'somewhere upper right', and put a parbox of width 60 mm at (25,25) containing 'A separate exercise file with the name `picture.tex` should be created for the exercises in this Chapter.'

Exercise 16.2: Repeat the picture processing with a value of 1.5 mm for `\unitlength` and with positioning arguments *t* and *b* for the parbox.

Picture boxes—rectangles

The box commands `\framebox`, `\makebox`, and `\savebox` (Section 5.1.1) are available in the `picture` environment but with an extended syntax. In addition, there is another box command `\dashbox`:

> `\makebox(`*x_dimen*`,`*y_dimen*`)[`*pos*`]{`*text*`}`
> `\framebox(`*x_dimen*`,`*y_dimen*`)[`*pos*`]{`*text*`}`
> `\dashbox{`*dash_len*`}(`*x_dimen*`,`*y_dimen*`)[`*pos*`]{`*text*`}`

The *dimensional* pair (*x_dimen*, *y_dimen*) defines the width and height of the rectangular box in units of `\unitlength`. The positioning argument *pos* determines how the *text* is located within the box. It may take on values:

[t] *top*   The input text appears—centered horizontally—*below* the *upper* edge of the box.

[b] *bottom*   The input text appears—centered horizontally—*above* the *lower* edge of the box.

[l] *left*   The input text *begins*—centered vertically—at the *left* edge of the box.

[r] *right*   The input text *ends*—centered vertically—at the *right* edge of the box.

[s] *stretch*   The input text is stretched horizontally to fill up the box and centered vertically.

Without the optional argument *pos*, the input text is centered vertically and horizontally within the box.

These positional values may be combined two at a time:

[tl] *top left*   The text appears at the *upper left.*

[tr] *top right*   The text appears at the *upper right.*

[bl] *bottom left*   The text appears at the *lower left.*

[br] *bottom right*   The text appears at the *lower right.*

The order of the values is unimportant: tl has the same effect as lt.

These box commands are to be used as *pic_elem* in the placement commands \put and \multiput. The box is so placed that its lower-left corner is at the position given by the coordinate pair in the placement command.

```
\put(1.5,1.2){\framebox(2.5,1.2){center}}
```

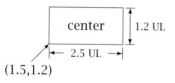

The arrow indicates the point (1.5,1.2), which is the position of the lower-left corner of the rectangle with width 2.5 units and height 1.2 units. The text 'center' is centered both horizontally and vertically. UL = 0.8 cm.

The effect of the text positioning argument is made clear with the following examples (UL = 1 cm):

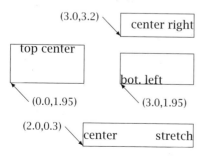

```
\put(0.0,1.95){\framebox(2,1.0)
               [t]{top center}}
\put(3.0,1.95){\framebox(2,0.8)
               [lb]{bot. left}}
\put(3.0,3.2){\framebox(2,0.6)
               [r]{center right}}
\put(2.0,0.3){\framebox(2,0.6)
      [s]{center\hfill stretch}}
```

The picture element \makebox is exactly the same as the \framebox command but without the rectangular frame. It is most often employed with the dimensional pair (0,0) in order to place text at a desired location. (See Section 5.1.1 for the effect of *zero* width boxes on the enclosed text.)

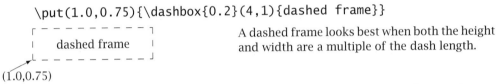

```
\put(3,1.6){\makebox(0,0){center center}}
\put(2,0.5){\makebox(0,0)[tr]{top right}}
\put(4,1.0){\makebox(0,0)[b]{bot center}}
\put(2,2.8){\makebox(0,0)[l]{flush left}}
```

The combination [lb] positions the text in exactly the same way as simply typing the text in as *pic_elem* without a box, as shown on page 300.

The picture element \dashbox also produces a framed box, but with a *dashed* line around it. The argument *dash_len* specifies the *dash length*.

```
\put(1.0,0.75){\dashbox{0.2}(4,1){dashed frame}}
```

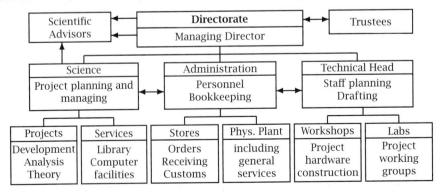

A dashed frame looks best when both the height and width are a multiple of the dash length.

Even in the above picture box commands, the entered *text* may be put into a vertical box (\parbox or minipage). Since vertical boxes themselves possess an optional positioning argument b or t, which must not conflict with that of the picture box, the following rule must be observed:

> If a picture box command contains the positioning argument b or t, then the same value must be applied to the enclosed vertical box. If the picture box command has no positioning argument or only r or l, then the vertical box must be used in the standard (no argument) form.

The positioning argument of a picture box has the same effect on the enclosed vertical box as it does on a line of text, because the whole box is treated as a single unit.

Exercise 16.3: *Reproduce the organization table below with the boxes and included text but without the horizontal and vertical lines and arrows. These will be part of the next exercise.*

Straight lines

In the `picture` environment, LATEX can draw straight lines of any length, horizontally and vertically as well as at a limited number of angles. The syntax for this picture element reads

$$\text{\textbackslash line}(\Delta x, \Delta y)\{length\}$$

For horizontal and vertical lines, *length* specifies how long the line is to be in length units. For lines at an angle, it has a somewhat more complicated meaning, as is explained below. The line begins at that spot given by the placement coordinates in the `\put` or `\multiput` command.

```
\thicklines
\put(0,0){\line(1,0){6}}
\put(0,0){\line(0,1){1}}
\put(6,0){\line(0,1){0.5}}
```

The angle at which the line is drawn is given by the *slope pair* $(\Delta x, \Delta y)$. The slope pair $(1,0)$, in which $\Delta x = 1$ and $\Delta y = 0$, produces a *horizontal* line, while the pair $(0,1)$ leads to a *vertical* line. This is illustrated in the above example.

In general $(\Delta x, \Delta y)$ has the following meaning:

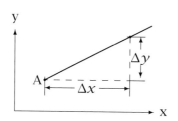

Beginning at a point A on the line and moving a distance Δx in the x direction (horizontally), Δy is the distance one must move in the y direction (vertically) in order to rejoin the line.

By specifying a slope pair $(\Delta x, \Delta y)$, a line is drawn at just that angle to fulfill the above conditions.

As mentioned already, the number of different slopes available is limited. This is because Δx and Δy may only take on values according to certain rules:

1. The number must be a whole integer (negative or positive).

2. Only the values 0, 1, ..., 6 are allowed.

3. The two numbers in the pair may not contain a common divisor.

Pairs such as $(3.5,1.2)$ (rule 1) and $(7,0)$ (rule 2) are thus forbidden. Similarly, $(2,2)$ and $(3,6)$ are invalid pairs by rule 3, since both numbers in the first pair are divisible by 2, and those in the second by 3. The same angles are achieved with the pairs $(1,1)$ and $(1,2)$ respectively. In all, there are 25 allowed slope pairs, including $(1,0)$ for horizontal and $(0,1)$ for vertical lines, as one can verify by writing down all the possibilities.

In addition, the numbers in the slope pair may be positive or negative, for example, $(0,-1)$, $(-2,-5)$. A negative Δx in the above diagram means motion to the left, and a negative Δy is for motion downwards. Thus `\put(2,3){\line(0,-1){2.5}}` draws a line starting at point $(2,3)$ and going 2.5 length units vertically downwards.

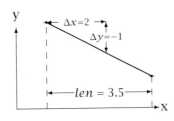

For lines at an angle, the argument *length* determines the projected distance along the x-axis. This is made clearer with the help of the diagram on the left.

`\put(1.0,2.75){\line(2,-1){3.5}}`

If one draws dashed lines straight down from the two end points, then that part of the x-axis between them is the projection of the line onto the x-axis.

Sloping lines must have a minimum length of about 10 pt or 3.5 mm, otherwise a warning is issued and no line is drawn.

Arrows

The *arrow* picture element is made with the command

$$\verb|\vector|(\Delta x,\Delta y)\{length\}$$

which functions exactly the same as the \line command as far as the arguments and their limitations are concerned. The command draws a line from the placement location given in the \put or \multiput command and places an arrowhead at the end.

Just as for lines, arrows also must have a length of at least 10 pt or 3.5 mm. Rules 1 through 3 apply to Δx and Δy as well, with the further restriction that the allowed numbers are limited to 0, 1, ..., 4. This makes a total of 13 possible angles for arrows, not counting changes in sign.

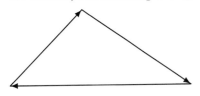

```
\begin{picture}(5,2)\thicklines
  \put(5,0){\vector(-1,0){5}}
  \put(0,0){\vector(1,1){2}}
  \put(2,2){\vector(3,-2){3}}
\end{picture}
```

Exercise 16.4: Complete the diagram in Exercise 16.3 by including the missing horizontal and vertical lines and arrows.

Exercise 16.5: Generate the figure at the right. The corner points are (0,5), (0,10), (5,15), (10,15), (15,10), (15,5), (10,0), and (5,0) and the length unit is 0.1 inch.

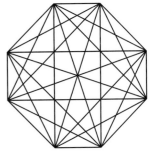

Circles

The *circle* picture element is produced with the commands

```
\circle{diameter}
\circle*{diameter}
```

With the *-form of the command, a solid filled-in circle is printed rather than just an outline as for the standard form. Only certain sizes are available, so LaTeX selects the one closest to the specified *diameter* entry. If the size is too small, a warning is output to the monitor and no circle is printed.

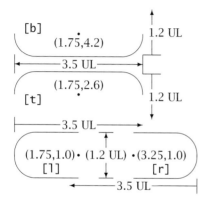

```
\begin{picture}(3,1.6)
    \put(1,1){\circle*{0.2}}
    \put(1,1){\circle{1.2}}
    \put(1,1){\vector(0,1){0.6}}
    \put(2.5,1){\circle*{0.5}}
\end{picture}
```

The placement location in the corresponding \put command refers to the center of the circle.

Ovals and rounded corners

The term *oval* is used here to mean a rectangle whose corners have been replaced by quarter circles; the largest possible radius is chosen for the circles such that the sides join together smoothly. The command to produce them is

```
\oval(x_dimen,y_dimen)[part]
```

The placement location in the corresponding \put command refers to the center of the oval.

```
\put(3.0,0.75){\oval(4.0,1.5)}
```

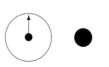

Here we have set the values $x\_dimen = 4.0$ UL and $y\_dimen = 1.5$ UL, whereby the unit length UL has been selected to be 0.8 cm. The center of the oval is at the placement coordinates in the \put command, (3.0,0.75).

The optional argument *part* takes on values t, b, l, or r, for making half ovals.

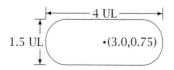

```
\put(1.75,4.2){\oval(3.5,1.2)[b]}
\put(1.75,2.6){\oval(3.5,1.2)[t]}
\put(1.75,1.0){\oval(3.5,1.2)[l]}
\put(3.25,1.2){\oval(3.5,1.2)[r]}
```

The width and height specifications for half ovals are always those of the *entire* figure even though only part of it is being drawn. Similarly, the placement coordinates in the corresponding \put command refer to the center of the complete oval. (Unit length here is UL = 1 cm.)

The argument *part* may also be one of the combinations tl, tr, bl, or br to
generate a quarter oval. The order of the two letters is unimportant, so that lt, rt,
lb, and rb are equally valid.

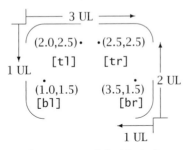

```
\put(2.0,2.5){\oval(3.0,1.0)[tl]}
\put(2.5,2.5){\oval(3.0,1.0)[tr]}
\put(1.0,1.5){\oval(1.0,2.0)[bl]}
\put(3.5,1.5){\oval(1.0,2.0)[br]}
```

Once again the size specifications refer to the
entire oval and not just to the part that is drawn,
and the placement coordinates in the \put command refer to the center of the complete oval.

Quarter and half circles may also be drawn as partial ovals with equal width
and height, but only up to a certain size. The following examples demonstrate that
sections of circles are possible up to a size of about 1.5 cm.

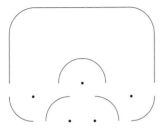

```
\put(2.0,1.0){\oval(4.0,4.0)[t]}
\put(2.0,1.0){\oval(1.5,1.5)[t]}
```

```
\put(0.75,0.75){\oval(1.5,1.5)[bl]}
\put(1.75,0.0){\oval(1.5,1.5)[tl]}
\put(2.25,0.0){\oval(1.5,1.5)[tr]}
\put(3.25,0.75){\oval(1.5,1.5)[br]}
```

Sections of ovals may be combined with other picture elements. The placement
coordinates in the \put command, however, require some serious consideration to
get them positioned properly.

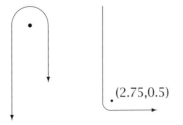

```
\put(0.5,2.5){\oval(1.0,1.0)[t]}
\put(0.0,2.5){\vector(0,-1){2.5}}
\put(1.0,2.5){\vector(0,-1){1.5}}
\put(0.5,2.5){\circle*{0.1}}
```

```
\put(2.5,0.5){\line(0,1){2.5}}
\put(2.75,0.5){\oval(0.5,0.5)[bl]}
\put(2.75,0.25){\vector(1,0){1.25}}
```

In all the above examples, the centers of the ovals have been marked with a black
dot to indicate where they are. They are not normally a part of the \oval picture
element.

UL=1 mm

*Exercise 16.6: Although the object pictured
here is very offensive, it does make an excellent exercise for the* picture *environment.
Hint: Sizing and positioning can be worked
out best by overlaying the illustration with
transparent graph paper.*

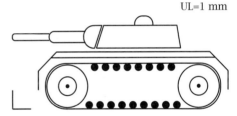

Vertically stacked text

It is sometimes necessary to write text vertically in a diagram, as in
the example here at the right. This is carried out with the command

$$\text{\textbackslash shortstack}[\textit{pos}]\{\textit{col}\}$$

The positioning argument can take on values l, r, or c. The standard
is c for centered. The command is similar to a tabular environment
with only one column. The text is entered as *col*, each row being
separated from the next by \\.

y
—
a
x
i
s

The \shortstack command is most frequently implemented for placing short
lines of text inside a framed box or for stacking single letters vertically. The individual
rows are separated from each other with the smallest possible vertical spacing. This
means that rows with letters sticking up or down (like *h* and *y*) will have larger
apparent gaps between them than rows without such letters. Adding \strut to each
line, as in the third example, equalizes the vertical spacing.

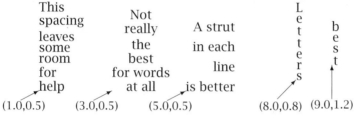

The placement coordinates of the corresponding \put command refer to the
lower-left corner of an imaginary box that contains the vertically stacked text. The
first of the above texts is left justified, the second centered, and the third right
justified. The last two on the right are centered. They were entered with

```
\put(1.0,0.5){\shortstack[l]{This\\spacing\\leaves\\some\\...}}
\put(3.0,0.5){\shortstack{Not\\really\\the\\best\\ ...}}
\put(5.0,0.5){\shortstack[r]{A strut\strut\\in each\strut\\...}}
\put(8.0,0.8){\shortstack{L\\e\\t\\t\\e\\r\\s}}
\put(9.0,1.2){\shortstack{b\\e\\s\\t}}
```

The \shortstack command may also be used outside of the picture environment within normal text. One possible application is for marginal notes, as in
Section 5.2.5.

Framed text

The \framebox command generates a frame of a predetermined size in which text
may be inserted at various positions (page 300). In text mode, there is the command
\fbox for drawing a frame around text that fits it exactly (Section 5.1.1). This
command is also available in the picture environment.

The amount of spacing between the box frame and the enclosed text is given
by the parameter \fboxsep. The placement of an \fbox by means of the \put
command occurs in an unexpected manner, as shown below:

```
\begin{picture}(5,2)
\setlength{\fboxsep}{0.25cm}
\put(0,0){\framebox(5,2){}}
\put(1,1){\fbox{fitted frame}}
\end{picture}
```

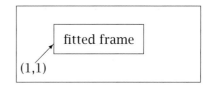

The additional frame spacing is often unwanted in a diagram, especially if the frame surrounds a picture object rather than text. In this case, the command

> \frame{*pic_elem*}

is used instead. The placement coordinate of the \put command then refers to the lower-left corner as usual.

```
\put(0.0,0.5){\frame{TEXT}}
\put(1.5,0.0){\frame{\shortstack{W\\O\\R\\D}}}
```

The contents of the \frame command can be any of the previous picture elements, and need not be merely text. However, in many cases the output comes out wrong.

```
\put(0,0){\frame{\vector(1,1){1.0}}}
\put(2,0){\frame{\circle{1.0}}}
```

The first example produces the correct result, while the second has failed. In such cases, one can try putting the picture object inside a \makebox of suitable size and positioning as argument for the \frame command. However, it would then make more sense to use the \framebox command itself in place of \frame{\makebox...}.

Curved lines

Curved lines may be drawn in the picture environment with the commands

> \qbezier[*num*]$(x_1,y_1)(x_2,y_2)(x_3,y_3)$

which draw a quadratic Bézier curve from point (x_1,y_1) to (x_3,y_3) with (x_2,y_2) as the extra Bézier point. The curve is actually drawn as *num* + 1 dots. The number of points *num* is an optional argument; if it is omitted, its value will be calculated to produce a solid-looking line.

The meaning of the extra point can be illustrated with the example at the right. The input is

```
\begin{picture}(40,20)
\qbezier(0,0)(20,20)(40,10)
\end{picture}
```

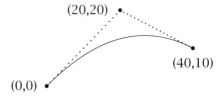

The curve is drawn from (0,0) to (40,10) such that the tangents at the endpoints (the dotted lines) intersect at the extra Bézier point (20,20). Another way of stating this is: As one moves from the first to the third point, one begins by heading directly

towards the second point, and on arrival at the destination, one is moving directly away from that second point again. The dotted lines in the above example, which are not drawn by the \bezier functions, illustrate this.

A dotted curve may be drawn by specifying the number of points *num*; some experimentation may be required to get just the right effect.

Line thickness

There is a choice of two line thicknesses for the picture elements \circle, \oval, and \vector, as well as for sloping lines. These may be selected with

> \thicklines   or   \thinlines

Each of these declarations remains in effect until countermanded by a call to the other one or until the end of the environment in which it was invoked. Initially, \thinlines is in effect.

The thickness of the horizontal and vertical lines may be set with the declaration

> \linethickness{*thickness*}

to any desired size. The argument *thickness* is a positive length specification. With \linethickness{1.5mm}, all subsequent horizontal and vertical lines will have a thickness of 1.5 mm.

Since frame boxes are constructed out of horizontal and vertical lines, the command \linethickness also affects the \framebox and \dashbox commands.

Saving parts of pictures

It is possible to store a combination of picture elements as a sub-picture under a certain name and to recall the whole set as often as one wants without having to reissue the individual commands every time.

First, each sub-picture must have a name reserved for it with

> \newsavebox{*sub_pic_name*}

which creates a box with the name *sub_pic_name* for storing the picture. Afterwards, the sub-picture is saved with

> \savebox{*sub_pic_name*}(*x_dimen*,*y_dimen*)[*pos*]{*sub_pic*}

where the arguments (*x_dimen*,*y_dimen*) and *pos* have the same meaning as for \makebox on page 300.

If the picture commands *sub_pic* are simply a piece of text, this command is exactly the same as the \makebox command except that the text is not printed but stored under the name *sub_pic_name*. The *sub_pic* may be set down anywhere within the main picture as a separate picture element.

> \usebox{*sub_pic_name*}

```
\newsavebox{\sub}
\savebox{\sub}(2,1)[br]{\small Sub-Pic}
....
\put(0.7,0.0){\frame{\usebox{\sub}}}
\put(3.0,1.0){\frame{\usebox{\sub}}}
```

This example may not seem very practical, since the \savebox and \usebox commands could have been replaced by a \framebox together with \multiput to achieve the same result with even less effort. However, the main advantage of these two commands is not for multiple setting of text but rather for more complex *sub_pic* compositions.

It should be pointed out that a \savebox command may be given outside of the picture environment, and even within the preamble. Such a sub-picture is then available in all picture environments throughout the document. However, if a \savebox is defined within an environment, it keeps its contents only until that environment comes to an end.

The picture elements inside a \savebox will be sized according to the value of \unitlength in effect at the time that the box is constructed. It will not be rescaled by a later change in \unitlength.

16.1.5 Making graph paper

Package: The package graphpap adds a new command for drawing gridded paper:
graphpap

$$\graphpaper[num](x,y)(lx,ly)$$

which places a grid with its lower-left corner at (x,y), which is *lx* units wide and *ly* units high. Grid lines are drawn for every *num* units, with every fifth one thicker and labeled. If *num* is not specified, it is assumed to be 10. All arguments must be integers, not decimal fractions. For example, \graphpaper(50,50)(200,100) produces

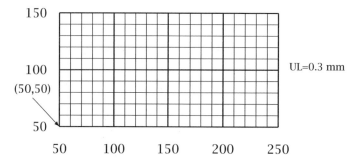

Exercise 16.7: *Produce a sheet of graph paper 10 cm by 15 cm with 2 mm separation between the lines. This sheet may be used to determine the positioning of picture elements when planning a new diagram.*

16.1.6 Shifting a picture environment

The generalized syntax of the `picture` environment contains a further coordinate pair as an optional argument

$$\begin{picture}(\textit{x\_dimen}, \textit{y\_dimen})(\textit{x\_offset}, \textit{y\_offset})$$
$$\textit{picture\_commands} \ \backslash\text{end\{picture\}}$$

In this form, (*x_offset*, *y_offset*) specifies the coordinates of the lower-left corner. This means that for all `\put` commands in the environment, the amounts *x_offset* and *y_offset* are effectively subtracted from the placement coordinates so that the entire picture is shifted by *x_offset* to the *left* and by *y_offset downwards*.

16.2 Extended pictures

16.2.1 The epic package

Package:
epic

With the intention of adding some higher-level commands and creating a more user-friendly interface to the `picture` environment, Sunil Podar released his `epic` package, adding new features and enhancements. One idea is to be able to draw multiple objects relative to each other, with only a limited number of absolute coordinates, making reuse and shifting much easier. Another goal is to simplify the drawing of lines.

This code was originally written for LaTeX 2.09, but functions just as well as a LaTeX 2_ε package. Thus it is implemented with

```
\usepackage{epic}
```

It makes the following new commands available to the user:

`\multiputlist`	`\matrixput`	`\grid`
`\dottedline`	`\dashline`	`\drawline`
`\jput`	`\picsquare`	`\putfile`

as well as the environments:

> dottedjoin dashjoin drawjoin

The `\multiputlist` command is a variation on the regular `\multiput` command; rather than placing the same element in several locations, it puts *different* elements at regularly spaced intervals.

$$\backslash\text{multiputlist}(x, y)(\Delta x, \Delta y)[\textit{pos}]\{\textit{Obj1, Obj2, \ldots, ObjN}\}$$

places the *N* picture elements *Obj1, ..., ObjN* at (x, y), $(x+\Delta x, y+\Delta y)$, and so on. They are actually put into a series of `\makebox(0,0)[pos]{}`, so that the optional *pos* argument specifies the location of the element relative to the plotted point (Section 16.1.4). The elements in the list are separated by commas, so they must be enclosed in {} if they themselves contain commas.

The `\matrixput` command is the 2-D equivalent of `\multiput`, creating an array of a single picture element. Its syntax is:

$\matrixput(x,y)(\Delta x_1,\Delta y_1)\{n_1\}(\Delta x_2,\Delta y_2)\{n_2\}\{Obj\}$

Thus, $\matrixput(0,0)(3,5)\{3\}(10,0)\{5\}\{\circle\{1.5\}\}$ produces

The \grid command is similar to the \graphpaper command, but it will also optionally label the axes.

$\grid(width,height)(\Delta width,\Delta height)[X_0,Y_0]$

draws a grid of size $width \times height$, with grid lines at intervals $\Delta width$ and $\Delta height$. If the optional argument is given, the grid lines are labeled starting at X_0, Y_0, which must be integers, incremented by $\Delta width$ and $\Delta height$, which must also be integers in this case. The \grid command must be placed inside a \put command to specify its lower-left corner: \put(0,0){\grid...}.

A set of points can be joined by a dotted line with the command

$\dottedline[dot\_char]\{dot\_gap\}(x_1,y_1)(x_2,y_2)...(x_n,y_n)$

where *dot_gap* is the spacing (in \unitlength units) between the dots and *dot_char* is the character used for the dot; if it is not specified, the \picsquare (see later in this section) is used by default, a small square. A near-solid line can be achieved by making *dot_gap* very small, but this could cause TeX to run out of memory.

To join a set of points with a dashed line, one uses

$\dashline[stretch]\{dash\_len\}\{dot\_gap\}(x_1,y_1)(x_2,y_2)...(x_n,y_n)$

where *dash_len* is the length of the dashes (in \unitlength units), which are constructed as a series of dots to produce a solid-looking dash. If the optional *dot_gap* is given, then the dashes are made as a series of dots with that separation. The optional *stretch* is a number between −100 and infinity. If it is 0 or missing, the number of dashes is chosen so that the gaps between them are the same length as the dashes: If *stretch* is positive, the number of dashes is increased by *stretch* percent; if negative, it is reduced by that amount. With various combinations of *stretch* and *dot_gap*, different dash patterns can be produced.

To draw a solid-looking line through a set of points, one uses

$\drawline[stretch](x_1,y_1)(x_2,y_2)...(x_n,y_n)$

which draws the lines as a series of line segments using the LaTeX line fonts. Since these have a limited number of angles, the result can appear fairly jagged. By increasing the optional *stretch* factor (again a percent), more segments are used and the appearance is improved; by decreasing it, the line can begin to look dashed.

As an example of these three line-drawing commands,

```
\begin{picture}(100,13)
  \dottedline[.]{3}(0,0)(10,10)(20,0)
  \dashline{3}(30,0)(40,10)(50,0)
  \drawline(60,0)(70,10)(80,0)
\end{picture}
```

produces

For each of the three line-drawing commands, there is a corresponding environment, named dottedjoin, dashjoin, and drawjoin, each taking the same set of optional and mandatory arguments as the commands, except for the set of coordinates. Within these environments, one gives a set of \jput commands, which behaves exactly like the regular \put, except that all its elements are joined by the selected line type. For example,

```
\begin{picture}(100,13)
  \begin{dottedjoin}{2}
    \jput(0,0){\circle{3}}
    \jput(20,8){\makebox(0,0){\Large$\star$}}
    \jput(40,3){\makebox(0,0)[lt]{\small Finish}}
  \end{dottedjoin}
  \begin{dashjoin}[20]{3}
    \jput(55,3){}
    \jput(70,10){\oval(10,5)}
    \jput(80,0){\circle*{2}}
  \end{dashjoin}
\end{picture}
```

produces:

Finish

Real-life data curves are generated by other software programs. These results can be imported into the picture environment by storing them in a data file, named say, mycurve.put, and then issuing

```
\putfile{mycurve.put}{\picsquare}
```

The data file contains a list of x y coordinates, one pair per line, with possible comments beginning with % as usual. The \putfile command places its second argument at all the points listed in the data file.

The default dot character for plotting all lines is the \picsquare, a black square that scales with the current line thickness. A different dot character may be used with \putfile if one wishes. It is also possible to specify the dot character for \dottedline, but the default is \picsquare.

The default values for the optional *stretch* argument in \dashline and \drawline are initially set to 0, but they may be changed at any time by redefining (with \renewcommand) \dashlinestretch and \drawlinestretch, respectively. This makes it possible to revise a whole set of curves with one command rather than manually changing each one.

16.2.2 The eepic package

Package:
eepic The epic commands are still subject to many of the limitations of the picture environment: limited number of slopes for lines, limited line thicknesses, and restrictions on circle sizes. This is because the picture environment uses LaTeX fonts to 'draw' inclined lines and circles, making the results portable to all output devices.

The eepic package, by Conrad Kwok, repairs these problems by employing graphic commands executed by the DVI driver itself. They are transmitted to the .dvi file by \special commands, which are driver-specific. Thus greater flexibility is achieved, but at the price of loss of portability. The package is therefore most suitable for use with the PostScript dvips driver as well as with the previewers xdvi and windvi. It does not work with pdfTeX, unfortunately; on the other hand, it has no problems with dvipdfm.

However, eepic not only recodes the features of epic, it also adds some additional functionality. If one wishes to invoke these extra features with a driver that does not recognize the graphics \specials, one can use the emulation package eepicemu instead. A comparison of the results with these two packages is shown in Figure 16.1 on the opposite page.

In either case, one must load epic with one of eepic or eepicemu:

        \usepackage{epic,eepic}   or   \usepackage{epic,eepicemu}

The following standard picture elements are modified by the eepic package:

\line(Δx,Δy){*length*} (page 303) where Δx and Δy may take on any positive or negative integer values, and not just those between ± 6.

\circle{*diameter*} (page 305) may have any value for *diameter*; the same for \circle*.

\oval (page 305) may have the maximum diameter of the corners set to any value; this is stored in the length \maxovaldiam, which the user may change; the default value is 40 pt.

Similarly, all the extra commands from epic package are also revised internally. The restrictions on slopes never apply directly to them, but lines of arbitrary slope are drawn with little segments at the nearest available slope, or as series of dots, requiring much computer time and overloading the output file. With eepic, these lines are drawn more efficiently.

Additional features added by eepic (and eepicemu, even if they do not work very well):

\allinethickness{*dimen*}
        sets the line thickness to *dimen* for *all* picture elements, including circles, ovals, and splines, not just for straight lines

\Thicklines
        sets the thickness of straight lines to 1.5 times that of \thicklines

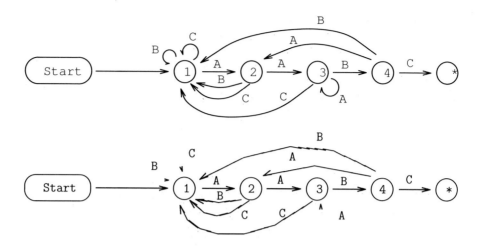

Figure 16.1: Comparison of results using the true `eepic` drawing functions (top) and those with the emulation in `eepicemu` (bottom). (This example is taken from the manual `eepic.tex` on the the the TeX Live CD in `texmf→doc→latex→eepic`.)

$\path(x_1,y_1)(x_2,y_2)\ldots(x_n,y_n)$
: is a fast version of `\drawline`, without the *stretch* option; a solid line is always drawn

$\spline(x_1,y_1)(x_2,y_2)\ldots(x_n,y_n)$
: draws a curve from the first to last point, with intermediate points as control points

`\ellipse(`*x_diam*`,`*y_diam*`)`
: draws an ellipse with horizontal and vertical sizes *x_diam*, *y_diam*, respectively; there is also *-form to produce a solid ellipse

`\arc{`*diameter*`}{`*start*`}{`*end*`}`
: draws the arc of a circle with *diameter* (in `\unitlength` units) from angle *start* to *end*, in radians, clockwise from 0 pointing to the right; *start* must be from 0 to 2π, and *end* from *start* to *start*$+2\pi$

16.3 Other drawing packages

16.3.1 The XY-pic package

As indicated at the beginning of this chapter, an exhaustive description of many other specialized packages, for drawing or using METAFONT fonts, can be found in *The LaTeX Graphics Companion* by Goossens et al. (1997). Most of these are designed for TeX in general, but they will also work with LaTeX. We mention two of these here just to show the possibilities.

The Xy-pic package can carry out general drawing entirely with extra METAFONT fonts, making it fully portable among all output drivers. The fonts are also available in type 1 coding (Section 13.1.6) so that the package works just as well with PDF output. It was created by Kristoffer H. Rose and then extended by Ross Moore and others.

Even an overview of Xy-pic is beyond the scope of this book. We recommend the package's *User's Guide* and more extensive *Reference Manual*, both to be found on the TeX Live CD in texmf→doc→generic→xypic. The descriptions and illustrations in Chapter 5 of Goossens et al. (1997) are especially helpful.

To give a flavor of the syntax in Xy-pic, we give the following examples:

```
\xymatrix{
U \ar@/_/[ddr]_y \ar@/^/[drr]^x \ar@{.>}[dr]|-{(x,y)} \\
& X \times_Z Y \ar[d]^q \ar[r]_p & X \ar[d]_r \\
& Y \ar[r]^g & Z}

\xy /r1.5pc/:,+<5pc,3pc>*+{P};p
  @(,+(2,2)*{+}@+, +(2,-2)*{+}@+
  ,+(2,2)*{+}@+, +(2,0)*+{C}="C"
  ,*\qspline{},"C",**\crvs{.}
  ,@i @)\endxy
```

that produce the diagrams:

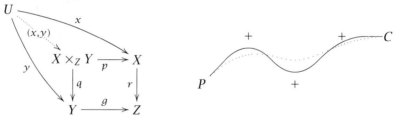

The first example, with \xymatrix, organizes its contents in rows and columns, not dissimilar to the tabular environment. In this case, the first row contains U in the first column, and the rest are empty; the second row has an empty first column (starts with &, the column separator) while the next two columns contain X \times_Z Y and X; the third row also has an empty first column, with entries Y and Z in the remaining columns. Everything else describes how these nodes are connected. For example, \ar@/_/[ddr]_y means 'draw an arrow, curving down to the node located two down and one right, and subscript it with y'... and so on for the other connections.

The second example, with \xy...\endxy gives more complicated drawing instructions, placing objects at given coordinates, joining them with arrows, lines, and curves. As can be seen from both of these examples, it takes some practice to learn the syntax and to exploit Xy-pic fully.

16.3.2 PSTricks

In Chapter 13 we describe how the PostScript language plays a very important role in TeX and LaTeX by making a wide spectrum of fonts available to complement the original Computer Modern fonts. But PostScript is also a powerful plotting language. It was to exploit the PostScript possibilities directly that Timothy van Zandt wrote the PSTricks package for direct use within TeX, and thus within LaTeX.

Actually, PSTricks consists of over a dozen packages. The complete functionality may be loaded with the package `pstricks`, or the individual packages may loaded separately. (Since PSTricks is really a TeX utility, the LaTeX package `pstricks.sty` does nothing more than load the `pstricks.tex` file containing the actual code.) Some of these packages and their uses are:

pst-3d	3-D drawing
pst-3dplot	a newer 3-D package
pst-blur	adding blurred shadows
pst-char	stroking and filling character paths
pst-coil	coil and zigzag objects
pst-eps	export objects to EPS files
pst-fill	adds \psboxfill command
pst-gr3d	drawing 3-D grids
pst-grad	gradient color fills
pst-lens	simulating effect of a lens
pst-node	placing and joining nodes
pst-osci	emulating oscilloscopes
pst-plot	plotting data
pst-poly	drawing polygrams
pst-slpe	improvement on pst-grad
pst-text	setting text along a path
pst-tree	tree commands

As with Xy-pic, it is beyond the scope of this book on document production with LaTeX to describe the extensive plotting features of PSTricks. We refer to Goossens et al. (1997), Chapter 4, for a description of most of these packages (some have been added since then) and otherwise to the manuals and documentation to be found on the TeX Live CD in texmf→source→generic→pstricks→doc.

<table>
<tr><td>

17

</td><td>

Presentation Material

</td></tr>
</table>

So far we have assumed that the output of a LaTeX project is to be printed on paper or an electronic document that looks like printed paper displayed on the computer monitor.

Another important type of output is *presentation material*, the visual support displayed in front of an audience during an oral presentation. Traditionally, this consisted of a set of slides to be projected onto a screen, but in more recent times this has been replaced by viewgraphs (or transparencies) and an overhead projector, giving the speaker much more interactive control over the presentation. However, the truly modern presentation is done electronically, with the entire presentation stored in a computer directly connected to the projector; there are no slides to fall out of the cassette or to be inserted the wrong way, no viewgraphs to spill out onto the floor. The only thing that can go wrong is that the computer refuses the connection, needs rebooting, or the necessary display program is missing. Such teething problems occur less frequently now that this form of presentation is becoming standard.

In spite of the change in medium away from the $2'' \times 2''$ pieces of film, a computer presentation is still called a *slide show*, a term that today presupposes the electronic medium. We will use the word *slide* more generally to mean a page of text and/or graphics for presentation, whether it is to be printed on paper and then photographically rendered to film or transparency, or to be directly projected from the computer. The preparation of such a slide with LaTeX is much the same regardless of the final projection method; direct projection does offer additional features, which we also address.

We start this chapter with the standard LaTeX method for slide preparation, the slides class, and then describe the far more advanced seminar and prosper classes, which are especially suitable for interesting PDF electronic presentations. We then illustrate pdfscreen, a package designed more for documents meant for electronic viewing but that can also produce slides. Finally, we show in Section 17.5 how PDF presentations may be enhanced with the help of a post-processor program.

17.1   Slide production with `slides` class

The `slides` class is the LaTeX2_ε successor to the old SLiTeX of LaTeX 2.09. This awkward and cumbersome device was needed then because of the way fonts were hardwired into the formats. This is no longer necessary: The entire functionality is now found within the `slides` class, much streamlined over the obsolete version, running under regular LaTeX or pdfLaTeX.

It is still fairly primitive compared to the more modern classes described in the following sections. We present it here because it is still part of the basic LaTeX and is the inspiration for those more sophisticated predecessors.

17.1.1   The `slides` class

Class:
`slides`

A slide is meant to be projected before an audience and is therefore something quite different from a sheet of paper to be read held in the hand. One could, of course, make up the text for slides with the normal LaTeX commands, but there would be problems getting the font size right, arranging overlays, making sure that the text does not change pages unexpectedly, and the question of whether book-style fonts are suitable for projection. The LaTeX class `slides` attempts to solve these.

A different set of fonts is used by this class, ones in which the lowercase letters are relatively larger than in the normal fonts, and with a much bigger base size. This has the effect of limiting the amount of text that fits on one page/slide, but this is, in fact, very good practice for presentation material. The text really should be restricted to keywords and abbreviated sentences. A full page of normal text projected onto a screen will not be read by the audience.

One is not obliged to use the built-in fonts; other (sans serif) font packages, such as `helvet` for Helvetica (Section 13.1.2), may still be selected. They will be used in larger sizes than usual.

Slides should also make use of color. The original SLiTeX had a complicated method for producing color overlays (in black and white, to be copied in color), which now is totally eliminated from the `slides` class. Instead, one simply makes use of the `color` package of Section 8.2.

Most of the formatting commands of regular LaTeX may be used with `slides`, except for the page breaking and sectioning commands. The special features that are unique to this class are described in the next sections.

17.1.2   The slide environments

The source file for producing slides is structured much the same as that for a normal document, except that the `slides` class is used, invoked as

```
\documentclass{slides}
    preamble text
\begin{document}
```

```
        slide text
     \end{document}
```

If colors are wanted, the `color` package of Section 8.2 must be added, for example, with

```
     \usepackage[pdftex]{color}
```

(You will have to specify your own driver as the option here, or rely on the local configuration to give it automatically, as is usually the case.)

The preamble may contain global specifications, for changing the paper size or selecting a page style, as usual. It may not contain any printable material.

Any text that appears after `\begin{document}` but before the special slide environments described below is output to an unnumbered *leading page* that comes before any slides. This may serve as a cover page for the slides.

There are three environments available for organizing different parts of a slide: the main *slide* itself, possible *overlays*, and additional *notes* to the slide.

Slides

A slide or viewgraph is created by means of the environment

```
     \begin{slide}   text and commands   \end{slide}
```

The contents of a `slide` environment may be any text that one pleases. Note that the `slides` class makes use of its own set of character fonts. The standard font in the normal size is roughly equivalent to the LaTeX sans serif font `\sffamily` in the size `\LARGE`. All the regular font commands and declarations of Section 4.1 are available, along with the other display and list environments of Chapter 4. However, there can be no page breaks within the environment, for the entire text is expected to fit on one page (slide or viewgraph). The successive `slide` environments will be numbered consecutively. If the page should overflow, a warning message is printed.

Any color commands from the `color` package may be employed if that package has been loaded.

Overlays

An *overlay* is an addition to a slide that can be laid on top of it to fill in certain gaps. The idea is to create suspense during a presentation, by filling in some keywords a few minutes later, or to be able to replace some text with alternatives.

The `slides` class generates overlays with the `overlay` environment, which functions exactly the same as the `slide` environment except that the numbering is done as a sub-number of the last slide. Thus the overlays following slide 6 are numbered 6-a, 6-b, and so on.

```
     \begin{overlay}   text and commands   \end{overlay}
```

The `slide` environment for a viewgraph that is to have overlays must come before the `overlay` environments that go with it. Both the slide and overlay should contain identical texts, except that certain parts are printed in 'invisible' ink by means of the two declarations

> `\invisible`   and   `\visible`

These two commands function just like font declarations. They may be set within curly braces {} to limit their scope or used to apply to the whole environment. Normally, in the `slide`, a few words might be made invisible, while in the corresponding `overlay`, `\invisible` is declared at the start and only those words that were blanked out in the slide are made visible.

Note: The `\invisible` command does not work with fonts other than the default ones, nor with pdfTeX. However, for pdfTeX, there are better methods to achieve the same results (Section 17.5.1).

One application for overlays is to present alternative text. One might, for example, show a table of cost estimates, with the figures on an overlay. By exchanging this overlay for another, new numbers that can be achieved by certain procedural changes may be fitted into the same table.

Notes

During a presentation, it is often necessary to refer to a list of keywords or other notes between the actual projected slides. The `slides` class has the `note` environment for producing such reminders for the speaker.

> `\begin{note}`   *text*   `\end{note}`

Like the overlays, notes are sub-numbered with respect to the previous slide, but with numbers instead of letters. Following slide 4, notes are numbered 4-1, 4-2, and so on.

17.1.3 Further features

Page styles

The LATEX command `\pagestyle{`*style*`}` may also be used with the `slides` class. The following styles are available:

`plain`   All slides, overlays, and notes have their number at the lower right corner.

`headings`
> The same as `plain` except that if the `clock` option is selected (see below), a time marker is printed in the lower left corner of the notes. This is the default page style.

`empty`   The sheets are printed with no page numbers.

In normal LaTeX, the command `\pagestyle` is issued in the preamble and is valid for the whole document. Individual pages may be given a different style by means of the `\thispagestyle` command, which remains in effect for only one page. This command should not be employed within one of the environments, but rather a new `\pagestyle` command may be given *outside* of the `slide`, `overlay`, and `note` environments.

Selective slide processing

During the construction of a slide show, one is likely to spend considerable time working on individual slides, ignoring the others for the time being. Complicated slides need to be corrected, processed, and viewed. One can speed this up by selecting only a few slides for processing, by placing the command

> `\onlyslides{`*slide_list*`}`

in the preamble. The *slide_list* stands for a list of slide numbers in ascending order, for example, `2,5,9-12,15`, specifying the slides, or range of slides, that are to be processed.

Nonexistent slide numbers may also appear in the *slide_list*. If the slide file contains, say, 20 slides, the command `\onlyslides{1,18-999}` will allow only slides 1 and 18–20 to be processed. Any overlays that belong to these slides will also be output.

Finally, the command

> `\onlynotes{`*note_list*`}`

in the preamble limits the notes that are output to those listed in *note_list*. If slide 5 has three `note` environments associated with it, `\onlynotes{5}` arranges for only the note pages 5-1, 5-2, and 5-3 to be printed.

17.2 Slide production with seminar

The `slides` class of the previous section provides some basic support for the production of presentation material. To improve on this, Timothy van Zandt has written the `seminar` class with many additional features. This was originally meant as a 'main style' for LaTeX 2.09, but has been upgraded to a LaTeX 2_ε class file by Sebastian Rahtz, with fixes by David Carlisle and Denis Girou. They only changed the interfacing so that it would work as a class file, leaving the functionality untouched.

Unfortunately, the supplied manual for `seminar` (`sem-user.tex`) has not been updated and is still couched in the language of LaTeX 2.09; in particular, it confuses packages and 'style options'. We try to correct this here.

If `seminar` is being used for PDF output, as for an electronic presentation, it is vital to include the `hyperref` package (Section 13.2.4), which detects the presence of `seminar` and adjusts the PDF page sizes accordingly. This should be done even if no other `hyperref` features are utilized. There are some other refinements to make `seminar` function smoothly with pdfTeX, explained in Section 17.2.7.

17.2.1 Overview

The seminar class is loaded as usual with

> \documentclass[*options*]{seminar}

Here we summarize its main features, which differ from the slides class:

- The slide material is put into the slide environment for landscape slides, and in slide* for portrait slides.

- Regular Roman fonts are used, but this can be changed. The options semhelv and semlcmss switch to sans serif family with the PostScript Helvetica and the standard slides fonts, respectively.

- Regular font sizes are used, with default 10 pt as usual. However, the slide text is magnified on output to make it more suitable for projection; the magnification factor can be set, but the default is a factor of 2, so the effective default font size is 20 pt.

- A slide is started automatically when the current one is full, or it may be forced with the \newslide command; the entire slide show could therefore be contained within a single slide environment.

- There is a choice of framing style for the slide text; the framing may be turned off with \slideframe{none} in the preamble.

- Everything outside of the slide or slide* environments counts as note text. The notes are printed on separate pages, numbered *n*.1, *n*.2, . . ., for those following slide number *n*.

- The options slidesonly, notes, and notesonly control whether only the slides, both slides and notes, or only the notes are printed. By default, both are printed.

- With the article option (not to be confused with the class of the same name), the slide show is printed in miniature form, two per page, appropriate for reviewing or as a handout. There is a notesonly* option to be used with article to indicate the missing slides.

We now explain these features in more detail.

17.2.2 Magnification and lengths

Rather than using enlarged fonts as does slides, seminar works with 'normal' sizes, which are then magnified at output. One can set the magnification step with \slidesmag{*num*} in the preamble, where *num* is an integer between -5 and 9. Step 0 is one-to-one, and each step indicates an additional factor of 1.2. The default is step 4 (factor 2).

By default, the basic font size is 10 pt, but this may be altered with the usual options 11pt and 12pt. All these are magnified on output. The font size can be changed at any point in the document with \ptsize{*pt*}, where *pt* can be either 8, 9, 10, 11, 12, 14, or 17. If this is given within a slide environment, it applies only within that environment.

The article option produces a handout, with two slides per page, using a separate magnification that is set with \articlemag{*num*}; the default step is 0, no magnification.

The output magnification applies to *all* sizes and lengths. This means that any lines drawn with \rule or spaces inserted with \hspace or \vspace are also magnified if they specify absolute units such as pt or in. The size of the slide itself remains unchanged by the magnification, since the purpose is only to increase the size of the contents relative to the slide. To set lengths to values that remain fixed relative to the slide dimensions, use \setslidelength and \addtoslidelength in place of \setlength and \addtolength. For example,

```
\newlength{\fixed}
\setslidelength{\fixed}{3in}
\addtoslidelength{\fixed}{1cm}
\rule{1pt}{\fixed}
```

draws a line of height 1 pt × magnification and of fixed length 3 in + 1 cm.

For the article output, there are the corresponding commands \setartlength and \addtoartlength.

The following length commands are slide lengths (do not magnify) and may be used wherever a length is required:

\semcm	1 centimeter
\semin	1 inch
\textwidth	width of the text area
\textheight	height of the text area
\linewidth	current width of text

These are particularly useful with the \includegraphics command and its options width= and height=.

17.2.3 Landscape and portrait slides

In contrast to slides, the seminar class allows landscape and portrait slides to be mixed. However, there are several aspects that need to be considered.

The slide and slide* environments determine whether the contents should be in landscape or portrait slides, but the actual placement will only be correct when it agrees with the orientation of the entire document, as specified by the options landscape and portrait. This means that when the landscape option is chosen, the landscape slides are properly formatted but the portrait ones are not. The reverse applies with the portrait option. One must print the landscape and portrait slides separately, each with the appropriate option, and with the `\landscapeonly` or `\portraitonly` command in the preamble.

When using the `dvips` driver, one can print the landscape and portrait slides together by including the option `semrot`, which ensures that the portrait slides are rotated into the landscape orientation. The entire document (slide show) can be printed in one go. The portrait sheets are then manually rotated to the correct orientation. This would not be acceptable for a PDF electronic presentation, where one wants the two orientations to be mixed in one file, with the text always upright. Another solution for pdfTeX is given in Section 17.2.7.

When printing both orientations together with the `semrot` option, the head and footlines will not normally be rotated with the text for portrait slides. This can be corrected by issuing `\rotateheaderstrue`. In this way, the output is the same as when one prints landscape and portrait slides separately.

Selecting landscape orientation in itself does not force the output printer to go into landscape mode; it only sets the page dimensions so that the text is written along the longer side. The printer is informed about the landscape intentions either by a switch when the file is sent to it or by an option to the DVI driver. Again, `dvips` can get around this, as explained on page 242. Using `seminar` and `dvips`, one should define

```
\renewcommand{\printlandscape}{\special{landscape}}
```

to allow the class to instruct the printer to go landscape *when necessary*. This also avoids the warning message on processing that the output must be printed in landscape mode.

17.2.4 Slide formatting

Here we describe the various ways to control the size, layout, and other formatting aspects of the slides.

Slide size

By default, the paper size is American letter size, 11×8.5 in, and the slide dimensions (slide writing area) are 8.5×6.3 in. By specifying the a4 option, the paper size becomes 29.7×21 cm and the slide dimensions 22.2×15.2 cm. (The **a4paper** option exists, but may cause an error.)

The slide size may be altered temporarily as optional arguments to the `slide` and `slide*` environments, as for example,

```
\begin{slide}[10cm,7cm]
\begin{slide*}[7cm,10cm]
```

Both of the above produce a slide 10 cm wide and 7 cm high.

Margins

Normally the material within a slide is centered vertically. The declaration commands

> `\centerslidefalse` and `\centerslidetrue`

turn this centering off and on, respectively. Without centering, the text is pushed to the top of the slide.

The text is left justified by default, with a ragged right margin. This can be changed with

> `\raggedslides[`*len*`]`

where *len* is the maximum space between the end of the line and the right margin. Omitting *len* produces a ragged right margin, while a value of 0 pt yields right justification; giving 2 em, say, creates a semi-ragged margin.

The margins between the slide area and the edge of the page are set with the commands

> `\slideleftmargin`   `\sliderightmargin`
> `\slidetopmargin`   `\slidebottommargin`

which are all set initially to 0.6 in. Since these are commands, not lengths, they must be changed with `\renewcommand`.

Framing

The slide area can be framed, the default being a rectangular box like that produced by `\fbox` (which is exactly what it is). The frame style can be chosen with

> `\slideframe[`*cmds*`]{`*style*`}`

The possible values for *style* are `plain` (the default) or `none`. The optional *cmds* are settings to adjust the frame parameters, such as `\fboxrule` and `\fboxsep`. By including the `fancybox` package, one also has `shadow`, `double`, `oval`, and `Oval` as allowed values for *style*, with their corresponding parameters (Section 5.1.9).

All frames make use of the lengths

> `\slideframewidth` and `\slideframesep`

for the frame thickness and separation from text. These may only be altered (with `\setlength`) outside the `\slideframe` command; in the optional *cmds*, one must alter `\fboxrule` and `\fboxsep` directly.

It is possible to define one's own frame style with

> `\newslideframe{`*new_style*`}[`*cmds*`]{\`*box_cmd*`{#1}}`

where *new_style* is the name of the new style (for use with `\slideframe`), *cmds* are box parameter settings, and `\`*box_cmd* is a box command, such as `\fbox` or `\shadowbox`.

There is a `semcolor` option for `seminar`, but this is not based on the LaTeX `color` package; rather, it depends on PostScript and the `dvips` driver. With the `color` package, one can make use of the `\color` and `\textcolor` commands for setting text in color as well as `\colorbox` and `\fcolorbox` for colored boxes and `\pagecolor` to color the whole page (page 166). Two examples for defining color frame styles are

```
\newslideframe{gplain}{\fcolorbox{green}{white}{#1}}
```

```
\newslideframe{rshadow}[\color{red}]%
        {\shadowbox{\color{black}#1\color{red}}}
```

The first makes use of the color frame box command `\fcolorbox`, while the second shows a trick to combine color commands with `\shadowbox`, which normally prints a black shadow box. The two `\color{red}` commands ensure that all sides of the box are in red, while the `\color{black}#1` puts the box's contents in black.

Page styles

Page styles determine how the running head and footlines appear on each page, just as in normal text. The regular LaTeX page style of Section 3.2 (`plain`, `empty`, `myheadings`, and `headings`) are all available, and the default is `plain`, with the page/slide number centered in the footline. A different page style may be selected with `\pagestyle{`*style*`}` at any time, or with `\thispagestyle{`*style*`}` for just the current page. There is also an additional page style `align` that puts + marks at the four corners.

You can define your own page styles with

```
\newpagestyle{style}{headline}{footline}
\renewpagestyle{style}{headline}{footline}
```

which is preferable to using the styles in the `fancyhdr` package of Section 3.2.2 since that cannot handle the magnified lengths correctly. For example, to define a page style with a centered text in the head, and a footline with a text at the left and the slide number at the right, give

```
\newpagestyle{mystyle}%
        {\hfill Report\hfill}%
        {March 20, 2004\hfill\thepage}
```

Note here that `\thepage` prints the number for the current page, whereas `\theslide` and `\thenote` refer to the latest slide and note numbers, respectively; `\thepage` is always set to whichever one is being printed.

Font commands can be included in the new definitions, but one should be aware that the commands `\slideheadfont` and `\slidefootfont` are always inserted into the head- and footlines. These are defined to be `\scriptsize`, but may be redefined by the user.

It is possible to select different page styles for the slides and notes. The `\pagestyle` command sets the style for both (as well as for the `article` output) while `\slidepagestyle` applies only to slides.

Page breaking

Unlike the `slides` class where each `slide` environment generates a single slide (and warnings if it is too big), the `seminar` package allows the text to break naturally into multiple slides just as normal text breaks into pages. A new slide may be forced with `\newslide`.

You can add some extra tolerance for the page breaking by specifying

> `\extraslideheight{`*len*`}`

where *len* is the additional height allowed before a break is automatically inserted. By setting this to be large, automatic page breaks never occur, and the user has full control, either with `\newslide` or by ending the environment. Setting it to 0 pt causes pages to be broken the same as for regular text. The default is 10 pt.

17.2.5 Selective output

One can select to output just the slides, or just the notes, or both, by adding one of the options `slidesonly`, `notesonly`, or `notes` to the `\documentclass` command. There is also a `notesonly*` option to print the notes alone in `article` output but with indicators for the slides.

A problem arises if `slidesonly` has been selected. Any global specifications issued after `\begin{document}` and outside of a `slide` environment will be ignored. One might want to redefine parameters in this way; including them inside the `slide` environment makes the changes local to that one environment. To avoid this, such global commands should be placed inside a `allversions*` environment. (If you actually want to include text and not just specifications, use the `allversions` environment instead.)

As for `slides`, one can output selected slides or notes. This is useful during development of the slide show, when one may spend much time designing a complicated slide and is constantly processing it to see the results; this can become tediously slow if the other completed slides are also complicated or include large graphics files. As for `slides` (page 323), the `\onlyslides{`*list*`}` command in the preamble ensures that only those slides whose numbers are included in *list* are processed. However, there is also a `\notslides{`*list*`}` command to exclude those slides in *list*.

The *list* a set of numbers in any order, separated by commas, or a range with a hyphen. It is even possible to include `\ref` commands for slides containing the corresponding `\label`, something that is very useful during development when the slide numbers are yet finalized. For example,

> `\onlyslides{4,2,\ref{sum},10-999}`

outputs slides 2, 4, the slide containing `\label{sum}`, and all from 10 to 999. Nonexistent numbers are ignored, so 10–999 really means '10 to the end' (unless there really are so many slides in the show).

17.2.6 Additional features

Counters

The `seminar` class provides all the standard LaTeX counters (Section 10.1) as well as `slide` and `note` counters, the values of which are printed with `\theslide` and `\thenote`. The page number is printed with `\thepage`, which is set to whichever of the others is current, or to the true page number for `article` output.

The `footnote` counter is the only one that is reset to 1 for each new slide. If you want other counters to be reset too, say, `equation`, specify this with

> `\slidereset{`*list*`}`   or   `\addtoslidereset{`*list*`}`

where *list* is a comma-separated list of counters. The first command overwrites the existing list of counters, the second adds to it.

The note environment

As an alternative to note pages being generated by all text outside of the `slide` environment, one can issue `\noxcomment` in the preamble, or select option `noxcomment` in `\documentclass`, and then place all the notes in `\begin{note}` ... `\end{note}` environments.

Overlays

Overlays for slides are produced by including the options `semlayer` and `semcolor`. These make use of PostScript coding and therefore only work with the `dvips` driver or equivalent.

The `\overlay{`*n*`}` indicates that the following text is to appear on overlay *n*; it remains in effect until the current scope is ended, at the end of the environment or `{..}` group, or when another `\overlay` command is issued.

Overlays are not so useful for a PDF electronic presentation. Instead, one creates the same effect by building the page successively. A method of doing this is explained in Section 17.5.1.

Adding a background image

Slide shows are made more effective with the use of color and with a background pattern or picture. A background color can be added with the `\pagecolor` command from the `color` package.

However, even more effective is a background image. If this is a graphics file named `mybg.png`, one can insert it as a background to all slides with the following trick. This does require the `fancybox` package for the `\fancyput` command.

```
\newlength\bgwidth
\newlength\bgheight
\ifportrait
```

```
    \setslidelength{\bgwidth}{\paperwidth}
    \setslidelength{\bgheight}{\paperheight}
  \else
    \setslidelength{\bgwidth}{\paperheight}
    \setslidelength{\bgheight}{\paperwidth}
  \fi
  \ifarticle\else
    \fancyput(-1\semin,1\semin){\raisebox{-\bgheight}
      {\includegraphics[totalheight=\bgheight,
                        width=\bgwidth]{mybg.png}}}
  \fi
```

First this defines and sets two new lengths, \bgwidth and \bgheight, to be the non-magnified size of the full page for the current orientation. The \fancyput command places its contents on each page, relative to a point 1 in from the upper-left corner; with the above coordinates, it is shifted exactly to the upper-left corner. The image file is inserted here, shifted down by the page height, and expanded/shrunk to fit the page exactly. One must design the image correctly so that any distortion is minimal. The \ifarticle construction prevents the background image from being included with article output.

This should work with any type of output, PostScript, PDF, or other. Of course, the type of graphics file must conform to those allowed by the DVI driver. For PostScript, it must be an .eps file, not .png.

See also page 341 for an alternative means of adding background images.

Local configuration

The seminar class reads in the file seminar.con if it exists. This gives the user the chance to write all the specifications and new definitions that he or she always employs to this file, so that they are automatically included in every seminar source file.

17.2.7 Using pdfTeX with seminar

Although the seminar class originated in the pre-LaTeX 2_ε days, and many of its extra features are coded for PostScript and the dvips driver without the modern graphics and color packages, there is no problem using it with today's LaTeX and those packages. This is particularly true for PDF output.

With pdfTeX itself, there are some extra length parameters \pdfpagewidth and \pdfpageheight that need to be properly set to get the correct output. This is most simply guaranteed by including the hyperref package (Section 13.2.4) even if none of its other features is needed.

Another difficulty arises if landscape and portrait slides are mixed. If the goal is only to print to paper or transparencies, then the two orientations may be processed and output separately, as explained above. However, for an electronic presentation, this would be most inconvenient. Certainly the ability to mix the two orientations is highly desirable.

The following code makes this possible. It revises the slide* environment to interchange the PDF page dimensions so that a true portrait page is produced. (This is not possible with printed output in which a single print job must have a fixed orientation.)

```
\@ifundefined{pdfoutput}{\endinput}{%
  \ifcase\pdfoutput \endinput \fi}
\newcommand*{\pdf@revpage}{%
  \@tempdima=\pdfpagewidth
  \pdfpagewidth=\pdfpageheight
  \pdfpageheight=\@tempdima
  \@tempdima=\paperwidth
  \paperwidth=\paperheight
  \paperheight=\@tempdima
}
\ifarticle \pdf@revpage \fi
\renewcommand{\printlandscape}{}

\expandafter\let\expandafter\slide@str
    \csname slide*\endcsname
\@namedef{slide*}{\pdf@revpage\slide@str}
```

Store this in a file named sempdftx.sty, which can be loaded with \usepackage. It is programmed to do nothing if pdfTEX is not being used. Alternatively, add a line \RequirePackage{sempdftx} to the local configuration file seminar.con to load it on every seminar run.

Note: This file can be copied from the enclosed CD in the directory books→Guide4, where a version of seminar.con is also available.

17.3   Slide production with the prosper class

Class:
prosper

There are many ongoing efforts to improve the generation of PDF presentation material with LATEX, or at least to simplify the input for more elaborate output. One of these, the prosper class, by Frédéric Goualard, exploits the seminar class and hyperref package, making extensive use of the PSTricks collection, to create very impressive slides fairly easily. Since PSTricks is based solidly on PostScript, it cannot be used with pdfTEX nor with dvipdfm, but must go the route DVI ⟶ PS ⟶ PDF.

Class options

The prosper class may be loaded with the following options:

draft   figures are indicated by a box, but are not inserted, and a slide caption indicates date and time of the processing

final   (default) for the final output

slideColor
        for a full set of colors

slideBW
        (default) for a reduced set, appropriate for printing in black and white

total   (default) the bottom caption display the slide number and the total number of slides

nototal
        only the current slide number is shown

colorBG
        for a color background depending on selected style

nocolorBG
        (default) for a white background

ps   for when the final output is to be PostScript for printing

pdf   for output that is converted to PDF for projecting

distiller
        when the conversion is done with the Acrobat Distiller program

troispoints
        the name of the default style; other supplied styles are named frames, lignesbleues, azure, contemporain, nuancegris, darkblue, alien, autumn, gyom, and rico; more may be added in time, and the user may define his or her own, using PSTricks. See the documentation and other style files.

Commands for setting things up

The following commands are used to enter various texts, set captions, logos, and font attributes:

\title{*text*}
        to enter the overall title

\subtitle{*text*}
        to enter a subtitle

\author{*text*}
        to give the author names

\institution{*text*}
        to enter the authors' affiliations

\slideCaption{*text*}
> for a caption that appears at the bottom of each slide; the title text will be used by default

\Logo(*x*,*y*){*logo_text*}
> places the logo defined by *logo_text* on each slide at a predefined position, or at (*x*,*y*) (in inches) from the bottom left, if this is given

\displayVersion
> turns on a draft caption containing file name, title, author, date and time of processing, even in final mode

\DefaultTransition{*trans*}
> sets the PDF page transition, where *trans* is one of the hyperref values on page 257; default is Replace

\FontTitle{*C*}{*BW*}
> defines font and color commands for setting titles, for color and black and white slides, respectively

\FontText{*C*}{*BW*}
> does the same for regular text

\fontTitle{*text*}
> sets *text* in the title font and color

\fontText{*text*}
> sets *text* in the text font and color

\ColorFoot{*col*}
> establishes the caption color

\PDFtransition{*trans*}
> sets the transition for the current slide

\myitem{*depth*}{*bullet*}
> redefines the bullet at itemization level *depth*

Making slides

The title slide is generated with the regular \maketitle command. An intermediate title slide can be inserted with

> \part[*trans*]{*text*}

where *text* is centered horizontally and vertically on the slide. This is used to break up the presentation into different parts.

The main environment for creating a slide with a heading and an optional page transition different from the default is

> \begin{slide}[*trans*]{*heading*}

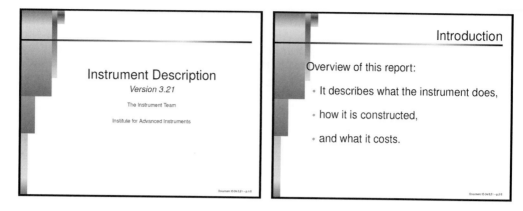

Figure 17.1: The title and first page from a sample prosper output

The itemize environment is redefined to yield a ragged right margin, while Itemize is the normal version of the environment.

The items in the itemstep environment are added one per page so that the slide is built up incrementally.

A slide may otherwise be built up incrementally by placing it inside the \overlays argument, as

```
\overlays{n}{
 \begin{slide}{...}
....
 \end{slide}}
```

This establishes n levels for the slide; the subsequent material within the slide can be assigned to different levels with the commands

```
\fromSlide{m}{content}
\onlySlide{m}{content}
\untilSlide{m}{content}
```

which place *content* on levels *m-n*, *m*, and *1-m*, respectively. Starred forms exist to place the contents in a box of zero size, suitable when they contain figures that replace each other. The different levels are in reality separate pages, which when sequenced produce the impression that material appears and/or disappears from the one slide.

The declarations \FromSlide{m}, \OnlySlide{m}, and \UntilSlide{m} act as switches, applying to all the text that follows them.

A sample output of prosper with the frames style is shown in Figure 17.1.

We stress once again that the prosper class cannot be used with pdfTEX nor with dvipdfm to generate PDF output. It must create a PostScript file that is then converted to PDF either with Acrobat Distiller or with Ghostscript, with its ps2pdf routine.

17.4 Electronic documents for screen viewing

Strictly speaking, this section is not about presentation material that is to be projected before an audience, but rather about documents that are deliberately intended to be read from a computer monitor. These have different requirements from printable documents: the page shape should be more like a monitor (that is, landscape instead of portrait) and navigation aids should be included, especially if the viewer's regular tool bars have been switched off. And, of course, internal links should be present, as well as links to external web sites and documents.

Package:
pdf-
screen

The `pdfscreen` package by C. V. Radhakrishnan is an effort to fulfill these requirements. But it is more flexible than that, for it also allows the entire document to be output in traditional print format. It even contains a `slide` environment for making projection material, so it does indeed belong to this chapter.

The supplied manual can be found in `texmf→doc→latex→pdfscreen`, in print and screen versions. The source file `manual.tex` can serve as a good example of how to use the package. Figure 17.2 on the opposite page demonstrates what a title page can look like, complete with navigation panel that appears on every page.

Parameters for pdfscreen

This package should be loaded with the `article` class and with the `hyperref` package. In fact, it should be considered to be an extension to `hyperref`. And it should be loaded last, right after `hyperref`.

The options that may be invoked with the `\usepackage` command are

`screen` to generate the output in the screen version, for online reading

`print` to generate the print version of the output

`panelleft`
      to place the navigation panel at the left

`panelright`
      to place the navigation panel at the right

`nopanel`
      to suppress the navigation panel

`paneltoc`
      to include a table of contents in the navigation panel

`nocfg` to ignore any local configuration file

`sectionbreak`
      to insert a new page at the start of sections

In addition, one can specify various color schemes for the panel and its buttons. Possible color options are `bluelace`, `blue`, `gray`, `orange`, `palegreen`, and `chocolate`. Also all the `babel` language options (Chapter 14) are recognized, for labeling the

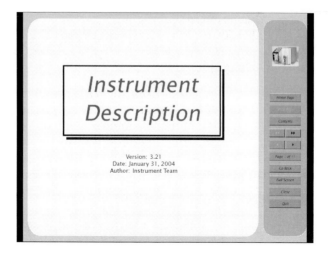

Figure 17.2: Title page of a pdfscreen document

navigation buttons, although only 15 are actually supported; the others default to English.

There are additional parameters that must be set by declarations:

\emblema{*image*}

> to set the name of the graphics file used for the logo in the navigation panel

\urlid{*url*}

> to set the web address (URL) of the home page button in the navigation panel

\screensize{*height*}{*width*}

> to set the dimensions of the screen; since there are no defaults, this must be given

\margins{*left*}{*right*}{*top*}{*bottom*}

> to set the margins for the document; again there are no defaults, so this must be given

The navigation panel

The navigation panel appears on each page and contains the buttons for changing pages and linking to the author's home page. A default panel is provided, but the user may redesign it as he or she pleases by redefining the \panel command. For example,

```
\renewcommand{\panel}{\colorbox{panelbackground}
{\begin{minipage}[t][\paperheight][b]{\panelwidth}
       . . . . .
```

```
\Acrobatmenu{FirstPage}
    {\addButton{.2in}{$\blacktriangleleft$}}
.  .  .  .  .
\end{minipage}}}
```

The \Acrobatmenu command is from the hyperref package (see page 259) while \panelwidth and \addButton are from pdfscreen. The \panelwidth length is by default 15% of the screen width and can be redefined. The \addButton{*wth*}{*text*} creates a button of width *wth* containing *text*. In the above example, clicking the button executes the viewer command to go to the first page.

There is also a command

```
\imageButton{wth}{ht}{image}
```

to insert the graphics file *image* as a button of width *wth* and height *ht*.

A row of small navigation buttons can be turned on at the bottom of the page with \bottombuttons and turned off with \nobottombuttons.

Background image

A graphics file can be inserted as a background image for the whole page with the command \overlay{*image*}, or a uniform background color can be selected with \backgroundcolor{*color*}.

The background color of the navigation panel is that previously defined as panelbackground, which the user may alter. Otherwise, the graphics file *image* may be inserted as the panel background with the command \paneloverlay{*image*}.

Making slides

There is a slide environment that places its contents centered vertically within a box the full size of the text area.

Local configuration

Any settings that you want to use for all documents with pdfscreen may be written to a file named pdfscreen.cfg, which is read in on loading if present.

Controlling print or screen output

The entire file can be processed either as a document to be printed in the traditional way or as an electronic document for reading on a monitor. This is switched by the options print and screen when loading the package.

Text and specifications that are meant exclusively for one output version must be enclosed in print or screen environments. This is especially important for the \screensize and \margins commands, which are inappropriate in print mode.

Other packages loaded

The pdfscreen package makes heavy use of several other packages, which it loads automatically. These must then also be installed on the system:

hyperref	graphicx	calc	shortvrb
comment	color	amssymb	fancybox
truncate	colortbl	amsbsy	

17.5 Special effects with PDF

There are many fancy features that one expects today from an electronic presentation: sounds and animation, text dancing in from the sides, fade-overs, and possibly fireworks. A PDF file can include many of these.

The pdfTeX program cannot (yet) generate these directly, but there is an auxiliary program called *PPower4*, written in Java by Klaus Guntermann and Christian Spannagel. This is a post-processor designed to take as input a PDF file specially prepared with pdfTeX with some extra packages and to create a new PDF file with the additional tricks.

For example, to build up a page containing an itemized list such that each item should pop up one at a time, one adds a \pause command after each item, runs pdfTeX, and processes the output with PPower4. It splits up the page into several pages, each one containing the text up to the next \pause. By stepping through these pages, the presenter 'constructs' the one slide before the eyes of the audience. In fact, PPower4 can do much more, making a very sophisticated electronic slide show from pure LaTeX input.

The PPower4 program and the necessary LaTeX support packages are on the TeX Live CD, but the latest versions can be obtained from http://www-sp.iti. informatik.tu-darmstadt.de/software/ppower4/. At the time of writing, it is still under development, but is already very impressive.

17.5.1 The PPower4 packages

The PPower4 post-processor is run with only two parameters: the names of the input and output files. There are no additional adjustments, controls, or options at processing time. Everything of that sort has already been placed in the LaTeX source text itself with the help of supplied packages. These instructional commands add comments to the resulting PDF file, which may be viewed and printed as normal. The post-processor then reads these comments and uses them as instructions for making up the new output file.

Here we describe these packages and the marker commands that they enable. The use of the hyperref package is presupposed, since many effects can be achieved directly with it.

Page transitions

Transitions from one page to another can be done in various ways to catch attention. The simplest is the plain replacement: the old page vanishes, the new one appears. Others involve effects that look like blinds opening, or like a box opening from or towards the center, or dissolving from one to the other. These can be set with the `hyperref` package with the option `pdfpagetransition` (page 257) or set to a different effect anywhere in the document by giving

> \hypersetup{pdfpagetransition={*pars*}}

where *pars* are the required parameters for the desired transition.

Marc van Dongen has prepared a file, `pagetrans.tex`, available with the PPower4 collection, that defines simpler commands to execute the above. (If this were renamed `pagetrans.sty`, it would be a package and could be loaded with `\usepackage`, but as is it must be included with the `\input` command.) These commands are:

`\Replace` pages are simply replaced, the default

`\Dissolve` one page 'dissolves' into the other in a mosaic fashion

`\VBlinds` several horizontal lines sweep vertically across the screen, like Venetian blinds

`\HBlinds` same as `\VBlinds`, but vertical lines move horizontally

`\HOSplit` two vertical lines sweep horizontally out from the center

`\HISplit` as above, but the lines move into the center

`\VOSplit` two horizontal lines sweep vertically out from the center

`\VISplit` as above, but the lines move into the center

`\OBox` a box opens out from the center

`\IBox` a box sweeps into the center

`\Wipe{`*angle*`}` a single line sweeps across the screen in the direction given by *angle*, which can be 0 (left to right), 90 (bottom to top), 180 (right to left), 270 (top to bottom)

`\pageTransitionGlitter{`*angle*`}` like `\Dissolve` but in a band that moves across the screen in the direction *angle*, which can be 0 (left to right), 270 (bottom to top), 315 (upper left to lower right)

We stress again, these declarations are simplifications of the `hyperref` commands and function without PPower4 post-processing. Once given, they remain in effect for all pages until a new transition command is declared.

Adding a background

We have already seen in Section 17.2.6 how a background image may be added with the help of the `fancybox` package and how a solid background color can be set with the `color` package.

These and other effects can also be achieved with the `background` package supplied with PPower4. This package provides the commands

> \hpagecolor[*color1*]{*color2*}   and
> \vpagecolor[*color1*]{*color2*}

that cause the background color to blend from *color1* to *color2* horizontally or vertically. If the optional *color1* is omitted, it is the intensity of *color2* that changes across the page. Both colors must be defined by the `color` package command \definecolor or be predefined colors. *This effect requires post-processing with PPower4!*

The package can also add background images, *without PPower4 post-processing*, if it is loaded with the option `bgadd`. This then includes the commands

> \bgadd{*image*}   and   \bgaddcenter{*image*}

to place *image* at the upper left corner or centered on the page. The *image* is an \includegraphics command with appropriate scaling to fit the page. These commands may be issued more than once to add further elements to the background. They may all be removed with \bgclear.

Note: The addition of background elements to the pages requires that the package `eso-pic` also be installed.

Building a page successively

The electronic equivalent to overlays is the successive building of a page of text. The PPower4 `pause` package introduces the \pause command that places markers in the PDF output which PPower4 then uses to break the page at that point, and to start a new page containing the previous contents plus whatever comes up to the next \pause or end of page. This works for both pdfTeX and dvipdfm.

For example, we could build a numbered list with

```
We proceed as follows:
\begin{enumerate}
  \item We write the list source text.\pause
  \item We add the pause markers.\pause
  \item We run pdf\TeX.\pause
  \item We run PPower4.\pause
\end{enumerate}
And there we have it!
```

The first PDF file generated will have a single page with a small colored block where each \pause command appears. (This may be suppressed if the package is loaded with the nomarkers option.) The resulting PDF file after post-processing will have five pages in place of this one, each one with an additional item. As the presenter steps through the pages, each new line appears to be added to a single page until the full page is complete.

Building with transitions

Rather than having the new line simply pop up out of nowhere, one can select the type of page transition at any step by giving a modified \pause with the name of one of the transition declarations from page 340. For example \pauseHBlinds is the same as \pause plus \HBlinds except that the transitions between main pages are not affected. Note that \pauseReplace is the default, causing the new text simply to appear. These remain in effect for the following \pause breaks until countermanded.

There is a \pauseGlitter{*angle*} command that is used as the equivalent to \pageTransitionGlitter{*angle*}, but all the others just attach the declaration name to \pause.

Building with levels

Even more sophistication can be added by assigning level numbers to the chunks of text between the \pause markers. In this way the page can be built up in any order, parts can be made to disappear or to be replaced, and the footline text at the bottom of the page can be visible from the beginning.

The level number corresponds to the sequence number of the views of the built-up page. Thus a chunk of text (that which comes between \pause commands) with level *n* will first appear in view *n*. By default, the level number starts at 1 and increases by 1 for each \pause. To ensure that the page footline is at level 1, we can write the last line of the above example as

```
And there we have it!\pause\pauselevel{=1}
```

The \pauselevel command sets the level number for the chunk in which it is located. There are several possibilities for its argument.

{=*n*} sets the level number absolutely to *n*

{=+*n*} increases it by *n*; bear in mind that the preceding \pause has already incremented it by 1

{=-*n*} decreases it by *n*

{=*n* -*d*} sets level number to *n* and makes the change in level number with \pause to be -*d*; this would be done with, say, {=10 -1} to make the chunks numbered backwards from 10, causing the page to be built from the bottom up

{:*m*} sets the maximum level to *m*; at higher levels, the text vanishes; with {=3 :4} the chunk is visible only at levels 3 and 4; the :*m* may also be set relatively as {:+*m*} or {:-*m*}

It is also possible to give multiple level specifications, as

```
\pause\pauselevel{=2 :2, =5 :6}Text\pause
```

to cause 'Text' to appear at level 2, to vanish for 3 and 4, and to reappear only for 5 and 6.

The level number may not be less than 1. Zero and negative numbers are treated as 1.

With some tricky playing around with level numbers and with the TeX overlap commands \rlap and \llap, it is possible to get text or images to be replaced. The two must be made to overlap, but at different level numbers. For example:

```
We now \rlap{alter}change this word
We now
  \pause\pauselevel{=1 :1}\rlap{alter}\pause
  change\pause\pauselevel{=1}
  this word
```

The first line shows the text without the \pause markers, in which 'alter' overlaps to the right over 'change'. The next lines show the same text with levels inserted: 'alter' belongs to level 1 and disappears after 1; 'change' belongs to 2 (automatic increment) and the remaining text is set back to level 1.

Highlighting instead of building

An alternative to building the page by pieces is to highlight the section of text being discussed. In this mode, the entire page is visible but printed in a dull color, like gray, while the chunk of text at the current level is in a bright color. When switching to the next view (level), that text becomes dull and the next chunk brightens.

To get this to work, one must inform PPower4 what the normal and highlight colors are to be, and one must further indicate what text should actually change. Clearly certain parts of the page are to remain as they always are, at least the head- and footlines, and possible titles. This is done with

\pausecolors{*textclr*}{*dullclr*}{*highclr*}

where *textclr* is a dummy color that is not otherwise being used. Only text indicated in this color will participate in the highlighting. For example:

```
\pausecolors{cyan}{gray}{red} ...
This is the \textcolor{cyan}{text to be highlighted}
  by the ...
```

The 'text to be highlighted' will normally appear in gray, but will turn red for that view corresponding to its level number. And only for that view! At the next view, it returns to gray. Note that the color cyan never appears; it is only a marker for PPower4. (Well, it does appear in the first PDF output, before post-processing.)

The highlighting mode is activated with \pausehighlight, which makes all text at all levels visible, but with this color-switching feature. The build mode can be reactivated with \pausebuild. In build mode, the color switching still takes place, but the text does not appear until the right view is reached. It will be highlighted only for this first view.

One can add the word highlight to the argument of \pauselevel to indicate a chunk that should always be visible even in build mode, and which participates in the color switching. In highlight mode, this has no effect.

Linking to first view

Package:
pp4link

An internal link made with the hyperref commands \hypertarget and \hyperlink (page 259) causes the target to be on the completed built-up page, on the last view. However, one probably wants to link to the first view, before the page is built up. The pp4link package can assist here. It defines the commands

$$\text{\textbackslash toplink}\{\textit{name}\}\{\textit{text}\} \quad \text{and} \quad \text{\textbackslash toptarget}\{\textit{name}\}$$

to establish *text* as a link to the target *name*.

This package tries to load hyperref on its own, without any options. If you try loading hyperref afterwards, with options, you will get a message about conflicting options and the options will be ignored. Therefore, load pp4link after hyperref.

17.5.2 The TEXPower collection

The only disadvantage of the PPower4 packages is that they require post-processing by another program, which can cause problems for some users. The TEXPower set of packages attempts to achieve the same ends by adhering exclusively to LATEX and pdfLATEX.

Package:
texpower

Written by Stephan Lehmke and Hans Fr. Nordhaug, the main package in the TEXPower collection is called texpower, which is intended to be used with any of the existing presentation classes. Since this is a fairly complicated package, which is still under development, we refer the user to the authors' documentation on TEX Live at texmf→doc→texpower→manual.pdf.

Letters

18

In addition to the three standard LaTeX document classes, there is a fourth one named `letter` for formatting correspondence. As provided, this class is intended for private letters without any frills, such as letterheads or business reference codes. However, local modifications are possible.

We first present the standard LaTeX `letter` class and then demonstrate how a house style can be written using our own institute style as an example. As always, it is highly recommended that each of these modifications be given its own file name so that `letter.cls` refers only to the provided LaTeX version.

18.1 The LaTeX `letter` class

Class:
letter

The `letter` document class is meant for writing letters. A single input file may contain the text for more than one letter and recipient, all from the same sender. Address labels may also be printed automatically if one wishes. Most of the normal LaTeX commands function as usual within the `letter` class. One exception, however, is the sectioning commands, which will lead to the error message ! `Undefined control sequence` when issued. It actually makes little sense to try to divide a letter up into chapters, sections, and so forth. On the other hand, there are a number of special commands that may be applied only within this style.

The input text for a letter begins as for every LaTeX document with

    \documentclass[*options*]{letter}

in which all the options listed in Section 3.1 may be given for *options* except for `twocolumn` and `titlepage`, which hardly make any sense within a letter.

Every letter must contain the name and address of the sender, which are set for all the letters in one file by including the commands

    \address{*sender_address*}
    \signature{*sender_name*}   or   \name{*sender_name*}

in the preamble. The *sender_address* normally consists of several lines, separated by \\ commands, as in the example

```
\address{Max-Planck-Institut f\"ur Aeronomie\\
         Max-Planck-Str.\ 2\\
         D--37191 Katlenburg--Lindau\\Germany}
```

The entry in the \name command will be used in the return address in the letterhead, if one has been programmed. The entry in the \signature command will be printed at the end of the letter below the space left blank for the writer's signature. If \signature has not been specified, the \name entry is inserted here instead. This allows a more formal \name to be used for the return address and a different form, perhaps with multiple lines, for the signature, as in

```
\name{Prof.\ M.\ Ostmann}
\signature{Martin Ostmann\\Project Leader}
```

When the above commands are issued in the preamble, they remain valid for all the letters in the document, except for those letters that contain new versions of these commands. Thus one letter might have a different \signature from the others. The scope of these entries extends only to the end of the environment in which they were called (see Section 10.5.4).

Two other sender entries are possible in standard LaTeX letter class. They are intended to be employed in local modifications for a house style. The idea is that if \address is *not* called, the preprogrammed company letterhead that might also contain the sender's room and/or telephone number is generated. Thus the commands

```
\location{room_number}   and   \telephone{tel_number}
```

are provided. In the standard letter class, the entries *room_number* and *tel_number* are printed at the bottom of the first page *only if* \address *is not issued*.

The preamble may also contain the \pagestyle command with the usual entries plain, empty, or headings. The first is the default, putting the page number centered at the bottom of all pages after the first. The headings page style adds the recipient's name, the date, and page number in a line at the top of all pages after the first.

After the preamble commands, the actual text begins as in all LaTeX files with the command \begin{document}. The text consists of one or more letters, each enclosed in a letter environment with the syntax:

```
\begin{letter}{recipient} text of letter \end{letter}
```

where *recipient* stands for the name *and* address of the recipient, divided into several lines separated by \\ commands.

```
\begin{letter}{Mr.\ Donald J. Burns\\
               Ontario Institute of Physics\\
               41 Adelaide St.\\
               London, Ontario\\Canada N4R 3X5}
```

The *text of letter* normally begins with the command \opening and ends with \closing, between which the body of the letter appears, mixed with whatever LaTeX commands are desired. The syntax of these two commands is

```
\opening{dear}
\closing{regards}
```

where *dear* is the salutation, such as `Dear Mr. Tibs`, and *regards* stands for the terminating text, for example `Yours sincerely,`. The `\opening` command could also contain other text, for example, a subject entry line, with the true salutation as part of the following body text.

LaTeX places the *sender's* name and address in the upper right corner of the first page with the current date set right justified below it. Then the *recipient's* name and address appear at the left margin, followed by the *salutation* and the body of the letter. The letter ends with the *terminating text* and the sender's *name* or *signature* left justified from the center of the line with sufficient vertical space between them for the handwritten signature.

After the `\closing`, a number of other commands may appear as part of the letter. One is `\cc` to produce a copy distribution list:

```
\cc{name1 \\ name2 \\ ... }
```

The text 'cc:' (or more correctly, the text defined in `\ccname`) is printed at the left margin, followed by an indented list of names of the copy recipients.

The second additional command is `\encl` for making a list of enclosures:

```
\encl{enclosure1 \\ enclosure2 \\ ... }
```

The word 'encl:' (actually the text in `\enclname`) is printed at the left margin and then the list of enclosures.

Finally, the command `\ps` may be used to add a postscript after the signature. The command itself does not generate any text, nor does it take an argument. The postscript text is everything located between the `\ps` and `\end{letter}` commands.

Normally the letter is dated automatically with the current date. However, if it is desired that the letter be back-dated or that the date be otherwise fixed in the text, it may be set with

```
\date{date_text}
```

in which case *date_text* appears where the current date would be placed.

A letter file may contain any number of `letter` environments, one per letter. As stated already, when `\address`, `\name`, and `\signature` have been specified in the preamble, they remain in force for all the letters in the file. It is possible to alter any one or more of these sender entries by reissuing the command within one of the letters, *before* the `\opening` command, but then this change is valid solely for that letter. If both `\name` and `\signature` have been declared, the latter is printed below the signature space.

The first page contains no page number. Subsequent pages have either a centered page number at the bottom (default) or a heading line with recipient, date, and page number at the top (page style `headings`).

The sample letter (Figure 18.1) was generated with the following input text.

Max–Planck–Institut für Aeronomie
Max–Planck-Str. 2
D-37191 Katlenburg–Lindau
Germany

September 8, 2003

TEXproof Ltd
P. O. Box 123
9876 Wordtown
Textland

Dear Sir;

We are most pleased to be able to answer your request for information about the use of LaTeX for general text processing at a scientific institute.

1. After some initial trepidation on the part of the secretarial staff, which was mainly due to their first experience with a non-WYSIWYG text system, the system is now fully accepted and appreciated.

2. Much to the surprise of many secretaries, they find that they are able to set the most complicated mathematical formulas in a reasonably short time without difficulties. The same applies to the production of detailed tables.

3. Creating cross-references and keyword indices no longer causes horror, even when the author is well known for demanding constant changes.

4. Finally, the high-quality appearance of the output has assisted in winning acceptance for LaTeX in our house.

An additional positive note is the ability to write business letters readily, making use of the `letter` class provided with LaTeX. In our institute, we have designed a special version to print our own letterhead, saving the need to have special letter paper printed.

Yours truly,

Patrick W. Daly

encl: Listing of our `mpletter.cls`
     Sample output

cc: H. Kopka
    B. Wand

Figure 18.1: A sample letter produced with the standard `letter` class

```
\documentclass[a4paper,11pt]{letter}
\name{Dr P. W. Daly}
\address{Max--Planck--Institut f\"ur Aeronomie\\
         Max--Planck--Str.\ 2\\
         D-37191 Katlenburg--Lindau\\Germany}
\signature{Patrick W. Daly}
\date{September 8, 2003}
\begin{document}
\begin{letter}{\TeX proof Ltd\\P.\,O. Box 123\\
               9876 Wordtown\\Textland}
\opening{Dear Sir;}
We are most pleased to be able to answer your request for
information about the use of \LaTeX{} for general text
processing at a scientific institute.
\begin{enumerate}
  \item
  After some initial trepidation on the part of the secretarial
  . . . . . . . . . . . . . . . . . . . . . . . . . . . . .
  in winning acceptance for \LaTeX{} in our house.
\end{enumerate}
An additional positive note is the ability to write business
  . . . . . . . . . . . . . . . . . . . . . . . . . . . . .
special paper printed.
\closing{Yours truly,}
\encl{Listing of our \texttt{mpletter.cls}\\Sample output}
\cc{H. Kopka\\B. Wand}
\end{letter}
\end{document}
```

By adding the command \makelabels in the preamble, the user can print out address stickers after all the letters have been output. The entries for the addresses are taken from the recipients' names and addresses in the argument to the letter environment. The standard LaTeX letter class is designed for a page of labels $4\frac{1}{4} \times 2$ inches, ordered in two columns. This could be altered for other formats. An address sticker without a corresponding letter may be printed by including an *empty* letter environment of the form

> \begin{letter}{*recipient*}\end{letter}

18.2 A house letter style

The sample letter on the facing page demonstrates the possibilities of the standard LaTeX letter class. The height and width of the text may easily be altered with appropriate declarations in the preamble. The use of explicit English words and date style is no problem for other languages since they are all contained in special commands that can be redefined.

The `letter` class has been designed so that if the `\address` command is omitted, a company letterhead will be printed instead. This presupposes that the file has been reprogrammed at the local installation for this purpose. Each employee using this house letter style will have certain personal entries to make, such as his or her room and/or telephone number. These commands have been provided for in the standard `letter` class.

We have such a house letter style at our institute, which we will illustrate here. However, it was necessary to add some more personal entries, such as 'Our Ref.', 'Your Ref.', and e-mail addresses. In addition, a command to print out 'Subject:' has also been added.

To distinguish our local house style from that of standard LaTeX, we have named it `mpletter`. It contains most of the features of `letter`, since it in fact reads in that class file and then makes its alterations and additions. The `\address` command is not necessary, since all letters are printed with the institute letterhead, including its address. The recipient's name and address are taken from the argument of the `letter` environment and are vertically centered in the space provided in the letterhead.

The writer's name and telephone extension are entered with

> `\name{`*author*`}`   and   `\telephone{`*ext_number*`}`

which, if given in the preamble, apply to all the letters in the file. If different letters have other authors, these commands must be made in the appropriate `letter` environment *before* the `\opening` command. New entry commands specific to `mpletter` are

> `\yref{`*your_code*`}`
> `\ymail{`*your_date*`}`
> `\myref{`*our_code*`}`
> `\subject{`*subj_text*`}`

which produce the words

> *Your Ref.:,   Your letter of:,   Our Ref.:,   Subject:*

properly positioned under the letterhead together with the corresponding text argument. If any of these commands are missing, their text will not appear in the letter.

Since ours is a German institute, there is an option `german` that translates all these words into their German equivalents. The entry commands have the same names, however.

As in the standard `letter` class, the current date is printed automatically but may be changed to any desired text with the command

> `\date{`*date_text*`}`

MAX–PLANCK–INSTITUT FÜR AERONOMIE   Max–Planck–Str. 2
                                     Katlenburg–Lindau
                                     GERMANY

MPI für Aeronomie, D–37191 Katlenburg–Lindau   Dr P. W. Daly
                                                    Tel.: 05556-401-279
                                                    E-mail:
Mr. George Murphy   daly @ linmpi.mpg.de
35 Waterville Rd.
Centertown, Middlesex
United Kingdom   May 10, 2003

Your Ref.: GFM/sdf   *Your letter from*: April 28, 2003   *Our Ref.*: PWD/sib

Subject: LaTeX information

Dear George,

Thank you for your inquiry about the latest version of the LaTeX installation and additional packages.

The entire TeX installation, with binaries and of course LaTeX, along with a large number of contributed packages, is distributed annually by the TeX Users Group, on their TeX Live CD.

I am sending you a copy of the current version of this CD, as you requested. In a separate directory named `bibtex` you will find the special bibliography formatting package files mentioned in 'A Guide to LaTeX'. I hope you will find these of use.

Do not hesitate to get in touch with me again if you have any further questions about the installation or running of the package.

Regards,

Patrick W. Daly

encl: 1 CD-ROM with TeXlive contents

cc: H. Kopka

Telephone	05556–401– 1	Bank		Train Station
Telefax	05556–401– 240	Kreis–Sparkasse Northeim		Northeim
Telex	9 65 527 aerli	41 104 449 (BLZ 262 500 01)		(Han.)

Figure 18.2: A sample letter produced using the authors' house style

if one wishes to back-date a letter or to fix the dating within the letter file itself. This is often handy if one only keeps electronic copies of the letters for the record. Otherwise, when a hard copy is run off months later, it will appear with the new current date and not with the original one.

The entry *author* that is given as the argument to the \name command appears in the letterhead as the name of the sender. It will also appear below the space left for the signature, unless it is overridden by the \signature command that specifies an alternative form of the name for this purpose.

The sample letter (Figure 18.2) has been generated with our house style, using the following input text.

```
\documentclass[12pt]{mpletter}
\name{Dr P. W. Daly} \signature{Patrick W. Daly}
\myref{PWD/sib}
\date{May 10, 2003}
\subject{\LaTeX{} information}
\telephone{279} \internet{daly}
\ymail{April 28, 2003} \yref{GFM/sdf}
\begin{document}
\begin{letter}{%
Mr.\ George Murphy\\35 Waterville Rd.\\
Centertown, Middlesex\\United Kingdom}
\opening{Dear George,}
Thank you for your inquiry about the latest version
of the \LaTeX{} installation and additional packages.
. . . . . . . . . . . . . . . . . . . . . . . . . .
Do not hesitate to get in touch with me again if you
have any further questions about the installation or
running of the package.

\closing{Regards,}
\encl{1 CD-ROM with \TeX{}live contents}
\cc{H. Kopka}
\end{letter}
\end{document}
```

The first page of our institute letter appears as shown, without a page number. If the text must continue beyond one page, the next page will have the heading

MAX–PLANCK–INSTITUT FÜR AERONOMIE

To Mr. George Murphy   *May 10, 2003*   *Page 2*

The recipient's name that appears in this heading is taken from the first line of the *recipient* argument in the \begin{letter}. This argument is split up by the LaTeX processing so that the first line is contained in the command \toname and the rest of the lines in \toaddress. The words 'To' and 'Page' are in the standard commands \headtoname and \pagename, and may be changed by an appropriate language adaptation option as shown in Section D.3.1.

18.3   A model letter customization

Adapting the letter.cls class file to the requirements of a company style should present few difficulties to an experienced LATEX programmer. Even a normal user may be able to make the necessary changes with the help of the example in this section.

We present here the class file mpletter.cls that was used to produce the sample letter in Figure 18.2. It makes heavy use of the LATEX programming features described in Appendix D. In order to understand it, one should be familiar with Section D.2. It will not be necessary to make any changes to the file letter.cls itself, since all modifications are in a separate class file that inputs the original.

The new class file is to be called mpletter.cls. It begins by specifying the TEX format that it requires and by identifying itself.

```
\NeedsTeXFormat{LaTeX2e}
\ProvidesClass{mpletter}
```

It will be necessary to execute conditionals, so we will need the ifthen package described in Section 10.3.5. We will want a flag to decide whether the letter is to be in German or not, determined by an option. Create the flag and define the option german to set it.

```
\RequirePackage{ifthen}
\newboolean{@german}
\setboolean{@german}{false}
\DeclareOption{german}{\setboolean{@german}{true}}
```

All other options that are valid in the standard letter class will also be accepted here, so simply pass them on to that class with the default option. Then process all options before loading letter itself with the a4paper option. We only have A4 paper in our institute.

```
\DeclareOption*{\PassOptionsToClass{\CurrentOption}{letter}}
\ProcessOptions
\LoadClass[a4paper]{letter}
```

This completes the preliminaries. So far, we have read in the standard letter class, along with the package ifthen, and defined a new option that is not present in the original class. Otherwise, all options and functions are unchanged, so far.

We now define the new 'name' commands to contain language-sensitive text, such as '*Subject*', which are not provided for in the basic class. The actual definitions will be executed by two commands, \englishnames and \germannames.

```
\newcommand{\englishnames}{%
\newcommand{\yrefname}{\textsl{Your Ref.}}
```

```
  \newcommand{\ymailname}{\textsl{Your letter from}}
  \newcommand{\myrefname}{\textsl{Our Ref.}}
  \newcommand{\subjectname}{\textsl{Subject}}
  \newcommand{\telephonename}{Telephone}
  \newcommand{\stationname}{Train Station}
  \newcommand{\germanname}{GERMANY}
  \newcommand{\telcode}{[49]-5556-401}
  \newcommand{\postcode}{D--37191}
}

\newcommand{\germannames}{%
. . . . . . . . . . . . . . . . . . . . . . .
 \newcommand{\telcode}{(05556) 401}
 \newcommand{\postcode}{37191}
}

\ifthenelse{\boolean{@german}}
   {\RequirePackage{german}\germannames}{\englishnames}
```

The last lines test whether the flag @german has been set (by the option german), and if so, the package german is loaded, and the German names are defined, otherwise the English names. The package german already translates the standard names commands \toname, \headtoname, and \pagename, so they are not included in \germannames.

Having settled the language problem, we now attack those commands for entering extra information in the header. Each of these stores its text argument in an internal command for future use. First, the internal storage commands must be created.

```
\newcommand{\@yref}{}      \newcommand{\@ymail}{}
\newcommand{\@myref}{}     \newcommand{\@subject}{}
\newcommand{\@internet}{}
```

```
\newcommand{\yref}[1]{\renewcommand{\@yref}{\yrefname: #1}}
\newcommand{\ymail}[1]{\renewcommand{\@ymail}{\ymailname: #1}}
\newcommand{\myref}[1]{\renewcommand{\@myref}{\myrefname: #1}}
\newcommand{\subject}[1]{\renewcommand{\@subject}
                           {\subjectname: #1}}
\newcommand{\internet}[1]{\renewcommand{\@internet}{#1}}
\newcommand{\INTERNET}{@linmpi.mpg.de}
```

Set the dimensions of the text on the page and its margins. These numbers are appropriate for A4 paper (which does make the a4paper option superfluous).

```
\setlength{\textheight}{215mm}  \setlength{\textwidth}{160mm}
\setlength{\oddsidemargin}{0pt} \setlength{\evensidemargin}{0pt}
\setlength{\topmargin}{-20pt}   \setlength{\headheight}{12pt}
\setlength{\headsep}{35pt}
```

The next step is to define some fixed fonts that are needed for the letterhead. We refer to the fonts with their explicit NFSS attributes; in this case they are all Computer Modern sans serif fonts in various sizes. These fonts will not change if totally different families are used for the body of the letter.

```
\DeclareFixedFont{\xviisf}{OT1}{cmss}{m}{n}{17}
\DeclareFixedFont{\xsf}{OT1}{cmss}{m}{n}{10}
\DeclareFixedFont{\viiisf}{OT1}{cmss}{m}{n}{8}
```

The letterhead itself is divided into two fields: The left one containing the institute name in large letters and the right one the address in a smaller font. Below the first horizontal line, the left field displays the name and address of the recipient, positioned to fit in the window of an envelope; the right one has the personal data of the letter writer, name, extension, and computer address. The widths of these fields are established.

```
\newlength{\leftfield}     \setlength{\leftfield}{117mm}
\newlength{\rightfield}    \setlength{\rightfield}{43mm}
```

The total width of these two fields equals 160 mm, which is the same as \textwidth. Next, we place the institute name and address in several saved boxes.

```
\newsavebox{\FIRM}         \newsavebox{\firmaddress}
\newsavebox{\firm}         \newsavebox{\firmreturn}

\sbox{\FIRM}
  {\parbox[t]{\leftfield}
      {\xviisf MAX--PLANCK--INSTITUT F\"UR AERONOMIE}}

\sbox{\firm}
  {\xsf MAX--PLANCK--INSTITUT F\"UR AERONOMIE}

\sbox{\firmreturn}
  {\viiisf\underline{MPI f\"ur Aeronomie,
                  \postcode{} Katlenburg--Lindau}}

\sbox{\firmaddress}
  {\parbox[t]{\rightfield}{\viiisf\baselineskip10pt
    Max--Planck--Stra\{\ss}e 2\\
    \postcode{} Katlenburg--Lindau\\\germanname}}
```

Using these boxes as building blocks, we put together the actual head and foot of the letterhead page in two further save boxes.

```
\newsavebox{\firmhead}     \newsavebox{\firmfoot}

\sbox{\firmhead}
  {\parbox{\textwidth}{\usebox{\FIRM}\raisebox{6pt}
```

```
        {\usebox{\firmaddress}}\\[3pt] \rule{\textwidth}{1pt}}}

    \sbox{\firmfoot}
      {\parbox{\textwidth}{\rule{\textwidth}{0.6pt}\\[5pt]
        \viiisf\setlength{\baselineskip}{12pt}%
        \begin{tabular}[t]{@{}ll}
          \underline{\telephonename}  & \telcode-1\\
          \underline{Telefax}         & \telcode-240\\
          \underline{Telex}           & 9\,65\,527 aerli
        \end{tabular}\hfill
        \begin{tabular}[t]{l}
          \underline{Bank}\\
          Kreis--Sparkasse Northeim\\
          41\,104\,449 (BLZ 262\,500\,01)
        \end{tabular}\hfill
        \begin{tabular}[t]{l@{}}
          \underline{\stationname}\\
          Northeim\\
          (Han.)
        \end{tabular} }}
```

The box \firmhead is fairly clear: It is a \parbox of width \textwidth containing the boxes \FIRM and \firmaddress side by side, with a line below. The foot \firmfoot is also a \parbox of the same width but containing three columns of general institute information, set in tabular environments.

It now remains to have the head and foot boxes placed on the first page. In the letter class, there is a special page style named firstpage that is always invoked for the first page of a letter. This must be redefined.

```
    \renewcommand{\ps@firstpage}
      {\setlength{\headheight}{41pt}\setlength{\headsep}{25pt}%
       \renewcommand{\@oddhead}{\usebox{\firmhead}}%
       \renewcommand{\@oddfoot}{\raisebox{-20pt}[0pt]
                                  {\usebox{\firmfoot}}}%
       \renewcommand{\@evenhead}{}\renewcommand{\@evenfoot}{}}
```

This page style must define the commands \@oddhead and \@oddfoot, which are always inserted at the top and bottom of odd pages, to place our special \firmhead and \firmfoot. The even pages are unimportant, since the first page is always odd. We must enlarge \headheight and \headsep to allow the big boxes to fit in.

Subsequent pages are set with the headings or plain page styles. We want to modify the former to include the firm address once more.

```
    \renewcommand{\ps@headings}
      {\setlength{\headheight}{41pt}%
       \renewcommand{\@oddhead}
         {\parbox{\textwidth}{\usebox{\firm}\\[5pt]
```

```
\slshape \headtoname{} \toname\hfill\@date\hfill
                              \pagename{} \thepage\\
\rule[3pt]{\textwidth}{1pt}}}
\renewcommand{\@oddfoot}{}
\renewcommand{\@evenhead}{\@oddhead}
\renewcommand{\@evenfoot}{\@oddfoot}}
```

One small problem remains: The first time one of these page style commands is executed, the head and foot commands may not yet exist, causing \renewcommand to complain. We ensure that they are there at the start by predefining them with \providecommand (Section 10.3.1).

```
\providecommand{\@evenhead}{}\providecommand{\@oddhead}{}
\providecommand{\@evenfoot}{}\providecommand{\@oddfoot}{}
```

Now make headings the active page style.

```
\pagestyle{headings}
```

There is only one last thing to do: Redefine the opening command that prints the recipient's address and the salutation. We add a bit more, including the personal data of the sender as well as the reference information. The address goes in the left field, the personal data to the right. The references go in a line below the rule, followed by the subject line. These entries are tested first and are only included if they are not blank. Several stored entry commands used here are part of the standard letter class, such as \toname and \toaddress. The \@date entry is either \today or whatever text was stored with \date.

```
\renewcommand{\opening}[1]{\thispagestyle{firstpage}%
  \parbox[t]{\leftfield}
     {\usebox{\firmreturn}}\\
      \parbox[b][3.5cm][c]{\leftfield}{\toname\\\toaddress}}%
  \parbox[t]{\rightfield}
     {\fromname
      \ifthenelse{\equal{\telephonenum}{}}
         {}{\\ Tel.: \telcode-\telephonenum}
      \ifthenelse{\equal{\@internet}{}}
         {}{\\{\viiisf E-mail: \@internet\INTERNET}}
      \\[5mm] \@date}
  \par
  \rule{\textwidth}{0.6pt}
  \makebox[\leftfield][l]
     {\ifthenelse{\equal{\@yref}{}}
        {\@ymail}{\@yref\hfill\@ymail\hfill}}
  \@myref\par
  \ifthenelse{\equal{\@subject}{}}
     {}{\@subject\par}
  \vspace{2\parskip} #1 \par\nobreak}
```

The result of this formatting can be seen on page 351. It should be possible to modify the coding as needed for other organizations without too much difficulty.

The field for the recipient's name and address has been positioned so that it will appear in the address window of an envelope when properly folded. The smaller return address will also be visible through this window. The printing of extra address stickers is thus superfluous.

Appendices

A — The New Font Selection Scheme

When TeX and LaTeX were invented, the fonts available for them were very limited in number. For this reason, the original LaTeX had an inflexible system of defining the fonts that were to be used, since it was not obvious that one might want to change them. The association between the high-level font commands such as `\large` and `\bf` and the external font name that is ultimately selected was rigidly fixed internally.

Today there are many additional fonts available, some of which should be used alongside the standard CM fonts and others that should replace them altogether. For example, the Cyrillic fonts of Section 15.4.2 should be added parallel to the Latin fonts, but to make them operate automatically under the LaTeX size commands was a complex procedure. (We know: We have done it!) Similarly, installing PostScript fonts involved calling intricate interface macros.

Another problem was the behavior of the font style and size commands. As explained in Section F.2.1, each of the font declarations `\rm`, `\bf`, `\sc`, `\sl`, `\it`, `\sf`, and `\tt` activates a particular font in the current size, overriding the previous declaration. One can select either a bold or an italic font, but there is no way to select a bold, italic one. Furthermore, selecting a new size automatically switches to `\rm`, an upright, Roman, medium font. That is, the attributes cannot be selected independently of each other.

In 1989 Frank Mittelbach and Rainer Schöpf proposed a New Font Selection Scheme (NFSS) for LaTeX, and a preliminary test package was ready in early 1990. A second release (NFSS2) was published mid-1993 with many substantial changes. With the official release of LaTeX 2_ε in June 1994, NFSS became firmly entrenched in the new standard. The new font declarations and commands are described in Sections 4.1.3 and 4.1.4. Here we explain the usage in more detail.

A.1 Font attributes under NFSS

According to the NFSS scheme, every character set can be classified by five attributes called *encoding*, *family*, *series*, *shape*, and *size*, which may be selected with the commands

\fontencoding{*encode*} \fontfamily{*fam*} \fontseries{*wt_wth*}
  \fontshape{*form*}   and   \fontsize{*sz*}{*line_sp*}

The *encode* attribute specifies the layout of the characters within the font. Possible values for it are listed in Table A.1. It is unlikely that one would want to change encoding within a document, except to activate Cyrillic fonts perhaps. This topic is dealt with further in Section A.3.

Package:
fontenc
However, before an encoding can be invoked, it is necessary to load the corresponding definition file. This is most easily done with the standard package fontenc, as for example

\usepackage[OT2,T1]{fontenc}

where the desired codings are listed as options in square brackets, the last of which is made to be the current one.

The argument *fam* in \fontfamily denotes a basic set of font properties. For the Computer Modern fonts, all the serif fonts belong to the family cmr. The family cmss includes all the sans serif fonts while cmtt contains the typewriter fonts. Table A.2 lists the CM fonts according to the family and other attributes.

The argument *wt_wth* in \fontseries designates the *weight* (=*boldness*) and *width* of the characters. These are specified by 1 to 4 letters as shown in Table A.3 on page 364.

The argument for \fontseries{*wt_wth*} consists of the letter or letters for the weight, followed by those for the width. Thus ebsc indicates weight *extrabold* and width *semicondensed* while bx means weight *bold* and width *expanded*. The letter m is omitted when combined with any non-normal weight or width; if both are to be normal, it is sufficient to give m alone.

In \fontshape, the argument *form* is one of the letter combinations n, it, sl, or sc for selecting normal (or upright), italic, slanted, or small caps.

The \fontsize attribute command takes two arguments, the first *sz* being the point size of the font (without the dimension pt explicitly given) and the second *line_sp* being the vertical spacing from one baseline to the next. The second argument becomes the new value of \baselineskip (Section 3.2.4). For example,

Table A.1: The NFSS encoding schemes

Encoding	Description	Sample Font	Page
OT1	Original text fonts from Knuth	cmr10	367
OT2	Univ. Washington Cyrillic fonts	wncyr10	
T1	The Cork (DC/EC) fonts	ecrm1000	370
TS1	Text Companion fonts	tcrm1000	372
T2	Cyrillic		
OML	TeX math letter fonts	cmmi10	368
OMS	TeX math symbol fonts	cmsy10	368
OMX	TeX math extended fonts	cmex10	
U	Unknown coding		

Table A.2: Attributes of the Computer Modern fonts

Series	Shape(s)	Examples of external names
	Computer Modern Roman (`\fontfamily{cmr}`)	
m	n, it, sl, sc, u	cmr10, cmti10, cmsl10, cmcsc10, cmu10
bx	n, it, sl	cmbx10, cmbxti10, cmbxsl10
b	n	cmb10
	Computer Modern Sans Serif (`\fontfamily{cmss}`)	
m	n, sl	cmss10, cmssi10
bx	n	cmssbx10
sbc	n	cmssdc10
	Computer Modern Typewriter (`\fontfamily{cmtt}`)	
m	n, it, sl, sc	cmtt10, cmitt10, cmsltt10, cmtcsc10

`\fontsize{12}{15}` selects a font size of 12 pt with interline spacing of 15 pt. (The second argument may be given a dimension, such as 15pt, but pt is assumed if no dimension is stated.)

Once all five attributes have been set, the font itself is selected with the command `\selectfont`. The new feature here is that the various attributes are independent of one another. Changing one of them does not alter the others. For example, if the selection

`\fontfamily{cmr} \fontseries{bx} \fontshape{n} \fontsize{12}{15}`

has been made for an upright, bold, expanded, Roman font of size 12 pt and interline spacing 15 pt, then when `\fontfamily{cmss}` is later selected for a sans serif font, the attributes weight and width bx, form n, and size 12(15pt) remain in effect when the next `\selectfont` is issued.

Alternatively, all attributes but the size may be specified and the font activated immediately with the command

`\usefont{`*code*`}{`*family*`}{`*series*`}{`*shape*`}`

Table A.2 (by F. Mittelbach and R. Schöpf) lists the classification of the Computer Modern character sets according to the attributes `\fontfamily`, `\fontseries`, and `\fontshape`. Having so many attribute combinations without a corresponding CM font may appear to be a weakness in the NFSS system, but recall that it is designed for the future. It may also be employed with the PostScript fonts, which are becoming ever more popular, to exploit their complete variability.

Formally it is possible to set any combination of attributes; however, there may not exist any font matching all the attributes selected. If that is the case, when

Table A.3: The NFSS *series* attributes

Weight class		Width class		
Ultralight	ul	Ultracondensed	50%	uc
Extralight	el	Extracondensed	62.5%	ec
Light	l	Condensed	75%	c
Semilight	sl	Semicondensed	87.5%	sc
Medium (normal)	m	Medium	100%	m
Semibold	sb	Semiexpanded	112.5%	sx
Bold	b	Expanded	125%	x
Extrabold	eb	Extraexpanded	150%	ex
Ultrabold	ub	Ultraexpanded	200%	ux

\selectfont is called, LaTeX issues a warning stating which font has been activated in its place. The font size attribute of the \fontsize command may normally take on values of 5, 6, 7, 8, 9, 10, 10.95, 12, 14.4, 17.28, 20.74, and 24.88, but other values may also be added. The second argument, the interline spacing, may take on any value since it is not something intrinsic to the font itself.

With the \begin{document} command, LaTeX sets the five attributes to certain preset default values. These are normally standard encoding OT1, family cmr, medium series m, normal shape n, and the base size selected. The user may change these initial values within the preamble, or they might be set differently by a special option, such as when a PostScript font has been selected.

A.2   Simplified font selection

The commands \fontencoding, \fontfamily, \fontseries, \fontshape, and \fontsize, together with the command \selectfont, are the basic tools in the New Font Selection Scheme. The user need not employ these commands directly, but rather may make use of the higher-level declarations presented in Sections 4.1.2 and 4.1.3. In fact, a font declaration such as \itshape is defined as \fontshape{it} \selectfont.

The high-level commands to select font sizes are:

\tiny	(5pt)	\normalsize	(10pt)	\LARGE	(17.28pt)
\scriptsize	(7pt)	\large	(12pt)	\huge	(20.74pt)
\footnotesize	(8pt)	\Large	(14.4pt)	\Huge	(24.88pt)
\small	(9pt)				

The sizes listed for the commands are those when 10pt (the default) has been selected as the basic size option in the \documentclass command; for 11pt and 12pt, they will all scale accordingly.

The family declarations and their standard family attribute values are:

\rmfamily (cmr)   \sffamily (cmss)   \ttfamily (cmtt)

which are the three Computer Modern families: Roman, Sans Serif, and Typewriter. The series declarations and their initial attribute values are:

\mdseries (m)   \bfseries (bx)

meaning that only a medium and a bold extended series are provided as standard. Finally, the shape declarations and their attribute values are:

\upshape   (n)   \itshape   (it)
\slshape   (sl)   \scshape   (sc)

to select upright, *slanted*, *italic*, and SMALL CAPS.

Note that there are no high-level declarations for the encoding attributes. This is because there is normally no need to change encoding within a document. An exception might be to use Cyrillic fonts (coding OT2), in which case one could define

\newcommand{\cyr}{\fontencoding{OT2}\selectfont}
\newcommand{\lat}{\fontencoding{OT1}\selectfont}

to be able to switch back and forth more conveniently.

The family, shape, and series attributes may be reset to their standard values at any time with the \normalfont command, which also activates that font in the current size.

For each of the above font attribute declarations there is also a corresponding font command (Section 4.1.4) that sets its argument in that font. Thus \textit{text} is almost the same as {\itshape text}, the only difference being that the command also contains the *italic correction* automatically. The complete list of such commands is:

Family: \textrm \textsf   \texttt
Series: \textmd \textbf
Shape: \textup \textit   \textsl \textsc
Other: \emph   \textnormal

The \emph command is described in Section 4.1.1; \textnormal sets its argument in \normalfont.

A.2.1   Default attribute values

We implied in Section A.2 that the font attribute declarations such as \itshape are defined as \fontshape{it}\selectfont, whereas in fact they make use of certain default attributes. Thus the true definition of \itshape is

\fontshape{\itdefault}\selectfont

The default commands available are

Family: \rmdefault \sfdefault \ttdefault
Series: \mddefault \bfdefault
Shape: \updefault \itdefault \sldefault \scdefault

and then `\itdefault` is defined to be the attribute `it`.

It is also necessary to define the standard attributes chosen when the command `\normalfont` is issued. These are contained in the four defaults

```
\encodingdefault  \familydefault  \seriesdefault
\shapedefault
```

All of this may sound like a complicated route linking the high-level commands to a particular font. However, it does provide flexibility and modularity. The author only needs to know that three families, two series, and four shapes are available, and does not care what they really are. A programmer defines these with the defaults at a lower level.

For example, to replace the standard fonts by the PostScript ones, it is only necessary to redefine the three family defaults. The package `times` (Section 13.1.2) contains only the lines

```
\renewcommand{\rmdefault}{ptm}
\renewcommand{\sfdefault}{phv}
\renewcommand{\ttdefault}{pcr}
```

This makes Times-Roman `ptm` the default Roman family, invoked with the command `\rmfamily`, Helvetica `phv` the default sans serif family (called by `\sffamily`), and Courier `pcr` the default typewriter family (activated by `\ttfamily`).

A.3   Font encoding

Computers work exclusively with numbers or, more precisely, only with bits that may be interpreted as numbers. They do not know the difference between the letter A and an apple, or that either even exists. For text processing, all symbols, both input and output, need to be represented as numbers somehow. The association between number and symbol is called the *encoding* or *layout*. The latter term derives from the common method of illustrating the encoding in the form of a table.

Encoding tables are by no means standard. The usual ASCII scheme is just one of several, and it is limited to 7 bits, or 128 characters. There are 8-bit (256 characters) versions as well; in fact, a large number exist, tailored to different computer systems and languages. The question of coding the input for LaTeX documents with more than 7 bits is addressed in Sections 2.5.9 and D.4.

A.3.1   Computer Modern fonts

Text fonts

When Donald E. Knuth invented the TeX program, he also provided it with an extensive set of character fonts, which he named *Computer Modern* (CM), rather than relying on the fonts available on any given printer. At that time, the printer fonts were not

	0	1	2	3	4	5	6	7
'00x	Γ 0	Δ 1	Θ 2	Λ 3	Ξ 4	Π 5	Σ 6	Υ 7
'01x	Φ 8	Ψ 9	Ω 10	ff 11	fi 12	fl 13	ffi 14	ffl 15
'02x	ı 16	ȷ 17	` 18	´ 19	ˇ 20	˘ 21	¯ 22	˚ 23
'03x	¸ 24	ß 25	æ 26	œ 27	ø 28	Æ 29	Œ 30	Ø 31
'04x	´ 32	! 33	" 34	# 35	$ 36	% 37	& 38	' 39
'05x	(40	) 41	* 42	+ 43	, 44	- 45	. 46	/ 47
'06x	0 48	1 49	2 50	3 51	4 52	5 53	6 54	7 55
'07x	8 56	9 57	: 58	; 59	¡ 60	= 61	¿ 62	? 63
'10x	@ 64	A 65	B 66	C 67	D 68	E 69	F 70	G 71
'11x	H 72	I 73	J 74	K 75	L 76	M 77	N 78	O 79
'12x	P 80	Q 81	R 82	S 83	T 84	U 85	V 86	W 87
'13x	X 88	Y 89	Z 90	[91	" 92	] 93	^ 94	. 95
'14x	` 96	a 97	b 98	c 99	d 100	e 101	f 102	g 103
'15x	h 104	i 105	j 106	k 107	l 108	m 109	n 110	o 111
'16x	p 112	q 113	r 114	s 115	t 116	u 117	v 118	w 119
'17x	x 120	y 121	z 122	— 123	— 124	ʺ 125	˜ 126	¨ 127

Font Layout 1: The character font `cmr10`. This is the standard character assignment for the OT1 encoding scheme

so good and certainly were not uniform. With the supplied fonts, TeX could produce identical, high-quality results on all printers.

LaTeX has inherited these fonts, which were once a trademark for documents produced by TeX or LaTeX. Of course, today LaTeX need not be married to any particular set of fonts, especially now that NFSS enormously simplifies font installation. The fonts used in this book, for example, are Lucida Bright, Lucida Sans, and Lucida Sans Typewriter, designed by Bigelow & Holmes and distributed by Y&Y Inc.

The encoding scheme used by the Computer Modern text fonts is essentially the 7-bit ASCII code, with the unprintable control characters replaced by Greek uppercase letters, ligatures, accents, and various dashes. The scheme is displayed in Font Layout 1, and is designated OT1 in NFSS, for *Original Text 1* (Table A.1).

In fact, the original Computer Modern fonts are not fully consistent with this scheme. The small caps and typewriter fonts deviate from pure OT1 in that the ligatures are replaced by extra symbols, and in the typewriter fonts the characters { | } are restored to their regular ASCII positions. The italic fonts differ from OT1 in that the pound sign £ replaces the dollar sign $.

The OT1 scheme is not limited to Computer Modern fonts. The TeX installations for PostScript fonts (Section 13.1.2) emulate this encoding so that LaTeX can function just as well with them without any internal character reassignments.

Math fonts

Since Knuth's primary concern was mathematical typesetting, he also developed a set of math fonts containing additional symbols required. These encodings have

'	0	1	2	3	4	5	6	7
'00x	Γ 0	Δ 1	Θ 2	Λ 3	Ξ 4	Π 5	Σ 6	Υ 7
'01x	Φ 8	Ψ 9	Ω 10	α 11	β 12	γ 13	δ 14	ϵ 15
'02x	ζ 16	η 17	θ 18	ι 19	κ 20	λ 21	μ 22	ν 23
'03x	ξ 24	π 25	ρ 26	σ 27	τ 28	υ 29	ϕ 30	χ 31
'04x	ψ 32	ω 33	ε 34	ϑ 35	ϖ 36	ϱ 37	ς 38	φ 39
'05x	↼ 40	↽ 41	⇀ 42	⇁ 43	` 44	' 45	▷ 46	◁ 47
'06x	0 48	1 49	2 50	3 51	4 52	5 53	6 54	7 55
'07x	8 56	9 57	. 58	, 59	$<$ 60	/ 61	$>$ 62	$\star$ 63
'10x	∂ 64	A 65	B 66	C 67	D 68	E 69	F 70	G 71
'11x	H 72	I 73	J 74	K 75	L 76	M 77	N 78	O 79
'12x	P 80	Q 81	R 82	S 83	T 84	U 85	V 86	W 87
'13x	X 88	Y 89	Z 90	$\flat$ 91	$\natural$ 92	$\sharp$ 93	$\smile$ 94	$\frown$ 95
'14x	ℓ 96	a 97	b 98	c 99	d 100	e 101	f 102	g 103
'15x	h 104	i 105	j 106	k 107	l 108	m 109	n 110	o 111
'16x	p 112	q 113	r 114	s 115	t 116	u 117	v 118	w 119
'17x	x 120	y 121	z 122	$\imath$ 123	$\jmath$ 124	$\wp$ 125	⃗ 126	⌢ 127

Font Layout 2: The font `cmmi10`, corresponding to the OML encoding scheme

'	0	1	2	3	4	5	6	7
'00x	$-$ 0	$\cdot$ 1	$\times$ 2	$*$ 3	$\div$ 4	$\diamond$ 5	$\pm$ 6	$\mp$ 7
'01x	$\oplus$ 8	$\ominus$ 9	$\otimes$ 10	$\oslash$ 11	$\odot$ 12	$\bigcirc$ 13	$\circ$ 14	$\bullet$ 15
'02x	$\asymp$ 16	$\equiv$ 17	$\subseteq$ 18	$\supseteq$ 19	$\leq$ 20	$\geq$ 21	$\preceq$ 22	$\succeq$ 23
'03x	$\sim$ 24	$\approx$ 25	$\subset$ 26	$\supset$ 27	$\ll$ 28	$\gg$ 29	$\prec$ 30	$\succ$ 31
'04x	$\leftarrow$ 32	$\rightarrow$ 33	$\uparrow$ 34	$\downarrow$ 35	$\leftrightarrow$ 36	$\nearrow$ 37	$\searrow$ 38	$\simeq$ 39
'05x	$\Leftarrow$ 40	$\Rightarrow$ 41	$\Uparrow$ 42	$\Downarrow$ 43	$\Leftrightarrow$ 44	$\nwarrow$ 45	$\swarrow$ 46	$\propto$ 47
'06x	$\prime$ 48	∞ 49	$\in$ 50	$\ni$ 51	$\triangle$ 52	$\triangledown$ 53	/ 54	$\mid$ 55
'07x	$\forall$ 56	$\exists$ 57	$\neg$ 58	$\emptyset$ 59	$\Re$ 60	$\Im$ 61	$\top$ 62	$\perp$ 63
'10x	$\aleph$ 64	$\mathcal{A}$ 65	$\mathcal{B}$ 66	$\mathcal{C}$ 67	$\mathcal{D}$ 68	$\mathcal{E}$ 69	$\mathcal{F}$ 70	$\mathcal{G}$ 71
'11x	$\mathcal{H}$ 72	$\mathcal{I}$ 73	$\mathcal{J}$ 74	$\mathcal{K}$ 75	$\mathcal{L}$ 76	$\mathcal{M}$ 77	$\mathcal{N}$ 78	$\mathcal{O}$ 79
'12x	$\mathcal{P}$ 80	$\mathcal{Q}$ 81	$\mathcal{R}$ 82	$\mathcal{S}$ 83	$\mathcal{T}$ 84	$\mathcal{U}$ 85	$\mathcal{V}$ 86	$\mathcal{W}$ 87
'13x	$\mathcal{X}$ 88	$\mathcal{Y}$ 89	$\mathcal{Z}$ 90	$\cup$ 91	$\cap$ 92	$\uplus$ 93	$\wedge$ 94	$\vee$ 95
'14x	$\vdash$ 96	$\dashv$ 97	$\lfloor$ 98	$\rfloor$ 99	$\lceil$ 100	$\rceil$ 101	$\{$ 102	$\}$ 103
'15x	$\langle$ 104	$\rangle$ 105	$\mid$ 106	$\parallel$ 107	$\updownarrow$ 108	$\Updownarrow$ 109	$\backslash$ 110	$\wr$ 111
'16x	$\surd$ 112	$\amalg$ 113	∇ 114	$\int$ 115	$\sqcup$ 116	$\sqcap$ 117	$\sqsubseteq$ 118	$\sqsupseteq$ 119
'17x	$\S$ 120	$\dagger$ 121	$\ddagger$ 122	$\P$ 123	$\clubsuit$ 124	$\diamondsuit$ 125	$\heartsuit$ 126	$\spadesuit$ 127

Font Layout 3: The font `cmsy10`, adhering to the OMS encoding scheme

been assigned the NFSS values of OML for *math letters* (Font Layout 2), OMS for *math symbols* (Font Layout 3), and OMX for *math extended*, for brackets and symbols that appear in several different sizes.

There are a number of other font families available in these encodings, most noticeably the MathTimes and Lucida math fonts for use with Times-Roman and Lucida Bright text fonts, respectively. Both of these may be purchased from Y&Y Inc.

A.3.2   Extended Computer fonts

Limitations of the CM fonts

Most of the diacritical marks (accents) used in European languages written with the Latin alphabet are contained in, or may be generated by, TEX's Computer Modern fonts. A basic set of naked accents is available for combination with other letters, such as the acute accent ´ with the letter *e* to make é. Other combinations may be constructed for diacritical marks that are not predefined in TEX or LATEX.

Fashioning diacritical characters as a combination of letters and special symbols has one great disadvantage for the TEX processing: Words containing such characters cannot take part in the automatic word division since the hyphenation patterns include only pure letters. The accented letters, such as those in German, French and most other languages, must be treated as *single* characters in the hyphenation patterns and must appear as single letters in the character set.

In addition to diacritical characters, a number of special letters are employed in some European languages, such as ß, Æ, æ, Œ, œ, Ø, and ø, which are provided in standard TEX with the CM fonts (Section 2.5.6). However, other special letters, such as Ð, ŋ, Þ, þ, and ð, are missing completely and cannot be easily constructed from existing ones.

The Cork proposal

At the 1990 International TEX Conference in Cork, Ireland, an extension of the Latin alphabet and its assignments within the 256 character positions was proposed and accepted. This extension includes the majority of special and diacritical letters as single characters for many languages written with the Latin alphabet. Hyphenation patterns for such languages may include the special and diacritical letters as single letters for optimal word division by TEX and LATEX.

Character fonts conforming to the Cork scheme are to bear the identifying letters ec in their names for *Extended Computer* in place of the cm for Computer Modern.

The Cork proposal for extending the TEX fonts to 256 characters was first implemented by Norbert Schwarz, who produced an initial set of METAFONT source files. He also selected the designation dc to emphasize that this was a preliminary realization of the EC fonts. Some work was still needed to fine-tune the design of several symbols.

After issuing versions 1.2 and 1.3 of the DC fonts in 1995 and 1996, Jörg Knappen released the first set of true EC fonts in January 1997. Font Layout 4 presents his font

	0	1	2	3	4	5	6	7
'00x	` 0	´ 1	^ 2	~ 3	¨ 4	ʺ 5	° 6	ˇ 7
'01x	˘ 8	¯ 9	˙ 10	ˎ 11	˛ 12	ˏ 13	‹ 14	› 15
'02x	" 16	" 17	„ 18	« 19	» 20	– 21	— 22	23
'03x	‰ 24	ı 25	ȷ 26	ff 27	fi 28	fl 29	ffi 30	ffl 31
'04x	32	! 33	" 34	# 35	$ 36	% 37	& 38	' 39
'05x	(40	) 41	* 42	+ 43	, 44	- 45	. 46	/ 47
'06x	0 48	1 49	2 50	3 51	4 52	5 53	6 54	7 55
'07x	8 56	9 57	: 58	; 59	< 60	= 61	> 62	? 63
'10x	@ 64	A 65	B 66	C 67	D 68	E 69	F 70	G 71
'11x	H 72	I 73	J 74	K 75	L 76	M 77	N 78	O 79
'12x	P 80	Q 81	R 82	S 83	T 84	U 85	V 86	W 87
'13x	X 88	Y 89	Z 90	[91	\ 92	] 93	^ 94	- 95
'14x	' 96	a 97	b 98	c 99	d 100	e 101	f 102	g 103
'15x	h 104	i 105	j 106	k 107	l 108	m 109	n 110	o 111
'16x	p 112	q 113	r 114	s 115	t 116	u 117	v 118	w 119
'17x	x 120	y 121	z 122	{ 123	| 124	} 125	~ 126	- 127
'20x	Ă 128	Ą 129	Ć 130	Č 131	Ď 132	Ě 133	Ę 134	Ğ 135
'21x	Ĺ 136	Ľ 137	Ł 138	Ń 139	Ň 140	Ŋ 141	Ő 142	Ŕ 143
'22x	Ř 144	Ś 145	Š 146	Ş 147	Ť 148	Ţ 149	Ű 150	Ů 151
'23x	Ÿ 152	Ź 153	Ž 154	Ż 155	IJ 156	İ 157	đ 158	§ 159
'24x	ă 160	ą 161	ć 162	č 163	ď 164	ě 165	ę 166	ğ 167
'25x	ĺ 168	ľ 169	ł 170	ń 171	ň 172	ŋ 173	ő 174	ŕ 175
'26x	ř 176	ś 177	š 178	ş 179	ť 180	ţ 181	ű 182	ů 183
'27x	ÿ 184	ź 185	ž 186	ż 187	ij 188	¡ 189	¿ 190	£ 191
'30x	À 192	Á 193	Â 194	Ã 195	Ä 196	Å 197	Æ 198	Ç 199
'31x	È 200	É 201	Ê 202	Ë 203	Ì 204	Í 205	Î 206	Ï 207
'32x	Đ 208	Ñ 209	Ò 210	Ó 211	Ô 212	Õ 213	Ö 214	Œ 215
'33x	Ø 216	Ù 217	Ú 218	Û 219	Ü 220	Ý 221	Þ 222	SS 223
'34x	à 224	á 225	â 226	ã 227	ä 228	å 229	æ 230	ç 231
'35x	è 232	é 233	ê 234	ë 235	ì 236	í 237	î 238	ï 239
'36x	ð 240	ñ 241	ò 242	ó 243	ô 244	õ 245	ö 246	œ 247
'37x	ø 248	ù 249	ú 250	û 251	ü 252	ý 253	þ 254	ß 255

Font Layout 4: The extended font `ecrm1000` with T1 encoding ecrm1000, the extended version of cmr10. The EC fonts are now considered to be stable in that neither their encoding nor their metrics (the .tfm files) will be changed in future. Thus their behavior as far as TeX and LaTeX are concerned is finalized. The actual printed characters might be modified slightly in later updates.

A parallel set of fonts called *text companion*, or TC, fonts is also provided, containing special symbols for text that are normally found in the CM math fonts, if at all, such as currency symbols and degree signs. These fonts are still somewhat experimental, so the symbol assignments are not yet stable. The current contents are shown in Font Layout 5.

Invoking the EC and TC fonts

The EC fonts correspond to the NFSS encoding scheme T1 (Table A.1). The simplest way to activate them is to place

> `\usepackage[T1]{fontenc}`

in the preamble of the document. This simply makes T1 the standard encoding by redefining `\encodingdefault` to be T1, and it loads the file tlenc.def, which redefines the accent and special letter commands

Package: textcomp — To obtain access to the symbols in the TC fonts, one can load the textcomp package, which not only redefines several existing symbol commands but also adds many new ones. For example, `\copyright`, which is normally defined to be `\textcircle{c}`, is changed to print character 169 from an appropriate TC font. Character 191 is the symbol for the European currency unit, the euro, printed with `\texteuro`; however, better ways of producing it are presented in Section 2.5.8.

Special character commands

Inspecting Font Layout 4, one notices that the EC fonts contain not only many single characters that are formed out of two CM symbols (like Ä = A + ¨) but also several characters that have no correspondence in the CM font layout at all. The first type is accommodated by internally redefining the action of accent and special character commands. The second set requires new commands that are recognized only when the T1 encoding is active. These are

> the ogonek accent `\k{o}`: ǫ

> special letters   `\DH` = Ð   `\DJ` = Đ   `\NG` = Ŋ   `\TH` = Þ
>   `\dh` = ð   `\dj` = đ   `\ng` = ŋ   `\th` = þ

> special symbols   `\guillemotleft` = «   `\guillemotright` = »
>   `\guilsinglleft` = ‹   `\guilsinglright` = ›
>   `\quotedblbase`   = „   `\quotesinglbase` = ‚
>   `\textquotedbl`   = "

When issued in OT1 encoding, these commands print an error message.

	0	1	2	3	4	5	6	7
'00x	` 0	´ 1	^ 2	~ 3	¨ 4	˜ 5	° 6	ˇ 7
'01x	˘ 8	¯ 9	˙ 10	˛ 11	¸ 12	، 13	14	15
'02x	16	17	‖ 18	19	20	— 21	— 22	23
'03x	← 24	→ 25	⌢ 26	⌢ 27	⌢ 28	⌢ 29	30	31
'04x	ƀ 32	33	34	35	$ 36	37	38	' 39
'05x	40	41	* 42	43	, 44	= 45	. 46	/ 47
'06x	0 48	1 49	2 50	3 51	4 52	5 53	6 54	7 55
'07x	8 56	9 57	58	59	⟨ 60	— 61	⟩ 62	63
'10x	64	65	66	67	68	69	70	71
'11x	72	73	74	75	76	℧ 77	78	◯ 79
'12x	80	81	82	83	84	85	86	Ω 87
'13x	88	89	90	⟦ 91	92	⟧ 93	↑ 94	↓ 95
'14x	` 96	97	★ 98	o|o 99	† 100	101	102	103
'15x	104	105	106	107	⊘ 108	∞ 109	♪ 110	111
'16x	112	113	114	115	116	117	118	119
'17x	120	121	122	123	124	125	~ 126	= 127
'20x	˘ 128	˘ 129	'' 130	`` 131	† 132	‡ 133	‖ 134	‰₀ 135
'21x	• 136	℃ 137	$ 138	¢ 139	f 140	₡ 141	W 142	N 143
'22x	₲ 144	P 145	£ 146	℞ 147	? 148	₺ 149	đ 150	™ 151
'23x	‰₀₀ 152	¶ 153	₿ 154	№ 155	℅ 156	℮ 157	° 158	℠ 159
'24x	{ 160	} 161	¢ 162	£ 163	¤ 164	¥ 165	¦ 166	§ 167
'25x	¨ 168	© 169	ª 170	↺ 171	¬ 172	℗ 173	® 174	‾ 175
'26x	° 176	± 177	² 178	³ 179	´ 180	µ 181	¶ 182	· 183
'27x	※ 184	¹ 185	º 186	√ 187	¼ 188	½ 189	¾ 190	€ 191
'30x	192	193	194	195	196	197	198	199
'31x	200	201	202	203	204	205	206	207
'32x	208	209	210	211	212	213	× 214	215
'33x	216	217	218	219	220	221	222	223
'34x	224	225	226	227	228	229	230	231
'35x	232	233	234	235	236	237	238	239
'36x	240	241	242	243	244	245	÷ 246	247
'37x	248	249	250	251	252	253	254	255

Font Layout 5: The text companion font `tcrm1000` with the TS1 encoding scheme

Note: The \guillemotleft and \guillemotright are not misprints even though the proper word for the French quotations marks is *guillemet*. The PostScript fonts contain these erroneous names for these symbols, and this mistake has been propagated to such an extent that it can never be removed from all the software that includes it. A *guillemot* is, in fact, an Arctic bird, not a French quotation mark.

B

Installing and Maintaining LATEX

In this appendix, we describe how the TEX program and LATEX files are installed, how they are organized, and what their roles are. Throughout this book we have given examples of contributed packages, but here we list those packages and other files that belong to the 'kernel', the essential installation. In Section B.6, we explain how LATEX ticks, what happens during a processing run, and what all the various file types mean.

B.1 Installing LATEX

We explain first LATEX installations in general before looking at the particular one provided on the enclosed TEX Live CD.

B.1.1 TEX implementations

One must have the TEX program and its auxiliaries (METAFONT, font files) before LATEX can be set up on top of it. Installing TEX is a somewhat daunting experience, but thankfully it need not be done very often and there are many ready-to-run implementations available for practically every computer operating system. These can be obtained from CTAN under the directory `systems` (Figure B.4 on page 384) or from the TEX Users Group (`www.tug.org`).

The system delivered with TEX Live is that originally written for Unix machines by Tomas Rokicki and Tim Morgan, known generically as *Web2c*. This name derives from the fact that it converts Donald Knuth's original TEX source files from his Web language (no relation to the World Wide Web, which it long predates) into the C programming language for subsequent compilation with a C compiler. The teTEX implementation, by Thomas Esser, extends Web2c to a fully functional ensemble, including `dvips`, BIBTEX, MakeIndex, and so on, while Fabrice Popineau's fpTEX does the same thing for the Win32 (Windows 95, 98, NT, 2000, XP) set of operating systems.

Another excellent TEX implementation for Windows is MikTEX by Christian Schenk, available from CTAN under `systems/win32/miktex`.

The implementation for DOS, emTeX by Eberhardt Mattes is still available from CTAN but is no longer appropriate for modern PCs. We used it to produce the first two editions of this book and found it superb for its time.

Commercial installations for TeX also exist: *PCTeX* (www.pctex.com) and *Y&Y TeX System* (Y&Y Inc., www.YandY.com) for Windows, and *Textures* for Macintosh (Blue Sky Research, www.bluesky.com). A 'what-you-see-is-what-you-get' TeX system is *Scientific Workplace*, which can be purchased from MacKichan Software Research (www.tcisoft.com).

It should be stressed that the TeX and pdfTeX programs in all the above implementations are identical (for the same version number). They provide ready-to-run executable programs from the same source code, which are necessarily different for different computer types. There are also minor variations as to how the programs are run.

The LaTeX files are all ASCII, so they are fully compatible with all systems. One uses the already installed TeX or pdfTeX program to generate the LaTeX formats (Section B.1.3). Even this task is normally done for you by the above implementations.

A graphics interface to TeX and LaTeX is not absolutely essential, but today it is almost unthinkable to do without one. This is an editor program for writing and managing the LaTeX source files, calling the various programs (LaTeX, BibTeX, MakeIndex), and invoking viewers by clicking icons. For Unix, the emacs is often used for this; for Windows, the two editor programs mentioned in Section 1.6.2, Winshell and WinEdt, can be highly recommended.

B.1.2   The TeX Live distribution

Each year, the TeX Users Group, TUG, along with other national users groups, distribute the latest TeX and LaTeX installations, with executable files for Win32, Linux, Macintosh, and many flavors of Unix. Up until 2001 this was on a single CD, but as of the 7th issue in 2002, it was necessary to split the contents over 2 CDs, separating the Unix versions from the others. Each CD is otherwise complete, missing only the executables of the other one.

The 2003 issue consists of one CD from which the TeX system may be run directly from Win32, Linux, and MacOSX, with as many packages as can fit on it; a second CD from which TeX may be installed to other machines with many more packages, but in compressed form that cannot be read directly; and a DVD with everything. It must be emphasized that the contents of the TeX Live distribution are contributions from dedicated users all around the world, and they are freely available.

The CD included with this book is a special version of the one for Win32, Linux, and MacOSX. Since the procedures for using it differ among the various operating systems, and may likely change in future issues, it is advisable to read the README.EN file in the top-level directory before starting. This will also point to further documentation and instructions on the CD.

We give here a brief outline of how to get started on Win32 systems.

The startup window in Figure B.1 should appear when you insert the CD into your computer. If the autorun function does not work, you can run the autorun.exe

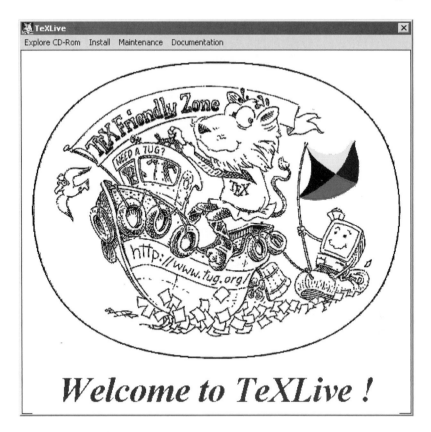

Figure B.1: The TEX Live welcome

program directly from the CD.

You then proceed with the installation by clicking Install on the upper bar. You then follow the instructions on the various pages that appear, making selections as you go.

If you elect to install only part of the system, you may still add further packages and support programs later by clicking maintenance. Or, you may run `texsetup --maintenance`, which does the same thing bypassing the Welcome window. Running `texsetup --help` produces a list of all the options.

You may also click Documentation→View TexLive doc to open the instruction manual for TEX Live, with details for all systems. (Or you can go directly to `texmf→doc→tldoc→english` and select `live.pdf` or `live.html`.)

Documentation for most of the packages and collections is available on the CD under `texmf→doc→...`, if the author has provided a description. We often refer to such manuals throughout this book, indicating more precisely where they are to be found. By clicking Documentation and then Run TeXDocTK, you may open a documentation browser (Figure B.2) to assist in finding descriptions for any module.

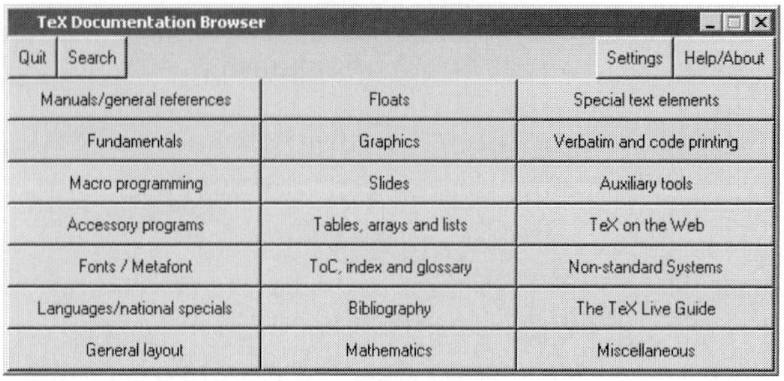

Figure B.2: The TeX Live documentation browser

The TeX Live installation program will do all the housekeeping for you, placing files in the right directories, setting up font-mapping files, and generating the formats. However, there might still be times when you want or have to do some of this yourself. This we explain in the next sections.

B.1.3   Making the LaTeX format

Adding or updating LaTeX onto an existing TeX installation by hand is relatively straightforward. One must obtain the source files, which on TeX Live are located at `texmf→source→latex→base` or on CTAN at `tex-archive→macros→latex→base`. At CTAN, instruction files with extension `.txt` are available for the various implementations, such as `miktex.txt` and `web2ctex.txt`, as well as the general instruction file `install.txt`.

These source files are a set of packed files consisting of a large number of .dtx files, the integrated source and documentation files. These are unpacked by running initex on the batch job file `unpack.ins`. This generates the necessary .cls, .sty, .clo, and other files. It also constructs the fundamental file `latex.ltx` that is needed to produce the format file. On CTAN, the unpacked files are already provided in a parallel directory `unpacked`.

The next step should be to run initex on the `latex.ltx` file to produce the LaTeX format `latex`. However, before doing that, there are a number of configuration aspects to be considered. At several points during the processing, certain files are read in, but if a file of the same root name with extension `.cfg` exists, it is loaded instead. This device permits one to configure the final format for local conditions or desires. The possible configuration files are:

`texsys.cfg` offers the possibility of adding some very machine-specific adjustments for older versions of TeX or for some peculiarities of the TeX installation; information is to be found in the specific `.txt` file or in `ltdirchk.dtx`.

`fonttext.cfg` is loaded in place of `fonttext.ltx` if it is present; this defines the fonts that are to be available for processing text; details can be found in `fontdef.dtx`.

`fontmath.cfg` is loaded in place of `fontmath.ltx` if it is present; this is the equivalent of `fonttext.cfg` for math fonts.

`preload.cfg` is loaded in place of `preload.ltx` if it is present; this determines which fonts are preloaded into the format; a number of other `preload` files may be extracted from `preload.dtx`, any one of which may be renamed to `.cfg` to be implemented.

`hyphen.cfg` is loaded in place of `hyphen.ltx` if it is present; this specifies the hyphenation patterns and their assignments; the patterns in `hyphen.tex` are loaded by default into language 0; the `babel` system provides such a configuration file (Section 14.1), which must be used if `babel` is to be incorporated into the format, in which case `language.dat` must be tailored to local requirements.

The only configuration file that you are likely to want to change is `hyphen.cfg`, especially if you are going to be using LaTeX for languages other than American English.

Once any configuration files have been set up and located where TeX can read them, initex may be run on `latex.ltx` with

```
initex latex.ltx    or
tex -ini latex.ltx
```

The resulting `latex.fmt` must be placed where format files are read. For fpTeX as installed by TeX Live, this is in `texmf-var→web2c`. Other unpacked files must be moved to `texmf→tex→latex→base`; these are:

- `latexbug.tex`, `testpage.tex`, `lablst.tex`, `idx.tex`, `nfssfont.tex`, `small2e.tex`, `sample2e.tex`, and `docstrip.tex`, and

- all files with extensions `.cls`, `.clo`, `.sty`, `.fd`, `.def`, and `.cfg`.

Files with extension `.ist` are moved to `texmf→makeindex→base`.

To make up the LaTeX format with pdfTeX, run instead

```
pdfinitex -fmt=pdflatex latex.ltx    or
pdftex -ini -fmt=pdflatex latex.ltx
```

This processes `latex.ltx` base file once more, but names the resulting format file `pdflatex.fmt` rather than `latex.fmt`. This is necessary because the format files may only be used with the program that generated them, so the two must be distinguished even though they both are essentially the same thing. Move this format to the format file directory also.

The actual commands to invoke TeX or pdfTeX with LaTeX (what we normally call 'running LaTeX or pdfLaTeX') are

```
tex &latex
pdftex &pdflatex
```

meaning 'run the TeX or pdfTeX program with the specified format file'. The system should have shortcuts named `latex` and `pdflatex` that translate to the above.

The web2c system, for which fpTeX is the Win32 implementation, has a different method. It stores all the necessary configuration information in a file named `texmf.cnf` located in the `texmf→web2c` directory. This sets up environments according to the name of the program being run and, in particular, adds the format name automatically for a TeX-like program. Thus a TeX program named `latex` will use the `latex.fmt` format file if none is specified. However, there is no real program named `latex`, so on Unix systems an alias with this name is established to point to the `tex` executable program. On Win32, the actual TeX executable code is in a dynamic link library `tex.dll`, and very small files named `tex.exe`, `latex.exe` exist to use this one library. These `.exe` files are in fact identical, and are really only there to ensure that different formats are invoked automatically when they are called. Similarly, there are `pdftex.dll`, `pdftex.exe`, and `pdflatex.exe`. If any additional formats are ever needed for these programs, one only needs to copy one of these `.exe` files to the new name.

B.1.4   Updating the database

TeX works with a very large number of files, for classes, packages, fonts, formats, and so on. A set of environments is used to indicate where the program should search for these files. With web2c, these are all defined in the `texmf.cnf` configuration file mentioned above. The user normally does not have to worry about this. However, to speed up the search, a database is prepared giving the exact location of all the files in the search paths. This database will be created and updated automatically if installation programs are used, such as that for TeX Live.

If the user should add a new package or font collection by hand, without going through an installation program, it will be necessary to update this database. Under web2c (and fpTeX), this is carried out with the command

    mktexlsr

Under MikTeX, one must run

    configure --update-fndb

or click 'refresh now' in the MikTeX options program.

It is not necessary to update the database if existing files are being replaced. It is only the names and locations of the files that go into the database, not their actual versions or sizes.

B.2   Obtaining the Adobe euro fonts

As pointed out in Section 2.5.8, the type 1 euro currency symbol fonts from Adobe Systems Inc. that are used with the `europs` and `eurosans` packages cannot be distributed on CDs such as TeX Live, nor on CTAN, since Adobe reserves the exclusive right to distribution, even though free of charge. TₑX Live and CTAN do provide all other files needed, such as the font metric .tfm and font definition .fd files.

You can obtain the Adobe euro .pfb files from www.adobe.com/type/eurofont. html, downloading the appropriate file for your computer type. They must be unpacked (on Windows, for example, you just execute the downloaded eurofont.exe) and then rename them as follows:

Windows	PostScript	TₑX
_1_____.PFB	EuroSans-Regular	zpeurs.pfb
_1I_____.PFB	EuroSans-Italic	zpeuris.pfb
_1B_____.PFB	EuroSans-Bold	zpeubs.pfb
_1BI____.PFB	EuroSans-BoldItalic	zpeubis.pfb
_3_____.PFB	EuroSerif-Regular	zpeur.pfb
_3I_____.PFB	EuroSerif-Italic	zpeuri.pfb
_3B_____.PFB	EuroSerif-Bold	zpeub.pfb
_3BI____.PFB	EuroSerif-BoldItalic	zpeubi.pfb
_2_____.PFB	EuroMono-Regular	zpeurt.pfb
_2I_____.PFB	EuroMono-Italic	zpeurit.pfb
_2B_____.PFB	EuroMono-Bold	zpeubt.pfb
_2BI____.PFB	EuroMono-BoldItalic	zpeubit.pfb

The first column is the name as unpacked on Windows, the second the internal PostScript name, and the third the name used by TₑX. The .pfb files must be renamed to those in the third column and placed in texmf→fonts→type1→adobe→euro (or better in texmf-local).

The font map file zpeu.map must also be added to the lists of font maps for dvips, dvipdfm, and pdfTₑX (Section 13.1.5). The TₑX Live installation does all this for you; you only need to get and store the .pfb files.

B.3 TₑX directory structure

The TₑX system, of which LATₑX is only one part, albeit a large one, requires a very large number of files for fonts, formats, classes, packages, bibliographies, and much more. Section B.6 lists the types of files and their extensions, at least for what concerns LATₑX. Other flavors of TₑX have their own types.

In the early days, anyone setting up a TₑX installation would try to create order of some sort by distributing the files into different directories (also called *folders*) according to their functions. However, everyone had their own ideas regarding how to do this. Thus changing from one installation to another required a completely new road map.

The TₑX Users Group, TUG, commissioned a working group to prepare a recommended standard, which published its initial results in 1994, with many updates since then. Version 1.0 was released in February 2003. The latest version of this

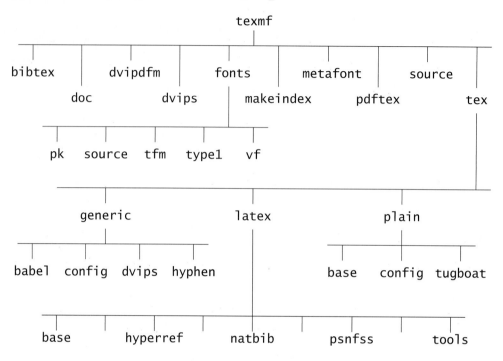

Figure B.3: The TDS directory tree

paper is on TeX Live at texmf→doc→tds in various formats. The TeX Directory Structure (TDS) described there can only be a recommendation, but it is fairly universally followed today. The TeX Live distribution certainly conforms to it.

Figure B.3 offers an overview of TDS. The top directory is named texmf to demonstrate that it holds the entire TeX and METAFONT systems. This may not be the absolute top directory on any installation. For example, if you install to a Windows hard disk, you might find it in program files→texlive→texmf. Furthermore, there might be parallel directories named texmf-var (where the system writes files it creates, such as font .pk files) and texmf-local for any private packages you install yourself. The idea is to keep the main texmf tree intact to let the TeX Live installation program manage it. These parallel trees should have the same structure, but may be incomplete.

The directories under texmf are the main subdivisions for the subsequent files, sorted mainly by program, such as BibTeX (Section 12.1), dvipdfm (Section 13.2.2), dvips (Section 13.1.1), MakeIndex (Section 11.4.3), METAFONT, and pdfTeX (Section 13.2.3). Others are

doc contains documentation of all sorts; its subdirectories are similarly structured to those under tex; most of the documentation files that we have referred to in this book are to be found here.

fonts is subdivided according to the types of files: pk for the pixel files (these usually go into `texmf-var`), `tfm` for the font metric files, `vf` for virtual font files, `source` for the METAFONT `.mf` sources, `type1` for the `.pfb` or `.pfa` PostScript outline font files; the contents of each of these directories are further sorted by supplier (`adobe`, `public`, ...), and then by font family (`times`, `cm`, ...).

`source` contains the delivery files for packages and collections; for LaTeX, these are the `.dtx` and `.ins` files, found under `latex→base`; similarly for packages, such as `latex→geometry` containing `geometry.dtx` and `geometry.ins`; these are not needed any more once installed; the subdirectories under `source` mirror those under `tex`.

`tex` is the main directory for files directly related to TeX; some of its subdirectories are

`generic` for files that apply to all TeX applications, such as hyphenation patterns;

`latex` for all the LaTeX-related files; this is further subdivided into directories for individual packages; only a handful are shown in Figure B.3; `base` contains the fundamental LaTeX files, the kernel; and

`plain` for Plain TeX, which is often just called TeX (Section 1.3.2).

This directory structure allows a user to locate what is needed—documentation, sources, package and collection files, and program support files—on all installations. The documentation and source files can readily be removed, or not copied at all from the CD, since they play no role during the processing. This structure makes it easy to remove such unnecessary branches of the tree.

B.4 The CTAN servers

The easiest way to obtain the LaTeX software not available on the TeX Live distribution is via one of the network servers supported by various educational institutions. They also provide the most up-to-date standard LaTeX installation, TeX extensions, programs for running TeX, collections of drivers for different printers, hyphenation patterns for other languages, and so on. Such a server is a treasure trove for the dedicated TeX and LaTeX user.

There are three main network servers for TeX and LaTeX located in the United States, Great Britain, and Germany, forming the Comprehensive TeX Archive Network, CTAN. They are not only kept up to date but also mirrored daily among themselves. They are all reachable via FTP on the Internet at

Country	Internet address
USA	`ftp://ctan.tug.org/tex-archive/`
UK	`ftp://ftp.tex.ac.uk/tex-archive/`
Germany	`ftp://ftp.dante.de/tex-archive/`

Alternatively, one can go to the HTTP interfaces at

www.ctan.org
www.tex.ac.uk
dante.ctan.org

In addition, there are many full and partial mirrors of these sites. See the TUG home page, www.tug.org, for details.

The directory structure is the same for all three servers. A sketch of the main parts of the directory tree is presented in Figure B.4.

The latest version of the LaTeX source files may be found under the subdirectories base or unpacked, where in the latter the files are already unpacked and latex.ltx is ready. The LaTeX extensions and general style files that have been contributed by other users are located in the subdirectory contrib, with each contribution in a subdirectory of its own. Extensions offered by the LaTeX3 Team, which include babel, graphics, tools, and so on, are found in the required subdirectory.

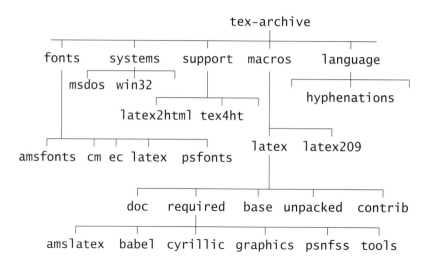

Figure B.4: Partial directory tree of CTAN servers

B.5   Additional standard files

Throughout this book we have pointed out and explained many contributed packages that expand LaTeX functionality. However, there are a number of service documents, additional classes, and packages that are delivered with the basic LaTeX installation, found in texmf→tex→latex→base. We list them all here, although some have been mentioned in other sections.

B.5.1 Special documents

The standard installation includes a number of special 'documents', files with the .tex extension. These are:

`small2e.tex` a short sample document;

`sample2e.tex` a longer sample document;

`lablst.tex` (Section 11.2.1) for printing out all the cross-reference labels, with translations and page numbers; it asks interactively the name of the document that is to be so listed;

`idx.tex` (page 224) listing the \index entries for a document, ordered in two columns, by page; it asks interactively the name of the document that is to be so listed;

`testpage.tex` which tests the positioning of the text on a page; this actually tests the printer driver to make sure that the margins are correct and that the scaling comes out properly;

`nfssfont.tex` a document to print out a font table, sample text, and various other tests; it asks for the name of the font interactively; the command \help prints out a list of commands that can be given; and

`docstrip.tex` which is more a program than a document; it is the basic tool for unpacking operating files from their documented source files; it not only removes comments but also includes alternative coding depending on various options.

B.5.2 Extra classes

In addition to the standard classes that have already been discussed (book, report, article, letter), the standard installation also contains

`proc` for producing camera-ready copy of conference proceedings; a variant of the two-column article class, it contains one extra command: \copyrightspace, which leaves blank space at the bottom of the first column for typing in a copyright notice;

`minimal` a bare-bones class for testing and debugging;

`slides` (Section 17.1) the former SliTeX, for producing presentation material; and

`ltxdoc` to produce class and package documentation.

B.5.3   Standard packages

The standard packages, some of which are described elsewhere, are:

alltt (Section 4.6.1) enables the `alltt` environment, which is much like `verbatim` except that \ { } behave as normal; this means that commands included in the text are executed and not printed literally;

doc provides many special features for documenting LaTeX packages;

exscale allows the mathematical symbols that appear in different sizes to scale with the font size option given in the \documentclass command; normally the size of these symbols is fixed, independent of the basic size of the text;

flafter (Section 9.2, page 171) ensures that floating objects (figures and tables) do not appear before their position in the text;

fontenc (Section A.1, page 362) declares font encodings by loading their .def files; the names of the encodings are listed as options;

graphpap (Section 16.1.5) provides the command \graphpaper, which produces coordinate grids in the `picture` environment;

ifthen (Section 10.3.5) allows text or command definitions depending on the state of various conditionals; one may test the state of a boolean switch, the value of a counter or length, or the text definition of a command;

inputenc (Section D.4) allows a LaTeX document file to be prepared with a system-dependent input encoding scheme for special characters;

latexsym loads the 11 special LaTeX symbols in the `lasy` fonts, which were part of LaTeX 2.09; this file is automatically read in in compatibility mode;

makeidx (Section 11.4.3) provides the commands that may be used with the MakeIndex program to generate a keyword index;

shortvrb (Section 4.6.1) simplifies the typing of literal text with the commands \MakeShortVerb and \DeleteShortVerb, which designate (and remove) a specified character as the equivalent of \verb. After \MakeShortVerb{\|} has been issued, |\cmd{x}| is equivalent to \verb|\cmd{x}|, producing \cmd{x};

showidx (page 225) makes the \index entries visible by printing them as marginal notes;

syntonly provides the command \syntaxonly, which, when given in the preamble, suppresses all output to the .dvi file but continues to issue errors and warnings; the job runs about four times faster than normal; this is used to check the processing when output is not immediately needed;

t1enc makes the T1 font encoding (Section A.3.2) the standard, for use with EC fonts;

textcomp makes the special symbols in the text companion fonts available in text mode (Section A.3.2); and

tracefnt is a diagnostic tool for checking NFSS font selections. The options given with \usepackage control its action:

debugshow writes considerably more information to the transcript file about every change of font; can produce a very large transcript;

errorshow suppresses all warnings and information messages to the monitor, which are still sent to the transcript file; only error messages are printed to the monitor;

infoshow (default option) sends font selection information to the monitor, which is normally only written to the transcript file;

loading shows the loading of external fonts;

pausing turns all warnings into error messages so that processing temporarily stops, awaiting user response; and

warningshow prints warnings and error messages on the monitor; this behavior is much the same as when the package is not used at all.

B.5.4 The tools packages

The members of the LaTeX3 Team, as individuals, have written a number of packages that they collectively make available; these are to be found in the texmf→tex→latex→tools directory. Although contributions, they are considered to be part of the standard installation.

Many of these have been described elsewhere in this book, but we list them all here.

afterpage (Section 9.1 on page 171) permits commands to be saved and executed at the end of the current page. This is useful for forcing stubborn floats to be output right away, with \afterpage{\clearpage}. If \clearpage were issued directly, a new page would be inserted at that point. With \afterpage, the command is reserved until the end of the page.

array (Section 6.2.4 on page 116) is a reimplementation of the tabular and array environments with several additional features.

bm permits individual math symbols to be printed in boldface with command \bm{\sym}. Thus $\alpha + \bm{\beta}$ produces $\alpha + \boldsymbol{\beta}$ without recourse to the \boldmath command, which would set the whole formula in boldface. There is also a command \DeclareBoldMathCommand{\name}{\sym} that defines \name to be \bm{\sym}.

calc reimplements the counter and length commands to allow 'normal' arithmetic with them, such as

```
\setlength{\mylen}{3cm + \textwidth}
\setcounter{page}{\value{section} * 3}
\parbox{\linewidth / \real{1.6}}{...}
```

Note that the arithmetical expressions can be used not only to set values but also as arguments to commands and environments.

dcolumn (Section 6.2.4) requires the array package; it allows decimal point alignment in the tabular tables.

delarray (Section 6.2.4) requires the array package; it permits large bracketing symbols to be put around array environments for making matrices of various sorts.

enumerate (Section 4.3.5, page 74) reimplements the enumerate environment so that an optional argument determines the numeration style.

fileerr.dtx when unpacked, produces a set of small files that may be used to reply to TeX when a file is not found; this makes the responses similar to those for error messages; the files are named h.tex, e.tex, s.tex, and x.tex; thus, replying x⟨return⟩ loads the last one, which terminates the input.

fontsmpl is a package to output a sample text, accents, and special characters for a given font; with the accompanying file fontsmpl.tex, a family such as cmr can be printed with all attributes and encodings.

ftnright puts footnotes in the right-hand column in two-column mode.

hhline requires the array package; it allows more flexibility in putting horizontal rules in tables.

indentfirst (Section 3.2.4 on page 49) indents the first paragraph of sections, which normally are not indented.

layout (Section 3.2.5 on page 50) defines the command \layout, which draws a diagram of the current page format with the values of the parameters printed.

longtable (Section 6.2.4 on page 117) makes tables that extend over several pages, with breaks occurring automatically.

multicol (Section 3.2.8) introduces the environment multicols, which switches to multicolumn output without a page break either before or after. It is called with

```
\begin{multicols}{num_cols}[header text][pre_space]
  Text set in num_cols columns
\end{multicols}
```

The optional *header text* is printed in a single column across the top of the multicolumn part. A \newpage is issued only if the remaining space on the current page is less than a certain value, stored in the length \premulticols; the optional length argument *pre_space* overrides this value if given. Similarly, the length \postmulticols determines whether a new page is inserted at the end of the multicolumn text. Column separation and possible rule are set by the standard LATEX lengths \columnsep and \columnseprule as for the \twocolumn command. The text in the multicolumn format is balanced; that is, the columns are all equally long.

showkeys prints out all the cross-reference keys defined by \label and \bibitem and used by \ref, \pageref, and \cite; these are marginal and interlinear notes for a draft only, to check the cross-referencing.

somedefs allows only selected commands to be defined in a package, depending on options in \usepackage.

tabularx (Section 6.2.4) defines a tabularx environment, which is like tabular*, a table of desired width, except that the column widths expand, not the inter-column spacing.

theorem provides extensions to the \newtheorem command for more flexible 'theorem-like' environments; it is very similar to the $\mathcal{A}_{\mathcal{M}}S$ amsthm package (Section 15.3.1).

varioref (Section 11.2.4) defines \vref and \vpageref commands, analogous to \ref and \pageref, which check whether the referenced object is only one page away and, if so, print text such as 'on the previous page'; the actual text printed can alternate between two variants.

verbatim (Section 4.6.1) is a reimplementation of the verbatim environment that prevents memory overflow for long texts; it also defines a command \verbatiminput to input a file and to print its contents literally, as well as a comment environment for a block comment in the input text.

xr (Section 11.2.3) is a package to allow \ref to cross-reference \label commands from other documents.

xspace (Section 10.3.1 on page 186) contains a device to fix the problem of command names swallowing up the blank that follows them; thus the command \PS, defined as

```
\newcommand{\PS}{PostScript\xspace}
```

may be used as \PS file without having to terminate the \PS command with \␣ or {}.

B.6   The various LaTeX files

A number of different files are used during the LaTeX processing: Some are read in while others are created to store information for the next run. They all consist of two parts:

> *root_name.extension*

For every LaTeX document, there is a *main* file, whose root name is used when the program LaTeX is called. It normally possesses the extension .tex, as do any other files that it might read in with \input or \include commands. (If they have a different extension, it must be given explicitly.)

The other files that are created during a LaTeX processing run normally have the same root name as the main file but with a variety of different extensions depending on their functions. If the main file contains \include commands, there will be additional files created having the same root names as the included .tex files but with the extension .aux.

Some of these files are created with every LaTeX run, whereas others appear only when certain LaTeX commands have been issued, such as \tableofcontents or \makeindex. The .aux files as well as those produced by special LaTeX commands may be suppressed by including the command \nofiles in the preamble. This command is useful if a document is being constantly corrected and reprocessed, so that the information in the special files is not yet finalized and may therefore be dispensed with. Files created at the TeX level of processing will always be generated.

Other extensions describe files that contain formatting information, additional instructions (coding), or databases. The root part of these file names is not associated with any document file. An example of this type is the article.cls file that defines the article class.

The rest of this section contains a list of the LaTeX file extensions with a short description of the role they play in the LaTeX processing.

.aux   This is the auxiliary file written by LaTeX, containing information for cross-references as well as some commands necessary for the table of contents and other lists. There will be one .aux file created (or recreated) for the main file, in addition to one for every file read in by an \include command.

The auxiliary .aux files may be suppressed by issuing \nofiles in the preamble.

.bbl   This file is not created by LaTeX, but by the program BibTeX. It has the same root name as the main file. BibTeX actually only reads the .aux file for its information. The .bbl file is read into the next LaTeX processing run by the command \bibliography and produces the list of literature references.

.bib   Bibliographic databases have the extension .bib. BibTeX reads them to extract the information it needs to generate the .bbl file. The root name describes the database and not (necessarily) any text file. The database name is included in the text by means of the \bibliography command.

.blg This is the transcript file from a BibTeX run. The root name is the same as that of the input file.

.bst This is a *bibliography style file* that is used as input to BibTeX to determine the format of the bibliography. The name of the .bst file is included in the text by means of the \bibliographystyle command.

.cfg Some classes permit local *configurations* for paper size or other requirements by putting specifications into a .cfg file of the same root name as the class.

.clo This is a *class option* file containing the coding for certain options that might apply to more than one class. There is no special command to input them.

.cls This is a *class* file defining the overall format of the document. It is read in by the \documentclass command. A .cls file may also be input from another one with the \LoadClass command.

.def Additional definition files of various types carry the .def extension. Examples are t1enc.def (to define the T1 encoding) and latex209.def (for compatibility mode between LaTeX 2_ε and 2.09).

.dtx These are documented source files for the LaTeX installation. If a .dtx file is processed directly, the documentation is printed. This is an explanatory manual and/or a detailed description of the coding. The class, package, .ltx, .fd, or other file(s) are extracted by processing the .dtx file with DocStrip, usually by running LaTeX or TeX on a supplied .ins file.

.dvi This is the TeX output file containing the processed text in a format that is independent of the output printer, hence a 'device-independent' file. It too is generated by every TeX process run and cannot be suppressed by \nofiles.

The .dvi file must be further processed by a *printer driver* program that converts it into the special commands for the desired output device (printer).

.fd Files containing the NFSS commands associating external font names with font attributes are *font description files*. The root names consist of the encoding and family designations, such as ot1cmr.fd. When a font of a given family is requested for the first time, the corresponding .fd file is automatically read in, if it exists.

.fdd Documented sources for .fd files have the extension .fdd and are nothing more than a special type of .dtx file. They may be processed for the documentation or have the .fd files extracted by DocStrip.

.fmt This extension belongs to a TeX *format* file that has been created with the special program initex (Section B.1.3). Format files contain all the basic instructions in a compact coding for quick loading. LaTeX is nothing less than TeX run with the format latex.fmt. (Plain TeX uses the format file plain.fmt.)

.glo This file is only generated when the command \makeglossary exists in the preamble. It has the same root name as the main file and contains only \glossaryentry commands that have been produced by \glossary commands in the input text. This file will be suppressed in spite of the presence of \makeglossary if the command \nofiles is issued in the preamble.

.gls This file is the glossary equivalent of the .ind file. It too is generated by the MakeIndex program, but with the .glo file as input. The input and output extensions must be explicitly given. There are no standard LaTeX commands to read in the .gls file. The doc package uses it to record a change history.

.idx This file is only generated when the command \makeindex exists in the preamble. It has the same root name as the main file and contains only \indexentry commands that have been produced by \index commands in the input text. This file will be suppressed in spite of the presence of \makeindex if the command \nofiles is issued in the preamble.

.ilg This is the transcript file from a MakeIndex run. The root name is the same as that of the input file.

.ind This file is generated by the MakeIndex program, with the .idx file as input. It is read in by the \printindex command, which is defined by the makeidx package. It contains a theindex environment, built up from the entries in the input file.

.ins To facilitate the DocStrip run on a .dtx file, the necessary commands (and options) are put into an *installation* file. The extraction is then accomplished simply by processing (with TeX or LaTeX) the appropriate .ins file.

.ist This is an *index style file* containing style settings for MakeIndex. The root name reflects the style and has no relationship to any text file. For the doc package, the files gind.ist and gglo.ist are provided for specialized index formatting.

.lof This file contains the information for the list of figures. It behaves exactly like the .toc file except that it is opened by the command \listoffigures instead of by \tableofcontents.

.log This is the transcript, or log file, containing the protocol of the TeX processing run, that is, all the messages that were sent to the monitor during the run as well as additional information that can be of use to TeX experts when errors occur. This file is always generated, even when \nofiles has been issued.

.lot This file contains the information for the list of tables. It behaves exactly like the .toc file except that it is opened by the command \listoftables instead of by \tableofcontents.

.ltx For LaTeX installation, certain files that are inputs to the initex program bear the extension .ltx. They form the basis for generating the format latex.fmt. The main such file is named latex.ltx.

.mf   METAFONT source files contain drawing instructions for the characters in a font. The METAFONT program converts these to bitmap .pk files in a given size and resolution for DVI driver programs.

.pk   Packed pixel, or bitmap, files contain images of the characters in a font. These are read in by the DVI drivers to print the characters either on paper or on the computer monitor.

.sty This is a *package* file to be loaded with \usepackage. A package contains additional LATEX commands to define new features or alter existing ones. It should not produce any printable text. It may be input by another package with the command \RequirePackage.

.tex The file containing the user's input text should have the extension .tex. For every LATEX document there is at least one .tex file. If there is only one .tex file, it is also the *main* file that determines the root name of all the others. If there are \input or \include commands within the input text, there are other files belonging to the document with different root names but all with the extension .tex. The main file is the one whose name appears when the program LATEX is called. It contains the highest level \input commands and is the only file that may have \include commands.

.tfm TEX font metric files contain all the font information that TEX needs to process a document: height, width, depth of each letter, ligature information, italic correction, and so on. The only thing that is missing is what the character looks like. This is provided by .pk files.

.toc This file contains the information for the table of contents. The command \tableofcontents reads in the .toc file, if it exists, and then outputs the table of contents. At the same time, a new .toc file is opened where all the contents information for the current processing run is written. This .toc file is closed by the \end{document} command so that if the LATEX run is interrupted before completion, the .toc file is lost.

      A .toc file is only generated if the document contains a \tableofcontents command and if the \nofiles command has not been issued. It has the same root name as the main file.

.vf   Virtual font files are read in in place of .pk files for fonts that do not really exist independently. For each character, there are instructions for the driver program, usually to take character *nn* from real font *xx*.

<table>
<tr><td>

┌─────────┐
│   │
│   C   │
│   │
└─────────┘

</td><td>

Error Messages

</td></tr>
</table>

Errors are bound to be made at times during the preparation of a long LaTeX document. The mistakes can be of various kinds, from simple typing errors for command names to forgetting that some commands must be paired or giving an incorrect syntax for a complicated command.

Errors during the LaTeX processing produce a list of messages on the monitor, which appear totally incomprehensible to the beginner. Even the advanced user can have difficulty figuring out a particular error message. However, these messages contain information about fundamental structures that can help an experienced TeX programmer to see much deeper into the heart of the problem.

In addition, the error messages contain useful information even for the beginner. It is the purpose of this chapter to explain some of these messages that can be of assistance to non-programmers.

Error messages are written both to the computer monitor and to the processing transcript file, with extension `.log`. One can examine this file if the messages on the monitor went by too fast.

C.1   Basic structure of error messages

Error messages have two sources: those from LaTeX and those from the underlying TeX program. The LaTeX messages are often followed by TeX messages since LaTeX operates at a higher level.

C.1.1   TeX error messages

We start with a simple error as an example.

```
\documentclass{article}
\begin{document}
The last words appear in \txetbf{boldface}.
\end{document}
```

Here the command \textbf has been mistakenly typed as \txetbf. During the
processing, LATEX assumes that the user wants to invoke a TEX command \txetbf.
Since LATEX does not know the TEX commands, it passes this text on to TEX, which
then decides that there is no such command in its repertoire. The following error
message is written to the monitor:

```
! Undefined control sequence.
1.3 The last words appear in \txetbf
                                     {boldface}.
?
```

 The program stops at this point and waits for a response from the user. This message
can be understood even by beginners. It consists of an error indicator that starts with
an exclamation point !. Here the indicator is: ! Undefined control sequence,
meaning that an *unknown command name* (control sequence) was the cause of
the error. Next comes a *pair of text lines*, the *first* of which is prefixed with 1.3,
meaning that the error occurred in 'line 3' of the input text. The error itself was
encountered at the last symbol printed in this *upper* line. The *lower* line shows the
continuation of the input line being processed when the error was found, here the
words {boldface}. Before continuing, TEX waits for a reaction from the user, as
indicated by the question mark in the last line of the message.
    Entering another ? and ⟨*return*⟩ as a response produces the following message:

```
Type <return> to proceed, S to scroll future error messages,
R to run without stopping, Q to run quietly,
I to insert something, E to edit your file,
1 or ... or 9 to ignore next 1 to 9 tokens of input,
H for help, X to quit
?
```

This is a list of the possible user responses:

1. ⟨*return*⟩: Simply typing the return key tells TEX to continue processing after
   making an attempt to handle the error according to some preprogrammed
   rules. In the case of an unknown command name, the error treatment is to
   ignore it.

2. S *scroll mode*: TEX continues the processing, writing further error messages to
   the monitor as they are encountered, but without stopping for a user response.
   This is as though ⟨*return*⟩ were pressed after all subsequent errors.

3. R *run mode*: TEX continues processing as with S, but does not even stop as it
   would in *scroll mode* if the file named in an \input or \include command is
   missing.

4. Q *quiet mode*: This is the same as with R except that no further error messages
   are printed to the monitor. They are, however, written to the .log file.

5. I *insert*: The mistake can be corrected by inserting the proper text. TEX puts the line of text entered from the keyboard into the processing in place of the error and then continues. Such a correction applies only to the processing: the original text in the .tex file is unchanged and must be altered with an editor. Typing in I\stop brings the program to a halt with the current page in the .dvi file.

6. 1 ...: Entering a number less than 100 will delete that many characters and commands from the subsequent text. The program then stops to await further response from the user.

7. H *help*: An extended account of the problem is printed to the monitor, which is more informative than the brief error indicator and which may contain tips for relieving the error.

8. X *exit*: The TEX processing is halted at this point. The current page does *not* appear in the .dvi file.

9. E *edit*: The process is halted as with X and a message is printed saying on which line of which file the error occurred. For some implementations, the editor may actually be called automatically, going directly to the faulty line.

The above response letters may be typed in either capitals or lowercase. The response does not take effect until after ⟨*return*⟩ is pressed.

Typing H or h for *help* on the previous sample error message produces the text:

```
The control sequence at the end of the top line
of your error message was never \def'ed. If you have
misspelled it (e.g., '\hobx'), type 'I' and the correct
spelling (e.g., 'I\hbox'). Otherwise just continue
and I'll forget about whatever was undefined.

?
```

The error is described in more detail: The command name at the end of the upper line is unknown; if this is simply a typing error, enter the proper text with the I response, in this case I\textbf. Otherwise, press ⟨*return*⟩ and the faulty command will be ignored. The line of text will be processed as though it had been The last word appears in boldface. Of course, no boldface can actually appear.

The basic structure of a TEX error message is summarized as:

Every error message begins with an error indicator, marked by a ! at the beginning of the first line. The indicator text is a brief description of the problem. Following are one or more lines of input text. The last symbol of the first of these lines is the one that has caused TEX to stop and print the error message. The last line contains the text or commands that are the next to be processed. TEX waits for a response from the user. If that response is the typing of an H for help, a more detailed description, with possible tips, is printed to the monitor, and TEX waits for a further response.

C.1.2   LaTeX error messages

As an example of a text with a LaTeX error, we take

```
\documentclass{article}
\begin{document}
\begin{qoute}\slshape
  Text indented at both ends
\end{quote}
\end{document}
```

Here the call \begin{quote} was incorrectly typed as qoute. The LaTeX processing writes the error message:

```
! LaTeX Error: Environment qoute undefined.

See the LaTeX manual or LaTeX Companion for explanation.
Type  H <return>  for immediate help.
 ...


l.3 \begin{qoute}
                 \slshape
?
```

The first line of this message states that LaTeX itself discovered this error, with a brief error indicator, in this case Environment qoute undefined. All LaTeX error messages begin with a line like this, followed by a reference to the LaTeX manuals for detailed explanation (which is also to be found in Section C.3 of this book). The third line of text is a reminder that the response H ⟨*return*⟩ will also type additional clarification.

!

The line of three dots ... indicates that there are more lines of internal coding that have been suppressed. Sometimes it is desirable to look deeper behind the error message, especially for practiced TeXperts who know how to interpret them. In this case, LaTeX can be made to output the missing lines of coding by setting

```
\setcounter{errorcontextlines}{num}
```

where *num* is the number of levels a macro will be decoded on an error. By default, *num* = −1. The knowledgeable user can set it to 99 to get more lines than he or she will ever be likely to want.

The next pair of lines shows just where the processing was halted when the error was detected. As for TeX messages, the current input line of text is broken at the error, with the processed part on the first line, here \begin{qoute}, and the remainder on the next line. Here this remainder is \slshape. The line indicator l.3 (small letter L, not number one) shows on which line (3) of the input file the error was found.

LaTeX now awaits a response from the user. Typing H ⟨*return*⟩ yields the additional information:

```
Your command was ignored.
Type I <command> <return> to replace it with another command,
```

```
or   <return>   to continue without it.
?
```

This means the last command in the upper line of the pair beginning with 1.3 has not been read into the processing. The mistake may thus be corrected *for the current process run only* with I\begin{quote} ⟨*return*⟩. The misspelling will still be in the text file, though, and needs to be removed by an editor run later.

However, if the processing is continued by pressing ⟨*return*⟩, then \begin{qoute} is ignored, as though this text were not in the source file. This leads directly to another error when the command \end{quote} is encountered, since now the matching \begin{quote} command is missing. The actual text of this second error message is:

```
! LaTeX Error: \begin{document} ended by \end{quote}.

See the LaTeX manual or LaTeX Companion for explanation.
Type  H <return>  for immediate help.
 ...

l.5 \end{quote}

?
```

The message again contains the standard LaTeX announcement, with error indicator, in the first line, followed by a reference to the manuals, and an invitation to type H for help. The error indicator in this case is

```
\begin{document} ended by \end{qoute}.
```

This arises because when LaTeX encountered \end{quote}, it checked the name of the current environment. Since \begin{quote} was missing, the matching \begin command is the \begin{document} statement, producing a mismatched \begin ...\end pair.

The last pair of lines again shows just how far the processing had progressed before the error was detected. In this case, the whole of the current line has already been taken in, so the remainder line is blank.

The response H ⟨*return*⟩ at this point leads to the same message as for the first error. A correction with an I entry will not do any good since the missing \begin{quote} can no longer be inserted ahead of the environment text. Entering I\begin{quote} will replace the \end{quote} with \begin{quote}, but that does not solve the real problem. The best response now is to type ⟨*return*⟩ so that the command \end{quote} is ignored and the processing continues.

Now both the faulty \begin{qoute} and correct \end{quote} commands are removed and the processing takes place as if the quote environment had never been in the input text at this point.

If the typing error qoute had been made in the \end instead of in the \begin command, the error message would have been:

```
! LaTeX Error: \begin{quote} on input line 3 ended by \end{qoute}
```

```
See the LaTeX manual or LaTeX Companion for explanation.
Type  H <return>  for immediate help.
 ...

l.5 \end{qoute}

?
```

The previous explanations should be enough for the user to understand what is now being said. The error indicator here is

```
\begin{quote} on input line 3 ended by \end{qoute}
```

and the last pair of lines indicate that the problem is in line 5 and that the troublesome command is \end{qoute}. The obvious thing to do now, and the H message encourages this conclusion, is to make a correction with I\end{quote}. However, now a new message appears on the monitor:

```
! Extra \endgroup.
<recently read> \endgroup
l.5 \end{qoute}

?
```

With the exception of the last pair beginning with l.5, this makes no sense at all. The error indicator ! Extra \endgroup is seemingly meaningless. That this is a TeX error message and not a LaTeX one is hardly any compensation.

The frustrated user is not really to blame. The response was perfectly reasonable even if it was wrong. Only experience could say that the best action at that point was to have just pressed ⟨return⟩. The quote environment is closed off anyway, although any special actions associated with \end{quote} would be left off.

The help message at this point is

```
Things are pretty mixed up, but I think the worst is over.
```

This is at least encouraging, and the user should not lose heart. The best thing is to just keep on pressing ⟨return⟩ to get through the run.

We give here two recommendations for choosing a response, one specific and one general. The specific one is:

If a false environment name appears in a \begin command, the proper correction of the error is

> I\begin{*right_name*}

If the misspelling has occurred in the \end command, the best way to handle this mistake is just to press ⟨return⟩. The environment will be closed and any local declarations or definitions will be terminated. However, if there are any commands to be executed or text to be printed by the \end command, these will be missing.

The general recommendation is:

> If the user knows how to correct the error with the help of the error message, this should be done with

> I *correction*

> Otherwise, one may give ⟨*return*⟩ and wait and see what happens. Even if more peculiar (TeX) error messages appear, one can keep on pressing ⟨*return*⟩ until the processing is finally at an end. The following print-out should indicate where the mistake was.

Instead of continually pressing ⟨*return*⟩, one may also enter S, R, or Q and ⟨*return*⟩ to speed up the error treatment (Section C.1.1). Here, as with the simple ⟨*return*⟩ entry, the faulty commands are not just ignored. TeX attempts to treat them by making assumptions about what the user wanted to do at this spot. Only when this is no longer possible will TeX ignore the command completely. For example, if the indicator reads

> `\begin{`*environment*`}` `ended` `by` `\end{`*environment*`}`

there was at least a `\begin` command with a valid environment name earlier. It could be assumed that the name of the environment in the `\end` command is wrong. LaTeX thus tries to execute this command using the name of the current environment.

C.1.3   Error messages from TeX macros

The majority of TeX commands and practically all the LaTeX commands are so-called TeX macros. These are combinations of primitive commands grouped together under a new command name, by which they may be called as a unit. TeX macros are structures similar to those that may be defined by the LaTeX command `\newcommand`. Up to nine arguments may be passed to them, just as for LaTeX commands. However, the corresponding TeX commands for generating macros are more general than `\newcommand`.

   In fact, of the approximately 900 Plain TeX commands available, only 300 are primitives, or fundamental commands. The remaining 600 are macros. If an error occurs within a macro, the other commands within it may also be affected.

   Here is an example for clarification. The command `\centerline` is a macro defined as

> `\def\centerline#1{\@@line{\hss#1\hss}}`

in which `\@@line` is itself a macro while `\hss` is a TeX primitive, a rubber length that can be infinitely stretched or shrunk. To avoid leading the user into the murky depths of TeX commands, we will simply point out that the above macro definition is more or less equivalent to the LaTeX command sequence

> `\newcommand{\centerline}[1]{\makebox[\textwidth][c]{#1}}`

Now take the following sample input text

```
\documentclass{article}
\begin{document}
\centerline{This is an \invalid command}
\end{document}
```

in which a \ has been placed before the word invalid, making a false command named \invalid. During the LaTeX processing, the following TeX error message appears:

```
! Undefined control sequence.
<argument> This is an \invalid
                              command
1.3 \centerline{This is an \invalid command}

?
```

This TeX message is now a bit more understandable. The error indicator is the same as for the example in Section C.1.1:

```
        ! Undefined control sequence.
```

The following pair of lines claim that the error was recognized after the 'command' \invalid was processed and that the next piece of text to be read in is the word command. At the same time, the <argument> at the beginning of the upper line says that this text is the argument of some other command.

The next pair of lines are familiar: The error occurred in line 3 of the input text, after the entire line, command and argument, had been read in for processing.

C.2   Some sample errors

C.2.1   Error propagation

The example with the incorrect \begin{qoute} environment showed that a simple response with the ⟨return⟩ key led to a second error message in spite of the fact that the \end{quote} command that produced it was correct. That one wrongly corrected error leads to further errors is more often the rule than the exception.

Let us look at the input text

```
\documentclass{article}
\begin{document}
\begin{itemie}
  \item This is the first point in the list
  \item And here comes the second
\end{itemize}
\end{document}
```

The only mistake in this text is the misspelled environment name `itemie` in place of `itemize`. The LaTeX processing first produces the same error message as for the incorrect `quote` environment earlier:

```
! LaTeX Error: Environment itemie undefined.

See the LaTeX manual or LaTeX Companion for explanation.
Type  H <return>  for immediate help.
 ...

1.3 \begin{itemie}

?
```

At this point, entering ⟨*return*⟩ leads to a new error message:

```
! LaTeX Error: Lonely \item--perhaps a missing list environment.

See the LaTeX manual or LaTeX Companion for explanation.
Type  H <return>  for immediate help.
 ...

1.4    \item T
              his is the first point in the list
?
```

What has happened here is that without the `\begin` command, the `\item` has been issued outside of a list environment, where it is rather meaningless. (Actually it is defined to print the above error message!) It is now too late to try to insert the missing start of the `itemize` environment. Typing H ⟨*return*⟩ for help yields

```
Try typing  <return>  to proceed.
If that doesn't work, type  X <return>  to quit.
?
```

Following this advice and pressing ⟨*return*⟩, one obtains the same error message once again, but this time on line 5, for the second `\item` command. Persevering further and pressing ⟨*return*⟩ once again, one is presented with

```
! LaTeX Error: \begin{document} ended by \end{itemize}.

See the LaTeX manual or LaTeX Companion for explanation.
Type  H <return>  for immediate help.
 ...

1.6 \end{itemize}

?
```

The `itemize` environment has now come to its end, but since it was never properly started, LaTeX complains about a mismatch of `\begin` and `\end` commands. Now at last, typing another ⟨*return*⟩ leads to a proper continuation of the processing. Of course, the itemized text will be incorrectly formatted, but the rest of the document will not be affected.

In this example, a single mistake in the input text generated three further error messages. This is by no means unusual. Some LaTeX errors can produce hundreds of such successive errors. It is even possible that the chain of errors never ceases and that the processing never advances. In this case, there is nothing else to do but to terminate the program. This should be done with the entry I\stop after the next error message. It may be necessary to give it several times before it takes effect. If this does not work, that is, if the same message appears every time, then the response X ⟨*return*⟩ will halt the program immediately.

It is better to stop the program with I\stop than with X, since then the output will include the last page being processed. This can be of assistance in trying to deduce what the source of the error was.

The final lesson of this section is simply this: *Even when faced with a host of error messages, don't panic! Continue to press the ⟨return⟩ key to advance the processing.*

Pressing S ⟨*return*⟩ instead will produce the same set of error messages on the monitor but without waiting for a user response in between (Section C.1.1).

C.2.2   Typical fatal errors

Occasionally it may happen that a user forgets to include one of the commands \documentclass or \begin{document}, or the entire preamble. The last can easily occur when a LaTeX file is to be read in with \input or \include but is mistakenly entered directly with the LaTeX program call. If a file with the text

```
This file has no preamble.
```

is put directly into the LaTeX processing, the following message appears on the monitor:

```
! LaTeX Error: Missing \begin{document}.

See the LaTeX manual or LaTeX Companion for explanation.
Type  H <return>  for immediate help.
 ...

1.1 T
     his file has no preamble.
?
```

with the accompanying help message after typing H ⟨*return*⟩:

```
You're in trouble here.  Try typing  <return>  to proceed.
If that doesn't work, type  X <return>  to quit.
?
```

One sees from the error message that LaTeX has discovered a mistake on reading the very first letter of the text. The help message is also not very encouraging. There is no point trying to continue the processing with ⟨*return*⟩. Rather, one should stop it with X or E right away, since nothing useful can be achieved here.

Even when the above example file contains the environment

```
\begin{document}
    This file has no preamble.
\end{document}
```

it is not possible to carry out a proper processing. The TEX error message now printed is

```
! LaTeX Error: The font size command \normalsize is not defined:
            there is probably something wrong with the class file.

See the LaTeX manual or LaTeX Companion for explanation.
Type  H <return>  for immediate help.
 ...

l.1 \begin{document}

?
```

The error indicator is rather peculiar since the command \normalsize never appears in the input. Only the last two lines of this message are easily understood. They state that the error was recognized on line 1 after \begin{document} was read in. The fact that this is the text of the first line is enough to show that no meaningful processing can take place, since the mandatory \documentclass command that must precede it is missing.

Here again there is no choice but to halt the program with X or E, since a continuation of the processing would be meaningless.

(The reason for the strange error indicator is that many formatting parameters are initiated by the \begin{document} statement, including the standard font. Here \normalfont is called internally, and this command must be defined in the class file, which is missing. Other initiating commands are defined in the LATEX format itself, and so they do not cause this error.)

If the name of the document class is wrongly typed, say, as

```
    \documentclass{fred}
```

the following message appears:

```
! LaTeX Error: File 'fred.cls' not found.

Type X to quit or <RETURN> to proceed,
or enter new name. (Default extension: cls)

Enter file name:
```

This message should be fairly clear: The program is looking for a file with the name fred.cls but cannot find it, so would the user be so kind as to enter an alternative name. If the new name has the same extension as that requested (.cls), it need not be explicitly given. In this case, the name of any standard LaTeX class, such as article, report, book, or letter, may be typed in, as well as that of any additional classes that you might have access to. Of course, it should be the class for which the document was written.

This same error message is printed whenever a file is to be read in that cannot be found on the system. The issuing command may be \input, \include, or \usepackage. If the file sought really does exist, perhaps it is not located where TeX is looking for files. Usually there is a system parameter set by the installation to point TeX to its files. If your file is somewhere else, you can trying entering its full name, with directory or path designations.

If LaTeX is asking for a file that you know does not exist, or which is totally unknown to you, you will want to halt the processing right away or tell LaTeX to skip the silly file. At this point, you have a problem. LaTeX insists on a valid file name. Typing X ⟨*return*⟩ only produces the message once again, this time stating that it cannot find the file x.*ext*. Some installations provide a dummy file named null.tex, while one of the extension packages available (Section B.5.4) offers a set of files named after the standard response letters x.tex, e.tex, r.tex, h.tex, and s.tex to emulate the responses to normal error messages.

Emergency stop: Sometimes one reaches a point where the program cannot be halted after an error, even with I\stop or X. In such a case, one has to apply the operating system's program interrupt, usually CTRL Z.

C.2.3   Mathematical errors

Surprisingly few errors occur as a result of incorrect application of mathematical formula commands themselves, even for a user with only a little experience. More often, the errors in mathematical formulas are fiddly ones, such as forgetting a closing brace } or neglecting to switch back to text mode. Another type of common error is to use a symbol in text mode that may only appear in math mode. We will point out a few typical examples here.

One wants to produce the text: 'The price is $3.50 and the order number is type_sample', and types the input text:

```
The price is $3.50 and the order number is type_sample.
```

This text contains two errors such that the first one cancels the second: The $ sign is the math mode switch for generating formulas within text (Section 7.1). The proper way to write a true dollar sign in text is as \$. Instead, in the sample text, the $ alone switches to math mode, setting everything that follows as a formula. However, the closing switch-back $ is missing, something that TeX will first notice at the end of the current paragraph.

```
! Missing $ inserted.
<inserted text>
                $
```

1.4

?

If ⟨*return*⟩ is simply pressed as a response, TEX inserts a $ at this point. For our sample text, this would be at the end of the text before the blank line. This means that the text from the first $ to the end of the paragraph will be set as a text formula:

The price is $3.50 and the order number ist ype_sample.$

This output should show the user right away what went wrong. Near the end of the line, there is a letter s printed as an index. This is the second error in the example. The underbar character _ is only permitted in math mode and should have been typed here as _. However, after the first $ had switched (incorrectly) into math mode, the _ sign became allowed, with the result that the following letter s was lowered.

If we now correct the text by replacing the $ sign with \$, then the _ symbol is no longer in math mode, producing the error message:

```
! Missing $ inserted.
<inserted text>
                $
1.5 ...ice is \$3.50 and the order number is type_
                                                sample.
?
```

Pressing ⟨*return*⟩ here tells TEX to recover from the error by inserting the apparently missing $ sign at this point before the math command _. The processing continues, and at some place before the end of the current paragraph TEX will notice again that the closing $ is not present. The same error message is printed as in the first case. The processing goes on with another ⟨*return*⟩ response, with the result:

The price is $3.50 and the order number is type_sample.$

In all three cases, asking for more help with H would type to the monitor:

```
I've inserted a begin-math/end-math symbol since I think
you left one out. Proceed, with fingers crossed.
```

The last sentence above is just what we recommend for mathematical error messages: *Keep on pressing ⟨return⟩ or S to get through to the end of the processing, and then look at the printed output to find the mistake.*

C.2.4   Errors from multifile texts

If the document text is split over many files that are to be read in with \input or \include commands, the line number in the error message refers to the file currently being read. A response with E ⟨*return*⟩ will call the editor program and open that file, going to the indicated line where the error was recognized. With the other responses, the editor has to be called separately, with the faulty file explicitly named.

It is possible to determine which file was being processed at the time of the error by examining the processing messages or the `.log` file. As the files are opened for reading, TeX writes an opening parenthesis (and the name of the file to the monitor and to the transcript `.log` file. When the file is closed, a closing parenthesis) is printed. Output page numbers are similarly written to both the monitor and transcript file in square brackets. For example, if the monitor shows the processing messages

```
..(myfile.tex [1] [2] [3] (part1.tex [4] [5]) (part2.tex [6] [7]
! Undefined control sequence
l.999 \finish
?
```

this can be interpreted as follows: A file `myfile.tex` was being read, and after pages 1, 2, and 3 had been output, the file `part1.tex` was read in with an `\input` or `\include` command inside the file `myfile.tex`. Pages 4 and 5 were output and `part1.tex` was closed, after which another file `part2.tex` was opened for input. An error was discovered in line 999 of this file. If this error is corrected from the keyboard or if the processing is otherwise continued, the monitor messages proceed as

```
[8] [9]) [10]
! Too many }'s
l.217 \em sample}
```

The closing parenthesis after page 9 indicates that the file `part2.tex` has been closed. The next error is on page 10 in the main file `myfile.tex`, since there is no closing) for it. The error was discovered on line 217 of this file.

C.3   List of LaTeX error messages

The LaTeX error messages are listed here, divided into general, package, or font error messages. Within each group, they are ordered alphabetically according to the error indicators. A description of the possible causes and solutions is also given.

C.3.1   General LaTeX error messages

The following error messages are those not involving font selection or definition, nor any of the special features for LaTeX programming class and package files (Appendix D).

! LaTeX Error: ... undefined.

The argument of a `\renewcommand` or `\renewenvironment` has not been previously defined. The corresponding `\new...` command should be used instead.

`! LaTeX Error: \< in mid line.`

The command `\<` in a `tabbing` environment occurred in the middle of a line. This command may only appear at the beginning of a line (Section 6.1.3).

`! LaTeX Error: Bad \line or \vector argument.`

The first argument of a `\line` or `\vector` command specifies the angle of the line or arrow. This message states that the selected angle entries are invalid. See pages 303–304.

`! LaTeX Error: Bad math environment delimiter.`

LaTeX has encountered a math switch command in the wrong mode: either a `\[` or `\(` command in math mode or the corresponding `\]` or `\)` in normal text mode. Either the math switches have been improperly paired or some braces `{...}` are incorrect.

`! LaTeX Error: \begin{...} on input line ... ended by \end{...}.`

LaTeX has encountered an `\end` command without a corresponding `\begin` of the same name. This may be due to a typing mistake in the name of the environment or to the omission of a previous `\end` command. A good way to avoid this error is always to enter the `\end` command immediately after the `\begin`, inserting the actual environment text with the editor in between the two. This is especially useful for long, nested environments. It also reduces the risk of typing the environment name incorrectly in the `\end` command.

`! LaTeX Error: Can be used only in preamble.`

Many commands may only be called within the preamble, such as `\documentclass`, `\usepackage`, `\includeonly`, `\makeindex`, `\makeglossary`, `\nofiles`, and several others. Certain commands that only have meaning within class or package files, such as `\ProvidesClass` and `\ProvidesPackage` (Section D.2.1), as well as many `\Declare..` and `\Set..` commands are also only allowed in the preamble. If one of these commands is issued after `\begin{document}`, this message is printed.

`! LaTeX Error: Command ... invalid in math mode.`

A command has been issued in math mode that only makes sense in text mode, such as `\item` or `\circle`. The font declarations `\itshape`, `\bfseries`, and so on, also produce this error in math mode, since the math alphabet commands `\mathit`, `\mathbf` should be used instead.

`! LaTeX Error: Command ... already defined.`

The user has tried to redefine an existing structure with one of `\newenvironment`, `\newcommand`, `\newtheorem`, `\newsavebox`, `\newfont`, `\newlength`, `\newcounter`, or `\DeclareMathAlphabet`. Either a different name must be selected or, in the case of commands and environments, the `\renew...` version must be employed. (Note that when an environment named `sample` is defined, the commands `\sample` and `\endsample` are also created.)

! LaTeX Error: Command ... undefined in encoding ....

The specified command has been defined with \DeclareTextCommand for a certain NFSS encoding (say OT1) but was executed while another encoding (for example, T1) for which there is no definition was active.

! LaTeX Error: Counter too large.

A counter that is to be printed as a letter contains a value greater than 26.

! LaTeX Error: Environment ... undefined.

LaTeX has encountered a \begin command with an unknown environment name. This is probably due to a typing mistake. It may be corrected during the processing with the response I followed by the correct name. (This does not alter the source file, where the error remains.)

! LaTeX Error: File '...' not found
Type X to quit or <RETURN> to proceed,
or enter new name. (Default extension: ...)
Enter file name:.

A file is to be loaded with one of the inputting commands, but it cannot be found. You may type a new file name, or quit, or proceed without it. If the file name has been given correctly, and it does exist, maybe it is not located where LaTeX looks for files. Make sure that it is in one of the right directories. The user is offered a chance to type in an alternative, or correctly typed, name via the keyboard. Type in the file name, with optional extension, and press ⟨return⟩. LaTeX proposes a default extension that is the same as that requested. There is no default for the main part of the file name.

! LaTeX Error: Float(s) lost.

A figure or table environment or a \marginpar command was given within a vertical box (\parbox or minipage environment), or these structures were issued within a LaTeX command that uses vertical boxes internally, such as a footnote. This error is first recognized by LaTeX when a page is output, so the actual cause could be many lines earlier in the text. A number of tables, figures, or marginal notes may have been lost as a result, but certainly not the one that triggered the problem.

! LaTeX Error: Illegal character in array arg.

A tabular or array environment contains an unknown column formatting entry (see Section 6.2.1) or the formatting entry in the second argument of a \multicolumn command is wrong.

! LaTeX Error: \include cannot be nested.

An attempt has been made to call \include from a file that has already been read in by an \include command. All \include commands must be issued in the main file (Section 11.1.2).

`! LaTeX Error: LaTeX2e command ... in LaTeX 2.09 document.`

This error occurs if a LaTeX 2_ε command is used in compatibility mode (Appendix F), that is, if the document uses \documentstyle instead of \documentclass. These can be \LaTeXe, \usepackage, \ensuremath, the lrbox environment, as well as the syntax for adding an optional argument with \newcommand and \newenvironment.

`! LaTeX Error: Lonely \item--perhaps a missing list environment.`

An \item command has been given outside of a list environment (Section 4.3). Either the environment name has been misspelled in the \begin command and not corrected by keyboard entry, or the \begin command has been forgotten.

`! LaTeX Error: Missing @-exp in array arg.`

The column formatting argument of a tabular or array environment contains an @ symbol without the necessary following text in curly braces { } that must go with it (Section 6.2.1 for @-expressions), or the same thing occurs in the second argument of a \multicolumn command.

`! LaTeX Error: Missing begin{document}.`

Either the \begin{document} command has been forgotten or there is printable text inside the preamble of the document. In the latter case, there could be a declaration with incorrect syntax, such as a command argument without curly braces { } or a command name without the backslash \ character.

`! LaTeX Error: Missing p-arg in array arg.`

The column formatting argument of a tabular or array environment contains a p symbol without the necessary width specification that must go with it (Section 6.2.1), or the same thing occurs in the second argument of a \multicolumn command.

`! LaTeX Error: No counter '...' defined.`

A \setcounter or \addtocounter command was called that referred to a counter name that does not exist. Most likely the name was typed incorrectly. If this error occurs while an .aux file is being read and if the name of the counter is indeed correct, the defining \newcounter command was probably given outside of the preamble. Therefore, it is highly recommended always to give the \newcounter commands inside the preamble. (If the other LaTeX counter commands are used with an undefined counter name, a long list of odd TeX error messages appears.)

`! LaTeX Error: No \title given.`

The \maketitle command has been given before \title has been declared.

`! LaTeX Error: Not in outer par mode.`

A figure or table environment or a \marginpar command was given within math mode or inside a vertical box (\parbox or minipage environment). In the first case, the math switch-back command was probably forgotten.

! LaTeX Error: Page height already too large.

The command \enlargethispage is trying to extend the vertical size of the page, which LaTeX already considers too large.

! LaTeX Error: \pushtabs and \poptabs don't match.

The number of \poptabs commands in a tabbing environment does not agree with the number of previous \pushtabs given (Section 6.1.4).

! LaTeX Error: Something's wrong--perhaps a missing \item.

The most likely cause of this error is that the text in a list environment (list, itemize, enumerate, or description) does not begin with an \item command. It will also occur if thebibliography environment is given without the argument {*sample_label*} (Section 11.3).

! LaTeX Error: Suggested extra height (...) dangerously large.

The command \enlargethispage is trying to extend the vertical size of the page more than LaTeX considers reasonable.

! LaTeX Error: Tab overflow.

The last \= command in a tabbing environment exceeded the maximum number of tab stops allowed by LaTeX.

! LaTeX Error: There's no line here to end.

The command \newline or \\ has been issued after a \par or blank line where it makes no sense. If additional vertical space is to be inserted here, this should be done with a \vspace command.

! LaTeX Error: This may be a LaTeX bug.

This message states that LaTeX is fully confused. This could be the result of a previous error after which the user response was to press ⟨*return*⟩. In this case, the processing should be brought to a halt with I\stop, X, or E and the earlier error corrected. It is also possible, although unlikely, that there is a bug in the LaTeX program itself. If this is the first error message in the processing and the text otherwise seems to be satisfactory, the file should be saved and submitted to the computing center for further investigation.

! LaTeX Error: Too deeply nested.

Too many list environments (description, itemize, enumerate, or list) have been nested inside one another. The maximum depth of such nesting is dependent on the installation but should always be at least four.

`! LaTeX Error: Too many columns in eqnarray environment.`

The `eqnarray` environment may only have three columns per line. You may have forgotten to start a new row with \\ or have placed an extra & in the line.

`! LaTeX Error: Too many unprocessed floats.`

This error may occur if there are too many \marginpar commands on one page. However, it is more likely that LaTeX is retaining more `figure` and `table` floats than it can hold. This happens if too many such float objects have been given before they can be output (Chapter 9). In this case, the last figure or table should be added later in the text. Another cause could be that the figure or table cannot be located on a normal text page, but rather on a special float page at the end of the text or after a \clearpage or \cleardoublepage command. Since the output sequence of figures and tables will be the same as that with which they were input, one such float can block the entire queue. A \clearpage or \cleardoublepage command can free the blockage.

`! LaTeX Error: Undefined tab position.`

A \>, \+, \-, or \< command in a `tabbing` environment has tried to move to a tabulator stop that does not exist (Section 6.1).

`! LaTeX Error: \verb ended by end of line.`

The text of an in-line verbatim command \verb+...+ extends over more than one line of text. This is forbidden in order to catch a common error: the missing terminating character. Make sure that the entire text between the initial and terminating characters is all on one input line.

`! LaTeX Error: \verb illegal in command argument.`

The \verb command may not be used in the argument of any other command, except \index and \glossary. It may not be used within section titles or footnotes, for example.

C.3.2   LaTeX package errors

The special programming commands for handling class and package files (Appendix D) have their own set of error messages. If one of these features issues a serious error, there is often little the user can do about it other than report the problem to the author of the file. On the other hand, some errors are due to the improper use of the file or of the options that it provides.

Often classes and packages contain their own error or warning messages with text and meanings that are peculiar to them. These are indicated as such, along with the name of the class or package that issued them. For example, the package `mypack` could print the error

```
Package mypack Error: cannot mix options 'good'
(mypack)                and 'bad'.
```

A help message should also be available when H is typed. Obviously, such error (and warning) messages cannot be explained here, since they depend entirely on the package in question.

! LaTeX Error: \LoadClass in package file.

A package file has called \LoadClass, which it is not allowed to do. A class file can only be loaded from another class file.

! LaTeX Error: Option clash for package ....

The specified package has been requested a second time with a different set of options. A package file will only be loaded once and a second attempt will be ignored. Thus, if two \usepackage or \RequirePackage commands load the same package with different options, there is a conflict. Try to arrange for a consistent set. Typing H for help after this message will print out the two sets of options.

! LaTeX Error: \RequirePackage or \LoadClass in Options Section.

These two commands may not appear in the definition of a class or package option made with the \DeclareOption command. Instead, the option should set some flag or other indicator that is later tested before calling the command in question.

! LaTeX Error: This file needs format '...' but this is '...'.

The \NeedsTeXFormat command specifies a different format from the one being used. The *format* is the prestored set of instructions that determine what type of TeX is being run. For LaTeX 2_ε, the format name specified must be LaTeX2e. This file cannot be processed at all with the current format in use.

! LaTeX Error: Two \documentclass or \documentstyle commands.

A document may contain only one \documentclass or \documentstyle command. If you can only see one in the main document file, check that other files being loaded do not contain an offending second one.

! LaTeX Error: Two \LoadClass commands.

The class file contains more than one \LoadClass command, something that is not allowed. The class file has been improperly written.

! LaTeX Error: Unknown option '...' for package '...'.

An option has been specified with \usepackage but it is not defined for that package. Check the instructions for the package or look for a misprint.

! LaTeX Error: \usepackage before \documentclass.

The \usepackage command may not appear before \documentclass. A class file must be loaded before any packages.

C.3.3 LaTeX font errors

The following error messages occur when defining or selecting fonts with the New Font Selection Scheme (Appendix A). Some of these messages indicate that the fonts have not been properly set up, in which case the font description files may be corrupted or contain mistakes. In either case, the system manager must see that a proper set of files are installed.

`! LaTeX Error: ... allowed only in math mode.`

A math alphabet command, such as \mathbf, has been used in text mode. Perhaps a $ has been forgotten.

`! LaTeX Error: Command ... not provided in base LaTeX2e.`

A number of symbols that were part of the basic LaTeX 2.09, but not in TeX, are no longer automatically included in LaTeX 2ε. Add one of the packages latexsym or amsfonts to include them.

`! LaTeX Error: Encoding scheme '...' unknown.`

A font declaration or selection command that refers to a nonexistent encoding scheme has been issued. There is probably a typing error involved here.

`! LaTeX Error: Font ... not found.`

The font with the specified attributes could not be found, nor could an adequate substitution be made. The font defined by \DeclareErrorFont is used instead.

`! LaTeX Error: The font size command \normalsize is not defined:`
`                there is probably something wrong with class file.`

It is necessary for class files to define \normalsize, the basic size of standard text in the document. If the class file does not do this, that is, if it only defines \@normalsize, then it must be repaired. This message is also printed if \documentclass is missing, for an empty class file is clearly a faulty one.

`! LaTeX Error: This NFSS system isn't set up properly.`

Something is wrong with the font descriptions in the .fd files, or there is no valid font declared by \DeclareErrorFont. This is a serious problem, which should be reported to the system manager.

`! LaTeX Error: Too many math alphabets used in version ....`

There is a limit of 16 math alphabets possible, a number set by TeX itself. Any additional math alphabet definitions are ignored.

C.4   T_EX error messages

This section contains a list of some of the most common T_EX error messages, ordered alphabetically according to the error indicator, together with a brief description of the possible cause. Each one begins with an exclamation point only.

`! Counter too large.`

As a T_EX error, this message refers to a footnote marked either with letters or symbols in which the counter has exceeded a value of 26 or 9. It may also occur if there are too many `\thanks` commands on a title page.

`! Double subscript.`

A mathematical formula contains two subscripts for the same variable, for example, `x_2_3` or `x_{2}_{3}`. The proper way to produce x_{2_3} is with `x_{2_3}` or `x_{2_{3}}` (Section 7.2.2).

`! Double superscript.`

A mathematical formula contains two superscripts for the same variable, for example, `x^2^3` or `x^{2}^{3}`. The proper way to produce x^{2^3} is with `x^{2^3}` or `x^{2^{3}}` (Section 7.2.2).

`! Extra alignment tab has been changed to \cr.`

A line in a `tabular` or `array` environment contains more & commands than there are columns defined. The error is probably due to a forgotten \\ at the end of the previous line.

`! Extra }, or forgotten $.`

In math mode, either an opening brace { has been left off or an extra closing brace } has been included by mistake. Another possibility is that a math mode switch command such as $, \[, or \(has been forgotten.

`! Font ... not loaded: Not enough room left.`

The text processing requires more character fonts to be loaded than T_EX can handle owing to memory limitations. If certain parts of the document need different fonts, you can try to split it up and process the parts separately.

`! Illegal parameter number in definition of ....`

This error message is probably due to a `\newcommand`, `\newenvironment`, `\renewcommand`, or `\renewenvironment` command in which the substitution character # has been applied incorrectly. This character may appear within the defining text only in the form #*n*, where *n* is a number between 1 and the number of arguments specified in the command. Otherwise the character # may only appear in the definition as `\#`. This error may also arise if the substitution character is applied within the last argument {*end_def*} (Section 10.4).

```
! Illegal unit of measure (pt inserted).
```
If this error message comes right after another error with the message
```
    ! Missing number, treated as zero.
```
the problem lies with this previous error (see below). Otherwise, the mistake is that TEX expects a length specification at this point but has only been given a number without a length unit. This occurs most often when a length is to be set to zero and 0 has been typed in instead of 0mm or 0pt. If this is the case, then responding with ⟨return⟩ produces the right result since for a zero value any unit specification is all right. This error may also occur if a length specification has been completely forgotten.

```
! Misplaced alignment tab character &.
```
The single character command & has been given in normal text outside of the `tabular` and `array` environments. Possibly the intention was to print &, in which case \& should be typed. This may still be achieved during the processing by responding with I\& to the error message.

```
! Missing control sequence inserted.
```
This error is most likely caused by a \newcommand, \renewcommand, \newlength, or \newsavebox command in which the backslash \ is missing from the first argument. Pressing ⟨return⟩ as response will complete the processing correctly since TEX assumes a backslash is missing and inserts it.

```
! Missing number, treated as zero.
```
This error is most likely due to a LATEX command that expects a number or length as argument, which is missing. It may also occur when a command that takes an optional argument is followed by text beginning with [. Finally, another cause can be a \protect command preceding a length or \value command.

```
! Missing { inserted.
! Missing } inserted.
```
TEX is totally confused when either of these error indicators is written. The line number printed will probably not be where the source of the error is to be found, which is a missing opening or closing brace. If the error is not obvious, continue the processing by pressing ⟨return⟩ and try to deduce where it might be from the printed output.

```
! Missing $ inserted.
```
Most likely a symbol or command that may only appear in math mode was used in normal text. Recall that all those commands described in Chapter 7 are only allowed in math mode unless otherwise stated. If an \mbox command is inserted within a math formula, its argument has temporarily exited from math to normal text mode. The message may also occur if a blank line appears within a math formula, signalling a new paragraph and the end of the formula without the necessary $ sign.

`! Not a letter.`

The word list in a `\hyphenation` command contains a character that is not recognized as a letter, for example, an accent command such as `\'{e}`. Such words can only be hyphenated by explicitly inserting the hyphenation possibilities (Sections 2.8.1 and 2.8.2).

`! Paragraph ended before ... was complete.`

The argument of a command contains a blank line or a `\par` command, something that is not allowed. Probably a closing brace } has been omitted.

`! TeX capacity exceeded, sorry [...].`

TeX sets up various storage buffers in the computer memory to carry out the text processing. This message appears when one of these buffers is full and can no longer be used. The name of the buffer and its maximum size are printed in the square brackets of the error indicator. With this message, the TeX processing is terminated. The source of this problem is rarely due to insufficient memory, no matter how much complicated text is being processed, but rather to an error in the text itself. The methods described in Section C.6 may be applied to try to detect the true error.

The following descriptions of the various buffers should help to decide whether the storage capacity allotted to TeX really is too small and to explain what one might do to correct this.

`buffer size` The problem here can be that the text in the argument of a sectioning, `\caption`, `\addcontentsline`, or `\addtocontents` command is too long. The message then normally appears when the `\end{document}` command is processed, but may also arise at one of `\tableofcontents`, `\listoffigures`, or `\listoftables`. The way to avoid this is to use the optional argument for the short form of the heading text (Sections 3.3.3 and 9.4). Indeed, such a long entry in the table of contents is a nuisance anyway and should be shortened. After the correction has been made in the input text, the previous LaTeX `.aux` file must be deleted before reprocessing.

This problem can occur on a PC if a word-processing program has been used to generate the input text instead of a text editor. Some of these programs put an entire paragraph into a single line even though the text on the monitor is broken up into lines.

`exception dictionary` The list of hyphenation exceptions that have been entered with the `\hyphenation` commands has become too large. Words used less frequently should be removed and their possible word divisions indicated explicitly with the `\-` command.

`hash size` The source file contains too many command definitions or uses too many cross-reference markers. This does not mean that the input text really needs all these commands, for it may be that the user has developed a large collection of private commands that are stored in a single file and read into every document, whether they are all applicable or not.

`input stack size` An overflow of this buffer is probably due to a mistake in a command definition. For example, the command defined with

```
\newcommand{\com}{One more \com}
```

produces `One more {One more {...One more \com}...}}` going on forever, since it continually calls itself. Actually, it does not go on forever, but only until this buffer is full.

`main memory size` This buffer contains the text for the page currently being processed. It also overflows if a recursively defined command has been called. However, the more usual reasons are: (1) a large number of very complicated commands have been defined on one page; (2) there are too many `\index` or `\glossary` commands on one page; (3) the page itself is too complex to fit within the allotted buffer space.

The solution to the first two situations is clear: Reduce the number of command definitions and/or `\index` and `\glossary` commands on that page. In the third case, the cause might be a long `tabbing`, `tabular`, `array`, or `picture` environment, or a stuck float (figure or table) waiting for an output command.

To find out whether the memory overflow is really due to an overly complex page, add the command `\clearpage` just before the spot where the overflow occurs. If the error message no longer appears on the next processing run, then this page was indeed too complicated for TeX. However, if the overflow still persists, the error is probably a mistake in the input text. If necessary, it may have to be located with the method explained in Section C.6.

If the page really is too complex for the TeX processing, it must be simplified. However, first recall that the entire last paragraph is processed before that page is output, even if the page break occurs near the beginning of the paragraph. Introducing a `\newpage` may solve the problem and should be tried out before attempting a tedious restructuring of the text. If the error is due to a stuck figure or table, it might be alleviated by moving the float object to later in the text or by changing the positioning argument (Section 9.1). If the whole text is not yet complete, one can try giving `\clearpage` for now in order to clear the blocked floats and then decide on a better ordering when the text is finalized.

`pool size` Most likely there are too many command definitions and/or labels, or their names are too long. Try shortening the names. This error may also occur if a closing right brace } has been forgotten in the argument of a counter command such as `\setcounter` or in a `\newenvironment` or `\newtheorem` command.

`save size` This buffer overflows when commands, environments, and the scope of declarations are nested too deeply, for example, if the argument of a `\multiput` command contains a `picture` environment, which in turn possesses a `\footnotesize` declaration with another `\multiput` command, and so on. Such a nesting must be simplified, unless the real problem is a forgotten closing brace } that merely makes the structure appear so complex.

`! Text line contains an invalid character.`

The input text contains a strange symbol that TeX does not recognize. This could be a problem with the editor itself, that it is inserting extra characters. If an examination of the source file does not reveal the strange symbol, consult the computing center for help.

```
! Undefined control sequence.
```

Every TeX user encounters this error message at some point. It is usually the result of an incorrectly typed command name. It may be amended during the processing by responding with I and the proper name of the command, plus ⟨*return*⟩. This does not alter the source file, which must be corrected separately after the LaTeX run. If the command name has been entered correctly in a LaTeX command, it may be that it was issued in an improper environment where it is not allowed (that is, not defined there).

```
! Use of ... doesn't match its definition.
```

If '...' is the name of a LaTeX command, it is likely that one of the picture commands from Sections 16.1.3 and 16.1.4 has been called with the wrong syntax for its arguments. If the name is \@array, there is a faulty @-expression (Section 6.2.1) in a tabular or array environment. Possibly a fragile command was given in the @-expression without the \protect command preceding it.

```
! You can't use 'macro parameter #' in ... mode.
```

The special symbol # has been used in normal text. Probably there should have been a \# in order to print # itself. This can be corrected during the processing with the response I\# and ⟨*return*⟩.

C.5 Warnings

TeX and LaTeX errors both bring the processing run to a temporary stop and wait for a reaction from the user, or they may halt the program completely. Warnings, on the other hand, merely inform the user that the processed output may contain some faults that he or she might want to correct. Warnings appear on the monitor along with the page number where they occur, without the program coming to a stop. They are also written to the .log file where they may be examined after the LaTeX processing and possible printing. Warnings may be issued either by LaTeX or by TeX itself.

C.5.1 General LaTeX warnings

LaTeX warnings are indicated by the words 'LaTeX Warning:' at their start, followed by the warning message itself.

```
LaTeX Warning: Citation '...' on page ... undefined on
               input line ....
```

The key in a \cite or other citation command has not yet been defined with a corresponding \bibitem command (Section 11.3). If this message does not disappear on the next run, then the bibliography is missing that defining \bibitem entry, either because B<small>IB</small>T<small>E</small>X has not been run or because that reference is not in any of the specified databases.

```
LaTeX Warning: Command ... has changed.
                Check if current package is valid.
```

The \CheckCommand statement is used to test whether a given command has a certain definition. This warning is issued if the test fails. This is used to be sure that a given package is doing what the programmer thinks it is doing.

```
LaTeX Warning: Float too large for page by ..pt on input line...
```

A float (figure or table environment) is too big to fit on the page. It will be printed anyway, but will extend beyond the normal page margins.

```
LaTeX Warning: 'h' float specifier changed to 'ht'.
```

The float placement specifier 'h' for 'here' (Section 9.1) permits the float to appear where the environment is given within the text, provided there is enough room remaining on the page for it, otherwise it appears at the top of the next available page. This message is a reminder of this fact.

```
LaTeX Warning: inputting '...' instead of obsolete '...'.
```

Some packages written for LaTeX 2.09 input certain files, such as article.sty, that have a new equivalent with a different name (in this case article.cls). Dummy files with the old names that issue this message and input the right file are provided.

```
LaTeX Warning: Label '...' multiply defined.
```

Two \label or \bibitem commands have defined keys with the same name (Sections 11.2.1 and 11.3). Even after the correction has been made, this message will be printed once more to the monitor since the information that led to it is to be found in the .aux file from the last processing run. On the run after that, it should be gone.

```
LaTeX Warning: Label(s) may have changed.
                Rerun to get cross-references right.
```

The printed outputs from the \ref, \pageref, and \cite commands may be incorrect since their values have been altered during the processing. LaTeX must be run once more so that the right values are used.

```
LaTeX Warning: Marginpar on page ... moved.
```

A marginal note on the given page has been shifted downwards to prevent it from being too close to another one. This means that it will not be beside the line of text where the \marginpar command was actually given.

```
LaTeX Warning: No \author given.
```

The \maketitle command has been issued without a previous \author command.

Unlike a missing `\title` command, this is not an error, but merely peculiar. The warning is printed just in case you did mean to specify an author.

`LaTeX Warning: Optional argument of \twocolumn too tall on page.`

The `\twocolumn` command (Section 3.2.7) starts a new page and switches to two-column formatting. The text in the optional argument is printed in one wide column above the double column text. If that text is too large to fit onto one page, this warning is printed.

```
LaTeX Warning: \oval, \circle, or \line size unavailable on
                input line ....
```

The size specified for an `\oval`, `\circle`, or slanted `\line` command in a `picture` environment is too small for LaTeX to print.

```
LaTeX Warning: Reference '...' on page ... undefined on
                input line ....
```

The marker name in a `\ref` or `\pageref` command has not been defined by a `\label` command in the previous processing run (Section 11.2.1). If this message does not disappear on the next run, the corresponding `\label` command is missing.

`LaTeX Warning: Text page ... contains only floats.`

This message points out that the float style parameters (Section 9.3) have excluded any regular text from appearing on the specified page. This is not necessarily bad, but you might want to check that page visually.

`LaTeX Warning: There were multiply-defined labels.`

This message is printed at the end of the LaTeX run if there were any `\label` or `\bibitem` commands that used the same marker name more than once. A warning is also printed near the beginning of the run for each repeated marker name.

`LaTeX Warning: There were undefined references.`

This message is printed at the end of the LaTeX run if there were any `\ref` or `\pageref` commands whose markers had not been defined during a previous run. A warning is also printed earlier for each undefined marker used. If it does not disappear on the next run, then the corresponding `\label` is missing, possibly due to a typing error in the marker text.

C.5.2   LaTeX package warnings

The class and package warnings are those that check the names and versions of the loaded files against those requested, or the use of options, or whether the `filecontents` environment has written some text to a file. The commands involved are described in Section D.2.9.

Classes and packages can also issue their own warnings, which are particular to them. These cannot be listed here, since they depend entirely on the class or package itself.

```
LaTeX Warning: File '...' already exists on the system.
                Not generating it from this source.
```

The filecontents environment is *not* extracting text from the main file because it has discovered a file of the same name already on the system.

```
LaTeX Warning: Unused global option(s):.
```

Options specified in the \documentclass statement are *global*, meaning they can apply to the class and/or to any following packages. However, if no class or package recognizes any of these options, this warning is printed, followed by a list of the unused options.

```
LaTeX Warning: Writing file '...'.
```

The filecontents environment (Section D.2.9) is extracting text out of the main file and writing it to a file of the given name.

```
LaTeX Warning: You have requested class/package '...',
                but the class/package provides '...'.
```

The name of the class or package as given by its internal identifying command \ProvidesClass or \ProvidesPackage does not agree with the file that was read in with \usepackage or \RequirePackage.

```
LaTeX Warning: You have requested, on input line ..., version
                '...' of class/package ...,
                but only version '...' is available.
```

The date of a class or package file, as given by its internal identifying command \ProvidesClass or \ProvidesPackage, is earlier than that asked for by the \usepackage or \RequirePackage command. The class or package may not have all the features that the inputting file expects.

```
LaTeX Warning: You have requested release '...' of LaTeX,
                but only release '...' is available.
```

The date of your LaTeX version is earlier than that specified for some input file in a \NeedsTeXFormat command (Section D.2.1). Your LaTeX may not provide all the features needed by that file.

C.5.3 LaTeX font warnings

Font warnings are those involving the NFSS commands (Appendix A). They are indicated by the text: LaTeX Font Warning: plus the warning text.

```
LaTeX Font Warning: Command ... invalid in math mode.
```

A command that should only appear in text mode has been given in math mode. The command is simply ignored. The commands `\boldmath`, `\unboldmath`, and `\em` lead to this message. There are other commands that produce an *error* message with the same text.

```
LaTeX Font Warning: Command \tracingfonts not provided.
(Font)              Use the 'tracefnt' package.
(Font)              Command found: on input line ....
```

The font-tracing diagnostic tool `\tracingfonts` may only be used if the `tracefnt` package (page 387) has been loaded. Otherwise, this command is ignored.

```
LaTeX Font Warning: Encoding '...' has changed to '...' for
(Font)              symbol font '...' in the math version '...'.
```

To make use of the specified symbol font in the given math version, it was necessary to change the font encoding temporarily.

```
LaTeX Font Warning: Font shape '...'in size <...> not available
(Font)              size <...> substituted.
```

No font has been defined for the size and shape requested, so a substitute size is used instead.

```
LaTeX Font Warning: Font shape '...' undefined
(Font)              using '...' instead.
```

The shape attribute that has been requested is unknown or has not been defined, so a substitute shape will be used instead.

C.5.4   TeX warnings

A TeX warning is recognized by the fact that it is not an error message (not prefixed with !) and that the processing is not halted. The most common TeX warnings are:

```
Overfull \hbox ....
```

TeX could not break this line in a reasonable way, so part of it will extend into the right margin. The rest of the information in the message can be of assistance.
   For example, with the complete warning message

```
Overfull \hbox (17.2122pt too wide) in paragraph at lines 4--6
[]\OT1/cmr/m/n/10 If T[]X can-not find an ap-pro-pri-ate
 spot to di-vide a word at the end of the line, as right
 here aaaaaaaaaaaaaaaaaaaaaaaaaaa
```

one knows that the line is about 17.2 pt (6 mm) too long and extends this amount into the right-hand margin. The line is part of the paragraph in lines 4 to 6. The font used is designated by its attributes `\OT1\cmr\m\n\10`. The text of the problem line is `If ... ... right here` aaaaaaaaaaaaaaaaaaaaaaaaaaa. Possible word divisions are shown with hyphens, such as di-vide. The last word cannot be divided, which is the cause of the problem.

A way around this is to include some suggested hyphenations with the \- command, such as aaaaaaaaa\-aaaaaaaaaaaaaa. Similarly, a \linebreak command before the problem word, or setting the whole paragraph in a sloppypar environment, will get rid of this warning message.

If a badly broken line extends only a tiny bit into the right margin, say 1 pt or less, in most cases this will hardly be noticed and may be left as it is. A sample output should be printed just to verify the appearance.

Overfull \vbox ....

This warning occurs very rarely. TeX could not break the page properly so that the text extends beyond the bottom of the page. More often TeX sets less text on a page than too much. Thus this warning arises only when the page contains a very large vertical box, higher than the value of \textheight, such as a long table.

Underfull \hbox ....

This is the opposite of the Overfull \hbox warning. It appears when TeX has filled a line right and left justified, but with so much interword spacing that it considers the appearance to be undesirable. This is often the result of a sloppypar environment, a \sloppy declaration, or a \linebreak command. It may also come about after an inappropriate application of a \\ or \newline command, such as two \\ commands one after the other. The additional information in the warning message contains the text of the badly formatted line plus an evaluation of the 'badness' of the word spacing.

If in the example of the Overfull \hbox a \linebreak is included in the text at the spot ..., as right\linebreak here, then the warning becomes

```
Underfull \hbox (badness 5504) in paragraph at lines 4--6
[]\OT1/cmr/m/n/10 If T[]X can-not find an ap-pro-pri-ate
 spot to di-vide a word at the end of the line, as right
```

which states that the paragraph in lines 4 to 6 contains an output line in which the interword spacing may be unacceptably wide. The text of this line reads If ... ..., as right and is set in the font \OT1/cmr/m/n/10. The evaluation badness 5504 is TeX's estimate of how unacceptable the spacing is: *The smaller this number, the better.*

Underfull \vbox ....

The page has been broken with head and foot justified, but TeX judges the amount of interparagraph spacing to be possibly unacceptable. The badness number here corresponds to the quantity with the same name from the Underfull \hbox warning.

C.6   Search for subtle errors

At some point or another you will encounter an error message for which you cannot identify any cause, try as you may. For such devious errors, we recommend the following search strategy:

1. Copy the file twice into a *previous* and a *working* copy (in addition to the original, which remains untouched during this search).

2. In the working copy, find the outermost environment where the error occurred and remove one or more inner environments. If there are no inner environments, shorten the remaining text. Process the file with LaTeX once more.

3. If the error still occurs, copy the shortened working copy to the previous copy and repeat step 2. If the outer environment in step 2 is \begin{document} ... \end{document}, the shortening may be carried out by simply inserting \end{document} at some earlier point.

4. If the error is no longer in the shortened working copy, copy the previous copy back to the working copy. The error is still present in this version. Remove less of the text than last time and repeat steps 2 to 4.

5. If the error is found to be in the next innermost environment, repeat the procedure for this environment with steps 2 to 4.

With this strategy, the error may be localized to one command or to the innermost environment with only a small remaining structure. If the error still cannot be identified in spite of its being precisely localized, seek help from a more experienced colleague or from the computing center. However, it is normally possible to recognize the mistake once the position of the error has been found.

It does happen that even though the error has been corrected, the same error message appears on the next LaTeX process run. This is because of the internal transfer in information through the LaTeX auxiliary files, which are always one run behind on the current situation. For example, if there is a mistake in one of the sectioning commands, then after it has been eliminated, the faulty entry still exists in the .toc file. If the document contains the \tableofcontents command, LaTeX will read in that .toc file on the next run and issue the error message once more, since a new .toc file is only created after a successful processing.

In this case, the .toc file should also be edited and the error removed. If that is not possible, the file should be erased and the corrected source file processed *twice* with LaTeX. If the error was in \caption, \addcontentsline, or \addtocontents, the same applies to the corresponding .lof or .lot file.

Occasionally the .aux file itself must be erased to prevent an error in it from being repeated even after the .tex file has been repaired. Here one must be careful that the command \nofiles has not been given in the preamble, for then a corrected .aux file will not be generated after a further LaTeX process run.

<table>
<tr><td>

```
┌─────────┐
│         │
│    D    │
│         │
└─────────┘
```

</td><td>

LATEX Programming

</td></tr>
</table>

In this appendix, we present the special commands that were designed for class and package files along with some convenient internal LATEX and TEX commands.

D.1 Class and package files

D.1.1 The LATEX concept, an open system

The wealth of contributed LATEX programming was probably never anticipated by Leslie Lamport when he released LATEX. It is now a fact of life, and indeed one of the great strengths of the system. The LATEX Team not only accommodates such 'foreign' extensions, it actually supports and encourages them, as witnessed by the copious presentations of such packages in *The LATEX Companion* (Mittelbach et al., 2004) as well as in this book.

And this is the way it should be. The extensions have been written by people who needed them, who realized that LATEX was missing something vital for them. On the other hand, to add all of them to the basic LATEX installation would overload it with features that 90% of the users would never require. The philosophy now is that LATEX provides a fundamental core, or kernel, which is extended first by the standard class files and then by the myriad of contributed packages and other classes.

It is the role of the LATEX Team to establish guidelines for programming, to ensure that packages do not clash needlessly with the kernel, or with each other, and to provide a basis of stability so that useful packages continue to operate through further updates to the kernel and the standard classes. These LATEX features for class and package control, together with a set of programming tools, offer an enhanced degree of reliability and durability, both among packages and against future updates of the kernel.

D.1.2 Levels of commands

There are a number of levels of commands with varying degrees of security for the future:

user commands (highest level) described in this and the other manuals, consisting of lower case letters, such as \texttt, are part of the LATEX external definition to be supported forever.

class and package commands with longish names of mixed upper- and lowercases (like \NeedsTeXFormat) are intended mainly for programmers, and are also guaranteed; most are preamble-only commands, but there is otherwise no real restriction to class and package files.

internal LATEX commands containing the character @ in their names can only be used in class and package files; they are not guaranteed forever, although many of them are indispensable for special effects; a programmer makes use of them at the risk that some day his or her package may become obsolete.

low-level TEX commands also have names with lowercase letters, and no @; they should be safe against future evolution of LATEX, but even this is not absolutely certain; they should be avoided where possible, as explained below.

internal private commands are those used within a contributed class or package file; it is recommended that they all be prefixed with some uppercase letters representing the package name and @ in order to avoid clashes with other packages; for example, \SK@cite, from the showkeys package.

A question that confronts LATEX programmers is to what extent the internal LATEX commands may be used in class and package files. There is always a danger that such commands may vanish in later versions, since they have never been documented in the official books (Lamport, 1985, 1994; Goossens et al., 1994). Like the TEX commands discussed in the next section, their use cannot be forbidden, but one must be aware that a certain degree of risk will accompany them.

The guidelines issued by the LATEX Team strongly recommend employing the high-level LATEX commands whenever possible.

- Use \newcommand and \renewcommand instead of \def; if one of the TEX defining commands must be used, because a template is required or because it must be \gdef or \xdef, issue a dummy \newcommand beforehand to test for a name clash. If it is unimportant whether the command name already exists, issue a dummy \providecommand followed by \renewcommand. The ability to define commands with one optional argument at the high level removes one reason for wanting to reach down to the lower ones.

- Use \newenvironment and \renewenvironment instead of defining \myenv and \endmyenv.

- Assign values to lengths and glues (rubber lengths) with the \setlength command, rather than by simply equating.

- Avoid the TEX box commands \setbox, \hbox, and \vbox; use instead \sbox, \mbox, \parbox and the like. With the extra LATEX optional arguments, the need for the TeX equivalents is greatly diminished, and the LaTeX versions are far more transparent. Moreover, the LaTeX boxes will function properly with the color package while the others are unpredictable.

- Issue error and warning messages with \PackageError and \PackageWarning rather than with \@latexerr or \@warning; the former also inform the user of the source of the message instead of labeling them all as LaTeX messages.

- There is no suggestion that one should exclusively use the \ifthenelse command from the ifthen package (Section 10.3.5) in place of the TeX conditionals. It seems that this package is offered to simplify employing conditionals, in a manner more consistent with LaTeX syntax. Although most of the examples in this book use it rather than the TeX versions, we never employ it ourselves in our own programming.

Adhering to these and similar rules will help ensure that a package will remain fit through future extensions of the LaTeX kernel.

D.1.3   TeX commands

Why should primitive TeX commands be shunned? To define commands with \def rather than \newcommand must be just as good and is often unavoidable. Is there really a chance that it might be removed from a future LaTeX version? The primitives are the building blocks on which all flavors of LaTeX are constructed. Surely they must remain!

This is not really the point. The primitive TeX commands form the bedrock of any format, and anything defined with them will always do exactly what the programmer expected. However, the equivalent LaTeX tools could actually do more as time goes on. The \newcommand checks for name clashes with existing commands, for example. It might even be possible that a debugging device that keeps track of all redefinitions could be added later; any commands defined with \def would be excluded from such a scheme. Even now there is something like this to keep track of all files input with middle- and high-level commands.

Another example of how low-level programming can go astray is the case of robust commands. Many commands are intrinsically fragile, meaning that they are prematurely interpreted when used as arguments of other commands, but they may be made robust by prefixing them with \protect. In LaTeX 2.09, several fragile commands were defined to be robust by including the \protect in the definition, as for the LaTeX logo command:

```
\def\LaTeX{\protect\p@LaTeX}
\def\p@LaTeX{...}
```

The true definition is in the internal \p@LaTeX, not the external \LaTeX. Since the original definition for the logo actually possessed some flaws, several packages included an improved version. Those that simply redefined \LaTeX itself made the command fragile; those that were cleverer only redefined \p@LaTeX, with the result that they are totally left behind in LaTeX 2_ε, where commands are made robust in a completely different (and much better) manner. (Incidentally, the internal definition of the LaTeX logo today has been greatly improved.)

In spite of the desirability of employing only official LaTeX commands, there are many occasions when either the internal LaTeX commands or the TeX primitives just must be used. The risk of future incompatibility must be taken in order to have a workable package now. However, one should not take this risk lightly where a high-level equivalent is available.

D.2   LaTeX programming commands

All the commands described in this section are new to LaTeX 2_ε. They are not essential to class and package files, but they do extend their usefulness and guarantee that they are employed properly.

D.2.1   File identification

Three commands test that the external environment in which the class or package has been inserted is correct. The first of these is

> \NeedsTeXFormat{*format*}[*version*]

The first statement in a class or package should be the declaration of the TeX format needed. Although there are existing formats with other names, only the one named LaTeX2e actually recognizes this statement. All others will immediately issue the error message

```
! Undefined control sequence.
1.1 \NeedsTeXFormat
                   {LaTeX2e}
```

which all by itself is fairly informative.

What is perhaps of more use is the optional *version* argument, which must contain the date of issue in the form yyyy/mm/dd. If a package makes use of features that were introduced in a certain version, its date should be given so that if it is used with an earlier version of LaTeX 2_ε, a warning is printed. For example, the command \DeclareRobustCommand did not exist in the preliminary test release of LaTeX 2_ε, but was first introduced with the official release of June 1, 1994. Thus any package containing this command should begin with

> \NeedsTeXFormat{LaTeX2e}[1994/06/01]

The form of the date is important, including the zeros and slashes.

This declaration is not limited to class and package files: It may also be issued at the start of the document itself to ensure that it is processed with the right LaTeX. It must, however, be given in the preamble.

The next two commands identify the class or package file itself:

> `\ProvidesClass{`*class*`}[`*version*`]`
> `\ProvidesPackage{`*package*`}[`*version*`]`

In both cases, the *version* consists of three parts: date, version number, and additional information. The date is in the same format as above, while the version number can be any designation without blanks, and the additional information is text with or without blanks. An example is

> `\ProvidesPackage{shortpag}[1995/03/24 v1.4 (F. Barnes)]`

Only the date part is actually checked by LATEX against the date specified in the calling `\usepackage` command. The version number and additional information are printed out if `\listfiles` has been requested. However, the above format is necessary for the `\GetFileInfo` command in the doc package.

Both the `\documentclass` and `\usepackage` commands (as well as `\LoadClass` and `\RequirePackage`) may take an optional argument to specify the earliest acceptable release date for the class/package. For example, with

> `\documentclass[12pt]{article}[1995/01/01]`

if the `article` class file loaded contains

> `\ProvidesClass{article}[1994/07/13 v1.2u`
>   `Standard LaTeX document class]`

a warning message is printed. The same procedure applies to the commands `\usepackage` and `\ProvidesPackage`.

This system of version checking allows a document to insist that suitable versions of the class and package files are loaded. It assumes, however, that all later versions are fully compatible with earlier ones.

There is a further identifying command for general files, those to be loaded with `\input`.

> `\ProvidesFile{`*file_name*`}[`*version*`]`

There is no checking of the name or version in this case, but both pieces of information will be printed by `\listfiles`.

D.2.2 Loading further classes and packages

In the main document file, classes are read in by the initializing `\documentclass` command and packages with `\usepackage`. Within class and package files, the commands

> `\LoadClass[`*options*`]{`*class*`}[`*version*`]`
> `\RequirePackage[`*options*`]{`*package*`}[`*version*`]`
> `\LoadClassWithOptions{`*class*`}[`*version*`]`
> `\RequirePackageWithOptions{`*package*`}[`*version*`]`

must be used instead. The first allows one class file to load another, with selected options, if desired; the second permits class and package files to load other packages. Only one \LoadClass command may appear within any class file; it may not be called from a package file. Neither command may be invoked in the document file. The *packages* argument may be a list of several package names, separated by commas.

The ...WithOptions variants load the class or package with all those options that were specified for the current one, something that is often required.

How the optional *version* arguments interact with the corresponding \Provides command has been explained in the previous section; how the *options* argument is treated is described below.

D.2.3   Processing options

Both classes and packages may take options that are defined with

\DeclareOption{*option*}{*code*}

where *option* is the name of the option and *code* is the set of instructions that it is to execute. Internally, a command named \ds@*option* is created. Often the code does nothing more than set flags or input an option file. (\RequirePackage may *not* be used within the option code!) Two examples from article.cls are

```
\DeclareOption{fleqn}{\input{fleqn.clo}}
\DeclareOption{twocolumn}{\setboolean{\@twocolumn}{true}}
```

A default option is defined with \DeclareOption*, which takes no option name, specifying the code to be executed for all requested options that are undefined.

There are two special commands that may be used only within the *code* of the default option definition:

\CurrentOption contains the name of the option being processed; and

\OptionNotUsed declares \CurrentOption to be unprocessed.

For example, to have a class file emulate LᴬTᴇX 2.09 behavior where all undefined options load a .sty file of the same name, define

```
\DeclareOption*{\InputIfFileExists{\CurrentOption.sty}%
                {}{\OptionNotUsed}}
```

which first checks whether there is a .sty file of the requested name, and if not declares the option to be unused. Requested options that have not been used (processed) are listed in a warning message.

The options are then processed with the commands

```
\ExecuteOptions{option_list}
\ProcessOptions
\ProcessOptions*
```

where \ExecuteOptions calls those commands defined for the options in *option_list*. This is normally done to establish certain options as being present by default. \ProcessOptions executes all the requested options *in the order in which they were defined* and then removes them from the list. Options are therefore executed only once by this command. The *-version is similar, except that the options are executed *in the order requested*.

It is also possible to transfer options to a class or package file with

```
\PassOptionsToClass{options}{class_name}
\PassOptionsToPackage{options}{package_name}
```

where *options* is a list of valid options recognized by the specified class or package file. These commands may be used within the definition of other options. The class or package named must later be loaded with \LoadClass or \RequirePackage.

If the default options for class and package files have not been altered by \DeclareOption*, the standard procedure for handling options that have been requested but are undefined is:

- All options requested in the \documentclass statement are designated *global*; they are considered to apply to all subsequent packages, but not to classes loaded with \LoadClass; if they are not defined in the class, no error or warning is issued.

- All options requested with other commands, including \LoadClass and the \PassOptionsTo.., are *local*; if they are not defined in that class or package, an error is issued.

- If there global options that are defined in neither the class nor any of the packages, a warning is issued.

- Options, global and local, are executed in the order in which they are defined in the class and packages, unless \ProcessOptions* has been called, in which case they are executed in the order in which they are listed.

D.2.4 Deferred processing

Sometimes, to achieve certain special effects or to avoid possible conflicts with other packages, it is desirable to have some commands executed at the end of the package or class, or at the beginning or end of the document. This can be accomplished with

```
\AtEndOfClass{cmds}
\AtEndOfPackage{cmds}
\AtBeginDocument{cmds}
\AtEndDocument{cmds}
```

The first two store away *cmds* to be carried out at the end of the class or package file. They can be used by local configuration files that are read in at the beginning but contain modifications that should be made at the end so that they are not overwritten by the defaults. The last two declarations store away the *cmds* to be executed with \begin{document} and \end{document}, respectively. All of these may be issued more than once, in which case the *cmds* are processed in the order in which they were issued.

The *cmds* stored with \AtBeginDocument are inserted into the processing stream effectively within the preamble, but after the command \begin{document} has done almost everything else that it does. Thus the *cmds* may be considered to be part of the main body but preamble-only commands are also allowed.

D.2.5   Robust commands

Commands may actually be *fragile*, meaning that if they are used in the arguments of other commands, they could be prematurely interpreted, causing unexpected problems. This happens with moving arguments, those that appear somewhere else other than where they were given: in the table of contents and in running headlines. Complex commands with conditionals or redefinitions are likely to be fragile.

Many intrinsic commands in LATEX 2.09 were fragile, and it was necessary to precede them with \protect when they appeared in the argument of a \section command, for example. In this case, the command name is transferred rather than its translation. Some commands could be made *robust* using the trick shown on page 429 for the \LaTeX command itself.

In today's LATEX, almost all regular commands are robust. However, the commands a user may define with \newcommand, \renewcommand, and \providecommand (Section 10.3) may very well be fragile. Alternatively, one can define the commands with

\DeclareRobustCommand{\com_name}[*narg*][*opt*]{*def*}

which has the same syntax as the other defining commands. If the command to be defined already exists, a message is written to the transcript file and the old definition is overwritten.

Another command with the same syntax simply checks the current definition of \com_name:

\CheckCommand{\com_name}[*narg*][*opt*]{*def*}

and issues a warning message if the actual definition is not the same as *def*, with the same number of arguments, and so on. This is used to ensure that the state of the system is as one expects and that no previously loaded packages have altered some important definition.

Both \DeclareRobustCommand and \CheckCommand may be called at any point in the document.

D.2.6   Commands with 'short' arguments

Normally, the arguments to user-defined commands are allowed to contain new paragraphs, with the \par command or with a blank line. In TEX jargon, these commands are said to be 'long'. This is not the standard behavior for commands created with the TeX \def command, where the arguments must be short in order to act as a test for forgotten closing braces.

With the version from December 1, 1994, LaTeX provides *-forms of all the defining commands:

```
\newcommand*              \renewcommand*
\newenvironment*          \renewenvironment*
\providecommand*
\DeclareRobustCommand*    \CheckCommand*
```

which create user-defined commands with 'short' arguments in the same way as does \def.

It is recommended that one should almost always take the *-version of these defining commands, unless there is some very good reason to expect that the possible arguments may be 'long', that is, contain new paragraphs. Long arguments should be the exception, not the rule.

D.2.7 Issuing errors and warnings

Classes and packages may be programmed to issue their own error messages and warnings. This is useful to indicate which file is responsible for the message.

Error messages are generated with

```
\ClassError{class_name}{error_text}{help}
\PackageError{package_name}{error_text}{help}
```

where *error_text* is the message printed to the monitor and to the transcript file and *help* is additional text printed after the user responds with H. If the texts contain command names that are to be printed literally, they must be preceded by \protect; spaces are generated with \space, and new lines with \MessageBreak. For example,

```
\PackageError{ghost}{%
    The \protect\textwidth\space is too large\MessageBreak
    for the paper you have selected}
    {Use a smaller width.}
```

produces the error message

```
! Package ghost Error: The \textwidth is too large
(ghost)                for the paper you have selected.

See the ghost package documentation for explanation.
Type  H <return>  for immediate help.
```

Typing H ⟨*return*⟩ produces

```
Use a smaller width.
```

after which LATEX halts again to wait for a response as described in Section C.1.

Warnings may also be issued from classes and packages in a similar way. The difference is that there is no *help* text, and the processing does not stop for a response. The line number of the input file where the warning occurred may be optionally suppressed.

```
\ClassWarning{class_name}{warning_text}
\ClassWarningNoLine{class_name}{warning_text}
\PackageWarning{package_name}{warning_text}
\PackageWarningNoLine{package_name}{warning_text}
```

For example, with the warning

```
\PackageWarning{ghost}
    {This text is haunted}
```

one obtains the message

```
Package ghost Warning: This text is haunted on input line 20.
```

and the processing continues. Warnings may be split into several lines with the \MessageBreak command, just like error texts.

Two last commands of this type are

```
\ClassInfo{class_name}{info_text}
\PackageInfo{package_name}{info_text}
```

which write their texts only to the transcript file, and not to the monitor. They are otherwise just like the corresponding NoLine warnings.

D.2.8   Inputting files

Files other than classes and packages may also be input, in which case it is often desirable to make sure that they exist beforehand. Or, alternative actions might be taken depending on the existence of a certain file. These goals are met with

```
\IfFileExists{file_name}{true}{false}
\InputIfFileExists{file_name}{true}{false}
```

Both these commands test for the presence of the specified *file_name* in the area that LATEX is looking for files and execute *true* if it is found, otherwise *false*. In addition, \InputIfFileExists reads in that file after executing *true*.

These commands are not restricted to the preamble, nor to class or package files. In fact, the regular \input command is defined in terms of them.

Many special classes make use of these commands to read in a local configuration file. For example, the class ltxdoc contains

```
\InputIfFileExists{ltxdoc.cfg}
    {\typeout{Local config file ltxdoc.cfg used}}
    {}
```

just before \ProcessOptions is called. This allows one to have a local configuration that might specify

> \PassOptionsToClass{a4paper}{article}

for a European installation without altering the files that are processed with the ltxdoc class.

D.2.9 Checking files

Although not really part of programming, two LATEX features to keep track of input files are described here. The first of these, already mentioned in Section 11.1.1, is the command

> \listfiles

which may be given in the preamble, even before \documentclass. It causes a list of all input files to be printed at the end of the processing, along with their version and release data. In this way, one has a record of just which files were included, something that may be of use when deciding to send a document file to another installation for processing there. Since any nonstandard files may also have to be included, these may be more readily identified from such a listing.

For example, the simple document file

```
\documentclass{article}
\usepackage{ifthen}
\listfiles
\begin{document}
  \input{mymacros}
    This is \te.
\end{document}
```

produces the listing

```
*File List*
 article.cls  2001/04/21 v1.4e Standard LaTeX document class
  size10.clo  2001/04/21 v1.4e Standard LaTeX file (size option)
  ifthen.sty  2001/05/26 v1.1c Standard LaTeX ifthen package
mymacros.tex
 ***********
```

In this case, the local file mymacros.tex contains no version information because it is missing a \ProvidesFile command.

What should one do if a local file, such as mymacros.tex above, is needed for the processing of a document file that is to be sent elsewhere? One could send it along with the main file, but that requires giving the recipient more instructions on what to do. Or, its contents could simply be included in the main file, for shipping purposes. For a package file, this is not so easy, since internal commands containing the @ sign would cause trouble, and the options would not be handled properly. For this purpose, we have the environment

```
\begin{filecontents}{file_name}
    file contents
\end{filecontents}
```

which is given at the very beginning of the document, before the \documentclass command. It tests to determine whether there is a file on the system with the name *file_name*, and if not, it writes its contents literally to a file of that name. This may be a package file that is subsequently input with \usepackage. In this way, the missing nonstandard files can be ported together with the main document file.

If we extend the above simple example by including at the very start

```
\begin{filecontents}{mymacros}
\newcommand{\te}{the end}
\end{filecontents}
```

the newly written file mymacros.tex contains

```
%% LaTeX2e file 'mymacros'
%% generated by the 'filecontents' environment
%% from source 'mydoc' on 2003/01/31.
%%
\newcommand{\te}{the end}
```

Note that the filecontents environment adds some comment lines to explain where the new file came from. If this is undesirable, the filecontents* environment may be used instead.

D.2.10 Useful internal commands

!

Notwithstanding the guidelines in Section D.1.2 that recommend avoiding internal LᴬTᴇX commands, there are a number that are fairly fundamental and indeed form many of the building blocks of the LᴬTᴇX kernel and many standard packages. Since they are still internal commands, they are not guaranteed for all future updates. However, if they were to vanish, many of the interesting extension packages provided by the LᴬTᴇX Team itself would have to be drastically overhauled. We merely present them briefly here for the sake of the bolder user.

```
\@namedef{cmd}{def}
\@nameuse{cmd}
```

define and execute a command named \cmd, where the backslash is not included in the command name. This name may contain any characters, even those normally forbidden in command names.

```
\@ifundefined{cmd}{true}{false}
```

executes *true* if the command \cmd does not exist, otherwise *false*. Again, the backslash is not included in *cmd*, and any characters may appear in the command name. This test is often used to define commands conditionally, a task that has been taken over by \providecommand. It may also be employed to determine whether the main class is article-like or not: \@ifundefined{chapter}{..}{..} tests for the existence of the \chapter command.

\@ifnextchar*char*{*true*}{*false*}

tests if the next character is *char*, and if so, executes *true*, otherwise *false*. This command
is traditionally used to define commands with optional arguments, where *char* is [. The
extended syntax of \newcommand offers a high-level means of achieving this.

\@ifstar{*true*}{*false*}

tests if the next character is a star *, and if so, executes *true*, otherwise *false*. It is used to
define *-forms of commands and environments, something that still cannot be done at the
high level.

\@for *obj* := *list* \do {*cmds*}

where *list* is a command that is defined to be a list of elements separated by commas, and
obj is successively set equal to each of these elements while the code *cmds* is executed once
for each element. For example,

```
\newcommand{\set}{start,middle,end}
\@for \xx:=\set \do {This is the \xx. }
```

prints 'This is the start. This is the middle. This is the end.'

D.2.11 Useful TEX commands

!

Many of the most sophisticated features of LATEX and its packages can only be programmed
with the help of Plain TEX commands. These are described not only in *The TEXbook* (Knuth,
1986a), but also in the excellent reference manual by Eijkhout (1992), *TEX by Topic, a
TEXnician's Reference*.

We do not intend this book to be a manual for TEX; nevertheless, there are a few common
TEX commands that appear in many packages, and even in the examples to follow. A brief
description of what they do will aid the understanding of these codings. A true TEXpert or
TEXnician can skip this section altogether.

\def*cmd*#1#2..{*definition*}

is the standard defining command in TEX. It is the equivalent of \newcommand* except that
there is no check for name clashes, and the arguments are specified differently. For example,
a command \Exp to write scientific notation can be defined as

```
        \def\Exp#1#2{\ensuremath{#1\times10^{#2}}}
or as  \newcommand*{\Exp}[2]{\ensuremath{#1\times10^{#2}}}
```

In both cases, \Exp{1.1}{4} produces 1.1×10^4. However, \def can go further: It can put
the arguments in a template, such as

```
\def\Exp#1(#2){\ensuremath{#1\times10^{#2}}}
```

to allow the more convenient notation \Exp1.1(4), something that cannot be produced with
\newcommand. The \def command is often used when a command is to be defined without
knowing (or caring) whether its name already exists or when a template is needed.

```
\gdef    \edef    \xdef
```

are variations on \def: The first makes a *global* definition, valid even outside the current environment or {..} bracketing; the second is an *expanded* definition, such that any commands in it have their meanings and not the command itself inserted in the definition; the last is a combination of the other two, expanded and global.

> \noexpand   \expandafter

control the expansion of commands in definitions and execution. Any commands in the definition part of \edef are expanded (their meanings inserted) unless they have \noexpand before them. The opposite is achieved with \expandafter, which jumps over the following command, expands the next one, and then executes the one skipped. This is very deep TeXnology and is best illustrated by an example with the \Exp command defined above.

> \newcommand*{\mynums}{1.1(4)} \expandafter\Exp\mynums

is identical to \Exp1.1(4), whereas \Exp\mynums is not; \mynums is expanded to 1.1(4) *before* \Exp is executed.

> \let\cmd_a = \cmd_b   or   \let\cmd_a\cmd_b

makes \cmd_a take on the *current* meaning of \cmd_b. This is often employed to save the current meaning of a command before redefining it, possibly using the older meaning too.

> \relax

does absolutely nothing, but it is often inserted in places where something should be but nothing is wanted.

> \if*cond* true_code \else *false_code* \fi

is the form of a TeX conditional. There are too many variations on the condition *cond* to explain here, but one common application is the equivalent of the LaTeX boolean switch commands:

\newif\if*flag*	=	\newboolean{*flag*}
*flag*true	=	\setboolean{*flag*}{true}
*flag*false	=	\setboolean{*flag*}{false}
\if*flag* ..\else..\fi	=	\ifthenelse{\boolean{*flag*}}{..}{..}

For those who are used to it, the TeX form is more compact but does not conform to the general LaTeX style of doing things.

> \ifcase *num* text_0 \or *text_1* \or ... \fi

executes one of the *text_num* according to the value of *num*.

> \endinput

terminates the current file being input. This is not really necessary, but it is considered good programming to end all files this way. The main document file does not need it since \end{document} has the same effect.

D.3   Changing preprogrammed text

D.3.1   Changing explicit names

There are a number of titles that appear automatically in LaTeX, such as 'Contents', 'Bibliography', and 'Chapter'. For works in languages other than English, it is necessary that they be replaced by their translations. And even in English, an author might prefer say 'Summary' in place of 'Abstract'. All such explicit words are to be found in certain name commands that may be redefined as one pleases.

These name commands are not defined in the basic LaTeX format itself, but rather in the various class files as they are needed. Thus \chaptername exists only in classes book and report, but not in article. This means that if a package were to redefine the word 'Chapter' for all classes, it must do so with something like

```
\providecommand*{\chaptername}{}
\renewcommand*{\chaptername}{Chapitre}
```

The standard set of name commands and their initial values are:

(defined in book, report, and article classes)

\contentsname	{Contents}
\listfigurename	{List of Figures}
\listtablename	{List of Tables}
\indexname	{Index}
\figurename	{Figure}
\tablename	{Table}
\partname	{Part}
\appendixname	{Appendix}

(defined in book and report classes)

\chaptername	{Chapter}
\bibname	{Bibliography}

(defined in article class)

\abstractname	{Abstract}
\refname	{References}

(defined in letter class)

\ccname	{cc}
\enclname	{encl}
\pagename	{Page}
\headtoname	{To}

(defined in makeidx package)

\seename	{see}
\alsoname	{see also}

(defined only in certain packages)

```
\prefacename       {Preface}
\glossaryname      {Glossary}
\proofname         {Proof}
```

The redefinition of these name commands is a fundamental part of the multi-lingual babel system (Chapter 14). The commands are not redefined directly but rather by means of certain \captions*language* such as \captionsgerman and \captionsenglish that allow for convenient switching back and forth between different languages. For example,

```
\newcommand*{\captionsgerman}{%
  \renewcommand*{\contentsname}{Inhaltsverzeichnis}
  ...
  \renewcommand*{alsoname}{siehe auch}}
```

D.3.2   The date

The \today command for the current date is another one that outputs explicit English words. Its standard definition conforms to the American style of giving dates, that is 'July 15, 2003'. If one wants to redefine this, either for the British style (15th July 2003) or for another language altogether, the best method is to follow the example of the other names commands: Do not redefine \today directly, but create commands that allow one to switch back and forth.

For example, we can define \dateUSenglish and \dateenglish making use of the internal TₑX counters \year, \month, \day and the TₑX \ifcase command (page 440).

```
\newcommand*{\dateUSenglish}{\renewcommand*{\today}{%
  \ifcase\month \or
  January\or February\or March\or April\or May\or June\or
  July\or August\or September\or October\or November\or
  December\fi \space\number\day, \number\year}}
```

```
\newcommand*{\dateenglish}{\renewcommand*{\today}{%
  \number\day \ifcase\day \or
  st\or nd\or rd\or th\or th\or th\or th\or th\or th\or th\or
  th\or th\or th\or th\or th\or th\or th\or th\or th\or th\or
  st\or nd\or rd\or th\or th\or th\or th\or th\or th\or th\or
  st\fi\space \ifcase\month \or
  January\or February\or March\or April\or May\or June\or
  July\or August\or September\or October\or November\or
  December\fi \space\number\year}}
```

Definitions for other languages can be modeled after these examples.

Note: It is probably more convenient to rely on the babel multilingual system (Chapter 14) to redefine all the captions and date outputs for you.

Table D.1: Input coding schemes for `inputenc` package

`ascii`	7-bit ASCII encoding, characters 32–127 only
`latin1`	ISO Latin-1 encoding (Western Europe)
`latin2`	ISO Latin-2 encoding (Eastern Europe)
`latin3`	ISO Latin-3 encoding (Catalan, Esperanto, Galacian, Maltese)
`latin4`	ISO Latin-4 encoding (Scandinavian, Greenland Inuit, Lappish)
`latin5`	ISO Latin-5 encoding (Turkish)
`latin9`	ISO Latin-9 encoding (with euro symbol)
`decmulti`	DEC Multinational encoding
`cp850`	IBM 850 code page (Western Europe)
`cp852`	IBM 852 code page (Eastern Europe)
`cp437`	IBM 437 code page (North America)
`cp437de`	Variant on 437, with German ß replacing Greek β in position 225
`cp865`	IBM 865 code page (Scandinavia)
`applemac`	Macintosh encoding
`next`	NeXt encoding
`ansinew`	Windows ANSI encoding
`cp1252`	Windows 1252 code page (same as `ansinew`)
`cp1250`	Windows 1250 code page, for Central and Eastern Europe

D.4 Direct typing of special letters

Package: inputenc In Section 2.5.9 we explained the `inputenc` package that permits direct typing of accented and special letters, provided one has an appropriate keyboard and display font. For example, on a German keyboard set up for Windows, typing the key marked 'ß' inserts character 223, which is displayed on the author's monitor as the 'eszet' letter for which the regular LaTeX input is \ss. The source file, however, receives only the code number 223, which LaTeX would normally reject as unknown. The `inputenc` package with the `ansinew` option tells it that character 223 is to be treated as \ss. This will have the same result even if the file is displayed on a monitor set up for a different coding.

Table D.1 lists the current set of encoding options for the package. Others may be added in the future. For each of these options, there is a corresponding `.def` file defining the extended characters with the commands

`\DeclareInputText{`*pos*`}{`*text*`}`   or
`\DeclareInputMath{`*pos*`}{`*math*`}`

which assign *text* or *math* coding to the character *pos*. For example, `ansinew.def` contains

`\DeclareInputText{223}{\ss}`

to translate the input character code 223 to the LaTeX command \ss.

Some TeX installations automatically contain such conversions for their own local input coding scheme; files written under such a system without the `inputenc` package will be processed correctly on their own system but will generate garbage

Table D.2: Alternative commands for special symbols in text mode

Command	Symbol	Replaces
Ligatures		
\textemdash	—	---
\textendash	–	--
\textexclamdown	¡	!`
\textquestiondown	¿	?`
\textquotedblleft	"	``
\textquotedblright	"	''
\textquoteleft	'	`
\textquoteright	'	'
Math symbols		
\textbullet	•	$\bullet$
\textperiodcentered	·	$\cdot$
\textbackslash	\	$\setminus$
\textbar	|	$\|$
\textless	<	$<$
\textgreater	>	$>$
Miscellaneous		
\textvisiblespace	␣	\verb*+ +
\textasciicircum	^	\verb+^+
\textasciitilde	~	\verb+~+
^{123}	123	^{123}
Special symbols		
\textcompwordmark		(ligature break)
\textregistered	®	
\texttrademark	™	
\textcircled{x}	ⓧ	

on another one. Thus this package should always be added when special symbols are directly typed in, especially if there is any possibility that the file may be processed on another computer system.

D.5   Alternatives for special symbols

A number of symbols in the text fonts cannot be addressed explicitly, but only as ligatures, for example, ¿ as ?`. Other symbols that one might want in text are only available in math mode. LaTeX provides some \text.. commands, listed in Table D.2, to print these and other characters directly.

D.6   Managing code and documentation

This section describes two additional advanced features for maintaining LaTeX code and its documentation. There is no need to employ these at all, for any home-written packages and classes will function just as well without them. They do add a degree of sophistication and security by tracing the history of the code's development and by including the current documentation within the code itself. Here 'documentation' means both the user's manual and the programmer's description of what each step of the code is doing.

The LaTeX installation files are written in this way. There are about 40 such files that are processed with the DocStrip utility (next section) to extract the code from these files and merge it into one file, `latex.ltx`. The documentation for each contributory file can be viewed alone, or a giant document can be created for the entire set. On the other hand, the standard class files, with much common coding, along with their option files, are all extracted from the one file `classes.dtx`, with a single documentation.

More practically, many packages are provided as `.dtx` files containing the package code plus user manual and programmer's documentation. A DocStrip batch job with extension `.ins` is also given, which when processed by LaTeX (or Plain TeX for that matter) extracts the actual `.sty` file, along with a drive `.drv` file. LaTeXing the driver file generates the documentation. This is usually superfluous since the `.dtx` file itself is constructed so that it behaves like a driver file. However, the `.drv` file can be edited to select, say, just the user manual and to suppress the programmer notes.

The next sections describe first the extraction program DocStrip, which can be used for many other applications as well (e.g., `custom-bib`, Section 12.3) and then the integrated documentation scheme in the following section.

D.6.1   The DocStrip utility

Since the TeX program is a programming as well as a text-formatting language, it can be exploited to provide a number of utility 'programs' to manipulate files. Such programs are immediately portable: If you have TeX, you can run them. One example of such a program is the DocStrip utility for extracting functioning code out of one or more source files containing documentation, as comments. The program was originally written by Frank Mittelbach and further developed by Johannes Braams, Denys Duchier, Marcin Woliński, and Mark Wooding.

The basic idea was to copy one file to another, leaving off all the comment lines. From this simple concept came two additional features that extended the application of DocStrip: Alternative lines of coding could be selectively suppressed or included depending on options chosen at processing time; and multiple files, or modules, could be input to form a single output file. This means that one source file can be the home of several different LaTeX packages and that a single package file can be constructed out of many different components, as for the main LaTeX file, `latex.ltx`, mentioned above.

Running interactively

The simplest way of running DocStrip on a file is to invoke it with TeX (or LaTeX, but TeX is faster), as

```
tex docstrip
```

which produces the response

```
*********************************************************
* This program converts documented macro-files into fast *
* loadable files by stripping off (nearly) all comments! *
*********************************************************
*****************************************************
* First type the extension of your input file(s):   *
\infileext=
*****************************************************
```

One replies by entering the input extension (usually .dtx); then one is asked in turn for the output extension, the options wanted, and finally, for the root name of the file(s) to be processed. Execution follows.

There are some limitations to this method, since the input and output files have the same root name, differing only in the extension, and initial and final comments added to the output are fixed. The more flexible means of running the utility is with a batch job.

Running as a batch job

A DocStrip batch job is a file containing instructions for the utility. For example, suppose we have a package named anchor that is to be put into a documented source file called anchor.dtx, and the actual package file anchor.sty is to be extracted with the option package, while a documentation driver file anchor.drv is obtained with option driver; the batch file, named anchor.ins, could look like

```
\input docstrip

\preamble
This is a stripped version of the original file.
\endpreamble

\postamble
This is the end of the stripped file.
\endpostamble

\declarepreamble\predriver
This is a documentation driver file.
\endpreamble

\declarepostamble\postdriver
End of documentation driver file.
\endpostamble
```

```
\keepsilent
\askforoverwritefalse

\generate{\file{anchor.sty}{\from{anchor.dtx}{package}}
        \file{anchor.drv}{\usepreamble\predriver
                                \usepostamble\postdriver
                                \from{anchor.dtx}{driver}}
        }
\endbatchfile
```

The first and last lines are vital: First the file `docstrip.tex` is loaded, defining all the special DocStrip commands; then after the instructions have been executed, `\endbatchfile` ensures an orderly termination.

The commands `\preamble` and `\postamble` allow one to insert explanatory comments at the beginning and end of the extracted file. The preamble is often a copyright notice and/or a caveat that the extracted file should never be distributed without the source. Additional labeled pre- and postambles may be declared with `\declarepreamble` and `\declarepostamble`, and activated with declarations `\usepreamble` and `\usepostamble`.

The instructions `\keepsilent` and `\askforoverwritefalse` are optional. The former suppresses processing information during the run while the latter turns off the warning that an existing file may be overwritten.

The main command is `\generate`, which specifies the files to be created with a series of `\file` commands, each taking two arguments: the name of the new file and a list of instructions for its production. These instructions can be declarations such as `\keepsilent` or `\usepreamble`, but the main one is the command `\from`. This again takes two arguments: the name of the input file and a list of the options to be applied. In the above example, each generated file has only a single input source, but multiple input files are possible with a series of `\from` commands.

The created `anchor.sty` file now contains

```
%%
%% This is file 'anchor.sty',
%% generated with the docstrip utility.
%%
%% The original source files were:
%%
%% anchor.dtx  (with options: 'package')
%% This is a stripped version of the original file.
%% Copyright (C) 2004 Simon J. Sawyer
\NeedsTeXFormat{LaTeX2e}

. . . . . . . . . . . . . . . . . . . . . . . .

\addtolength{\topmargin}{-1in}
%% This is the end of the stripped file.
%%
```

```
%% End of file 'anchor.sty'.
```

It is possible to have a master batch job to process individual ones, in which case the master must input them with \batchinput and not with \input.

Rules for removing lines

The \generate and \file commands cause the input file(s) to be transferred to the output file, line by line, according to the following rules:

1. Any lines beginning with a *single* % sign are removed.

2. Any lines beginning with double %% signs are retained.

3. Any line beginning with %<opt> (or %<+opt>) will have the rest of its text transferred if opt is one of the selected options; otherwise it is removed.

4. Any line beginning with %<!opt> (or %<-opt>) will have the rest of its text transferred if opt is *not* one of the selected options; otherwise it is removed.

5. All lines between %<*opt> and %</opt> are retained or removed depending on whether opt is a selected option or not.

Options can be combined logically, negated, and grouped:

```
a&b       (a and b);
a|b       (a or b);
!a        (not a);
(a|b)&c (c and one of a or b)
```

For more information on DocStrip, see the documentation that can be obtained by processing docstrip.dtx with LATEX.

D.6.2   Documenting LATEX coding

Package: doc

The documenting of software products is extremely important: On the one hand it provides a manual for the user, and on the other, details about the coding for the programmer. The original LATEX styles, as well as the basic latex.tex file, were heavily commented by Leslie Lamport, but only with straightforward, normal text. It was Frank Mittelbach's doc package that first allowed sophisticated, integrated documentation of the source codes.

By *integrated* documentation, we mean that the descriptions and the coding are to be found merged together in a single source file. Thus two processes are necessary: One to extract the actual coding on its own (the DocStrip utility of Section D.6.1) and another to print the documentation (the doc package). The basic idea behind this package is that the comments are in fact regular LATEX text, with some extra features to allow automatic indexing and to record the program's development. The coding itself appears in a special type of verbatim environment.

The documentation is produced by running a special driver file through LATEX. Such a driver for a source file named anchor.dtx would be, in its simplest form,

```
\documentclass{article}
\usepackage{doc}
\begin{document}
  \DocInput{anchor.dtx}
\end{document}
```

The \DocInput command reads in the specified file, but it first alters the function of the % character from 'comment' to 'do nothing'. This means all comment lines in anchor.dtx become real text to be processed!

We describe some of the extra features that the doc package makes available for the 'comments' in the .dtx files, illustrated by a sample source file, anchor.dtx, for the dummy anchor package. As usual, a more complete manual can be acquired by processing doc.dtx.

The description part

The documentation consists of two parts: the *description*, which is a manual for the end user, and the *coding*, a detailed explanation of how the software works, including the lines of code themselves. It is possible to suppress the coding part and to print only the description by issuing

```
\OnlyDescription
```

in the preamble.

Special commands for the description part are:

```
\DescribeMacro{\macro_name}
\DescribeEnvironment{env_name}
```

which are placed at the start of the text that illustrates a new high-level command (macro) or environment. These commands do two things: They place the macro or environment name in a marginal note at that location (for easy reference when reading) and they insert an entry in the index.

Because documentation needs to use the \verb command frequently for printing input text, some abbreviations are provided with

```
\MakeShortVerb{\c}   and   \DeleteShortVerb{\c}
```

which first turn the character c into shorthand for \verb$c$ and then restore its normal use. For example, after \MakeShortVerb{\|}, |\mycom| prints \mycom. (These commands can be made available for any document by loading the package shortvrb, which is actually extracted from the doc package.)

If the comment character % has been deactivated, how can one put comments into the documentation text? One way is to make use of the TeX conditional \iffalse to form a block, or *meta* comment, as

```
% \iffalse
%     These lines are ignored even when the
%     percent character is inactive
% \fi
```

The other method is to use ˆˆA in place of %, a special doc feature.

The description part is terminated with

\StopEventually{*final text*}

where *final text* is to appear at the very end of the article; if only the description part is printed, *final text* is printed immediately and the documentation is ended.

The coding part

The coding part should normally contain the more specialized material that is of no interest to the everyday user. The special commands that may be used here are

\begin{macro}{*macro_name*} *text and code* \end{macro}
\begin{environment}{*env_name*} *text and code* \end{environment}

both of which again insert a marginal note and make an entry in the index. They also organize any \changes commands, as explained below.

The most important environment in the coding part is macrocode, which prints its contents as in verbatim, optionally with a code line number. The form of this environment is somewhat special:

␣␣␣␣\begin{macrocode}
lines of code
␣␣␣␣\end{macrocode}

The four spaces before the \end{macrocode} are obligatory; those before the \begin are not necessary, but it is good practice to insert them for symmetry. This environment also counts all the backslashes within it for a checksum test and makes an index entry for every command name that it finds. So it is something more than a mere verbatim environment!

The coding part is brought to an end with

\Finale

which carries out the checksum test and then inserts the *final text* stored from the \StopEventually command. There may actually be more text following it, which is only printed when both description and coding parts are output.

Index of macros and record of changes

The doc package makes automatic entries into an index by means of the two \Describe*xxx* commands and the two environments presented above. In addition, all commands that appear in the coding are indexed. However, the indexing is turned on only if one of

\CodelineIndex ␣␣␣ or ␣␣␣ \PageIndex

is given in the preamble. The first references the indexed commands to the number of the code line where they appear, the second to the page number. In the second case, the code lines are not numbered, unless the declaration `\CodelineNumbered` is also issued.

Since not all commands in the coding really need to be indexed, especially those that are part of standard LATEX and TEX, the command

    `\DoNotIndex{`*list of command names*`}`

is given, often repeatedly, near the beginning, to exempt the listed commands from being indexed.

The automatic indexing of all the commands in the code slows down the processing considerably. Once the index `.idx` file has been produced, future runs do not need to repeat this effort (unless there have been changes to the code). The command

    `\DisableCrossrefs`

will suppress this indexing, but it may be negated by an earlier `\EnableCrossrefs` that neutralizes the disabling command.

The text of the index is generated from the `.idx` data file by the MakeIndex program (Section 11.4.3), which must be run with the special indexing style `gind.ist` as

    `makeindex -s gind.ist` *filename*

The indexing style file `gind.ist` can be extracted from `doc.dtx`.

To print the index, the command

    `\PrintIndex`

is placed where it should appear. Often this is in the *final text* in `\StopEventually`. An up-to-date index can only appear after MakeIndex has been run between two LATEX processings.

A record of changes to the software can be made by inserting

    `\changes{`*version*`}{`*date*`}{`*text*`}`

throughout the documentation, in both the description and coding parts. To form the change history list, the command

    `\RecordChanges`

must be placed in the preamble. This enables the change entries to be placed in a glossary file, which is then processed by MakeIndex as

    `makeindex -s gglo.ist -o` *filename*`.gls` *filename*`.glo`

(The indexing style file `gglo.ist` is also extracted from `doc.dtx`.) The change history is then printed in the documentation where

    `\PrintChanges`

is located, again often as part of *final text*. The texts of the `\changes` commands are ordered, first by version number and then by the name of the macro or environment in which they appear.

Integrity tests

If the source file is to be sent over electronic networks, there is a danger that it might be corrupted or truncated. Two tests are possible to check for this. By placing

> \CheckSum{*num*}

near the start of the documentation (before the coding anyway), all the backslashes in the `macrocode` environments will be added up and the total compared with the number *num* by the \Finale command. If *num*=0, the true total will be printed on the monitor; otherwise, if the sum does not agree with *num*, an error is printed, with the two values.

The other test checks that the character set has not been corrupted by passing through computer systems with different character codes.

```
\CharacterTable
{Upper-case     \A\B\C\D\E\F\G\H. . .
.  .  .  .  .
.  .  .  .  .    Tilde     \~}
```

The argument must agree exactly with that expected by doc (except for inactive % signs and multiple spaces). It should be copied from the doc.sty or doc.dtx files.

Obtaining the file information

File information may be obtained with the command

> \GetFileInfo{*filename*}

which defines \filename, \filedate, \fileversion, and \fileinfo from the optional release information to be found in the \Provides*xxx* command identifying the specified file (Section D.2.1). The idea is that the .dtx file should contain this information once, and only once, but it needs to be known to print it in the title of the article. These \file*xxx* commands may be used for this purpose. The release information must conform to the sequence *date*, blank, *version*, blank, *text*.

The ltxdoc class

Class: ltxdoc

A special class called ltxdoc is provided to assist running the doc package. It invokes the article class with the doc package, and then issues commands

```
\AtBeginDocument{\MakeShortVerb{\|}}
\CodelineNumbered
\DisableCrossrefs
```

and defines a number of other useful commands for aiding the documentation. See the description by processing ltxdoc.dtx. It also provides for local configuration: If ltxdoc.cfg exists, it is read in. This can pass paper size or other formatting options to article, issue \OnlyDescription by means of \AtBeginDocument, and so on.

A sample .dtx file

To illustrate these features, we show part of the source file anchor.dtx. The initial lines ensure that all the files that can be extracted from it (the package .sty and the documentation driver .drv) receive their proper identifying commands. The date and version information appears only once, but is transferred to both extracted files.

```
% \iffalse       (This is a meta-comment)
%% Copyright (C) 2004 Simon J. Sawyer
\NeedsTeXFormat{LaTeX2e}
%<*dtx>
\ProvidesFile           {anchor.dtx}
%</dtx>
%<package>\ProvidesPackage{anchor}
%<driver>\ProvidesFile{anchor.drv}
% \fi
%\ProvidesFile{anchor}
                [2004/02/15 1.1 (SJS)]
```

The last \ProvidesFile{anchor} enables the proper functioning of \GetFileInfo; the first one is only a dummy to absorb the information line when the .dtx file is read directly.

Next, the driver part is given. This is what LaTeX sees when it processes the file directly.

```
%\iffalse
%<*driver>
\documentclass[a4paper,11pt]{article}
\usepackage{doc}
\EnableCrossrefs
\RecordChanges
\CodelineIndex
\begin{document}
    \DocInput{anchor.dtx}
\end{document}
%</driver>
%\fi
```

Now the checksum and list of commands that are not to be indexed are given, followed by the start of the article.

```
% \CheckSum{73}
% \DoNotIndex{\addtolength,\boolean,\ExecuteOptions}
% \DoNotIndex{\newboolean,\newlength,\ProcessOptions}
% \DoNotIndex{\RequirePackage,\setboolean,\setlength}
% \changes{1.0}{1999 Oct 25}{Initial version}
% \changes{1.1}{2004 Feb 15}{Next revision}
```

```
% \GetFileInfo{anchor}
% \title{\bfseries A Package to weigh anchors}
% \author{Simon J. Sawyer}
% \date{This paper describes package \texttt{\filename}\\
%        version \fileversion, from \filedate}
% \maketitle
% \MakeShortVerb{\|}
%
% \section{Purpose}
% To raise anchors . . .
% . . . . . .
```

We advance to the end of the description and start of the coding part.

```
% \StopEventually{\PrintIndex\PrintChanges}
%
% \section{The Coding}
% The first thing is to read in the \texttt{ifthen} package,
% if it is not already there.
%     \begin{macrocode}
%<*package>
\RequirePackage{ifthen}
%     \end{macrocode}
%
% \begin{macro}{\DeclareOption}
% \begin{macro}{\AN@weight}
% Define the options with help of the length |\AN@weight|. The
% options |large| and |small| select the anchor size.
%     \begin{macrocode}
\newlength{\AN@weight}
\DeclareOption{large}{\setlength{\AN@weight}{50}}
\DeclareOption{small}{\setlength{\AN@weight}{100}}
%     \end{macrocode}
% \end{macro}
```

The end of the file finishes the coding and calls \Finale.

```
. . . . . . .
%</package>
%     \end{macrocode}
% \end{macro}\end{macro}
% \Finale
```

E | LATEX and the World Wide Web

Today it is no longer sufficient to produce professional-looking printed output on paper; one has to be able to get it online as well, that is, make it available in electronic form of some kind. To some extent, PostScript output fulfills this requirement in that it may be considered electronic paper. However, as we point out in Section 17.4, true electronic documents are something quite different.

The Internet used to be a nice, quiet neighborhood where academics could exchange simple, plain text e-mails or obtain known files by FTP, until it was invaded by the rowdy *World Wide Web* with its corporate identities, slick advertising, energetic yuppies, anarchists, and revolutionaries. In other words, it went cosmopolitan. Here in this glittering marketplace electronic documents have to compete for attention.

An electronic document is not something that is simply sent to a printer or leisurely viewed on a monitor: It is interactive—it guides the reader to other parts of itself or to other documents located anywhere else on the Web. With these *links*, the viewer can jump to other relevant passages with a mere mouse click. Colored illustrations are naturally part of such documents, but so are sounds and movies, as well as means of sending feedback to the author. This is a totally new medium for information exchange, almost as radical as the Gutenberg revolution from handwritten manuscripts to printed books.

In Section 1.2 we explain the structural similarities between LATEX and the Web languages HTML and XML. Here we point out the possibilities for conversion from LATEX to the others and then how TEX can be used as an engine to render XML documents in LATEX formats. Detailed descriptions of the conversion programs are to be found in the supplied documentation and in the *LATEX Web Companion* (Goossens and Rahtz, 1999). This topic is far too extensive to be covered in this book.

E.1 Converting to HTML

E.1.1 The LATEX2HTML program

The LATEX2HTML translator, written by Nikos Drakos with additions by a large number of contributors, is a comprehensive Perl script that converts a LATEX source file into HTML with the help of several other programs, notably LATEX itself, `dvips`, Ghostscript, and the `netpbm` library of graphics utilities.

When LATEX2HTML processes a LATEX file, it creates a new subdirectory with the same name as that file, to which it writes the resulting HTML output and any generated images as `.gif` files. The program interprets the LATEX input text in the same way as LATEX itself does, but instead of producing typesetting instructions in the `.dvi` file, it writes appropriate HTML code to an `.html` file. For example, `\section{Introduction}` is interpreted as `<H1>Introduction</H1>` for the output.

This means that LATEX2HTML is essentially duplicating the LATEX processing, an enormous undertaking. Since the document classes contain varying commands or have common ones behaving differently, there must be Perl scripts for each one (`article.perl`, and so on) to program these commands properly. Additional packages loaded with `\usepackage` can also define new commands or alter the functionality of existing ones; the translator must be informed about these by means of corresponding Perl scripts. For example, the `natbib` package described in Section 11.3.4 defines citation commands `\citet` and `\citep`, which need to be made available to LATEX2HTML in a file `natbib.perl`. Most of the tools packages of Section B.5.4 are included as Perl scripts, as are many other popular contributed packages. In other words, the entire LATEX2HTML installation must mirror the LATEX one.

This process is somewhat simplified by the fact that both formats are markup languages written in pure typewriter text. However, this similarity soon reaches its limits with the many LATEX features not available in HTML, such as complex math, included figures, and cross-referencing. In the other direction, HTML exhibits hyperlinks, both internally and to external documents, something not provided by normal LATEX.

LATEX2HTML attempts to reproduce math with the limited HTML possibilities, but failing that, formulas are handled the same as figures and other environments that cannot be directly rendered: They are converted to GIF image files along the route `.tex` → `.dvi` → `.ps` → `.pbm` → `.gif`, which are then included in the HTML file as in-line images.

Cross-references and citations are automatically provided with hyperlinks to their targets; the keyword index also links back to the text. Other features of HTML can be included by means of special commands defined in the `html.sty` package. Examples are:

- explicit hyperlinks, internal and external,
- conditional text for the HTML or LATEX versions only,
- raw HTML code,
- segmentation of the HTML output,
- finer image control.

This package thus provides the LATEX writer with a more convenient interface for producing hypertext documents; furthermore, the same document can still be processed with LaTeX to generate the 'paper' version at any time. The conditional text mentioned above allows the electronic and paper versions to exhibit some differences.

LaTeX2HTML is available on the CTAN servers (Figure B.4 on page 384) under the `support` directory. It can also be downloaded from the LaTeX2HTML home page

    http://cbl.leeds.ac.uk/nikos/tex2html/doc/latex2html/latex2html.html

where more information as well as a manual can be obtained.

E.1.2 The TeX4ht program

An alternative program is that by Eitan M. Gurari, called TeX4ht. It produces much the same results as LaTeX2HTML but by a different route. Rather than trying to interpret the LaTeX input text itself, it processes the `.dvi` file to extract the HTML output. It is therefore applicable both to LaTeX and Plain TeX, as its name implies.

In reality, it is not as simple as that. Since the DVI output is normally only a list of typesetting instructions containing no logical markup information at all, it is necessary to process the LaTeX input with the matching `TeX4ht.sty` package that redefines all the regular LaTeX commands to write appropriate code to the `.dvi` file. This is accomplished by means of the `\special` command, a basic TeX command for writing instructions to a particular DVI driver. In this case the driver is the TeX4ht program; no other driver will be able to process this `.dvi` file.

The TeX4ht processor writes the HTML output according to various options specified in the LaTeX input. For example, the HTML output can be segmented by chapters or sections, tables of contents may be added to each segment, and links are automatically established for cross-references. As with LaTeX2HTML, manual links to external documents or internal points can be made, raw HTML coding included, and explicit images included. It is also possible to turn off the HTML conversion in order to produce a normal `.dvi` file; conditional input for whether HTML is on or off is also available.

Any symbols, tables, equations, or imported figures that cannot be directly rendered in HTML are written to a new DVI file, with extension `.idv`, one item per page. Finally, a log file is written containing conversion instructions for each such object; this file is constructed to act as a script, or batch job, for creating GIF images. Just how this conversion is realized and how the instructions are formatted depend on the local installation and can be configured by the user. However, the usual route is something like `.idv` → `.ps` (dvips) → `.ppm` (Ghostscript) → `.gif` (pbm). An example of TeX4ht output with a GIF representation of a math equation can be seen in Figure E.1 on the next page.

Since TeX4ht needs to redefine all the LaTeX markup commands, one could argue that it too is duplicating LaTeX just like LaTeX2HTML. To some extent this is true, although there is a very important difference: Only the markup, not the formatting commands, needs to be massaged. Most classes and additional packages will need no extra configuring to be processed by TeX4ht. A package like `natbib` that adds new citation commands `\citet` and `\citep` will totally confuse LaTeX2HTML without the additional Perl script `natbib.perl`, whereas under TeX4ht these commands will

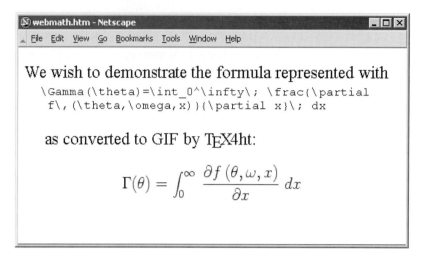

Figure E.1: Example of a math formula converted to HTML by TeX4ht, as a GIF image

produce the correct output text in the HTML file without any additional definitions. (However, the automatic links between the citations and list of references will be missing since this is a markup feature, but the printed text will be all right.)

TeX4ht is available from the TeX Live CD, or from `http://www.cis.ohio-state.edu/~gurari/TeX4ht/mn.html`.

LaTeX2HTML and TeX4ht are only two examples of procedures for creating HTML output from LaTeX. In both cases, one should not try to convert arbitrary LaTeX files, but should view them as a means of producing normal LaTeX and HTML output from a common source file. This source file must be constructed accordingly, possibly with conditional texts for the two outputs, with manual hyperlinks, formatting options for HTML, and so on.

The use of GIF bitmap images for rendering items not readily available in HTML, while producing the visual features on screen, does not allow these objects to be searched for or otherwise further processed. Such images also do not participate in automatic font size changes and other Web manipulations.

E.2   The Extensible Markup Language: XML

It has long been recognized that HTML has many severe limitations. Its simplicity may have been responsible for its rapid rise in popularity, but that simplicity also restricts it to the type of documents for which it was originally intended. Today the Web is offering much more than at the beginning, with databases, search engines, and data verification. HTML is not programmable, so browser suppliers have found it necessary to add additional features of their own that only function with their browser. Standardization is thus destroyed.

What is needed is a means of adding new features to an HTML file so that the browser can be informed of what they mean. This would be like adding new features to a LaTeX file by means of a package. It is to this end that the Web Consortium began the development in 1996 of the *Extensible Markup Language*, or XML.

However, XML is not so much a language as a specification for defining languages in a standard manner. An XML interpreter must be able to determine whether an XML document conforms to the general rules (mainly that all tags are properly closed), in which case it is considered to be *well-formed*, and to the specific syntax of the tags that it uses (as defined in a DTD, Document Type Definition), in which case it is also *valid*. There remains the question of how those tags are to be rendered (how are sections formatted, what to do with cross-references, how to include graphics), which is relegated to *style sheets* documented in the *Extensible Stylesheet Language*, XSL. Here we have true separation between content and format, between logical and typographical markup.

If all this sounds overwhelming, it is! Furthermore, the DTDs are considered too cumbersome and various alternatives have been developed, themselves conforming to XML (which the DTDs do not). This whole area is in transition, but the rewards will be high when a reliable standard for electronic data exchange is achieved. *Data* in this sense is very generic and includes textual documents. We recommend the books by (Marchal, 2000) and (Williamson, 2001), or one can check the Web Consortium home page at `http://www.w3.org/`.

E.2.1   XML and LaTeX

What does all this have to do with LaTeX? Just as the similarity between LaTeX and HTML allows relatively easy conversion, so does the essential similarity with XML. The TeX4ht system has already done the real work of converting LaTeX structure into HTML tags; it is therefore simply a matter of changing the output for each of those tags, something that is put into corresponding configuration files.

Since XML itself is not a language with defined tags, how do we know what those tags are to be? Here we rely on existing DTDs for textual documents. These can be the DocBook DTD developed for software user manuals and other computer documentation, or the TEI DTD, the *Text Encoding Initiative*, meant essentially for general text, including images and sounds.

The TeX4ht collection on the TeX Live CD includes configurations for producing XML output from LaTeX for both of these DTDs. The preamble to the LaTeX source file should then include

```
\usepackage[html]{tex4ht}              for HTML output
\usepackage[xhtml,docbook]{tex4ht}     for XML, DocBook output
\usepackage[xhtml,tei]{tex4ht}         for XML, TEI output
```

One might ask why the author doesn't write an XML file directly as the source document. First, one might very well want to convert older documents recorded in LaTeX to XML. Second, one might find it simpler to write in LaTeX (not everyone agrees) since no one would write an XML file by hand (everyone agrees) but would rely on some application to do it behind the scenes. Certainly LᴬTᴇX source text is easier to read, even when interspersed with commands, than an XML file.

E.2.2   MathML and LᴬTᴇX

One of the strengths of TᴇX, and thus LᴬTᴇX, over other text-processing systems is the ability to handle mathematics in a way that is acceptable to mathematicians. HTML has never been able to even begin to compete in this area. The only way conversion programs like LᴬTᴇX2HTML and TᴇX4ht can render equations like that in Figure E.1 is to convert it to an image file. This is hardly a satisfactory solution.

The MathML project attempts to define an XML language to encode mathematics. We refer to Chapter 8 of the *LᴬTᴇX Web Companion* (Goossens and Rahtz, 1999) for a description. TᴇX4ht can produce output in MathML by specifying

```
\usepackage[xhtml,mathml]{tex4ht}
```

Symbols that do not exist in the browser fonts will still be converted to image files, but instructions are inserted to carry out the placement for fractions and superscripts and subscripts. Unfortunately, most browsers do not recognize MathML (yet). Again, once this becomes established there will be a standard for recording and exchanging documents with complex mathematics.

E.2.3   Rendering XML with TᴇX/LᴬTᴇX

Another role that LᴬTᴇX, or more properly the TᴇX program, can play in the XML world is to translate it to a form that can be viewed or printed as a finished document. This is known as *rendering*.

David Carlisle has written macros in a file `xmltex.tex` to act as an XML parser for output in TᴇX or LᴬTᴇX. Sebastian Rahtz has written an additional macro package, *PassiveTᴇX*, to incorporate an XSL style sheet for the TEI DTD into `xmltex`. With this combination, one can produce DVI or PDF output from a TEI-coded XML file.

There are a number of ways to go about this. The simplest is to write a 'wrapper' file for processing `document.xml` as

```
\def\xmlfile{document.xml}
\input xmltex.tex
```

and then to process this with either LᴬTᴇX or pdfLᴬTᴇX. The PassiveTᴇX macros will be found automatically if they are on the system.

Another means is to generate an `xmltex` format, as described in Section B.1.3. This would be done with

```
initex &latex xmltex.tex        or
tex -ini &latex xmltex.tex
```

to generate a format named `xmltex.fmt`. One can then invoke it with

```
tex &xmltex document.xml
```

or simply with `xmltex document.xml` if an alias or batch file for the command `xmltex` has been defined to equate to the real command.

Instead of using the TeX program, one can also use pdfTeX to generate PDF rather than DVI output.

F

Obsolete LATEX

Since 1994, LATEX 2_ε has replaced LATEX 2.09 as the official version. Although the newer version is backward compatible with the previous one, this is only to allow older source files written for LATEX 2.09 to be processed under LATEX 2_ε; it is not intended that newer files should use the obsolete syntax.

Human nature being conservative as it is, many authors continued to use the commands they were familiar with, and do so even today. The purpose of this chapter is to explain those commands for users who may come across such legacy documents and to indicate to traditional LATEX users which commands they should no longer be employing. It is not meant to be a guide for using LATEX 2.09!

At first sight, the differences seem very slight indeed. In fact, the real changes are mainly internal, allowing packages to be handled more systematically and fonts to be dealt with in a more flexible manner. The advantages of LATEX 2_ε for class and package writers are considerable, as explained in Appendix D. Regular users benefit indirectly by being able to employ these extensions and by being able to activate fonts other than the original Computer Modern families.

F.1 The 2.09 preamble

As for LATEX 2_ε, the document preamble in LATEX 2.09 contains overall specifications for the entire document, including general layout.

F.1.1 Style instead of class

LATEX 2.09 works with *style* rather than class files, so the first command in the source file is

`\documentstyle[`*options*`]{`*style*`}`

rather than \documentclass. Possible values for *style* are article, report, book, or any other main style files that might exist locally. These styles may have various options associated with them, such as 11pt, twoside, and so on, which can be listed in the set of *options*. Not all of the options available with the LaTeX 2_ε class files are recognized by the style files.

The *options* list has an additional function in LaTeX 2.09: For any option in the list that is not recognized by the style file, a file with that name and extension .sty is loaded, if it exists. The original idea of this mechanism was to allow certain options applicable to all styles to have the common coding stored in an extra file rather than repeating it within each main style file. This idea later led to the concept of *packages*.

There is no \usepackage command in LaTeX 2.09; packages can only be loaded with the *options* list, and no options may be specified for the packages.

To start a document with the article style and 12pt option, with the parskip and makeidx packages, one gives

```
\documentstyle[12pt,parskip,makeidx]{article}
```

F.1.2   Compatibility mode

LaTeX 2_ε is designed to be able to process older LaTeX documents with exactly the same output as with LaTeX 2.09. To do this, it recognizes the \documentstyle command that switches it into *compatibility* mode, changing the functionality of many LaTeX 2_ε features. For example, the \usepackage command becomes inoperable, issuing an error message.

With a true LaTeX 2.09 installation, the above \documentstyle example would load the files article.sty, parskip.sty, and makeidx.sty. Under LaTeX 2_ε, in compatibility mode, it first tries to load the main style as a class file with the extension .cls, in this case article.cls, but if that fails it then looks for the extension .sty. This is to handle local main style files that have no class file equivalent. The packages parskip.sty and makeidx.sty are loaded as well. However, they too may recognize the compatibility mode and behave differently from how they would with regular LaTeX 2_ε.

F.2   Font selection

The other major difference between the two versions is font selection. The New Font Selection Scheme (NFSS) and font attributes described in Section 4.1.3 are missing in LaTeX 2.09, as are the font commands \textbf, \texttt, and so on, and the font attribute declarations such as \bfseries and \ttfamily. (They are still available even in LaTeX 2_ε compatibility mode.)

F.2.1   Old font declarations

In LaTeX 2.09, only the two-letter font declarations that originally came from Plain TeX are possible.

\rm	Roman	\it	*Italic*	\sc	Sᴍᴀʟʟ Cᴀᴘs
\bf	**Boldface**	\sl	*Slanted*	\sf	Sans Serif
\tt	Typewriter				

These are all declarations, changing the font until another font declaration is given or until the current environment is ended. They are normally used as {\bf boldface} to yield **boldface**.

The emphasizing declaration \em also belongs to this group, but it has been taken over as part of LATEX 2ε proper.

These old declarations behave differently than their NFSS counterparts: They rigidly select a particular font instead of altering only one attribute, while retaining the current size. Compare:

```
{\sl slanted {\bf bold}}        ⇒   slanted bold
{\slshape slanted {\bfseries bold}}  ⇒   slanted bold
```

It is not possible to obtain slanted or italic boldface with LATEX 2.09 even though such fonts are available.

These two-letter declarations are also retained in the standard LATEX 2ε classes, not just in compatibility mode. Note carefully that wording: They are not part of LATEX 2ε itself, but are only included as part of the standard class files. This means other class files might not provide them, or they might even be removed in some later version (although this is most unlikely). Therefore, their use is not to be encouraged at all.

F.2.2   Font size declarations

In LATEX 2.09, the font-size declarations reset all other font attributes (Section 4.1.3) to their defaults, that is, Roman, upright, medium weight. In LATEX 2ε these attributes remain unchanged. Compare the results of {\sl slanted {\Large larger}}:

LATEX 2.09:   *slanted* larger
LATEX 2ε: *slanted larger*

In LATEX 2ε compatibility mode, the size declarations behave as they do in LATEX 2.09.

F.3   Obsolete means obsolete

Many features have been added to LATEX 2ε, and a number of commands have been given extended syntax in the form of additional optional arguments. We have no intention of indicating them anymore because this book is for the newer version only. (Previous editions did make a distinction.)

Apart from the restrictions pointed out in the above sections, all of the LATEX 2ε features will work in compatibility mode. Nevertheless, we stress once more that compatibility mode is only intended for the processing of older source files. Every effort has been undertaken to ensure that the results are identical to those of processing with the true LATEX 2.09 itself.

Compatibility mode (\documentstyle in place of \documentclass) issues a very strong warning:

```
         Entering LaTeX 2.09 COMPATIBILITY MODE
**********************************************************
    !!WARNING!!     !!WARNING!!     !!WARNING!!     !!WARNING!!

This mode attempts to provide an emulation of the LaTeX 2.09
author environment so that OLD documents can be successfully
processed. It should NOT be used for NEW documents!

New documents should use Standard LaTeX conventions and start
with the \documentclass command.

Compatibility mode is UNLIKELY TO WORK with LaTeX 2.09 style
files that change any internal macros, especially not with
those that change the FONT SELECTION or OUTPUT ROUTINES.

Therefore such style files MUST BE UPDATED to use
         Current Standard LaTeX: LaTeX2e.
If you suspect that you may be using such a style file, which
is probably very, very old by now, then you should attempt to
get it updated by sending a copy of this error message to the
author of that file.
**********************************************************
```

Take this message seriously, and stick to \documentclass.

Command Summary

This appendix contains a brief description of all the LaTeX commands, in alphabetical (ASCII) order, neglecting the leading backslash \\, along with some TeX commands that have been explained in this book. In the following section, the commands are presented in their logical grouping in a number of tables and figures.

G.1 Brief description of the LaTeX commands

For each command in the following summary, the section and page number are given where it is introduced and described in detail. The numbers are shown in the form: '(*Section*) – *Page*': for example (2.5.1) – 13 means 'Section 2.5.1, page 13'.

The following notations may be added to the commands:

[m] those permitted in math mode only,

[a] those belonging to $\mathcal{A}_{\mathcal{M}}S$-LaTeX, and

[p] those allowed only in the preamble.

\␣ . . . . (2.1), (2.7.1) – 22, 32

Normal space between words after a command without arguments or after a period that is not the end of a sentence.

! . . . . (11.4.2) – 223

Field separation character within the \index command. For example: With \index{command!fragile} one produces an index subentry 'fragile' under the main entry 'command'.

!' produces ¡ . . . . (2.5.6) – 27

\! [m] . . . . (7.5.1) – 146

In math mode, a negative space of $-1/6$ quad: xx\!x = xxx.

" . . . . (2.5.2), (11.4.2), (12.2) – 26, 224, 229

1. In normal text, this produces the double closing quote ".

    2. Literal sign for MakeIndex, in order to print one of the special characters !, @, |, or ". Example: \index{"!} to enter character ! without it being interpreted as a separation character.

    3. Delimiter for a text field in BibTeX. Example:
      AUTHOR = "Donald E. Knuth".

\" . . . . (2.5.7) – 27

Produces an umlaut accent: \"{a} = ä.

. . . . (10.3.2), (10.4.2) – 187, 196

Argument replacement character in a user-defined command or environment.

. . . . (10.5.6) – 202

Replacement character for an *internal* argument within a *nested* user-defined command or environment.

\# . . . . (2.5.4) – 27

Command to produce a hash symbol: \# = #.

$ . . . . (7.1) – 121

Toggle character for switching between text and in-line math modes. On the first appearance (text to math) it behaves the same as \(or \begin{math}, while the second call (math to text) is as \) or \end{math}.

\$ . . . . (2.5.4) – 27

Command to produce a dollar sign: \$ = $.

% . . . . (4.7) – 83

Comment character. The rest of the line of text following % is ignored by the TeX processing.

\% . . . . (2.5.4) – 27

Command to produce a percent sign: \% = %.

& . . . . (6.2.1) – 106

Indicates a new column in array and tabular environments.

\& . . . . (2.5.4) – 27

Command to produce an ampersand symbol: \& = &.

\' . . . . (2.5.7), (6.1.4) – 27, 103

    1. Command to produce an acute accent: \'a = á.

    2. Within the tabbing environment, a command to jump to the end of the current column.

( ) . . . . (12.2), (16.1.2) – 230, 298

For a picture command in picture environment, specifies a coordinate pair. In BibTeX, is an alternative form for the outermost grouping of the entry type.

\(. . . . (7.1) – 121

Switches from text to in-line math mode to produce formulas within a line of text. It functions the same as \begin{math} and as a $ sign in text mode.

\) . . . . (7.1) – 121

Switches back from in-line math mode to text mode. It functions the same as \end{math} and as a $ sign in math mode.

\+ . . . . (6.1.3) – 102

Within the tabbing environment, increments the left margin by one tab stop (moves it to the right).

\, ... (2.7.1), (7.5.1) – 32, 146

Small space, the size of 1/6 quad, for use in text and math mode: xx\,x = $xx\,x$.

¯ . . . . (2.5.3) – 26

As -, produces the hyphen - for compound words and word division, as --, the en dash –, and as ---, the em dash —.

\- . . . . (2.8.1), (6.1.3) – 38, 102

1. Denotes possible word division. If a word contains at least one \- the normal word division rules are suspended for that word and division may occur *only* at those locations.

2. Within the tabbing environment, decrements the left margin by one tab stop (moves it to the left).

\. . . . . (2.5.7) – 27

Command to produce a dot accent: \.o = ȯ.

\/ . . . . (2.5.10) – 30

Command to break up ligatures: shelf\/ful = shelfful.

\: [m] . . . . (7.5.1) – 146

In math mode, a medium space, the size of 2/9 quad: xx\:x = $xx\:x$.

\; [m] . . . . (7.5.1) – 146

In math mode, a large space, the size of 5/18 quad: xx\;x = $xx\;x$.

\< . . . . (6.1.3) – 102

Within the tabbing environment, moves to the left by one tab stop.

\= . . . . (2.5.7), (6.1.1) – 27, 101

1. Command to produce a macron accent: \=o = ō.

2. Within the tabbing environment, sets a tab stop at the current position within the line.

\> . . . . (6.1.1) – 101

Within the `tabbing` environment, moves right to the next tab stop.

?' produces ¿ . . . . (2.5.6) – 27

@ . . . . (11.4.2), (12.2) – 223, 229

1. In MakeIndex, separates an entry in an `\index` command into a lexical (for alphabetization) and printing part. Example: `\index{sum@$\sum$}` means that the entry appears in the index at the location of the word 'sum', but what is printed is the summation sign $\sum$.

2. In BibTeX, denotes the *entry type*. Example: @BOOK indicates that the following literature entries correspond to those of a book.

\@ . . . . (2.7.1) – 32

Extra space at the end of a sentence ending with a capital letter.

[ ] . . . . (2.1) – 22

After commands or environment calls, specifies an optional argument.

\[. . . . (7.1) – 122

Switches from text mode to displayed math mode for putting a formula on a line by itself. Has the same effect as `\begin{displaymath}` or $$ in text mode.

\\[*space*] . . . . (2.7.2) – 34

Ends the current line (without right justifying it). The optional argument [*space*] inserts additional vertical spacing of length *space* before the next line.

*[*space*] . . . . (2.7.2) – 34

The same as \\ but prevents a page break from occurring between the current and next line.

\] . . . . (7.1) – 122

Switches back from displayed math mode to text mode. Has the same effect as `\end{displaymath}` or $$ in math mode.

^ [m] . . . . (7.2.2) – 123

Exponents and superscripts in equations: $x^2 = x^2$, $x^{-2n} = x^{-2n}$.

\^ . . . . (2.5.7) – 27

Command to produce a circumflex accent: $\^o = \hat{o}$.

_ [m] . . . . (7.2.2) – 123

Subscripts in equations: $a_n = a_n$, $a_{i,j,k} = a_{i,j,k}$.

_ . . . . (2.5.4) – 27

Command to produce the underbar sign: $t\_v = t_v$.

\` . . . . (2.5.7), (6.1.4) – 27, 103

    1. Command to produce a grave accent: \`o = ò.

    2. Within the `tabbing` environment, pushes the following text up against the right margin of the line.

{ } . . . . (2.1), (2.2), (12.2) – 22, 23, 229

    1. After a command or environment call, specifies a mandatory argument.

    2. Grouping a section of text to create a nameless environment.

    3. In BIBTEX, delimiting the name of an entry type, as well as an alternative delimiter for the text field.

\{ produces a left curly brace: \{ = { . . . . (2.5.4) – 27

| [m] produces | . . . . (7.3.4), (7.4.1) – 128, 134

| . . . . (11.4.2) – 224

    In MakeIndex, the command character within a \index command.

    1. After the command \newcommand{\ii}[1]{\textit{#1}} has been defined, \index{entry|ii} produces the page number for 'entry' in the index in italic type.

    2. The cross-reference command \see from `makeidx.sty` can be invoked with \index{bison|see{buffalo}} to produce cross-references within the index.

\| [m] produces || . . . . (7.3.6) – 129

\} produces a right curly brace: \} = } . . . . (2.5.4) – 27

~ . . . . (2.7.1) – 32

    A normal space between words, but without the possibility that the line will be broken there. Example: Prof.~Jones ensures that 'Prof.' and 'Jones' both remain on the same line.

\~ . . . . (2.5.7) – 27

    Command to produce a tilde accent: \~n = ñ.

\a= . . . . (6.1.4) – 103

    Produces a macron accent within `tabbing` environment: \a=o = ō.

\a' . . . . (6.1.4) – 103

    Produces an acute accent within `tabbing` environment: \a'o = ó.

\a\` . . . . (6.1.4) – 103

    Produces a grave accent within `tabbing` environment: \a\`o = ò.

`\AA` produces Å . . . . (2.5.6) – 27

`\aa` produces å . . . . (2.5.6) – 27

`\abovedisplayshortskip` [m] . . . . (7.5.4) – 149

> Vertical space between a *short* displayed equation and the preceding line of text. A new value may be assigned with the `\setlength` command as in the above example.

`\abovedisplayskip` [m] . . . . (7.5.4) – 149

> Vertical space between a *long* displayed equation and the preceding line of text. A new value may be assigned with the `\setlength` command:
>
> `\setlength{\abovedisplayskip}{10pt plus2pt minus5pt}`

`\abstractname` . . . . (D.3.1) – 441

> Command containing the heading for the abstract. In English, this is 'Abstract', but may be altered for adaptation to other languages.

`\acute{x}` [m] . . . . (7.3.9) – 131

> Acute accent over math variable *x*: `\acute{a}` = á

`\addcontentsline{`*file*`}{`*format*`}{`*entry*`}` . . . . (3.4.3), (3.4.4) – 61, 62

> Manual addition of *entry* into the list file `.toc`, `.lof`, or `.lot`, according to the value of *file*, to be formatted as the heading of a sectioning command, as given by *format*; for example
>
> `\addcontentsline{toc}{section}{References}`

`\address{`*sender*`}` . . . . (18.1) – 345

> In the `letter` document class, enters the sender's address. Multiple lines in *sender* are separated by `\\`.

`\addtocontents{`*file*`}{`*entry*`}` . . . . (3.4.3), (3.4.4) – 61, 62

> Manual addition of *entry* into the list file `.toc`, `.lof`, or `.lot`, according to the value of *file*. Example:
>
> `\addtocontents{lof}{\protect\newpage}`

`\addtocounter{`*counter*`}{`*number*`}` . . . . (10.1.3) – 182

> Adds *number* to the current value of the number stored in *counter*.

`\addtolength{`*length_name*`}{`*length*`}` . . . . (10.2) – 184

> Adds the quantity *length* to the current value of the length command `\`*length_name*.

`\addvspace{`*length*`}` . . . . (10.2) – 184

> Inserts vertical spacing of amount *length* between paragraphs at the point where the command is given. If other vertical spacing exists, the total will not exceed *length*.

With the amsmath package, allows automatic page breaks to occur within multiline math formulas. If *num* is present, it takes a value of 0-4 to increase the ease with which page breaks occur. Without this command, a manual page break can be made at the end of any formula line with \displaybreak.

Prints the current value of *counter* as a capital letter.

Prints the current value of *counter* as a lowercase letter.

Command for use in the makeidx package. It prints the text for a command \seealso. In English, this is 'see also', but it may be altered for adaptation to other languages.

Used to separate author names within the \author command for generating a title page with \maketitle.

Command containing the heading for the appendix. In English, this is 'Appendix', but may be altered for adaptation to other languages.

Prints the current value of *counter* as an Arabic number.

Command to produce the function name 'arccos' in equations.

Command to produce the function name 'arcsin' in equations.

Command to produce the function name 'arctan' in equations.

\arg [m] . . . . (7.3.8) – 130

Command to produce the function name 'arg' in equations.

\arraycolsep . . . . (6.2.2) – 107

Half the width of the intercolumn spacing in the array environment. Value is assigned with the LaTeX command \setlength:

    \setlength{\arraycolsep}{3mm}

\arrayrulewidth . . . . (6.2.2) – 107

The thickness of vertical and horizontal lines in the array and tabular environments. Its value is assigned to a length with \setlength:

    \setlength{\arrayrulewidth}{0.5mm}

\arraystretch . . . . (6.2.2) – 108

Factor to change the spacing between lines in a table, normal value being 1. Spacing is multiplied by this factor, which is set to a new value with \renewcommand{\arraystretch}{*factor*}.

\ast [m] produces $*$ . . . . (7.3.3) – 127

\asymp [m] produces $\asymp$ . . . . (7.3.4) – 128

\AtBeginDocument{*code*} [p] . . . . (D.2.4) – 433

Stores the *code* to be inserted into the processing stream when \begin{document} is executed. Commands that are only allowed in the preamble may be part of *code*. A package might include coding in this way to ensure that it is not overwritten by another package.

\AtEndDocument{*code*} [p] . . . . (D.2.4) – 433

Stores the *code* to be inserted into the processing stream when \end{document} is executed. A package might include coding in this way to have additional features printed automatically at the end of the document.

\AtEndOfClass{*code*} [p] . . . . (D.2.4) – 433

Stores the *code* to be inserted into the processing stream when the current class file has finished being read. May only be given in a class file or in another file that is read by a class file. May be used by a local configuration file to overwrite defaults in the class file itself.

\AtEndOfPackage{*code*} [p] . . . . (D.2.4) – 433

Stores the *code* to be inserted into the processing stream when the current package file has finished being read. May only be given in a package file or in another file that is read by a package file. May be used by a local configuration file to overwrite defaults in the package file itself.

\author{*name*} . . . . (3.3.1) – 55

Enters the author name(s) for a title page produced by the \maketitle command.

\b{x} . . . . (2.5.7) – 27

> Command to produce an underbar accent: \b{o} = o̲.

\backmatter . . . . (3.3.5) – 60

> In the book class, introduces the material that comes at the end (bibliography, index) by turning off the chapter numbering of the \chapter command.

\backslash [m] produces \ . . . . (7.3.6) – 129

\bar{x} [m] . . . . (7.3.9) – 131

> Macron accent over the math variable x: \bar{a} = $\bar{a}$.

\baselineskip . . . . (4.1.2) – 65

> Interline spacing within a paragraph. Every font has its own internal line spacing. A new value (a rubber length) may be assigned with \setlength:
>
>   \setlength{\baselineskip}{12pt plus2pt minus1pt}

\baselinestretch . . . . (3.2.4), (4.1.2) – 49, 65

> A factor with the normal value of 1 by which the internal length \baselineskip is multiplied to produce the actual interline spacing. May be changed with:
>
>   \renewcommand{\baselinestretch}{*factor*}
>
> The new value takes effect after the next change in font size!

\begin{*envrnmnt*} . . . . (2.2) – 23

> Start of an environment with the name *envrnmnt*. This command must be coupled with \end{*envrnmnt*} to terminate the environment. The environment name in both these commands must be identical.

\begin{abstract} . . . . (3.3.2) – 57

> Start of the environment abstract to produce an abstract. With document class article, font size \small and the quotation environment are selected. With report, the abstract appears on a separate page with normal font size and line width. In both cases, the heading **Abstract** is centered above the text.

\begin{align} [a] . . . . (15.2.6) – 285

> With the amsmath package, switches to displayed math mode to produce a set of aligned equations. Line are terminated by \\ commands. The lines are split into columns aligned on the first, third, fifth . . . & characters. Each line receives an equation number unless the *-form of the environment has been selected.

\begin{alignat}{*num*} [a] . . . . (15.2.6) – 286

> Is the same as the align environment except that no spacing is inserted automatically between the column pairs. The argument *num* is the number of column pairs = $(1 + n_\&)/2$ where $n_\&$ is the number of & signs in one row. Explicit spacing may be placed between column pairs, especially if the left part of that pair is otherwise empty.

`\begin{aligned}`[*pos*] [m][a]   . . . .   (15.2.6) – 287

With the `amsmath` package, is like the `align` environment but is used as an element within math mode. The optional argument *pos* determines the vertical positioning relative to neighboring elements: t or b for top or bottom, no argument for centering.

`\begin{appendix}`   . . . .   (3.3.4) – 59

Start of the environment `appendix` to produce an appendix. The main section counter is reset to zero and its numbering appears as capital letters.

`\begin{array}`[*pos*]{*col*} [m]   . . . .   (6.2.1), (7.4.3) – 105, 135

Start of the environment `array` to produce matrices and arrays in math mode. The column definition *col* contains a formatting character for each column. Thus `\begin{array}{lcr}` produces an array with three columns: one *left justified*, one *centered*, and one *right justified*. The optional parameter *pos* determines how the array is aligned vertically with text outside it on the same line: t with the top line, b with the bottom line, while the default is with the center. See also `\begin{tabular}`.

`\begin{center}`   . . . .   (4.2.1) – 67

Start of the environment `center`. Each line of text terminated by \\ appears centered. See also `\centering`.

`\begin{`*command_name*`}`   . . . .   (2.2) – 23

Most declaration commands, such as the font styles and sizes, can be used as environment names. For example, `\begin{small}` switches to font size `\small` until the terminating `\end{small}` is given.

`\begin{alltt}`   . . . .   (4.6.1) – 82

When the `alltt` package has been loaded, this environment prints out original text in typewriter typeface, maintaining line breaks, special symbols, and so on, except for \ { }, which function as usual. This allows commands to be executed within the typewriter text.

`\begin{bmatrix}` [m][a]   . . . .   (15.2.4) – 277

Like the `matrix` environment, but enclosed in square brackets [].

`\begin{Bmatrix}` [m][a]   . . . .   (15.2.4) – 277

Like the `matrix` environment, but enclosed in curly braces { }.

`\begin{cases}` [m][a]   . . . .   (15.2.6) – 288

With the `amsmath` package, writes math expressions on several lines, terminated by \\, in left-justified columns, separated by &, with a curly brace enclosing all lines at the left, the whole command being centered vertically.

`\begin{description}`   . . . .   (4.3.3) – 71

Start of the environment `description` to produce an indented list with labels. The label text is the argument *label* in the command `\item[`*label*`]`.

`\begin{displaymath}` . . . . (7.1) – 122
   Switches from text to displayed math mode for producing a formula on a line by
   itself. Functions the same as `\[`.

`\begin{document}` . . . . (1.5.2) – 12
   Start of the outermost environment of a text document. This command terminates the preamble. It is obligatory for every LaTeX document, as is its counterpart
   `\end{document}` for ending the document.

`\begin{enumerate}` . . . . (4.3.2) – 70
   Start of the environment `enumerate` to produce a numbered, indented listing.
   The style of numbering depends on the depth of nesting; at the first level, it
   consists of a running Arabic number that is incremented with each call to `\item`.

`\begin{eqnarray}` [m] . . . . (7.4.7) – 140
   Switches from text to displayed math mode to produce a set of equations or
   a multiline formula in the form of a three-column table `{rcl}`. The individual
   lines of the formula are ended with the command `\\`; the fields within a line
   are separated by & characters. Each line is given a sequential equation number
   unless the command `\nonumber` appears within it.

`\begin{eqnarray*}` [m] . . . . (7.4.7) – 140
   Is the same as the `eqnarray` environment except that no equation numbers are
   printed.

`\begin{equation}` [m] . . . . (7.1) – 122
   Switches from text to displayed math mode to produce a formula on a line by
   itself, including an automatic sequential equation number.

`\begin{falign}` [a] . . . . (15.2.6) – 286
   With the `amsmath` package, is the same as the `align` environment except that
   spacing is inserted between the column pairs to fill up the entire line.

`\begin{figure}`[*loc*] . . . . (9.1) – 169
   Float environment for entering text for a figure. The optional argument *loc* can be
   any combination of the letters h, t, b, and p to determine the various positioning
   possibilities. Default is tbp. The character ! may additionally be given to ignore
   all float spacing and number restrictions set by the float style parameters.

`\begin{figure*}`[*loc*] . . . . (9.1) – 169
   The same as the `figure` environment except that the figure is inserted over the
   width of two columns when the option `twocolumn` or the command `\twocolumn`
   has been selected. The standard form `figure` will only fill the width of one
   column.

`\begin{filecontents}{`*file_name*`}` [p] . . . . (D.2.9) – 438
   An environment that may be given only before `\documentclass`, it writes its
   lines literally to a file of the specified name if that file does not already exist. It
   also adds comment lines stating its source. In this way, nonstandard files may be
   included in the main document file for shipment to other installations. If a file
   with the stated name already exists, it is not overwritten, but a warning message
   is issued.

`\begin{filecontents*}{`*file_name*`}` [p] . . . . (D.2.9) – 438

> Is the same as the `filecontents` environment except that no comment lines are written to the file. The file will contain exactly the contents of the environment and nothing more.

`\begin{flushleft}` . . . . (4.2.2) – 68

> Start of the `flushleft` environment in which each line of text is left justified; that is, it begins flush with the left margin but is not expanded to match the right edge. The equivalent declaration is `\raggedright`.

`\begin{flushright}` . . . . (4.2.2) – 68

> Start of the `flushright` environment in which each line of text is right justified; that is, the right-hand side is flush with the right margin, but the line is not expanded to start exactly at the left edge. The equivalent declaration is `\raggedleft`.

`\begin{gather}` [a] . . . . (15.2.6) – 284

> With the `amsmath` package, switches to displayed math mode to produce several lines of equations, all centered with no alignment. Lines are terminated by `\\` commands. Each line receives an equation number unless the *-form of the environment has been selected.

`\begin{gathered}[`*pos*`]` [m][a] . . . . (15.2.6) – 287

> With the `amsmath` package, is like the `gather` environment but is used as an element within math mode. The optional argument *pos* determines the vertical positioning relative to neighboring elements: t or b for top or bottom, no argument for centering.

`\begin{itemize}` . . . . (4.3.1) – 70

> Start of the `itemize` environment for producing labeled, indented listings. The type of label depends on the depth of nesting; at the first level it is a • generated by each `\item` command.

`\begin{letter}{`*recipient*`}` . . . . (18.1) – 346

> Start of a letter with the document class `letter`. Name and address of the *recipient* are given within the second pair of brackets; lines of text within this argument are ended with the command `\\`.

`\begin{list}{`*standard_label*`}{`*list_decl*`}` . . . . (4.4) – 74

> Start of a generalized list environment. The label is defined by *standard_label*, which is generated by each `\item` command. The desired list declarations are contained in *list_decl* (see page 75).

`\begin{longtable}` . . . . (6.2.4) – 117

> With the `longtable` package, begins a table with the same syntax as `tabular` but which will continue to other pages as necessary. The head- and footlines on the continued pages can be specified, terminated with `\endhead`, `\endfirsthead`, `\endfoot`, `\endlastfoot`.

`\begin{lrbox}{\`*boxname*`}`   . . . . (5.1.1) – 87

Functions in a way similar to the command `\sbox` except that the text of the environment is stored in the LR box named `\`*boxname*, which has previously been created with `\newsavebox{\`*boxname*`}`. The contents of the box may be printed as often as desired with `\usebox{\`*boxname*`}`.

`\begin{math}`   . . . . (7.1) – 121

Switches from text to in-line math mode to produce formulas within a line of text. This environment has the same effect as `\(` or `$` in text mode.

`\begin{matrix}` [m][a]   . . . . (15.2.4) – 277

With the `amsmath` package, is the same as the `array` environment except that the column specifier argument may be omitted, without which up to 10 centered columns may be entered. This maximum may be changed with the counter `MaxMatrixCols`. The environments `pmatrix`, `bmatrix`, `Bmatrix`, `vmatrix`, and `Vmatrix` function the same as `matrix` but are enclosed in braces (), [], {}, | |, and ‖ ‖, respectively.

`\begin{minipage}` [*pos*] [*height*] [*inner_pos*] {*width*}
. . . . (5.1.3), (5.1.5) – 88, 90

Environment to format text within a 'minipage' of width *width*. Its vertical positioning with respect to the surrounding text is determined by the optional argument *pos*: t for alignment with its top line, b with its bottom line, and centered with no argument. The other two optional arguments are *height* to give the total height and *inner_pos* to specify how the text is to be positioned inside it. Possible values are t for top, b for bottom, c for centered, and s to be stretched out to fill the whole vertical space. The default is the value of the external positioning *pos* option. The *height* argument may contain the parameters `\height`, `\depth`, `\width`, and `\totalheight`.

`\begin{multicols}{`*num_cols*`}` [*header*] [*pre_space*]
. . . . (3.2.8), (B.5.4) – 54, 388

This environment is provided by the `multicol` package in the tools collection (Section B.5.4). It switches to printing the text in *num_cols* columns, with *header* printed in one column across the top. A new page is inserted only if the remaining space on the current page is less than `\premulticols` or the optional argument *pre_space*. A new page is inserted at the end if the remaining space is less than `\postmulticols`. The columns on the last page are balanced. Column separation and rule are set by the lengths `\columnsep` and `\columnseprule`.

With the starred version `multicols*`, the columns of text are not balanced on the last page of the environment.

`\begin{multline}` [a]   . . . . (15.2.6) – 282

With the `amsmath` package, switches to displayed math mode to produce a single equation over several lines. Line breaks are forced by `\\` commands. The first line is to the far left, the last to the right, all others centered. With `\shoveleft{`*form*`}` and `\shoveright{`*form*`}`, single lines consisting of *form* may be pushed to the

left or right. The single equation number appears at the right of the last line
or at the left of the first line, depending on class options `reqno` (default) and
`leqno`, respectively. With the *-form of the environment, the equation number is
suppressed.

`\begin{note}` . . . . (17.1.2) – 322

In `slides` class, the environment for producing a note for the current slide.
Notes are numbered with the current slide number followed by a hyphen and
running number, for example 8-1, 8-2, and so on.

`\begin{overlay}` . . . . (17.1.2) – 321

In `slides` class, the environment for producing an overlay for the current slide.
Overlays are numbered with the current slide number followed by a lowercase
letter, for example 3-a, 3-b, and so on. See also `\begin{slide}`.

`\begin{picture}`(x_dimen, y_dimen) . . . . (16.1.2) – 298

Environment to generate a picture with the width x_dimen and height y_dimen,
where the unit of length has previously been specified by the declaration
`\unitlength`.

`\begin{picture}`(x_dimen, y_dimen)(x_offset, y_offset) . . . . . (16.1.6) – 311

Most general form of the call to the `picture` environment. The picture is displaced to the left by x_offset and downwards by y_offset.

`\begin{pmatrix}` [m][a] . . . . (15.2.4) – 277

Like the `matrix` environment, but enclosed in round parentheses ().

`\begin{quotation}` . . . . (4.2.3) – 68

Start of the `quotation` environment in which text is indented on both sides
relative to the normal page margins. Paragraphs within the environment are
marked with an additional indentation of the first line.

`\begin{quote}` . . . . (4.2.3) – 68

The same as the `quotation` environment except that the first line of a paragraph
is not indented; instead, additional line spacing comes between paragraphs.

`\begin{slide}` . . . . (17.1.2), (17.2.1) – 321, 324

In `slides` and `seminar` classes, the main environment for producing a slide.

`\begin{sloppypar}` . . . . (2.8.3) – 39

Inside this environment word spacings are allowed to stretch more generously
than usual so that paragraphs are broken up into lines with fewer word divisions.
See also `\sloppy`.

`\begin{split}` [m][a] . . . . (15.2.6) – 283

With the `amsmath` package, this is used within a math environment such as
`equation` to write a formula over several lines. Line breaks are forced with `\\`
commands, and the lines are horizontally aligned on the & alignment marker.
Any equation number is generated by the outer environment, its position being
determined by class options `centertags`, `tbtags`, `reqno`, and `leqno`.

\begin{subarray}{*pos*}{*1st line*\\..*last line*} [m][a] . . . . . (15.2.2) – 273

With the amsmath package, sets multiline text for superscripts and subscripts, such as \substack, but the parameter *pos* may take on values c or l for centered or left-justified lines.

\begin{subequations} [a] . . . . (15.2.7) – 289

With the amsmath package, numbers equations within it with a fixed main number and sequence of lowercase letters attached, as 7a, 7b, 7c, and so forth.

\begin{tabbing} . . . . (6.1.1) – 101

Start of the tabbing environment in which special tabbing commands become operational: \= sets a tab stop, \> jumps to the next stop, \< goes back a stop, \\ terminates and starts a new line, \+ sets the left margin one tab stop further, and \- moves the left margin back one stop.

\begin{table}[*loc*] . . . . (6.2.5), (9.1) – 118, 169

Float environment for entering text for a table. The optional argument *loc* can be any combination of the letters h, t, b, and p to determine the various positioning possibilities. Default is tbp. The character ! may additionally be given to ignore all float spacing and number restrictions set by the float style parameters.

\begin{table*}[*loc*] . . . . (9.1) – 169

The same as the table environment except that the table is inserted over the width of two columns when the option twocolumn or the command \twocolumn has been selected. The standard form table will only fill the width of one column.

\begin{tabular}[*pos*]{*cols*} . . . . (6.2.1) – 105

Start of the tabular environment for producing tables. The argument *cols* contains a formatting character for each column in the table: c for centered text, l for left, r for right justification, or p{*wd*} for a column of width *wd* in which the text may extend over several lines.

When the entry @{*text*} appears between any two of the above column formatting characters, *text* is inserted in every row between those two columns. Where the character | appears, a vertical line is drawn in every row.

The optional argument *pos* specifies how the table is to be vertically aligned with the surrounding text: With no argument, it is centered; otherwise, with t the top line is aligned with the external baseline, with b, the bottom line.

The text entries of the individual columns are separated by &, and the rows are terminated by \\.

\begin{tabular*}{*width*}[*pos*]{*cols*} . . . . (6.2.1) – 105

The same as \begin{tabular} except that the total width of the table is given by the argument *width*. This may only be achieved successfully if there is rubber spacing between the columns. This may be added with @{\extracolsep\fill} somewhere within the *cols* format definition.

`\begin{thebibliography}{`*sample_label*`}` . . . . (11.3.1) – 215

Environment to generate a list of literature references. The *sample_label* is the longest reference marker that will appear. Each entry in the bibliography starts with the command `\bibitem`, which prints the marker for that entry; lines after the first are indented by an amount equal to the width of *sample_label*.

`\begin{theindex}` . . . . (11.4.1) – 222

Environment to produce a keyword index in two-column format. Entries are made with the `\item`, `\subitem`, `\subsubitem`, or `\indexspace` commands.

`\begin{`*theorem_type*`}[`*extra_title*`]` . . . . (4.5) – 80

Environment to invoke a theorem-like structure that has previously been defined by the user with the `\newtheorem` command. The name of the environment, *theorem_type*, something like `theorem` or `axiom`, is the first argument of the `\newtheorem` command. The *extra_title* is text that is added after the name and number of the structure in () parentheses.

`\begin{titlepage}` . . . . (3.3.1) – 57

Environment to produce a title page without a page number. The user has total control over the composition of this page.

`\begin{trivlist}` . . . . (4.4.5) – 79

Environment to generate a trivial list *without* a sample label and list declarations. The parameters `\leftmargin`, `\labelwidth`, and `\itemsep` are all set to 0 pt while `\listparindent` = `\parindent` and `\parsep` = `\parskip`.

`\begin{verbatim}` . . . . (4.6) – 81

Environment to print out source text, that is, as from a typewriter. Blank lines, line breaking, and commands are all output literally without any interpretation or formatting.

`\begin{verbatim*}` . . . . (4.6) – 81

The same as the `verbatim` environment except that blanks are printed as ␣ to make them visible.

`\begin{verse}` . . . . (4.2.4) – 69

Environment for setting rhymes, poems, verses, and so on. Stanzas are separated by blank lines, individual lines by the `\\` command.

`\begin{vmatrix} [m][a]` . . . . (15.2.4) – 277

Like the `matrix` environment but enclosed in vertical lines | |.

`\begin{Vmatrix} [m][a]` . . . . (15.2.4) – 277

Like the `matrix` environment but enclosed in double vertical lines ‖ ‖.

`\belowdisplayshortskip [m]` . . . . (7.5.4) – 150

Vertical spacing between a *short* displayed formula and the following text. Value is set with the `\setlength` command as in the above example.

`\belowdisplayskip` [m] . . . . (7.5.4) – 149

Vertical spacing between a *long* displayed formula and the following text. A new value may be assigned with the `\setlength` command:

`\setlength{\belowdisplayskip}{\abovedisplayskip}`

which sets `\belowdisplayskip` to the same value as `\abovedisplayskip`. See further examples under `\abovedisplayskip`.

`\beta` [m] produces β . . . . (7.3.1) – 127

`\bfdefault` . . . . (A.2.1) – 365

This command defines the series attribute that is selected with the `\bfseries` command. It may be redefined with `\renewcommand`:

`\renewcommand{\bfdefault}{b}`

`\bfseries` . . . . (4.1.3), (A.2) – 66, 365

This declaration switches to a font in the current family and shape but with the **bold** series attribute.

`\bibitem`[*label*]{*key*} *entry_text* . . . . (11.3.1), (11.3.4) – 215, 218

Command to enter the text for a literature reference in the `thebibliography` environment. The reference word *key* is used in the main body of the text with citation commands to refer to this entry. In standard LATEX, the bibliography list will be sequentially numbered except for those entries with an optional *label*, in which case *label* replaces the number. In author-year bibliographies, the *label* must have a special form to transfer author and year texts to the citation commands.

`\bibliography`{*file_list*} . . . . (11.3.2), (12.1) – 217, 227

For producing a bibliography with the aid of the BIBTEX program; *file_list* is the root name of one or more files containing the literature databases to be searched.

`\bibliographystyle`{*style*} . . . . (11.3.2), (12.1) – 216, 228

In conjunction with the BIBTEX program, this command selects the style in which the bibliography entries are to be written. Choices for *style* are `plain`, `unsrt`, `alpha`, and `abbrv`, or `plainnat`, `unsrtnat`, `abbrvnat` with `natbib`. Many other contributed styles also exist.

`\bibname` . . . . (D.3.1) – 441

Command containing the heading for the bibliography in `book` and `report` document classes. In English, this is 'Bibliography', but it may be altered for adaptation to other languages.

`\big`*br_symbol* [m] . . . . (7.5.3) – 149

A bracket symbol larger than normal but smaller than `\Big`. Example: `\big(`.

`\Big`*br_symbol* [m] . . . . (7.5.3) – 149

A bracket symbol larger than `\big` but smaller than `\bigg`. Example: `\Big[`.

> A bracket symbol larger than `\Big` but smaller than `\Bigg`. Example: `\bigg|`.

> The largest bracket symbol. Example: `\Bigg\langle`.

> Inserts large vertical spacing of the amount `\bigskipamount`. See also `\medskip` and `\smallskip`.

`\bigskipamount`

> Standard value for the amount of vertical spacing that is inserted with the command `\bigskip`. May be changed with the `\setlength` command:
>
>   `\setlength{\bigskipamount}{5ex plus1.5ex minus2ex}`

> With the amsmath package, prints a binomial expression:
>
>   `\[\binom{n}{k}\]` yields $\binom{n}{k}$.

> Command to produce the function name 'mod' in the form
>
>   `a\bmod b` = $a \bmod b$

> Switches to boldface for math mode. This command must be given in text mode, however, before going into math mode. To set only part of a formula in boldface, use `\mbox{\boldmath$...$}` to return temporarily to text mode.

\boldsymbol{*symbol*} [m][a] . . . . (15.2.1) – 270

> When one of the packages amsmath or amsbsy has been loaded, this command prints *symbol* in boldface. Unlike \mathbf, it also affects math symbols and lowercase Greek letters.

\bot [m] produces ⊥ . . . . (7.3.6) – 129

\botfigrule . . . . (9.3) – 173

> A command that is executed before a float at the bottom of a page. It is normally defined to do nothing, but may be redefined to add a rule between the float and the main text. It must not add any net vertical spacing.
>
>   \renewcommand{\botfigrule}{\vspace*{-.4pt}
>   \rule{\columnwidth}{.4pt}}

\bottomfraction . . . . (9.3) – 172

> Maximum fraction of a page that may be taken up by floats at the bottom. May be set to a new value with:
>
>   \renewcommand{\bottomfraction}{*decimal_frac*}.

bottomnumber . . . . (9.3) – 171

> Maximum number of floats that may appear at the bottom of a page. Set to a new number with \setcounter{bottomnumber}{*num*}.

\bowtie [m] produces ⋈ . . . . (7.3.4) – 128

\Box [m] produces □ . . . . (7.3.3) – 127

\boxed{*formula*} [m][a] . . . . (15.2.5) – 281

> With the amsmath package, sets the mathematical *formula* in a box.

\breve{*x*} [m] . . . . (7.3.9) – 131

> Breve accent over the math variable x: \breve{a} = $\breve{a}$.

\bullet [m] produces • . . . . (7.3.3) – 127

\c{*x*} . . . . (2.5.7) – 27

> Produces a cedilla under x: \c{C} = Ç.

\cap [m] produces ∩ . . . . (7.3.3) – 127

\caption[*short_form*]{*caption_text*} . . . . (9.4) – 173

> Produces a numbered title or caption with the text *caption_text* within the float environments figure or table. The *short_form* is the abbreviated text appearing in the list of figures or tables, which is the same as the *caption_text* if it is omitted.

\captions*language* . . . . (14.1), (D.3.1) – 267, 442

> A command used in several language adaptations to redefine the headings of special sections, such as 'Chapter' and 'Contents'. It occurs in packages like german as well as in the babel system. This command is normally part of the definition of the \selectlanguage command.

Command within document class `letter` to generate 'cc:', copies, followed by a
list of names *list* at the end of the letter.

Command in the `letter` document class containing the word to be printed by
the \cc command. In English, this is 'cc', but it may be altered for adaptation to
other languages.

Declaration to switch to centered lines of text, each input line being terminated
by \\. See also \begin{center}.

An additional TeX command that sets *text* centered on a horizontal line by itself.

With the `amsmath` package, produces a continued fraction. The optional argument
pos may be l or r to have the numerator left or right justified on the horizontal
rule; otherwise it is centered.

Starts a new chapter on a new page, with an automatic sequential chapter number
and *title* as header. If the optional *short title* is given, it appears in place of *title*
in the table of contents and in the running head at the top of the pages.

Starts a new chapter on a new page, with *title* as header, but without a chapter
number. The entry does not appear in the table of contents.

Command containing the chapter heading. In English, this is 'Chapter', but it
may be altered for adaptation to other languages.

Háček accent over the math variable x: \check{a} = $\check{a}$.

Tests that the current definition of *com_name* is as expected. If not, an error
message is issued. This is used to ensure that important commands have not
been altered by other packages.

Picture element command to produce a circle with diameter *diameter* in the
`picture` environment. To be used as an argument in a \put or \multiput
command.

\circle*{*diameter*} . . . . (16.1.4) – 305

Like \circle but produces a solid circle, filled in black.

\cite[*note*]{*key*} . . . . (11.3.3), (12.1) – 217, 227

Literature citation using the identifier *key* to produce a reference label in the text. The optional *note* text is included with the label.

\citep[*pre-note*][*post-note*]{*key*} . . . . (11.3.4) – 218

With the natbib package, inserts a parenthetical literature citation as '[Jones et al., 1999]', using the identifier *key*. The optional note texts are included within the parentheses, before and after; if only one is present, it is a *post-note*. In numerical citation mode, the citation number is printed as '[21]', just as with the standard \cite command. Multiple keys may be given.

\citet{*key*} . . . . (11.3.4) – 218

With the natbib package, inserts an in-text literature citation as 'Jones et al. [1999]', using the identifier *key*. In numerical citation mode, it prints the author's name before the citation number, as 'Jones et al. [21]'.

\ClassError{*class_name*}{*error_text*}{*help*} [p] . . . . (D.2.7) – 435

Writes an error message *error_text* to the monitor and transcript file, labeled with the class name, and halts processing, waiting for a user response as for a LaTeX error. If H⟨*return*⟩ is typed, the *help* text is printed. Both *error_text* and *help* may contain \MessageBreak for a new line, \space for a forced space, and \protect before commands that are to have their names printed literally and not interpreted.

\ClassInfo{*class_name*}{*info_text*} [p] . . . . (D.2.7) – 436

Is like \ClassWarningNoLine except that the text *info_text* is only written to the transcript file, not to the monitor.

\ClassWarning{*class_name*}{*warning_text*} [p] . . . . (D.2.7) – 436

Writes *warning_text* to the monitor and transcript file, labeled with the class name and the current line number of the input file. Processing continues. The *warning_text* is formatted in the same way as for \ClassError.

\ClassWarningNoLine{*class_name*}{*warning_text*} [p] . . . . (D.2.7) – 436

Is like \ClassWarning except that the current line number of the input file is not printed.

\cleardoublepage . . . . (2.7.4) – 37

Ends the current page and outputs all unprocessed floats on to one or more float pages. The next page will be a *right-hand* one, with an odd page number.

\clearpage . . . . (2.7.4) – 37

Ends the current page and outputs all unprocessed floats on to one or more float pages.

`\cline{`*n-m*`}` . . . . (6.2.1) – 107

In `tabular` environment, produces a horizontal rule from the beginning of column *n* to the end of column *m*. Example: `\cline{2-5}`.

`\closing{`*regards*`}` . . . . (18.1) – 346

End of the text in the `letter` environment; *regards* stands for the desired terminating text.

`\clubsuit` [m] produces ♣ . . . . (7.3.6) – 129

`\color` *col_spec* . . . . (8.2) – 166

A command made available with the `color` package. It is a declaration that switches the color in which the text is printed to that specified. It remains in effect until the end of the current environment or until countermanded by another `\color` command. The *col_spec* is either the name of a color defined (or predefined) by `\definecolor` or of the form [*model*]{*specs*}, where the arguments have the same meaning as they do for `\definecolor`. Examples:

    `\color[rgb]{0.5,0.5,0}`   `\color{magenta}`

`\colorbox` *col_spec*`{`*text*`}` . . . . (8.2) – 166

A command made available with the `color` package. The *text* is set in an LR box with the specified color as the background color. The *col_spec* is the same as for `\color`.

`\columnsep` . . . . (3.1.1) – 43

Declaration for the amount of intercolumn spacing in two-column page formatting. May be changed with the `\setlength` command:

    `\setlength{\columnsep}{1pt}`

`\columnseprule` . . . . (3.1.1) – 44

Declaration for the thickness of the vertical rule separating the columns in two-column page formatting. Value is set with the `\setlength` command:

    `\setlength{\columnseprule}{1pt}`

`\cong` [m] produces ≅ . . . . (7.3.4) – 128

`\contentsline{`*sec_type*`}{\numberline{`*sec_num*`}`*title_text*`}{`*page*`}`

Command that appears in the `.toc` file for every entry in the table of contents, which is read when the `\tableofcontents` command is given. Such commands may be altered or added to the `.toc` file by means of the text editor. The entry *sec_type* stands for the sectioning level, such as `section`, while *sec_num* is its number (for example, 2.3), and *page* is the page number where the entry appears.

`\contentsname` . . . . (D.3.1) – 441

Command containing the heading for the table of contents. In English, this is 'Contents', but it may be altered for adaptation to other languages.

\coprod [m] produces $\coprod$ . . . . (7.3.7) – 129

\copyright produces © . . . . (2.5.5) – 27

\cos [m] . . . . (7.3.8) – 130

> Command to produce the function name 'cos' in formulas.

\cosh [m] . . . . (7.3.8) – 130

> Command to produce the function name 'cosh' in formulas.

\cot [m] . . . . (7.3.8) – 130

> Command to produce the function name 'cot' in formulas.

\coth [m] . . . . (7.3.8) – 130

> Command to produce the function name 'coth' in formulas.

\csc [m] . . . . (7.3.8) – 130

> Command to produce the function name 'csc' in formulas.

\cup [m] produces $\cup$ . . . . (7.3.3) – 127

\CurrentOption [p] . . . . (D.2.3) – 432

> A command that may only be used in the definition of options, especially for default options. It contains the name of the option being processed.

\d{x} . . . . (2.5.7) – 27

> Produces a 'dot under' accent: \d{o} = o̦.

\dag produces † . . . . (2.5.5) – 27

\dagger [m] produces † . . . . (7.3.3) – 127

\dashbox{dash}(x_dimen,y_dimen)[pos]{text} . . . . (16.1.4) – 300

> Picture element command to produce a dashed frame with width x_dimen and height y_dimen, using a dash length of dash in the picture environment. Without the optional pos, the contents text are centered within the frame, otherwise they are positioned at the left (l), right (r), top (t), or bottom (b), or a combination thereof, such as lt. This command is used as an argument in a \put or \multiput command.

\dashv [m] produces ⊣ . . . . (7.3.6) – 129

\date{date_text} . . . . (3.3.1), (18.1) – 55, 347

> 1. The command \maketitle normally prints the current date on the title page. The declaration \date will replace the date with whatever text is given in date_text.
>
> 2. Prints the text date_text instead of the automatic current date in a letter.

\date*language* . . . . (14.1) – 267

A command used in several language adaptations to redefine the \today command according to the requirements of *language*. It occurs in german package as well as in the babel system. It may also be used for 'dialects', such as \dateUSenglish and \dateenglish. This command is normally part of the definition of the \selectlanguage command.

\dbinom{*over*}{*under*} [m][a] . . . . (15.2.3) – 276

With the amsmath package, produces a binomial as \binom does but set in \displaystyle size.

\dblfigrule . . . . (9.3) – 173

A command that is executed after a two-column float at the top of a page. It is normally defined to do nothing but may be redefined to add a rule between the float and the main text. It must not add any net vertical spacing.

```
\renewcommand{\dblfigrule}{\vspace*{-.4pt}
  \rule{\textwidth}{.4pt}}
```

\dblfloatpagefraction . . . . (9.3) – 172

For two-column page formatting, the fraction of a float page that must be filled with floats before a new page is called. A new value is assigned with

```
\renewcommand{\dblfloatpagefraction}{decimal_frac}
```

\dblfloatsep . . . . (9.3) – 172

For two-column page formatting, the vertical spacing between floats that extend over both columns. A new value is set with the \setlength command:

```
\setlength{\dblfloatsep}{12pt plus 2pt minus 4pt}
```

\dbltextfloatsep . . . . (9.3) – 172

For two-column page formatting, the vertical spacing between floats extending over both columns at the top of the page and the following text. A new value is set with the \setlength command.

\dbltopfraction . . . . (9.3) – 172

For two-column page formatting, the maximum fraction of a page that may be occupied at the top by floats extending over both columns. A new value is assigned with

```
\renewcommand{\dbltopfraction}{decimal_frac}.
```

dbltopnumber . . . . (9.3) – 172

For two-column page formatting, the maximum number of floats that may appear at the top of a page extending over both columns. A new value is assigned with

```
\setcounter{dbltopnumber}{num}.
```

\ddag produces ‡ . . . . (2.5.5) – 27

\ddagger [m] produces ‡ . . . . (7.3.3) – 127

\dddot{*x*} [m][a] . . . . (15.2.2) – 274

With the amsmath package, a triple dot accent in math formulas: \dddot{a} = $\dddot{a}$.

With the amsmath package, a four-dot accent in math formulas: \ddddot{a} = $\ddddot{a}$.

A double-dot accent in mathematical formulas: \ddot{a} = $\ddot{a}$.

Establishes the list of default extensions for graphics files that can be imported with the \includegraphics command and the graphics or graphicx packages; *ext_list* is a comma-separated list of file extensions, such as .eps, .ps.

Associates a graphics file extension *ext* with a graphics file type and a file extension (*bb*) where the bounding box information is to be read, and an operating command (*cmd*) that is to be executed on the file to make it available for importation. For example:

```
\DeclareGraphicsRule{.eps.gz}{eps}
    {.eps.bb}{`gunzip -c #1}
```
Here the command must be prefixed with `, and #1 represents the name of the file to be processed.

In a class or package file, this command defines the set of commands (*code*) that is to be associated with the given *option*. These commands are executed when \ExecuteOptions or \ProcessOptions is called. After the latter, all definitions are erased to save memory. The *code* is internally stored in a command named \ds@*option*.

In a class or package file, this command defines the default set of commands that is associated with every undefined option. Special commands that may be used within *code* are \CurrentOption (the name of the option) and \OptionNotUsed. Example:

```
\DeclareOption*{\InputIfFileExists
    {\CurrentOption.sty}{}{\OptionNotUsed}}
```

Defines or redefines the command \cmd in the same way as \newcommand except that the result is robust: It may be used in the argument of another command without a \protect command before it.

The same as \DeclareRobustCommand except that the arguments to \cmd must be 'short', not containing any new paragraphs.

`\definecolor{`*name*`}{`*model*`}{`*specs*`}` . . . . (8.2) – 166

A command made available with the `color` package. It associates the name of a color (*name*) with the specifications *specs* according to a certain *model*. Possible values for *model* are `rgb` (red, green, blue), `cmyk` (cyan, magenta, yellow, black), `gray`, and `named`. In each case, *specs* is a comma-separated list of numbers between 0 and 1 specifying the strength of the relevant component. In the case of the `named` model, *specs* is an internal name for the color that is known by the driver program. Examples:

> `\definecolor{litegrn}{cmyk}{0.25,0,0.75.0}`
> `\definecolor{brown}{named}{RawSienna}`

A number of colors are predefined in all color drivers: `red`, `green`, `blue`, `yellow`, `cyan`, `magenta`, `black`, and `white`.

`\deg` [m] . . . . (7.3.8) – 130

Command to produce the function name 'deg' in formulas.

`\DeleteShortVerb{\c}` . . . . (4.6.1, B.5.3) – 82, 386

When the standard package `shortvrb` has been loaded, this command counteracts the effects of a previous `\MakeShortVerb{\c}`, allowing the character *c* to have its original meaning once more.

`\Delta` [m] produces Δ . . . . (7.3.1) – 127

`\delta` [m] produces δ . . . . (7.3.1) – 127

`\depth` . . . . (5.1.1) – 86

A length parameter equal to the depth of a box (baseline to bottom); it may only be used in the *width* specification of `\makebox`, `\framebox`, or `\savebox`, or in the *height* specification of a `\parbox` or `minipage` environment.

> `\framebox[20\depth]{text}`

`\det` [m] . . . . (7.3.8) – 130

Command to produce the function name 'det' in formulas. Can be combined with a lower limit by means of the subscript command.

`\dfrac{`*numerator*`}{`*denominator*`}` [m][a] . . . . (15.2.3) – 275

With the `amsmath` package, produces a fraction as `\frac` does but set in `\displaystyle` size.

`\DH` . . . . (A.3.2) – 371

When T1 encoding is active, prints the character Đ.

`\dh` . . . . (A.3.2) – 371

When T1 encoding is active, prints the character ð.

`\Diamond` [m] produces $\Diamond$ . . . . (7.3.3) – 127

`\diamond` [m] produces $\diamond$ . . . . (7.3.3) – 127

`\diamondsuit` [m] produces $\blacklozenge$ . . . . (7.3.6) – 129

`\dim` [m] . . . . (7.3.8) – 130

Command to produce the function name 'dim' in formulas.

`\discretionary{`*before*`}{`*after*`}{`*without*`}` . . . . (2.8.1) – 38

Hyphenation suggestion within a word. The word may be divided such that *before* is at the end of one line and *after* at the start of the next line. If no division occurs, *without* is printed.

`\displaybreak[`*num*`]` [m][a] . . . . (15.2.7) – 289

With the `amsmath` package, allows a manual page break in a multiline math formula when given just before `\\`; if *num* is present, it takes on values of 0–4 with increasing encouragement for a break, where 4 is the same as no value, a forced page break. Automatic page breaks are impossible in multiline formulas unless `\allowdisplaybreaks` has been issued in the preamble.

`\displaystyle` [m] . . . . (7.5.2) – 147

Switches to font size `\displaystyle` as the active font within a math formula.

`\div` [m] produces ÷ . . . . (7.3.3) – 127

`\DJ` . . . . (A.3.2) – 371

When T1 encoding is active, prints the character Đ.

`\dj` . . . . (A.3.2) – 371

When T1 encoding is active, prints the character đ.

`\documentclass[`*options*`]{`*class*`}` [*version*] [p] . . . . (3.1) – 41

Normally the first command in a LaTeX document, determining the overall characteristics. Standard values for *class* are:

`article, report, book, letter,` and `slides`

of which only one may be selected. In addition, various options may be chosen, their names separated by commas. Possibilities are:

`10pt, 11pt, 12pt,`
`letterpaper, legalpaper, executivepaper,`
`a4paper, a5paper, b5paper, landscape,`
`onecolumn, twocolumn,`
`oneside, twoside,`
`notitlepage, titlepage,`
`leqno, fleqn, openbib,`
`draft, final`

These and any additional options are all global, meaning that they also apply to any packages specified with a following `\usepackage` command.

The optional *version* is a date, given in the form *yyyy/mm/dd*, as, for example, 1994/08/01. If the date of the class file read in is earlier than this, a warning message is printed.

`\dot{`*x*`}` [m] . . . . (7.3.9) – 131

A dot accent in mathematical formulas: `\dot{a}` = $\dot{a}$.

`\doteq` [m] produces $\doteq$ . . . . (7.3.4) – 128

`\dotfill` . . . . (2.7.1) – 34

Fills up the space in a line with a dotted leader: . . . . = `\dotfill`.

\dots produces ... . (7.2.6) – 125

\dots [m][a] . . . . (15.2.2) – 275

> With the amsmath package, places continuation dots in math mode automatically at a height determined by the following symbol.

\dotsb [m][a] produces dots for binary operator: ⋯ . . . . . . (15.2.2) – 275

\dotsc [m][a] produces dots for commas: ... . (15.2.2) – 275

\dotsi [m][a] produces dots for integral signs: ⋯ . . . . (15.2.2) – 275

\dotsm [m][a] produces dots for multiplication: ⋯ . . . . (15.2.2) – 275

\doublebox{*text*} . . . . (5.1.9) – 94

> With the fancybox package, is a variant of \fbox, drawing a doubled box around *text*; the thicknesses and separation of the lines depend on the length \fboxrule.

\doublerulesep . . . . (6.2.2) – 107

> The distance between double rules inside the tabular and array environments. New value assigned with \setlength outside of the environment.

\Downarrow [m] produces ⇓ . . . . (7.3.5) – 129

\downarrow [m] produces ↓ . . . . (7.3.5) – 129

\ell [m] produces ℓ . . . . (7.3.6) – 129

\em . . . . (4.1.1) – 64

> This declaration switches to an emphatic font, one that has the current family and series but with a different shape attribute. It normally toggles between an upright and an italic shape.

\emph{*text*} . . . . (4.1.1) – 64

> This command sets its argument in an emphatic font, one that has the current family and series but with a different shape attribute. It normally toggles between an upright and an italic shape.

\emptyset [m] produces ∅ . . . . (7.3.6) – 129

\encl{*enclosures*} . . . . (18.1) – 347

> Command in the document class letter to add the word 'encl:' with the list *enclosures* at the end of a letter.

\enclname . . . . (D.3.1) – 441

> Command in the letter document class containing the word to be printed by the \encl command. In English, this is 'encl', but it may be altered for adaptation to other languages.

\end{*environment*} . . . . (2.2) – 23

> Command to terminate an environment started with a \begin{*environment*} command.

\endfirsthead   . . . . (6.2.4) – 117

> Within the longtable environment of the longtable package, this command ends those specifications that are to be added to the top of the table (the head) on the first page only.

\endfoot   . . . . (6.2.4) – 117

> Within the longtable environment of the longtable package, this command ends those specifications that are to be added at the bottom of the table (the foot) before it is continued to other pages.

\endhead   . . . . (6.2.4) – 117

> Within the longtable environment of the longtable package, this command ends those specifications that are to be added to the top of the table (the head) when it is continued to other pages.

\endlastfoot   . . . . (6.2.4) – 117

> Within the longtable environment of the longtable package, this command ends those specifications that are to be added at the bottom of the table (the foot) on the last page.

\enlargethispage{*size*} . . . . (2.7.4) – 37

> The \textheight parameter is temporarily increased by the length *size* in order to improve a bad page break. On the following pages, \textheight will have its normal value once more.

\enlargethispage*{*size*} . . . . (2.7.4) – 37

> Is the same as \enlargethispage except that any additional spacing between the lines is removed as necessary to maximize the amount of text on the page.

\ensuremath{*math cmds*}   . . . . (10.3.1) – 186

> Sets *math cmds* in math mode; may be called in both text and math modes. Its main use is to define new commands that require math mode but can be called from either mode.

\epsilon [m] produces ϵ . . . . (7.3.1) – 127

\eqref{*marker*} [a]   . . . . (15.2.7) – 289

> With the amsmath package, is a variation on the \ref command, and prints the equation number defined with \label{*marker*} in parentheses, as (5.6).

\equiv [m] produces $\equiv$ . . . . (7.3.4) – 128

\eta [m] produces η . . . . (7.3.1) – 127

\euro   . . . . (2.5.8) – 28

> With the eurosym package, prints the euro symbol € from the eurosym META-FONT fonts. With the eurosans package, it prints the symbol from the Adobe (PostScript) euro fonts. In both cases, the symbol is sans serif but changes to boldface or slanted to match the current font.

`\EUR` . . . . (2.5.8) – 28

With the europs package, prints the euro symbol € from the Adobe (PostScript) euro fonts such that it matches the font family and other attributes. `\EURofc` prints the invariable symbol €.

`\evensidemargin` . . . . (3.2.5) – 51

Sets the left margin for the even-numbered pages. It is effective in the document class book and, when the option twoside has been selected, in the other classes. A new value is assigned with the `\setlength` command:

  `\setlength{\evensidemargin}{2.5cm}`

`\ExecuteOptions{`*option_list*`} [p]` . . . . (D.2.3) – 432

In a class or package file, this command executes all the option definitions in *option_list*. This is normally invoked just prior to `\ProcessOptions` to establish certain options as default.

`\exists` [m] produces ∃ . . . . (7.3.6) – 129

`\exp` [m] . . . . (7.3.8) – 130

Command to produce the function name 'exp' in formulas.

`\extracolsep{`*extra_width*`}` . . . . (6.2.1) – 105

Tabular command for setting extra spacing between all the following columns in a table. This command is inserted as an @-expression into the column definition field of the tabular environment:

  `\begin{tabular}{lr@{\extracolsep{2.5mm}}lcr}`

`\fancypage{`*cmds1*`}{`*cmds2*`}` . . . . (5.1.9) – 95

With the fancybox package, places a framed box around the contents of all subsequent pages; *cmds1* exclude the head and footlines, *cmds2* includes them. The arguments set box parameters such as `\fboxrule` but must end with a box command such as `\shadowbox`. Usually one set of *cmds* is left blank.

`\fbox{`*text*`}` produces a frame around ⊡text⊡ . . . . (5.1.1) – 86

`\fboxrule` . . . . (5.1.8) – 93

The line thickness for the frames drawn by `\fbox` and `\framebox` commands. A new value is assigned with the `\setlength` command:

  `\setlength{\fboxrule}{1pt}`

`\fboxsep` . . . . (5.1.8) – 93

The distance between the frame and text in the `\fbox` and `\framebox` commands. A new value is assigned with the `\setlength` command:

  `\setlength{\fboxsep}{1mm}`

\fcolorbox *col_spec1 col_spec2*{*text*} . . . . (8.2) – 166

A command made available with the color package. Like \colorbox, the *text* is set in an LR box with the *col_spec2* as the background color but with a frame of color *col_spec1* around it. The *col_spec*s are either both defined names or employ the same model. Examples:

```
\fcolorbox[rgb]{1,0,0}{0,1,0}{Text}
\fcolorbox{red}{green}{Text}
```

\figurename . . . . (D.3.1) – 441

Command containing the name for a figure caption. In English, this is 'Figure', but it may be altered for adaptation to other languages.

\fill . . . . (2.4.2) – 25

A rubber length with a natural size of zero that can stretch to any size necessary to fill up the horizontal or vertical space available.

\flat [m] produces ♭ . . . . (7.3.6) – 129

\floatpagefraction . . . . (9.3) – 172

The fraction of a float page that must be filled with floats before a new page is called. A new value is assigned with

```
\renewcommand{\floatpagefraction}{decimal_frac}
```

\floatsep . . . . (9.3) – 172

The vertical spacing between floats that appear at the top or bottom of a page. A new value is set with the \setlength command:

```
\setlength{\floatsep}{12pt plus 2pt minus 4pt}
```

\flushbottom . . . . (3.2.5) – 51

A declaration that puts vertical spacing between paragraphs so that the last line on every page is at the same position. Is the standard for the book document class and for the twoside option.

\fnsymbol{*counter*} . . . . (10.1.4) – 183

Prints the current value of the given *counter* as a 'footnote symbol':
* † ‡ § ¶ ‖ ** †† ‡‡

\fontencoding{*enc*} . . . . (A.1) – 362

This command selects the font encoding scheme. Possible values of *enc* are OT1 for the standard and T1 for the Cork encodings. Other values are also possible.

\fontfamily{*fam*} . . . . (A.1) – 362

This command selects the 'family' of fonts. Possible values of *fam* for standard LaTeX with the Computer Modern fonts are cmr, cmss, cmtt, and cmfi.

\fontseries{*ser*} . . . . (A.1) – 362

This command selects the 'series' of fonts within a 'family'. Possible values of *ser* for standard LaTeX are m (medium) and bx (bold extended).

`\fontshape{`*form*`}` . . . . (A.1) – 362

> This command selects the 'shape' of fonts. Possible values of *form* are n (normal), it (italic), sl (slanted), sc (small caps), and u ('unslanted' italic).

`\fontsize{`*sz*`}{`*line_sp*`}` . . . . (A.1) – 362

> This command selects the font size. The argument *sz* specifies the size of the characters in points (without the dimension pt) and *line_sp* determines the value of the interline spacing (\baselineskip), with an explicit dimension. Example: \fontsize{12}{14pt}.

`\footnote[`*num*`]{`*footnote_text*`}` . . . . (5.2.1), (5.2.2) – 95, 96

> Produces a footnote containing the text *footnote_tex*. The optional argument *num* will be used as the footnote number in place of the next number in the automatic sequence.

`\footnotemark[`*num*`]` . . . . (5.2.3) – 96

> Produces a footnote marker in the current text. The optional argument *num* will be used as the footnote number in place of the next number in the automatic sequence. May be used within structures where \footnote is not normally permitted, such as LR boxes, tables, and math formulas.

`\footnoterule` . . . . (5.2.6) – 100

> This is an internal command to produce the horizontal rule between the regular text on a page and the footnote text at the bottom. May be changed with, for example,
>
> > \renewcommand{\footnoterule}
> > {\rule{*wdth*}{*hght*}\vspace{-*hght*}}

`\footnotesep` . . . . (5.2.6) – 99

> The vertical spacing between two footnotes. A new value is assigned with the \setlength command:
>
> > \setlength{\footnotesep}{6.5pt}

`\footnotesize` . . . . (4.1.2) – 64

> Switches to the font size \footnotesize, which is smaller than \small but larger than \scriptsize.

`\footnotetext[`*num*`]{`*footnote_text*`}` . . . . (5.2.3) – 96

> Produces a footnote with the text *footnote_text* but without generating a marker in the current text. The marker that is used for the footnote itself at the bottom of the page derives from the current value of the counter footnote, which remains unchanged, or from the value of the optional argument *num*. This command may be used together with the \footnotemark command to insert footnotes into structures where they are otherwise not allowed, such as LR boxes, tables, and math formulas. The \footnotetext command must be given *outside* of that structure.

`\footskip` . . . . (3.2.5) – 51

The distance from the bottom edge of the text body to the lower edge of the footline. A value is assigned with the `\setlength` command:

`\setlength{\footskip}{25pt}`

`\forall` [m] produces ∀ . . . . (7.3.6) – 129

`\foreignlanguage{`*language*`}{`*text*`}` . . . . (14.1) – 266

In the `babel` system, sets a short *text* in the selected *language*.

`\frac{`*numerator*`}{`*denominator*`}` [m] . . . . (7.2.3) – 123

Math command for generating fractions.

`\frame{`*text*`}` . . . . (16.1.4) – 308

Produces a frame without any intervening spacing around ⬚*text*⬚. Mainly used as a picture element in a `\put` or `\multiput` command within the `picture` environment.

`\framebox[`*width*`][`*pos*`]{`*text*`}}` . . . . (5.1.1) – 86

Produces a frame of width *width* around *text*. By default, the text is centered within the frame but may be left or right justified by giving the optional argument *pos* as l or r. It may also have the value s to stretch the text to the given width.

`\framebox(`*x_dimen*`,`*y_dimen*`)[`*pos*`]{`*text*`}` . . . . (16.1.4) – 300

Picture element command to produce a frame of width *x_dimen* and height *y_dimen* within the `picture` environment. Without the optional argument *pos*, the text is centered vertically and horizontally. The text may be left or right justified, and/or aligned at the top or bottom, by setting *pos* to a combination of the letters l, r, t, and b, such as tr for top, right; *pos* may also contain s to stretch the text to the full width. The command is to be used as the argument of a `\put` or `\multiput` command.

`\frenchspacing` . . . . (2.7.1) – 32

After this command has been given, no additional horizontal spacing is inserted at the end of a sentence. The counter command is `\nonfrenchspacing`.

`\frontmatter` . . . . (3.3.5) – 60

In the `book` class, introduces the material that comes at the beginning (preface, table of contents) by turning off the chapter numbering of the `\chapter` command and switching to Roman numbers for the pagination.

`\frown` [m] produces ⌢ . . . . (7.3.4) – 128

`\fussy` . . . . (2.8.3) – 39

Counter command of `\sloppy` that allows larger interword spacings than normal. After `\fussy` has been given, the normal spacings apply once more.

\Gamma [m] produces Γ . . . . (7.3.1) – 127

\gamma [m] produces γ . . . . (7.3.1) – 127

\gcd [m] . . . . (7.3.8) – 130

Command to produce the function name 'gcd' in formulas. A lower limit may be given as a subscript.

\ge [m] produces ≥ . . . . (7.3.4) – 128

\genfrac{*left*}{*right*}{*thkns*}{*mathsz*}{*over*}{*under*} [m][a]

. . . . (15.2.3) – 276

With the amsmath package, produces a generalized fraction with delimiters *left* and *right*, line thickness *thkns*, math font size *mathsz* 0–3, and with *over* on top of *under*. If *mathsz* is empty, the sizing is automatic.

\geq [m] produces ≥ . . . . (7.3.4) – 128

\gets [m] produces ← . . . . (7.3.5) – 129

\gg [m] produces ≫ . . . . (7.3.4) – 128

\glossary{*glossary_entry*} . . . . (11.4.4) – 226

Write a \glossaryentry command to the .glo file if \makeglossary has been issued in the preamble; otherwise it does nothing.

\glossaryentry{*glossary_entry*}{*page_number*} . . . . (11.4.4) – 226

The form in which the entry is written to the .glo file by the \glossary command.

\graphpaper[*num*]$(x, y)(lx, ly)$ . . . . (16.1.5) – 310

A command added with the graphpap package for use in the picture environment. It plots a labeled grid system with the lower left corner at (x, y), *lx* wide and *ly* high. Grid lines are drawn every *num* units, with the fifth ones thicker. If *num* is not specified, it is assumed to be 10. All arguments must be integers, not decimal fractions.

\grave{*x*} [m] . . . . (7.3.9) – 131

A grave accent over the math variable x: \grave{a} = $à$.

\guillemotleft . . . . (A.3.2) – 371

When T1 encoding is active, prints the symbol «.

\guillemotright . . . . (A.3.2) – 371

When T1 encoding is active, prints the symbol ».

\guilsinglleft . . . . (A.3.2) – 371

When T1 encoding is active, prints the symbol ‹.

\guilsinglright . . . . (A.3.2) – 371

When T1 encoding is active, prints the symbol ›.

\H{x} . . . . (2.5.7) – 27

Hungarian double acute accent: \H{o} = ő.

\hat{x} [m] . . . . (7.3.9) – 131

Circumflex over the math variable x: \hat{a} = $\hat{a}$.

\hbar [m] produces $\hbar$ . . . . (7.3.6) – 129

\headheight . . . . (3.2.5) – 51

The height of the head at the top of each page. A new value is assigned with the \setlength command:

        \setlength{\headheight}{25pt}

\headsep . . . . (3.2.5) – 51

Vertical spacing between the lower edge of the page head and the top of the main text. A new value is assigned with the \setlength command:

        \setlength{\headsep}{0.25in}

\headtoname . . . . (D.3.1) – 441

Command in the letter document class containing the text that precedes the recipient's name in the headline after the first page. In English, this is 'To', but it may be altered for adaptation to other languages.

\heartsuit [m] produces $\heartsuit$ . . . . (7.3.6) – 129

\height . . . . (5.1.1) – 86

A length parameter equal to the natural height of a box (distance from the baseline to the top); it may only be used in the *width* specification of \makebox, \framebox, or \savebox, or in the *height* specification of a \parbox or a minipage environment.

        \framebox[6\height]{text}

\hfill . . . . (2.7.1) – 33

A horizontal rubber spacing with a natural length of zero that can be stretched to any value. Used to fill up a horizontal line with blank spacing. This command is an abbreviation for \hspace{\fill}.

\hline . . . . (6.2.1) – 106

Produces a horizontal line in the array and tabular environments over the width of the entire table.

\hoffset 554, 555

Horizontal offset of the output page from the printer border set by the printer driver. This printer border is normally 1 inch from the left edge of the paper. The standard value of \hoffset is 0 pt so that the left reference margin of the page is identical with the printer margin. A new value is assigned with the \setlength command:

        \setlength{\hoffset}{-1in}

\hom [m] . . . . (7.3.8) – 130

    Command to produce the function name 'hom' in formulas.

\hookleftarrow [m] produces ↩ . . . . (7.3.5) – 129

\hookrightarrow [m] produces ↪ . . . . (7.3.5) – 129

\hrulefill . . . . (2.7.1) – 34

    Fills up the space in a line with a rule: _____= \hrulefill.

\hspace{*width*} . . . . (2.7.1) – 33

    Produces horizontal spacing of length *width*. It is ignored if it occurs at the beginning or end of a line.

\hspace*{*width*} . . . . (2.7.1) – 33

    Produces horizontal spacing of length *width* even at the beginning or end of a line.

\huge . . . . (4.1.2) – 64

    Switches to the font size \huge, which is smaller than \Huge but larger than \LARGE.

\Huge . . . . (4.1.2) – 64

    Switches to the largest font size available \Huge, which is larger than \huge.

\hyperlink{*name*}{*link*} . . . . (13.2.4) – 259

    With the hyperref package, makes the contents of *link* to be a link to the target with the name *name*, established with the \hypertarget command. The *link* may be text, a symbol, or a graphic loaded with \includegraphics. The link is framed with a colored box unless the option colorlinks has been set to true, in which case the *link* is set in a text color determined by the option linkcolor.

\hypersetup{*key* = *value*, . . . } . . . . (13.2.4) – 253

    With the hyperref package, allows parameters (*key*) to be assigned values (*value*); the parameters may also be set as options in the \usepackage loading command; with \hypersetup, these values may be changed within the document. The list of possible keys and values is given on pages 254-258.

\hypertarget{*name*}{*text*} . . . . (13.2.4) – 259

    With the hyperref package, prints the *text* argument as normal, but makes it a target for internal links, named *name*. The *text* may be empty.

\hyphenation{*hyphenation_list*} [p] . . . . (2.8.2) – 38

    Sets up a list of hyphenation exceptions. The *hyphenation_list* consists of a collection of words containing hyphens at the places where word division may occur: hy-phen-a-tion per-mit-ted.

Tests whether the file *file_name* can be found in the places where LaTeX looks for files; if so, the code *true* is executed; otherwise, *false*. This is like \InputIfFileExists except that the file is not input.

In the multilingual babel system, tests if *language* is the currently selected language and if so, executes *yes_text*, otherwise *no_text*.

A conditional command available when the standard package ifthen has been loaded. If the logical statement *test* evaluates to ⟨*true*⟩, then *then_text* is inserted, otherwise *else_text*. The logical statement may be relational (two numbers with one of < = > between them), an even-odd test (\isodd{*number*}), a comparison of two texts (\equal{*text1*}{*text2*}), a comparison of two lengths (\lengthtest{*length1* op *length2*}, *op* is one of < = >), or a test of a boolean switch (\boolean{*switch*}). Switches are created with \newboolean{*switch*} and set with \setboolean{*switch*}{*value*}, where *value* is true or false. Logical statements may be combined with logical operators \and, \or, and \not, and grouped with \(and \).

Inserts the contents of the file with the root name *file* and extension .tex into the current text at the point where the command appears. A new page is always started! Together with \includeonly, this command allows portions of the document to be processed as though the rest of the text were present.

A command made available with the graphics package that imports external graphics stored in the file *file_name*. The coordinates of the bounding box are given by *llx, lly* (lower left corner) and by *urx, ury* (upper right corner). The contents of this bounding box are used for further manipulation, such as scaling and rotating. It is also the (manipulated) bounding box that is used to reserve space in the text; any graphics that extend beyond the limits of this box will also be printed, but overlapping any other material that may be beside it.

The bounding box coordinates may have units attached to them; the default units are big points bp (72 per inch).

If the bounding box coordinates are omitted, the information is obtained in some other manner depending on the type of graphics file. For an encapsulated PostScript file, this information is taken from the graphics file itself.

If *llx* and *lly* are not specified, they are assumed to be 0. That is, if only one set of optional coordinates are given, they refer to the upper-right corner.

\includegraphics*[*llx,lly*][*urx,ury*]{*file_name*} . . . . (8.1.2) – 155

The same as \includegraphics except that any graphics extending beyond the bounding box are *not* included: the figure is clipped.

\includegraphics[*key=value*,...]{*file_name*} . . . . (8.1.3) – 157

With the graphicx package, this command has a different syntax in which the scaling, rotating, and clipping are affected through *key=value* pairs such as width=7cm, angle=90, and scale=.5.

\includeonly{*file_list*} [p] . . . . (11.1.2) – 207

Only those files whose names are in *file_list*, separated by commas, will be read in by the \include commands. The \include commands for other file names are ignored. Nevertheless, all the auxiliary files are read in so that the page and section numbers will be correct, as are the cross-reference markers.

\indent . . . . (3.2.4) – 49

The first line of the *next* paragraph is to be indented.

\index{*index_entry*} . . . . (11.4.2) – 223

Writes a \indexentry command to the.idx file if the \makeindex command has been issued in the preamble; otherwise it does nothing. The MakeIndex program (Section 11.4.3) can process this file if the entries are in the forms

\index{*main_entry*}
\index{*main_entry*!*sub_entry*}
\index{*main_entry*!*sub_entry*!*sub_sub_entry*}

making up a theindex environment with the entries alphabetically ordered and organized with \item, \subitem, and \subsubitem commands.

\indexentry{*index_entry*}{*page_number*} . . . . (11.4.2) – 223

The form in which the entry is written to the .idx file by the \index command.

\indexname . . . . (D.3.1) – 441

Command containing the heading for the index. In English, this is 'Index', but it may be altered for adaptation to other languages.

\indexspace . . . . (11.4.1) – 222

Command within theindex environment to produce a blank line.

\inf [m] . . . . (7.3.8) – 130

Command to produce the function name 'inf' in formulas. A lower limit may be set as a subscript.

\infty [m] produces ∞ . . . . (7.3.6) – 129

\input{*file*} . . . . (11.1.1) – 205

Inserts the contents of the file with the root name *file* and extension .tex into the current text at the point where the command appears. The file that is read in may also contain further \input commands.

\InputIfFileExists{*file_name*}{*true*}{*false*} . . . . (D.2.8) – 436

Tests whether the file *file_name* can be found in the places where LaTeX looks for files; if so, the code *true* is executed and the file is input; otherwise, *false* is executed.

\int [m] produces ∫ . . . . (7.2.5) – 124

\iint [m][a] produces ∬ . . . . (15.2.2) – 272

\iiint [m][a] produces ∭ . . . . (15.2.2) – 272

\iiiint [m][a] produces ⨌ . . . . (15.2.2) – 272

\intertext{*insert_text*} [m][a] . . . . (15.2.1) – 271

When the package amsmath is loaded, this command inserts text as a left-justified line between lines of an equation without affecting their horizontal alignment.

\intextsep . . . . (9.3) – 172

The vertical spacing between floats in the middle of a page and the surrounding text. A new value is assigned with the \setlength command:

```
\setlength{\intextsep}{10pt plus2pt minus3pt}
```

\invisible . . . . (17.1.2) – 322

In slides class, is a declaration that makes the following text be printed in 'invisible ink', that is, it takes up as much space as though it were there. It remains in effect until the end of the environment, or the end of the curly braces, in which it was issued, or until \visible is given. It is used for making overlays.

\iota [m] produces ι . . . . (7.3.1) – 127

\itdefault . . . . (A.2.1) – 365

This command defines the shape attribute that is selected with the \itshape command. It may be redefined with \renewcommand:

```
\renewcommand{\itdefault}{it}
```

\item[*label*] . . . . (4.3), (4.4.1) – 70, 75

Produces a label and the start of an item text in a list environment. Without the optional argument, the label is generated according to the type of environment, for example, numbers for the enumerate environment. The optional argument inserts *label* in place of this standard item label.

\item . . . . (11.4.1) – 222

Produces a main entry in theindex environment.

\itemindent . . . . (4.4.2) – 77

The amount by which the label and the text of the first line after each \item is indented in a list environment. The standard value is 0 pt but a new value may be assigned with the \setlength command:

```
\setlength{\itemindent}{1em}
```

\itemsep . . . . (4.4.2) – 76

> The amount of vertical spacing in addition to \parsep that is inserted between the \item texts in a list environment. A new value may be assigned with the \setlength command:
>
>   \setlength{\itemsep}{2pt plus1pt minus1pt}

\itshape . . . . (4.1.3), (A.2) – 66, 365

> This declaration switches to a font in the current family and series but with the *italic* shape attribute.

\j produces ȷ . . . . (2.5.7) – 28

\jmath [m] produces $\jmath$ . . . . (7.3.6) – 129

\Join [m] produces ⋈ . . . . (7.3.6) – 129

\jot . . . . (7.5.4) – 149

> The amount of vertical spacing between the formula lines of an eqnarray or eqnarray* environment. Standard value is 3 pt. A new value may be assigned with the \setlength command:
>
>   \setlength{\jot}{4.5pt}

\k{x} . . . . (A.3.2) – 371

> When T1 encoding is active, prints the ogonek accent \k{A} = Ą.

\kappa [m] produces κ . . . . (7.3.1) – 127

\ker [m] . . . . (7.3.8) – 130

> Command to produce the function name 'ker' in formulas.

\kill . . . . (6.1.2) – 102

> Removes the preceding sample line in a tabbing environment that was given only to set the tabs and not to be printed at this point.

\L produces Ł . . . . (2.5.6) – 27

\l produces ł . . . . (2.5.6) – 27

\label{*marker*} . . . . (11.2.1) – 211

> Sets a marker in the text at this position with the name *marker*. It may be referred to either earlier or later in the document with the command \ref{*marker*} to output the counter that was then current, such as the section, equation, or figure number, or with the command \pageref{*marker*} to print the page number where the marker was set.

`\labelenum`*n* . . . . (4.3.5) – 73

A set of commands to produce the standard labels for the nesting levels of the enumerate environments, where *n* is one of i, ii, iii, or iv. For example,

`\renewcommand{\labelenumii}{\arabic{enumii}.)}`

changes the standard labels of the second-level enumerate environment to be 1.), 2.), and so on.

`\labelitem`*n* . . . . (4.3.5) – 73

A set of commands to produce the standard labels for the nesting levels of the itemize environments, where *n* is one of i, ii, iii, or iv. For example,

`\renewcommand{\labelitemi}{$\Rightarrow$}`

changes the standard labels of the outermost itemize environment to ⇒.

`\labelsep` . . . . (4.4.2) – 77

In a list environment, the distance between the label box and the list text. A new value is assigned with the `\setlength` command:

`\setlength{\labelsep}{5pt}`

`\labelwidth` . . . . (4.4.2) – 77

In a list environment, the width of the box reserved for the label. A new value is assigned with the `\setlength` command:

`\setlength{labelwidth}{2.2cm}`

`\Lambda` [m] produces Λ . . . . (7.3.1) – 127

`\lambda` [m] produces λ . . . . (7.3.1) – 127

`\langle` [m] produces $\langle$ . . . . (7.4.1) – 134

`\language{`*num*`}` . . . . (14.1) – 267

In TeX versions 3.0 and later, activates the set of hyphenation patterns number *num*. The patterns must be previously loaded into the format file by an initex run in which `\language{`*num*`}` was given before those patterns were read in.

`\large` . . . . (4.1.2) – 64

Switches to the font size `\large`, which is smaller than `\Large` but larger than `\normalsize`.

`\Large` . . . . (4.1.2) – 64

Switches to the font size `\Large`, which is smaller than `\LARGE` but larger than `\large`.

`\LARGE` . . . . (4.1.2) – 64

Switches to the font size `\LARGE`, which is smaller than `\huge` but larger than `\Large`.

`\LaTeX` produces LaTeX . . . . (2.1) – 22

> Adjusts the size of the bracket symbol *lbrack* to fit the height of the formula between the \left ... \right pair; for example, \left[. If there is to be no matching bracket, the \left and \right commands must still be given to specify the part of the formula to be sized, but the missing bracket is given as a period; for example, \right. for a dummy right bracket.

> A command inside the eqnarray environment that outputs its argument as though it had zero width, thus having no effect on the column widths. It is used mainly for the first row of a multirow formula.

> In a list environment, the amount by which the left edge of the text is indented relative to the surrounding text. A new value is assigned with the \setlength command. For nested list environments, different values for the indentation can be specified by adding i ... vi to the declaration name, such as
>
>   \setlength{\leftmarginiii}{0.5cm}

> With the amsmath package, used in the index to a \sqrt command to shift it slightly to the left. The *shift* is a number specifying how many units to move it. Example:
>
>   \sqrt[\leftroot{-1}\uproot{3}\beta]{k}

> Command to produce the function name 'lg' in formulas.

\lhd [m] produces ◁ . . . . (7.3.3) – 127

\lim [m] . . . . (7.3.8) – 130

Command to produce the function name 'lim' in formulas. A lower limit may be set as a subscript.

\liminf [m] . . . . (7.3.8) – 130

Command to produce the function name 'lim inf' in formulas. A lower limit may be set as a subscript.

\limits [m] . . . . (7.2.5), (7.3.7) – 125, 130

Places the upper and lower limits above and below the appropriate symbols whereas these would normally go just after them.

\limsup [m] . . . . (7.3.8) – 130

Command to produce the function name 'lim sup' in formulas. A lower limit may be set as a subscript.

\line ($\Delta x, \Delta y$) {*length*} . . . . (16.1.4) – 303

A picture element command within a picture environment for drawing horizontal and vertical lines of any length as well as slanted lines at a limited number of angles. For horizontal and vertical lines, the *length* argument is the actual length in units of \unitlength. For slanted lines, *length* is the length of the projection on to the x-axis (horizontal displacement). The slope is determined by the ($\Delta x, \Delta y$) arguments, which take on integral values such that $-6 \le \Delta x \le 6$ and $-6 \le \Delta y \le 6$. This command is the argument of a \put or \multiput command.

\linebreak[*n*] . . . . (2.7.2) – 35

A recommendation to break the line of text at this point so that it fills the horizontal space available (left and right justified). The urgency of the recommendation is given by the integral number *n* between 0 and 4, with the higher numbers meaning a stronger recommendation. A value of 4 is the same as the command without the optional argument and means an obligatory line break.

\linethickness{*thickness*} . . . . (16.1.4) – 309

Sets the thickness of the horizontal and vertical lines in the picture environment. The argument *thickness* is a length specification with units, for example, 1.2mm.

\linewidth . . . . (3.2.5) – 50

A length that is set to the current text line width, whether in one column of a two-column page, or in a minipage or parbox. This must never be changed, but is used when that width is needed, say, to set the width of an included graphics with

        \includegraphics[width=0.8\linewidth]{..}

\listfigurename . . . . (D.3.1) – 441

Command containing the heading for the list of figures. In English, this is 'List of Figures', but it may be altered for adaptation to other languages.

\listfiles [p] . . . . (11.1.1), (D.2.9) – 206, 437

> When given in the preamble, causes a list of all files read in during the processing to be printed to the monitor and to the transcript file at the end of the run. The list includes version number, date, and any additional information entered with one of the \Provides... commands.

\listoffigures . . . . (3.4.4) – 62

> Produces a list of figures with the entries from all the \caption commands in figure environments.

\listoftables   . . . . (3.4.4) – 62

> Produces a list of tables with the entries from all the \caption commands in table environments.

\listparindent . . . . (4.4.2) – 77

> Depth of indentation for the first line of a paragraph inside a list environment. A new value may be assigned with the \setlength command:
>
>   \setlength{\listparindent}{1em}

\listtablename . . . . (D.3.1) – 441

> Command containing the heading for the list of tables. In English, this is 'List of Tables', but it may be altered for adaptation to other languages.

\ll [m] produces ≪   . . . . (7.3.4) – 128

\ln [m] . . . . (7.3.8) – 130

> Command to produce the function name 'ln' in formulas.

\LoadClass[options]{class}[version] [p] . . . . (D.2.2) – 431

> This command may only be invoked within a class file to load another class file. It may only be called once within any class file. The file loaded must have the extension .cls. Any options specified in the \documentclass command are *not* passed over as global options.
>
> The optional *version* is a date given in the form *yyyy/mm/dd*, as, for example, 1994/08/01. If the date of the class file is earlier than this, a warning message is printed.

\LoadClassWithOptions{class}[version] [p] . . . . (D.2.2) – 431

> Like \LoadClass except all the currently specified options are automatically passed to *class*.

\location{number} . . . . (18.1) – 346

> In the letter document class, enters the sender's room number. In the standard LaTeX letter class, *number* is only output if \address has not been called. It is intended to be used in company letterheads classes such as mpletter.

\log [m] . . . . (7.3.8) – 130

> Command to produce the function name 'log' in formulas.

`\mainmatter` . . . . (3.3.5) – 60

In the book class, introduces the main body of text after the front matter by resetting the page numbering to 1 with Arabic numbers and by reactivating the chapter numbering with the \chapter command. It undoes the effects of \frontmatter.

`\makebox` [*width*] [*pos*] {*text*} . . . . (5.1.1) – 86

Produces a box of width *width* containing *text* centered horizontally unless *pos* is given to specify that it is to be left (l) or right (r) justified. It may also have the value s to stretch the text to *width*.

`\makebox` (*x_dimen*, *y_dimen*) [*pos*] {*text*} . . . . (16.1.4) – 300

Picture element command to produce a box of width *x_dimen* and height *y_dimen* within the picture environment. Without the optional argument *pos*, the text is centered vertically and horizontally. The text may be left or right justified, and/or aligned at the top or bottom, by setting *pos* to a combination of the letters l, r, t, and b, such as tr for top, right; *pos* may also contain s to stretch the text to the full width. The command is used as the argument of a \put or \multiput command.

`\makeglossary` [p] . . . . (11.4.4) – 226

Command to activate the \glossary commands in the text.

`\makeindex` [p] . . . . (11.4.2) – 223

Command to activate the \index commands in the text.

`\makelabel` {*text*} . . . . (4.4.1) – 75

An internal command that is called by the \item command to produce the actual label *text* within a list environment.

`\makelabels` . . . . (18.1) – 349

Produces address labels in the letter document class using the entries from the \begin{letter} environment.

\MakeLowercase{*text_cmd*}

>   Converts *text_cmd* (text and commands) to lowercase.

\MakeShortVerb{\c} . . . . (4.6.1, B.5.3) – 82, 386

>   When the standard package shortvrb has been loaded, this command makes the character *c* a shorthand form for \verbc: Everything that appears between two occurrences of *c* is printed literally, in typewriter type. With \DeleteShortVerb{\c}, the character is restored to its normal meaning. Example: \MakeShortVerb{\|}

\maketitle . . . . (3.3.1) – 56

>   Produces a title page using entries in the \author and \title commands and, optionally, those in the \date and \thanks commands.

\MakeUppercase{*text_cmd*}

>   Converts *text_cmd* (text and commands) to uppercase.

\mapsto [m] produces ↦ . . . . (7.3.5) – 129

\marginpar[*left_text*]{*right_text*} . . . . (5.2.5) – 99

>   Produces a marginal note at the right of the text containing *right_text*. With two-sided formatting, the marginal note goes into the left margin on the even pages, in which case the optional *left_text* will be written instead. For two-column text, the marginal notes always go into the 'outer' margin and, again, *left_text* will be used for the left margin.

\marginparpush . . . . (5.2.6) – 100

>   The minimum vertical separation between two marginal notes. A new value may be assigned with the \setlength command.

\marginparsep . . . . (5.2.6) – 100

>   The spacing between the edge of the text and a marginal note. A new value may be assigned with the \setlength command.

\marginparwidth . . . . (5.2.6) – 100

>   The width of the box reserved for marginal notes. A new value may be assigned with the \setlength command.

\markboth{*left_head*}{*right_head*} . . . . (3.2.1) – 46

>   Sets the text entries for the left- and right-page headlines in two-sided formatting when the page style myheadings has been selected or when the automatic entries of page style headings are to be changed.

\markright{*head*} . . . . (3.2.1) – 46

>   Sets the text entry for the page headline when the page style myheadings has been selected or when the automatic entry of page style headings is to be manually changed. In two-sided formatting, only the right headline is set with this command.

\mathbf{*text*} [m] . . . . (7.4.2) – 134

This command sets *text* in a bold font (\bfseries) within math mode. Spaces are ignored as usual.

\mathcal{*text*} [m] . . . . (7.3.2), (7.4.2) – 127, 134

This command sets *text* in calligraphic letters within math mode:
$\mathcal{ABC}$ = $\mathcal{ABC}$.

\mathindent . . . . (3.1.1) – 43

The indentation of displayed formulas from the left margin when the option fleqn has been selected. A new value may be assigned with the \setlength command:
\setlength{\mathindent}{25pt}

\mathit{*text*} [m] . . . . (7.4.2) – 134

This command sets *text* in a text italic font (\itshape) within math mode. It differs from \mathnormal in that the spacing between the letters is as in regular text. Compare *mathit* and *mathnormal*.

\mathnormal{*text*} [m] . . . . (7.3.1), (7.4.2) – 126, 134

This command sets *text* in the normal (italic) math font within math mode. In this font, capital Greek letters are also set in italics:
$\Gamma\mathnormal{\Gamma}$ = $\Gamma\Gamma$.

\mathring{*x*} [m] . . . . (7.3.9) – 131

A ring accent in mathematical formulas: \mathring{a} = $\mathring{a}$.

\mathrm{*text*} [m] . . . . (7.4.2) – 134

This command sets *text* in a Roman font (\rmfamily) within math mode. Spaces are ignored as usual.

\mathsf{*text*} [m] . . . . (7.4.2) – 134

This command sets *text* in a sans serif font (\sffamily) within math mode. Spaces are ignored as usual.

\mathtt{*text*} [m] . . . . (7.4.2) – 134

This command sets *text* in a typewriter font (\ttfamily) within math mode. Spaces are ignored as usual.

\max [m] . . . . (7.3.8) – 130

Command to produce the function name 'max' in formulas. A lower limit may be set as a subscript.

\mbox{*text*} produces an LR box around *text* . . . . (5.1.1) – 86

\mddefault . . . . (A.2.1) – 365

This command defines the series attribute that is selected with the \mdseries command. It may be redefined with \renewcommand:
\renewcommand{\mddefault}{m}

\mdseries . . . . (4.1.3), (A.2) – 66, 365

> This declaration switches to a font in the current family and shape, but with the medium series attribute.

\medskip . . . . (2.7.3) – 36

> Inserts large vertical spacing of the amount \medskipamount. See also \bigskip and \smallskip.

\medskipamount

> Standard value for the amount of vertical spacing that is inserted with the command \medskip. May be changed with the \setlength command:
>
> \setlength{\medskipamount}{3ex plus1ex minus1ex}

\medspace [m][a] . . . . (15.2.5) – 280

> With the amsmath package, this is an alias for \:, a medium space in a math formula.

\MessageBreak . . . . (D.2.7) – 435

> Forces a new line in the texts of error, warning, and information messages. These are the only places where it may be invoked, otherwise it does nothing.

\mho [m] produces ℧ . . . . (7.3.6) – 129

\mid [m] produces ∣ . . . . (7.3.4) – 128

\min [m] . . . . (7.3.8) – 130

> Command to produce the function name 'min' in formulas. A lower limit may be set as a subscript.

\mod{*arg*} [m][a] . . . . (15.2.5) – 279

> With the amsopn or amsmath packages, command to produce the function name 'mod' in formulas in the form:
>
> $y\mod{a+b} = y \mod a + b$

\models [m] produces ⊨ . . . . (7.3.4) – 128

\mp [m] produces ∓ . . . . (7.3.3) – 127

\mspace{*mu*} [m][a] . . . . (15.2.5) – 281

> With the amsmath package, inserts spacing in math formulas; *mu* is a math space in units of mu (=1/18 em): \mspace{-4mu}.

\mu [m] produces μ . . . . (7.3.1) – 127

\multicolumn{*n*}{*col*}{*text*} . . . . (6.2.1) – 107

> Merges the next *n* columns in the array and tabular environments, formatting the text entry *text* according to the single-column definition *col*, which may be l, c, r, as well as |.

\multiput$(x,y)(\Delta x,\Delta y)${n}{*pic_elem*} . . . . (16.1.3) – 299

Multiple positioning command in the picture environment. The object *pic_elem* is placed n times, at (x,y), $(x+\Delta x, y+\Delta y), \ldots (x+(n-1)\Delta x, y+(n-1)\Delta y)$.

\multlinegap [m][a] . . . . (15.2.6) – 283

A length that determines the left and right margins of formulas produced with the $\mathcal{AMS}$-LaTeX multline environment; initial value is 10 pt but may be reset by the user.

\nabla [m] produces ∇ . . . . (7.3.6) – 129

\name{*sender*} . . . . (18.2) – 350

In the letter document class, enters the sender's name.

\natural [m] produces $\natural$ . . . . (7.3.6) – 129

\nearrow [m] produces $\nearrow$ . . . . (7.3.5) – 129

\NeedsTeXFormat{*format*}[*version*] [p] . . . . (D.2.1) – 430

Declares the TeX format that is necessary for processing the file. This should be the first statement in the file. At the moment, the only legitimate value for *format* is LaTeX2e. The *version*, if included, must be given as a date in the form *yyyy/mm/dd*, specifying the earliest possible release date of the format that is consistent with all the features employed in the file. Example:

    \NeedsTeXFormat{LaTeX2e}[1994/06/01]

\neg [m] produces $\neg$ . . . . (7.3.6) – 129

\negmedspace [m][a] . . . . (15.2.5) – 280

With the amsmath package, this inserts a negative medium space in a math formula.

\negthickspace [m][a] . . . . (15.2.5) – 280

With the amsmath package, this inserts a negative thick space in a math formula.

\negthinspace [m][a] . . . . (15.2.5) – 280

With the amsmath package, this is an alias for \!, a negative thin space in a math formula.

\neq [m] produces $\neq$ . . . . (7.3.4) – 128

\newboolean{*switch*} . . . . (10.3.5) – 193

Requires the standard LaTeX package ifthen. Creates a new boolean switch. The value of the switch is set with \setboolean{*switch*}{*value*}, where *value* is true or false. Its value is tested with \boolean{*switch*}, which may be used as a logical statement in the *test* part of \ifthenelse and \whiledo.

`\newcommand{`*com_name*`}[`*narg*`][`*opt*`]{`*def*`}` . . . . (10.3) – 185

Defines a user command with the name `\`*com_name* to be *def.* The first optional argument *narg* ≤ 9 specifies how many variable arguments the command is to have, which appear in the *def* as the replacement characters #1 to #*narg*. If the second optional argument is present, the first argument of the new command is optional and takes on the value *opt* if it is not explicitly given.

`\newcommand*{`*com_name*`}[`*narg*`][`*opt*`]{`*def*`}` . . . . (D.2.6) – 435

The same as `\newcommand` except that the arguments to `\`*com_name* must be 'short', not containing any new paragraphs.

`\newcounter{`*counter_name*`}[`*in_counter*`]` . . . . (10.1.2) – 182

Establishes a new counter with the name *counter_name*. The optional argument *in_counter* is the name of an existing counter which, when incremented, resets the new counter to zero; that is, the new counter is a subcounter of *in_counter*.

`\newenvironment{`*env_name*`}[`*narg*`][`*opt*`]{`*beg_def*`}{`*end_def*`}`

. . . . (10.4) – 194

Defines a user environment with the name *env_name*, which has the `\begin` definition *beg_def* and the `\end` definition *end_def*. The optional argument *narg* ≤ 9 specifies how many variable arguments the environment is to have, which appear in the *beg_def* as the replacement characters #1 to #*narg*. If the second optional argument is present, the first argument of the `\begin` command is optional and takes on the value *opt* if it is not explicitly given.

`\newenvironment*{`*env_name*`}[`*narg*`][`*opt*`]{`*beg_def*`}{`*end_def*`}`

. . . . (D.2.6) – 435

The same as `\newenvironment` except that the arguments to `\begin{`*env_name*`}` must be 'short', not containing any new paragraphs.

`\newfont{\`*font_cmd*`}{\`*font_name* `scaled` *size*`}` . . . . (4.1.5) – 67

Establishes the relation between the font file name *file_name* magnified by the scaling factor *size* and a font selection command `\`*font_cmd*. After `\`*font_cmd* has been called, `\baselineskip`, the interline spacing, still has its previous value.

`\newlength{\`*length_cmd*`}` . . . . (10.2) – 184

Creates a new length command with the name `\`*length_cmd* and initializes it to 0 pt. New values may be assigned as for all length commands with the `\setlength` command:

   `\setlength{\`*length_cmd*`}{`*length*`}`

The quantity *length* must have units (such as cm, pt) and may be a rubber length.

`\newline` . . . . (2.7.2) – 34

Terminates and starts a line of text *without* right justifying it.

`\newpage` . . . . (2.7.4) – 36

Terminates and starts a new page, leaving the rest of the page blank.

\newsavebox{\boxname}   . . . . (5.1.1) – 87

Creates a storage box with the name \boxname in which LR boxes may be saved with the \savebox command.

\newtheorem{type}[num_like]{title}
\newtheorem{type}{title}[in_ctr]   . . . . (4.5) – 80

Defines a new theorem-like environment named *type* which when called prints a theorem declaration with the name *title* in **boldface**, followed by an automatic sequential number and the actual text of the environment in *italic*. The optional argument *num_like* is the name of another theorem structure that is to share the same numbering counter. The other optional argument, *in_ctr*, is the name of a sectioning counter, such as chapter, which is to reset the theorem counter every time it is incremented. That is, the theorem counter is a subcounter of *in_ctr*. Only one of the optional arguments may be given.

\NG   . . . . (A.3.2) – 371

When T1 encoding is active, prints the character Ŋ.

\ng   . . . . (A.3.2) – 371

When T1 encoding is active, prints the character ŋ.

\ni [m] produces ∋ . . . . (7.3.4) – 128

\nocite{key}   . . . . (12.1) – 228

The entry in the literature database with the keyword *key* will be included in the bibliography without any citation (reference) in the text. With \nocite{*}, *all* entries in all databases will be included.

\nofiles [p] . . . . (B.6) – 390

Issued in the preamble, this command suppresses the output of the auxiliary files .aux, .glo, .idx, .lof, .lot, and .toc.

\noindent   . . . . (3.2.4) – 49

The first line of the *next* paragraph will *not* be indented.

\nolimits [m]   . . . . (7.3.7) – 130

Places the upper and lower limits after the appropriate symbols whereas these would normally go just above or below them.

\nolinebreak[n]   . . . . (2.7.2) – 35

A recommendation *not* to break the line of text at this point. The urgency of the recommendation is given by the integral number *n* between 0 and 4, with the higher numbers meaning a stronger recommendation. A value of 4 is the same as the command without the optional argument and means absolutely no line break here.

\nonfrenchspacing   . . . . (2.7.1) – 32

Countermands \frenchspacing, switching back to the standard formatting in which extra word spacing is inserted at the end of a sentence.

`\nonumber` [m]   . . . .   (7.4.7) – 140

> The formula line in an `eqnarray` environment in which this command appears will *not* contain an equation number.

`\nopagebreak[`*n*`]`   . . . .   (2.7.4) – 36

> A recommendation *not* to break the page at this point. The urgency of the recommendation is given by the integral number *n* between 0 and 4, with the higher numbers meaning a stronger recommendation. A value of 4 is the same as the command without the optional argument and means absolutely no page break here.

`\normalcolor`   . . . .   (8.2) – 166

> A command that normally does nothing. However, if the `color` package has been loaded, it resets the color for text to be the color that was in effect at the end of the preamble, normally black. A `\color` command in the preamble can alter this 'standard' color.
>
> This command is called by many internal LaTeX macros to reset the text color when printing headlines and headings. Other packages should also use it so that they are consistent with the `color` package.

`\normalfont`   . . . .   (4.1.3), (A.2) – 66, 365

> This declaration switches to the font with the default family, shape, and series attributes.

`\normalmarginpar`   . . . .   (5.2.5) – 99

> Countermands `\reversemarginpar`, switching back to the standard placement of marginal notes in the 'outer' margin.

`\normalsize`   . . . .   (4.1.2) – 64

> Switches to the font size `\normalsize`, the size selected by the option in the `\documentclass` or `\documentstyle` commands. It is smaller than `\large` but larger than `\small`.

`\not` [m]   . . . .   (7.3.4) – 128

> Changes the following comparison symbol into its negative counterpart:
>
> $\not\cong$ = $\ncong$

`\notag{`*mark*`}` [m][a]   . . . .   (15.2.6) – 282

> Within one of the $\mathcal{A}_{\mathcal{M}}S$-LaTeX alignment environments, suppresses the automatic equation number.

`\notin` [m] produces $\notin$ . . . .   (7.3.4) – 128

`\nu` [m] produces ν . . . .   (7.3.1) – 127

`\numberwithin{`*ctr*`}{`*in_ctr*`}` [a]   . . . .   (15.2.7) – 288

> With the amsmath package, redefines the counter *ctr* to be a subcounter of *in_ctr*, meaning it is reset every time *in_ctr* is incremented. The value of *in_ctr* is printed with that of *ctr*. This is normally used to make equations in an article to be numbered within sections:
>
> `\numberwithin{equation}{section}`

Sets the left margin for the odd-numbered pages in document class book or when the option twoside has been selected for other classes. In all other cases, it sets the left margin for *all* pages. A new value is assigned with the \setlength command:

```
\setlength{\evensidemargin}{1.5cm}
```

Starts a new page and switches from two-column to one-column page formatting.

In slides class, a command to be issued in the preamble to generate only those notes whose numbers appear in *note_nums*. The command behaves the same as \onlyslides for slides.

In slides class, a command to be issued in the preamble to generate only those slides whose numbers appear in *slide_nums*. The numbers are separated by commas and may include a range with a hyphen: \onlyslides{4,10-13,23}.

In the letter environment of the letter class, this sets the form of the salutation at the start of the letter text, for example, \opening{Dear George,}.

A command that may only be used in the definition of options, especially default options. It declares the \CurrentOption to be unprocessed. This is used if the processing of a default option should fail, say, because some file is missing. LaTeX is then informed that this requested option is still outstanding.

\oslash [m] produces ⊘ . . . . (7.3.3) – 127

\otimes [m] produces ⊗ . . . . (7.3.3) – 127

\oval (*x_dimen*, *y_dimen*) [*part*] . . . . (16.1.4) – 305

> Picture element command to produce an oval with width *x_dimen* and height *y_dimen* in the picture environment. The optional *part* argument may take on values of t, b, l, and r to draw only the top, bottom, left, or right halves of the oval. A combination of these values may be given to draw only a quarter of the oval, such as tl or lt for the top left part. To be used as an argument in a \put or \multiput command.

\ovalbox{*text*} . . . . (5.1.9) – 94

> With the fancybox package, is a variant of \fbox, drawing a framed box with round corners around *text*; the thickness of the lines is given by \thinlines.

\Ovalbox{*text*} . . . . (5.1.9) – 94

> With the fancybox package, is the same as \ovalbox but the thickness of the lines is given by \thicklines.

\overbrace{*sub_form*} [m] . . . . (7.4.4) – 137

> Produces a horizontal curly brace over the math formula *sub_form*. Any following superscript will be placed centered above the horizontal brace.

$$\overbrace{a+b} = \overbrace{a+b}$$

$$\overbrace{x+y+z}^{\xi\eta\zeta} = \overbrace{x+y+z}^{\xi\eta\zeta}$$

\overleftarrow{*expr*} [m][a] . . . . (15.2.2) – 274

> With the amsmath package, places a long leftward-pointing arrow over the mathematical expression *expr*.

\overleftrightarrow{*expr*} [m][a] . . . . (15.2.2) – 274

> With the amsmath package, places a long double arrow over the mathematical expression *expr*.

\overline{*sub_form*} [m] . . . . (7.4.4) – 137

> Produces a horizontal bar over the math formula *sub_form*:
> $$\overline{a-b} = \overline{a-b}$$

\overrightarrow{*expr*} [m][a] . . . . (15.2.2) – 274

> With the amsmath package, places a long rightward-pointing arrow over the mathematical expression *expr*.

\overset{*char*}{*symbol*} [m][a] . . . . (15.2.2) – 273

> With the amsmath package, places *char* over the math symbol *symbol* in superscript size.

Writes an error message *error_text* to the monitor and transcript file, labeled with the package name, and halts processing, waiting for a user response as for a LaTeX error. If H⟨*return*⟩ is typed, the *help* text is printed. Both *error_text* and *help* may contain \MessageBreak for a new line, \space for a forced space, and \protect before commands that are to have their names printed literally and not interpreted.

Is like \PackageWarningNoLine except that the text *info_text* is only written to the transcript file and not to the monitor.

Writes *warn_text* to the monitor and transcript file, labeled with the package name and the current line number of the input file. Processing continues. The *warn_text* is formatted in the same way as for \PackageError.

Is like \PackageWarning except that the current line number of the input file is not printed.

A recommendation to break the page at this point. The urgency of the recommendation is given by the integral number *n* between 0 and 4, with the higher numbers meaning a stronger recommendation. A value of 4 is the same as the command without the optional argument and means an obligatory page break.

A command made available with the color package. Sets the background color starting with the current page. All following pages have the same background color until \pagecolor is called once more. The *col_spec* is the same as for \color.

Command in the letter document class containing the text for page numbers after the first page. In English, this is 'Page', but it may be altered for adaptation to other languages.

Determines the style of the page numbering and resets the page counter to 1. Possible values for *style* are: arabic, roman, Roman, alph, and Alph.

Prints the number of the page where *marker* has been set by a \label{*marker*} command.

`\pagestyle{`*style*`}` [p] . . . . (3.2) – 46

> Determines the page style, that is, the contents of the head- and footlines on every page. Possible values for *style* are: `plain`, `empty`, `headings`, and `myheadings`.

`\paperheight` . . . . (3.2.5) – 51

> The total height of the page as specified by the page size option in the `\documentclass` command line. With the default `lettersize` option, this is 11 in; with a4paper, it is 29.7 cm. The additional option `landscape` interchanges the values of `\paperwidth` and `\paperheight`.

`\paperwidth` . . . . (3.2.5) – 51

> The total width of the page as specified by the page size option in the `\documentclass` command line. With the default `lettersize` option, this is 8.5 in; with a4paper, it is 21 cm. The additional option `landscape` interchanges the values of `\paperwidth` and `\paperheight`.

`\par` . . . . (2.5.1) – 26

> Ends the current paragraph and begins a new one. This command is equivalent to a blank line.

`\paragraph[`*short title*`]{`*title*`}` . . . . (3.3.3) – 58

> The second to last command in the sectioning hierarchy, coming between `\subsubsection` and `\subparagraph`. It formats *title* with the current subsubsection number and an automatic sequential paragraph number. If the optional *short title* is given, it appears in place of *title* in the table of contents.

`\paragraph*{`*title*`}` . . . . (3.3.3) – 58

> The same as `\paragraph` but without a number or an entry in the table of contents.

`\parallel` [m] produces ∥ . . . . (7.3.4) – 128

`\parbox[`*pos*`][`*height*`][`*inner_pos*`]{`*width*`}{`*text*`}` . . . . (5.1.3), (5.1.5) – 88, 90

> Produces a vertical box of width *width* in which *text* is set in lines that are left and right justified to this width. The vertical positioning with respect to the surrounding text is determined by the optional argument *pos*: t for alignment with its top line, b with its bottom line, and centered with no argument. The two additional optional arguments are: *height* to give the total height and *inner_pos* to specify how the text is to be positioned inside it. Possible values are t for top, b for bottom, c for centered, and s to be stretched out to fill the whole vertical space. The default is the value of the external positioning *pos* option. The *height* argument may contain the parameters `\height`, `\depth`, `\width`, and `\totalheight`.

`\parindent` . . . . (3.2.4) – 49

> The amount of indentation for the first line of a paragraph. A new value may be assigned with the `\setlength` command:
>
>   \setlength{\parindent}{1.5em}

`\parsep` . . . . (4.4.2) – 76

The vertical spacing between paragraphs within a `list` environment. A new value may be assigned with the `\setlength` command:

    \setlength{\parsep}{2pt plus1pt minus1pt}

`\parskip` . . . . (3.2.4) – 49

The vertical spacing between paragraphs. A new value may be assigned with the `\setlength` command:

    \setlength{\parskip}{3pt plus1pt minus2pt}

`\part`[*short title*]{*title*} . . . . (3.3.3) – 58

The highest command in the sectioning hierarchy. It begins a new 'Part' with an automatic sequential part number and the heading *title*. The following sectioning numbers are not influenced by the part number. If the optional *short title* is given, it appears in place of *title* in the table of contents.

`\part`*{*title*} . . . . (3.3.3) – 58

The same as `\part` but without a number or an entry in the table of contents.

`\partial` [m] produces ∂ . . . . (7.3.6) – 129

`\partname` . . . . (D.3.1) – 441

Command containing the part heading. In English, this is 'Part', but it may be altered for adaptation to other languages.

`\partopsep` . . . . (4.4.2) – 76

The additional vertical spacing at the beginning and/or end of a listing when a blank line precedes or follows the environment commands. A new value may be assigned with the `\setlength` command:

    \setlength{\partopsep}{2pt plus1pt minus1pt}

`\PassOptionsToClass`{*options*}{*class*} [p] . . . . (D.2.3) – 433

Assigns the options in the list *options* to the specified class file, which is later loaded with `\LoadClass`. This command must be called from a class file or from another file input by a class file. It may be used in the definition of options or in a configuration file to activate options.

`\PassOptionsToPackage`{*options*}{*package*} [p] . . . . (D.2.3) – 433

Assigns the options in the list *options* to the specified package file, which is later loaded with `\RequirePackage`. This command may be called from a class or package file. It may be used in the definition of options or in a configuration file to activate certain options.

`\path`{*directory*} . . . . (4.6.2) – 83

With the `url` package, prints *directory* literally, in typewriter font, with line breaks after non-letters, without hyphens. It functions much the same as the `\url` command but is *logically* distinct since it is encoding something different.

\perp [m] produces ⊥ . . . . (7.3.4) – 128

\Phi [m] produces Φ . . . . (7.3.1) – 127

\phi [m] produces φ . . . . (7.3.1) – 127

\Pi [m] produces Π . . . . (7.3.1) – 127

\pi [m] produces π . . . . (7.3.1) – 127

\pm [m] produces ± . . . . (7.3.4) – 128

\pmb{*symbol*} [m][a] . . . . (15.2.1) – 270

> When one of the packages amsmath or amsbsy has been loaded, this command prints *symbol* in simulated boldface. This is done by printing it several times slightly displaced.

\pmod{*arg*} [m] . . . . (7.3.8), (15.2.5) – 130, 279

> Command to produce the function name 'mod' in formulas in the form:
> $$y\backslash\text{pmod\{a+b\}} = y \pmod{a + b}$$

\pod{*arg*} [m][a] . . . . (15.2.5) – 279

> With the amsopn or amsmath packages, command to produce the function name 'mod' in formulas in the form:
> $$y\backslash\text{pod\{a+b\}} = y \; (a + b)$$

\poptabs . . . . (6.1.4) – 103

> Restores the last set of tabular stops in the tabbing environment that has been saved with \pushtabs.

\pounds produces £ . . . . (2.5.5) – 27

\Pr [m] . . . . (7.3.8) – 130

> Command to produce the function name 'Pr' in formulas. A lower limit may be set as a subscript.

\prec [m] produces ≺ . . . . (7.3.4) – 128

\preceq [m] produces ≼ . . . . (7.3.4) – 128

\prime [m] produces ′ (identical to the ′ symbol) . . . . (7.3.6) – 129

\printindex . . . . (11.4.3) – 225

> A command defined in the makeidx.sty file that generates theindex environment after the program MakeIndex has processed the .idx file.

\ProcessOptions [p] . . . . (D.2.3) – 432

> In a class or package file, this command processes the requested options by executing the \ds@ commands for each one *in the order in which they were defined*. The \ds@ commands are then erased.

\ProcessOptions* [p] . . . . (D.2.3) – 432

> This is the same as \ProcessOptions except that the \ds@ commands are executed *in the order in which the options were requested*.

\prod [m] produces $\prod$ . . . . (7.3.7) – 129

\propto [m] produces $\propto$ . . . . (7.3.4) – 128

\protect   . . . . (D.2.5) – 434

> Fragile commands may be used in moving arguments when they are preceded
> by the \protect command. For example:
>
>   \section{The \protect\pounds{} Sign}.

\providecommand{*com_name*} [*narg*] [*opt*] {*def*}   . . . . (10.3.1) – 186

> The same as \newcommand except that if a command with the name *com_name*
> already exists, the new definition is ignored.

\providecommand*{*com_name*} [*narg*] [*opt*] {*def*}   . . . . (D.2.6) – 435

> The same as \providecommand except that the arguments to *com_name* must
> be 'short', not containing any new paragraphs.

\ProvidesClass{*class*} [*version*] [p]   . . . . (D.2.1) – 431

> At the beginning of a class file, this statement declares the name of the class and
> its version, to be checked against the name and version in the \documentclass
> or \LoadClass command that input it. The *version* specification, if present,
> consists of three parts: date, version number, and additional information. For
> example:
>
>   \ProvidesClass{thesis}[1995/01/25 v3.8 U of Saigon]

\ProvidesFile{*file_name*} [*version*]   . . . . (D.2.1) – 431

> At the beginning of a general file, this statement declares its name and version.
> No checking is done when the file is read in with \input, but the information is
> printed out if \listfiles has been activated. This command is not limited to
> the preamble as the other \Provides.. commands are.

\ProvidesPackage{*class*} [*version*] [p]   . . . . (D.2.1) – 431

> At the beginning of a package file, this statement declares the name of the
> package and its version, to be checked against the name and version in the
> \usepackage or \RequirePackage command that input it. The *version* specifi-
> cation, if present, consists of three parts: date, version number, and additional
> information. For example:
>
>   \ProvidesPackage{notes}[1995/02/13 1.2 G. Smith]

\ps *text*   . . . . (18.1) – 347

> Adds a postscript to a letter in the letter document class.

\Psi [m] produces Ψ . . . . (7.3.1) – 127

\psi [m] produces ψ . . . . (7.3.1) – 127

\pushtabs   . . . . (6.1.4) – 103

> Saves the current set of tabulator stops in the tabbing environment. It may be
> recalled with the \poptabs command.

\put(x,y){*pic_elem*} . . . . (16.1.3) – 299

The positioning command within a picture environment. The picture element *pic_elem* is placed with its reference point at the location (x,y).

\qbezier[*num*](x_1,y_1)(x_2,y_2)(x_3,y_3) . . . . (16.1.4) – 308

This command can be given within the picture environment to draw a quadratic Bézier curve from point (x_1,y_1) to (x_3,y_3), using (x_2,y_2) as the extra Bézier point. The curve is drawn as $num + 1$ dots if the optional argument *num* is given, otherwise *num* is calculated automatically to produce a solid line. It is the same as \bezier except that *num* is optional.

\qquad . . . . (2.7.1) – 33

Inserts horizontal spacing of size 2 em.

\quad . . . . (2.7.1) – 33

Inserts horizontal spacing of size 1 em.

\quotedblbase . . . . (A.3.2) – 371

When T1 encoding is active, prints the symbol „.

\quotesinglbase . . . . (A.3.2) – 371

When T1 encoding is active, prints the symbol ‚.

\r{*x*} . . . . (2.5.7) – 27

Produces a circle accent: \r{o} = o̊.

\raggedbottom . . . . (3.2.5) – 51

The standard page formatting for article, report, and letter document classes when the twoside option has *not* been selected. The spacing between paragraphs is fixed so that the last line will vary from page to page. The opposite command is \flushbottom.

\raggedleft . . . . (4.2.2) – 68

After this declaration, the lines of text will only be right justified and the left margin will be uneven. The individual lines are terminated by \\. See also \begin{flushright}.

\raggedright . . . . (4.2.2) – 68

After this declaration, the lines of text will only be left justified and the right margin will be uneven. The individual lines are terminated by \\. See also \begin{flushleft}.

\raisebox{*lift*}[*height*][*depth*]{*text*} . . . . (5.1.2) – 87

An LR box containing *text* is raised an amount *lift* above the current baseline. If *lift* is negative, the box is lowered. The optional arguments state that it is to be treated as though it extended by *height* above and by *depth* below the baseline regardless of its true extents.

`\raisetag{`*len*`}` [m][a] . . . . (15.2.6) – 282

Within one of the $\mathcal{A}_{\mathcal{M}}S$-LATEX alignment environments, raises the equation number or marker by *len* above its normal position.

`\rangle` [m] produces ⟩ . . . . (7.4.1) – 134

`\rceil` [m] produces ⌉ . . . . (7.4.1) – 134

`\Re` [m] produces ℜ . . . . (7.3.6) – 129

`\ref{`*marker*`}` . . . . (11.2.1) – 211

Prints the number of the section, equation, figure, or table where *marker* has been set by a `\label{`*marker*`}` command.

`\reflectbox{`*text*`}` . . . . (8.1.2) – 156

A command made available with the `graphics` package that reflects the contents *text* as an LR box so that left and right are reversed.

`\refname` . . . . (D.3.1) – 441

Command containing the heading for the bibliography in `article` document class. In English, this is 'References', but it may be altered for adaptation to other languages.

`\refstepcounter{`*counter*`}` . . . . (10.1.3) – 182

Increases the value of the number stored in *counter* by one, the same as `\stepcounter`, but also makes the specified counter the relevant one for the `\label`-`\ref` cross-referencing commands.

`\renewcommand{`*com_name*`}[`*narg*`][`*opt*`]{`*def*`}` . . . . (10.3) – 185

The same as `\newcommand` except that the command `\`*com_name* must already exist, otherwise an error message is printed.

`\renewcommand*{`*com_name*`}[`*narg*`][`*opt*`]{`*def*`}` . . . . (D.2.6) – 435

The same as `\renewcommand` except that the arguments to `\`*com_name* must be 'short', not containing any new paragraphs.

`\renewenvironment{`*env*`}[`*narg*`][`*opt*`]{`*beg*`}{`*end*`}` . . . . (10.4) – 194

The same as `\newenvironment` except that the environment *env* must already exist, otherwise an error message is printed.

`\renewenvironment*{`*env*`}[`*narg*`][`*opt*`]{`*beg*`}{`*end*`}` . . . . . . (D.2.6) – 435

The same as `\renewenvironment` except that the arguments to `\begin{`*env*`}` must be 'short', not containing any new paragraphs.

`\RequirePackage[`*options*`]{`*packages*`}[`*version*`]` [p] . . . . (D.2.2) – 431

This command is the equivalent of `\usepackage` within a class or package file. It loads one or more package files with the extension `.sty`. More than one package may be specified in *packages*, the names being separated by commas. Any *options* listed will be applied to all packages. Furthermore, any options listed in the `\documentclass` command will also be applied to the package files.

The optional *version* is a date given in the form *yyyy/mm/dd*, as, for example, 1994/08/01. If the date of the package file is earlier than this, a warning message is printed.

\RequirePackageWithOptions{*package*}[*version*] [p] . . . . . . (D.2.2) – 431

Like \RequirePackage except all the currently specified options are automatically passed to *package*.

\resizebox{*h_length*}{*v_length*}{*text*} . . . . (8.1.2) – 156

A command made available with the graphics package that scales the contents *text* as an LR box such that the horizontal size becomes *h_length* and the vertical size *v_length*. If either size is given as !, the one scale factor is applied to both dimensions.

\resizebox*{*h_length*}{*v_length*}{*text*} . . . . (8.1.2) – 156

The same as \resizebox except that the vertical size *v_length* refers to the total height plus depth of the LR box.

\reversemarginpar . . . . (5.2.5) – 99

Changes the placement of marginal notes from the standard (right or 'outer' margin) to the opposite side. Can be countermanded with \normalmarginpar.

\rfloor [m] produces ⌋ . . . . (7.4.1) – 134

\rhd [m] produces ▷ . . . . (7.3.3) – 127

\rho [m] produces ρ . . . . (7.3.1) – 127

\right*rbrack* [m] . . . . (7.4.1) – 133

Adjusts the size of the bracket symbol *rbrack* to fit the height of the formula between the \left ... \right pair. For example, \right]. If there is to be no matching bracket, the \left and \right commands must still be given to specify the part of the formula to be sized, but the missing bracket is given as a period (for example, \left.).

\Rightarrow [m] produces ⇒ . . . . (7.3.5) – 129

\rightarrow [m] produces → . . . . (7.3.5) – 129

\rightharpoondown [m] produces ⇁ . . . . (7.3.5) – 129

\rightharpoonup [m] produces ⇀ . . . . (7.3.5) – 129

\rightleftharpoons [m] produces ⇌ . . . . (7.3.5) – 129

\rightmargin . . . . (4.4.2) – 77

In a list environment, the amount by which the right edge of the text is indented relative to the right side of the surrounding text. Standard value is 0 pt. A new value is assigned with the \setlength command:

    \setlength{\rightmargin}{0.5cm}

\rmdefault . . . . (A.2.1) – 365

This command defines the family attribute that is selected with the \rmfamily command. It may be redefined with \renewcommand:

    \renewcommand{\rmdefault}{ptm}

\rmfamily . . . . (4.1.3), (A.2) – 66, 364
> This declaration switches to a font in the current series and shape, but with the Roman family attribute.

\Roman{*counter*} . . . . (10.1.4) – 183
> Prints the current value of the *counter* as an uppercase Roman numeral.

\roman{*counter*} . . . . (10.1.4) – 183
> Prints the current value of the *counter* as a lowercase Roman numeral.

\rotatebox{*angle*}{*text*} . . . . (8.1.2) – 156
> A command made available with the graphics package that rotates the contents *text* as an LR box through the *angle* expressed in degrees. The rotation is counterclockwise about the left-hand end of the baseline of the box.

\rule[*lift*]{*width*}{*height*} . . . . (5.1.6) – 91
> Produces a black rectangle of width *width* and height *height*, raised above the baseline by an amount *lift* if this optional argument is given. A value of '0 pt' for either the *width* or *height* creates an invisible horizontal or vertical *strut* that may be used to make spacing.

\rvert [m][a] produces | (right delimiter) . . . . (15.2.5) – 281
\rVert [m][a] produces ‖ (right delimiter) . . . . (15.2.5) – 281

\S produces § . . . . (2.5.5) – 27
\SS produces SS, the uppercase version of \ss, ß . . . . (2.5.6) – 27
\savebox{*boxname*}[*width*] [*pos*]{*text*} . . . . (5.1.1) – 87
> Functions the same as the \makebox command except that the box contents are not output but saved under the name *boxname*, which has been previously defined with \newsavebox. The box may be set any place in the text as often as desired with the command \usebox{*boxname*}.

\savebox{*boxname*}(*x_dim*, *y_dim*) [*pos*]{*sub_pic*} . . . . . . (16.1.4) – 309
> In the picture environment, a sub-picture *sub_pic* may be stored as a box of width *x_dim* and height *y_dim* under the name *boxname*, which has been previously defined with \newsavebox. The *pos* argument functions as it does for the picture \makebox. The box may be set any place in the picture environment with the command \usebox{*boxname*}.

\sbox{*boxname*}{*text*} . . . . (5.1.1) – 87
> Stores *text* in an LR box named *boxname* that has previously been created with \newsavebox{*boxname*}. The contents of the box may be printed as often as desired with \usebox{*boxname*}.

\scalebox{*h_scale*}[*v_scale*]{*text*} . . . . (8.1.2) – 155
> A command made available with the graphics package that scales the contents *text* as an LR box with the horizontal factor *h_scale* and optionally with the (different) vertical factor *v_scale*. If *v_scale* is missing, it is the same as *h_scale*.

`\scdefault` . . . . (A.2.1) – 365

This command defines the shape attribute that is selected with the `\scshape` command. It may be redefined with `\renewcommand`:

    \renewcommand{\scdefault}{sc}

`\scriptscriptstyle` [m] . . . . (7.5.2) – 147

Switches to font size `\scriptscriptstyle` as the active font inside a math formula.

`\scriptsize` . . . . (4.1.2) – 64

Switches to the font size `\scriptsize`, which is smaller than `\footnotesize` but larger than `\tiny`.

`\scriptstyle` [m] . . . . (7.5.2) – 147

Switches to font size `\scriptstyle` as the active font inside a math formula.

`\scshape` . . . . (4.1.3), (A.2) – 66, 365

This declaration switches to a font in the current family and series, but with the CAPS AND SMALL CAPS shape attribute.

`\searrow` [m] produces ↘ . . . . (7.3.5) – 129

`\sec` [m] . . . . (7.3.8) – 130

Command to produce the function name 'sec' in formulas.

`\section`[*short title*]{*title*} . . . . (3.3.3) – 58

Begins a new section, formatting *title* with the current chapter number (`book` and `report` classes only) and an automatic sequential section number. If the optional *short title* is given, it appears in place of *title* in the table of contents and the running head at the top of the pages.

`\section*`{*title*} . . . . (3.3.3) – 58

The same as `\section` but without a number or an entry in the table of contents.

`\see`{*reference*} . . . . (11.4.2) – 224

A command defined in the `makeidx` package for use with the MakeIndex program. It is called within an `\index` command to refer to another entry in the keyword index as 'see *reference*'. Given in the form:

    \index{entry|see{reference}}

Note: The above text is correct with | in place of \ for |see.

`\seealso`{*reference*} . . . . (11.4.2) – 224

Like `\see`, but will print the text 'see also *reference*' in the index. More precisely, it prints the text stored in the command `\alsoname`. Requires the `makeidx` package.

A command defined in the package makeidx containing the text for the command \see. In English, this is 'see', but it may be altered for adaptation to other languages.

Activates the font with the current set of attributes, making it the current font in which text is set. It should normally follow an attribute selection command. For example:

    \fontshape{sl}\selectfont

Command in multilanguage packages such as german and in the babel system, for changing the language. The names of titles, the form of the date command \today, special language-specific commands, and the hyphenation patterns are all changed. For example:

    \selectlanguage{english}

Requires the standard LaTeX package ifthen. Sets the value of a boolean switch to ⟨*true*⟩ or ⟨*false*⟩ depending on *value*, which must be true or false. The switch must have been created with \newboolean{*switch*}. Its value is tested with \boolean{*switch*}, which may be used as a logical statement in the *test* part of \ifthenelse and \whiledo.

Assigns the integral number *value* to the counter *counter*.

The length command with the name *length_cmd* is assigned the length value *length_spec*, which may be a fixed or rubber length.

The length command with the name *length_cmd* is assigned a value equal to the depth of *text* below the baseline.

The length command with the name *length_cmd* is assigned a value equal to the height of *text* above the baseline.

The length command with the name *length_cmd* is assigned a value equal to the length of *text* as it would be set in an LR box.

`\sfdefault` . . . . (A.2.1) – 365

> This command defines the family attribute that is selected with the `\sffamily` command. It may be redefined with `\renewcommand`:
>
>   \renewcommand{\sfdefault}{phv}

`\sffamily` . . . . (4.1.3), (A.2) – 66, 364

> This declaration switches to a font in the current series and shape, but with the sans serif family attribute.

`\shadowbox{`*text*`}` . . . . (5.1.9) – 94

> With the fancybox package, is a variant of `\fbox`, drawing a shadowed box around *text*; the thickness of the shadow is given by the length `\shadowsize`.

`\sharp` [m] produces ♯ . . . . (7.3.6) – 129

`\shortstack[`*pos*`]{`*text*`}` . . . . (16.1.4) – 307

> Formats the *text* into a single column, where the individual rows are terminated by `\\`. The optional positioning argument *pos* takes on values of l or r to set the text left or right justified, otherwise it is centered. For example:
>
>   \shortstack{aa\\bbb\\cc\\x\\yy\\zzz}

```
aa
bbb
cc
x
yy
zzz
```

`\sideset{`*pre*`}{`*post*`}\`*symbol* [m][a] . . . . (15.2.2) – 273

> With the amsmath package, places superscripts and subscripts snugly before (*pre*) and after (*post*) the math symbol `\`*symbol*. For example:
>
> $\sideset{_\dag^*}{_\dag^*}\prod$ yields $\overset{*}{\underset{\dagger}{\prod}}\overset{*}{\underset{\dagger}{}}$

`\Sigma` [m] produces Σ . . . . (7.3.1) – 127

`\sigma` [m] produces σ . . . . (7.3.1) – 127

`\signature{`*name*`}` . . . . (18.1) – 345

> In the `letter` document class, supplies the name of the writer that should go below the signature if this is different from the entry in `\name`.

`\sim` [m] produces ∼ . . . . (7.3.4) – 128

`\simeq` [m] produces ≃ . . . . (7.3.4) – 128

`\sin` [m] . . . . (7.3.8) – 130

> Command to produce the function name 'sin' in formulas.

`\sinh` [m] . . . . (7.3.8) – 130

> Command to produce the function name 'sinh' in formulas.

`\sldefault` . . . . (A.2.1) – 365

> This command defines the shape attribute that is selected with the `\slshape` command. It may be redefined with `\renewcommand`:
>
>   \renewcommand{\sldefault}{sl}

`\sloppy` . . . . (2.8.3) – 39

> After this command has been given, word spacings are allowed to stretch more generously than usual so that paragraphs are broken up into lines with fewer word divisions. It is countermanded by `\fussy`. See also `\begin{sloppypar}`.

`\slshape` . . . . (4.1.3), (A.2) – 66, 365

> This declaration switches to a font in the current family and series, but with the *slanted* shape attribute.

`\small` . . . . (4.1.2) – 64

> Switches to the font size `\small`, which is smaller than `\normalsize` but larger than `\footnotesize`.

`\smallskip` . . . . (2.7.3) – 36

> Inserts large vertical spacing of amount `\smallskipamount`. See also `\medskip` and `\bigskip`.

`\smallskipamount`

> Standard value for the amount of vertical spacing that is inserted with the command `\smallskip`. May be changed with the `\setlength` command:
>
> `\setlength{\smallskipamount}{1ex plus0.5ex minus0.3ex}`

`\smash[`*pos*`]{`*text*`}` [m][a] . . . . (15.2.5) – 280

> With the `amsmath` package, this TEX command acquires an optional argument *pos* that may be b or t, to effectively zero the depth or height of the *text*. With no *pos*, both height and depth are zeroed.

`\smile` [m] produces ⌣ . . . . (7.3.4) – 128

`\spadesuit` [m] produces ♠ . . . . (7.3.6) – 129

`\sqcap` [m] produces ⊓ . . . . (7.3.3) – 127

`\sqcup` [m] produces ⊔ . . . . (7.3.3) – 127

`\sqrt[`*n*`]{`*arg*`}` [m] . . . . (7.2.4) – 124

> Basic math command to produce a root sign. The height and length of the sign are made to fit the contents *arg*. The optional argument *n* is the degree of the root: `\sqrt[3]{2}` = $\sqrt[3]{2}$, `\sqrt{2}` = $\sqrt{2}$.

`\sqsubset` [m] produces ⊏ . . . . (7.3.4) – 128

`\sqsubseteq` [m] produces ⊑ . . . . (7.3.4) – 128

`\sqsupset` [m] produces ⊐ . . . . (7.3.4) – 128

`\sqsupseteq` [m] produces ⊒ . . . . (7.3.4) – 128

`\ss` produces ß . . . . (2.5.6) – 27

`\stackrel{`*upper*`}{`*lower*`}` [m] . . . . (7.4.5) – 138

> Places one mathematical symbol *upper* on top of another *lower*, such that the upper one appears in a smaller typeface:
>
> `\stackrel{\alpha}{\longrightarrow}` = $\stackrel{\alpha}{\longrightarrow}$

`\star` [m] produces ⋆   . . . . (7.3.3) – 127

`\stepcounter{`*counter*`}`   . . . . (10.1.3) – 182

> Increases the value of the number stored in *counter* by one.

`\stretch{`*decimal_num*`}`   . . . . (10.2) – 184

> A rubber length with a natural value of 0 pt but with a stretchability that is *decimal_num* times that of `\fill`.

`\subitem{`*sub_entry*`}`   . . . . (11.4.1) – 222

> In `theindex` environment, a command to produce a second-level entry after an `\item` command.

`\subparagraph[`*short title*`]{`*title*`}`   . . . . (3.3.3) – 58

> The last command in the sectioning hierarchy, coming after `\paragraph`. It formats *title* with the current paragraph number and an automatic sequential subparagraph number. If the optional *short title* is given, it appears in place of *title* in the table of contents.

`\subparagraph*{`*title*`}`   . . . . (3.3.3) – 58

> The same as `\subparagraph` but without a number or an entry in the table of contents.

`\subsection[`*short title*`]{`*title*`}`   . . . . (3.3.3) – 58

> The command in the sectioning hierarchy that comes between the `\section` and `\subsubsection`. It formats *title* with the current section number and an automatic sequential subsection number. If the optional *short title* is given, it appears in place of *title* in the table of contents.

`\subsection*{`*title*`}`   . . . . (3.3.3) – 58

> The same as `\subsection` but without a number or an entry in the table of contents.

`\substack{`*1st line*`\\..\\`*last line*`}` [m][a]   . . . . (15.2.2) – 272

> With the `amsmath` package, produces centered multiline indices or limits; it must immediately follow ˆ or _ and be enclosed in { }.

`\subsubitem{`*sub_sub_entry*`}`   . . . . (11.4.1) – 222

> In `theindex` environment, a command to produce a third-level entry under a `\subitem` command.

`\subsubsection[`*short form*`]{`*title*`}`   . . . . (3.3.3) – 58

> The command in the sectioning hierarchy coming between `\subsection` and `\paragraph`. It formats *title* with the current subsection number and an automatic sequential sub-subsection number. If the optional *short title* is given, it appears in place of *title* in the table of contents.

\subsubsection*{*title*} . . . . (3.3.3) – 58

The same as \subsubsection but without a number or an entry in the table of contents.

\subset [m] produces ⊂ . . . . (7.3.4) – 128

\subseteq [m] produces ⊆ . . . . (7.3.4) – 128

\succ [m] produces ≻ . . . . (7.3.4) – 128

\succeq [m] produces ⪰ . . . . (7.3.4) – 128

\sum [m] produces ∑ . . . . (7.2.5) – 124

\sup [m] . . . . (7.3.8) – 130

Command to produce the function name 'sup' in formulas. A lower limit may be set as a subscript.

\suppressfloats[*loc*] . . . . (9.2) – 171

Any floats given between this command and the end of the current page will be suspended at least until the next page. If the optional *loc* is given as one of t or b (not both), only floats with that placement parameter are suspended.

\supset [m] produces ⊃ . . . . (7.3.4) – 128

\supseteq [m] produces ⊇ . . . . (7.3.4) – 128

\surd [m] produces √ . . . . (7.3.6) – 129

\swarrow [m] produces ↙ . . . . (7.3.5) – 129

\t{*xy*} . . . . (2.5.7) – 27

Produces a 'tie-after' accent over two letters: \t{oo} = o͡o.

\tabbingsep . . . . (6.1.4) – 103

Determines the spacing between the text *ltext* and the current tabular stop when *ltext*\' is given in a tabbing environment. A new value may be assigned with the \setlength command.

\tabcolsep . . . . (6.2.2) – 107

Determines the half-column spacing in the tabular environment. A new value may be assigned with the \setlength command:

    \setlength{\tabcolsep}{3mm}

\tableofcontents . . . . (3.4.2) – 61

Prints the table of contents from information in the sectioning commands and additional entries.

\tablename . . . . (D.3.1) – 441

Command containing the name for a table caption. In English, this is 'Table', but it may be altered for adaptation to other languages.

`\tabularnewline[`*len*`]` . . . . (6.2.1) – 107

Terminates a row in the `tabular` or `array` environments, adding vertical spacing *len* if it is specified. This is equivalent to `\\[`*len*`]` except that there is no ambiguity as to whether it is terminating a row in the table or a line of text within a column entry. If something like `\raggedright` is given in the last column, then this command *must* be used in place of `\\`.

`\tag{`*mark*`}` [m][a] . . . . (15.2.6) – 282

Within one of the $\mathcal{A}_{\mathcal{M}}$S-LaTeX alignment environments, prints *mark* in place of the equation number, in parentheses. The *-form prints it without parentheses.

`\tan` [m] . . . . (7.3.8) – 130

Command to produce the function name 'tan' in formulas.

`\tanh` [m] . . . . (7.3.8) – 130

Command to produce the function name 'tanh' in formulas.

`\tau` [m] produces τ . . . . (7.3.1) – 127

`\tbinom{`*over*`}{`*under*`}` [m][a] . . . . (15.2.3) – 276

With the `amsmath` package, produces a binomial as `\binom` does, but in `\textstyle` size.

`\telephone{`*number*`}` . . . . (18.1), (18.2) – 346, 350

In the `letter` document class, enters the sender's telephone number. In the standard LaTeX `letter.sty`, *number* is only output if `\address` has not been called. It is intended to be used in company letter styles such as `mpletter`.

`\TeX` produces TeX . . . . (2.1) – 23

`\text{`*short_text*`}` [m][a] . . . . (15.2.1) – 271

When one of the packages `amsmath` or `amstext` has been loaded, this command prints *short_text* as normal text within a math formula. If used in subscripts or superscripts, automatic sizing takes place.

`\text`*sym_name* . . . . (D.5) – 444

An alternative means to produce certain special symbols that otherwise are only available in math mode or through ligature combinations: `\textbullet` (•); `\textemdash` (—); `\textendash` (–); `\textexclamdown` (¡); `\textperiodcentered` (·); `\textquestiondown` (¿); `\textquotedblleft` ("); `\textquotedblright` ("); `\textquoteleft` ('); `\textquoteright` ('); `\textvisiblespace` (␣) `\textasciicircum` (^); `\textasciitilde` (˜); `\textbackslash` (\); `\textbar` (|); `\textgreater` (>); `\textless` (<)

`\textbf{`*text*`}` . . . . (4.1.4) – 67

This command sets its argument in a font in the current family and shape, but with the **bold** series attribute. It is equivalent to {`\bfseries` *text*}.

Produces the specified character in a circle: `\textcircled{s}` = Ⓢ.

A command made available with the `color` package. The *text* is set in the specified color. The *col_spec* is the same as for `\color`.

Prints an invisible character that may be used to break ligatures:

f`\textcompwordmark` i = fi

The vertical spacing between floats at the top of the page and the following text or between text and floats at the bottom of the page. A new value is set with the `\setlength` command.

   `\setlength{\textfloatsep}{20pt plus 2pt minus 4pt}`

The minimum fraction of a page containing text and floats that must be filled with text. A new value is set with

   `\renewcommand{\textfraction}{`*decimal_frac*`}`

The total height reserved for the text on each page, excluding head and footlines. A new value may be assigned with the `\setlength` command:

   `\setlength{\textheight}{45\baselineskip}`

This command sets its argument in a font in the current family and series, but with the *italic* shape attribute. It is equivalent to {`\itshape` *text*}.

This command sets its argument in a font in the current family and shape, but with the medium series attribute. It is equivalent to {`\mdseries` *text*}.

This command sets its argument in the font with the default family, series, and shape attributes. It is equivalent to {`\normalfont` *text*}.

When T1 encoding is active, prints the symbol ".

Sets *text* in a font in the current series and shape, but with the Roman family attribute. It is equivalent to {`\rmfamily` *text*}.

`\textsc{`*text*`}` . . . . (4.1.4) – 67

Sets *text* in a font in the current family and series, but with the CAPS AND SMALL CAPS shape attribute. It is equivalent to {`\scshape` *text*}.

`\textsf{`*text*`}` . . . . (4.1.4) – 67

Sets *text* in a font in the current series and shape, but with the sans serif family attribute. It is equivalent to {`\sffamily` *text*}.

`\textsl{`*text*`}` . . . . (4.1.4) – 67

Sets *text* in a font in the current family and series, but with the *slanted* shape attribute. It is equivalent to {`\slshape` *text*}.

`\textstyle` [m] . . . . (7.5.2) – 147

Switches to font size `\textstyle` inside a math formula.

`\textsuperscript{`*char*`}` . . . . (D.5) – 444

Produces a superscript in the current text, rather than math, font: `\textsuperscript{12}` = ^{12}.

`\texttrademark` produces ™ . . . . (D.5) – 444

`\texttt{`*text*`}` . . . . (4.1.4) – 67

Sets *text* in a font in the current series and shape, but with the `typewriter` family attribute. It is equivalent to {`\ttfamily` *text*}.

`\textup{`*text*`}` . . . . (4.1.4) – 67

Sets *text* in a font in the current family and series, but with the upright shape attribute. It is equivalent to {`\upshape` *text*}.

`\textwidth` . . . . (3.2.5) – 51

The total width reserved for the text on a page. For two-column formatting, this is the width of both columns plus the gap between them. A new value may be assigned with the `\setlength` command.

`\tfrac{`*numerator*`}{`*denominator*`}` [m][a] . . . . (15.2.3) – 275

With the `amsmath` package, produces a fraction as `\frac` does, but in `\textstyle` size.

`\TH` . . . . (A.3.2) – 371

When T1 encoding is active, prints the character Þ.

`\th` . . . . (A.3.2) – 371

When T1 encoding is active, prints the character þ.

`\thanks{`*footnote_text*`}` . . . . (3.3.1) – 56

Produces a footnote to an author's name on the title page when `\maketitle` is called.

\the*counter* . . . . (10.1.4) – 183

> Internal commands for formatting and printing counter values, making possible use of other counters. For example, \thesubsection might be defined to be \thesection.\roman{subsection}. A new definition may be made with \renewcommand{\the*counter*}{*def*}.

\Theta [m] produces Θ . . . . (7.3.1) – 127

\theta [m] produces θ . . . . (7.3.1) – 127

\thicklines . . . . (16.1.4) – 309

> In the picture environment, this command sets all the sloping lines and arrows, circles, and ovals to be drawn with thicker-than-normal lines.

\thickspace [m][a] . . . . (15.2.5) – 280

> With the amsmath package, this is an alias for \;, a thick space in a math formula.

\thinlines . . . . (16.1.4) – 309

> In the picture environment, resets the line thickness for sloping lines and arrows, circles, and ovals back to the standard value after \thicklines has been given.

\thinspace [m][a] . . . . (15.2.5) – 280

> With the amsmath package, this is an alias for \,, a thin space in a math formula.

\thisfancypage{*cmds1*}{*cmds2*} . . . . (5.1.9) – 95

> With the fancybox package, places a framed box around the contents of the current page only; *cmds1* excludes the head and footlines, *cmds2* includes them. The arguments set box parameters such as \fboxrule but must end with a box command like \shadowbox. Usually one set of *cmds* is left blank.

\thispagestyle{*style*} . . . . (3.2) – 46

> Changes the page style for the current page only. Possible values for *style* are: plain, empty, headings, and myheadings.

\tilde{*x*} [m] . . . . (7.3.9) – 131

> Produces a tilde (squiggle) over the math variable x: \tilde{a} = $\tilde{a}$.

\tiny . . . . (4.1.2) – 64

> Switches to the smallest font size available \tiny, smaller than \scriptsize.

\times [m] produces × . . . . (7.3.3) – 127

\title{*text*} . . . . (3.3.1) – 55

> Enters the *text* for the title page that is produced by \maketitle.

\to [m] produces → . . . . (7.3.5) – 129

\today . . . . (2.5.11), (D.3.2) – 30, 442

> Prints the current date in the American fashion. This form may be changed to British or to that of other languages by redefining the command with the help of the internal TeX commands \day, \month, and \year.

`\top [m]` produces ⊤ . . . . (7.3.6) – 129

`\topfigrule` . . . . (9.3) – 172

A command that is executed after a float at the top of a page. It is normally defined to do nothing, but may be redefined to add a rule between the float and the main text. It must not add any net vertical spacing.

```
\renewcommand{\topfigrule}{\vspace*{-.4pt}
   \rule{\columnwidth}{.4pt}}
```

`\topfraction` . . . . (9.3) – 172

The maximum fraction of a page that may be occupied at the top by floats at the top of the page. A new value is assigned with

```
\renewcommand{\topfraction}{decimal_frac}
```

`\topmargin` . . . .(3.2.5) – 51

The size of the margin from the top of the page to the page head. A new value may be assigned by the `\setlength` command:

```
\setlength{topmargin}{0.5in}
```

`topnumber` . . . . (9.3) – 171

The maximum number of floats that may appear at the top of a page. A new value is assigned with:

```
\setcounter{topnumber}{num}
```

`\topsep` . . . . (4.4.2), (7.5.4) – 76, 150

The extra vertical spacing, in addition to `\parskip`, inserted at the beginning and end of a listing environment. When document class option `fleqn` has been chosen, it is also inserted at the beginning and end of displayed math formulas. A new value may be assigned with the `\setlength` command:

```
\setlength{\topsep}{4pt plus2pt minus2pt}
```

`\topskip` . . . . (3.2.5) – 51

The vertical distance from the top of the page body to the baseline of the first line of text. A new value may be assigned with the `\setlength` command:

```
\setlength{\topskip}{12pt}
```

`\totalheight` . . . . (5.1.1) – 86

A length parameter equal to the total natural height of a box (height plus depth); it may only be used in the *width* specification of `\makebox`, `\framebox`, or `\savebox`, or in the *height* specification of a `\parbox` or a `minipage` environment.

```
\framebox[6\totalheight]{text}
```

`totalnumber` . . . . (9.3) – 171

The total number of floats that may appear on a page regardless of their positions. A new value is assigned with:

```
\setcounter{totalnumber}{num}
```

\triangle [m] produces △ . . . . (7.3.6) – 129

\triangleleft [m] produces ◁ . . . . (7.3.3) – 127

\triangleright [m] produces ▷ . . . . (7.3.3) – 127

\ttdefault . . . . (A.2.1) – 365

> This command defines the family attribute that is selected with the \ttfamily command. It may be redefined with \renewcommand:
>
> > \renewcommand{\ttdefault}{pcr}

\ttfamily . . . . (4.1.3), A.2) – 66, 364

> This declaration switches to a font in the current series and shape, but with the typewriter family attribute.

\twocolumn[*text*] . . . . (3.2.7) – 54

> Begins a new page and switches to two-column page format. The optional *text* is set in one column extending over the two columns.

\typein[*cmd*]{*message*} . . . . (11.1.3) – 209

> Prints the *message* to the monitor and stops the program, waiting for a reply from the user. The text of the response is assigned to the LaTeX command named \@typein or to *cmd* if the optional argument has been given. After the return key is pressed, the processing continues. The typed-in text is inserted in place of \@typein if the optional argument was not given; otherwise, it may be inserted as one pleases with the *cmd* command.

\typeout{*message*} . . . . (11.1.3) – 209

> Prints the *message* to the monitor and continues the processing. The *message* is also written to the .log file.

\u{*x*} . . . . (2.5.7) – 27

> Produces a breve accent: \u{o} = ŏ.

\unboldmath . . . . (7.4.9) – 144

> Countermands the \boldmath command. It must be given outside of the math mode. Afterwards, formulas are set in standard '*math italics*' once more.

\underbrace{*sub_form*} [m] . . . . (7.4.4) – 137

> Produces a horizontal curly brace beneath the math formula *sub_form*. Any following subscript will be placed centered below the horizontal brace.
>
> > \underbrace{a+b}: $\underbrace{a+b}$
> >
> > \underbrace{x+y+z}_{\xi\eta\zeta}: $\underbrace{x+y+z}_{\xi\eta\zeta}$

\underleftarrow{*expr*} [m][a] . . . . (15.2.2) – 274

> With the amsmath package, places a long leftward-pointing arrow beneath the mathematical expression *expr*.

`\underleftrightarrow{`*expr*`}` [m][a] . . . . (15.2.2) – 274

> With the `amsmath` package, places a long double arrow beneath the mathematical expression *expr*.

`\underline{`*text*`}` . . . . (7.4.4) – 137

> Underlines the *text* in both math and normal text modes: `\underline{Text}` = Text.

`\underrightarrow{`*expr*`}` [m][a] . . . . (15.2.2) – 274

> With the `amsmath` package, places a long rightward-pointing arrow beneath the mathematical expression *expr*.

`\underset{`*char*`}{\`*symbol*`}` [m][a] . . . . (15.2.2) – 273

> With the `amsmath` package, places *char* below the math symbol `\`*symbol* in subscript size.

`\unitlength` . . . . (16.1.1) – 298

> Defines the unit of length for the following `picture` environments. A value is assigned with the `\setlength` command:
>
>   \setlength{\unitlength}{1.2cm}

`\unlhd` [m] produces $\unlhd$ . . . . (7.3.3) – 127

`\unrhd` [m] produces $\unrhd$ . . . . (7.3.3) – 127

`\Uparrow` [m] produces $\Uparrow$ . . . . (7.3.5) – 129

`\uparrow` [m] produces $\uparrow$ . . . . (7.3.5) – 129

`\updefault` . . . . (A.2.1) – 365

> This command defines the shape attribute that is selected with the `\upshape` command. It may be redefined with `\renewcommand`:
>
>   \renewcommand{\updefault}{n}

`\Updownarrow` [m] produces $\Updownarrow$ . . . . (7.3.5) – 129

`\updownarrow` [m] produces $\updownarrow$ . . . . (7.3.5) – 129

`\uplus` [m] produces $\uplus$ . . . . (7.3.3) – 127

`\upshape` . . . . (4.1.3), (A.2) – 66, 365

> This declaration switches to a font in the current family and series, but with the upright shape attribute.

`\Upsilon` [m] produces Υ . . . . (7.3.1) – 127

`\upsilon` [m] produces υ . . . . (7.3.1) – 127

`\uproot{`*shift*`}` [m][a] . . . . (15.2.5) – 280

> With the `amsmath` package, used in the index to a `\sqrt` command to shift it slightly upwards. The *shift* is a number specifying how many units to move it. Example:
>
>   \sqrt[\leftroot{-1}\uproot{3}\beta]{k}

\url{*address*} . . . . (4.6.2) – 83

With the ur1 package, prints *address* literally, normally in typewriter font, with line breaks after non-letters, without hyphens. Intended for Internet and e-mail addresses. With the hyperref package, *address* becomes an active link in a PDF file. The *address* argument may be delimited either by curly braces as usual or by some other character, as is done with \verb. Examples:
\url{w_smith@xyz.com} or \url|w_smith@xyz.com|

\urlstyle{*style*} . . . . (4.6.2) – 83

With the ur1 package, sets the typeface for subsequent \url commands, where *style* is one of tt, rm, sf, or same, for typewriter, Roman, sans serif, or unchanged font, respectively.

\usebox{*boxname*} . . . . (5.1.1) – 87

Inserts into the text the contents of the box that was saved with the \sbox or \savebox command under the name *boxname*, which has been previously created with the \newsavebox command.

\usecounter{*counter*} . . . . (4.4.1) – 75

Command in the list environment that specifies which counter is to be employed in the standard labels with the \item commands. This counter is incremented by one with each \item call.

\usefont{*code*}{*fam*}{*ser*}{*shp*} . . . . (A.1) – 363

Activates the font with the given set of attributes in the current size. Is equivalent to selecting the given font attributes and then calling \selectfont.

\usepackage[*options*]{*packages*}[*version*] [p] . . . . (3.1.2) – 45

Loads one or more package files containing additional LATEX or TEX definitions. The files have the extension .sty. More than one package may be specified in *packages*, the names being separated by commas. Any *options* listed will be applied to all packages. Furthermore, any options listed in the \documentclass command will also be applied to the package files.

The optional *version* is a date given in the form *yyyy/mm/dd*, as, for example, 1994/08/01. If the date of the package file is earlier than this, a warning message is printed.

Example:
\usepackage{bezier,ifthen}[1994/06/01]

\v{*x*} . . . . (2.5.7) – 27

Produces háček accent: \v{o} = ǒ.

\value{*counter*} . . . . (10.1.3) – 182

The current value of the number stored in *counter* for use with commands that require a number. It does *not* output this number. For example, \setcounter{*counter1*}{\value{*counter2*}} sets *counter1* to the same value as that of *counter2*.

A vector symbol over the variable x: \vec{a} = $\vec{a}$.

A picture element command within a picture environment for drawing horizontal and vertical arrows of any length as well as slanted arrows at a limited number of angles. For horizontal and vertical arrows, the *length* argument is the actual length in units of \unitlength. For slanted arrows, *length* is the length of the projection on to the x-axis (horizontal displacement). The slope is determined by the ($\Delta x,\Delta y$) arguments, which take on integral values such that $-4 \le \Delta x \le 4$ and $-4 \le \Delta y \le 4$. This command is the argument of a \put or \multiput command.

Everything that comes between the |...| symbols is output in the typewriter font exactly as is with no interpretation of special symbols or commands. Any symbol other than * may be used as the switch character, illustrated here as |, as long as it does not appear in *source_text*.

The same as \verb except that blanks are made visible with the symbol $\sqcup$.

A vertical rubber spacing with a natural length of zero that can be stretched to any value. Used to fill up parts of a page with blank spacing. This command is an abbreviation for \vspace{\fill}.

`\visible` . . . . (17.1.2) – 322

In `slides` class, a declaration that countermands a previous `\invisible` command, making text printed again. It remains in effect until the end of the environment, or end of the curly braces, in which it was issued, or until `\invisible` is given. It is used for making overlays.

`\vline` . . . . (6.2.1) – 107

Prints a vertical rule within the column entry of a table in the `tabular` environment.

`\voffset` 554, 555

Vertical offset of the output page from the printer border set by the printer driver. This printer border is normally 1 inch from the top edge of the paper. The standard value of `\voffset` is 0 pt so that the top reference margin of the page is identical with the printer margin. A new value is assigned with the `\setlength` command:

    `\setlength{\voffset}{-1in}`

`\vpageref[`*current*`][`*non-current*`]{`*key*`}` . . . . (11.2.4) – 213

With the `varioref` package, this is equivalent to on page `\pageref{`*key*`}` unless `\label{`*key*`}` is on the current or adjacent page, in which case appropriate text is automatically substituted, for example, 'on the next page'. The first optional argument is inserted for the current page, the second for other pages.

`\vref{`*key*`}` . . . . (11.2.4) – 213

With the `varioref` package, this is equivalent to `\ref{`*key*`}` on page `\pageref{`*key*`}` unless `\label{`*key*`}` is on the current or adjacent page, in which case appropriate text is automatically substituted for the page specification, for example, 'on the next page'.

`\vspace{`*height*`}` . . . . (2.7.3) – 35

Produces vertical spacing of length *height*. It is ignored if it occurs at the beginning or end of a page.

`\vspace*{`*height*`}` . . . . (2.7.3) – 35

Produces vertical spacing of length *height* even at the beginning or end of a page.

`\wedge` [m] produces ∧ . . . . (7.3.3) – 127

`\whiledo{`*test*`}{`*do_text*`}` . . . . (10.3.5) – 192

A conditional command available when the standard package `ifthen` has been loaded. The *do_text* is inserted repeatedly as long as the logical statement *test* evaluates to ⟨*true*⟩. The logical statement may be relational (two numbers with one of < = > between them), an even–odd test (`\isodd{`*number*`}`), a comparison of two texts (`\equal{`*text1*`}{`*text2*`}`), a comparison of two lengths (`\lengthtest{`*length1* op *length2*`}`, *op* is one of < = >), or a test of a boolean switch (`\boolean{`*switch*`}`). Switches are created with `\newboolean{`*switch*`}` and set with `\setboolean{`*switch*`}{`*value*`}`, where *value* is `true` or `false`. Logical statements may be combined with logical operators `\and`, `\or`, and `\not`, and grouped with `\(` and `\)`.

\widehat{*xyz*} [m] . . . . (7.3.9) – 131

> Produces a wide \hat symbol over several characters: \widehat{xyz} = $\widehat{xyz}$.

\widetilde{*xyz*} [m] . . . . (7.3.9) – 131

> Produces a wide \tilde symbol over several characters: \widetilde{xyz} = $\widetilde{xyz}$.

\width . . . . (5.1.1) – 86

> A length parameter equal to the natural width of a box; it may be used only in the *width* specification of \makebox, \framebox, or \savebox, or in the *height* specification of a \parbox or a minipage environment.
>
> > \framebox[2\width]{text}

\wp [m] produces $\wp$ . . . . (7.3.6) – 129

\wr [m] produces $\wr$ . . . . (7.3.3) – 127

\Xi [m] produces Ξ . . . . (7.3.1) – 127

\xi [m] produces ξ . . . . (7.3.1) – 127

\xleftarrow[*below*]{*above*} [m][a] . . . . (15.2.2) – 274

> With the amsmath package, draws a leftward-pointing arrow with *above* printed over it in superscript size and, optionally, *below* beneath it in subscript size.

\xrightarrow[*below*]{*above*} [m][a] . . . . (15.2.2) – 274

> With the amsmath package, draws a rightward-pointing arrow with *above* printed over it in superscript size and, optionally, *below* beneath it in subscript size.

\zeta [m] produces ζ . . . . (7.3.1) – 127

G.2   Summary tables and figures

Table G.1   Font attribute commands   (4.1.3) – p. 66.

\rmfamily	\textrm{*text*}	Roman
\sffamily	\textsf{*text*}	sans serif
\ttfamily	\texttt{*text*}	typewriter
\upshape	\textup{*text*}	upright
\itshape	\textit{*text*}	*italic*
\slshape	\textsl{*text*}	*slanted*
\scshape	\textsc{*text*}	SMALL CAPS
\mdseries	\textmd{*text*}	medium
\bfseries	\textbf{*text*}	**boldface**

Table G.2   Math alphabet commands   (7.4.2) – p. 134.

\mathrm{*text*}	Roman
\mathsf{*text*}	sansserif
\mathnormal{*text*}	$normal$
\mathtt{*text*}	typewriter
\mathit{*text*}	*italic*
\mathbf{*text*}	**boldface**
\mathcal{*text*}	$\mathcal{CAL}$

Table G.3   Font sizes   (4.1.2) – p. 64.

\tiny	smallest
\scriptsize	very small
\footnotesize	smaller
\small	small
\normalsize	normal
\large	large
\Large	larger
\LARGE	even larger
\huge	still larger
\Huge	largest

Table G.4   LATEX 2.09 font declarations   (F.2.1) – p. 464.

\rm	Roman	\it	*Italic*	\sc	SMALL CAPS
\bf	**boldface**	\sl	*Slanted*	\sf	Sans Serif
\tt	Typewriter	\mit	$\Gamma\Pi\Phi$	\cal	$\mathcal{CAL}$

Table G.5   Dimensions   (2.4.1) – p. 25.

mm	millimeter	bp	big point (1 in = 72 bp)
cm	centimeter	dd	(1157 dd = 1238 pt)
in	inch (1 in = 2.54 cm)	cc	cicero (1 cc = 12 dd)
pt	point (1 in = 72.27 pt)	sp	(1 pt = 65536 sp)
pc	pica (1 pc = 12 pt)		

em	The current width of a capital M
ex	The current height of the letter x

Table G.6   Accents   (2.5.7) – p. 27.

ò =\'{o}	ó=\'{o}	ô=\^{o}	ö=\"{o}	õ=\~{o}
ō =\={o}	ȯ=\.{o}	ǒ=\u{o}	ǒ=\v{o}	ő=\H{o}
ȏo=\t{oo}	ǫ=\c{o}	ọ=\d{o}	o̲=\b{o}	o̊=\r{o}

Table G.7   Special letters from other languages   (2.5.6) – p. 27.

œ={\oe}	Œ={\OE}	æ={\ae}	Æ={\AE}	å={\aa}	Å ={\AA}	¡=!'
ø ={\o}	Ø ={\O}	ł ={\l}	Ł ={\L}	ß={\ss}	SS={\SS}	¿=?'

Table G.8   Special symbols   (2.5.5) – 27.

† \dag   § \S   © \copyright   ‡ \ddag   ¶ \P   £ \pounds

Table G.9   Command symbols   (2.5.4) – 27.

$ \$ % \%   { \{   _ _   & \&   # \#   } \}

Table G.10   Greek letters   (7.3.1) – p. 126.

Lowercase letters

α	\alpha	θ	\theta	o	o	τ	\tau
β	\beta	ϑ	\vartheta	π	\pi	υ	\upsilon
γ	\gamma	ι	\iota	ϖ	\varpi	ϕ	\phi
δ	\delta	κ	\kappa	ρ	\rho	φ	\varphi
ϵ	\epsilon	λ	\lambda	ϱ	\varrho	χ	\chi
ε	\varepsilon	μ	\mu	σ	\sigma	ψ	\psi
ζ	\zeta	ν	\nu	ς	\varsigma	ω	\omega
η	\eta	ξ	\xi				

Uppercase letters

Γ	\Gamma	Λ	\Lambda	Σ	\Sigma	Ψ	\Psi
Δ	\Delta	Ξ	\Xi	Υ	\Upsilon	Ω	\Omega
Θ	\Theta	Π	\Pi	Φ	\Phi		

Table G.11   Binary operation symbols[*]   (7.3.3) – p. 127.

±	\pm	∩	\cap	∘	\circ	○	\bigcirc
∓	\mp	∪	\cup	•	\bullet	□	\Box
×	\times	⊎	\uplus	◇	\diamond	◇	\Diamond
÷	\div	⊓	\sqcap	◁	\lhd	△	\bigtriangleup
·	\cdot	⊔	\sqcup	▷	\rhd	▽	\bigtriangledown
∗	\ast	∨	\vee	⊴	\unlhd	◁	\triangleleft
⋆	\star	∧	\wedge	⊵	\unrhd	▷	\triangleright
†	\dagger	⊕	\oplus	⊘	\oslash	\	\setminus
‡	\ddagger	⊖	\ominus	⊙	\odot	≀	\wr
⨿	\amalg	⊗	\otimes				

[*]The underlined commands can only be used with packages latexsym or amsfonts.

Table G.12   Relational symbols[*]   (7.3.4) – p. 128.

≤ \le \leq		≥ \ge \geq		≠ \neq		~ \sim
≪ \ll		≫ \gg		≐ \doteq		≃ \simeq
⊂ \subset		⊃ \supset		≈ \approx		≍ \asymp
⊆ \subseteq		⊇ \supseteq		≅ \cong		⌣ \smile
⊏ \sqsubset		⊐ \sqsupset		≡ \equiv		⌢ \frown
⊑ \sqsubseteq		⊒ \sqsupseteq		∝ \propto		⋈ \bowtie
∈ \in		∋ \ni		≺ \prec		≻ \succ
⊢ \vdash		⊣ \dashv		⪯ \preceq		⪰ \succeq
⊨ \models		⊥ \perp		∥ \parallel |			\mid	

[*]The underlined commands can only be used with packages latexsym or amsfonts.

Table G.13   Negated relational symbols   (7.3.4) – p. 128.

≮	\not<	≯	\not>	≠	\not=
≰	\not\le	≱	\not\ge	≢	\not\equiv
⊀	\not\prec	⊁	\not\succ	≁	\not\sim
⋠	\not\preceq	⋡	\not\succeq	≄	\not\simeq
⊄	\not\subset	⊅	\not\supset	≉	\not\approx
⊈	\not\subseteq	⊉	\not\supseteq	≇	\not\cong
⋢	\not\sqsubseteq	⋣	\not\sqsupseteq	≭	\not\asymp
∉	\not\in	∉	\notin		

Table G.14   Brackets   (7.4.1) – p. 134.

(	(	)	)	⌊	\lfloor	⌋ \rfloor
[	[	]	]	⌈	\lceil	⌉ \rceil
{	\{	}	\}	⟨	\langle	⟩ \rangle
|	|	‖	|	↑	\uparrow	⇑ \Uparrow
/	/	\	\backslash	↓	\downarrow	⇓ \Downarrow
				↕	\updownarrow	⇕ \Updownarrow

Table G.15   Arrows[*]   (7.3.5) – p. 129.

← \leftarrow	\gets	⟵ \longleftarrow		↑ \uparrow	
⇐ \Leftarrow		⟸ \Longleftarrow		⇑ \Uparrow	
→ \rightarrow	\to	⟶ \longrightarrow		↓ \downarrow	
⇒ \Rightarrow		⟹ \Longrightarrow		⇓ \Downarrow	
↔ \leftrightarrow		⟷ \longleftrightarrow		↕ \updownarrow	
⇔ \Leftrightarrow		⟺ \Longleftrightarrow		⇕ \Updownarrow	
↦ \mapsto		⟼ \longmapsto		↗ \nearrow	
↩ \hookleftarrow		↪ \hookrightarrow		↘ \searrow	
↼ \leftharpoonup		⇀ \rightharpoonup		↙ \swarrow	
↽ \leftharpoondown		⇁ \rightharpoondown		↖ \nwarrow	
⇌ \rightleftharpoons		⤳ \leadsto			

[*]The underlined commands can only be used with packages latexsym or amsfonts.

Table G.16   Miscellaneous symbols[*]   (7.3.6) – p. 129.

ℵ \aleph	′ \prime	∀ \forall	□ \Box
ℏ \hbar	∅ \emptyset	∃ \exists	◇ \Diamond
ι \imath	∇ \nabla	¬ \neg	△ \triangle
ȷ \jmath	√ \surd	♭ \flat	♣ \clubsuit
ℓ \ell	∂ \partial	♮ \natural	♦ \diamondsuit
℘ \wp	⊤ \top	♯ \sharp	♥ \heartsuit
ℜ \Re	⊥ \bot	‖ |	♠ \spadesuit
ℑ \Im	⊢ \vdash	∠ \angle	⋈ \Join
℧ \mho	⊣ \dashv	\ \backslash	∞ \infty

[*]The underlined commands can only be used with packages latexsym or amsfonts.

Table G.17   Mathematical symbols in two sizes   (7.3.7) – p. 129.

Σ ∑	\sum	∩ ⋂	\bigcap	⊙ ⨀	\bigodot
∫ ∫	\int	∪ ⋃	\bigcup	⊗ ⨂	\bigotimes
∮ ∮	\oint	⊔ ⨆	\bigsqcup	⊕ ⨁	\bigoplus
Π ∏	\prod	∨ ⋁	\bigvee	⊎ ⨄	\biguplus
∐ ∐	\coprod	∧ ⋀	\bigwedge		

Table G.18   Function names   (7.3.8) – p. 130.

\arccos	\cosh	\det	\inf	\limsup	\Pr	\tan
\arcsin	\cot	\dim	\ker	\ln	\sec	\tanh
\arctan	\coth	\exp	\lg	\log	\sin	
\arg	\csc	\gcd	\lim	\max	\sinh	
\cos	\deg	\hom	\liminf	\min	\sup	

Table G.19   Math accents   (7.3.9) – p. 131.

$\hat{a}$ \hat{a}	$\breve{a}$ \breve{a}	$\grave{a}$ \grave{a}	$\bar{a}$ \bar{a}
$\check{a}$ \check{a}	$\acute{a}$ \acute{a}	$\tilde{a}$ \tilde{a}	$\vec{a}$ \vec{a}
$\dot{a}$ \dot{a}	$\ddot{a}$ \ddot{a}	$\mathring{a}$ \mathring{a}	

The symbols in the following tables are made available with the package amssymb.

Table G.20 $\mathcal{AMS}$ arrows

⇢	\dashrightarrow	⇠	\dashleftarrow
⇇	\leftleftarrows	⇆	\leftrightarrows
⇚	\Lleftarrow	↞	\twoheadleftarrow
↢	\leftarrowtail	↩	\looparrowleft
⇋	\leftrightharpoons	↶	\curvearrowleft
↺	\circlearrowleft	↰	\Lsh
⇈	\upuparrows	↿	\upharpoonleft
⇃	\downharpoonleft	⊸	\multimap
⇜	\leftrightsquigarrow	⇉	\rightrightarrows
⇄	\rightleftarrows	⇉	\rightrightarrows
⇄	\rightleftarrows	↠	\twoheadrightarrow
↣	\rightarrowtail	↪	\looparrowright
⇌	\rightleftharpoons	↷	\curvearrowright
↻	\circlearrowright	↱	\Rsh
⇊	\downdownarrows	↾	\upharpoonright
⇂	\downharpoonright	⇝	\rightsquigarrow

Negated arrows

↚	\nleftarrow	↛	\nrightarrow
⇍	\nLeftarrow	⇏	\nRightarrow
↮	\nleftrightarrow	⇎	\nLeftrightarrow

Table G.21 $\mathcal{AMS}$ binary operation symbols

∔	\dotplus	╲	\smallsetminus
⋒	\Cap	⋓	\Cup
⊼	\barwedge	⊻	\veebar
⩞	\doublebarwedge	⊟	\boxminus
⊠	\boxtimes	⊡	\boxdot
⊞	\boxplus	⍟	\divideontimes
⋉	\ltimes	⋊	\rtimes
⋋	\leftthreetimes	⋌	\rightthreetimes
⋏	\curlywedge	⋎	\curlyvee
⊖	\circleddash	⊛	\circledast
⊚	\circledcirc	·	\centerdot
⊤	\intercal		

Table G.22 $\mathcal{A}_{\mathcal{M}}\mathcal{S}$ Greek and Hebrew letters

F	\digamma	$\varkappa$ \varkappa	
$\beth$ \beth		$\daleth$ \daleth	$\gimel$ \gimel

Table G.23 $\mathcal{A}_{\mathcal{M}}\mathcal{S}$ delimiters

$\ulcorner$ \ulcorner	$\urcorner$ \urcorner	$\llcorner$ \llcorner	$\lrcorner$ \lrcorner

Table G.24 $\mathcal{A}_{\mathcal{M}}\mathcal{S}$ relational symbols

≦ \leqq		⩽ \leqslant	
⋜ \eqslantless		≲ \lesssim	
⪅ \lessapprox		≊ \approxeq	
⋖ \lessdot		⋘ \lll	
≶ \lessgtr		⋚ \lesseqgtr	
⪋ \lesseqqgtr		≑ \doteqdot	
≓ \risingdotseq		≒ \fallingdotseq	
∽ \backsim		⋍ \backsimeq	
⊆ \subseteqq		⋐ \Subset	
⊏ \sqsubset		≼ \preccurlyeq	
⋞ \curlyeqprec		≾ \precsim	
⪷ \precapprox		◁ \vartriangleleft	
⊴ \trianglelefteq		⊨ \vDash	
⊪ \Vvdash		⌣ \smallsmile	
⌢ \smallfrown		≏ \bumpeq	
≎ \Bumpeq		≧ \geqq	
⩾ \geqslant		⋝ \eqslantgtr	
≳ \gtrsim		⪆ \gtrapprox	
⋗ \gtrdot		⋙ \ggg	
≷ \gtrless		⋛ \gtreqless	
⪌ \gtreqqless		≖ \eqcirc	
≗ \circeq		≜ \triangleq	
∼ \thicksim		≈ \thickapprox	
⊇ \supseteqq		⋑ \Supset	
⊐ \sqsupset		≽ \succcurlyeq	
⋟ \curlyeqsucc		≿ \succsim	
⪸ \succapprox		▷ \vartriangleright	
⊵ \trianglerighteq		⊩ \Vdash	
∣ \shortmid		∥ \shortparallel	
≬ \between		⋔ \pitchfork	
∝ \varpropto		◀ \blacktriangleleft	
∴ \therefore		϶ \backepsilon	
▶ \blacktriangleright		∵ \because	

Table G.25 $\mathcal{A}_\mathcal{M}\mathcal{S}$ negated relational symbols

≮	\nless	≰	\nleq
≰	\nleqslant	≨	\nleqq
≨	\lneq	≨	\lneqq
≨	\lvertneqq	⋦	\lnsim
⪹	\lnapprox	⊀	\nprec
⋠	\npreceq	⋨	\precnsim
⪹	\precnapprox	≁	\nsim
∤	\nshortmid	∤	\nmid
⊬	\nvdash	⊭	\nvDash
⋪	\ntriangleleft	⋬	\ntrianglelefteq
⊈	\nsubseteq	⊊	\subsetneq
⊊	\varsubsetneq	⊊	\subsetneqq
⊊	\varsubsetneqq	≯	\ngtr
≱	\ngeq	≱	\ngeqslant
≩	\ngeqq	≩	\gneq
≩	\gneqq	≩	\gvertneqq
⋧	\gnsim	⪺	\gnapprox
⊁	\nsucc	⋡	\nsucceq
⋡	\nsucceq	⋩	\succnsim
⪺	\succnapprox	≇	\ncong
∦	\nshortparallel	∦	\nparallel
⊮	\nvDash	⊯	\nVDash
⋫	\ntriangleright	⋭	\ntrianglerighteq
⊉	\nsupseteq	⊉	\nsupseteqq
⊋	\supsetneq	⊋	\varsupsetneq
⊋	\supsetneqq	⊋	\varsupsetneqq

Table G.26   Miscellaneous $\mathcal{A}_\mathcal{M}\mathcal{S}$ symbols

ℏ	\hbar	ℏ	\hslash
△	\vartriangle	▽	\triangledown
□	\square	◇	\lozenge
Ⓢ	\circledS	∠	\angle
∡	\measuredangle	∄	\nexists
℧	\mho	⅃	\Finv
⅁	\Game	𝕜	\Bbbk
`	\backprime	∅	\varnothing
▲	\blacktriangle	▼	\blacktriangledown
■	\blacksquare	◆	\blacklozenge
★	\bigstar	∢	\sphericalangle
∁	\complement	ð	\eth
╱	\diagup	╲	\diagdown

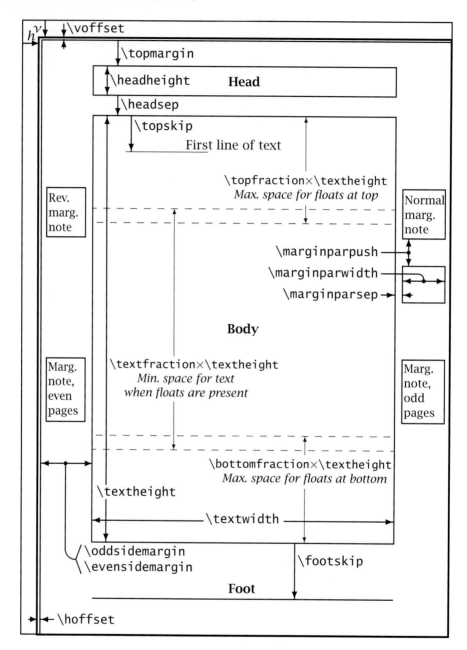

Figure G.1   Single-column page format
(3.2.5), p. 51 – (5.2.6), p. 100 – (9.3), p. 172

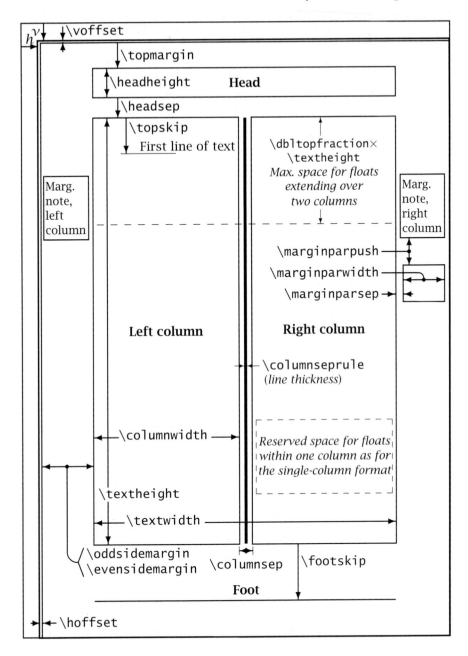

Figure G.2 Double-column page format
(3.2.5), p. 51 – (3.1.1), p. 43 – (5.2.6), p. 100 – (9.3), p. 172

Remarks on the page format figures

The reference margins in the LaTeX processing are shifted from the *logical* margins by the amounts \hoffset and \voffset. These in turn are displaced from the *physical* margins by h and v in the DVI driver. The default values for \hoffset and \voffset are 0 pt, so the reference margins are equal to the *logical* ones. The usual values for h and v are 1 inch. Thus the logical page margins on the left and at the top are shifted 1 inch from the physical edge of the paper. The user may alter this by changing the values of \hoffset and \voffset.

LaTeX 2_ε recognizes the parameters \paperwidth and \paperheight, which contain the full dimensions of the paper, including the 1-inch margins. These are set by the paper size option to the class specification.

The parameter \footheight was specified but never used in LaTeX 2.09; it has been dropped from LaTeX 2_ε.

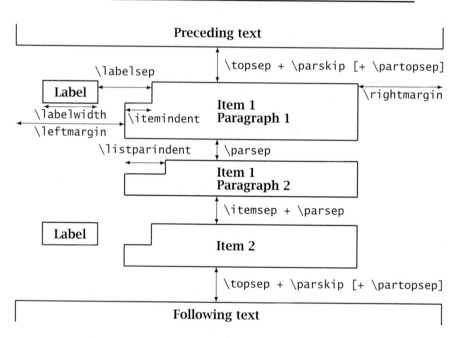

Figure G.3   Format of the `list` environment   (4.4.2) – p. 75

Note 1: The default values are 0 pt for the three parameters, \itemindent, \listparindent, and \rightmargin.

Note 2: The default values in the `trivlist` environment are 0 pt for \itemindent, \leftmargin, \rightmargin, and \labelwidth; on the other hand, \parsep and \listparindent are assigned the respective values of \parskip and \parindent.

Bibliography

Abrahams P. W., with Hargreaves K. A. and Berry K. (1990). *T_EX for the Impatient*. Reading, MA: Addison-Wesley.

Beccari C. (1997). Typesetting mathematics for science and technology according to ISO 31/XI. *TUGboat*, **18**(1), 39-48.

Botway L. and Biemesderfer C. (1985). *LaT_EX Command Summary*. Providence, RI: T_EX Users Group.

Eijkhout V. (1992). *T_EX by Topic, a T_EXnician's Reference*. Harlow: Addison-Wesley. Available online at www.eijkhout.net/tbt/.

Flynn P. (1995). HTML & T_EX: Making them sweat. *TUGboat*, **16**(2), 146-150.

Haralambous Y. and Rahtz S. (1995). LaT_EX, hypertext and PDF, or the entry of T_EX into the world of hypertext. *TUGboat*, **16**(2), 162-173.

Goossens M. and Saarela J. (1995). From LaT_EX to HTML and back. *TUGboat*, **16**(2), 174-214.

Goossens M., Mittelbach F. and Samarin A. (1994). *The LaT_EX Companion*. Reading, MA: Addison-Wesley.

Goossens M., Rahtz S. and Mittelbach F. (1997). *The LaT_EX Graphics Companion*. Reading, MA: Addison-Wesley.

Goossens M. and Rahtz S. (1999). *The LaT_EX Web Companion*. Reading, MA: Addison-Wesley.

Knuth D. E. (1986a). *The T_EXbook*, Computers and Typesetting, Vol. A. Reading, MA: Addison-Wesley.

Knuth D. E. (1986b). *T_EX: The Program*, Computers and Typesetting, Vol. B. Reading, MA: Addison-Wesley.

Knuth D. E. (1986c). *The METAFONTbook*, Computers and Typesetting, Vol. C. Reading, MA: Addison-Wesley.

Knuth D. E. (1986d). *METAFONT: The Program*, Computers and Typesetting, Vol. D. Reading, MA: Addison-Wesley.

Knuth D. E. (1986e). *Computer Modern Typefaces*, Computers and Typesetting, Vol. E. Reading, MA: Addison-Wesley.

Lamport L. (1985). *LaTeX—A Document Preparation System*. Reading, MA: Addison-Wesley.

Lamport L. (1994). *LaTeX—A Document Preparation System*, 2nd ed. for LaTeX2_ε. Reading, MA: Addison-Wesley.

Marchal B. (2000). *XML by Example*. Indianapolis, IN: Que-Programming.

Merz T. (1997). *PostScript & Acrobat/PDF*. Berlin: Springer-Verlag.

Merz T. (1998). *Web Publishing with Acrobat/PDF*. Berlin: Springer-Verlag.

Mittelbach F., Goossens M., Braams J., Carlisle D. and Rowley C. (2004). *The LaTeX Companion, Second Edition*. Boston, MA: Addison-Wesley.

Rokicki T. (1985). Packed (PK) font file format. *TUGboat*, **6**(3), 115-20.

Reckdahl K. (1996a). Using EPS graphics in LaTeX2_ε documents, part 1: The `graphics` and `graphicx` packages. *TUGboat*, **17**(1), 43-53.

Reckdahl K. (1996b). Using EPS graphics in LaTeX2_ε documents, part 2: Floating figures, boxed figures, captions, and math in figures. *TUGboat*, **17**(3), 288-310.

Samuel A. L. (1985). *First Grade TeX: A Beginner's TeX Manual*. Providence, RI: TeX Users Group.

Schwarz N. (1990). *Introduction to TeX*. Reading, MA: Addison-Wesley.

Snow W. (1992). *TeX for the Beginner*. Reading, MA: Addison-Wesley.

Sojka P., Thành H. T. and Zlatuška J. (1996). The joy of TeX2PDF—Acrobatics with an alternative to DVI format. *TUGboat*, **17**(3), 244-251.

Spivak M. (1990). *The Joy of TeX*, 2nd edition. Providence, RI: American Mathematical Society.

Taylor P. (1996). Computer typesetting or electronic publishing? New trends in scientific publication. *TUGboat*, **17**(4), 367-381.

Urban M. (1986). *An Introduction to LaTeX*. Providence RI: TeX Users Group.

Williamson H. A. (2001). *XML from A to Z*. Redmond WA: Redmond Technology Press.

Index

For purposes of alphabetization, the backslash character \ is ignored at the start of an entry. Otherwise, the ordering is by the ASCII sequence.

Bold page numbers indicate the place where the command or concept is introduced, explained, or defined. Slanted page numbers refer to the Command Summary, Appendix G.

The keyword index is set up with main and two subentries. If a keyword cannot be found as a main entry, one should try to find it as a subentry to some more general term. Such major topics are

$\mathcal{AMS}$-LaTeX, bibliographic database, bibliography, box, command, command (user-defined), cross-reference, error messages, exercises, file types, float, fonts, footnote, formula, hyphenation, LaTeX, LaTeX counters, letter, line breaking, lists, package, page breaking, page formatting, page numbering, page style, picture, PostScript, programming, sectioning, slides, spacing, style parameter, symbols, tabbing, table, table examples, TeX, text.

TOOLS AND TECHNIQUES FOR COMPUTER TYPESETTING

Frank Mittelbach, Series Editor

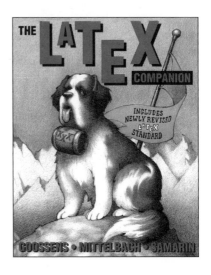

http://www.awprofessional.com

inform IT

Register
Your Book

at www.awprofessional.com/register

You may be eligible to receive:

- Advance notice of forthcoming editions of the book
- Related book recommendations
- Chapter excerpts and supplements of forthcoming titles
- Information about special contests and promotions throughout the year
- Notices and reminders about author appearances, tradeshows, and online chats with special guests

Contact us

If you are interested in writing a book or reviewing manuscripts prior to publication, please write to us at:

Editorial Department
Addison-Wesley Professional
75 Arlington Street, Suite 300
Boston, MA 02116 USA
Email: AWPro@aw.com

Visit us on the Web: http://www.awprofessional.com

CD-ROM Warranty

Addison-Wesley warrants the enclosed disc to be free of defects in materials and faulty workmanship under normal use for a period of ninety days after purchase. If a defect is discovered in the disc during this warranty period, a replacement disc can be obtained at no charge by sending the defective disc, postage prepaid, with proof of purchase to:

Editorial Department
Addison-Wesley Professional
Pearson Technology Group
75 Arlington Street, Suite 300
Boston, MA 02116
Email: AWPro@awl.com

Addison-Wesley makes no warranty or representation, either expressed or implied, with respect to this software, its quality, performance, merchantability, or fitness for a particular purpose. In no event will Addison-Wesley, its distributors, or dealers be liable for direct, indirect, special, incidental, or consequential damages arising out of the use or inability to use the software. The exclusion of implied warranties is not permitted in some states. Therefore, the above exclusion may not apply to you. This warranty provides you with specific legal rights. There may be other rights that you may have that vary from state to state. The contents of this CD-ROM are intended for personal use only.

More information and updates are available at:
http://www.awprofessional.com/